Glossary
(continued)

Cash discounts Price reductions to encourage buyers to pay their bills promptly.

Catalog retailers Sell several lines out of a catalog and display showroom—with backup inventories.

Central markets Convenience places where buyers and sellers can meet to exchange goods and services.

Chain store A member of a group which works together to operate more efficiently.

Channel captain One who helps direct the activities of a whole channel.

Channel of distribution A series of marketing firms from producer to final user or consumer.

Cold-storage warehouses Store perishable products such as grain, apples, butter, and furs.

Combination export manager A blend of manufacturers' agent and selling agent—handling the entire export function for several manufacturers of non-competing lines.

Combiners Try to increase the size of their target markets by combining two or more submarkets.

Commission merchants Agent middlemen who handle goods shipped to central markets by sellers, complete the sales, and send the money—minus their commissions—to the sellers.

Commodity warehouses Store perishable products such as grain, apples, butter, and furs.

Common carriers Such as railroads and major truck lines—must maintain regular schedules and accept goods from any shipper.

Communication process Shows how a source tries to reach a receiver with a message.

Community shopping centers A planned shopping center which has some shopping stores as well as the convenience stores found in neighborhood shopping centers.

Comparative advertising Makes brand comparisons—using actual product names.

Competitive advertising Advertising which tries to develop selective demand, i.e., demand for a specific brand.

Competitive environment The number and types of competitors the marketing manager must face and how they might behave.

Component parts and materials Expense items which have had more processing than raw materials.

Consumer cooperative A group of consumers who buy together.

Consumer goods Products meant for the final consumer.

Consumerism A social movement seeking to increase the rights and powers of consumers.

Contract carriers Transporters who work for anyone for an agreed sum and for any length of time.

Contract farming The farmer gets supplies and perhaps working capital from local middlemen or manufacturers who agree to buy the farmer's output—sometimes at guaranteed prices.

Contract manufacturing Turning over production to others while retaining the marketing process.

Convenience (food) stores A variation of the conventional limited-line food stores, offering convenience not assortment.

Convenience goods Consumer goods the customer needs but isn't willing to spend much time shopping for.

Convenience store A convenient place to shop.

Cooperative advertising Middlemen and producers sharing the cost of ads.

Cooperative chains Retailer-sponsored groups which run their own buying organizations.

Copy thrust *What* is to be communicated by the written copy and illustrations in an advertisement.

Corrective advertising Ads to correct deceptive advertising.

Cost of goods sold The total value (at cost) of all the goods sold during the period of an operating (profit and loss) statement.

Cues Products, signs, ads, and other stimuli existing in the environment.

Cultural and social environment The surroundings and attitudes that affect how and why people live and behave as they do.

Culture The whole set of values, beliefs, attitudes, and ways of doing things of a similar group of people.

Cumulative quantity discounts Quantity discounts which apply to purchases over a given time period, normally increasing as .the quantity purchased increases.

(continued on p. 489)

ESSENTIALS OF MARKETING

The Irwin Series in Marketing

Consulting Editor
GILBERT CHURCHILL
University of Wisconsin, Madison

About the author . . .

E. Jerome McCarthy received his Ph.D. from the University of Minnesota in 1958. Since then, he has been deeply involved in teaching and developing new teaching materials. Now 50 years old, Dr. McCarthy is active making presentations to academic conferences and business meetings. He has worked with groups of teachers throughout the country, and has addressed international conferences in South America, South Africa, and India.

Dr. McCarthy was voted one of the "top five" leaders in Marketing Thought in 1975 by marketing educators. He was also a Ford Foundation Fellow in 1963–64, doing independent research on the role of marketing in economic development. In 1959–60, he was a Ford Foundation Fellow at the Harvard Business School working on mathematical methods in marketing.

Besides his academic interests, Dr. McCarthy is involved in consulting for and guiding the growth of several businesses. He has also been director of several for-profit and not-for-profit organizations. His primary interests, however, are in (1) teaching marketing and marketing strategy planning, and (2) preparing teaching materials to help others do the same. This is why he has continued to spend a substantial part of his time working on *Basic Marketing* and *Essentials of Marketing*. This is a continuing process, and this book incorporates the newest thinking in the field.

ESSENTIALS OF MARKETING

E. Jerome McCarthy, Ph.D.
Michigan State University

With the assistance of
A. A. Brogowicz, Ph.D.
University of Illinois, Chicago Circle Campus

RICHARD D. IRWIN, INC. Homewood, Illinois 60430
Irwin-Dorsey Limited Georgetown, Ontario L7G 4B3

ISBN 0-256-02142-2
Library of Congress Catalog Card No. 78–70938

Printed in the United States of America

1 2 3 4 5 6 7 8 9 0 K 6 5 4 3 2 1 0 9

PREFACE

This book presents the "essentials" of marketing. A basic objective has been to make it easy for the average student to grasp these very important "essentials."

Essentials of Marketing is a shortened version of my *Basic Marketing*—a book that has been widely used in the marketing course. While cutting the material to *Essentials,* much time and effort was spent on carefully defining terms and finding the "right" word to speed understanding. Similarly, figures, pictures, and illustrations were selected and created to help today's more visual student "see" the material better.

The point of all this editing and illustrating was to try to make sure that the student really does get a good feel for a market-directed system and how he or she can help it and the company they are in run better.

A special feature of this book is that it is possible to rearrange the use of the chapters in many ways to fit various needs. *Essentials of Marketing* retains the marketing strategy planning emphasis—seeing marketing through the marketing manager's eyes. It begins with three chapters on the nature of marketing and its environment. Then four chapters are concerned with selecting target markets. Included here are chapters on marketing research, customer behavior, segmenting markets, and forecasting sales. The bulk of the book is concerned with developing a marketing mix—out of four ingredients, called the four Ps: Product, Place (that is, channels and institutions), Promotion, and Price. These sections are concerned with developing the "right" Product and making it available at the "right" Place with the "right" Promotion and the "right" Price—to satisfy target customers and still meet the objectives of the business. These chapters are presented in a logical way to help the student see the "big picture."

Chapter 18 applies the ideas in the text to international marketing. While there is a multinational emphasis throughout the text, this separate chapter is provided for those wishing special emphasis on international marketing.

The final chapter considers how efficient the marketing process is. Here we discuss many criticisms of marketing and evaluate the effectiveness of both micro- and macro-marketing—considering whether any changes are needed. This final analysis is important. Marketing people must be concerned about their impact on the economy and how they can help our system work more effectively. After this chapter, the student might want to look at Appendix C, concerning career opportunities in marketing, now that he can see what marketing is all about.

Some text books treat currently "hot" topics such as "social responsibility" and "consumerism" as a basis for separate chapters. This is not done in this text. Instead, they are treated in their proper places. That is, these matters are not only treated at the beginning and end of the text, but also are woven into the text to emphasize that marketing managers must be continually concerned with and work within their environment. Isolating such materials in a separate chapter could lead to an unfortunate "compartmentalization" of ideas. In fact, a marketing manager must give continual consideration to these issues.

It is hoped that, in this framework, marketing will be looked upon by more students as a useful, fascinating, and very necessary function in our American economy.

Really understanding marketing and how to plan marketing strategies can build self-confidence and make a student more ready to take an active part in the business world.

By making the "essentials" more interesting and accessible, we hope to help more students see marketing as the challenging and rewarding area that it is.

These materials can be studied in a number of ways. *One,* the text can be supplemented by lectures and class discussion of the materials and perhaps additional readings. A separate volume, *Readings in Basic Marketing,* can provide additional complementary materials. *Two,* understanding the text material can be deepened by discussion of conventional questions and problems at the end of each chapter and/or the cases at the end of the book. Further, a separate *Study Guide* offers additional opportunities to obtain a deeper understanding of the material. This *Study Guide* includes not only exercises, but also true-false and multiple-choice questions (*with answers*). *Three,* thought-provoking questions included at the end of the chapters can be used to encourage the student to investigate the marketing process and organize an individual way of thinking about it. Some of the questions and exercises from the *Study Guide* also can be used to accomplish this objective.

To help the student see what is coming in each chapter, behavioral objectives are included on the first page of each chapter. And to speed student understanding, important new terms are shown in color and defined right there. They are also listed in the *Study Guide*. Further, a glossary of these terms is presented inside the front and back covers. It is hoped these aids will help the student understand important concepts and speed review before examinations.

Finally, feedback—from both students and instructors—is encouraged. It is my intention to prepare the best teaching materials I can. Learning should not only be fun, but should accomplish specific objectives. Any suggestions for improving the learning process in the marketing area will be greatly appreciated.

March 1979   E. Jerome McCarthy

ACKNOWLEDGMENTS

This book is the result of the blending of my experience in business and in various academic institutions, including Northwestern University, Michigan State University, and the Universities of Minnesota, Oregon, and Notre Dame. Many people have had an influence on this text. My colleagues at the University of Notre Dame greatly affected my thinking during the years we were developing a beginning course emphasizing marketing management. And more recently, Professor Yusaku Furuhashi of the University of Notre Dame has made numerous suggestions and provided on-going counsel on the multinational emphasis. Similarly, Professor Andrew A. Brogowicz of the University of Illinois, Chicago Circle, has been extremely helpful, suggesting changes and actually drafting text materials. Persons who supplied helpful criticisms and comments for the sixth edition of *Basic Marketing* from which this *Essentials* was developed as a shortened version are acknowledged there. It is important to recognize their contribution, however, because many of those suggestions helped us see what was "essential" and how it would be possible to create a shortened version which would still cover the essential points.

Joanne and Barbara McCarthy provided invaluable editorial assistance—making the text more readable and accessible to more students. And Mary McCarthy provided the visual emphasis—identifying where visual aids were needed and then actually selecting or creating appropriate ones. Peter S. Sheldon, Bruce Malsberger, and Andrew Schreiner helped with many of the pictures. Thomas McCarthy provided research assistance. And Patricia Vermeer was a great help handling transcription and typing of the sometimes illegible manuscript. Finally, I must thank my wife, Joanne, for considerable patience and advice throughout the process and then for assistance during the final proofreading which occurs under typically chaotic conditions. Also helpful in this process were several of our children mentioned above as well as our daughter Anne. To all these persons and to the many publishers who graciously granted permission to use their material, I am deeply grateful. Responsibility for any errors or omissions is certainly mine, but the book would not have been possible without the assistance of many others. My sincere appreciation goes to everyone who helped in their own special way.

E. J. McC.

A NOTE TO STUDENTS (BOTH MALE AND FEMALE) REGARDING GRAMMATICAL MATTERS AND ROLES IN MARKETING

The English language makes it very difficult for an author—even a well-meaning author—not to appear "sexist." I have struggled long and hard on this matter and decided that there is really no solution satisfactory to everyone until some changes are made in the language.

The reality is that our world is filled with both males and females who can fill most of the roles in our society, but an author must use either male or female words to refer to an individual. Trying to recognize that both males and females can and do play various roles in business, however, results in "semantic gymnastics" if an author tries to use devices such as he/she, he or she, she and he, s/he, person, or various plural forms such as them, their, persons, or people. Excessive preoccupation with semantics not only deadens and lengthens the text, it risks losing sight of what marketing is all about. Marketing is concerned with satisfying people, but people buy one at a time. Buyers and sellers interact as individuals, not as groups of "them." Further, we are trying to put the student in the position of a decision maker—a "marketing manager"—and this individual is responsible for making decisions.

So, in the interest of personalizing and humanizing this text, I have deliberately tried to "de-sex" it while at the same time continuing to use masculine singular pronouns wherever necessary to be sure that the student continues to put himself (or herself) in the role of marketing manager. It is hoped that female students will not feel discriminated against and male students will not feel that all the "good" managerial jobs are reserved for them. This is simply not true.

Besides referring to individual business people as he or him, it is sometimes practical to refer to corporations and business institutions in the same way, because they are persons. Similarly, it is practical to refer to individual consumers as he or him. The intent is not to discriminate, but to get individual students to feel that their decisions will make a difference and that they will have to make them as individuals. By the end of the text, I hope to have brought you to the point where you will feel confident that you *can* make decisions that make a difference.

In summary, I chose to try to humanize and personalize the text, in the hope it will make the text more interesting and help make you a better marketer. I hope it accomplishes these goals without offending females or misleading or raising "false hopes" in too many males.

E. J. McC.

CONTENTS

ESSENTIALS OF MARKETING

When you finish this chapter, you should:

1 Know what marketing is and why you should learn about it.
2 Know why and how macro-marketing systems develop.
3 Know why and how marketing specialists—including middlemen—develop.
4 Recognize the important new terms shown in red.

MARKETING'S ROLE IN SOCIETY

You are probably reading this book because you have to. It's required reading in a course you have to take. Therefore, we want to tell you why you should study this book.

MARKETING AND YOU

Why you should study marketing

One reason for studying marketing is that—as a consumer—you pay for marketing activities. It's estimated that marketing costs about 50 percent of each consumer's dollar.[1]

Another important reason for learning about marketing is that marketing affects almost every part of your daily life. The products you buy. The stores where you shop. All that advertising you are exposed to. They are all a part of marketing. Even your job resumé is part of a marketing campaign to sell yourself to some employers.

Another reason for studying marketing is that there are many exciting and rewarding career opportunities in marketing. Marketing is often the road to the top. Throughout this book—and in Appendix C—you will find information about opportunities in various areas of marketing.

Those of you who are looking for nonmarketing positions in business will have to work with marketing people. Knowing something about marketing will help you understand them better. It will also help you do your own job better. Remember, a company that cannot successfully sell its products won't need accountants, computer programmers, financial managers, personnel managers, production managers, and so on. It's often said, "Nothing happens unless the cash register rings."

Even if you are not planning a business career, marketing ideas and methods will be very useful for you. Nonprofit organizations are beginning to realize this. The same approaches used to sell soap can also be used to "sell" ideas, politicians, mass transportation, health care services, energy conservation, and museums.

A final and even more basic reason for studying marketing is that marketing plays a big part in economic growth and development. Marketing stimulates research and change—resulting in new products. If these products attract customers, this can lead to fuller employment, higher incomes, and a higher standard of living. An effective marketing system is important, therefore, to the future of our nation—and all nations.

MARKETING—WHAT'S IT ALL ABOUT?

If you are a typical student taking your first course in marketing, it's a pretty safe bet that you have little, if any, idea of what marketing is all about. Don't worry—you're not alone! Few Americans really understand what marketing is. In fact, even some business managers would have a hard time giving an exact definition of marketing.

Marketing is more than selling or advertising

If forced to define marketing, most people would probably say that marketing means "selling" or "advertising." But this is not true. It is very important for you to see that selling and advertising are only *part* of marketing. Marketing is much more than selling and advertising.

How did all those tennis racquets get here?

Let's think about the marketing of tennis racquets. None of us was born with a tennis racquet in our hand. Nor do we make our own tennis racquets. Instead, they are made by firms like Wilson, Spaulding, Slazenger, Davis, Head, and Bancroft.

Most tennis racquets look pretty much alike. All are intended to do the same thing—hit the ball over the net. Even so, a tennis player can choose among a wide assortment of racquets. There are different weights, handle sizes, materials, and strings. You can spend less than $10 on a prestrung racquet or more than $100 for just a frame! This variety in sizes and materials complicates the production and sale of tennis racquets. The following list is just some of the many things a firm should do when it decides to manufacture tennis racquets.

1. Estimate how many people will be playing tennis over the next several years and how many tennis racquets they will buy.
2. Predict exactly when people will want to buy tennis racquets.
3. Determine which handle sizes and weights people will want and how many of each.
4. Decide what materials to use as well as where and how to get them.
5. Estimate what price different tennis players will be willing to pay for their racquets.
6. Determine where these tennis players will be and how to get the firm's racquets to them.

7. Decide which methods of promotion should be used to tell potential customers about the firm's tennis racquets.
8. Estimate how many other firms will be manufacturing tennis racquets, how many racquets they will produce, what kind, at what prices, and so on.

The above activities are *not* part of manufacturing. Rather, they are part of a larger process—called marketing—which can provide needed direction for manufacturing and help to be sure that the right products find their way to interested consumers. You can see that this includes far more than selling or advertising. As you move through the book, you will learn much more about these activities. For now, however, it is important to see that marketing plays a necessary role in providing consumers with goods and services that satisfy their needs.

HOW MARKETING RELATES TO MANUFACTURING

Manufacturing is a very important economic activity. Whether for lack of skill, resources, or just lack of time, most people don't make most of the products they use. Picture yourself, for example, building a ten-speed bicycle, a color television, or a digital watch—starting from scratch! Clearly, the high standard of living that most Americans enjoy would not be possible without modern manufacturing know-how.

Tennis racquets, like mousetraps, don't sell themselves

Although manufacturing is a necessary economic activity, some people tend to overrate its importance in relation to marketing. Their attitude is reflected in the old saying: "If a man . . . makes a better mousetrap . . . the world will beat a path to his door."

"Ralph, no one is going to beat a path to your door if they don't even know about them . . . at least advertise!"

The mousetrap theory probably wasn't true in your grandfather's time—and it certainly is not true today. In modern economies, the grass grows high on the path to the Better Mousetrap Factory—if the new mousetrap is not properly marketed. We have already seen, for example, that there is a lot more to selling tennis racquets than simply manufacturing them. This is true for most products.

The point is that manufacturing and marketing are both important parts of an economic system aimed at providing consumers with need-satisfying goods and services. Together they provide the four basic economic utilities—form, time, place, and possession utility—which are commonly needed to provide consumer satisfaction. Here, **utility** means the power to satisfy human needs.

Tennis racquets do not automatically provide utility

Form utility is provided when a manufacturer makes something (say a tennis racquet) out of other materials. But contrary to those who believe in the mousetrap theory, just making tennis racquets does not result in consumer satisfaction. Time, place, and possession utility must also be provided.

Time utility means having the product available *when* the customer wants it. And **place utility** means having the product available *where* the customer wants it. For example, how much satisfaction would a tennis player in California get from a tennis racquet in a manufacturer's warehouse in Pennsylvania? That tennis racquet wouldn't win many games unless it were available *when* (time utility) and *where* (place utility) the tennis player wanted it. And to have the legal right to use the tennis racquet, the tennis player would have to pay for it before enjoying possession utility. **Possession utility** means completing a transaction and gaining possession so that one has the right to use the product.

Stated simply, the job of manufacturing is to create form utility, while marketing's job is to provide time, place, and possession utility. And marketing information may help decide what products to produce. So it can also be argued that marketing helps create form utility.

You can see that successful manufacturing depends on successful marketing. How marketing creates time, place, and possession utility will be explored later in this chapter. First, we must define marketing—something we have avoided until now.

HOW SHOULD WE DEFINE MARKETING?

As noted earlier, most people would probably define marketing as selling or advertising. On the other hand, one famous marketing expert called marketing: "The creation and delivery of a standard of living."[2]

Micro- or macro-marketing?

There is a big difference between these two definitions. The first definition focuses on the activities of an individual firm. The second focuses on the economic welfare of the entire society.

Which view is correct? Is marketing a set of activities performed by individual organizations, or is it a social process?

Society needs a marketing system to organize production to satisfy consumers' many needs.

To answer this question, let's go back to our tennis racquet example. We saw that a manufacturer of tennis racquets would have to perform several customer-related activities besides simply producing racquets. The same would be true for an art museum or a welfare agency. This supports the idea of marketing as a set of activities performed by individual organizations.

On the other hand, people cannot live on tennis racquets and art museums alone! In an advanced economy like ours, it takes thousands of goods and services to satisfy the many needs of society. A large supermarket may handle as many as 10,000 items. A typical K mart stocks 15,000 different items. A society needs some sort of marketing system to organize all the producers needed to satisfy the needs of all its citizens. So it would appear that marketing is an important social process.

The answer to our question then is that marketing is *both* a set of activities performed by organizations *and* a social process. Therefore, we will present two definitions of marketing—one for micro-marketing and another for macro-marketing. The first looks at customers and organizations. The second one takes a broad view of our whole production-distribution system.

MICRO-MARKETING DEFINED

Micro-marketing is the performance of activities which seek to accomplish a firm's objectives by anticipating customer needs and directing a flow of need-satisfying goods and services from producer to customer. Let's look at this definition.

Marketing should result in a customer who is ready to buy.

Applies to profit and nonprofit organizations

This definition applies to both profit and nonprofit organizations. The customers (or clients) may be individual consumers, business firms, nonprofit organizations, government agencies, or even foreign nations. While most of the customers will have to pay for the goods and services they receive, others get them free.

What activities are included in micro-marketing? Certainly personal selling and advertising are marketing activities. Unfortunately, many managers would limit marketing to selling and advertising. They feel that the job of marketing is to "get rid of" the product that has been produced and priced by the production, accounting, and finance people.

This narrow view of marketing should be rejected. As noted management consultant Peter Drucker has stated:

> There will always, one can assume, be need for selling. But the aim of marketing is to make selling [unnecessary]. The aim of marketing is to know and understand the customer so well that the product or service sells itself.
>
> Ideally, marketing should result in a customer who is *ready* to buy. All that should be needed then is to make the product or service available. . . .[3]

So, when we define micro-marketing as those activities which *direct* the flow of goods and services, we mean just that: direct.

Marketing should begin with a customer not with a production process. Marketing—not production—should decide what products are to be made and what prices should be charged. Marketing should set credit and collection policies, as well as transporting and storing policies. Marketing should decide when and how the products are to be advertised and sold. Warranty and service policies should be decided by marketing, too.

This does *not* mean that marketing should take over the traditional production, accounting, and financial activities. Rather, it means that marketing—by understanding customers' needs—should provide direction for these activities. After all, the purpose of a business or nonprofit organization is to satisfy customer or client needs. It is *not* to supply goods or services which are convenient to produce or which *might* sell.

THE FOCUS OF THIS TEXT—BUSINESS-ORIENTED MICRO-MARKETING

Assuming that you are preparing for a business career, the main focus of this text will be on micro-marketing. We will see marketing through the eyes of the marketing manager. Much of this material will also be useful for those who plan to work for nonprofit organizations.

It is very important, however, that marketing managers never forget that their organizations are just small parts of a larger macro-marketing system. Therefore, for the rest of this chapter we will look at the macro—"the big picture"—view of marketing. Let's begin by defining macro-marketing and then reviewing some basic concepts.

MACRO-MARKETING DEFINED

Macro-marketing is a social process which directs an economy's flow of goods and services from producers to consumers in a way which effectively matches supply and demand and accomplishes the objectives of society.

Like micro-marketing, macro-marketing is concerned with the flow of need-satisfying goods and services from producer to consumer. When we talk about macro-marketing however, the emphasis is not on the activities of *individual* organizations. Rather, the emphasis is on how the *whole system* works.

EVERY SOCIETY NEEDS AN ECONOMIC SYSTEM

All societies must provide for the material needs of their members. Therefore, each society needs some economic system to arrange for the production and distribution of goods and services to satisfy the people.

How an economic system operates depends upon a society's goals and its political system. But, all economic systems must decide *what and how much* is to be produced *by whom and when* and distributed *to whom.* How these decisions are made may vary from nation to nation—but the macro-level objectives are basically the same: to create goods and services and make them available when and where they are needed to maintain or improve each nation's output.

HOW ECONOMIC DECISIONS ARE MADE

There are two basic kinds of economic systems: planned systems and market-directed systems. Actually, no economy is *entirely* planned or market-directed. Most developing or advanced economies are a mixture of the two.

The assortment of goods and services may be limited in a planned economy.

Government planners may make the decisions

A **planned economic system** is one in which government planners decide what and how much is to be produced and distributed by whom, when, and to whom. Producers generally have very little choice concerning product design. Their main job is to meet their assigned production quotas. Prices are set by government planners and tend to be very rigid—not changing according to supply and demand. Consumers usually have some freedom of choice. It is impossible to control every single detail! But the assortment of goods and services may be quite limited. Activities such as market research, branding, and advertising may receive little emphasis—and sometimes are not done at all.[4]

Government planning may work fairly well as long as the economy is simple and the variety of goods and services is small. It may even be necessary under certain conditions—during wartime, for example. However, as economies become more complex, government planning becomes more difficult. It may even break down. Planners may face too many complex decisions. And consumers may lose patience if the planners don't meet their needs.

A market-directed economy runs itself

A **market-directed economic system** is one in which the individual decisions of the many producers and consumers make the macro-level decisions for the whole economy.

A pure market-directed economy is free from the government controls that go with government planning. Consumers make a society's production decisions when they make their choices in the marketplace. They decide what is to be produced and by whom—through their dollar "votes." The prices in the marketplace serve roughly as a measure of the social importance of goods and services. If consumers are willing to pay the market prices, then apparently they feel they are getting at least their money's worth.

Whenever a new consumer need arises, an opportunity is created for some profit-minded business. All consumer needs which can be served profitably will encourage producers to meet those needs. Ideally, control of the economy is completely democratic. Power is spread throughout the economy.

GREATEST FREEDOM OF CHOICE

Consumers in a market-directed economy enjoy maximum freedom of choice. They are not forced to buy any goods or services except those that must be provided for the good of society—things like national defense, schools, police and fire protection, mass transportation, and public health services. These are provided by the community, and citizens are taxed to pay for them.

In a market-directed economy, people nave free choice in finding work that is satisfying to them. Producers are free to produce whatever they wish, providing that they stay within the rules of the game established by government *and* that they receive sufficient dollar votes from consumers. If they do their job well, they will earn a profit and stay in business. But profit, survival, and growth are not guaranteed.

The American economy is largely but not completely market-directed. For example, in addition to setting and enforcing the rules of the game, the federal government controls interest rates and the supply of money, sets import and export restrictions, regulates radio and TV broadcasting, alternately restricts and stimulates agricultural production, sometimes controls prices and wages, and so on. Some of these activities may be necessary to reach short-run goals. But some may get in the way of accomplishing long-run goals. For example, increasing government interference could affect the survival of our market-directed system—and the economic and political freedom that goes with it.[5]

DO ALL ECONOMIES NEED MACRO-MARKETING SYSTEMS?

In general, no economic system—whether planned or market directed—can achieve its objectives without an effective macro-marketing system. To explain why this is true, we will look at marketing in primitive economies. Then we will see how macro-marketing tends to become more and more complex in advanced economic systems.

Marketing involves exchange

In a pure subsistence economy, each family unit produces all the goods that it consumes. There is no need to exchange goods and services. Each producer-consumer unit is totally self-sufficient. Marketing would not take place—because marketing does not occur unless there are two or more parties who want to exchange something for something else.

Almost all economies have gone beyond the pure subsistence stage. There is a need to exchange things.

The term "marketing" comes from the word "market." A **market** is a

Central markets help exchange

group of sellers and buyers bargaining the terms of exchange for goods and services. This can be done face-to-face at some physical location (e.g., a farmers' market). Or it can be done indirectly through a complex network of middlemen who link buyers and sellers who are far apart.

In primitive economies, markets tend to be located in central places. **Central markets** are convenient places where buyers and sellers can meet face-to-face to exchange goods and services. We can understand macro-marketing better by seeing how and why central markets develop.

Imagine a small village of five families. Each has some special skill for producing some need-satisfying product. After meeting basic needs, each family might decide to specialize. It is easier for one family to make two pots and another to make two baskets than it is for each one to make one pot and one basket. Specialization makes labor more efficient and more productive. It can increase the total amount of form utility created.

If these five families specialize in one product each, they will have to trade with each other. As Figure 1–1 shows, it would take the five families ten separate trips and exchanges to obtain some of each of the products. If the families live near each other, the exchange process would be relatively simple. But if they are far apart, traveling back and forth will take time. Who would do the traveling and when?

Faced with this problem, the families can agree to come to a central market and trade on a certain day. Then, each family would need to make only one trip to the market to trade with all the others. This will reduce the total number of trips to five. This would make exchange easier, leave more time for production and consumption, and provide for social gatherings. In total, much more time, place, possession, and even form utility would be enjoyed by each of the five families.

Money system speeds trading

While a central meeting place would simplify exchange, the individual bartering transactions would still take much time. Bartering requires another

Figure 1–1
Ten exchanges required when a central market is not used[6]

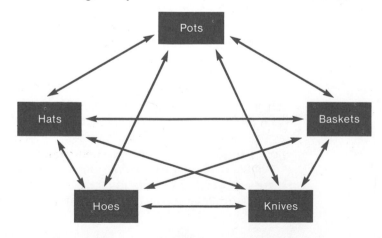

person who wants what you have and vice versa. Each trader must find others who have products of about equal value. After trading with one group, a family might find itself with some extra hats, knives, and pots. Then it would have to find others willing to trade for these products.

A money system would change all of this. A seller would merely find a buyer who can either use or sell his product, agree on a price, and be free to spend his money to buy whatever he wants.

Middlemen help exchange even more

The development of a central market and a money system would simplify the exchange process among the five families in our imaginary village. But a total of ten separate transactions would still be required—once the families arrived at the central market. Thus, it would still take a lot of time and effort to carry out exchange among the five families.

This clumsy exchange process could be made much simpler by the appearance of a **middleman**—someone who specializes in trade rather than production. He would be willing to buy each family's output and then sell each family whatever goods it needs. This middleman would charge for his service, of course. But this charge might be more than offset by a savings in time and effort.

In our simple example, using the services of a middleman at a central market would reduce the number of transactions for all families from ten to five. See Figure 1–2. Each family would have more time for production, consumption, and visits to other families. Also, each family could specialize in production—creating greater form utility. Meanwhile, by specializing in trade, the middleman could provide additional time, place, and possession utility. In total, all the villagers might enjoy greater economic utility and greater satisfaction by using a middleman in the central market.

You can see that the reduction in transactions that results from using a middleman in a central market becomes more important as the number of families increases. For example, if the population of our imaginary village

Figure 1–2
Only five exchanges are required when a middleman in a central market is used[7]

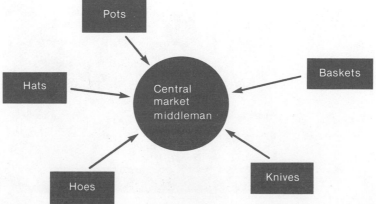

were to increase from five to ten families, 45 transactions would be required without a middleman. Using a middleman would reduce the necessary number of transactions to ten—one for each family.

Today, such middlemen—offering permanent trading facilities—are known as wholesalers and retailers. The advantages of working with middlemen increase as the number of producers and customers, their distance apart, and the number and variety of competing products increase. That is why there are so many wholesalers and retailers in modern economies.

THE ROLE OF MARKETING IN ECONOMIC DEVELOPMENT

Modern economies have advanced well beyond the five-family village— but the same ideas still apply. The basic purpose of markets and middlemen is to make exchange easier and allow greater time for production, consumption, and other activities—including leisure.

Effective marketing is necessary for economic development

Although it is tempting to decide that more effective macro-marketing systems are the result of greater economic development, just the opposite is true. An effective macro-marketing system is necessary for economic development. In fact, management expert Peter Drucker has suggested that marketing may even be the key to growth in less-developed nations.[8]

Breaking the vicious circle of poverty

Without an effective macro-marketing system, the less-developed nations may not be able to escape the "vicious circle of poverty."[9] They can't leave their subsistence way of life to produce for the market, because there are no buyers for any goods they might produce. And there are no buyers because everyone else is producing for his own needs. Breaking this vicious circle of poverty may require a major change in the micro- and macro-marketing systems that are typical in less-developed nations.

CAN MASS PRODUCTION SATISFY A SOCIETY'S CONSUMPTION NEEDS?

The growth of cities brings together large numbers of people. They must depend on others to produce most of the goods and services they

An effective macro-marketing system encourages growth in an economy.

need to satisfy their basic needs. Also, many consumers have higher incomes. They can afford to satisfy higher-level needs as well. A modern economic system has a big job satisfying all these needs.

Economies of size mean lower costs

Fortunately, advanced economies can take advantage of mass production with its **economies of size.** This means that as a company produces larger numbers of a particular product, the cost for each of these products goes down. For example, a one-of-a-kind, custom-built car would cost *much* more than a mass-produced standard model.

Modern manufacturing skills can help produce great quantities of goods and services to satisfy large numbers of consumers. But mass production alone can't solve the problem of satisfying a society's needs. Effective marketing is needed also.

Effective marketing is needed to link producers and consumers

Effective marketing means delivering the goods and services that consumers need and want. And it means getting the goods to them at the right time, in the right place, and at a price they're willing to pay. This is no easy job, especially if you think about the big variety of goods a highly developed economy can produce—and the many kinds of goods and services consumers want.

Effective marketing in an advanced economy is more difficult because producers are separated from consumers in several ways—as Figure 1–3 shows.[10] It is also complicated by ''discrepancies of quantity'' and ''discrepancies of assortment'' between producer and consumers. This means that individual producers specialize in producing and selling large amounts of a narrow assortment of goods and services, but each consumer wants only small quantities of a wide variety of goods and services.

Mass production offers economies of size.

16

Figure 1–3
Marketing facilitates production and consumption[11]

PRODUCTION SECTOR
Specialization and division of labor result in heterogeneous supply capabilities

MARKETING
Needed
to
overcome

SPATIAL SEPARATION . . . . Producers and consumers are separated geographically. Producers tend to cluster together by industry in a few concentrated locations, while consumers are located in many scattered locations.

SEPARATION IN TIME . . . . Consumers may not want to consume goods at the time they are produced, and time may be required to transport goods from producer to consumer.

SEPARATION OF INFORMATION . . . . . . Producers do not know who needs what, where, when, and at what price. Consumers do not know what is available from whom, where, when, and at what price.

SEPARATION IN VALUES . . . . Producers value goods and services in terms of costs and competitive prices. Consumers value goods and services in terms of economic utility and ability to pay.

SEPARATION OF OWNERSHIP . . . . Producers hold title to goods and services which they themselves do not want to consume. Consumers want to consume goods and services which they do not own.

DISCREPANCIES OF QUANTITY . . . . Producers prefer to produce and sell in large quantities. Consumers prefer to buy and consume in small quantities.

DISCREPANCIES OF ASSORTMENT . . . Producers specialize in producing a narrow assortment of goods and services. Consumers need a broad assortment.

CONSUMPTION SECTOR
Heterogeneous demand for form, time, place, and possession utility to satisfy needs and wants

Universal marketing functions must be performed

The purpose of a macro-marketing system is to overcome these separations and discrepancies. The "universal functions of marketing" do this.

The **universal functions** of marketing are: buying, selling, transporting, storing, standardization and grading, financing, risk-taking, and market information. These marketing functions are *universal* in the sense that they must be performed in *all* macro-marketing systems. *How* these functions are performed by *whom* may differ among nations and economic systems, but they are needed in any macro-marketing system. Let's take a closer look at them now.

The **buying function** means looking for and evaluating products and services. The **selling function** is the promotion of the product. It would include the use of personal selling, advertising, and other mass selling methods. This is the best known, and some people feel the only function of marketing.

Transporting function means the movement of goods from one place to another. The **storing function** involves holding goods.

Standardization and grading involve sorting products according to size and quality. This simplifies buying and selling by reducing the need for inspection and sampling. **Financing** provides the necessary cash and credit to manufacture, transport, store, promote, sell, and buy products. **Risk-taking** involves bearing the uncertainties that are a part of the marketing process. A firm can never be sure that customers will want to buy its products. And the products could also become damaged, stolen, or outdated. The **market information** function involves the collection, analysis, and distribution of information needed to plan, carry out, and control marketing activities.

WHO PERFORMS MARKETING FUNCTIONS?

Producers, consumers, and marketing specialists

From a macro-level viewpoint, these functions are all part of the marketing process and must be done by someone. None of them can be skipped or eliminated. In a planned economy, some of the functions might be performed by government agencies. Others might be left to individual producers and consumers. In a market-directed economy, these marketing functions are performed by producers, consumers, and various marketing specialists.

Earlier in this chapter, we saw that adding a middleman to a simple five-family village of producers and consumers made exchange easier and increased the total amount of economic utility. This effect is even greater in a large, complicated economy. This helps explain why most of the products sold in the United States are distributed through wholesalers and retailers—instead of directly from producers to consumers.

You saw how producers and consumers benefited when a marketing specialist (middleman) helped in buying and selling. Producers and consumers also benefit when marketing specialists perform the other marketing functions. So we find marketing functions being performed by a variety of other specialists. These include advertising agencies, marketing research firms, independent product-testing laboratories, public warehouses, transportation firms, and banks. Through specialization and economies of size, specialists are often able to perform the marketing functions at a lower cost than producers or consumers could. This allows producers and consumers to spend more time on production and consumption.

Functions can be shifted and shared

From a macro viewpoint all of the marketing functions must be performed by someone. But from a micro viewpoint not every firm must perform all of the functions. Some marketing specialists perform all the functions. Others specialize in only one or two. For example, marketing research firms specialize only in the market information function.

Sometimes several specialists are used between producer and consumer. Then some of the marketing functions may be performed several times. But the key point to remember is this: Responsibility for performing the marketing functions can be shifted and shared in a variety of ways, but no function can be completely eliminated!

HOW WELL DOES OUR MACRO-MARKETING SYSTEM WORK?

It connects remote producers and consumers

A macro-marketing system does more than just deliver goods to consumers—it allows mass production with its "economies of size." Also, with mass communication and transportation, our system allows the products of our farms and factories to be shipped where they are needed. Oranges from California are found in Minnesota stores—even in December—and coal from West Virginia heats homes in Massachusetts.

It encourages growth and new ideas

In addition to making mass production possible, our market-directed macro-marketing system encourages new ideas. Competition for the consumers' dollars forces firms to think of new and better ways of satisfying consumer needs.

"Who's right? Some complain we're encouraging materialism while others complain that we don't supply enough jobs."

It has its critics   In trying to explain marketing's role in society, we have emphasized the good points of our macro-marketing system. In general, we feel this approach is right because our macro-marketing system has provided us with one of the highest standards of living in the world. We have to admit, however, that marketing—as we know it in the United States—has many critics. Marketing activity is especially open to criticism because it is the part of business most visible to the public. There is nothing like a pocket-book issue for getting consumers excited!

Typical complaints about marketing include:

Advertising is annoying, dishonest, and wasteful.

Product quality is terrible—they just don't build things like they used to!

Marketing makes people too materialistic—it motivates them toward the "almighty dollar" instead of social needs.

Easy consumer credit makes people buy things they don't need and can't really afford.

Too many unnecessary products are offered.

Packaging and labeling are often confusing and deceptive.

Middlemen add to the cost of distribution and raise prices without providing anything in return.

Marketers are destroying our environment.

Advertising is corrupting the minds of children and putting too much sex and violence on TV.

Greedy business people create monopolies which limit output and raise prices.

Distribution costs are too high.

Retailers are cheating the public.

There are too many unsafe products on the market.

Marketing serves the rich and exploits the poor.

Such complaints cannot and should not be taken lightly. They show that many Americans aren't happy with some part of our marketing system. The strong public support that consumer advocates like Ralph Nader have received shows that not all consumers feel they are being treated like kings and queens. If business people ignore these complaints, there could be strong pressure for the government to reshape our macro-marketing system. Already, some of our nation's leaders are calling for national economic planning instead of depending on a market-directed system.[12]

Conclusion

In this chapter we have defined two levels of marketing: micro-marketing and macro-marketing. A close review of the complaints against marketing suggests that there are basically two levels of criticism also. Some are concerned with marketing's overall role in society (macro-marketing). Others are concerned with the activities of individual organizations (micro-marketing).

This chapter has gone into macro-marketing in some detail because marketing managers should not forget that their organizations are just small parts of a bigger macro-marketing system. We saw how economic decisions are made—in both planned and market-directed economies. We talked about the nature of markets and how and why central markets develop. Finally, the role of marketing in economic development and in mass production was considered. The importance of the universal marketing functions was emphasized.

Although the major emphasis in this chapter was on macro-marketing, the emphasis of this book is on micro-marketing. We believe that most criticisms of marketing are the result of ineffective decision making at the micro level. Therefore, the best way to answer some of this criticism is to educate future business people, like you, to be more efficient and socially responsible decision makers. This will help improve the performance of individual organizations. Eventually, it should also make our macro-marketing system work better.

The effect of micro-level decisions on society will be discussed throughout the text. Then, in Chapter 19—after you have begun to understand how and why producers and consumers think and behave the way they do—we will return to macro-marketing. We will try to evaluate how well both macro-marketing and micro-marketing perform in our market-directed economic system.

Questions for discussion

1 It is fairly easy to see why people do not beat a path to the mousetrap manufacturer's door, but would they be similarly indifferent if some food processor developed a revolutionary new food product which would provide all necessary nutrients in small pills for about $100 per year per person?

2 Distinguish between macro- and micro-marketing. Then explain how they are interrelated, if they are.

3 Distinguish between how economic decisions are made in a centrally planned economy and in a market-directed economy.

4 Explain *(a)* how a central market facilitates exchange and *(b)* how the addition of a middleman facilitates exchange even more.

5 Identify a "central market" in your own city and explain how it facilitates exchange.

6 Discuss the nature of marketing in a socialist economy. Would the functions that must be provided and the development of wholesaling and retailing systems be any different?

7 Describe a recent purchase you have made and indicate why that particular product was available at a store and, in particular, at that store.

8 Explain, in your own words, why the emphasis in this text is on micro-marketing.

9 Why is satisfying consumers apparently considered of equal importance with satisfying an organization's objectives in the text's definition of micro-marketing?

10 On the streets of cities in many developing countries, one sees old women and small boys selling cigarettes one at a time. The price per cigarette is higher than if the customer purchased a package or carton, as is typical in the United States. Some Americans are appalled at the unhygienic aspects of this method of distribution. Some are also appalled at the "inefficiency" of this method of distribution. Is this an inefficient method of distribution? Are consumers getting "ripped off"? If so, by whom? Who is benefiting?

Suggested cases

2 Mike's Home Service
28 "Save-A-Life" Franchise

When you finish this chapter, you should:

1 Know what the marketing concept is and how it should affect a firm's strategy planning.
2 Understand what a marketing manager does.
3 Know what marketing strategy planning is and why it will be the focus of this book.
4 Be familiar with the four Ps in a marketing mix
5 Recognize the important new terms shown in red.

MARKETING'S ROLE IN THE FIRM

Marketing and marketing management are important in our society—and in business firms. As you saw in Chapter One, marketing is concerned with anticipating needs and directing the flow of goods and services from producers to consumers. This is done to satisfy the needs of consumers and accomplish both the economy's (the macro view) and the firm's (the micro view) objectives.

To get a better understanding of both macro- and micro-marketing, we are going to emphasize micro-marketing. That is, we are going to look at things from the point of view of the marketing manager—the one who makes a company's important marketing decisions.

THE MARKETING CONCEPT—A MODERN VIEW OF BUSINESS

In a modern economy, marketing management is very important. But this hasn't always been true. It is only recently that more and more producers, wholesalers, and retailers have begun to see the importance of marketing planning. These companies used to think mainly about making a product. Now they focus on customers and try to aim the company's total effort toward satisfying them.

From the production era to the marketing era

The story of this change was told very well by R. J. Keith—a top executive of Pillsbury, Inc.—a manufacturer of flour, cake mixes, and animal feeds.[1]

FROM THE PRODUCTION TO THE SALES ERA

The marketing concept was a long time coming to Pillsbury. The company was formed in 1869 and continued until about 1930 in what Keith called the production era. The **production era** was a time when few manufactured products were available and the company's focus was on production. Beginning in 1930, the company went into the sales era. The **sales era** was a time when the company emphasized selling to its middlemen and final consumers. Competition was increasing, and Pillsbury became aware that it was very important to attract both its middlemen and the middlemen's customers.

TO THE MARKETING DEPARTMENT ERA

The sales era continued until about 1950. By then, Pillsbury had developed many new products. Sales were growing rapidly. Someone was needed to tie together the efforts of production, research, purchasing, and sales. As Pillsbury faced up to this job, the sales era was replaced by the marketing department era. The **marketing department era** was a time when there was heavy emphasis on short-run policy planning—to tie together the firm's activities. Finding people trained in short-run marketing policy making was difficult. For three or four years the company worked at learning how to turn ideas into products and products into profits.

TO THE MARKETING COMPANY ERA

In a relatively few years, Pillsbury had developed a staff with a marketing management approach. Then, in 1958, the company went all the way—into the marketing company era. The **marketing company era** is a time when—in addition to short-run marketing planning—the total company effort is guided by the marketing concept. Now, Pillsbury's marketing specialists look and plan three to ten years ahead.

What does the marketing concept mean in business?

The **marketing concept** means that a firm aims all its efforts on satisfying its customers—at a profit. This is really a new idea in business. It replaces the production-oriented way of thinking. **Production orientation** means making products which are easy to produce, and *then* trying to sell them. **Marketing orientation** means trying to carry out the marketing concept.

The marketing concept calls for changing the firm's ways of doing things. Instead of trying to get customers to buy what the firm has produced, a marketing-oriented firm would try to produce what customers want.

Those who believe in the marketing concept feel that customers' needs should be the firm's main focus. They feel that the firm's resources should be organized to satisfy those needs.

Three basic ideas are included in the definition of the marketing concept:

1. A customer orientation.
2. A total company effort.
3. Profit—not just sales—as a goal of the firm.

"If the customer wants ice cream with mustard sauce, then that's what we're serving!"

Carrying out the marketing concept, therefore, might require three related changes:

1. A change in management attitudes.
2. A change in the firm's organization structure.
3. A change in its management methods and procedures.

Changes in all three areas would probably be needed if the firm really wanted to adopt the marketing concept.

The typical production orientation is a road block

Give the customers what they need—this may seem so obvious and logical that it may be hard for you to understand why the marketing concept is such a new idea. However, people haven't always done the logical and obvious. In a typical company, production managers thought mainly about getting out the product. Accountants were interested only in balancing the books. Financial people looked after the company's cash position. And sales people were mainly concerned with getting orders. Each person saw the rest of the business working around him. No one was concerned with whether the whole system made sense. As long as the company made a profit, each department went merrily on—"doing its own thing." Unfortunately, this is still true in most companies today.

"Production orientation" refers to the typical lack of a central focus in a business firm. To be fair to the production people, however, it also is seen in sales-oriented sales representatives, advertising-oriented agency people, finance-oriented finance people, and so on. We will use "production orientation" to cover all such narrow thinking.

Figure 2–1A
A business as a box (most departments have high fences)

Figure 2–1B
Total system view of a business (implementing marketing concept; still have departments but all guided by what customer wants)

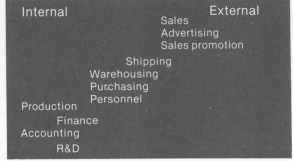

It should be a "sharing" situation

Ideally, all managers should work together because the output from one department may be the input to another. But managers in production-oriented firms tend to build "fences" around their own departments—as seen in Figure 2–1A. Each department runs its own affairs for its own benefit. There may be committees to try to get them to work together. But usually each department head comes to such meetings with the idea of protecting his department's interests.

It's easy to slip into a production orientation

It is very easy to slip into a production-oriented way of thinking. Production managers, for example, might prefer to have long production runs of easy-to-produce, standardized products. And retailers might prefer only daytime weekday hours—avoiding nights, Saturdays, and Sundays, when many customers would prefer to shop. Differences in outlook between production-oriented and marketing-oriented managers are shown in Figure 2–2.

Work together . . . do a better job

In a firm that has accepted the marketing concept, however, the fences come down. There are still departments, of course, because there are efficiencies in specialization. But the total system's effort is guided by what customers want—instead of what each department would like to do.

In such a firm, it is more realistic to view the business as a box with both an internal and an external section. See Figure 2–1B. Here, there are some internal departments concerned mainly with affairs inside the firm—production, accounting, and research and development (R&D). And there are external departments concerned with outsiders—sales, advertising, and sales promotion. Finally, there are departments that must be concerned with both the internal and the external sections—warehousing, shipping, purchasing, finance, and personnel. The efforts of *all* of these departments are aimed at satisfying some market needs—at a profit.

Figure 2–2
Some differences in outlook between adopters of the marketing concept and the typical production-oriented managers[2]

Marketing orientation	Attitudes and procedures	Production orientation
Customer needs determine company plans	← Attitudes toward customers →	They should be glad we exist, trying to cut costs and bring out better products
Company makes what it can sell	← Product offering →	Company sells what it can make
To determine customer needs and how well company is satisfying them	← Role of marketing research →	To determine customer reaction, if used at all
Focus on locating new opportunities	← Interest in innovation →	Focus is on technology and cost cutting
A critical objective	← Importance of profit →	A residual, what's left after all costs are covered
Seen as a customer service	← Role of customer credit →	Seen as a necessary evil
Designed for customer convenience and as a selling tool	← Role of packaging →	Seen merely as protection for the product
Set with customer requirements and costs in mind	← Inventory levels →	Set with production requirements in mind
Seen as a customer service	← Transportation arrangements →	Seen as an extension of production and storage activities, with emphasis on cost minimization
Need-satisfying benefits of products and services	← Focus of advertising →	Product features and quality, maybe how products are made
Help the customer to buy if the product fits his needs, while coordinating with rest of firm—including production, inventory control, advertising, etc.	← Role of sales force →	Sell the customer, don't worry about coordination with other promotion efforts or rest of firm

Marketing concept forces change

The marketing concept is really very powerful if taken seriously. It forces the company (1) to think through what it is doing, and why, and then (2) to develop a plan for accomplishing its objectives. Where the marketing concept has been wholeheartedly accepted and carried out, it has led to major changes in the way the firm operates—and often to higher profits.

THE MARKETING CONCEPT IS USEFUL FOR NONPROFIT ORGANIZATIONS, TOO

Most of this book will focus on how to apply the marketing concept in a business firm. But the same general principles can be applied directly to nonprofit organizations. The Red Cross, art museums, and government agencies are all seeking to satisfy some consumer groups. The objectives are different but the marketing concept works here, too![3]

THE MANAGEMENT JOB IN MARKETING

Hitting the target customers

The marketing manager wants to satisfy the needs of a particular group of customers—the target—with a particular good or service. Out of all the products offered to customers, the marketing manager wants to be sure that *his* product will succeed. How can he do this?

First, the marketing manager is a manager. So let's see first what a manager does.

The marketing management job is continuous

The **marketing manager's job** consists of three basic tasks: planning, implementing, and control. See Figure 2–3. The planning job consists of two parts: (1) finding attractive opportunities and (2) developing marketing strategies. The marketing manager can't be satisfied with only planning present strategies. In a competitive marketplace, he is always looking for new opportunities and making plans for new strategies. Developing marketing strategies is the main focus of this book. Without a well-defined strategy, there are no guidelines for implementing or control.

Only after the basic strategy is developed can managers begin to carry out (implement) that strategy (personnel selection, salary administration, retailer selection, and so on). Making the plan work may, in fact, take a greater part of the manager's time.

We will discuss control, too, since it provides feedback that may lead to changing marketing strategies. The tools most frequently used by the marketing manager are data processing, marketing research, and accounting.

All marketing jobs require planning

At first, it might seem that planning should concern only the top management of large companies. This isn't true. Even the smallest farmer, retailer, or wholesaler must plan a strategy.

Figure 2–3
The marketing management process

FINDING ATTRACTIVE OPPORTUNITIES

Most people have unsatisfied needs. Alert marketers can find opportunities all around them. But *attractive* opportunities will depend on (1) the firm's own resources and objectives and (2) what competition is doing or planning to do. Let's see the kinds of opportunities which may be found. Figure 2–4 shows that there are four possibilities: market penetration, market development, product development, and diversification.

Figure 2–4
Four basic types of opportunities

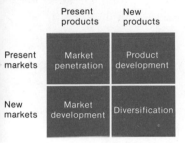

Market penetration means a firm tries to increase sales of its present products in its present markets—probably through a more aggressive effort. Research might show that there is a chance to increase the customer's rate of use. New promotion appeals might be effective. McDonald's could have "Ronald McDonald" invite the kids in for a special offer. Or more stores could be added in an area—to make it convenient for present customers to buy more. Obviously, effective planning would be aided by a real understanding of why some people are buying now and what might encourage them to buy more.

Market development means a firm tries to increase sales by selling its present products in new markets. This might involve, for example, McDonald's adding new stores in new areas—perhaps in downtown locations, in schools or hospital lobbies, or even in foreign countries. Or it might only mean advertising in different media to reach new customers.

Product development means the firm offers new or improved products for present markets. Here, the company understands its market's needs and sees the possibility of adding or modifying product features to satisfy the present market better. For example, McDonald's added breakfast for adults and cookies for kids.

Diversification means moving into totally different lines of business. This might mean introducing entirely new products or entering new markets.

Which opportunities come first?

Most firms tend to think first of greater market penetration. If they already have as big a share as they can get in their present markets, then they may think of market development—finding new markets for their present products.

Marketers who have a good understanding of their present markets may see opportunities in product development—especially because they already have a way of reaching their present customers.

The most challenging opportunities are in diversification. Here, both new products and new markets are involved. The farther the new idea is from what the firm is doing now, the more attractive it may look. But it will be harder to evaluate. And opportunities far from a firm's current operations usually mean much higher risks.

WHAT IS MARKETING STRATEGY PLANNING?

Marketing planning means finding attractive opportunities and developing profitable marketing strategies. But what is a "marketing strategy"?

We have used these words rather casually so far. Now let's see what they really mean.

What is a marketing strategy?

A **marketing strategy** is a "big picture" of what a firm will do in some market. It consists of two parts:

1. A **target market**—a fairly homogeneous (similar) group of customers to whom a company wishes to appeal.
2. A **marketing mix**—the controllable variables which the company puts together to satisfy this target group.

The importance of target customers in this process can be seen in Figure 2–5, where the customer—the "C" in the center of the diagram—is surrounded by the controllable variables which we call the "marketing mix." A typical marketing mix would include some product or service offered at a price, with some promotion to tell potential customers about the availability of the product.

Strategy planning takes place within a framework

A marketing manager's strategy planning does not take place in a vacuum. Instead, the manager works within a framework with many uncontrollable variables. He has to consider these variables even though he can't

Figure 2–5
Marketing manager's framework

Cultural and social environment

Political and legal environment

THE MARKETING MIX

C

Resources and objectives of firm

Economic environment

Competitive environment

Controllable variables

Uncontrollable variables

A marketing manager must plan within an uncontrollable environment.

control them. Figure 2–5 illustrates this framework. It shows that the typical marketing manager has to be concerned about the cultural and social environment, the political and legal environment, the economic environment, the competitive environment, and the resources and objectives of the firm. We will talk about these uncontrollable variables in more detail in Chapter 3.

SELECTING A MARKET-ORIENTED STRATEGY IS TARGET MARKETING

Target marketing is not mass marketing

It is important to see that a marketing strategy focuses on some target customers. We will call this market-oriented approach "target marketing"— to distinguish it from "mass marketing." **Target marketing** focuses on some specific target customers. **Mass marketing**—the typical production-

Figure 2–6
Production-oriented and marketing-oriented managers have different views of the market

Production-oriented manager sees everyone as basically similar and practices "mass marketing"

Marketing-oriented manager sees everyone as different and practices "target marketing"

oriented approach—focuses on "everyone." Production-oriented managers just assume that everyone is the same and will want whatever their firms offer. They don't try to find out what *some* customers might want. Instead, everyone is considered a potential customer. See Figure 2–6.

"MASS MARKETERS" MAY DO TARGET MARKETING

Commonly used terms can be confusing here. The words "mass marketing" and "mass marketers" do not mean the same thing. Far from it! "Mass *marketing*" means selling to "everyone" as explained above—while "mass *marketers*" like General Electric, Procter & Gamble, and Sears, Roebuck are *not* aiming at "everyone." They do aim at clearly defined target markets. The confusion with "mass marketing" occurs because their target markets usually are large and spread out.

We'll use the words "strategy planning" to mean "marketing strategy planning" and "target marketing." We want to avoid "mass marketing."

DEVELOPING MARKETING MIXES FOR MARKETING STRATEGIES

There are many marketing mix variables

There are many possible ways to satisfy the needs of target customers. A product can have many different features, colors, and appearances. The package can be of various sizes, colors, or materials. The brand names and trademarks can be changed. Services can be adjusted. Various advertising media (newspapers, magazines, radio, television, billboards) may be used. A company's own sales force or other sales specialists can be used. Different prices can be charged, and so on. With so many variables available, the question is: Is there any way of simplifying the selection of marketing mixes? And the answer is yes.

The four "Ps" make up a marketing mix

It is useful to reduce the number of variables in the marketing mix to four basic ones:

Product
Place
Promotion
Price

**Figure 2–7
A marketing strategy**

It helps to think of the four major parts of a marketing mix as the "four Ps." Figure 2–7 emphasizes their relationship and their focus on the customer—"C."

CUSTOMER IS NOT PART OF THE MARKETING MIX

The customer is shown surrounded by the four Ps in Figure 2–7. This has led some students to think that the customer is part of the marketing mix. This is not true. The customer should be the target of all marketing efforts. The customer is placed in the center of the diagram to show this—the C stands for the target market.

Table 2–1
Strategic decision areas

Product	Place	Promotion	Price
Features	Channels	Promotion blend	Flexibility
Accessories	Market exposure	Kind of sales people	Level
Installation	Kinds of middlemen	Selection	Introductory pricing
Instructions	Who handles storing	Motivation	Discounts
Service	and transporting	Kind of advertising	Allowances
Warranty	Service levels	Media type	Geographic terms
Product lines		Copy thrust	
Package			
Brand name			

Table 2–1 shows some of the variables in the four Ps which will be discussed in later chapters. For now, let's just describe each P briefly.

Product—the right one for the target

The Product area is concerned with developing the right "product" for the target market. This product may involve a physical product and/or service. The important thing to remember in the Product area is that your product—or service—should satisfy some customers' needs.

Under Product we will cover problems connected with developing products and product lines. We will also talk about the characteristics of various kinds of products so that you will be able to make generalizations about product classes. This will help you develop whole marketing mixes more quickly. Although most of this text will be concerned with physical products, the principles also apply to services. This is important because the service side of our economy is large and growing.

Place—reaching the target

Place is concerned with getting the right product to the target market. A product isn't much good to a customer if it isn't available when and where it's wanted. In the Place area, we will see where, when, and by whom the goods and services can be offered for sale.

Goods and services move to consumers through channels of distribution. A **channel of distribution** is any series of firms from producer to final user or consumer. A channel can include several kinds of middlemen. Marketing managers work with these channels. So our study of Place is very important to marketing strategy planning.

Sometimes a channel system is quite short. It may run directly from a producer to a final user or consumer. Usually, it is more complex—involving many different kinds of middlemen. And if a marketing manager has several different target markets, several channels of distribution might be needed. See Figure 2–8.

Figure 2–8
Four possible (basic) channels of distribution for consumer goods

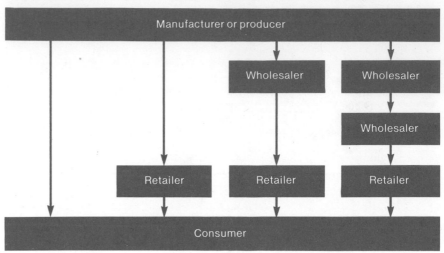

**Promotion—telling and
selling the customer**

Price—making it right

The third P, Promotion, is concerned with telling the target market about the "right" product. Promotion includes personal selling, mass selling, and sales promotion. It is the marketing manager's job to blend these methods.

Personal selling involves direct face-to-face relationships between sellers and potential customers. Personal selling lets the salesperson adapt the firm's marketing mix to each potential customer. But this individual attention comes at a price. Personal selling can be very expensive. Often this personal effort has to be blended with mass selling and sales promotion.

Mass selling is communicating with large numbers of customers at the same time. **Advertising** is any paid form of nonpersonal presentation of ideas, goods, or services by an identified sponsor. It is the main form of mass selling.

Sales promotion refers to those promotion activities—other than personal selling and mass selling—that encourage customers to buy. This can involve designing and arranging for the distribution of novelties, point-of-purchase materials, store signs, catalogs, and circulars. Sales promotion people try to help the personal selling and mass selling specialists.

In addition to developing the right Product, Place, and Promotion, marketing managers must also decide the right Price. In setting a price, they must consider the nature of competition in the target market. They must also try to estimate customer reaction to possible prices. Besides this, they also must know current practices as to markups, discounts, and other terms of sale. Further, they must be aware of legal restrictions on pricing.

If customers won't accept the Price, all of the planning effort will be wasted. So you can see that Price is an important area for the marketing manager.

Relative importance of the four Ps

All four Ps are needed in a marketing mix. In fact, they should all be tied together. But is any one more important than the others? Generally speaking, the answer is no. When a marketing mix is being developed, all decisions about the Ps should be made at the same time. That's why the four Ps are arranged around the customer (C) in a circle—to show that they all are equally important.

Strategy guides implementing

Let's sum up our discussion of marketing mix planning this far. We develop a *Product* that we feel will satisfy the target customers. We find a way *(Place)* to reach our target customers. *Promotion* tells the target customers about the availability of the product that has been designed for them. Then, the *Price* is set after estimating expected customer reaction to the total offering and the costs of getting it to them.

These ideas can be seen more clearly with an example in the home decorating market.

A BRITISH PAINT MANUFACTURER LOOKS AT THE HOME DECORATING MARKET

The experience of a paint manufacturer in England illustrates the strategic planning process and how strategic decisions help decide how the plan is carried out.

First, this paint manufacturer's marketing manager interviewed many potential customers and studied the various needs for the products he could offer. By combining several kinds of customer needs and some available demographic data, he came up with the view of the market shown in Figure 2–9. In the following description of these markets, note that useful marketing mixes come to mind immediately.

There turned out to be a large market for "general-purpose paint"— about 60 percent of the potential for all kinds of paint products. The manufacturer did not consider this market because he was not a large producer. Further, he did not want to compete "head-on" with the many companies already in this market. The other four markets—which were placed in the four corners of a market diagram simply to show that they were different markets—he called Helpless Housewife, Handy Helper, Crafty Craftsman, and Cost-Conscious Couple.

The Helpless Housewife—the manufacturer found out—really didn't know much about home painting or specific products. She needed a helpful paint retailer who could supply not only paint and other supplies but also much advice. And the retailer who sold her the paint would want it to be of fairly good quality so that she would be satisfied with the results.

The Handy Helper was a jack-of-all-trades who knew a great deal about paint and painting. He wanted a good-quality product and was satisfied

Figure 2–9
The home decorating market (paint area) in England[4]

"We could diversify into toys . . . we wouldn't be too far from what we already know!"

to buy from an old-fashioned hardware store or lumber yard—which usually sells mainly to men. Similarly, the Crafty Craftsman was willing to buy from a retailer who would not attract female customers. In fact, these older men didn't want to buy paint at all. They wanted pigments, oils, and other things to mix their own paint.

Finally, the Cost-Conscious Couple was young, had low income, and lived in an apartment. In England, an apartment dweller must paint the apartment during the course of the lease. This is an important factor for at least some tenants as they choose their paint. If you were a young apartment dweller with limited income, what sort of paint would you want? Some couples in England—the manufacturer discovered—did not want very good paint! In fact, something not much better than whitewash would do fine.

The paint manufacturer decided to cater to "Cost-Conscious Couples" with a marketing mix flowing from the description of that market. That is, knowing what he did about them, he offered a low-quality paint (Product), made it available in lower-income apartment neighborhoods (Place), aimed his price-oriented ads at these areas (Promotion), and, of course, offered an attractive low price (Price). The manufacturer has been extremely successful with this strategy—giving his customers what they really want, even though the product is of low quality.

THE IMPORTANCE OF MARKETING STRATEGY PLANNING

Most of our emphasis in this book will be on the planning phase of the marketing manager's job—for a good reason. The "one-time" strategy decisions—the decisions that decide what business the company is in and the general strategy it will follow—may be more important than has been realized. In fact, an extremely good plan might be carried out badly and still be profitable, while a poor but well-executed plan can lose money. The case histories that follow show the importance of planning and why we are going to emphasize strategy planning throughout this text.

Sears Roebuck found its own market

Sears Roebuck has had success since World War II because of a good new plan. While other large retailers were concentrating downtown, Sears tried a new strategy—developing stores with their own parking in suburban areas where the population was growing fast. Some conventional retailers predicted Sears would fall. But the company knew what it was doing. Sears placed its new units away from competition. It provided ample parking space and built stores so large and well stocked that customers could do all their shopping under one roof.

Instead of trying to meet competition head on, Sears developed a strategy for reaching *some* target markets that had not been completely satisfied before. At the same time, people were shifting to the suburbs.

Henry Ford's strategy worked—until General Motors caught up

Henry Ford is remembered for developing the mass production techniques that produced a car for the masses. His own view of his approach, however, is that mass production developed *because* of his basic decision to build a car for the masses. In those days, cars were almost custom-built for the wealthy, the sports drivers, and other specialty buyers. Ford decided on a different strategy. He wanted to produce a car that could appeal to the majority of potential buyers.

Henry Ford saw a market for millions of cars.

Certainly, new production ideas were needed to carry out Ford's strategy. But the really important decision was the initial *market-oriented* decision that there was a market for millions of cars in the $500 price range. Much of what followed was just carrying out this decision. Ford's strategy to offer a low priced car was an outstanding success and millions of Model Ts were sold in the 1910s and 1920s. But there was a defect in his strategy. To keep the price down, a very basic car was offered with "any color you want as long as it's black."

In the 1920s, General Motors' management felt that there was room for a new strategy. Their basic decision was to add colors and styling—even if this meant raising prices. They also hit upon the idea of looking at the market as having several segments (based on price and quality), and then offering a full line of cars with entries at the top of each of these price ranges. They planned to appeal to quality-conscious consumers—always offering good values. The General Motors strategy was not an immediate success. But they stuck with their plan through the 1920s and slowly caught up with Ford. Finally, in May 1927, Ford closed down his assembly line for 18 months and switched his strategy to meet the new competition. He stopped producing the long-successful Model T and introduced the more market-oriented Model A. But General Motors was already well on its way to the commanding market position it now holds.[5]

The watch industry sees new strategies

The conventional watchmakers—both domestic and foreign—had always aimed at customers who thought of watches as high-price, high-quality symbols to mark special events like graduation, retirement, and so on. These manufacturers produced expensive watches and stressed their symbolic appeal in advertising. Their promotion was heavily concentrated in the gift-buying seasons of Christmas and graduation time. Jewelry stores were the main retail outlets—charging large markups.

This commonly accepted strategy of the major watch companies ignored those who just wanted to tell the time and were interested in low-priced watches that kept time reasonably well. So the U.S. Time Company developed a successful strategy around its "Timex" watches and became the world's largest watch company.[6]

U.S. Time completely upset the watch industry—both foreign and domestic—by not only offering a good product (with a one-year guarantee) at a lower price, but also by using new, lower-cost channels of distribution. Its watches are widely available in drug stores, discount houses, and nearly any other retail outlet which will carry them.

Now, Timex itself faces competition from the digital watchmakers. Texas Instruments Company and other electronics firms have entered the market with an entirely new time-keeping idea. They have also been cutting prices drastically, while following Timex's lead into widespread distribution. Some of the traditional watchmakers are closing their factories. Even Timex is threatened because it is not deeply involved in electronics. Here, technological improvements combined with modern marketing strategy planning may completely change this whole industry in only a few years.[7]

Creative strategy planning needed for survival

Such dramatic shifts in strategy may surprise conventional production-oriented managers. But they are becoming much more common—especially in industries where some of the firms have accepted the marketing concept.

What all this means is that a marketing manager and his firm may have to pay less attention to finding ways to use a company's present resources—a typical production-oriented approach—and pay more attention to locating new market opportunities. By looking for breakthrough opportunities, a company may find profit possibilities which might otherwise be missed.

Creative strategy planning is becoming even more important because profits no longer can be won just by spending more money on plant and equipment. Moreover, domestic and foreign competition threatens those who can't create more satisfying goods and services. New markets, new customers, and new ways of doing things must be found if companies are to operate profitably in the future—and contribute to our macro-marketing system.

STRATEGIC PLANS AND PROGRAMS MUST BE DEVELOPED—EVENTUALLY

Our focus has been, and will continue to be, on developing marketing strategies. But it is also important to see that eventually marketing managers must develop strategic plans and marketing programs. However, detailed study of these ideas is beyond the scope of this book. We can only discuss them briefly here. See Figure 2–10.

What is a strategic plan?

A strategy is a "big picture" of what a firm will do in some market. A strategic plan goes farther. A **strategic plan** includes the time-related

A strategic plan includes the details for carrying out a strategy.

Figure 2–10
Elements of a firm's marketing program

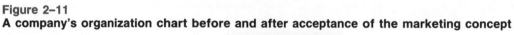

$$\left.\begin{array}{c}\text{Target market}\\+\\\text{Marketing}\\\text{mix}\end{array}\right\} = \begin{array}{c}\text{Marketing}\\\text{strategy}\end{array} + \begin{array}{c}\text{Time related}\\\text{details and}\\\text{control}\\\\\text{procedures}\end{array} = \left.\begin{array}{c}\text{Strategic}\\\text{plan}\\+\\\text{Other}\\\text{strategic}\\\text{plans}\end{array}\right\} \begin{array}{c}\text{A firm's}\\\text{marketing}\\\text{program}\end{array}$$

details for carrying out a strategy. It should spell out the following in detail: (1) what marketing mix is to be offered to whom (i.e., the target market), and for how long; (2) what company resources (shown as costs) will be required, at what rate (month by month, perhaps); and (3) what results are expected (sales and profits, perhaps month by month). It should also

Figure 2–11
A company's organization chart before and after acceptance of the marketing concept

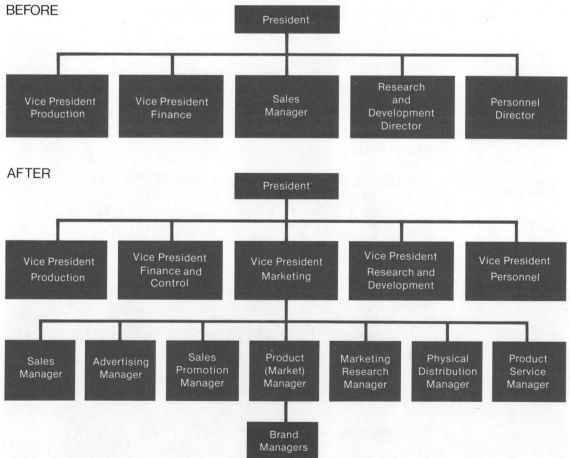

include some control procedures so that whoever is to carry out the plan will know when things are going wrong. This might be something as simple as comparing actual sales against expected sales—with a "warning flag" to be raised whenever total sales fall below a certain level.

Several plans make a program

Most companies have more than one strategic plan at the same time. Typically, they aim at several target markets and prepare different marketing mixes for each one. A **marketing program** blends all of a firm's strategic plans into one "big" plan. This program, then, is the responsibility of the whole company.

ORGANIZING TO PLAN AND IMPLEMENT MARKETING STRATEGIES

Pointing the company toward its goal

The first and most important step in applying the marketing concept is a serious commitment to a customer orientation. Without acceptance of this idea—at least by top management—any change in the organization structure won't really matter.

Some organization helps

After top management has accepted the marketing concept, some formal reorganization is usually desirable. The product planning function is often under the production or R&D (research and development) department. Pricing is under the finance or accounting department. And sales and advertising are often separate departments.

All these activities involve the customer, so they should be under the direction of the marketing manager. The marketing manager should report directly to top management—along with the heads of production, R&D, finance, and accounting. The arrangement of a particular marketing department depends on the strategies of that company and the personalties involved. Organization charts in one company before and after adoption of the marketing concept are shown in Figure 2–11.

Who should organize and run the total system?

Top management is responsible for developing and running a *total system* designed to meet the needs of target customers. Ideally, the whole

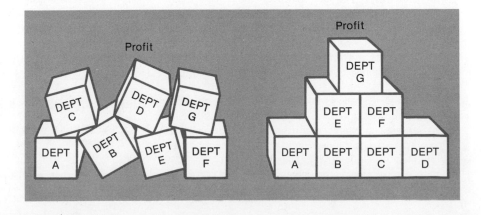

company becomes customer-oriented. All departments pull together to reach its objectives. We will still have departments—because there are advantages in job specialization. But instead of battles between various departments, a marketing-oriented system would do some marketing research, perhaps run some market tests, and figure potential costs and *company* (not departmental) profits for possible strategies. Then it would decide what is best for the *firm*—not just what is best for any one department.

In such a system, the marketing manager would help develop this "total system" attitude within the firm. He must work regularly with customers and is in an ideal position to tie things together.

Who is suited to lead a marketing-oriented company?

Many marketing managers probably will come out of sales management because they are more likely to be familiar with target customers. But this isn't always true. The marketing manager and a marketing-oriented president could come from any specialty. In one cosmetic company—as might be expected in this type of business—the advertising and sales promotion manager gradually assumed major planning and coordinating responsibilities. In another firm, however—which produced highly technical custom-built products—the production manager was the leader in applying the marketing concept.

The most important point is that the prospective marketing manager and top manager accept the marketing concept.

Conclusion

Marketing's role within a marketing-oriented firm is to tie the company together. The marketing concept provides direction. It stresses that the firm's efforts should be focused on satisfying some target markets—at a profit. Production-oriented firms tend to forget this. Often, the various departments within such a firm let their natural conflicts of interest lead to building "fences" around their areas. Then, even coordinating committees may not be able to redirect the firm's efforts.

Complete acceptance of the marketing concept would probably lead to new organization arrangements. But the really important matter is acceptance by top management of the marketing concept. Without this, new arrangements probably won't make much difference.

The job of marketing management is one of continuous planning, implementing, and control. The marketing manager must constantly study the environment—seeking attractive opportunities. And new strategies must be planned continually. Potential target markets must be matched with marketing mixes that the firm can offer.

Then attractive strategies are chosen for implementation. Controls are needed to be sure that the plans are carried out successfully. If anything goes wrong along the way, this continual feedback should cause the process to be started over again—with the marketing manager planning more attractive marketing strategies.

A marketing mix has four variables—the four Ps: Product, Place, Promotion, and Price. Most of this text is concerned with developing profitable marketing mixes for clearly defined target markets. So, after several chapters on selecting target markets, we will discuss each of the four Ps in greater detail.

Questions for discussion

1 Define the marketing concept in your own words, and then explain why the notion of profit is usually included in this definition.

2. Define the marketing concept in your own words,

and then suggest how acceptance of this concept might affect the organization and operation of your college.

3. Distinguish between production orientation and marketing orientation, illustrating with local examples.

4. Explain why a firm should view its internal activities as part of a "total system." Illustrate your answer for *(a)* a large grocery products manufacturer, *(b)* a plumbing wholesaler, and *(c)* a department store chain.

5. Does the acceptance of the marketing concept almost require that a firm view itself as a "total system"?

6. Explain the major differences among the four basic types of opportunities discussed in the text, and cite examples for two of these types.

7. Explain how new opportunities may be seen by defining a firm's markets more precisely. Illustrate for a situation where you feel there is an opportunity—i.e., an unsatisfied market segment—even if it is not very large.

8. Explain why a firm might want to pursue a market penetration opportunity before pursuing one involving product development or diversification.

9. Distinguish clearly between a marketing strategy and a marketing mix. Use an example.

10. Distinguish clearly between mass marketing and target marketing. Use an example.

11. Why is the customer placed in the center of the four Ps in the text diagram of a marketing strategy? Explain, using a specific example from your own experience.

12. Explain, in your own words, what each of the four Ps involves.

13. Discuss the importance of planning to implementing and controlling.

14. Distinguish between a strategy and a strategic plan.

15. Distinguish between a strategic plan and a marketing program.

16. Outline a marketing strategy for each of the following new products:

a. A radically new design for a haircomb.
b. A new fishing reel.
c. A new "wonder drug."
d. A new industrial stapling machine.

17. Recently the Federal Trade Commission (FTC) accused Sears, Roebuck of dealing unfairly with customers. The FTC argued that Sears' print and television campaign for Lady Kenmore dishwashers between 1972 and 1975 was misleading because it suggested that the appliances would remove all food residue without presoaking. Part of the FTC's evidence came from Sears' owner's manual, which suggests that one scour baked-on foods before putting dishes in the machine. Assuming the FTC is correct in its argument, how could this situation come about? That is, how is it that a company could say one thing in one place and another in another place?

Suggested cases

1 Taylor Incorporated

3 Modern Manufacturing Company

30 Auto Specialties Manufacturing Company

ECONOMICS FUNDAMENTALS

When you finish this
appendix, you should:

1 Understand the "law of diminishing demand."
2 Know what a market is.
3 Understand demand and supply curves—and how they set the size of a market and its price level.
4 Know about elasticity of demand and supply.
5 Recognize the important new terms shown in red.

A marketing manager should be an expert on markets and the nature of competition in different kinds of markets. The economists "demand and supply" analysis gives us useful tools for studying the nature of demand. In particular, you should master the ideas of a demand curve and demand elasticity. A firm's demand curve shows how the target customers see the firm's offering. And the effect of both demand and supply curves helps set the size of the market and the market price. These ideas are discussed more fully in the following sections.

PRODUCTS AND MARKETS AS SEEN BY CUSTOMERS AND POTENTIAL CUSTOMERS

Economists provide useful insights

The way potential customers (not the firm) see a firm's good or service has an important effect on how much they are willing to pay for it, where it should be made available, and how eager they are to obtain it. In other words, it has a very direct effect on marketing strategy planning.

Economists have been concerned with these basic problems for years. Their tools can be quite helpful in showing how customers view products and how markets behave.

Economists see individual customers choosing among alternatives

Economics is sometimes called the "dismal" science because it shows that customers just can't buy everything they want. Since most customers have a limited income over any period of time, they must balance their needs and the costs of various products.

Economists usually assume that customers have a fairly definite set of preferences. When they are given a set of alternatives, it is assumed that they evaluate these alternatives in terms of whether they will make them feel better (or worse) or in some way improve (or change) their situation.

But what exactly is the nature of the customer's desire for a particular product?

Usually the argument is given in terms of the extra utility (value) the customer can get by buying more of a particular product or how much utility would be lost if he had less of the product. (Students who wish more discussion of this approach should refer to indifference curve analysis in any standard economics text.)

Utility is a theoretical idea. It may be easier to understand if we look at what happens when the price of one of the customer's usual purchases changes.

The law of diminishing demand

Suppose that a consumer were buying potatoes in 10-pound bags at the same time he bought other foods—such as meat and vegetables. If the consumer is mainly interested in buying a certain amount of foodstuffs, and the price of potatoes drops, it seems reasonable to expect that he will switch some of his food money to potatoes—and away from some other foods. But if the price of potatoes goes up, you would expect our consumer to buy fewer potatoes and more of other foods.

The general relation of price and quantity shown by this example is called the **law of diminishing demand**—which says that if the price of a product is raised, a smaller quantity will be demanded—and if the price of a product is lowered, a greater quantity will be demanded.

A group of customers makes a market

A market has a group of consumers who buy in a similar way. If price drops, the total quantity demanded by the group will increase. But if the price rises, the quantity demanded will decrease. "Real world" data supports this reasoning—especially for general product classes or "commodities" like potatoes.

The relationship between price and quantity demanded in the market for potatoes is shown in Table A–1. It is an example of what economists call a "demand schedule." Notice that as the price decreases, the quantity demanded increases. Total dollar sales or total revenue of the potato market is shown in the third column. Notice, however, that as prices go lower, the total *unit* sales increases—but the total revenue (total dollar sales) decreases. It is suggested that you fill in the missing blanks and watch the behavior of total revenue—an important figure for the marketing manager. We will explain what you should have seen—and why—a little later.

The demand curve— usually downsloping

If your only interest is seeing at which price customers would be willing to pay the greatest total revenue, the demand schedule may be enough. But a demand curve may be more helpful. A **demand curve** is a "picture"

Table A–1
Demand schedule for potatoes

Point	(1) Price of potatoes per bag (P)	(2) Quantity demanded (bags per month) (Q)	(3) Total revenue per month (P × Q = TR)
A	$0.80	8,000,000	$6,400,000
B	0.65	9,000,000	
C	0.50	11,000,000	5,500,000
D	0.35	14,000,000	
E	0.20	19,000,000	

of the relationship between price and quantity in a market—assuming that all other things stay the same. It is a graph of the demand schedule. Figure A–1 shows the demand curve for potatoes—really just a plotting of the demand schedule. It shows how many potatoes would be demanded by potential customers at various possible prices. This is known as a "downsloping demand curve."

Most demand curves are downsloping. It just shows that if prices were lowered, the quantity that customes will buy would increase.

Note that the demand curve only shows how customers would react to various prices. Usually, in a market, we see only one price at a time—not all of these prices. The curve just shows what quantities will be demanded—depending upon what price is set. You can see that most business people would like to set the price at a point where the resulting income was large.

Figure A–1
Demand curve for potatoes (10-pound bags)

Table A–2
Demand schedule for refrigerators

Point	(1) Price per refrigerator (P)	(2) Quantity demanded per year (Q)	(3) Total revenue per year (P × Q = TR)
A	$300	20,000	$ 6,000,000
B	250	70,000	17,500,000
C	200	130,000	26,000,000
D	150	210,000	31,500,000
E	100	310,000	31,000,000

Before talking about this, however, we should think about the demand schedule and curve for another product—to get a better picture of demand curves.

A refrigerator demand curve looks different

A different kind of demand curve is the one for refrigerators shown in Table A–2. Column (3) shows the total revenue that would be earned at various possible prices and quantities. Again, as the price of refrigerators goes down, the quantity demanded goes up. But here, unlike the potato example, total revenue increases—at least until the price drops to $150.

Every market has a demand curve—for some time period

These general demand relationships are true for all products. But each product has its own demand curve in each potential market—no matter how small the market. In other words, a particular demand curve has meaning only when tied to a particular market. We can think of demand curves for individuals, regions, and even countries. And the time period

Figure A–2
Demand curve for refrigerators

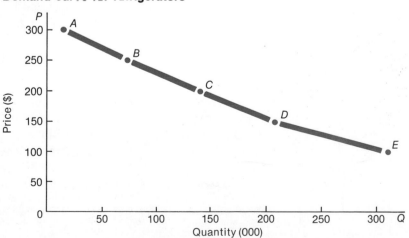

covered really should be stated. This is often ignored, however, because monthly or yearly periods are usually implied.

The difference between elastic and inelastic

The demand curve for refrigerators—see Figure A–2—is downsloping. But note that it is "flatter" than the curve for potatoes. It is quite important that you understand what this flatness means.

We will look at the flatness in terms of total revenue—since this is what interests business managers.*

When you filled in the total revenue column for potatoes, you should have noticed that total revenue would continue to decrease if the price were reduced. This is bad from a manager's point of view, and shows inelastic demand. **Inelastic demand** means that although the quantity demanded would increase if the price were decreased, the quantity demanded would not "stretch" enough—that is, it is not elastic enough—to increase total revenue.

In contrast, **elastic demand** means that if prices were dropped, the quantity demanded would stretch enough to increase total revenue. The upper part of the refrigerator demand curve is an example of elastic demand.

But note that if the refrigerator price were dropped from $150 to $100, total revenue would *decrease*. We can say, therefore, that between $150 and $100, demand is inelastic—that is, total revenue would decrease if price were lowered to $100.

Thus, elasticity is defined in terms of changes in total revenue. If total revenue would *increase* if price were lowered, then demand is said to be elastic. If total revenue would *decrease* if price were lowered, then demand is said to be inelastic.

TOTAL REVENUE MAY DECREASE OR INCREASE IF PRICE IS RAISED

A point that is often missed in talking about demand is what happens when prices are raised instead of lowered. With elastic demand, total revenue will decrease if the price is raised. With inelastic demand, total revenue would increase if the price is raised. If total revenue remains the same when prices change, then we have a special case known as "unitary elasticity of demand."

The possibility of raising price and increasing total revenue at the same time should be of special interest to managers. This occurs if the demand curve is inelastic—and is an attractive situation because total costs probably would not increase and might actually go down at smaller quantities!

The ways total revenue changes as prices are raised are shown in

* Strictly speaking, two curves should not be compared for flatness if the graph scales are different, but for current purposes we will do so to illustrate the idea of "elasticity of demand." Actually, it would be more correct to compare two curves for one commodity—on the same graph. Then, both the shape of the demand curve and its position on the graph would be important.

Figure A–3
Changes in total revenue as prices increase

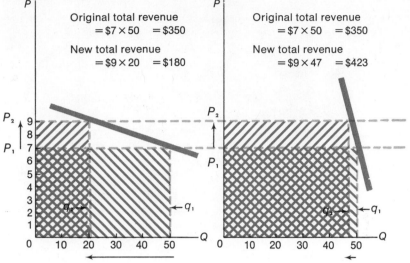

Figure A–3. Here, total revenue is shown as a rectangular area formed by a price and its related quantity.

P₁ is the original price here. The total potential revenue with this original price is shown by the area with the diagonal lines slanted down from the left. The possible total revenue with the new price, P₂, is shaded—with lines running diagonally upward from the left. At both prices, there is some overlap. So the important areas are those with only a single shading. Note that in the left-hand figure—where demand is elastic—the revenue added when price is increased is less than the revenue lost. (Compare only the single-shaded areas.) When demand is inelastic, however, only a small single-shaded revenue area is given up for a much larger one when price is raised.

An entire curve is not elastic or inelastic

It is important to see that it is wrong to talk about a whole demand curve as elastic or inelastic. Instead, elasticity for a particular curve refers to the change in total revenue between two points on a curve—and not along the whole curve. The change from elastic to inelastic can be seen in the refrigerator example.

Generally, however, nearby points are either elastic or inelastic. So it is common to refer to a whole curve by the elasticity of the curve in the price range that normally is of interest—the relevant range.

Demand elasticities affected by availability of substitutes and urgency of need

At first, it may be hard to see why one product should have an elastic demand and another an inelastic demand. Many things—such as the availability of substitutes, the importance of the item in the customer's budget, and the urgency of the customer's need and its relation to other needs—

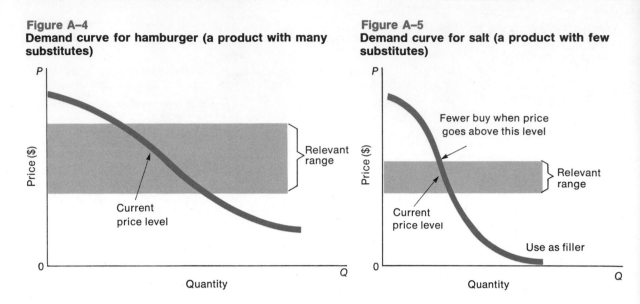

Figure A–4
Demand curve for hamburger (a product with many substitutes)

Figure A–5
Demand curve for salt (a product with few substitutes)

affect demand for a particular product. By looking at one of these factors—the availability of substitutes—we should better understand why demand elasticities vary.

Substitutes are goods or services that offer a choice to the buyer. The greater the number of good substitutes available, the greater the elasticity of demand will be. The term "good" here refers to the amount of similarity that customers see. If they see the products as extremely different—then a particular need cannot be satisfied by easily exchanging them—and the demand for the most satisfactory product may be quite inelastic.

For example, if the price of hamburger is lowered—and other prices stay the same—the quantity demanded will increase a lot. And so will total revenue. The reason is that not only will regular hamburger users buy more hamburger, but those consumers who used to buy hot dogs, steaks, or bacon probably will buy hamburger too. But if the price of hamburger rises, the quantity demanded will decrease—perhaps sharply—depending on how much the price has risen, their individual tastes, and what their guests expect. See Figure A–4.

In contrast to a product which has many "substitutes"—such as hamburger—consider a product with few or no substitutes. Its demand curve will tend to be inelastic. Salt is a good example. Salt is needed to flavor food. Yet no one person or family uses great quantities of salt. And even with price changes within a reasonable range, it is not likely that the quantity of salt wanted will change much. Of course, if the price dropped to an extremely low level, manufacturers might buy more—say for low-cost filler instead of clay or sand. See Figure A–5. Or, if the price rose to a very high figure, many people would have to do without. But these extremes are outside of the relevant range.

MARKETS AS SEEN BY SUPPLIERS

Demand curves are introduced here because the elasticity of demand shows how potential customers feel about the product—and especially whether there are substitutes for the product. But to get a better understanding of markets, we must study the supply side of "demand and supply." Customers may want a product, but if suppliers aren't willing to offer it, then there is no market.

Note: economists often use the kind of analysis we are discussing here to explain pricing in the marketplace. We aren't trying to do that. Here we are interested in markets and the relation between customers and potential suppliers. The discussion in this appendix does not explain how individual firms set prices. We'll talk about that in Chapters 16 and 17.

Supply curves reflect supplier thinking

Generally speaking, suppliers' costs affect the quantity of products they are willing to offer during any time period. In other words, their costs affect their supply curves. While a demand curve shows the quantity of goods customers would be willing to buy at various prices, a **supply curve** shows the quantity of goods that would be offered at various possible prices by all suppliers together. With a demand curve, it shows the attitudes and probable behavior of buyers and sellers toward a particular product in a particular market.

Some supply curves are vertical

We usually assume that supply curves slope upward—that is, that suppliers will be willing to offer greater quantities at higher prices. If a product's market price is very high, you can see why producers will want to produce more of the product. They might even put workers on overtime or perhaps hire additional workers to increase the quantity they can offer. To go further, it seems likely that producers of other products will switch their resources— farms, factories, and labor—to the product that is in great demand.

If, however, a very low price is being offered for a particular product, you might expect producers to switch to other products—reducing supply.

A supply schedule (Table A–3) and a supply curve (Figure A–6) for potatoes illustrate these ideas. This supply curve shows how many potatoes would be produced and offered for sale at each possible market price in a given month.

In the very short run—say, over a few hours, a day, or a week—suppliers may not be able to increase the supply at all. So we would see a vertical supply curve. This situation is often important in the market for fresh fruits and vegetables. Fresh strawberries, for example, will spoil and suppliers want to sell them quickly—hopefully at a higher price—but they want to sell them at any price.

If the product is a service, it may not be easy to expand the supply. And there is no way to "store" it either. Additional barbers or medical doctors are not quickly trained and licensed. And they only have so much time to give each day. When the day is done, the unused "supply" is lost. Further, the hope of much higher prices in the near future will not

Table A–3
Supply schedule for potatoes

Point	Possible market price per 10-lb. bag	Number of bags sellers will supply per month at each possible market price
A	$0.80	17,000,000
B	0.65	14,000,000
C	0.50	11,000,000
D	0.35	8,000,000
E	0.20	3,000,000

Note: This supply schedule is for a month to emphasize that farmers might have some control over when they delivered their potatoes. There would be a different schedule for each month.

expand the supply of many services. A good play or an "in" restaurant or nightclub may be limited in the amount of "product" it can offer at a particular time.

Elasticity of supply

The term elasticity also is used to describe supply curves. An extremely steep or almost vertical supply curve—often found in the short run—is called **inelastic supply**—the quantity supplied does not stretch much (if at all) if the price is raised. A flatter curve is called **elastic supply**—the quantity supplied does stretch if the price is raised. A slightly upsloping supply curve is typical of longer-run market situations. Given more time, suppliers have a chance to change their offerings and competitors may enter or leave the market.

Figure A–6
Supply curve for potatoes (10-pound bags)

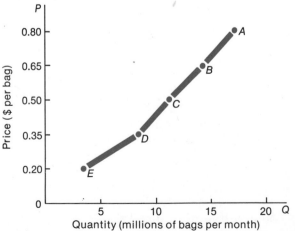

Figure A–7
Equilibrium of supply and demand for potatoes

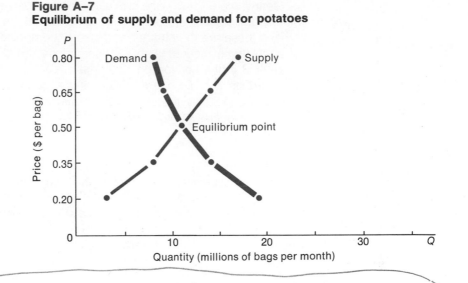

DEMAND AND SUPPLY INTERACT TO ESTABLISH THE SIZE OF THE MARKET AND PRICE LEVEL

We have talked about demand and supply forces separately. Now we must bring them together to show their relationship. The intersection of these two forces decides the size of the market and the market price. At this point, the market is said to be in equilibrium (balanced).

The intersection of demand and supply is shown in Figure A–7 for the potato data discussed above. In this potato market, the demand is inelastic—the total revenue of all the potato producers would be greater at higher prices. But the market price is at the **equilibrium point**—where the quantity and the price that sellers are willing to offer are equal to the quantity and price that buyers are willing to accept. The $0.50 equilibrium price for potatoes gives a smaller total revenue to potato producers than would a higher price. This lower equilibrium price comes about because the many producers are willing to supply enough potatoes at the lower price. Demand is not the only fact that decides price level! Cost also must be considered—via the supply curve.

DEMAND AND SUPPLY HELP UNDERSTAND THE NATURE OF COMPETITION

The elasticity of demand and supply curves and their interaction help predict the kind of competition a marketing manager is likely to meet. For example, extremely inelastic demand curves together with the usual upsloping supply curves mean that the firm will have much choice in its strategy planning. Apparently customers like the product and see few substitutes. They are willing to pay higher prices before cutting back too much on their use of the product.

Clearly, the elasticity of a firm's demand curves is important for strategy planning. But there are other facts which affect the nature of competition. Among these are the number and size of competitors and the uniqueness of each firm's marketing mix. These ideas are discussed more fully in Chapter 3 in the section on "competitive environment." That discussion is based on a real understanding of the contents of this appendix. So now you should be ready to handle that and later material dealing with pricing—especially Chapters 16 and 17.

Conclusion

The economist's traditional demand and supply analysis provides useful tools for studying the nature of demand and market situations. It is important that you master the ideas of a demand curve and demand elasticity. The way demand and supply act together helps set the size of a market and its price level. It also helps explain the kind of competition in different market situations. These ideas are discussed in Chapter 3 and then built upon throughout the text. So careful study of this appendix will build a good foundation for later work.

Questions for discussion

1 Explain in your own words how economists look at markets and arrive at the "law of diminishing demand."

2 Explain what a demand curve is and why it is usually downsloping.

3 What is the length of life of the typical demand curve? Illustrate your answer.

4 If the general market demand for men's shoes is fairly elastic, how does the demand for men's dress shoes compare with it? How does the demand curve for women's shoes compare with the demand curve for men's shoes?

5 If the demand for fountain pens were inelastic above and below the present price, should the price be raised? Why or why not?

6 If the demand for steak is highly elastic below the present price, should the price be lowered?

7 Discuss what factors lead to inelastic demand and supply curves. Are they likely to be found together in the same situation?

When you finish this chapter, you should:

1 Be aware of the uncontrollable variables the marketing manager must work with.
2 Be familiar with population and income trends.
3 Know why you could go to prison by ignoring the legal environment.
4 Know the effect of the different kinds of market situations on strategy planning.
5 Understand how the economic environment as well as the resources and objectives of the firm can affect strategy planning.
6 Recognize the important new terms shown in red.

STRATEGY PLANNING IN AN UNCONTROLLABLE ENVIRONMENT

Figure 3–1
Marketing manager's framework

Marketing managers do not plan strategies in a vacuum. They have to work with several uncontrollable variables when choosing target markets and developing the four Ps. As we saw in Chapter 2—see Figure 3–1—these variables fall in the following areas:

1. Cultural and social environment.
2. Political and legal environment.
3. Economic environment.
4. Competitive environment.
5. Resources and objectives of the firm.

Let's see how these uncontrollable variables add to the challenge of marketing management.

CULTURAL AND SOCIAL ENVIRONMENT

The **cultural and social environment** deals with how and why people live and behave as they do. This variable is very important because it has a direct effect on customer buying behavior.

Markets consist of real people—with money to spend. But the location of these people is pretty much set. And, many of their attitudes and behavior patterns are fixed—or changing only slowly. Let's take a look at what we already know about our cultural and social environment.

Figure 3–2
Map showing each state's area in proportion to its population

Many people are already born

We already have over 200 million people living in the United States. And population experts know how long the people in various age groups will live and—at least roughly—where they will live.

The map in Figure 3–2 shows that Americans are not spread out equally across the country. The map shows the area of each state in relation to its population. Notice the importance of the midwestern states and the southern states when taken as a group. These regions are often seen as very good target markets by marketers wanting to avoid the competitive east and west coast markets. Note, too, the small number of people in the Plains and Mountain states. This explains why some "national" marketers pay less attention to these areas. Yet these states can provide an opportunity for an alert marketer looking for less competitive markets.

Population will keep growing, but . . .

It seems certain that our population will continue to grow—at least for another 50 years or more—because of the number of young people already born. The big questions are: "How much and how fast?" The birth rate is going down and may continue to drop. In fact, the "baby boom" of the 1950s and 1960s turned into the "baby bust" of the 1970s. The **fertility rate**—number of children per woman—fell from a post-war high of 3.8 children per woman in 1957 to 1.8 in 1976. This means there will be less need for baby food, toys, teachers, and child-oriented recreation.[1]

Many people are already born.

AVERAGE AGE WILL RISE

Although our population may continue to grow, there will be a major change in our society. The average age is going to rise for many years because the post–World War II baby boom—lasting roughly from 1947 to 1957—produced about 43 million children. This is about one fifth of our present population. This large group crowded into the schools in the 1950s and 1960s. Then they moved into the job market in the 1970s. By the 1980s and 1990s they will be middle-aged. And early in the 21st century, they will reach retirement—still a large group in the total population. According to one population expert, "it's like a goat passing through a boa constrictor."

The effect of the falling birth rate *and* the post-war babies moving through their life cycle can be seen in Figure 3–3. The average age will continue to rise as there are fewer young people and more older people. The figure shows that the traditional population triangle with many more young people at the bottom will turn into a rectangle. All generation groups will be about the same size.

FERTILITY RATE SHOULD BE WATCHED

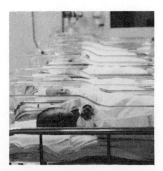

Some of these population forecasts may be changed by new attitudes towards marriage, family size, and family planning.

New births could rise fast because there are so many potential mothers around. Only a small increase in the fertility rate would mean a large number of babies. This could happen, because many women say they want to have a family. They have only delayed the decision.

So fertility figures should be watched carefully. They obviously affect future market sizes. For now, however, it is clear that population will continue to grow—although not as fast as in the past. Further, most of this population growth will be in already crowded urban areas.

Figure 3–3
An aging population[2]

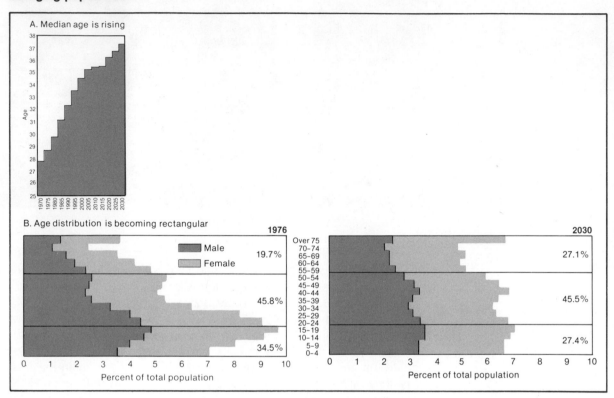

A. Median age is rising

B. Age distribution is becoming rectangular

People live in urban areas

Migration from rural to urban areas has continued in the United States since 1800. In 1920, about half the population lived in rural areas. By 1975 it had dropped to almost 4 percent.

Since World War II, there has been a race to the suburbs. By 1970, more people were living in the suburbs than in central cities. This may be changing, however. Some families have become discouraged with the suburban dream. They're tired of commuting, yard and house work, rising local taxes, and gossipy neighbors. This movement back to the cities is more common among older and sometimes wealthier families. These older families are showing more interest in apartments close to downtown or other areas with shopping, recreation, and office facilities.

Developing a new concept of the urban area

These population shifts mean that the usual way of reporting population by cities and counties may not be helpful to marketers. They are more interested in the size of homogeneous (similar) market areas than in the number of people within political boundaries. To meet this need, the U.S. Census Bureau developed a new population category—the Standard Metropolitan Statistical Area. Much data is available on the people in these areas.

A **Standard Metropolitan Statistical Area (SMSA)** is an economic and social unit with a fairly large population at the center. Usually, a SMSA contains one city of at least 50,000 people, or "twin cities" with a combined population of at least 50,000. The SMSA includes the county of such a central city or cities and nearby counties that are urban in character and economically and socially tied to the central city.

Figure 3–4 shows the location of the nation's biggest urban areas. 276 SMSAs account for over two thirds of the country's population. Notice that this map also shows the concentration of population in certain areas.

Some national marketers aim only at these big urban areas. Large numbers of possible customers are within easy reach of their major distribution facilities. Table 3–1 shows the size of the top 15 SMSAs in 1976.

The mobile ones are an attractive market

Americans are very mobile. Nearly 20 percent of Americans move each year. These "mobiles" are an important market. Their moves are often caused by promotions and job transfers. They have money to spend. Many decisions have to be made fairly quickly after they move. They must find new sources of food, clothing, medical and dental services, and household goods. Alert marketers should try to find these people and tell them about their products.

The income pyramid has turned over

Unless people have money to spend, they aren't very attractive customers. Income comes from producing and selling goods or services.

Family incomes in the United States have been increasing steadily for about 100 years. Even more important to marketers is the change in income

Table 3–1
Rank and population of top 15 Standard Metropolitan Statistical Areas in 1976

Rank and SMSA	Population
1 New York, NY–NJ	9,561,000
2 Chicago, IL	7,015,300
3 Los Angeles–Long Beach, CA	6,986,900
4 Philadelphia, PA–NJ	4,807,000
5 Detroit, MI	4,424,400
6 San Francisco–Oakland, CA	3,140,300
7 Washington, DC–MD–VA	3,021,800
8 Boston, MA	2,890,400
9 Nassau–Suffolk, NY	2,656,800
10 Dallas–Ft. Worth, TX	2,527,200
11 St. Louis, MO–IL	2,366,500
12 Pittsburgh, PA	2,322,200
13 Houston, TX	2,286,200
14 Baltimore, MD	2,147,900
15 Minneapolis–St. Paul, MN–WI	2,010,800

Source: *Statistical Abstract of the United States,* 1977, pp. 426–31.

**Figure 3-4
Standard Metropolitan Statistical Areas**

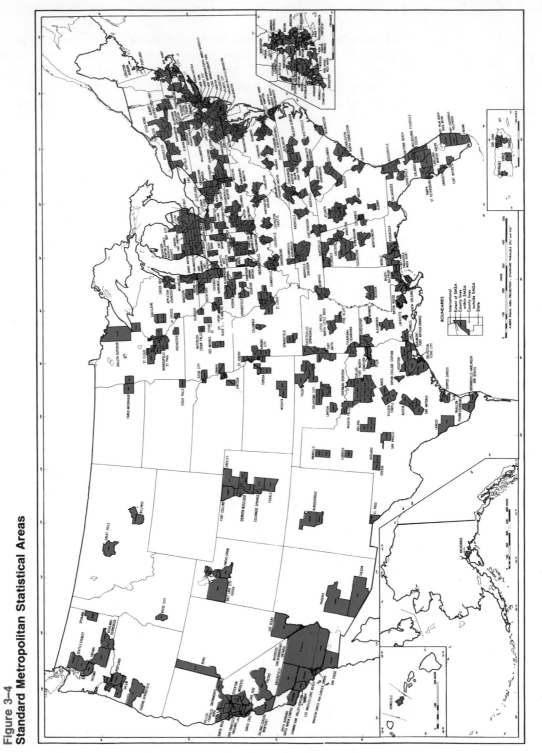

Source: *Standard Metropolitan Statistical Areas—1975*, revised edition, U.S. Department of Commerce.

Americans are mobile.

distribution. Many more families are now in the middle and upper income levels.

Figure 3–5 shows that as recently as 1930, most U.S. families were bunched together at lower income levels. The income distribution looked something like a pyramid. By the 1970s, real incomes (buying power) had risen so much that the pyramid had turned over! Before this upward shift in real income, most markets had a large number of people at the bottom of the income distribution and a relative handful forming an "elite" market at the top. The shift is a real revolution—it has created an attractive "mass market"—and drastically changed our marketing system.

HIGHER INCOME GROUPS GET A BIG SHARE

Although the income pyramid has turned over, higher income groups do receive a large share of the total income and are attractive markets—especially for "luxury" items. Figure 3–6 shows that less than 15 percent of the U.S. households have incomes over $25,000—but they receive more than 35 percent of the total income of the nation.

At the lower end, almost 18 percent of the households receive less than 4 percent of total income. Even so, they are good markets for some basic commodities—especially food and clothing.

The American "melting pot" is not homogenized

There are many other differences among Americans. We are called a friendly people. But actually, this varies by region. People on the West Coast, for example, tend to be more open and friendly. This may be because many have moved west to find a new life. They wanted to leave behind the more tradition-bound social structures of the Midwest and East.

Figure 3–5
There has been a revolution in the distribution of buying power

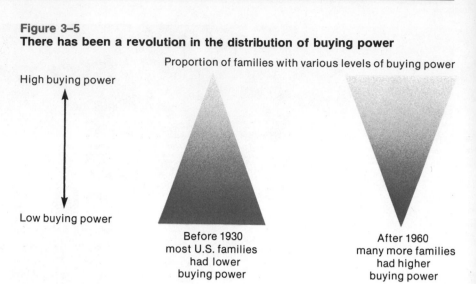

Proportion of families with various levels of buying power

High buying power

Low buying power

Before 1930
most U.S. families
had lower
buying power

After 1960
many more families
had higher
buying power

Source: Based on study in *Business Week,* October 16, 1965; and other data showing real incomes continuing to rise.

Figure 3–6
Total household income distribution by income levels in 1976[3]

Household income level	Number of households (millions)	Percent of total households	Percent of total income
$25,000 and over	10.8	14.6	35.2
$15,000–24,999	20.1	27.1	35.0
$10,000–14,999	14.2	19.1	15.8
$5,000–9,999	15.8	21.3	10.5
Under $5,000	13.2	17.9	3.5
Total	74.1	100.0	100.0

Mean household income equal to $14,922.

Even eating habits vary in different regions and within urban areas. Biscuits and grits are much more popular in the South, for example. And Mexican food has long been favored in the Southwest. Within the large cities, we still find ethnic and religious groups which are separate markets for some goods and services. Large urban areas often have neighborhoods of Irish, Italians, Poles, Jews, Puerto Ricans, Hispanics, and Blacks. Some have newspapers, radio stations, restaurants, grocery stores, and record shops which aim at these culturally defined markets.

Growing interest in the "quality of life" may lead to a slower-paced life.

**Women are being
liberated**

The last ten years has seen a shift in thinking about women's roles in our culture. Women are now free to seek any kind of job they want—and many are doing so. Greater financial freedom is making many women less dependent on marriage as a career. More women are not marrying at all or marrying later. They plan to have fewer children as we saw already. This is having an effect on manufacturers of housing, baby foods, convenience foods, clothing, and cosmetics.

It is clear that this is a big shift in American thinking which must be considered in strategy planning. It will affect not only what is offered to consumers, but also how and by whom. We will see many more women in manager positions. Others will have important selling and advertising jobs. Ineffective and untrained males are in for some real shocks as more women get business training and go out to compete as equals. They will take jobs which once might have gone to less able males. This is happening already.

**Work and growth are
important to some**

We also have to consider changing attitudes toward life and work. The American culture encourages the idea that hard work leads to achievement and material rewards. Americans are willing to work. But they also expect rewards and material comforts. This has led us to place great emphasis on growth, and producing and distributing goods and services. Much of our study of U.S. markets will be within this cultural framework.

In some other societies, however, more importance is placed on leisure and enjoyment of life. More holidays are built into the working year. The output of such economies may not be quite as high, but the people don't feel that they are suffering because of this.

Our growing interest in the "quality of life" may reflect a desire for less goods-oriented solutions to our problems. This may lead to reducing our productivity and income. In time, we may learn to live a slower paced, less goods-oriented life. This obviously will affect marketers.

Changes come slowly

It is important to see, however, that changes in basic values come slowly. An individual firm could not hope to encourage big changes in the short run. Instead, it should identify these attitudes and plan accordingly.

Sometimes, however, strong outside forces—such as energy shortages, riots, or boycotts—may force more rapid changes in the cultural and social environment. And these may affect the political and economic environments.

POLITICAL ENVIRONMENT

The attitudes of people, social critics, and governments are becoming more important to the marketing manager. They all affect the political environment.

Consumerism is here and basic

Consumerism is a social movement seeking to increase the rights and powers of consumers and buyers. Its recent growth is due to a change in thinking which was captured by President Kennedy's "Consumer Bill of Rights." Although they did not become law, they have affected people's thinking—including government agencies and some courts.

President Kennedy's "Consumer Bill of Rights" includes the following:

The right to safety.
The right to be informed.
The right to choose.
The right to be heard.

Kennedy did not include "the right to a clean and safe environment"— probably because the environment had not yet become a public concern. But most people are concerned with such a right. More government pressure is being applied on everyone—including businesses and government units—to improve our waste handling and clean our chimneys and motor exhaust systems. This is probably the outstanding recent example of a rapid change in cultural values which was turned into action by the political authorities.

These consumer "rights" are generally not as easy to obtain as the antipollution moves. Instead, individual firms and government agencies must make basic changes in their attitudes about what is "right" and "wrong." This doesn't happen quickly. So there may be an ongoing need for consumerists to help make sure that the "little guy" is not ignored by business or government. The consumerism movement is not likely to die overnight.

Consumerist Ralph Nader.

NOT MEETING CONSUMERS EXPECTATIONS COULD BE DRASTIC

A 1977 poll showed the business community "out of step" with the American public on consumerism issues. Generally, the public seems to like what the consumerists are trying to do.[4] Marketers shouldn't forget that the role of businesses is to satisfy consumers. No firm has a God-given right to operate anyway it wants to.

This means that the marketing manager—as well as top management—should pay more attention to consumers' attitudes in marketing planning. Ignoring the consumer movement could be fatal. The rules governing business could change. Specific businesses might be told they could not operate. Or they might face such heavy fines that they would be forced out of business. And, in an "antibusiness" environment, fines could be quite large. A Utah family was awarded $450,000 when the court ruled that the Ford Bronco was a dangerous vehicle—and was, in part, the cause of a fatal accident.[5] Such an award against a small company could wipe it out. For a large company, it opens the door to additional law suits which could be costly and damage its reputation.

Clearly, more attention must be paid to product design and safety in our social and political environment. The old, production-oriented ways of doing things are no longer acceptable.

Political environment may offer new opportunities

The political environment is not always antibusiness. Governments may decide that encouraging business is good for their people. Foreign governments often do this to encourage outside investors. The U.S. government has special programs and financial incentives to encourage urban redevelopment and minority business. State and local governments also try to attract and hold business—sometimes with tax incentives.

LEGAL ENVIRONMENT

U.S. legislative developments: Encouraging competition

American economic and legislative thinking has been based on the idea that competition among many small firms will make the economy work better. Therefore, attempts by businesses to limit competition are thought to be against the public interest.

As industries grew larger after the Civil War, some became monopolies controlled by wealthy businessmen—often called "robber barons." This made it hard for smaller producers to survive. As a result, there was a movement—especially among midwestern farmers—to control monopolists.

Beginning in 1890, a series of laws were passed that were basically antimonopoly or procompetition. They are aimed mainly at attempts to monopolize or limit trade. The names and dates of these laws are shown in Figure 3–7.

Antimonopoly law and marketing mix planning

Specific application of antimonopoly law to the four Ps will be presented in later chapters. To round out our discussion here, you should know

Figure 3–7
Outline of federal legislation now affecting competition in marketing

Year	Antimonopoly (procompetition)	Anticompetition	Antispecific practices
1890	Sherman Act		
1914	Clayton Act Federal Trade Commission Act		Clayton Act
1936	Robinson-Patman Act	Robinson-Patman Act	Robinson-Patman Act
1938			Wheeler-Lea Amendment
1950	Antimerger Act		Antimerger Act
1975	Magnuson-Moss Act		Magnuson-Moss Act

what kind of proof government must have to obtain a conviction under each of the major laws. You should also know which of the four Ps have been most affected by each law. Figure 3–8 provides such a summary—with a phrase following each law to show what must be proved to obtain a conviction. Note how the wording of the laws is moving to the side of protecting consumers.

PROSECUTION IS A SERIOUS MATTER—ONE CAN GO TO JAIL

Business and business managers must obey both criminal and civil laws. Penalties for breaking civil laws are limited to blocking or forcing certain actions—along with fines. Where criminal law applies, jail sentences can be imposed. For example, the Sherman Act now provides for fines of up to $1 million for corporations, as well as fines of up to $100,000 and/or up to three years in prison for individuals!

Antimonopoly laws are serious business. In recent years some business managers have gone to jail or received suspended jail sentences because they broke the criminal part of these laws. Recently, for example, several packaging company managers were given prison terms and fines up to $35,000.[6] Clearly, government is becoming more serious about antimonopoly legislation.

Small business managers should take special note of these laws. They have ignored them because they felt that they were "too small for the government to worry about." But they may be in for a shock.[7] The government is now applying the laws to large and small alike. This new seriousness should cause marketing managers to pay more attention to the political and legal environment in the future.

Some businessmen have already gone to jail.

Consumer protection laws are not new

There is more to the legal environment than just the antimonopoly laws. Some consumer protections were built into English and U.S. law from the beginning. A seller had to tell the truth (if asked a direct question),

KNOW TABLE

Figure 3–8
Focus (mostly prohibitions) of federal antimonopoly laws on the four Ps

MOST IMPORTANT

Law	Product	Place	Promotion	Price
Sherman Act (1890) Monopoly or conspiracy in restraint of trade *(AGAINST MONOPOLIES)*	Monopoly or conspiracy to control a product	Monopoly or conspiracy to control distribution channels		Monopoly or conspiracy to control prices
Clayton Act (1914) Substantially *STRENGTH* lessen competition *(SHERMAN ACT)*	Forcing sale of some products with others—tying contracts	Exclusive dealing contracts (limiting buyers' sources)		Price discrimination by manufacturers
Federal Trade Commission Act (1914) Unfair methods of *(DECEPTION)* competition		Unfair policies	Deceptive ads	Deceptive pricing
Robinson-Patman Act (1936) Tends to injure competition *(YOU MUST CHARGE ALL WHOLESALERS THE SAME PRICE)*		Prohibits paying allowances to "direct" buyers in lieu of middlemen costs (brokerage charges)	Prohibits "fake" advertising allowances or discrimination in help offered	Prohibits price discrimination on goods of "like grade and quality" without cost justification, and quantity discounts limited
Wheeler-Lea Amendment (1938) Unfair or deceptive practices *(AMENDS F.T.C.A—1914)*	Deceptive packaging or branding		Deceptive ads or selling claims	Deceptive pricing
Antimerger Act (1950) Lessen competition *(CONTINUATION OF CLAYTON ACT)*	Buying competitors	Buying producers or distributors		
Magnuson-Moss Act (1975) Unreasonable practices *(CONTINUATION OF F.T.C.A)*	Product warranties			

meet contracts, and stand behind the firm's product (to some reasonable extent). But beyond this, it was expected that vigorous competition would protect consumers—*as long as they were careful.*

Focusing only on competition did not protect consumers very well in some areas, however. So the government has found it necessary to pass other laws—usually involving specific types of products.

FOODS AND DRUGS ARE CONTROLLED

Consumer protection laws go back at least to 1906. The Pure Food and Drug Act was passed then. Colorful exposés of unsanitary meat-packing practices in the Chicago stockyards caused consumer interest in this act. After much debate, it was decided to pass a general law to control the quality and labeling of foods and drugs in interstate commerce. This was a major victory for consumer protection. Before this, it was assumed that common law and the old warning "let the buyer beware" would take care of consumers.

Figure 3–9
Selected consumer protection legislation[8]

Year	Law
1906	Pure Food and Drug Act—prohibited the adulteration and misbranding of foods and drugs; set up the Food and Drug Administration (FDA).
1906	Meat Inspection Act—required that meat shipped in interstate commerce be processed under sanitary conditions.
1938	Food, Drug, and Cosmetic Act—expanded the responsibility of the Food and Drug Administration to include cosmetics and therapeutic devices, by amending the 1906 act.
1938	Wheeler-Lea Amendment to FTC Act—expanded the FTC's responsibility to include unfair or deceptive acts or practices, and gave it the power to take action whenever it is in the public interest, even where there is no proof of competitive injury.
1939	The Wool Products Labeling Act—required that products containing wool carry labels showing the fiber content.
1951	Fur Products Labeling Act—required that all fur products carry labels correctly describing their contents.
1953	Flammable Fabrics Act—prohibited the manufacture or sale of fabrics or wearing apparel which were dangerously flammable.
1958	Food Additives Amendment (Delaney Act)—as an amendment to the Food, Drug, and Cosmetic Act of 1938, required that food additives be limited to those which do not cause cancer in humans or animals.
1960	Hazardous Substances Labeling Act—required proper labeling on packages of hazardous household products.
1962	Kefauver-Harris Amendment to Food, Drug, and Cosmetic Act (1938)—required that all drugs be tested for safety and efficacy.
1966	Fair Packaging and Labeling Act—permitted the voluntary adoption of industry-accepted uniform packaging standards and required clearer labeling of consumer goods.
1966	National Traffic and Motor Vehicle Safety Act—provided for the establishment of compulsory standards for automobiles and new and used tires.
1966	Child Protection Act of 1966—amended the Hazardous Substances Labeling Act (1960) to ban all hazardous substances and prohibit sales of potentially harmful toys and other articles used by children.
1966	Cigarette Labeling Act—required health warnings on all cigarette packages.
1968	Consumer Credit Protection Act (Truth in Lending)—required full disclosure of the terms and rates charged for loans and credit.
1970	Poison Prevention Packaging Act—provided for standards for child-resistant packaging of hazardous substances.
1972	Consumer Product Safety Act—established the Consumer Product Safety Commission and empowered it to set safety standards for a broad range of consumer products and to impose penalties for failure to meet these standards.
1975	Magnuson-Moss Act—established disclosure requirements and minimum federal standards for written warranties.

Some loopholes in the law were corrected in following acts. The law now bans the shipment of unsanitary and poisonous products and requires much testing of drugs. The Food and Drug Administration (FDA) attempts to control manufacturers of these products. It has the power to seize products that violate its rules. It also has regulations on branding and requires that food shipped in interstate commerce contain labels which correctly describe the contents. In general, it has done a good job. But the outcry over a recent proposal to completely ban the use of saccharin may force the government to decide how much protection consumers really want. In this case, there were many users who felt that the government should first ban the use of many other products whose bad effects had already been more thoroughly proved—for example, alcohol and cigarettes. Clearly, more thinking is needed in this area.

A variety of other laws protect consumer interests. See Figure 3–9 for a list of selected consumer protection laws. Some deal with labeling and/or production of products such as wool, furs, and flammable fabrics. A truth-in-lending law requires a statement of the true interest rates being charged for loans and credit.

PRODUCT SAFETY IS CONTROLLED

The Consumer Product Safety Act (of 1972) is another important consumer protection law. It sets up the Consumer Product Safety Commission to control product safety. This group has broad power to set safety standards and penalties for failure to meet these standards. Again, there is some question as to how much safety consumers want. The Commission found the bicycle the most hazardous product under its control!

But given that the Commission has the power to force a product off the market, it is obvious that safety must be considered in product design. This is an uncontrollable variable which must be treated seriously by business managers.[9]

"I know they're plastic, lady, but I just got sued for selling real flowers during hay fever season."

(Let the seller beware!)

State and local laws affect strategy planning, too

Besides federal legislation which affects interstate commerce, marketers must be aware of state and local laws. There are state and city laws regulating minimum prices and price setting; regulations for starting up a business (licenses, examinations, and even tax payments); and in some communities, regulations banning certain activities—such as door-to-door selling or selling on Sundays or during evenings.

Consumerists and the law say "let the seller beware"

The old rule about buyer-seller relations was "let the buyer beware." Now it seems to be shifting to "let the seller beware." The number of consumer protection laws has been increasing. These laws and court decisions suggest that there is more interest now in protecting consumers instead of protecting competition. This may upset production-oriented managers. But they will just have to adapt to the new political and legal environment. Times have changed.

ECONOMIC ENVIRONMENT

National income changes make a difference

A well-planned marketing strategy may fail if the country goes through a rapid business decline. As consumers' incomes go down, people have to shift their spending patterns. They may completely eliminate some types of purchases. During the U.S. recession of 1969–70, for example, some firms offering luxury goods were badly hurt. But retailers such as K mart, J. C. Penney, and Woolworth had sales gains.

The recession of 1973–74 hit harder, however. Even producers and retailers of lower-priced goods were hurt. Finally, the largest retail bankruptcy in U.S. history was announced by the W. T. Grant (general merchandise) chain in 1976. And the Robert Hall chain—selling lower-priced clothing—went bankrupt in 1977. Other firms had to cut product lines or change strategies to avoid similar fates.[10]

Resource shortages may limit opportunities

The growing shortage of some natural resources—and in particular energy resources—may cause real upsets. Plastics manufacturers, for example, use oil-based resources. Their costs are rising so high that they are priced out of some markets. Rising gasoline prices may make consumers less interested in the larger, more profitable (to the auto industry) cars. Further, important shifts in auto buying patterns will affect the whole economy. The auto industry is a major buyer of metals, plastics, fabrics, and tires.

Higher fuel prices may cut economic growth

The continued economic growth that we have come to accept may be slowed or stopped by higher fuel costs. We are big energy users *and* energy importers. Higher fuel costs for imported oil have shifted income out of the United States and reduced our real income. Even lower real incomes are possible in the future because of technological factors. Much of our plant and equipment now depends on lots of low-cost energy. Industrial processes that were profitable with low energy prices are now less profitable. So it is possible that the average job in the future will use

A shortage in one area may affect other areas.

less machinery and be less productive. In effect, rising energy costs will increase real incomes in a few countries with large energy reserves. But the balance of the world may see lower real incomes. This means U.S. consumers and industries will have to adjust their spending patterns.

Inflation can change mixes

Inflation is a major influence in many economies. The marketing manager must understand this when setting prices. When inflation becomes a way of life, people buy and sell accordingly. Some countries have had 25–100 percent inflation per year for years. In contrast, the 6–10 percent level reached in the United States in the 1970s was small. Still, inflation must be considered in strategy planning. It can lead to government policies which will reduce income, employment, *and* consumer spending.

The technological base affects opportunities

Underlying any economic environment is the **technological base**—the technical skills and equipment which affect the way the resources of an economy are converted to output. In tradition-bound societies, relatively little technology is used. And the output is small. In modern economies on the other hand, aggressive competitors continually seek better ways of doing things. They copy the best methods quickly.

Technological developments certainly affect marketing. The modern automobile, for example, lets farmers come to town and urban people go wherever they want. This has destroyed the local "monopolies" of some retailers and wholesalers. Modern trucks and airplanes have opened up national and international markets. Electronic developments have made possible mass promotion by radio, TV, and telephone. Soon we may be able to shop in the home with a combination TV-computer system—eliminating the need for some retailers and wholesalers.

As we move through the text, you should see that some of the big advances in business have come from early recognition of new ways to do things. Marketing managers should help their firms see such opportunities by trying to understand the "why" of present methods—and what is keeping their firms from doing things more effectively. Then, as new developments come along, they will be alert to possible uses and see how opportunities can be turned into profits.

Further, marketers can help decide what technical developments would be acceptable to society. With the growing concern about environmental pollution, the quality of life, working conditions, and so on, it is possible that some potentially attractive developments should be rejected because of their long-run effects. Perhaps what might be good for the firm and the economy's *economic* growth might not fit with the cultural and social environment—or the political and legal environment. The marketing manager's closeness to the market could give him a better feel for what people are thinking—and help him to help the firm avoid bad mistakes.[11]

THE COMPETITIVE ENVIRONMENT

(Note: The following materials assume some familiarity with economic analysis and especially the nature of demand curves and demand elasticity. For those wishing a review of these materials, see Appendix A, which follows Chapter 2.)

The **competitive environment** refers to the number and types of competitors the marketing manager must face and how they might behave. Although these factors can't be controlled by the marketing manager, he can choose strategies which will avoid head-on competition.

A marketing manager will have to operate in one of four kinds of market situations. We will talk about three kinds: pure competition, oligopoly, and monopolistic competition. A fourth type—monopoly—is not found very often and is like monopolistic competition anyway.

Understanding these market situations is quite important because the freedom of a marketing manager—especially his control over price—is greatly reduced in some situations. The important aspects of these kinds of competition are outlined in Figure 3–10.

When competition is pure

MANY COMPETITORS OFFER THE SAME THING

Pure competition is a market situation which develops when a market has:

1. Homogeneous (similar) products.
2. Many buyers and sellers who have full knowledge of the market.
3. Ease of entry for buyers and sellers, i.e., new firms have little difficulty starting in business and new customers can easily come into the market.

More or less pure competition is found in many agricultural markets. In the potato industry, for example, there are tens of thousands of producers and they are in pure competition. Let's look more closely at these small producers.

Figure 3–10
Some important dimensions regarding marketing competition

Important dimensions / Types of situations	Pure competition	Oligopoly	Monopolistic competition	Monopoly
Uniqueness of each firm's product	None	None	Some	Unique
Number of competitors	Many	Few	Few to many	None
Size of competitors (compared to size of market)	Small	Large	Large to small	None
Elasticity of demand facing firm	Completely elastic	Kinked demand curve (elastic and inelastic)	Either	Either
Elasticity of industry demand	Either	Inelastic	Either	Either
Control of price by firm	None	Some (with care)	Some	Complete

Note: Some economists identify a "differentiated oligopoly" situation but we will ignore this one because the marketing mixes are differentiated, some anyway, and therefore the situations can be treated as monopolistic competition.

In pure competition, these many small producers see almost a perfectly flat demand curve facing each one of them. The relation between the industry demand curve and the demand curve facing the individual farmer in pure competition is shown in Figure 3–11. Although the potato industry as a whole has a downsloping demand curve, each individual potato producer has a demand curve that is perfectly flat at the going market price—the equilibrium price.

To explain this more clearly, let's look at the demand curve for the individual potato producer. Assume that the equilibrium price for the industry is 50 cents. This means the producer can sell as many potatoes as he chooses at 50 cents. The quantity that all producers choose to sell makes up the supply curve. But acting alone, a small producer can do almost anything he wants to do.

If this individual farmer raises 1/10,000th of the quantity offered in the market, for example, you can see that there will be little effect on the market if he goes out of business or doubles his production.

The reason an individual's demand curve is flat in this example is that the farmer probably could not sell any potatoes above the market price. And there is no point in selling below 50 cents.

Not many markets are *purely* competitive. But many are close enough to allow us to talk about "almost" pure competition situations—ones in which the marketing manager has to accept the going price.

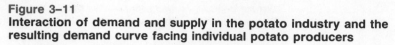

Figure 3–11
Interaction of demand and supply in the potato industry and the resulting demand curve facing individual potato producers

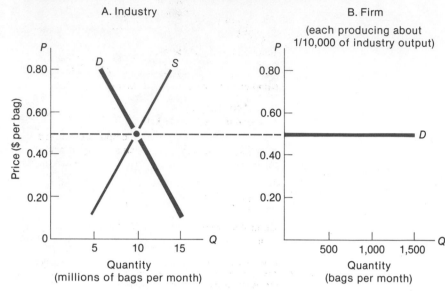

SQUEEZE ON THE ORANGE GROWERS

Florida orange growers, for example, have basically homogeneous products. They have no control over price. When there is a very large supply, prices drop rapidly and are beyond the producers' control. When supplies are short, the reverse happens. During one year, the crop was 50 percent larger than the previous crop—and most growers sold their oranges below their costs. Oranges "on the tree" which cost 75 cents a box to grow were selling for 35 cents a box. Supply turned around the next year, however, and oranges were selling for $2.40 to $2.60 a box.[12]

PROFIT SQUEEZE IS ON IN MANY MARKETS

Such highly competitive situations are not limited to agriculture. Wherever many competitors sell basically homogeneous products—such as some chemicals, plastic parts, lumber, coal, printing, and laundry services—the demand curve for each producer tends to be flat.

Markets tend to become more competitive. In pure competition, prices and profits may be pushed down until some competitors are forced out of business. Eventually, the price level is only high enough to keep enough firms in the market. That is, none of them makes a profit. Each just covers all its costs.

When competition is oligopolistic

Not all markets move toward pure competition. Some become oligopoly situations.

FEW COMPETITORS OFFERING SIMILAR THINGS

Oligopoly situations are special market situations which develop when a market has:

1. Essentially homogeneous products—such as basic industrial chemicals or gasoline.
2. Relatively few sellers, or a few large firms and many smaller ones who follow the lead of the larger ones.
3. Fairly inelastic industry demand curves.

4. NO PRICE COMPETITION.

The demand curve facing each firm is especially interesting in an oligopoly situation. Although the industry demand curve can be inelastic throughout the relevant range, the demand curve facing each competitor looks "kinked." See Figure 3–12. The current market price is at the kink.

There is a "market price" because the competing firms watch each other carefully and know it is wise to be at the kink. Each marketing manager must expect that raising his own price above the market for such a homogeneous product would cause a big loss of sales. Few, if any, competitors would follow his price increase. So, his demand curve would be relatively flat above the market price. But if he lowers his price, he must expect competitors to follow. Therefore, given inelastic industry demand, his own demand curve would be inelastic at lower prices. Since lowering prices along such a curve would drop total revenue, he probably should not do it. That is, he should leave his price at the kink—the market price.

Actually, however, there are price fluctuations in oligopolistic markets. Sometimes this is due to firms who don't understand the market situation and cut their prices to get business. In other cases, substantial increases in demand or supply change the basic nature of the situation and lead to price cutting. Sometimes the price cuts are drastic, such as Du Pont's Dacron price cut of 25 percent. This happened when Du Pont decided

Figure 3–12
Oligopoly—kinked demand curve—situation

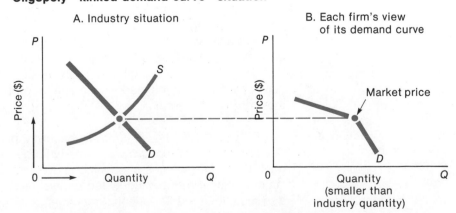

A. Industry situation

B. Each firm's view of its demand curve

that industry production capacity already exceeded demand and more was due to start into production.[13]

PRICE WARS ARE SOMETIMES STARTED

A common example of price fluctuations can be seen in retail gasoline marketing at a major intersection where there are several obvious competitors. Apparently enough final consumers think of gasoline as homogeneous to create oligopoly conditions. And oligopoly-type "price wars" are common. These usually start when some gasoline discounter successfully attracts "too much" business—perhaps by cutting his prices one cent a gallon below his usual price. The war proceeds for a time—with everyone losing money—until one of the dealers calls a meeting and suggests that they all "get a little sense." Sometimes these price wars will end immediately after such a meeting—with prices returning to a "reasonable and proper" level.

When competition is monopolistic—A price must be set

You can see why firms would want to avoid pure competition or oligopolistic situations. They would prefer a market in which they have more control.

Monopolistic competition is a market situation which develops when:

1. A market has different (heterogeneous) products—in the eyes of some consumers,
2. Sellers feel they do have some competition in this market.

The word *monopolistic* means that each firm is trying to get its own little monopoly. But the word *competition* means that there are still substitutes. The vigorous competition of the purely competitive market is reduced. Each firm has its own downsloping demand curve. But the shape of the curve depends on the similarity of competitors' products and marketing mixes. Each monopolistic competitor has freedom—but not complete freedom—in its own little "industry."

JUDGING ELASTICITY WILL HELP SET THE PRICE

Since a firm in monopolistic competition has its own downsloping demand curve, it must make a price decision as part of its strategy planning. Here, estimating the elasticity of the firm's own demand curve is helpful. If it is highly inelastic, the firm may decide to raise prices to increase total revenue. But if demand is highly elastic, this may mean many competitors with acceptable substitutes. Then the price may have to be set near "competition." And the marketing manager probably should try to develop a better marketing mix.

Why some products are offered in pure competition

Why would anyone compete in basically profitless pure competiton? One reason is that the firm was already in the industry. Or the firm enters without knowing what is happening and then must stick it out until it runs out of money. Production-oriented people seem more likely to make such a mistake than market-oriented managers.

Avoiding pure competition seems wise. It certainly fits with our emphasis on target marketing.

COMPANY RESOURCES MAY LIMIT SEARCH FOR OPPORTUNITIES

A smart marketing manager knows that his firm has some resources—hopefully some unique resources—which will help it develop a good strategy. As a result of the firm's own history, experience, and personnel, it should have strengths and weaknesses that make it different from other firms. Attractive opportunities should take advantage of these strong points. Resources that should be considered when looking for attractive opportunities are discussed in the following sections.

Financial strength

Some industries (such as steel and public utilities) need large amounts of capital to gain economies of size. For them, the cost of production per unit goes down as the quantities produced increase. Therefore, smaller producers would be at a great disadvantage if they tried to compete in these lines. On the other hand, large companies often have difficulties when they enter low-investment businesses. For example, a large chemical processor tried to make and sell decorated shower curtains because it was producing the basic plastic sheets. It lost heavily on the experiment, however. The smaller shower curtain manufacturers and wholesalers were much more flexible—changing their styles and price policies more rapidly. Here, financial strength was an asset in the basic plastic sheet business, but not where style and flexibility in adapting to customer needs was important.

Raw material reserves

Firms that own or have dependable sources of basic raw materials have a head start in businesses that need these resources. But companies—large or small—that don't have this advantage may have difficulty even staying in these businesses. Chemical and paper manufacturers, for example, usually try to control timber supplies. And the metals and oil companies have controlled their own resources. Now that we see a growing shortage of raw materials, it probably would be desirable for a firm to be sure of supplies before building a marketing strategy which depends upon raw materials.

Physical plant

Some kinds of business require large physical plants which must be owned by the firm. If these are well located, this may be an asset. On the other hand, badly located or out-of-date factories or wholesale or retail facilities may be real handicaps. The existing physical plant can affect marketing strategy planning. One of the firm's objectives probably will be to use the existing plant as fully as possible.

Patents

Patents are most important to manufacturers. A patent owner has a 17-year "monopoly" to develop and use its new product, process, or material as it chooses. If a firm has a patent on a basic process, potential competitors may be forced to use second-rate processes—and they may fail. Clearly, if a firm has such a patent, it is a resource. But if its competitors have it, it may be a handicap which cannot be overcome with other parts of a marketing mix.

Public acceptance

If a firm has developed a **customer franchise**—a loyal following of customers for its product or service—others may have trouble breaking into its market. A strong customer franchise is a valuable asset that a marketing manager should use in developing his marketing strategy.

Skill of personnel

Some firms deliberately pay high wages to attract and hold skilled workers—so they can offer high-quality products or services. A skilled sales force is also an asset. But lack of good sales people may limit strategy planning. Skilled workers may be able to produce a new product, but the sales force may not have the contacts or know-how to sell it. This often happens when a firm moves into new markets.

Management attitudes

The attitudes toward growth are important in strategy planning—especially in developing new products.

The president of a New England manufacturing company was excited about the prospects of a new product. But after looking at the attitudes of his company personnel, and especially his management people, he dropped his plans for the product. Why? He found that his employees had no ambition or interest in growth![14]

OBJECTIVES MAY LIMIT THE SEARCH FOR OPPORTUNITIES

A company's objectives should direct the operation of the whole business. If it has already decided that the firm is to stay small so the owner has plenty of time for golf, then this objective will obviously limit the firm's opportunities. (Actually, of course, it probably wouldn't even be looking for opportunities!) On the other hand, if a large aggressive firm seeks to maximize profit wherever it can, then the range of opportunities expands quickly.

Objectives should set firm's course

Objectives are important to marketing strategy planning. A business should know where it is going or it is likely to fall into the trap: "Having lost sight of our objectives, we redoubled our efforts."[15]

In spite of their importance, objectives are seldom stated clearly. They may even be stated after the strategies are carried out!

Setting objectives that really guide the present and future development of a company is a soul-searching process. It forces top management to look at the entire business and relate its present needs and resources to the external environment. Then it can decide what it wants to do in the future.

"Uh . . . sure J. B. uh . . . if *you* think we should expand to Alaska. Uh . . . we'll do it."

THREE BASIC OBJECTIVES PROVIDE GUIDELINES

The following three objectives provide a useful starting point for setting objectives for a firm. These three objectives could be stated in many ways. But they should be aimed at together because, in the long run, a failure in even one of the three areas could lead to total failure of the business.

1. Engage in some specific business activity that will perform a socially and economically useful function.
2. Develop an organization to stay in business and carry out its strategies.
3. Earn enough profit to survive.[16]

Shortsighted top management may straitjacket marketing

We are assuming that it is the marketing manager's job to work within the framework of objectives provided by the top executives. But some of these objectives may limit marketing strategies—perhaps hurting the whole business. This is why the marketing manager should help set the company's objectives.

A few examples will show how the marketing manager might have to choose undesirable strategies.

A quick return on investment is sometimes sought by top management. This might influence the marketing manager to select marketing strategies that would result in quick returns in the short run but kill the "customer franchise" in the long run.

Top management might decide on entering new businesses—diversification. This might force the marketing manager to choose strategies that are poorly suited to the company's resources.

Some top managements want a large sales volume or a larger market share—just for its own sake. Ampex (an electronics firm) almost went out of business seeking growth for its own sake. And Ford Motor Company, RCA, and Westinghouse shifted their objectives toward *profitable* sales growth when they realized that the two do not necessarily go together.[17]

OBJECTIVES SHOULD GUIDE MARKETING DEPARTMENT PLANNING

Ideally, the marketing manager should be involved in setting company objectives. But even if he isn't, these objectives should guide the search for opportunities and planning of specific marketing strategies. Particular marketing objectives should be set within the framework of these overall objectives. So, in later chapters, we will discuss specific marketing objectives and the policies needed to carry them out.

Conclusion

This chapter has been concerned with the forces which—while beyond the marketing manager's control—affect strategy planning. Some uncontrollable variables can change faster than others. But all can change—requiring adjustments in plans. Ideally, possible changes would be included in the planning.

We have seen that a marketer must develop marketing mixes suited to the customs of his target markets.

He also must be aware of legal restrictions and be sensitive to changing political climates. The consumer movement may force many changes.

The economic environment—the chance of recession or inflation—also will affect the choice of strategies. And the marketer must consider the competitive environment. How well established are competitors? What action can they be expected to take? What is the nature of competition: pure, oligopolistic, or monopolistic?

The firm's own resources and objectives may limit the search for attractive opportunities. Ideally, the marketing manager would be involved in setting company-wide objectives. But regardless, these objectives should guide marketing strategy planning.

Developing good market-oriented strategies in an uncontrollable environment is not easy. You can see that marketing management is a challenging job.

Questions for discussion

1 Discuss how slower population growth, and especially a decline in the number of babies, will affect the businesses in your local community.

2 Discuss the impact of our aging culture on marketing strategy planning.

3 Explain why the concept of the Standard Metropolitan Statistical Areas was developed. Would it be the most useful breakdown for retailers?

4 Explain how the continuing mobility of consumers should affect marketing strategy planning. Be sure to consider the impact on the four Ps.

5 Explain how the redistribution of income has affected marketing planning thus far and its likely impact in the future.

6 Explain the meaning of consumerism in your own words. How long do you feel this movement will continue?

7 What and whom is the government attempting to protect in its effort to preserve and regulate competition?

8 Are consumer protection laws really new? Discuss the evolution of consumer protection. Is more such legislation likely?

9 Discuss the probable impact on your hometown of a major technological breakthrough in air transportation that would permit foreign producers to ship into any U.S. market for about the same transportation cost that domestic producers incur.

10 If a manufacturer's well-known product is sold at the same price by many retailers in the same community, is this an example of pure competition? When a community has many small grocery stores, are they in pure competiton? What characteristics are really needed in order to have a purely competitive market?

11 List three products that are sold in purely competitive markets and three sold in monopolistically competitive markets. Do any of these products have anything in common? Can any generalizations be made about competitive situations and marketing mix planning?

12 Cite a local example of an oligopoly, explaining why it is an oligopoly.

13 Explain how a firm's resources might limit its search for opportunities. Cite a specific example for a specific resource.

14 Discuss how a company's financial strength might have a bearing on the kinds of products it produces

15 Explain how a firm's objectives might affect its search for opportunities.

16 Specifically, how would various company objectives affect the development of a marketing mix for a new type of baby shoe? If this company were just being formed by a former shoemaker with limited financial resources, list the objectives he might have and then discuss how they will affect the development of the marketing strategy.

17 Discuss the relative importance of the uncontrollable variables, given the speed with which these variables move. If some must be neglected because of a shortage of manager time, which would you recommend for neglect?

18 For a new design of haircomb, or one of the items mentioned in Question 16 of Chapter 2, discuss the uncontrollable factors that the marketing manager will have to consider.

Suggested cases

1 Taylor Incorporated

5 Inland Steel Company

When you finish this chapter, you should:	1 Understand a scientific approach to marketing research.
	2 Know how to go about defining and solving marketing problems.
	3 Know about getting secondary and primary data.
	4 Know about marketing information systems.
	5 Recognize the important new terms shown in red.

4

GATHERING INFORMATION FOR MARKETING DECISION MAKING

Marketing managers need information to plan successful marketing strategies. Ideally, they would like (1) information about potential target markets and how they might react to various marketing mixes, and (2) information about competition and other uncontrollable factors. Marketing research is needed to help the marketing manager gather the information needed to make wise decisions. This is not an easy job because potential customers and competitors are not very predictable. It is a very necessary job though. Without good information, managers can only guess about potential markets. In our fast-changing, competitive economy, this almost guarantees failure.

MARKETING RESEARCHERS HELP SUPPLY MARKETING INFORMATION

Marketing research gathers and analyzes data to help marketing managers make decisions. One of the important jobs of a marketing researcher is to help management get the "facts" and understand them. Marketing research is much more than a bunch of techniques or a group of specialists in survey design. Good marketing researchers must keep marketing *and* management in mind—to be sure that their research focuses on real problems.

Managers must know what researchers do

Marketing research details can be handled by staff or outside specialists. But marketing managers must be able to explain the kinds of problems

85

"Ok, you researchers, why isn't it selling? Everyone is blaming everyone else—I want to know the real problem!"

they are facing—and the kinds of information which will help them make decisions. They also must be able to communicate with specialists in *their* language. Marketing managers may only be "consumers" of research, but they have to be able to explain what they want. For this reason, our emphasis won't be on mechanics, but rather on how to plan and evaluate the work of marketing researchers.

OUR STRATEGIC PLANNING FRAMEWORK CAN GUIDE MARKETING RESEARCH

Marketing researchers work on all kinds of problems—from developing wholly new strategies to evaluating current strategies. An important part of their job is providing "feedback"—which may lead to new plans. Marketing research is a continuing process—involving a wide range of possible jobs.

Finding the right problem level almost solves the problem

The strategic planning framework introduced early in the text can be especially useful here—helping the researcher to see where the real problem lies. Do we really know enough about target markets? If so, do we know enough to work out all of the four Ps?

The importance of understanding the nature of the problem and then trying to solve it can be seen more clearly in the following example of a manufacturer of a new easy-to-use baking mix. Top management had selected apartment dwellers, younger couples, and the too-busy-to-cook crowd as the target market—because it seemed "logical" that the convenience of the new product should appeal to them. A little research on the size of this market indicated that—if these consumers responded as expected—there were enough of them to create a profitable baking mix market. The company decided to aim at this market and developed a logical marketing mix.

WHY DIDN'T THIS BAKING MIX SELL?

During the first few months, sales results were disappointing. The manufacturer "guessed" that something was wrong with the product since the promotion seemed to be adequate. At this point, a consumer survey was done—with surprising results. The product was apparently satisfactory, but the target customers just weren't interested in convenience for this kind of product. Instead, the best market turned out to be families who did lots of cooking! They liked the convenience of the mix—especially when they needed a dish in a hurry.

In this case, the original strategy planning was sloppy. The choice of target market was based on guesswork by top management. This led to a poor strategy and wasted promotion money. Just a little research on consumers—about their needs and attitudes—might have avoided this costly error. Both marketing research and management fumbled the ball by not studying the target market. Then, when sales results were poor, the company fumbled again by assuming that the product was at fault instead of checking consumers' real attitudes about the product. Fortunately, research finally uncovered the real problem. Then the overall strategy was changed quickly.

The moral of this story is that our strategic planning framework can be useful for guiding marketing research efforts. Without a logical approach, marketing researchers can waste time working on the wrong problem.

Quick answers are often needed

Marketing research often has to supply information quickly. But researchers still should use the best methods possible. For this reason, we will show that a scientific approach to solving marketing problems makes sense. This scientific approach—combined with our strategic planning framework—can help marketing managers make better decisions—even if they have to be made quickly.

THE SCIENTIFIC METHOD AND MARKETING RESEARCH

Managers want to make the best decisions possible. The scientific method helps them do this. It forces researchers to follow steps that reduce the chances for sloppy work or guesswork.

The **scientific method** is a research approach which consists of four stages:

1. Observation.
2. Developing hypotheses.
3. Prediction of the future.
4. Testing the hypotheses.

With this method, researchers try to develop **hypotheses**—educated guesses about the relationships between things or what will happen in the future. Then they test each hypothesis. A formal hypothesis statement

The scientific method starts with careful observation.

might be: "There is no significant difference between brands A and B in the minds of consumers."

The scientific approach to pain

To illustrate these stages in a simple nonmarketing case, consider a college student who develops a painful, swollen ankle after a skiing accident. The ankle could be bruised, sprained, or broken. What should he do? If he goes to a doctor, he will probably find the doctor following the scientific method:

1. Observation: Pain seems to increase if foot is twisted, but pain is not unbearable.
2. Developing an hypothesis: Since a sprain would be more painful than this, the ankle is broken.
3. Prediction of the future: Pain and swelling will reduce, but bone may heal improperly if not set.
4. Testing the hypothesis: X-ray the ankle; don't wait to see if hypothesis is correct in this case!

Now let's use the same framework to show how a marketing manager might use this method.

The scientific approach to offering shirt wrappers

A manufacturer of men's shirts wanted to develop new opportunities. The approach taken is shown here:

1. Observation: Notice some competitors' sales increasing and many competitors shifting to a new plastic wrapping.
2. Developing hypotheses: Assume (a) that plastic wrapping is the main cause of competitors' sales increases and (b) that the firm's products are similar.

3. Prediction of the future: Firm's sales ought to increase if it shifts to the new wrapping.
4. Testing hypotheses: Produce some shirts in the new package and test them in the market.

The market test revealed that the prediction was correct—sales did increase. But what if they had not? Here is one important benefit of the scientific approach. Through careful control—making certain that the test was correctly designed and run—and evaluation of results, we should be able to see exactly where the hypotheses were wrong.

In this case, either one of the hypotheses could have been wrong. Either increased sales by competitors were not caused by the new wrapping, or this manufacturer's products were not similar.

Assuming that the first hypothesis was wrong, further research might show that competitors' sales increased because their promotion was better. Or, if the second hypothesis was wrong, it might find out how the products differed and change the product.

FOUR-STEP APPROACH TO SOLVING MARKETING PROBLEMS

In marketing research, there is a four-step application of the scientific method: (1) definition of the problem, (2) situation analysis, (3) informal investigation, and (4) formal research project.

Observation—the first stage in the scientific method—is used during the first three marketing research steps. Once the problem is defined, developing hypotheses takes place. Prediction of the future occurs any time before a formal research project is planned. Testing the hypotheses

Table 4-1
Relation of scientific method to marketing research

Scientific method stages	*Used during the following marketing research steps*
Observation	Definition of problem Situation analysis Informal investigation Formal research
Formulation of hypotheses	Situation analysis Informal investigation Formal research (planning)
Prediction of the future . . . . (action implications)	Situation analysis Informal investigation Formal research (planning)
Testing hypotheses	Formal research (unless management is satisfied with an earlier but more intuitive solution)

is completed in the formal research project unless, as often happens, informal investigation solves the problem.

You can see that the scientific method is an important part of marketing research. Table 4–1 may help you see the relationships. The exact meaning of these terms is explained in the following pages.

DEFINITION OF THE PROBLEM—STEP ONE

Defining the problem is the most important and often the most difficult job of the marketing researcher. It is slow work. It requires careful observation. Sometimes it takes over half the time spent on a research project. But it is time well spent if the problem is precisely defined. The best research job on the wrong problem is wasted effort. It may even lead to more costly mistakes—the introduction of a poor product or the use of an ineffective advertising approach.

Don't confuse problems with symptoms

Problem definition sounds simple, and that's the danger. It is easy to confuse symptoms with the problem. For example, suppose that a firm's continuing sales analysis shows that the company's sales are decreasing in certain territories—while expenses remain the same—with a resulting decline in profits. Will it help to define the problem by asking: How can we stop the sales decline? Probably not. This would be like asking how to lower a patient's temperature instead of first trying to find the cause of the fever.

The real problem may be hard to discover. The marketing manager can start with the strategic planning framework and evaluate what is known

A library is a good source of data for a situation analysis.

about the target market and whether the marketing mix seems to make sense. If there are doubts about one or more of these factors, these problem areas can be explored. But without further evidence, the marketing manager should not assume too quickly that he has defined the real problem. Instead, he should take his list of possible problems and go on to the next step—trying to discover which is the basic cause of the trouble.

SITUATION ANALYSIS—STEP TWO

No talks with outsiders

In a situation analysis, researchers try to size up the situation—but without talking to outsiders. They talk to informed people within the company. They study internal company records. They also search libraries for available material.

This research is important since researchers have to know the environment in which they work. They should study information about their own company and its products. They should know the industry—and the specific markets in which it operates. They must understand their middlemen, the firm's own promotion, and its competitors' activities. Once the researchers have begun to focus on possible problems, they can look for specific kinds of information.

Unless they know what they are looking for, researchers may be confused by all the information available in their own company or in libraries. Let's take a look at the type of information we're talking about.

Secondary data is available *now*

A situation analysis evaluates **secondary data**—information which is already published. **Primary data** is information which is gathered specifically to solve a current problem. Gathering primary data is discussed later. But it must be emphasized now that too often researchers rush out to gather primary data when there is already plenty of secondary information. And this data may be available immediately—at little or no cost!

One of the first places a researcher should look for secondary data is a good library. Often your local library has the answer you need. Librarians can be a big help. Ask! They're glad to help you.

GOVERMENT SOURCES

Federal and state governments publish data on almost every subject. The federal government publishes a monthly guide to its current publications. But it is more practical to refer to federal government summary publications to obtain leads to more detailed documents.

The most useful of these summaries—the *Statistical Abstract of the United States*—is like an almanac. It is issued each year and lists more than 1,000 summary tables from work published by various federal agencies and other groups. References to world markets are included. Detailed footnotes are a guide to more specific detail on a topic.

PRIVATE SOURCES

Many private research groups, advertising agencies, newspapers, and magazines publish useful data. A good business library is valuable here for sources such as *Sales and Marketing Management, Industrial Marketing, Advertising Age,* and the publications of the National Industrial Conference Board. Some information is available at low cost as a customer service to clients of advertising agencies. For example, the J. Walter Thompson Co. advertising agency and the *Chicago Tribune* maintain continuing panels of consumers for research purposes. These panels help researchers to spot trends—giving them market knowledge hard to get in one-time surveys.

RESEARCH BY SUBSCRIPTION

Some research firms specialize in supplying data that will aid the marketing manager in situation analysis. The best-known organization specializing in continuing research is A. C. Nielsen Co. It checks 2,200 stores to supply information on product movement through food and drug stores. Nielsen also provides additional information about competitors' use of retail displays, 2-for-1 sales, and other activities. Subscribers often learn more about the activities and sales of their competitors than some of these competitors know about themselves. Nielsen now offers similar services in other countries, including Canada, Mexico, Japan, and most Western European countries.

Trade associations can also be a good source of information about a particular industry. They gather data from and for their members. They also publish magazines that report on the problems and important topics in the industry. Some of these magazines are found in large business libraries.

PROBLEM MAY BE SOLVED DURING THE SITUATION ANALYSIS.

If the problem is clear-cut, it can sometimes be solved at this point—without additional expense. Perhaps someone else already has done a study that answers almost exactly the same question.

The fact that further research may not be necessary is important. Too often researchers rush out a questionnaire to 100 or even several thousand persons or firms. This gives the impression that they are really "doing something." An effective situation analysis, unfortunately, is less impressive. If a supervisor asks the researcher what he is doing, about all he can say is, "I'm sizing up the situation" or "I'm studying the problem."

Actually, the situation analyst is really trying to discover the exact nature of the situation *and* the problem. The person who rushes out all the questionnaires may be doing this too—although he may not even know it. The point is that when the results of the questionnaire come in, he may finally see the problem. But he still won't have the answer. He will have to go on to the next step in analysis—just like the more "scientific" researcher.

"It's not fair! I break my back doing surveys while she mumbles about analyzing the situation, and *she* gets the promotion."

INFORMAL INVESTIGATION—STEP THREE

During the informal investigation, the researcher is still trying to define the problem and develop hypotheses. But now the idea is to get outside the company and the library—to talk to informed people. By informed people, we mean intelligent and efficient retailers, wholesalers, and customers. No formal questionnaire is used. The researcher is not yet testing hypotheses—except informally.

When developing machine tools, for example, it would make sense to talk to a few machine operators, plant managers in more efficient factories, design engineers at independent research organizations or universities, and perhaps a few good wholesalers who have close contact with potential customers.

Fast, informative, inexpensive

These talks would be informal, but they should help the researcher zero in on the problem and develop useful hypotheses. By this time, the researcher should have the problem area narrowed down. This is important—asking informed people to discuss general problems would be a waste of time.

An informal investigation takes little time but can be very informative. Also, it is cheaper than a large-scale survey.

On the basis of the information gathered in a situation analysis and informal investigation, the researcher should now be developing some definite hypotheses. And he may be able to decide on an answer to the problem without further research.

If management has to make a decision quickly—if it can't wait for a formal test—then well-considered hypotheses may lead to a practical solution. In such cases, care in the early steps may now be well worth the extra time and effort spent on more "scientific" research.

PLANNING THE FORMAL RESEARCH PROJECT—STEP FOUR

Gathering primary data

If the researcher has failed to solve the problem by this time, the next step is a formal research project—usually to gather primary data. Three basic methods can be used: (1) the observation method, (2) the survey method, or (3) the experimental method.

The **observation method** involves observing potential customers' behavior. This method avoids face-to-face interviews—because asking direct questions may not get very good results. Sometimes, however, asking questions can't be avoided. Then, the **survey method**—which asks potential customers questions—may be helpful. Telephone, mail, or personal interviews can be used for surveys. The **experimental method** uses experiments to test hypotheses. Either the observation method or the survey method or both could be used. But usually control groups are needed.

Managers should share in research design

The actual design of a research project is beyond the scope of this text, but it is very important to the final results. Therefore, marketing managers should be involved in the process. At least, they should be familiar with some of the design details. Then they will be able to evaluate the quality of the research and be sure that the results will be useful.

Some researchers may imply a great deal about the reliability of their research methods. They may be using samples which are not representative—yet try to pass off the results as reliable. An experienced manager would not be fooled by such sloppy work. He would understand that technical matters such as research design and the size and representativeness of samples do have relevance for the quality of the results.

EXECUTION AND INTERPRETATION OF THE RESEARCH PROJECT

We can't discuss here how to conduct and interpret a formal research project. This involves training a field staff and tabulating, interpreting, and presenting results. It also means following through to make sure results are used effectively. Such matters are explained in most marketing research texts.[1]

Marketing manager and researcher should work together

Marketing research involves some technical details. But it should be obvious that the marketing researcher and the marketing manager should work together to be sure that they really do solve the problems facing the firm.[2]

When the researcher and the manager have not worked closely together, the interpretation step becomes extremely important. While managers may not be research specialists, they have to be able to evaluate research

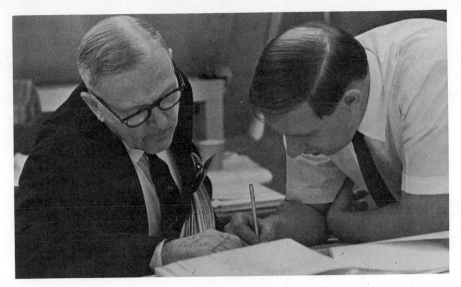

Managers should share in research design.

results. If the research methods and the reliability of the data are not clearly explained, the marketing manager must use even greater judgment in evaluating the data. In fact, if the researcher doesn't explain his methods and then suggest specific action, he should not be surprised if the marketing manager ignores the work. This stresses, again, the importance of the two working together to solve problems.

REAL PROBLEM SOLVING MAY REQUIRE ALL FOUR STEPS

Logical flow of steps may help

Marketing research usually must combine several steps to do a good job. This is illustrated by an example of a manufacturer interested in expanding its market for interior decorating products.

The company wanted to increase its sales. But it didn't know how many interior decorators were in the market—or how much money consumers spent on the company's product type (definition of the problem). A review of U.S. Census of Business data indicated that there were approximately 1,300 interior decorators. According to their own sales records (situation analysis), this would not leave much room for expansion of sales volume with their present line. Management considered branching out into other lines (hypothesis that business would improve by producing other products for this or other markets).

Before doing this, the company decided to do additional research in its present market area. They interviewed the company's sales reps and checked the circulation data of an interior decorators' magazine (more situation analysis). They also made a limited mail survey to check on the size of the market (a formal research project to test the hypothesis that there were more potential customers).

This revealed that there were actually 9,700 interior decorators who spent some $75 million on the company's type of product alone. For some reason (probably their small size) the decorators had not all been included in the published census data. It was clear at this point that the company's biggest and best market was the one which they were already selling.

In this case, no research at all or a too sketchy situation analysis would have led to a wrong answer. But further analysis—along with an informal investigation and a limited survey—got results that proved very satisfactory.[3] This type of research is within the reach of even small firms. You should now be able to understand and help in such an effort.

COST AND ORGANIZATION OF MARKETING RESEARCH

Relatively little—perhaps too little—is spent on the typical marketing research department. Often the research department's budget is about 0.2 percent of sales—$100,000 for a company with a $50 million annual sales volume![4] This is in contrast to research and development budgets that frequently run 5 to 10 percent of sales. Unfortunately, this sometimes leads to the development of products with little or no market potential.

Shortcuts cut cost, add risk

Even on small budgets, however, good research work can be done.[5] When a problem is carefully defined, formal research projects may not be necessary. This is especially true for industrial markets—because of the relatively small number of manufacturers. But taking shortcuts increases the risk.

More dependable research can become expensive. A large-scale survey could easily cost from $10,000 to $100,000. And the continuing research available from companies such as A. C. Nielsen can cost a company from $25,000 to $100,000 or more a year.

Who does the work

Most large companies have a separate marketing research department to plan and conduct research projects. Even these departments, however, often use outside specialists—such as interviewing services—to handle specific jobs.

Few companies with sales of less than $2.5 million have separate marketing research departments. They depend on sales personnel or top executives for what research they do.[6]

HOW MUCH RESEARCH SHOULD BE DONE?

No firm can afford to do without marketing research

Most companies do some marketing research—whether they know it or not. Most marketing executives would agree with the manager of marketing research for Dow Chemical Co., who states:

I feel that it is impossible to run a company today without market research, whether it is done by the president, the sales manager, or a separate group set up specifically to perform the function. Few companies are small enough to afford the luxury of having their market research done by the president. No company can afford not to do market research at all.[7]

What is the value of information?

The high cost of good research must be balanced against its probable value to management. You never get all the information you would like to have. Very detailed surveys or experiments may be "too good" or "too expensive" or "too late" if all that is needed is a rough sampling of retailer attitudes about a new pricing plan *by tomorrow*.

Marketing managers must take risks because of incomplete information. This is part of their job and always will be. They might like more data. But they must compare the cost of getting it against its likely value. If the risk is not too great, the cost of getting more or better information may be greater than the potential loss from a poor decision. A decision to expand into a new territory with the present marketing mix, for example, might be made with more confidence of success after a $5,000 survey. But simply sending a sales rep into the territory for a few weeks to try to sell the potential customers would cost less than $5,000. And—if successful—the answer is in and so are some sales.

Faced with many risky decisions, the marketing manager should seek help from research only for problems where he feels the risk can be greatly reduced at a reasonable cost.[8]

SOME FIRMS ARE BUILDING COMPUTER-AIDED MARKETING INFORMATION SYSTEMS

In some companies, marketing researchers have high status and are deeply involved in major marketing decisions. In other companies, they may be just data collectors. They have not managed to sell the idea that good information (not just data) will improve decision making.

Separate department may be needed

Some companies are setting up marketing information systems to improve the quality and quantity of information available to their managers. A **marketing information system (MIS)** is an organized way of gathering

Researchers must try to balance the cost and value of more information.

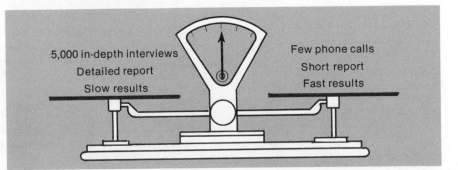

5,000 in-depth interviews
Detailed report
Slow results

Few phone calls
Short report
Fast results

Figure 4–1
A diagram of a marketing information system showing various inputs to a computer and outputs to managers

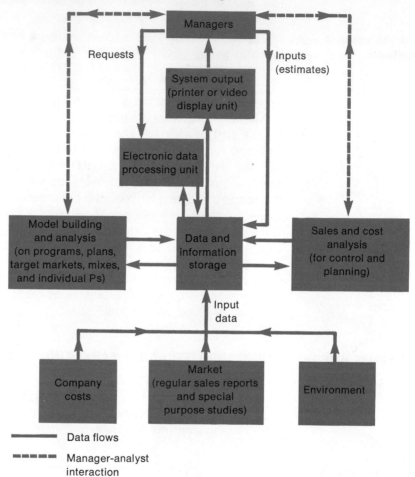

and analyzing data to obtain information to help marketing managers make decisions. Sometimes this means expanding the job of the marketing research department. In other companies, this information function is separated into a new department. Management wants to make sure that it does not get buried in the data-collection activities of the marketing research department.

Information may make managers greedy

Once marketing managers see how a working MIS can help their decision making, they are eager for more information. They see that they can improve all of their planning. They can check strategies—comparing results and making necessary changes more quickly. Figure 4–1 shows how the parts in a MIS work together.

Interest in developing information systems is growing because companies are beginning to see that better information can improve profits. It may also encourage what may seem like "daring" actions. After a series of experiments and careful data analysis, for example, Anheuser-Busch felt that they better understood how advertising affected their sales. So they cut their advertising budget from $14.8 million down to $10 million a year. While reducing advertising, sales continued to grow and the cost of advertising per barrel dropped in half. Obviously, this had a good effect on profits.[9]

We probably will see more and better marketing information systems as researchers become more experienced and computer costs continue to go down. The biggest problem may be marketing managers—not asking for more useful information or failing to use it in their decision making. Unfortunately, modern decision-making techniques are not used very much in most companies. There is still lots of room in marketing for able people who are willing to apply research techniques to solving real marketing problems.

Conclusion

In this chapter, we saw that marketing research is not a mystery understood only by statisticians. It is a management tool that helps the marketing manager make better decisions based—not on "feel" and guesswork—but on useful information. The marketing researcher should work with the marketing manager—helping him to solve real problems. Without this teamwork, the output of a marketing research department may be useless. And the department may become just a collector of data.

Marketing research should use the scientific method to solve marketing problems. Some organized approach is desirable because very often a researcher does not have the time or money to complete a full research project. If the early stages of the research effort have been done effectively, he may be able to solve the problem early in the process. A scientific approach to solving marketing problems involves four steps: definition of the problem, a situation analysis, an informal investigation, and, if necessary, a formal research project.

The text's strategic planning framework can be a big help in identifying the real problem. By focusing on the real problem, a researcher may be able to move quickly to a useful solution without the cost and problems of a formal research project. If the manager has more time and money, then he may be able to afford the luxury of a more detailed analysis. Some firms have even developed computer-aided marketing information systems which help them to learn a great deal about their market areas. This, in turn, helps them to make better decisions.

Questions for discussion

1 Marketing research entails expense—sometimes a considerable expense. Why does the text recommend the use of marketing research even though a highly experienced marketing manager is available?

2 Explain the steps in the general scientific method and then show how the steps in marketing research are similar.

3 How is situation analysis different from informal investigation? Could both be done at the same time to obtain answers sooner? Is this wise?

4 Explain how you might use each of the research methods (observation, survey, and experiment) to forecast market reaction to a new kind of margarine that is to receive no promotion other than what the retailer will give it. Further, it should be assumed that the new margarine's name will not be associated with other known products. The product will be offered at competitive prices.

5 If a firm were interested in determining the distribution of income in the state of Ohio, how could it proceed? Be specific.

6 If a firm were interested in sand and clay production in Georgia, how could it proceed? Be specific.

7 Go to the library and find (in some government publication) three marketing-oriented "facts" which you did not know existed or were available. Record on one page and show sources.

8 Discuss the concept that some information may be too expensive to obtain in relation to its value. Illustrate.

9 Discuss the concept of a marketing information system and how its output would differ from the output of the typical marketing research department.

10 Discuss what will be needed before marketing information systems become common. Also, discuss the problem facing the marketer in a small firm that is not likely to be able to afford the development of a marketing information system.

11 McDonald's was seriously considering upgrading its offering to the "dinner market" in 1978. Its objective was to increase profits. It was test marketing a chopped beefsteak sandwich selling for about $1.40—to be served from 4:00 P.M. to 9:00 P.M. McDonald's felt that increasing dinner-time sales would be one way of dealing with problems such as higher hamburger costs, the rising minimum wage, and increased competition from other hamburger-restaurant chains. Expanding its offering to the dinner market follows a successful effort to appeal to the "breakfast market." McDonald's found that it now attracts older customers for breakfast than it does for lunch or dinner. And it knows that the company's weakest appeal has been to customers over 45 years of age. Evaluate the likelihood of success of McDonald's new product. Is this a new strategy?

Suggested cases

4 Recco, Incorporated

6 Rocco's Place

7 Wallis Properties, Inc.

When you finish this chapter, you should:

1 Know how final consumer spending is related to population, income, family life cycle, and other variables.

2 Know how to estimate likely consumer purchases for broad classes of products.

3 Understand how the intra- and inter-personal variables affect an individual's buying behavior.

4 Have some "feel" for how all the behavioral variables and incoming stimuli are handled by a consumer.

5 Recognize the important new terms shown in red.

FINAL CONSUMERS AND THEIR BUYING BEHAVIOR

How can marketing managers predict how much consumers will spend on various kinds of goods? How can they predict which specific products will be purchased? In what quantities?

This chapter shows that basic data on consumer spending patterns can help forecast trends in consumer buying. But predicting which specific products and brands will be bought requires a deeper understanding of consumer buying behavior. That's what most of this chapter is about.

CONSUMER SPENDING PATTERNS RELATED TO POPULATION AND INCOME

Markets are made up of people with money to spend. So consumer spending patterns are related to population and income.

Consumer budget studies show that most consumers spend their incomes as part of a family or household unit. The family members usually pool their incomes when planning family purchases. So it makes sense for us to talk about how households or families spend their incomes.

Spending data gives specific numbers

We have much detailed information on consumer spending patterns. The patterns are the important thing—rather than the specific dollar figures—because these patterns stay pretty much the same over time. So even as this data gets older, the relationships will help us see how families spend their incomes. Continuing inflation will, of course, require some adjusting of this data.

Table 5-1
Family spending by family income level

	All families	Under $3,000	$3,000 to $3,999	$4,000 to $4,999	$5,000 to $5,999	$6,000 to $6,999	$7,000 to $7,999	$8,000 to $9,999	$10,000 to $11,999	$12,000 to $14,999	$15,000 to $19,999	$20,000 to $24,999	$25,000 and over
Food	$1,554	$ 739	$ 943	$1,071	$1,126	$1,157	$1,288	$1,392	$1,563	$1,750	$2,010	$2,293	$2,651
Housing	2,435	1,310	1,539	1,614	1,709	1,818	1,964	2,128	2,342	2,591	3,027	3,495	4,682
Clothing	653	218	311	310	394	427	493	517	617	692	867	1,082	1,564
Transport	1,629	508	631	783	892	1,096	1,257	1,422	1,697	1,956	2,257	2,712	3,202
Health care	486	227	309	381	387	410	423	456	482	508	578	697	887
Personal care	101	36	53	59	69	77	77	81	96	105	130	159	226
Education	98	14	17	25	18	27	33	35	53	74	132	253	425
Reading	49	17	23	24	31	32	38	36	47	54	67	82	108
Recreation	657	174	238	241	334	288	371	470	586	683	896	1,297	1,834
Alcohol	78	25	39	45	50	52	65	63	84	79	106	117	177
Tobacco	129	72	77	90	96	108	119	135	142	155	172	172	148
Personal insurance	257	55	84	84	103	109	135	175	236	277	370	459	771
Retirement, pensions	595	239	279	261	291	334	354	392	557	626	820	1,071	1,480
Gifts, contributions	432	128	157	175	210	280	268	311	314	403	492	669	1,604

Source: Consumer Expenditure Survey Series: Interview Survey, 1972 and 1973, Report 455–3, pp. 19–23.

Table 5–1 shows the average annual spending by families for major kinds of purchases. These figures should keep you from making wild guesses based only on your own experience. The amount spent on food, housing, clothing, transport, and so on does vary by income level. The relationships make sense when you realize that many of the purchases are for "necessities."

Estimating how potential customers spend their money

Data such as in Table 5–1 can help a marketing manager understand how potential target customers spend their money. For example, if he is seriously considering consumers in the $15,000–$19,999 income group, he can analyze how families in this group spend their money. Then he can consider how they would have to rearrange spending to buy his product. A swimming pool manufacturer could see that such families spend about $896 on recreation of all kinds. If a particular pool costs $600 a year, including depreciation and maintenance, the average family in this income category would have to make a big change in life-style if it bought the pool.

Of course, this data will not tell the pool maker whether these potential customers *will* buy the pool. But it does supply useful input to help the manager's planning. If a manager feels that more information is needed— perhaps about these people's attitudes toward recreation products—then some marketing research may be necessary. For example, a manager may want to make a budget study on consumers who already have swimming pools—to see how they adjusted their spending patterns—and how they felt before and after the purchase.

Income has a direct effect upon spending patterns. But there are other facts that should not be ignored in any careful analysis of potential markets.

Stage of family life cycle affects spending

Two demographic dimensions—age and number of children—affect spending patterns. Put together, these dimensions are concerned with the life cycle of a family. See Figure 5–1 for a summary of life cycle and buying behavior.

YOUNG PEOPLE AND FAMILIES ACCEPT NEW IDEAS

Younger people seem to be more open to new products and brands. But they are also careful shoppers. One study of 14–25 year olds showed that 74 percent of them compared prices and brands before buying. The average income of these younger people is lower than that of older groups. But they spend a greater part of their income on "discretionary" items. They do not yet have big expenses for housing, education, and raising a family.[1] Although many are marrying later—or deciding not to—some young people *are* getting married. These younger families (especially those with no children) are still buying durable goods such as automobiles and furniture. They need less food. It is only as children begin to arrive and grow that the family spending shifts to furniture, clothing, and services—

Figure 5–1
Stages in the family life cycle[2]

Stage	Characteristics and buying behavior
1. Singles: Unmarried people living away from parents	Feel "affluent" and "free." Buy basic household goods. More interested in recreation, cars, vacations, clothes, cosmetics and personal care items.
2. Divorced or separated	May be financially squeezed to pay for alimony or maintaining two households. Buying may be limited to "necessities"—especially for women who had no "job skills."
3. Newly married couples: No children	Both may work and so they feel financially well-off. Buy durables: cars, refrigerators, stoves, basic furniture—and recreation equipment and vacations.
4. Full nest I: Youngest child under six	Feel squeezed financially because they are buying homes and household durables—furniture, washers, dryers, and TV. Also buying child-related products—food, medicines, clothes and toys. Really interested in new products.
5. Full nest II: Youngest child over five	Financially are better off as husband earns more and/or wife goes to work as last child goes to school. More spent on food, clothing, education, and recreation for growing children.
6. Full nest III: Older couples with dependent children	Financially even better off as husband earns more and more wives work. May replace durables and furniture, and buy cars, boats, dental services, and more expensive recreation and travel. May buy bigger houses.
7. Empty nest: Older couples, no children living with them, head still working	Feel financially "well-off." Home ownership at peak and house may be paid for. May make home improvements or move into apartments. And may travel, entertain, go to school, and make gifts and contributions. Not interested in new products.
8. Sole survivor, still working	Income still good. Likely to sell home and continue with previous life style.
9. Senior citizen I: Older married couple, no children living with them, head retired	Big drop in income. May keep home but cut back on most buying as purchases of medical care, drugs, and other health-related items go up.
10. Senior citizen II: Sole survivor, not working	Same as senior citizen I, except likely to sell home, and has special need for attention, affection, and security.

such as education, medical, and personal care. This usually occurs when the household head reaches the 35–44 age bracket.

TEENAGERS MEAN SHIFTS IN SPENDING

Once the children become teenagers, further shifts in spending occur. Teenagers eat more. Their clothes become more expensive. And they develop recreation and education needs that are hard on the family budget. The parents may be forced to change their spending to cover these costs—spending less on durable goods such as appliances, automobiles, furniture, and houses.

Many teenagers do earn much or all of their own spending money—

Young people spend money on "discretionary" items.

so they are an attractive market. But marketers who have aimed at teenagers are beginning to notice the aging of the population. Motorcycle manufacturers, for example, have already been hurt—as teenagers are their heaviest buyers.[3]

SELLING TO THE "EMPTY NESTERS"

An important group within the 50–64 age category is sometimes called the "empty nesters." Their children are grown. They are now able to spend their money in other ways. It is the "empty nesters" who move back into the smaller, more luxurious apartments in the city. They may also be more interested in travel, small sports cars, and other things they couldn't afford before. Much depends on their income, of course. But this is a high-income period for many workers—especially white-collar workers.

SENIOR CITIZENS ARE A BIG NEW MARKET

Finally, the "senior citizen" market should not be neglected. The number of people over 65 is now over 10 percent of the population—and growing.

Although older people generally have reduced incomes, many do have money and very different needs. Some firms are already catering to the senior citizen market. Gerber, for example—faced with a declining baby market—began producing foods for older people.[4] Some firms have gone into special diet supplements and drug products. Others have designed housing developments to appeal to older persons.

Do ethnic groups buy differently?

America may be called the "melting pot," but there are still distinct ethnic groups that require special consideration.

It is in this area that stereotype thinking is the most common and where a marketer may need to do some original marketing research. All blacks, for example, do not drive big cars. In fact, black consumers spend less on automobile transportation than do whites with comparable incomes.[5] And those of Irish descent do not eat just corn beef and cabbage, just as those of Italian descent buy food products other than pasta.

Some minority groups seem to be striving for what they believe to be white middle-income standards in material goods. Current products may be quite acceptable to them. Others have rejected this goal in favor of their own set of values. Separate strategies may be needed for these nationality or racially defined markets.

When the wife earns, the family spends

A relatively new trend that deserves attention is the growing number of married women who have jobs. In 1950, only 24 percent of wives worked outside the home. This rose to 44 percent by 1976.[6]

In families where the wife works, she contributes about 30 percent of all the family spending power.[7] This is why the average family income is as high as it is.

When the wife works outside the home, it seems to have little effect on the nutrition value of her family's food. But working wives do spend more for food. And they do choose more expensive types of food. Families with working wives also spend more on clothing, alcohol and tobacco, house furnishings and equipment, and automobiles.

In short, when a wife works, it affects the spending habits of the family. This fact must be considered when analyzing markets.

THE BEHAVIORAL SCIENCES HELP US UNDERSTAND CONSUMERS

Consumer spending patterns are useful for forecasting basic trends and relationships. Unfortunately, however, when many firms sell similar products, this data is of little value in predicting which specific products and brands will be purchased. Yet this is very important to a marketing manager.

To find better answers, we need to understand people better. For this reason, many marketers have turned to the behavioral sciences for help. For the rest of this chapter, we'll be looking at the thinking in psychology, sociology, and the other behavioral sciences.

Buying in a black box

A simplified way of summing up the way some behavioral scientists see consumer buying behavior is shown in Figure 5–2. Potential customers are exposed to various stimuli—including the marketing mixes of competitors. Somehow, an individual interprets these stimuli. (This person is usually shown in a mysterious "black box" that we can't see into. (See Figure 5–2.) Then, for some reason, he responds to the stimuli and may buy a marketer's product or service.

This is the classical model of buyer behavior. This **stimulus-response**

Figure 5–2
Simplified buyer behavior model

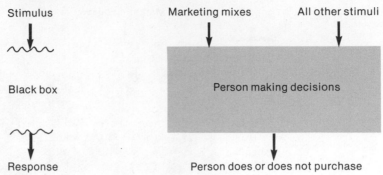

model says that people respond in some predictable way to a stimulus. The model does not predict *why* they behave the way they do—only that there is a predictable response to a stimulus. This is the model we were using when discussing spending patterns. There, we hoped to find some relationship between demographic characteristics of customers in the black box, product categories (stimulus), and the customer's buying behavior (response). We did find some relationships. Now we want to go even deeper. This requires a better understanding of how consumer decision making works.

There are many black boxes

Depending on a person's behavioral science training, we find many descriptions of how the black box works. These different theories lead to different forecasts about how consumers will behave.

How the economist views the black box

The economist typically assumes that consumers are **economic men**—people who logically weigh choices in terms of cost and value received—to obtain the greatest satisfaction from spending their time, energy, and money. Therefore, the economist collects and analyzes demographic data when trying to predict consumer behavior. It was a logical extension of the economic-man theory which led us to look at consumer spending patterns earlier in the chapter. There is value in this approach. Consumers must at least have income to be in the market. But other behavioral scientists suggest that the black box works in a more complicated way than the economic-man model.

How we will view the black box

Consumers have many dimensions. Let's try to combine their various dimensions into a better model of how consumers make decisions. Figure 5–3 presents a more detailed view of the black box model. Here, we see both intra-personal and inter-personal variables affecting the person making decisions.

These topics will be discussed in the next few pages. Then, we will look at the consumer's problem-solving process.

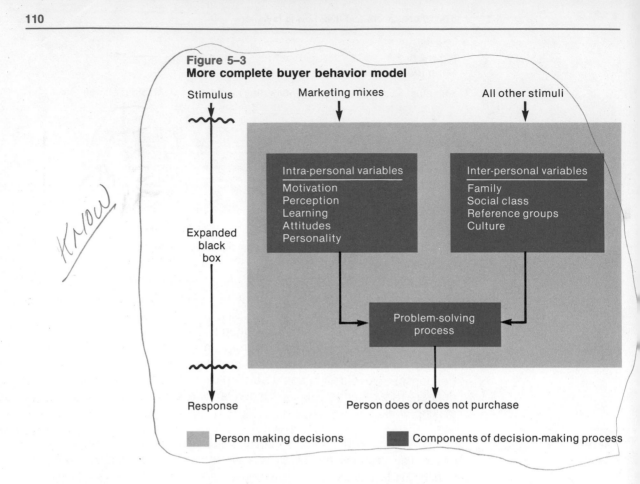

Figure 5–3
More complete buyer behavior model

Stimulus   Marketing mixes   All other stimuli

Expanded
black
box

Intra-personal variables
Motivation
Perception
Learning
Attitudes
Personality

Inter-personal variables
Family
Social class
Reference groups
Culture

Problem-solving
process

Response   Person does or does not purchase

Person making decisions   Components of decision-making process

INTRA-PERSONAL VARIABLES FOCUS ON THE INDIVIDUAL

**Motivation determines
what is wanted**

Everybody is motivated by needs and wants. **Needs** are the basic forces which motivate an individual to do something. Some needs are concerned with a person's physical body. Other needs are concerned with the individual's view of himself and his relationship with others. Wants are less basic. **Wants** are "needs" which are learned during an individual's life. For example, everyone has a basic need for food, but some people also have a learned want for a "Big Mac."

When a need or want is not satisfied, it leads to a drive. The food need, for instance, leads to a hunger drive. A **drive** is a strong stimulus which causes a tension that the individual tries to reduce by finding ways of satisfying this drive. Drives are, in effect, the reasons behind certain behavior patterns.

ARE THERE HIERARCHIES OF NEEDS?

Some psycholgists see a hierarchy of needs. Maslow is well known for his five-level hierarchy. But we will discuss a similar four-level hierarchy which is easier to apply. It is supported by more recent reseach on human

"The trouble is, my stomach's full after salad and fish, but my mind isn't full until after chocolate cake."

Figure 5–4
The PSSP hierarchy of needs

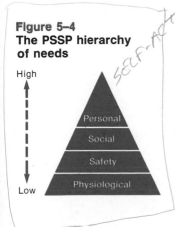

SELF-ACTUALIZATION

High

Personal

Social

Safety

Physiological

Low

Unit pricing may help satisfy economic needs.

motivation.[8] The four levels are illustrated in Figure 5–4. The lowest-level needs are physiological. Then come safety, social, and personal needs. For easy recall, think of the "PSSP needs."

The **physiological needs** are concerned with satisfying hunger, thirst, rest, sex, and other biological needs. The **safety needs** are concerned with protection and physical well-being (perhaps involving health, food, drugs, and exercise). The **social needs** are concerned with love, friendship, status, and respect. These are all things that involve a person's interaction with others. The **personal needs,** on the other hand, are concerned with the need of an individual to gain personal satisfaction—unrelated to what others think or do. Examples here include self-respect, accomplishment, fun, freedom, and relaxation.

Motivation theory suggests that humans never reach a state of complete satisfaction. As soon as lower-level needs are reasonably satisfied, those at higher levels become more dominant. It is important to see, however, that a particular physical good or service might satisfy more than one need at the same time. A hamburger in a friendly environment, for example, might satisfy not only the physiological need to satisfy hunger, but also some social need.

ECONOMIC NEEDS AFFECT HOW WE SATISFY BASIC NEEDS

The four basic needs can help explain *what* we buy. The economic needs help explain *how* we buy and *why* we want specific product features.

Economic needs are concerned with making the best use of a customer's limited resources—as the customer sees it. Some people look for the best price. Others want the best quality, almost regardless of price. And others settle for the best value. It's helpful to think of eight economic needs:

ECONOMIC NEEDS

KNOW

1. Convenience.
2. Efficiency in operation or use.
3. Dependability in use.
4. Reliability of service.
5. Durability.
6. Improvement of earnings.
7. Improvement of productivity of property.
8. Economy of purchase or use.

With economic needs, measurable factors can be emphasized. These might include specific dollar savings, differences in weight, or length of product life.

Perception determines what is seen and felt

DECIDE

All kinds of stimuli are aimed at consumers. But they may not hear or see anything. This is because we unconsciously apply the following selective processes:

1. **Selective exposure**—our eyes and mind notice only information that interests us.
2. **Selective perception**—we can screen out or modify ideas, messages, and information that conflict with previously learned attitudes and beliefs.
3. **Selective retention**—we remember only what we want to remember. These selective processes help explain why some people are not at all affected by some advertising—even offensive advertising. They just don't see or remember it.

A person's attitudes affect these selective processes. Further, decisions that the consumer is currently making and typically concerned about will affect which attitudes are important. If a consumer is thinking about buying an automobile, for example, then he may become quite interested in available cars, people's attitudes toward them, and car advertising. At the same time, if a house purchase is not being considered at all, housing-related stimuli may be completely screened out.

When planning strategies, it would be useful to know how potential customers perceive their problems, what kind of information they are looking for, and what standards they are using. This would help an advertiser catch the attention of potential buyers as they are receiving the incoming stimuli.

Perception skills are improved by learning. This is why some marketers pay special attention to the learning process.

Learning determines what is remembered

Learning theorists have described a number of steps in the learning process. They define a "drive" as a strong stimulus that motivates an individual. Depending on the **cues**—products, signs, ads, and other stimuli existing in the environment—an individual chooses some specific response. A **response** is an effort to satisfy a drive. The specific response chosen depends on the cues and the person's past experience.

Reinforcement of the learning process occurs when a response is followed by satisfaction—that is, reducing the drive tension. Reinforcement

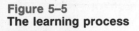

Figure 5–5
The learning process

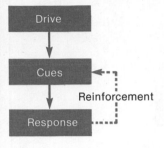

strengthens the relationship between the cue and the response. And it may lead to a similar response the next time the drive occurs. Repeated reinforcement leads to the development of a habit—making the decision process routine for the individual. The relationships of the important variables in the learning process are shown in Figure 5–5.

The learning process can be illustrated by a hungry person. The hunger drive could be satisfied in a variety of ways. But if the person happened to be driving around and saw a McDonald's sign—a cue—he might satisfy the drive by buying a McDonald's hamburger—the response. If the experience is satisfactory, reinforcement would occur. Our friend might be quicker to satisfy this drive in the same way in the future. This emphasizes the importance of developing good products which live up to the promises of the firm's advertising. Note, people could learn to like *or dislike* McDonald's hamburgers. Learning works both ways.

Good experiences can lead to positive attitudes about a firm's product. Bad experiences can lead to negative attitudes—which may be difficult or impossible to change with promotion. In fact, the subject of attitudes is very important to marketers. We'll discuss this more fully in a following section.

ARE NEEDS LEARNED?

Trying to separate learned from unlearned needs is not very useful. But brief consideration of the idea is desirable because some critics feel that marketing "creates" many needs.

It can be argued that people are born with all the basic needs. A small child develops strong desires for "things"—certainly before advertisers have had a chance to influence him.

Even the need for status—which some marketing critics feel is related to the influence of advertising—is found among animals and in human societies where there is no advertising. Studies of birds show that there is a definite pecking order in flocks. In a study of jackdaws, for instance, it was found that the female—upon mating—takes on the status of her mate. African villagers raise domesticated cattle and goats purely as signs of wealth and social status. For food, they hunt wild animals.[9]

WANTING A HAMBURGER IS LEARNED BEHAVIOR

Some needs may be culturally (or socially) determined, however. When human babies are born, their needs are simple. But as they grow, they learn complex behavior patterns—to satisfy the drives arising from these needs. As their needs become more sophisticated and specific, the needs can be described as wants. The need for food, for instance, may lead to many specific food wants. The resulting hunger drive may be satisfied only by the specific food desired. The people of Western nations like beef. And their children learn to like it. In India, however, Hindus regard the cow as sacred and will not eat beef. Hindu children learn to eat and like other foods. Many foods, in other words, can satisfy the hunger drive.

Drive   Cue   Response   Reinforcement

But in a particular culture, an individual might want a hamburger. And the hunger drive might not be fully satisfied until he has eaten one.

Attitudes limit what decisions are made

Attitudes are an important topic for marketers because they affect the selective processes. Attitudes also affect learning—and eventually buying decisions. **Attitudes** are reasonably permanent points of view about an object or class of objects. Attitudes are things people believe strongly enough to be willing to take some action. Opinions and beliefs are not so action-oriented. It would be possible to have a belief—say that the world was round—without having an attitude about the world.

Attitudes are not the same thing as buying intentions. A person might have a positive attitude toward a Cadillac, for example, without ever intending to buy one. So attitudes must be used with care when trying to predict buying behavior.

Consumers' attitudes—both positive and negative—are learned from experiences with a product, exposure to the attitudes of others, or promotion which affects their own attitudes. If a marketer can learn the attitudes of the firm's potential target markets, he can know whether there are positive attitudes to appeal to. Or maybe he must change existing attitudes. Or perhaps he must create new attitudes. Each of these jobs would require a slightly different approach.

Marketers generally try to understand the attitudes of their potential customers and work with them—perhaps directing positive attitudes toward the firm's own brand. This is much easier and more economical than trying to change attitudes. Changing present attitudes—especially negative ones—is probably the most difficult job that marketers face. If very negative attitudes are held by the target market, it may be more practical to try another strategy.[10]

Personality affects how people see things

Much research has been done on how personality affects people's behavior. The results have been disappointing to marketers. Certainly, personality traits influence how individual people behave. But right now we do not have *general* principles about personality which help us much in strategy planning.

LIFE-STYLE ANALYSIS MAY HELP

Some marketers have tried to find meaning in sets of consumer-related dimensions. These include consumers' demographics, as well as their Activities, Interests, and Opinions—which could include personality characteristics. The last three sets are referred to as the "AIO variables." Typical life-style dimensions are shown in Table 5–2.

The basic idea behind this kind of analysis is that the more you know about your potential customers, the better you can plan strategies to reach them.

Life-style analysis usually includes many items—perhaps questionnaires as long as 25 pages—because several statements must be answered for each of the AIO variables to get a real understanding of potential customers. For example, if a marketer wanted to learn whether his target market included "sports spectators" he could list statements such as:

"I like to watch or listen to baseball or football games."
"I usually read the sports pages in the daily paper."
"I thoroughly enjoy conversations about sports."
"I would rather go to a sporting event than a dance."[11]

Potential customers would be asked how strongly they agreed with the statements—from "definitely agree" to "definitely disagree." Hundreds of such statements are used. And then a computer tries to find patterns among all of the answers.

Life-style research can provide helpful information about markets. But

Table 5–2
Life-style dimensions

Activities	*Interests*	*Opinions*	*Demographics*
Work	Family	Themselves	Age
Hobbies	Home	Social issues	Education
Social events	Job	Politics	Income
Vacation	Community	Business	Occupation
Entertainment	Recreation	Economics	Family size
Club membership	Fashion	Education	Dwelling
Community	Food	Products	Geography
Shopping	Media	Future	City size
Sports	Achievements	Culture	Stage in life cycle

Source: Joseph T. Plummer, "The Concept and Application of Life-Style Segmentation," *Journal of Marketing,* January 1974, pp. 33–37.

so far, the results have been special purpose—no general principles have been found. A specific analysis, for example, might isolate clearly defined segments such as swingers, conservatives, etc.

The answers to the AIO questions provide the marketer with an in-depth view of how these markets think and buy specific products. Sometimes it will show that changing products or target markets is needed. White Stag, for example, modified its missy-size sportswear lines when a life-style study showed that what the firm thought was the "missy market" was really five different kinds of women with varied life-styles. This led to new lines for the various submarkets and new promotion to consumers and retailers.[12]

INTER-PERSONAL VARIABLES AFFECT THE INDIVIDUAL'S BUYING BEHAVIOR

So far we have been discussing findings from psychology. Yet consumer behavior may be determined not only by a person's particular personality and drives, but also by his relations with others.

Social psychologists and sociologists see market behavior as a response to the attitudes and behavior of others. Let's look at their thinking about the interaction of the individual with family, social class, reference groups, and culture.

Family considerations may overwhelm personal ones

Most decisions are made within a framework developed by experience within a family. An individual may go through much thinking about his own preference for various products and services. But this analysis may be only one of the influences in the final decision. Social processes— such as power, domination, and affection—may be involved, too. This decision-making behavior is often the result of much social learning.

A BOAT FOR FATHER OR A TV FOR MOTHER

The interaction of various social forces can be illustrated by a choice between two products: a television set and a boat with outboard motor.

The husband in a family might be interested in the boat and motor for his camping and fishing trips. Weekend pleasure outings with the family would be secondary. But in his arguments, he can present his preference in the desirable terms of family wants and uses. At the same time, his wife might want a new television set. It would add to the beauty of her home and also could be used as entertainment for herself, her husband, and the children. She, too, could argue that this purchase is for the family.

The actual outcome in such a situation is unpredictable. It depends on: the strength of the husband's and the wife's preferences; their individual degree of dominance of the family; who contributes the most money to the family's income; the need for affection; and the response of other family members. Yet an individual retail sales clerk in direct contact with the family might sense how the family operates and be able to adjust the sales presentation to fit.

Families make decisions together.

WHO IS THE REAL DECISION MAKER?

Although one person in the family often makes the purchase, in planning strategy it is important to know who is the real decision maker.

Traditionally, the wife has been considered the family purchasing agent. She had the time to shop and run the errands. So, most promotion has been aimed at women. But the situation may be changing as more women work—and as night and Sunday shopping become more popular. Men now have more time for—and interest in—shopping.

THE NATURE OF THE PRODUCT MAKES A DIFFERENCE

The husband is usually concerned with buying decisions that involve functional (mechanical or technical) items. Of the two, he tends to be more concerned with matters external to the family. The wife is more likely to make those buying decisions that have expressive values. She is more concerned with internal matters. These distinctions may apply even if the user of a purchased product is the other person. For example, a wife may buy the husband's clothing accessories. The husband might buy household appliances.

The husband and wife may work together where the usual husband-wife roles overlap. Husbands and wives may share in home improvements, for example, because they involve both functional and internal matters.[13]

SOME BUY FOR THEMSELVES OR OTHERS

The question of spending by the family is not limited to wives and husbands. As the life-cycle stages of the family change, children begin to spend more money.

In many cases, the person doing the shopping is just acting as an agent for others. And they may have specified which products should be bought. Small children may want specific brands of cereals. A teenager may want a certain brand of shampoo.

Social class affects buying of specifics

Up to now, we have been concerned with the individual and his relation to his family. Now let's consider how society looks at an individual and the family—in terms of social class. **Social class** is concerned with how an individual fits into the social structure.

Just mentioning "social class" raises negative reactions in some people. But sociological research shows that a class structure does exist in the United States.

In discussing class structure, we will use the traditional technical terms: "upper," "middle," and "lower." These words seem to suggest "superior" and "inferior." But no value judgment is meant. In fact, it is not possible to say that a particular class is "better" or "happier" than any other. Some people try to enter a different class because they find that class more attractive. But others are quite comfortable in their own class—and prefer to remain there. A marketer should learn the characteristics and typical buying patterns of each class—not pass judgments.

CHARACTERISTICS OF THE U.S. CLASS SYSTEM

The U.S. class system is an individual and a family system. While a child is a member of a family, his social class will depend on the class of his family. But grown children often "join" a different class than their parents. This happens when they reach higher education levels or take different occupations than their parents.

The U.S. class system is usually measured by occupation, education, and housing arrangements. The *source* of income is related to these variables. *But there is* not *a direct relation between* amount *of income and social class.* Some blue-collar workers earn much more than some white-collar workers, but they are usually placed in a "lower" class.

The early work on social class in the United States was done for cities in the 10,000–25,000 population range. Later, the *Chicago Tribune* developed a population breakdown for Chicago—which is probably typical of a big industrial city. Many of the findings are interesting to marketing managers. Let's look at the *Chicago Tribune*'s breakdown first, and then consider some of the findings.

1. **Upper Class** (0.9 percent of the total population): This was defined as wealthy old families **(upper-upper class)** and the socially prominent new rich **(lower-upper class).** This group has been the traditional leader in the American community. Most large manufacturers, bankers, and top marketing people belong to it. It represents, however, less than 1 percent of the population. Being so small, the two upper classes are often merged into one.
2. **Upper-Middle Class** (7.2 percent of population): These are the successful business people, professionals, and top sales people. The advertising professional usually is part of this class—reflecting the tastes and codes of the first two groups. Yet, together, groups 1 and 2 still represent only 8.1 percent of the population!

3. **Lower-Middle Class** (28.4 percent of population): These are the white-collar workers—small business people, office workers, teachers, technicians, and most sales people. The American moral code and the emphasis on hard work have come from this class. This has been the most conforming, church-going, morally serious part of society. We speak of America as a middle-class society. But the middle-class value system stops here. *Two thirds of our society is not middle class.*

4. **Upper-Lower Class** (44.0 percent of population): These are the factory production line workers, the skilled workers, the service workers—the "blue-collar" workers—and the local politicians and union leaders who would lose their power if they moved out of this class.

5. **Lower-Lower Class** (19.5 percent of population): This group includes unskilled laborers and people in nonrespectable occupations.[14]

WHAT DO THESE CLASSES MEAN?

The *Chicago Tribune* class studies suggest that an old saying—"A rich man is simply a poor man with more money"—is not true. It appears that a person belonging to the lower class—given the same income as a middle-class person—handles himself and his money very differently. The various classes shop at different stores. They would prefer different treatment from sales people. They buy different brands of products—even though their prices are about the same—and they have different spending-saving attitudes. Some of these differences are shown in Figure 5–6.

The impacts on strategy planning are most interesting. Selection of advertising media should be related to social class, for example. Customers

Figure 5–6
A comparison of attitudes and characteristics of middle and lower social classes[15]

Middle class	Lower class
1. Pointed to the future.	1. Pointed to the present and past.
2. Viewpoint embraces a long expanse of time.	2. Lives and thinks in a short expanse of time.
3. More urban identification.	3. More rural identification.
4. Stresses rationality.	4. Nonrational essentially.
5. Has a well-structured sense of the universe.	5. Vague and unclear structuring.
6. Horizons vastly extended or not limited.	6. Horizons sharply defined and limited.
7. Greater sense of choice making.	7. Limited sense of choice making.
8. Self-confident, willing to take risks.	8. Very much concerned with security and insecurity.
9. Immaterial and abstract in thinking (idea-minded).	9. Concrete and perceptive in thinking (thing-minded).
10. Sees himself tied to national happenings.	10. World revolves around family.

in the lower classes would have little interest in *Fortune, Holiday, Vogue,* or *Ladies Home Journal.* The middle and upper classes probably would have little desire to read *True Story, Modern Romances,* or *True Confessions.*

Class should also affect product design—and the kinds of goods carried by retailers. The *Chicago Tribune* studies found that lower class people preferred overstuffed or "flashy" house furnishings. Those in the middle and upper classes preferred plain, functional styles. Further, those in the lower classes seemed to be confused by variety and had difficulty making choices. As a result, such buyers looked on furniture sales people as friends and advisors. The middle-class buyers, on the other hand, were more self-confident. They knew what they wanted. They preferred the sales clerk to be an impersonal guide.

Reference groups are important too

A **reference group** is the people to whom the individual looks when forming attitudes about a particular topic. A person normally has several reference groups—for different topics. Some he meets face-to-face. Others he may just wish to copy. In either case, he may take his values from "them" and make buying decisions based on what he feels they would accept. *Playboy* magazine editors, for instance—and the "in" people who read it—might be a reference group for *some Playboy* readers.

The importance of reference groups depends on the product and whether anyone else will be able to "see" which product and which brand is being used. Figure 5–7 suggests the relationships. For example, an individual may smoke cigarettes because his reference group smokes. And the group's preference may even decide the brand he chooses. At the other extreme, most people in our society use laundry soap. But which brand is used is not easily seen. In this case, reference group influence may be small.

Figure 5–7
Reference-group influence[16]

Brand type \ Product class	Weak	Strong
Weak	Canned peaches Laundry soap Refrigerator (brand) Radios	Air conditioners* Instant coffee* TV (black and white)
Strong	Clothing Furniture Magazines Refrigerator (type) Toilet soap	Cars* Cigarettes* Beer (premium versus regular)* Drugs*

*Classification by the extent to which reference groups influence their purchase based on actual experimental evidence. Other products listed are classified speculatively on the basis of generalizations derived from the sum of research in this area and confirmed by the judgment of seminar participants.

Reaching the opinion leaders who are buyers

Opinion leaders are people who influence others. Opinion leaders are not necessarily wealthier or better educated. And opinion leaders on one subject are not necessarily opinion leaders on another subject. Home-makers with large families may be consulted for advice on cooking. Young girls may be leaders in new clothing styles and cosmetics. This may occur within the various social classes—with different opinion leaders in the various classes.[17]

Culture surrounds the whole decision-making process

Culture is the whole set of values, beliefs, attitudes, and ways of doing things of a similar group of people. We can think of the American culture, the western Canadian culture, the French culture, or the Latin American culture. People in these cultural groupings would be more similar in outlook and behavior than those in other groups. And sometimes it is useful to think of subcultures within such groups. For example, within the American culture there are various religious and ethnic subcultures.

From a target marketing point of view, marketers would probably want to aim at people within one culture. So, if a firm developed strategies for two cultures, two different strategies would be needed.[18]

The values, attitudes, and beliefs within a culture change slowly. So once a manager develops a good understanding of the culture for which he is planning, he can focus on the more dynamic variables discussed above.

CONSUMERS USE PROBLEM-SOLVING PROCESSES

Behavioral scientists generally agree that people are problem solvers. How the individual solves a particular problem depends on his own intra-personal and inter-personal variables. However, a common problem-solving process seems to be used by most consumers.

The basic problem-solving process consists of five steps:

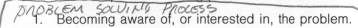

1. Becoming aware of, or interested in, the problem.
2. Gathering information about possible solutions.
3. Evaluating alternative solutions, perhaps trying some out.
4. Deciding on the appropriate solution.
5. Evaluating the decision.[19]

A larger version of this basic process is presented in Figure 5–8.

Three levels of problem solving are useful

The basic problem-solving process shows the steps a consumer might go through while trying to find a way to satisfy his needs. But it does not show how long he will take—or how much thought he will give each step.

It is helpful, therefore, to recognize three levels of problem solving: extensive problem solving, limited problem solving, and routinized re-sponse behavior.[20] These problem-solving approaches might be used for any kind of product or service.

Figure 5–8
Consumer's problem-solving process

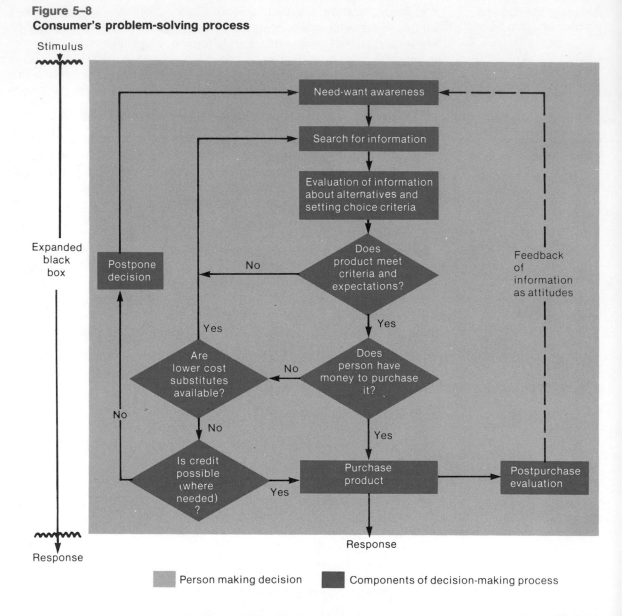

Extensive problem solving is involved when a need is completely new to a person—and much effort is taken to understand the need and how to satisfy it. A new college student, for example, may have feelings of loneliness, a need for companionship, a need for achievement, and so on. It may take him some time to figure out how and what he wants to do.

Limited problem solving involves *some* effort to understand a person's need and how best to satisfy it. Our college student, for example, might have tried various ways of satisfying his needs and come up with several fairly good choices. So limited problem solving would mean deciding which choice would be best at a particular time.

Routinized response behavior involves mechanically selecting a particular way of satisfying a need whenever it occurs. When our college student feels the need for companionship, for example, it might be quickly solved by meeting with friends in familiar surroundings. A daily trip to the local "hang out" might become the answer to this problem.

New ideas need an adoption process

Really new ideas present a problem solver with a harder job—the adoption process. The **adoption process** means the steps which individuals go through on the way to accepting or rejecting a new idea. Note how promotion could affect the adoption process.

The adoption process for individuals moves through some definite stages, as follows:

1. Awareness—The potential customer comes to know about the product but lacks details. He may not even know how it works or what it will do.
2. Interest—If he becomes interested, he gathers general information and facts about the product.
3. Evaluation—He begins to make a mental trial, applying the product to his own situation.
4. Trial—The customer may buy the product so that he can try it. A product that is either too expensive to try or can't be obtained for trial may have trouble being adopted.
5. Decision—The customer decides on either adoption or rejection. A satisfactory experience may lead to adoption of the product and regular use. According to learning theory, reinforcement will lead to adoption.
6. Confirmation—The adopter continues to think over his decision and searches for support for his choice, i.e., further reinforcement.[21]

DISSONANCE MAY SET IN AFTER THE DECISION

After a decision has been made, a buyer may have second thoughts. He may have had to choose from among several attractive choices— weighing the pros and cons and finally making a decision. Later doubts, however, may lead to **dissonance**—a form of tension growing out of uncertainty about the rightness of a decision. Dissonance may lead a buyer to search for more information to confirm the wisdom of the decision and help reduce his tension. You can see how important it is to provide information the consumer might want at this stage. Without this confirmation, the adopter might buy something else next time. Further, he would not give very positive comments to others.[22]

Several processes are related and affect strategy planning

The relation between the problem-solving process, the adoption process, and learning can be seen in Figure 5–9. It is important to see that they can be changed by promotion. Also, note that the problem-solving behavior of potential buyers would affect the design of distribution systems.

Dissonance may occur after a purchase.

If they are not willing to travel far to shop, then more facilities may be needed if you want their business. Their attitudes may also decide what price to charge. Clearly, a knowledge of how a target market handles problem solving would make strategy planning easier.

Figure 5–9
Relation of problem-solving process, adoption process, and learning (given a problem and drive tensions)

Problem-solving steps	Adoption process steps	Learning steps
1. Becoming aware of or interested in the problem.	Awareness and interest	Drive
2. Gathering information about possible solutions.	Interest and evaluation	Cues
3. Evaluating alternative solutions, perhaps trying some out.	Evaluation, maybe trial	
4. Deciding on the appropriate solution.	Decision	Response
5. Evaluating the decision.	Confirmation	

Reinforcement

INTEGRATING THE BEHAVIORAL SCIENCE APPROACHES

We have been studying the impact of many variables on a consumer's problem-solving behavior. Now—to tie this all together—we will show the various processes in one diagram. Then, we will suggest how it might help you plan better marketing strategies and understand new research findings.

Integrated model can aid strategy planning

The integrated buyer behavior model in Figure 5–10 can be useful for predicting the problem-solving behavior the target customers are likely to use in a specific market.

Extensive problem solving may be necessary if there isn't much information at some of the decision-making steps. Then the consumer must get the needed information and apply it. Routine buying behavior, on the other hand, could result if the consumer was familiar with the incoming stimuli, understands them correctly (at least in his own mind), and has already learned that a particular product will be very satisfactory.

Running through this model could help a marketing manager focus on what he knows and does not know about his target customers' buying processes. If he doesn't know how they search for information, for example, he might do some marketing research to be sure he understands how they behave.

If the target customers don't see the product correctly, a promotion effort might try to change the information entering the buyer's "black box." Of if there is confusion about how to use all the information, advertising or personal selling efforts might be designed to help potential customers choose among the various offerings.

Model can help use new findings

Finally, this model gives marketing managers a way to handle new research findings in a useful way. Instead of just saying, "Well, that's very interesting"—and wondering how it all fits—they can organize their thoughts within the model. This may mean changing their understanding of whichever variables are involved in the research findings.

Intuition and judgment are still needed

The present state of our knowledge of consumer behavior is such that we still must use intuition and judgment to describe the "why" of consumer behavior in specific markets. By applying our model, however, "guesses" should be limited to areas where knowledge is lacking. There is no excuse for "guessing" about the impact of things which have already been well researched.

Some people feel that understanding consumers is just "common sense." Actually they are using some model—perhaps a very simple one. As we have seen, economists tend to use the "economic man" model. Some very price-oriented retailers depend on this model. But, consumer behavior is much more complicated. Better strategies will probably result

Figure 5–10
Integrated buyer behavior model

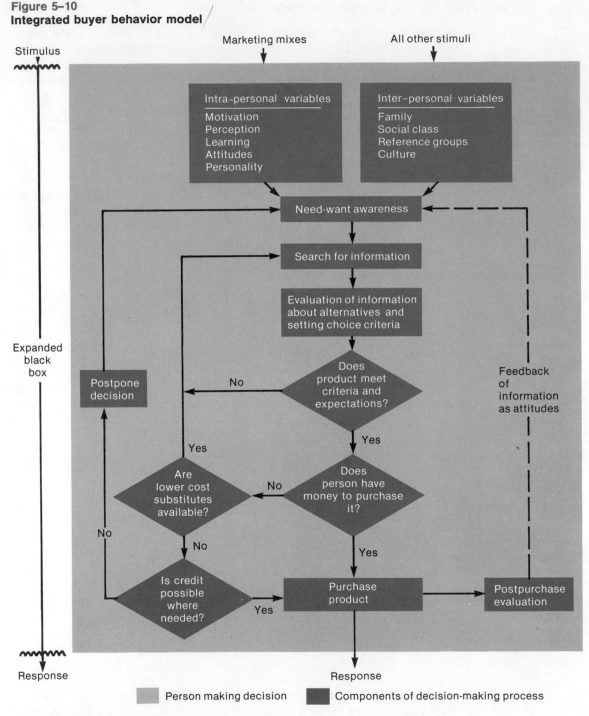

from making informed judgments about how the intra-personal and inter-personal variables affect the target customers' problem solving in a particular market.

Conclusion

In this chapter, we studied consumer spending patterns. We saw that they can be helpful for understanding general relationships. But for predicting which specific products or brands will be bought, we need to know more about how individual consumers buy.

We looked at the individual consumer as a problem solver who is influenced by intra-personal and inter-personal variables. Understanding this material is important to marketing strategy planning. The assumption that everyone behaves the way you do—or even like your family or friends do—can lead to serious marketing errors.

An integrated buyer behavior model was shown to help you tie together the present findings and any new data which you might get from marketing research. As of now, the behavioral sciences can only offer theories which the marketing manager must blend with intuition and judgment when developing marketing strategies.

Marketing research may have to be used to answer specific questions. But if neither the time nor the money is available for research, then management will have to depend on the available descriptions of present behavior and "guesstimates" about future behavior. We have more information on consumer behavior than is generally used by business managers. Using this information may help *you* develop better marketing strategies.

Questions for discussion

1 Some demographic characteristics are likely to be more important than others in determining market potential. For each of the following characteristics, identify two products for which this characteristic is *most* important: *(a)* size of geographic area, *(b)* population, *(c)* income, *(d)* stage of life cycle.

2 What behavioral science concept underlies the "black box" model of consumer behavior? Does this concept have operational relevance to marketing managers; i.e., if it is a valid concept, can they make use of it?

3 Explain what is meant by a hierarchy of needs and provide examples of one or more products that enable *you* to satisfy each of the four levels of need.

4 Cut out two recent advertisements: one full-page color ad from a magazine and one large display from a newspaper. Indicate which needs are being appealed to in each case.

5 Explain how an understanding of consumers' learning processes might affect marketing strategy planning.

6 Explain life-style analysis. Explain how this might be useful for planning marketing strategies to reach college students as compared with the "average" consumer.

7 How should the social class structure affect the planning of a new restaurant in a large city? How might the four Ps be adjusted?

8 What social class would you associate with each of the following phrases or items?
a. Sport cars.
b. *True Story, True Romances*, etc.
c. *New Yorker*.
d. *Playboy*.
e. People watching "soap operas."
f. TV bowling shows.
g. Families that serve martinis, especially before dinner.
h. Families who dress formally for dinner regularly.
i. Families that are distrustful of banks (keep money in socks or mattress).
j. Owners of French poodles.

In each case, choose one class, if you can. If you are not able to choose one class, but rather feel that several classes are equally likely, then so indicate. In those cases where you feel that all classes would be equally interested or characterized by a particular item, choose all five classes.

9 Illustrate how the reference group concept may apply in practice by explaining how you personally are influenced by some reference group for some product. What are the implications of such behavior for marketing managers?

10 Illustrate the three levels of problem solving with an example from your own personal experience.

11 On the basis of the data and analysis presented in Chapters 3 and 5, what kind of buying behavior would you expect to find for the following products: *(a)* canned peas, *(b)* toothpaste, *(c)* ballpoint pens, *(d)* baseball gloves, *(e)* sport coats, *(f)* dishwashers, *(g)* encyclopedias, *(h)* automobiles, and *(i)* motorboats? Set up a chart for your answer with products along the left-hand margin as the row headings and the following factors as headings for the columns: *(a)* how consumers would shop for these products, *(b)* how far they would go, *(c)* whether they would buy by brand, *(d)* whether they would wish to compare with other products, and *(e)* any other factors they should consider. Insert short answers—words or phrases are satisfactory—in the various grid boxes. Be prepared to discuss how the answers you put in the chart would affect each product's marketing mix.

12 The trend toward more people "eating out" has continued in recent years. Now over one third of the meals in the United States are eaten outside of the home. And this number may go to one half of the meals sometime in the 1980s. Many of these meals are eaten in "fast food" outlets. Given that population is not increasing very fast, this has a direct impact on food sales through supermarkets. In an effort to increase their sales, supermarkets and some of their suppliers have decided that in order to compete with the fast-food industry, they will have to offer more fast food. Some are promoting fast-food meals that consumers can cook in their own kitchens and eat in their own homes. And to meet the "restaurant-hamburger tastes," products are being designed to taste like those people are buying at the fast-food outlets. Clearly, hamburgers, french fries, fried chicken, pizzas, milk shakes, and soft drinks have become *the* foods for some Americans—especially the younger ones. An example of a food processor seeking to cater to the "new consumer" is a South Carolina firm that offers frozen cheeseburgers, frozen hot dogs, and a frozen "breakfast on a bun" that is very similar to McDonald's Egg McMuffin. Evaluate the likelihood of supermarkets and food processors reversing the trend toward eating out.

Suggested cases

6 Rocco's Place

8 Polar Ice Palace

9 Betty's Shop

When you finish this chapter, you should:

1 Know about the buying behavior of intermediate customers.
2 Understand the problem-solving behavior of manufacturers' purchasing agents.
3 Know the basic methods used in industrial buying.
4 Know how buying by retailers, wholesalers, farmers, and governments are similar to—and different from—industrial buying.
5 Recognize the important new terms shown in red.

INTERMEDIATE CUSTOMERS AND THEIR BUYING BEHAVIOR

Who are intermediate customers anyway? Most purchases are made by "intermediate customers." In this chapter, we'll talk about them. Who they are. Where they are. And how they buy.

There are great marketing opportunities in serving intermediate customers. A student aiming for a business career has a good chance of working with these customers.

INTERMEDIATE CUSTOMERS ARE DIFFERENT

Intermediate customers are any buyers between the owners of basic raw materials and final consumers. The various types and their number are shown in Table 6–1. There are only about 12 million intermediate customers in the United States. Compare this to the more than 200 million final consumers. But intermediate customers do a wide variety of jobs. Many different market dimensions are needed to describe all these different markets.

The emphasis in this chapter will be on the buying behavior of manufacturers, because we know the most about them. Other intermediate customers seem to behave much the same way.

Even small differences are important

Understanding how and why intermediate customers buy is very important. Competition is often tough in intermediate markets. Even small differences may affect the success of a marketing mix.

131

Table 6–1
Kind and number of intermediate customers

Agriculture, forestry, and fisheries	3,561,000
Service industries	3,524,000
Retailers	2,356,000
Contract construction	1,145,000
Wholesalers	580,000
Manufacturers	456,000
Governmental units	78,000
Others	2,135,000

Source: *Statistical Abstract of the United States,* 1977.

Sellers usually approach each intermediate customer directly—through a sales rep. This makes it possible to adjust the marketing mix for each individual customer. It is even possible that there will be a special marketing mix for each individual customer. This is carrying target marketing to its extreme! But when the customer's sales volume is large, it may be worth it.

Now, let's see how these intermediate customers behave.

MANUFACTURERS ARE IMPORTANT CUSTOMERS

There are not many big ones

There are very few manufacturers compared to final consumers. Most manufacturers are quite small. See Table 6–2. The owners may also be the buyers in these small plants. They are more informal about the buying process than the buyer in the relatively few large plants.

Larger plants, however, employ the majority of workers—and produce a big share of the value added by manufacturing. See Table 6–2. Plants with 250 or more employees were only 4.3 percent of the total—yet they employed 57 percent of the production employees and produced 63 percent of value added by manufacturers. You can see these large plants are an important market.

Customers cluster in geographic areas

Besides concentration by size, industrial markets are concentrated in certain geographic areas. The Middle West, Middle Atlantic states, and California are important industrial markets. So are the big urban areas.

The buyers for some of these large manufacturers are even further concentrated in home offices—often in big cities. One of the large building material manufacturers, for example, does most of its buying for more than 50 plants from its Chicago office. In such a case, a sales rep may be able to sell all over the country without leaving his home city. This makes selling easier for competitors also—and the market may be very competitive.

Concentration by industry

Manufacturers also concentrate by industry. Manufacturers of advanced electronics systems are centered in the Boston and New York areas and

Table 6–2
Size distribution of manufacturing establishments

Size in terms of number of employees	Number of establish-ments	Value added by manufacturing ($ million)	Total number of employees (000)	Percent of firms	Percent of value added	Percent of employees
1–4	112,289	3,752.9	196.8	35.9	1.06	1.09
5–9	46,696	5,248.5	312.0	14.9	1.48	1.7
10–19	43,735	10,126.1	605.4	13.9	2.86	3.35
20–49	49,892	25,625.8	1,568.5	15.9	7.2	8.69
50–99	25,628	29,244.4	1,787.1	8.19	8.26	9.9
100–249	20,800	56,466.7	3,232.0	6.65	15.95	17.9
250–499	8,032	51,426.0	2,785.2	2.56	14.5	15.4
500–999	3,481	48,496.9	2,370.0	1.1	13.7	13.1
1,000–2,499	1,527	50,488.2	2,248.6	0.48	14.26	12.46
2,500 and over ..	582	73,097.7	2,926.8	0.18	20.65	16.2

Source: 1972 Census of Manufactures.

on the West Coast. The steel industry is heavily concentrated in the Pittsburgh, Birmingham (Alabama), and Chicago areas.

Much data is available on industrial markets by SIC codes

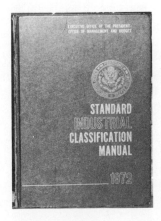

In industrial markets, marketing managers can focus their attention on a relatively few clearly defined markets and be near most of the business. Their efforts can be aided by some very detailed information collected by the federal government. The data shows the number of firms, their sales volume, and how many people they employ—broken down by industry, county, and SMSA. The data is reported for Standard Industrial Classification code industries (SIC codes). These codes make market analysis easier.

SIC code breakdowns start with such general industry categories as food and related products (code 20), tobacco products (code 21), textile mill products (code 22), apparel (code 23), and so on.

Within each two-digit industry breakdown, much more detailed data is often available. Within the apparel (23) industry, for example, there is industry 232—men's, youths', and boys' furnishings and work clothing. This is broken down into the following four-digit industries: shirts, collars, and night wear (2321), underwear (2322), neckwear (2323), separate trousers (2327), work clothing (2328), and NEC (not elsewhere classified) (2329).

If companies working in industrial markets know who their targets are, this easily available data—organized by SIC codes—can be very valuable.

INDUSTRIAL BUYERS ARE PROBLEM SOLVERS

Some people think of industrial buying as entirely different from consumer buying. But there are many similarities. In fact, it appears that the problem-solving framework introduced in Chapter 5 can be applied here.

Figure 6–1
Decision network diagram of the buying situations: Special drill[1]

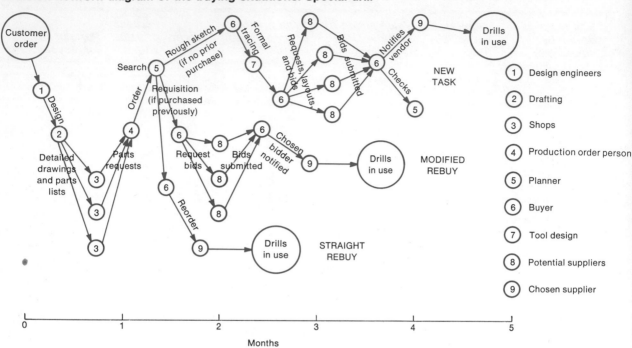

Three buying processes are useful

In Chapter 5, we discussed three kinds of buying by consumers: extended, limited, and routine buying. In industrial markets, it is useful to change these ideas a little and work with three buying processes: a new-task buying process, a modified rebuy process, or a straight rebuy.[2]

NEW-TASK BUYING

New-task buying occurs when a firm has a new need and the buyer wants a lot of information. New-task buying can include setting product specifications and sources of supply.

MODIFIED REBUY BUYING

A **modified rebuy** is the in-between buying process where some review of the buying situation is done—though not as much as in new-task buying.

STRAIGHT REBUY BUYING

A **straight rebuy** is a routine repurchase which may have been made many times before. Buyers probably would not bother looking for new information or even new sources of supply. Most of a company's purchases might be this type. But they would take a small amount of a good buyer's time.

The fact that a particular product or service might be bought in any of the three ways is very important. Careful market analysis is needed to learn how the firm's products are bought, and by whom. A new-task buy will take much longer than a straight rebuy and give much more chance for promotion impact by the seller. This can be seen in Figure 6–1. It shows the time and the many influences involved in buying a special drill.

Industrial buyers are becoming specialists

The large size of some manufacturers has led to buying specialists. **Purchasing agents** are buying specialists for manufacturers. These experts in buying usually must be seen first—before any other employee is contacted. Purchasing agents have a lot of power. In large companies, they may become very specialized—by specific product area. These buyers expect information that will help them buy wisely. They like to know about new products and possible price changes, strikes, and other changes in business conditions. Most industrial buyers are intelligent and well educated. A sales rep should treat them accordingly.

Basic purchasing needs are economic

Industrial buyers are usually less emotional in their buying habits than final consumers. They tend to look for specific product characteristics; including economy, productivity, uniformity, purity, and ability to make the buyer's final product better.

In addition to product characteristics, buyers consider the dependability of the seller, cooperativeness, ability to provide speedy maintenance and repair, and, of course, fast delivery.

SUPPLY SOURCES MUST BE DEPENDABLE

The matter of dependability is really important. There is nothing worse for a purchasing agent and a production manager than shutting down a production line because sellers have not delivered their goods. Product quality is important, too. The cost of a small item may have little to do with its importance. If it causes the breakdown of a larger unit, it may cause a large loss—much greater than its own value.

Emotional needs are relevant, too

Industrial purchasing does have an emotional side, however. Buyers are human, and want friendly relationships with suppliers. Some buyers seem eager to copy progressive competitors. Some want to be the first to try new products. Such "innovators" might deserve special attention when new products are being introduced.

Buyers also want to protect their own position in the company. "Looking good" is especially hard for purchasing agents. They often have to buy a wide variety of products from many sources. They must make decisions involving many factors beyond their control. A new source may deliver low-quality materials, for example, and the buyer may be blamed. Or late delivery may reflect on his ability. Any product or service or sales rep, therefore, that helps the buyer look good to higher-ups has a definite appeal. In fact, this might make the difference between a successful and an unsuccessful marketing mix.

"You can count on lots of orders from me now—when *you* delivered and no one else did, *I* got a bonus!"

A seller's marketing mix should satisfy both the buyer's company needs and the buyer's emotional needs. Therefore, it helps to find some common area where both can be satisfied.

Multiple influence on buying

Most purchases of the typical purchasing agent are straight rebuys which he handles himself. But in some situations—especially in new-task buying—a multiple buying influence may be important. **Multiple buying influence** means the buyer shares the purchasing decision with several managers—perhaps even top management. Each of these buying "influencers" may be interested in different topics.

The sales rep might have to talk to every one of these possible influencers—stressing different matters. This not only complicates the promotion job, but also lengthens it. Approval of a routine order may take anywhere from a week to several months. On very important purchases—say, the puchase of a new computer system or major equipment—the selling period may stretch out to a year or more.

BASIC METHODS IN INDUSTRIAL BUYING

Should you inspect, sample, describe, or negotiate?

Industrial buyers—really, buyers of all types, including final consumers—can use four basic ways to evaluate and buy products: inspection, sampling, description, and negotiated contracts.

In modern economies, most products are purchased by description or negotiated contracts. In contrast, most buying is done by inspection or sampling in less-developed economies. The reason is doubt about quality—or lack of faith in the seller. Understanding the "when" and "why" of these buying methods is important in strategy planning.

INSPECTION LOOKS AT EVERYTHING

Inspection buying means looking at every item. It is used for products that are not standardized—for example, fruits and vegetables, livestock, used buildings, and cars. These products are often sold in open markets or at auctions. Potential buyers inspect the merchandise and either bargain over price with the seller or bid against competitors.

SAMPLING LOOKS AT SOME

Sampling buying means looking at only part of a potential purchase. As products become more standardized (perhaps because of more careful grading and better quality control) buying by sample becomes possible. The general price level may be set by demand and supply factors—but the actual price may be adjusted according to the quality of a specific sample. This kind of buying is used when buying truck or railcar loads of wheat or corn, for example.

DESCRIPTION JUST DESCRIBES ACCURATELY

Description buying means buying from a written (or verbal) description of the product. The goods are not inspected. This method is used when quality can be controlled and described—as with many branded products. In recent years, more wholesale and retail buyers have come to accept government grading standards for fruits and vegetables. Now, most of these products are packed in the fields and sold without any further inspection or sampling. This, of course, reduces the cost of buying and is used by buyers whenever possible.

NEGOTIATED CONTRACTS EXPLAIN HOW TO HANDLE RELATIONSHIPS

Negotiated contract buying means writing a contract that allows for changing the purchase arrangements.

Sometimes, the buyer knows roughly what is needed but can't describe it exactly. Perhaps the specifications or total requirements may change as the job is being done. Or maybe some of the details can't be anticipated. This is found, for example, in research and development work and in building special-purpose machinery and buildings. In such cases, the general project is described. Then, a basic price may be agreed upon—with allowance for adjustments both upward and downward. The whole contract may even be subject to bargaining as the work proceeds.

Buyers may favor loyal, helpful suppliers

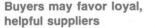

To be assured of dependable quality, a buyer may develop loyalty to certain suppliers. This is especially important when buying nonstandardized products. When a friendly relationship is developed over the years, the supplier almost becomes a part of the buyer's organization.

Most buyers have a sense of fair play. When a seller suggests a new idea that saves the buyer's company money, the seller is usually rewarded with orders. This encourages future suggestions.

In contrast, buyers who use a bid system exclusively may not be offered much beyond the basic products. They are interested mainly in price. Marketing managers who have developed better products and services may not seek such business—at least with their better mixes.

But buyers must spread their risk—seeking several sources

Even if a firm has the most ideal marketing mix possible, it probably will not get all the business of its industrial customers. Purchasing agents usually seek several dependable sources of supply. They must protect themselves from unpredictable events—such as strikes or other problems in their suppliers' plants. Still, a good marketing mix is likely to win a larger share of the total business.

Most buyers try to routinize buying procedure

Most firms use a buying procedure that tries to routinize the process. When some department wants to buy something, a **requisition**—a request to buy something—is filled out. After approval by a supervisor, the requisition is forwarded to the buyer for placement with the "best" seller. Now the buyer is responsible for issuing a purchase order and getting delivery by the date requested.

ORDERING MAY BE ROUTINE AFTER REQUISITIONING

Requisitions are converted to purchase orders as quickly as possible. Straight rebuys are usually made the day the requisition is received—by choosing from a list of acceptable suppliers. New task and modified rebuys take longer. But if time is important, the buyer may place the order by telephone.

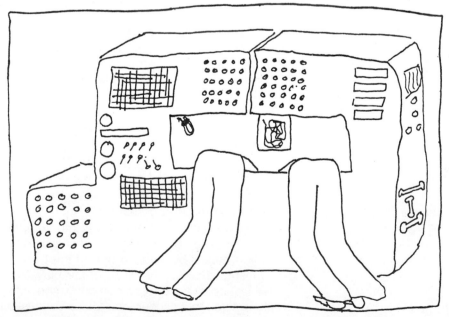

"Now what I need is a cylinder that will fit in here and let this thing slide back and forth. Can you make it cheaply?"

(Some purchases are negotiated.)

IT PAYS TO KNOW THE BUYER

Notice the importance of being one of the regular sources of supply. Buyers do not even call potential suppliers for straight rebuys.

Further, note that if a particular sales rep has won a favorable image, it is likely that he might achieve a slightly larger share of the orders. Moving from a 20 percent to a 30 percent share may not seem like much from the buyer's point of view. But for the seller it represents a 50 percent increase in sales!

SOME BUY BY COMPUTER

Some buyers have been able to turn over a large part of their routine order placing to computers. They develop decision rules that tell the computer how to order and leave the details of following through to the machine. If economic conditions change, the buyers may modify the instructions to the computer. When nothing unusual happens, however, the computer system can continue to routinely rebuy as needs develop—printing out new purchase orders to the regular suppliers.

It is extremely important, then, for a supplier to be in the computer's "memory." In such a situation, the critical thing is to be one of the regular suppliers. Obviously, this is a big "sale." It requires an attractive marketing mix—perhaps for a whole line of products—not just a lower price for a particular order.

Paying taxes affects spending decisions

How the cost of a particular purchase affects profits may have a big effect on the buyer. If the cost of a large machine can be charged to the current year's expenses, the company may be more willing to buy it.

There are two general methods of charging costs—as capital and as expense items. Both are determined primarily by U.S. Internal Revenue Service regulations.

CAPITAL ITEMS ARE DEPRECIATED

Capital items are durable goods—such as large machinery or factories—which are charged off over many years, i.e., depreciated. The depreciation period could be 2 to 50 years, depending on the item.

Managers do look at capital investments differently than at expense items. The purchase of capital items is likely to lead to "new-task" purchasing. The purchase of capital items is, in effect, a long-term claim against future revenues. Mistakes can affect many years' profits. So, managers are hesitant to make quick decisions. Further, there is little agreement on the best approach to capital expenditure decisions.[3] So emotional considerations may become important in strategy planning.

EXPENSE ITEMS ARE EXPENSED

In contrast to capital items, **expense items** are short-lived goods and services which are charged off as they are used—usually in the year of purchase. The potential value is more easily forecast and can be compared with the cost. Since the company is not spending against its future when it buys these items, it tends to be less concerned about these costs. This is especially true if business is good.

The multiple-buying influence is less here. Straight rebuys are more common.

Inventory policy may determine purchases

Industrial firms generally try to maintain an adequate inventory—at least enough to be sure that production lines keep moving. There is nothing worse than to have a production line close down.

Adequate inventory is often stated in number of days' supply—for example, a 60- or 90-day supply. But what a 60- or 90-day supply is, depends upon the demand for the company's products. If the demand rises sharply—say by 10 percent—then total purchases will expand by *more* than 10 percent to maintain regular inventory levels and meet the new needs. On the other hand, if sales decrease by 10 percent, actual needs and inventory requirements decrease. Buying may even stop while the inventory is being "worked off." During this time, a seller would probably have little success with trying to stimulate sales. The buyer is just "not in the market."

Reciprocity helps sales, but . . .

Reciprocity means trading sales for sales—i.e., "If you buy from me, I'll buy from you." If a company's customers also sell products which the firm buys, then the sales departments of both buyer and seller may try to "trade" sales for sales. Purchasing agents usually resist reciprocity. But often it is forced upon them by their sales departments.

Reciprocal buying and selling are common in some industries—paints, chemicals, and oil. When both prices and product qualities are competitive, it's hard to ignore the pressures from the sales departments. An outside supplier can only hope to become an alternate source of supply. He has to wait for the "insiders" to let quality slip or prices rise.

The U.S. Justice Department frowns upon reciprocity. It tries to block reciprocal buying on the grounds that it injures competition. This may force those firms that depend on reciprocity to rethink their marketing strategies.

RETAILERS AND WHOLESALERS ARE PROBLEM SOLVERS, TOO

They must buy for their customers

Most retail and wholesale buyers see themselves as purchasing agents for their target customers. They believe the old saying: "Goods well bought are half sold." They do *not* see themselves as sales agents for manufacturers. They buy what they think they can sell. They do not try to make value judgments about the desirability of what they are selling. Instead, they focus on the needs and attitudes of their target customers.

Sales reps should have something to do when they call.

They must buy too many items

Most retailers carry a large number of items—drugstores up to 12,000, hardware stores up to 25,000, and grocery stores up to 10,000. They just don't have time to pay close attention to each item. Wholesalers, too, handle so many items that they can't give constant attention to each one of them. A grocery wholesaler may stock up to 20,000 items and a drug wholesaler up to 125,000 items.

You can see why retailers and wholesalers buy most of their products as straight rebuys. Sellers should recognize the difficulty of the buyer's job. Many of these buyers are annoyed by the number of sales reps who call on them with little to say about only one of the many items they carry. Sales reps should have something useful to say and do when they call. For example, besides just improving relationships, they might take inventory or arrange shelves—while looking for a chance to talk about specific products.

In larger firms, buyers spend more time on individual items. They may even specialize in certain goods. Some large chains even expect buyers to get out of their offices and find additional and lower-cost sources of supply.[4]

They watch inventories and computer output

The large number of items stocked by wholesalers and retailers makes it necessary to watch inventories carefully. Most modern retailers and wholesalers try to maintain a selling stock and *some* reserve stock. Then they depend on a continual flow through the channel.

Increasingly, even small firms are moving to automatic inventory control methods. Large firms use complicated computer-controlled inventory systems. Large retail discounters have even moved to unit control systems to quickly pinpoint sales of every product on their shelves. As one discounter put it, ''We are not satisfied to know what we are selling in a thousand-foot area—we want to know quickly what we are selling on each table.[5]

Buyers who watch their inventory this closely know their needs. They become more demanding about dependable delivery. They also know how goods move and what promotion help might be needed.

Some are not always "open to buy"

Just as manufacturers sometimes try to reduce their inventory and are ''not in the market,'' retailers and wholesalers may stop buying for similar reasons. No special promotions or price cuts will make them buy.

In retailing, another fact affects buying. A buyer may be controlled by a fairly strict budget. This is a miniature profit and loss statement for each department or merchandise line. In an effort to make a profit, the buyer tries to forecast sales, merchandise costs, and expenses. The figure for ''cost of merchandise'' is the amount the buyer has to spend over the budget period. If the money has not yet been spent, the buyer is **open to buy**—that is, the buyer has budgeted funds which he can spend in the current time period.

''Tell me how to get rid of all this—*then* I'll buy from you.''

Owners or professional buyers may buy

The buyers in small stores—and for many wholesalers—are the owners or managers. There is a very close relationship between buying and selling. In larger operations, buyers may specialize in certain lines. But they still may supervise the sales people who sell what they buy. These buyers, therefore, are in close contact with their customers *and* their sales people. The sales people are sensitive to the success of the buyer's efforts—especially when they are on commission. A buyer may even buy some items to satisfy the preferences of sales people. They should not be ignored in a seller's promotion effort. The multiple buying influence may make the difference.

As sales volumes rise, a buyer may specialize in buying only and have no responsibility for sales. Sears is an extreme case, to be sure. But it has a buying department of more than 3,000 people—supported by a staff department of over 1,400. These are professional buyers who may know more about prices, quality, and trends in the market than their suppliers. Obviously, these are big potential customers and should be approached differently than the typical small retailers.[6]

Resident buyers may help a firm's buyers

Resident buyers are independent buying agents who work in central markets for several retailer or wholesaler customers in outlying markets. They work in cities like New York, Chicago, Los Angeles, and San Francisco. They buy new styles and fashions—and fill-in items—as their customers run out of stock during the year. Resident buying organizations may buy everything (except furniture, shoes, and food) for their stores. Some resident buyers have hundreds of employees and buy more than $1 billion worth of goods a year.

Resident buying organizations fill a need for the many small manufacturers who cannot afford large selling organizations. Resident buyers usually are paid an annual fee based on the amount they buy.

Committee buying happens, too

In some large companies, especially in those selling foods and drugs, the major buying decisions may be made by a buying committee. The seller still must contact the buyer. But the buyer does not have final responsibility. The buyer prepares a form summarizing the proposal for a new product. The seller may help complete this form—but he probably won't get to present his story in person to the buying committee.

This rational, almost cold-blooded, approach has become necessary because of the flood of new products. Consider the problem facing grocery chains. In an average week, up to 250 new items are presented to the buying offices of the larger food chains. If all were accepted, 10,000 new items would be added during a single year. This might be more than their present stock! Obviously, buyers must be hard-headed and impersonal. About 90 percent of the new items presented to food stores are rejected.

Clearly, marketing managers must develop good marketing mixes when buying becomes so organized and competitive.

Committee buying reduces impact of personal selling.

THE FARM MARKET

Farmers are the largest group of intermediate customers. But the number of farms has really dropped in recent years. From 1940 to 1975, the total dropped from more than 6 million to less than 3 million farms. The remaining farms have taken over some of this acreage. During the same time period, the average farm increased in size from about 200 acres to 400 acres.

Just as in manufacturing, there are still many small units—but the large farms produce most of the output. About half the farmers produce almost 90 percent of the total farm output.

The owners of large farms tend to run their farms as a business. They are impressed by sales presentations stressing savings and increases in productivity. Further, they are well-informed and open to change. And, they may have the money to act on their decisions.

Many farmers are unwilling to shop around for the lowest price—preferring the convenience of the nearest farm implement or feed dealer. There is some keeping up with the neighbors, too—especially in the purchase of farm machinery. A farmer's home and place of business are the same. A new tractor may offer just as much status as a new car would to an urban resident!

Fitting products to customers' specialization

Another important factor is that farmers are tending to specialize in one or a few products (such as wheat alone, fruit, or eggs) rather than a full range of "foods." These farmers are interested in very specific kinds of products.

Some farmers are becoming more businesslike as their farms grow.

Marketing mixes may have to be planned for each individual farmer—and in some cases this is happening. Fertilizer producers have moved far beyond selling an all-purpose bag of fertilizer. Now they are able to blend the exact type needed for each farm. Then they load it directly onto fertilizer spreaders. Some producers, in fact, are working directly with farmers, providing a complete service—including fertilizing, weeding, and debugging—all fitted to each individual farmer's needs.[7]

Agriculture is becoming agribusiness

Of growing importance is the tendency for farmers to go into contract farming. **Contract farming** means the farmer gets supplies and perhaps working capital from local middlemen or manufacturers who agree to buy the farmer's output—sometimes at guaranteed prices. The farmer becomes, in effect, an employee. Such arrangements are found in raising chickens and turkeys and in growing fresh vegetables for commercial canning. These arrangements give security to the farmer. But they also limit the markets for sellers. It is all part of **agribusiness**—the move toward bigger and more businesslike farms.

Where contract farming is found, marketing managers will have to adjust their marketing mixes. They may have to sell directly to large manufacturers or middlemen who are handling the arrangements—instead of to the farmer.

In summary, the modern farmer is becoming more businesslike. He seems willing to accept help and new ideas. But only when he's sure they will help improve production.

THE GOVERNMENT MARKET

Size and variety

Government is the largest customer in the United States. Over 20 percent of the U.S. national income is spent by various government units. Governments buy almost every kind of product. They run schools, police departments, and military organizations. They also run supermarkets, public utilities, research laboratories, offices, hospitals, and liquor stores. Government buying cannot be ignored by an aggressive marketing manager.

Bid buying is common

Many government customers buy by description, using a required bidding procedure which is open to public review. Often the government buyer is forced to accept the lowest bid. His biggest job—after deciding generally what is wanted—is to correctly describe the need so that the description is clear and complete. Otherwise, the buyer may find sellers bidding on a product he doesn't even want. By law, the buyer might have to accept the low bid—for an unwanted product!

Negotiated contracts are common, too

Bargaining is often necessary when products are not standardized. Unfortunately, this is exactly where "favoritism" and "influence" can slip in. Nevertheless, bargaining (negotiating) is an important buying method in government sales. Here, a marketing mix must emphasize more than just low price.

Learning what government wants

Since most government contracts are advertised, marketers should focus on the government agencies they want to sell to and learn their bidding procedures. The U.S. government offers a purchasing directory that explains its procedures. Various state and local governments also offer help. There are trade magazines and trade associations providing information on how to reach schools, hospitals, highway departments, park departments, and so on. These are unique target markets. They must be treated as such when developing marketing strategies.

Conclusion

In this chapter we have considered the number, size, location, and buying habits of intermediate customers. We tried to identify logical dimensions for potential target markets. We saw that the nature and size of the buyer—as well as the buying situation—are important. We saw that the problem-solving models of buyer behavior introduced in Chapter 5 can be used here, with modifications.

The chapter emphasized buying in the industrial market because more is known about manufacturers' buying behavior. Some specific differences in buying by retailers and wholesalers were discussed. The trend toward fewer, larger, more productive farms with better informed and more progressive farmers was emphasized. The government market was described as an extremely large, complex set of markets—which requires much market analysis.

A clear understanding of intermediate customer buying behavior can make marketing strategy planning easier. And since there are fewer intermediate customers than final customers, it may even be possible to develop a special marketing mix for each potential customer.

Questions for discussion

1 Discuss the importance of thinking "target marketing" when analyzing intermediate customer markets. How easy is it to isolate homogeneous market segments in these markets?

2 Explain how SIC codes might be helpful in evaluating and understanding industrial markets.

3 Compare and contrast the problem-solving approaches used by final consumers and by industrial buyers.

4 Describe the situations that would lead to the use of the three different buying processes for a particular product, such as computer tapes.

5 Compare and contrast the buying needs of final consumers and industrial buyers.

6 Distinguish among the four methods of evaluating and buying (inspection, sampling, etc.) and indicate which would probably be most suitable for furniture, baseball gloves, coal, and pencils, assuming that some intermediate customer is the buyer.

7 Discuss the advantages and disadvantages of reciprocity from the industrial buyer's point of view. Are the advantages and disadvantages merely reversed from the seller's point of view?

8 Is it always advisable to buy the highest-quality product?

9 Discuss how much latitude an industrial buyer has in selecting the specific brand and the specific source of supply for that product, once a product has been requisitioned by some production department. Consider this question with specific reference to pencils, paint for the offices, plastic materials for the production line, a new factory, and a large printing press. How should the buyer's attitude affect the seller's marketing mix?

10 How does the kind of industrial good affect manufacturers' buying habits and practices? Consider lumber for furniture, a lathe, nails for a box factory, and a sweeping compound.

11 Considering the nature of retail buying, outline the basic ingredients of promotion to retail buyers. Does it make any difference what kinds of products are involved? Are any other factors relevant?

12 Discuss the impact of the decline in the number of commercial farmers on the marketing mixes of manufacturers and middlemen supplying this market. Also consider the impact on rural trading communities that have been meeting the needs of farmers.

13 The government market is obviously an extremely large one, yet it is often slighted or even ignored by many firms. "Red tape" is certainly one reason, but there are others. Would you advise a firm to try to cater to the government market? Explain.

Suggested cases

3 Modern Manufacturing Company
5 Inland Steel Company

When you finish this chapter, you should:

1 Understand how to segment markets into submarkets.
2 Know some dimensions which have been useful for segmenting markets.
3 Know a seven-step approach to segmenting which you can do yourself.
4 Know the difference between market segmentation and market combination.
5 Understand several approaches to forecasting target market potential.
6 Recognize the important new terms shown in red.

7

SEGMENTING MARKETS AND FORECASTING SALES

You have to aim at somebody—not just everybody—to make a profit. This is the big difference between production-oriented managers and target marketers. Production-oriented managers think of their markets in terms of *products* and aim at everybody. They think of the "women's clothing" market or the "car" market. Target marketers think of their markets in terms of *customers' needs*. They segment (split up) such markets into submarkets as they look for attractive opportunities.

In this chapter, we'll talk about segmenting markets and forecasting sales in these markets. It's important to see that segmenting markets is not just a classroom exercise. If a product isn't aimed at a specific target market, all the effort may be wasted.

MARKET SEGMENTING HELPS FIND TARGET MARKETS

Target marketers almost automatically realize that what some people think of as one market may actually be many smaller, more homogeneous (similar) markets. Let's look at this idea more closely.

Segmenting assumes submarkets

Market segmenting assumes that any market consists of submarkets which might need separate marketing mixes. So target marketers try to find ways to describe these submarkets. The dimensions they choose for submarkets should help guide marketing mix planning. Table 7–1 shows some of the kinds of dimensions we have been talking about in the last

Table 7–1

Potential target market dimensions	*Affects on decision areas*
1. Geographic location and other demographic characteristics of potential customers	Affects size of *Target Markets* (economic potential) and *Place* (where products should be made available) and *Promotion* (where and to whom to advertise)
2. Behavioral needs, attitudes, and how present and potential goods or services fit into customers' consumption patterns	Affects *Product* (design, packaging, length or width of product line) and *Promotion* (what potential customers need and want to know about the product offering, and what appeals should be used)
3. Urgency to get need satisfied and desire and willingness to compare and shop	Affects *Place* (how directly products are distributed from producer to consumer, how extensively they are made available, and the level of service needed) and *Price* (how much potential customers are willing to pay)

several chapters and their probable effect on the four Ps. Ideally, we would like to describe any potential market in terms of all three types of dimensions—because these dimensions will help us develop better marketing mixes.

WHY SOME SEGMENTING EFFORTS HAVE BEEN DISAPPOINTING

Segmenting does not mean "breakdown"

Some "first-time" segmenting efforts are very disappointing because beginners often start with the whole "mass market." Then they try to find one or two demographic characteristics to explain differences in customer buying behavior. Typically, they get little because they are trying to work with too few or the wrong dimensions.

Sometimes many different dimensions are needed to describe the different submarkets. This was the case in the home decorating market example we used in Chapter 2. Recall that the British paint manufacturer finally settled on the "cost-conscious couple" as its target market. In that case, four possible target markets with very different dimensions were placed in the four corners of a market diagram. This is the kind of segmenting we want to do.

Segmenting is a gathering process

Target marketers think of **segmenting** as a gathering process. They start with the idea that each person is "one of a kind" and can be described by a special set of dimensions. Using these sets of dimensions, the segmenter tries to gather similar customers together.

Gathering loses detail   Once the gathering is started, some details of each individual are ignored as we look for similarities. This can be seen in Figure 7–1, where the many dots show each person's position in a market with respect to two dimensions: status and dependability. To get three (an arbitrary number) relatively homogeneous groups, the segmenter might gather these people into three groups—A, B, and C. Group A might be called "Status Oriented" and group C "Dependability Oriented." Members of group B want both and might be called the "Demanders."

Each group should represent a homogeneous set of people—a market segment. The larger the group is made, the less homogeneous it becomes. At some point, the segmenter has to decide: "This is the boundary of this group."

One of the difficult things about segmenting is that some potential customers just don't "fit" neatly into market segments. Not everyone in Figure 7–1 was put into one of the three groups. They could be *forced* into one of the groups—but this wouldn't really be segmenting. Additional segments could be created—but they might be small and hard to describe. Some people may be too "special." It may not be possible to group them with anyone else.

Figure 7–1
Every individual has his or her own unique position in the market—those with similar positions can be gathered into potential target markets

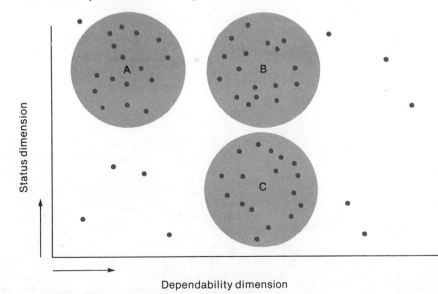

HOW FAR SHOULD THE GATHERING GO?

There is no point in treating each individual in a market as a separate market segment if they all are basically the same. Usually, however, there are some important differences and segmenting is helpful. In fact, in very competitive markets, even small variations can make a big difference in how well a firm does against tough competitors.

Basically, profit-oriented firms would probably want to continue gathering potential customers into a larger market as long as a marketing mix could satisfy those customers—at a profit.

Standards for segmenting markets

Ideally, "good" market segments would meet the following standards:

1. Homogeneous (similar) within—the people in a market segment should be as homogeneous as possible with respect to their needs and attitudes and their likely responses to the marketing mix variables.
2. Heterogeneous (different) between—buying behavior, not just customer characteristics, should be different from segment to segment.
3. Substantial—be big enough to be profitable.
4. Operational—their dimensions should be useful for deciding on marketing mix variables. There is no point in having a dimension that isn't usable.

Number 4 is especially important because it is possible to find dimensions which are useless—even though they are related to past buying behavior. A personality trait like moodiness, for example, might be found among the traits of particularly heavy buyers of a product—but how could you use it? Personal sales people would have to give a personality test to each buyer—clearly an impossible task. Similarly, advertising media buyers or copywriters could not make much use of this information. So, although "moodiness" might be related in some way to previous purchases, it would not be a useful dimension for segmenting.

"I'm sure there is a segment of crazy lovelorn spinsters, but I really don't think it's large enough for this love potion."

Figure 7–2
Types of segmenting dimensions

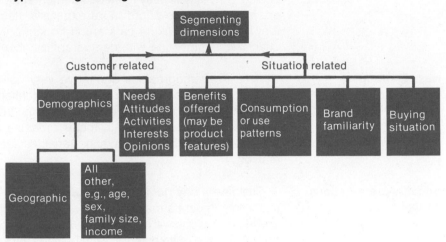

TYPES OF SEGMENTING DIMENSIONS WHICH ARE USED

Consumers have many dimensions—and several may be useful for segmenting a market. We discussed many possibilities in the last several chapters. Figure 7–2 shows the major types that have been used for final consumer markets. As the figure shows, there are customer-related dimensions and situation-related factors—which are more important in some markets. When all competitors in a market are imitating each other, for example, then some product feature may be *the important dimension*. Or the degree of brand loyalty or even whether the brand is in a store when it is wanted (i.e., the buying situation) may decide which product is purchased. Let's look at these potential dimensions now—to see which ones will be the most useful.

Geographic dimensions can be useful

Geographic dimensions are a sensible basis for segmenting because consumers in different areas do have different life-styles and needs. Further, customers in different areas may have to be served by different middlemen and reached with different media. In fact, this is such a basic segmenting dimension, that it may be more practical to use it in the title of a market rather than as a segmenting dimension, for example, the "West Coast market for. . . ."

Using geographic dimensions usually leads to a quick split of a market, but it does not give the detail needed for planning a marketing strategy. So more segmenting of each geographic market is usually necessary.

Other demographic dimensions are useful, too

Demographic variables (such as age, sex, family size, income) have been popular segmenting dimensions because they are easy to measure and data is easy to get. These reasons, however, are not good reasons for using demographics. Often, product choice—and especially brand choice—are only slightly related to demographics. Higher-income consumers may be able to afford more expensive items, but that doesn't mean they'll buy them. Luxury cars aren't bought only by the wealthy. So, mechanically segmenting with demographics should be avoided.

Needs, attitudes, activities, interests, and opinions affect buying

Because demographics don't give very good answers, behavioral dimensions have been getting increasing attention. Sometimes two or three need or attitude dimensions can help segment a market. But generally, life-style specialists work with many variables at the same time (maybe 25 to 100). And different sets of variables are found useful in different markets.

Benefits are why some people buy

Customers buy goods or services to satisfy needs. So it is sometimes useful to segment a market based on the benefits sought or being offered. These dimensions will obviously be specific to a market—the benefits from buying skis are quite different from buying snack foods. Segmenting based on benefits can be tricky. Not everyone may be interested in the same benefits. Nevertheless, product features or benefits can provide understanding about how customers see a market. For example, "high-performance" athletic equipment—like some snow skis—may give status to those who can really use them, but make fools of beginners who buy them to impress others.[1]

Consumption or use patterns—related to how much is bought

Segmenting by whether people are current product users and at what rate—heavy, medium, light—has helped some target marketers. Research often shows, for example, that a small group of "heavy users" accounts for a large part of sales. The firm may want to aim at these heavy users

"Well, I'm looking for something to give me status yet won't make me appear stuck-up."

to make sure they keep on buying. Alternately, the present nonusers or light users might be attractive target markets.

Brand familiarity affects brand choice

Some firms segment their markets by how familiar present customers are with the various brands. This approach can be interesting—especially if some brand has reached the stage where customers demand it. This may suggest that competitors should change their focus to people less attached to a particular brand.

Buying situation—is the product in the store?

Some people have segmented markets based on how consumers behave in different buying situations. In a small convenience food store, for example, consumers may do less brand and price comparison than when on their weekly shopping trip to a supermarket. They may be willing to pay higher prices for convenience. This obviously affects marketing strategy planning.

Possible buying-situation dimensions include the kind of store, its depth of assortment, whether it is leisurely or rushed buying, or whether it is a "serious" or "browsing" shopping trip. Obviously, using these dimensions requires real knowledge of the market.

A SEVEN-STEP APPROACH TO SEGMENTING MARKETS

We have discussed the ideas behind segmenting and some dimensions which are often used. Now let's look at a seven-step approach which can be used without expensive marketing research or computer analysis. More complicated methods are discussed later, but this approach works and has led to successful strategies.

So that you can understand this approach better, we will list each step separately, explain its importance, and use a common example to show how each step works. The example we will use is rental housing—in particular, the apartment market in a big urban area.

1. Select the market to be considered After the firm has defined its objectives, it must decide what market it wants to serve. If it is already in some market, this might be a good starting point. If it is just starting out, then many more choices are open—although the available resources, including human and financial, will limit the possibilities.

Example: The firm might be building small utility apartments for low-income families—basically just satisfying physiological needs. A narrow view of the market—that is, considering only products now being produced—might lead the firm to thinking only in terms of more low-income families. A bigger view—considering more market needs—might see these compact apartments as only a small part of the total apartment or total rental housing, or even the total housing market in the firm's area. Taking an even bigger view, the firm could consider expanding to additional geographic areas—or moving out of housing into other construction markets.

Idea-gathering can start with
the PSSP hierarchy of needs.

Of course, there has to be some balance between defining the market too narrowly (same old product, same old market) and defining it too broadly (the whole world and all its needs is our market). Here, the firm looked at the whole apartment market in one urban area—because this is where the firm had some experience and wanted to work.

2. List all needs that all potential customers may have in this market This is an "idea gathering" step. We want to write down as many needs as we can—as quickly as possible. The list doesn't have to be complete. The idea here it to get enough ideas to stimulate thinking in the next several steps. Some need dimension which is just "thrown in" now may be the most important dimension for a market segment. If that need were not included at this time, it is possible that this market segment would be missed.

Possible need dimensions can be identified by starting with the PSSP hierarchy of basic needs (see Chapter 5) to be sure that all potential dimensions have a chance of being considered. Expanding these four basic needs into more specific needs can be done by thinking about why some people buy the present offerings in this market.

Example: In the rental apartment market, it is fairly easy to list the following needs—which start with but move beyond the basic needs: basic shelter, parking, play space, safety and security, distinctiveness, economy, privacy, convenience (to something), enough living area, attractive interiors, and good supervision and maintenance to assure trouble-free and comfortable living.

3. Form possible market segments Assuming that some market segments will have different needs than others, select out of the above list the most important ones for yourself, then for a friend, then for several acquaintances from widely different demographic groups. Form one segment around yourself or an obvious user, and then go on gathering others into other segments until three or more market segments emerge. Be sure you know the customer-related characteristics of the segments so it will be possible to name them later.

There is obviously some guess work here—but you should have some thoughts about how you behave. Given that you are "one-of-a-kind," you can see that others have different needs and attitudes. Once this is accepted, it is really remarkable how good your judgment becomes about how others behave. We all may have different preferences, but well-informed observers do tend to agree at least roughly on how and why people behave. Market-related experience and judgment are needed to screen all the possible dimensions. But at the least, the geographic, demographic, and behavioral topics discussed in earlier chapters should be considered when forming these market segments.

Example: A college student living off campus would probably want an apartment to provide basic shelter, parking, economy, convenience to school and work, and enough room somewhere to have parties. An older married couple, on the other hand, might have quite different needs—perhaps for basic shelter and parking, but also privacy and good supervision so they would not have to put up with rowdy parties—which might appeal to the student. Someone with a family would also be interested in shelter and parking, but might not have much money. So they would want economy while getting enough room for the children.

4. Look for segmenting dimensions Review the lists of dimensions in each market segment and remove any that appear in each segment. They may be important dimensions, but they are not the segmenting dimensions which we are seeking now.

A potential dimension such as low price or good value may be important for *all* potential customers. It may be an extremely important dimension which will have to be satisfied in *any* marketing mix. But for segmenting purposes, it should be removed at this stage.

Example: With our "apartment hunters," the needs for basic shelter, parking, and safety and security appear to be common. Therefore, in this step, we will remove them from our list of potential segmenting dimensions.

5. Name the possible market segments Review the remaining dimensions, segment by segment, and give each segment a name—based on the dominant segmenting dimension(s).

Here is where creativity and judgment are needed—to compare the relative importance of the remaining dimensions. This should lead to giving each market segment a "people-related" name.

Example: We can identify the following apartment segments at this time: swingers, sophisticates, family, job-centered, home-centered, and urban-centered. Each segment has a different set of product features which follow directly from the people types and the needs they have. See the legend at the bottom of Figure 7–3.

6. Seek better understanding of possible market segments After naming the segments as we did in Step 5, more thought about what is already known about each segment is needed—to help you understand

Figure 7–3
Market for apartment dwellers in a metropolitan area[2]

Swingers

Family

Job centered

Sophisticates

Home centered

Newly married

Urban centered

Name of market segment	People characteristics	Determining product features
Swingers	Young, unmarried, active, fun-loving, party-going	Economy Common facilities Close-in location
Sophisticates	Young, but older than swingers, more mature than swingers, more income and education than swingers, more desire for comfort and individuality	Distinctive design Privacy Interior variety Strong management
Newly married ...	No longer swingers, want a home but do not yet have enough money, wife works so economy not necessary	Privacy Strong management
Job centered	Single adults, widows, or divorcees, not much discretionary income and want to be near job	Economy Close-in location Strong management
Family	Young families with children and not enough income to afford own home	Economy Common facilites Room size
Home centered ..	Former homeowners who still want some aspects of suburban life	Privacy Room size Interior variety
Urban centered ..	Former homeowners in the suburbs, who now want to be close to attractions of city	Distinctive design Close-in location Strong management

how and why these markets behave the way they do. This may help explain why some present offerings are more successful than others. It also can lead to splitting and renaming some segments.

Example: Newly married couples might have been treated as "swingers" in Step 5 if the "married" dimension was ignored. But, with more thought, we see that while some newly married couples are still swingers at heart, others have shifted their focus to buying a home. For these "newly married," the apartment is only a temporary place. Further, they are not like the "sophisticates" (as shown at the bottom of Figure 7–3) and probably should be treated as a separate segment. The point here is that these market differences might only be discovered in Step 6. It would be at this point that the "newly married" segment would be named.

7. Tie each segment to demographic and other customer-related characteristics, if possible, and then draw a "picture" of the whole market to show their relative sizes Eventually, we are looking for profitable opportunities. So now we must try to tie our market segments to demographic data—so it will be easier to estimate the sizes of the segments. We aren't trying to estimate market potential here. Now we only want to provide the basis for later forecasting and marketing mix planning. The more we know about different target markets, the easier those jobs will be.

Fortunately, much demographic data is available. And bringing in demographics adds a note of economic reality. It is possible that some market segments will have almost no market potential. Without some hard facts, the risks of aiming at such markets are great.

Finally, to help understand the whole market and explain it to others, it is useful to draw a "picture" of the market with boxes that give some idea of the size of the various market segments. This will help the company aim toward larger and perhaps more attractive markets.

Example: It is possible to tie the "swingers" to demographic data. Most of them are young—in their 20s. And the U.S. Census Bureau has very detailed information about age. Given age data and an estimate of what percentage are swingers, it would be easy to estimate the number of swingers in an urban area.

Market dimensions suggest a good mix

Once we have followed all seven steps, we should be able to see the outlines (at least) of the marketing mixes which would appeal to the various market segments. Let's take a look.

We know that "swingers" are active, young, unmarried, fun-loving, and party-going. The housing needs shown at the bottom of Figure 7–3 show what the swingers want in an apartment. (As an aside, it is interesting to note what they do *not* want—strong management. Most college students will probably understand why!)

A very successful appeal to the swingers in the Dallas, Texas, area includes a complex of apartments with a swimming pool, a putting green, a night club that offers jazz and other entertainment, poolside parties,

"I'm sorry, sir—I think you misunderstood our ad."

receptions for new tenants, and so on. To maintain their image, management insists that tenants who get married move out shortly so that new swingers can move in.

As a result, apartment occupancy rates were extremely high. At the same time, other builders were having trouble filling their apartments—mostly because their units were just "little boxes" with few uniquely appealing features.

COMPUTER-AIDED MARKETING RESEARCH CAN HELP IN SEGMENTING

The seven-step approach is logical, practical—and it works. But a marketing manager is no longer limited to this approach. Some computer-aided methods can help.

Market judgment is still needed

The basic aim of these methods is to try to find similar patterns within sets of data. This data could include such things as demographics, attitudes toward the product or life in general, and past buying behavior. The computer searches among all the data for homogenous groups of people. When they are found, the dimensions of the people in the groups must be studied to find why the computer grouped them together. If the results make some sense, they may suggest new and perhaps better marketing strategies.

A computer analysis of the toothpaste market, for example, might show that some people buy toothpaste for its sensory satisfaction (the sensory segment), while others are concerned with the effect of clean teeth on their social image (the sociables). Others are worried about decay (the worriers), and some are just interested in the best value for their money (the economic men). Each of these market segments calls for a different marketing mix—although some of the four Ps may be similar. Finally, a marketing manager would have to decide which one (or more) of these segments would be the firm's target market(s).

It should be clear that computer-aided methods are only an aid to the manager. Judgment is still needed to develop an original list of possible dimensions and then to name the resulting groups.[3]

Segmenting applies to services, too

These computer methods can be used for both goods and services—and consumer goods and industrial goods.

In a study of the commercial banking market, for example, six different groups were found. These groups were called the "nonborrowers," "value seekers," nonsaving convenience seekers," "loan seekers," "one-stop bankers," and an "other" group (which was not particularly different on any dimension). Because of this study, changes were made in the bank's whole program—aiming at each of the markets and treating them as the basis for separate strategies. Instead of the old—"we are friendly people"—advertising campaign, the bank focused on its various products and services to try to appeal to the different markets. The "nonborrowers" were appealed to with messages about the bank's checking account, bank charge card, insurance, and investment counseling. For the "convenience seekers," on the other hand, the bank talked about its teller service, express drive-in windows, overnight drop boxes, and deposit-by-mail accounts. To try to reach the "loan seekers," the promotion stressed auto-loan checking accounts, mail-loan request forms, and loan programs through automobile dealers.[4]

MARKET SEGMENTATION VERSUS MARKET COMBINATION

Every firm has some kind of a strategy—even if it's just an unplanned "mass marketing" strategy. So our concern here is with developing better market-oriented strategies.

Target marketers aim at specific targets

There are three basic ways of developing market-oriented strategies for a general market area: (1) segmenting the market and selecting one of the homogeneous submarkets as the target market, (2) segmenting the market and selecting two or more homogeneous submarkets as the basis for different strategies, or (3) combining two or more homogeneous submarkets into one larger target market as the basis for one strategy. Both combiners and segmenters are target marketers—they aim at specific and clearly defined target markets. See Figure 7–4.

Figure 7–4
Target marketers have specific aims

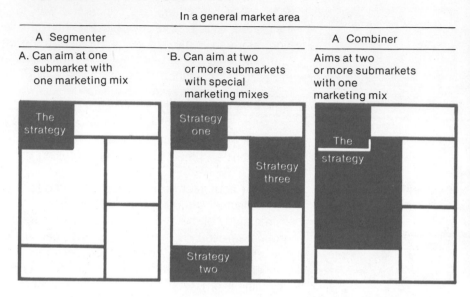

In a general market area

A Segmenter		A Combiner
A. Can aim at one submarket with one marketing mix	B. Can aim at two or more submarkets with special marketing mixes	Aims at two or more submarkets with one marketing mix

Combiners try to satisfy "pretty well"

Combiners try to increase the size of their target markets by combining two or more submarkets. They look at the similarities among many possible customers. Then they try to improve their basic offering to appeal to these "combined" customers with just one marketing mix. See Figure 7–5. Combiners may try a new package, a new brand, new features, new flavors. But even if physical changes are made, their aim is *not* at small submarkets. Instead, combiners try to improve the general appeal of their marketing mix to appeal to their bigger "combined" target market.

Combiners depend heavily on promotion because product differences are often small. But these little differences—in color, texture, or ease of use—may be *very* important to some customers. Also, the many different customers combined into one target market may be interested in different features of the same product. In the cosmetics market, the same product may have different meanings and fill different needs for different customers. For example, some women may be concerned with cleanliness, others with beauty, and others with glamour. One cosmetic advertisement for one product might appeal to all of them—but for different reasons. A combiner might see that the firm might be able to serve *all* these needs at the same time. If they aren't too different, this may be not only possible, but also economically sensible for the firm.

Segmenters try to satisfy "very well"

Segmenters, on the other hand, aim at one homogeneous subset of a market (at a time) and try to develop a marketing mix that will satisfy that smaller market very well.

Figure 7–5
How different kinds of competitors develop strategies and compete over time

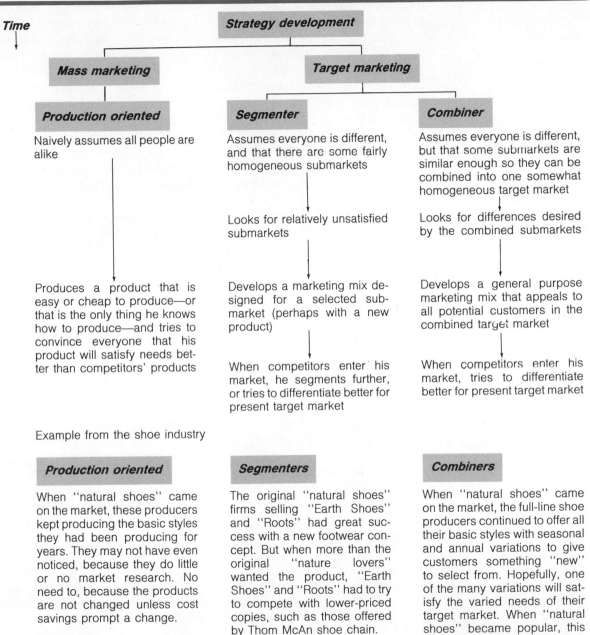

Time

Strategy development

Mass marketing

Target marketing

Production oriented

Naively assumes all people are alike

Produces a product that is easy or cheap to produce—or that is the only thing he knows how to produce—and tries to convince everyone that his product will satisfy needs better than competitors' products

Segmenter

Assumes everyone is different, and that there are some fairly homogeneous submarkets

Looks for relatively unsatisfied submarkets

Develops a marketing mix designed for a selected submarket (perhaps with a new product)

When competitors enter his market, he segments further, or tries to differentiate better for present target market

Combiner

Assumes everyone is different, but that some submarkets are similar enough so they can be combined into one somewhat homogeneous target market

Looks for differences desired by the combined submarkets

Develops a general purpose marketing mix that appeals to all potential customers in the combined target market

When competitors enter his market, tries to differentiate better for present target market

Example from the shoe industry

Production oriented

When "natural shoes" came on the market, these producers kept producing the basic styles they had been producing for years. They may not have even noticed, because they do little or no market research. No need to, because the products are not changed unless cost savings prompt a change.

Segmenters

The original "natural shoes" firms selling "Earth Shoes" and "Roots" had great success with a new footwear concept. But when more than the original "nature lovers" wanted the product, "Earth Shoes" and "Roots" had to try to compete with lower-priced copies, such as those offered by Thom McAn shoe chain.

Combiners

When "natural shoes" came on the market, the full-line shoe producers continued to offer all their basic styles with seasonal and annual variations to give customers something "new" to select from. Hopefully, one of the many variations will satisfy the varied needs of their target market. When "natural shoes" became popular, this style was simply added as "another" new style to satisfy their target market's desire for a selection of new styles.

With a market segmentation approach, more basic changes in marketing mixes—perhaps in the physical product itself—are made to aim at smaller, more homogeneous target markets. Each submarket would be seen as needing a separate marketing mix. A segmenter would worry that trying to appeal to *several* submarkets at the same time with the same mix might confuse the customers about the nature of the product. For example, some of the early entries in the "instant breakfast" market failed with combination appeals to dieters (as a low-calorie meal), harried commuters (as a breakfast substitute), working mothers (for a quick, complete, nutritious breakfast for kids), and housewives (as a nutritious snack between meals.) Now, some segmenters have aimed at the "nutritious snack" market and succeeded with "crunchy granola" bars. It is interesting to note that while their direct appeal is to the snack market, they are also getting some of the "quick lunch" and "fast breakfast" customers.

Segmenting may produce bigger sales

It is very important to understand that a segmenter is not settling for a smaller sales potential. Instead, by focusing the firm's efforts on only a part of a larger market, the segmenter expects to get a much larger share of his target market(s). In the process, total sales may be larger. The segmenter may even get almost a monopoly in "his" market(s).

A segmenter may be able to separate himself from extremely competitive market conditions. For example, the Wolverine World Wide Company came out with "Hush Puppies"—a casual, split-pigskin shoe that moved the firm into the very competitive U.S. shoe market with spectacular success—while conventional small shoe manufacturers were offering just "shoes" and facing tough competition. "Earth Shoes" and "Roots" shoes had similar success.

Should you segment or combine?

Which approach should be used? It depends on the market. What one firm would see as one market, another might see as many markets and design products—and marketing mixes—to satisfy only *some* of them. Which firm wins will depend on how the market(s) respond(s) to the competing mixes. If there really are differences which are satisfied, then the segmentation effort may be more profitable. But if the whole market really is more or less the same, then combination efforts may be just as successful—perhaps at lower cost.

With our present knowledge of consumer behavior, moving directly to combination may be the "safe" way. But it probably will lead one into fairly direct competition with others using the same "safe" approach. "Safety" may be bought at the price of the attractive profits which usually go with marketing breakthroughs.

FORECASTING TARGET MARKET POTENTIAL AND SALES

Estimates of target market potential and likely sales volumes are necessary for effective strategy planning. But a manager can't forecast *sales* without some possible plans. Sales are *not* just "out there for the taking." Market opportunities may be there—but whether a firm can change these opportunities into sales depends on the strategy it selects. Much of our discussion in this chapter, therefore, will be concerned with estimating market potential. We may have to estimate the potential before we can talk about what share of that potential a firm *may* be able to win. In other cases—say when economic conditions are steady and no strategy changes are planned—sales may be forecasted directly.

TWO APPROACHES TO FORECASTING

Many methods are used in forecasting potential and sales—but they can be grouped under two basic approaches: (1) extending past behavior and (2) predicting future behavior. The large number of methods may seem confusing at first, but in fact this variety is an advantage. Forecasts are so important that management often prefers to develop forecasts in two or three different ways—and then compare the differences before preparing a final forecast.

TREND EXTENSION CAN MISS IMPORTANT TURNING POINTS

Extending past behavior

When we forecast for existing products, we usually have some past data to go on. The basic approach—called **trend extension**—extends past sales experience into the future. See Figure 7–6.

Ideally—when extending past sales behavior—one should decide why sales vary. This is a difficult and time-consuming part of sales forecasting. Usually we can gather a lot of data about the product or market—or about the economic environment. But unless the *reason* for past sales variations is known, it's hard to predict in what direction and by how much, sales will move. Graphing the data and statistical techniques—including correlation and regression analysis—can be useful here. These techniques are beyond our scope. They are discussed in beginning statistics courses.

Once we know why sales vary, it usually is easy to develop a specific

Figure 7–6
Straight-line trend projection—extends past sales into the future

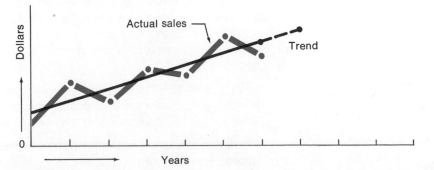

"I see sales increasing by 42% because . . . your competitor goes to Bermuda and leaves a half-wit in charge."

(Better methods are available.)

forecast. Sales may be moving directly up as population grows, for example. So we can just get an estimate of how population is expected to grow and then project the impact on sales.

The big limitation of the trend-extension method is that it assumes past conditions will continue unchanged into the future. In fact, the future is not always like the past. And, unfortunately, trend-extension will be wrong whenever there are important variations. For this reason—although they may extend past behavior for one estimate—most managers look for another way to help them forecast sharp economic changes.

Predicting future behavior takes judgment

When we try to predict what will happen in the future—instead of just extending the past—we have to use other methods and add a bit more judgment. Some of these methods, to be discussed later, include juries of executive opinion, sales people's estimates, surveys, panels, and market tests.

THREE LEVELS OF FORECAST ARE USEFUL

We are interested in forecasting the potential in specific market segments. To do this, it helps to make several kinds of forecasts.

Some economic conditions affect the entire economy. Others may influence only one industry. And some may affect only one company or one product's sales potential. For this reason, a common approach to sales forecasting is to:

1. Develop a *national income forecast* and use this to . . .
2. Develop an *industry sales forecast,* which then is used to . . .
3. Develop *specific company* and *product forecasts.*

Generally, a marketing manager does not have to make forecasts for the national economy or his industry. This kind of forecasting—basically trend projecting—is a speciality in itself. Fortunately, these forecasts are available in business and government publications. So managers can simply use one source's forecast or combine several together. Unfortunately, however, the more "targeted" the marketing managers' previous segmenting efforts were, the less likely that available industry data will fit the firms' target markets. So the managers will have to move directly to estimating potential for their own company and specific products. This topic is discussed next.

FORECASTING COMPANY AND PRODUCT SALES BY EXTENDING PAST BEHAVIOR

Past sales can be extended

At the very least, a marketing manager ought to know what the firm's markets look like and what it has sold to them in the past. A detailed sales analysis—for products and geographic areas—gives such facts for projecting future results.

Simply extending past sales into the future may not seem like much of a forecasting method. But it is better than just assuming that next year's *total* sales will be the same as this year's.

Factor method includes more than time

Simple extension of past sales gives one forecast. But it usually is desirable to tie future sales to something more than the passage of time. The factor method tries to do this.

The **factor method** tries to find a relation between the company's sales and some other factor (or factors). The basic formula is: something (past sales, industry sales, etc.) *times* some factor *equals* sales forecast.

AN EXAMPLE FOR BREAD

The following example for a bread manufacturer shows how forecasts can be made for many geographic market segments using the factor method and available data. This general approach can be useful for any firm—manufacturer, wholesaler, or retailer.

Analysis of past sales relationships showed that a particular bread manufacturer regularly sold one half of 1 percent (0.005) of the total retail food sales in its various target markets—this is a single factor. By using this single factor, estimates of the manufacturer's sales for the coming period could be obtained by multiplying a forecast of expected retail food sales by 0.005.

Retail food sales estimates are made each year by *Sales & Marketing Management* magazine. Figure 7–7 shows the kind of geographically detailed data available each year in its "Survey of Buying Power" issues.

Let's carry this bread illustration further using the data in Figure 7–7 for Evanston, Illinois—which has 0.0347 of U.S. population—and a larger share, 0.0465, of buying power. Evanston's food sales were $44,171,000 for the previous year. By simply accepting last year's food sales as an estimate of next year's sales and multiplying the food sales estimate for Evanston by the 0.005 factor (the firm's usual share in such markets)

Figure 7–7
Sample of pages from *Sales & Marketing Management's* "Survey of Buying Power"[5]

ILL.					POPULATION—12/31/76					RETAIL SALES BY STORE GROUP 1976					
METRO AREAS COUNTIES CITIES	Total Pop (Thousands)	% Of U.S	Median Age Of Pop	% Of Population By Age Group				House-holds (Thousands)	Total Retail Sales ($000)	Food ($000)	Eating & Drinking Places ($000)	General Mdse ($000)	Furnit.-Furnish Appl ($000)	Auto-motive ($000)	Drug ($000)
				18–24 Years	25–34 Years	35–49 Years	50 & Over								
CHAMPAIGN - URBANA - RANTOUL	166.1	.0770	23.7	29.5	17.0	12.4	15.3	52.1	548,556	77,046	58,516	95,780	33,881	108,058	20,631
Champaign	166.1	.0770	23.7	29.5	17.0	12.4	15.3	52.1	548,556	77,046	58,516	95,780	33,881	108,058	20,631
• Champaign	58.6	.0271	23.8	34.3	15.5	11.8	16.6	19.0	264,793	27,493	30,308	48,350	20,850	67,302	11,267
• Rantoul	26.2	.0121	22.1	33.6	18.7	11.5	6.1	6.5	66,625	8,001	6,472	6,840	4,459	24,318	1,270
• Urbana	34.6	.0160	23.7	38.9	16.5	10.1	15.9	10.8	77,283	13,937	2,278	17,188	4,697	1,976	3,147
SUBURBAN TOTAL	46.7	.0218	26.1	14.6	18.3	15.4	18.3	15.8	139,855	27,615	9,458	23,402	3,875	14,462	4,947
CHICAGO	7,003.8	3.2442	29.5	12.1	15.8	16.7	24.6	2,394.6	24,706,798	4,492,479	2,315,671	3,525,393	1,288,892	4,202,897	859,446
Cook	5,347.7	2.4771	30.1	12.1	15.8	16.5	25.8	1,883.3	18,355,861	3,397,210	1,781,393	2,374,227	969,603	2,744,766	656,850
Arlington Heights	75.2	.0348	27.3	9.0	16.6	21.4	15.8	22.6	248,170	50,647	18,851	13,348	14,302	79,746	12,843
Berwyn	48.0	.0222	41.5	10.3	12.6	15.3	41.3	19.9	190,271	28,610	13,039	28,921	10,464	36,554	12,401
• Chicago	3,110.6	1.4409	30.7	12.6	15.6	15.6	27.7	1,152.7	9,689,814	1,721,330	1,000,535	1,160,790	532,758	1,087,532	349,815
Chicago Heights	39.3	.0182	27.4	12.0	16.0	16.0	21.8	12.5	191,371	25,023	20,700	28,382	8,272	65,253	5,774
Cicero	61.8	.0286	35.0	12.4	15.2	15.5	34.5	24.9	157,492	33,455	20,237	7,757	4,152	38,819	4,109
Des Plaines	56.1	.0260	29.2	10.2	16.8	19.0	21.3	18.0	201,714	54,053	23,936	15,973	4,191	26,272	9,022
Evanston	74.9	.0347	31.9	16.4	16.2	14.3	30.7	27.8	267,370	44,171	12,576	24,207	16,645	89,294	6,907

ILL.			EFFECTIVE BUYING INCOME 1976					METRO AREAS COUNTIES CITIES			EFFECTIVE BUYING INCOME 1976				
METRO AREAS COUNTIES CITIES	Total EBI ($000)	Median Hsld EBI	% Of Hslds By EBI Group (A) $8,000-$9,999 (B) $10,000-$14,999 (C) $15,000-$24,999 (D) $25,000 & Over				Buying Power Index		Total EBI ($000)	Median Hsld EBI	% Of Hslds By EBI Group (A) $8,000-$9,999 (B) $10,000-$14,999 (C) $15,000-$24,999 (D) $25,000 & Over				Buying Power Index
			A	B	C	D					A	B	C	D	
CHAMPAIGN - URBANA - RANTOUL	946,751	14,748	7.6	19.4	30.9	18.1	.0806	CHICAGO (cont.)							
Champaign	946,751	14,748	7.6	19.4	30.9	18.1	.0806	Arlington Heights	620,545	25,625	1.8	6.6	33.1	52.8	.0446
• Champaign	350,552	14,915	6.6	15.9	31.2	18.5	.0323	Berwyn	355,290	16,890	5.4	16.9	36.8	21.2	.0282
• Rantoul	95,359	10,100	17.3	26.0	20.4	4.3	.0095	• Chicago	18,892,070	14,391	7.2	19.3	30.5	17.1	1.5305
• Urbana	195,775	13,374	6.9	19.6	24.4	19.6	.0150	Chicago Heights	224,864	16,717	5.8	19.2	35.0	21.4	.0219
SUBURBAN TOTAL	305,065	17,564	5.1	20.8	39.1	22.5	.0238	Cicero	416,725	16,056	5.7	19.6	38.7	15.7	.0306
CHICAGO	47,497,764	17,823	5.3	15.8	34.3	25.9	3.7880	Des Plaines	436,935	22,778	2.8	10.0	39.1	40.6	.0329
Cook	35,888,710	17,071	5.8	16.6	33.2	24.1	2.8533	Evanston	644,919	19,198	5.5	15.1	29.5	33.4	.0465

Buying Power Index is a weighted average of each market's strength. Each market's share of U.S. population is multiplied (weighted) by 2, its income by 5, and its retail sales share by 3. The resulting sum is divided by 10 (the total weighting) to give the BPI.

the manager would have an estimate of his next year's bread sales in Evanston. That is, last year's food sales estimate ($44,171,000) times 0.005 equals this year's bread sales estimate of $220,855.

The factor method is not limited to using just one factor—like in the food example. Several factors can be used together. For example, *Sales and Marketing Management* regularly gives a "buying power index" as a measure of the potential in different geographic areas. See Figure 7-7. This index combines the population in a market with the income and retail sales in that market. But whether one or several factors are included, the same basic approach is used with the factor method.

PREDICTING FUTURE BEHAVIOR CALLS FOR MORE JUDGMENT AND SOME OPINIONS

The methods discussed above make use of quantitive data—projecting past experience and assuming that the future will be somewhat like the past. But this may be risky in competitive markets. Usually, it is desirable

Jury approach combines opinions of experienced managers.

to add judgment to hard data to obtain other forecasts—before making the final forecast.

Jury of executive opinion adds judgment

One of the oldest and simplest methods of forecasting—the **jury of executive opinion**—combines the opinions of experienced executives—perhaps from marketing, production, finance, purchasing, and top management. Basically, each executive is asked to estimate market potential and sales for the coming years.

The main advantage of the jury approach is that it can be done quickly and easily. On the other hand, the results may not be very good. There may be too much extending of the past. Some of the executives may have little contact with outside market influences. At the best, however, it could alert the forecasters to important changes in customer demand or competition.

Estimates from sales people can help, too

Using sales people's estimates to forecast is like the jury approach. But sales people are more likely than home office managers to be familiar with customer reactions and what competitors are doing. Their estimates are especially useful in industrial markets—where a limited number of customers may be well known to the sales people. But this approach is useful in any type of market. Good retail clerks have a "feel" for the market—their opinions should not be ignored.

Three limitations concerning the use of sales people's estimates should be kept in mind.

First, sales people usually don't know about possible changes in the national economic climate—or even about changes in the company's marketing mix.

Second, sales people may have little to offer if they change jobs often. Finally, care is needed if the estimates are used for other purposes. If bonuses are based on these estimates, for example, the estimates may be low. But, if the promotion money given to each territory is based on sales prospects, the estimates may be high. In both cases, it is only human for sales people to suit their forecasts to their own advantage.

With these limitations in mind, sales people's estimates can provide another forecast for comparison before the final forecast is made.

Surveys, panels, and market tests

Special marketing research surveys of final buyers, retailers, and wholesalers can be useful. Some firms use panels of stores or final consumers to keep track of buying behavior. This helps them decide just when extending past behavior is not enough.

Survey methods are sometimes combined with market tests when the company wants to estimate the reaction of customers to possible changes in the marketing mix. A market test might show that a product increased its share of the market by 10 percent when its price was dropped 1 cent below competition. But this extra business might be quickly lost if the price were increased 1 cent above competition.

Such market experiments can help the marketing manager make good estimates of future sales when one or more of the four Ps are changed.

ACCURACY OF FORECASTS

The accuracy of forecasts varies a lot. Annual forecasts of national income may be accurate within 5 percent. Industry sales forecasts are usually accurate within 10 percent.

When estimates are made for individual products, there is even more chance for errors. Where style and new ideas are involved, forecast errors of 10 to 20 percent for established products are common. The accuracy of specific new-product forecasts is even lower! Many new products fail completely.[6]

Conclusion

This chapter discusses the process of segmenting markets—to find potentially attractive target markets. Some people try to segment markets by breaking them down into smaller submarkets. But this can lead to poor results. Instead, segmenting should be seen as a gathering process. The more similar customers' needs, the larger the market segments can be. Four standards for evaluating market segments were presented.

Ways of developing better strategies—segmenting and combining—were discussed. Segmenting aims the firm's efforts at smaller, more homogeneous target markets. Combining, on the other hand, builds up the size of a firm's target market by combining smaller homogeneous submarkets into one larger target market.

We also talked about several approaches to forecasting market potential and sales. The most common approach is to extend past behavior into the future. Reasonably good results can be obtained if market conditions are fairly stable. Methods here include extension of past sales data and the factor method. We saw that projecting the past into the future is risky when big market changes are likely. To make up for this possible weakness, marketers must use their own experience and judgment. They also may be able to bring in the judgment of others—using the jury of executive opinion method and sales people's estimates. They may also use surveys, panels, and market tests.

We saw that the accuracy of forecasts depends on

how general a forecast is being made—with the most error when specific forecasts for products, and especially new products, are made.

Even though forecasts are subject to error, they are still necessary to help the firm choose among alternative strategic plans. Sloppy forecasting could lead to poor strategies. No forecasting at all is stupid!

Questions for discussion

1 Explain the basic concept underlying the segmenting of markets.

2 Explain why first-time segmentation efforts may be disappointing.

3 Illustrate the concept that segmenting is a gathering process by referring to the apparent admissions policies of your own college and a nearby college or university.

4 (*a*) Evaluate how "good" the seven markets identified in the market for apartments (Figure 7–3) are with respect to the four standards for selecting good market segments. (*b*) Same as (*a*) but evaluate the four corner markets in the British home decorating market (Figure 2–9).

5 Review the types of segmenting dimensions listed in Figure 7–2 and Table 7–1 and select the ones you feel should be combined to fully explain the market you, personally, would be in if you were planning to buy a new automobile today. Do not hesitate to list several dimensions, but when you have done so, then attempt to develop a shorthand name, like "swinger," to describe your own personal market. Try to estimate what proportion of the total automobile market would be accounted for by your market.

6 Apply the seven-step approach to segmenting consumer markets to the college-age market for off-campus recreation, which can include eating and drinking. Then, evaluate how well the needs in these market segments are being met in your geographic area. Is there an obvious breakthrough opportunity waiting for someone?

7 Apply the seven-step approach to segmenting industrial markets for a new "super glue" which can be useful for basic production processes as well as almost any kind of repair job, because it can bond together almost any kinds of surfaces.

8 Distinguish between market segmentation and market combination. Which is best? Why and when?

9 Explain the difference between a forecast of market opportunities and a sales forecast.

10 Suggest a plausible explanation for sales fluctuations for (*a*) bicycles, (*b*) baby food, (*c*) motor boats, (*d*) baseball gloves, (*e*) wheat, (*f*) woodworking tools, and (*g*) latex for rubber-based paint.

11 Discuss the relative accuracy of the various forecasting techniques. Explain why some are more accurate than others.

12. Explain (in your own words) what the factor method is and how to use it.

13 Given the following annual sales data for a company that is not planning any spectacular marketing strategy changes, forecast sales for the coming year (7) and explain your method and reasoning.

(a)		(b)	
Year	**Sales (in 000s)**	**Year**	**Sales (in 000s)**
1	$200	1	$160
2	230	2	155
3	210	3	165
4	220	4	160
5	200	5	170
6	220	6	165

14 Discuss the relative market potential of Cicero and Evanston, Illinois, for: (*a*) prepared cereals, (*b*) automobiles, and (*c*) furniture.

Suggested cases

4 Recco, Incorporated

6 Rocco's Place

8 Polar Ice Palace

When you finish this chapter, you should:

1 Understand what "Product" really means.
2 Know the differences among the various consumer and industrial goods classes.
3 Understand how the goods classes can help a marketing manager plan marketing strategies.
4 Understand how product life cycles should affect strategy planning.
5 Recognize the important new terms shown in red.

PRODUCTS AND MARKETING MIX PLANNING

Product involves developing the right product—which then can be put in the right *place*—and sold with the right *promotion* and *price*.

To help you understand marketing strategy planning better, we will talk about some goods classes. The consumer goods and industrial goods classes introduced in this chapter should be studied carefully. They can speed your development as a marketing strategy planner.

Developing the right product isn't easy. Customer needs and attitudes are always changing. Competition forces products through life cycles—from introduction to decline.

WHAT IS A PRODUCT?

Customers buy satisfaction, not parts

First, we have to decide what we mean by a "product."

If we sell an automobile, are we selling a certain number of nuts and bolts, some sheet metal, an engine, and four wheels?

If we sell a detergent to be used in a washing machine, are we selling several chemical raw materials?

If we sell a delivery service, are we selling so much wear and tear on a delivery truck and so much operator fatigue?

The answer to all these questions is *no*. Instead, what we are really selling is the satisfaction, use, or profit the customer wants.

All the customers ask is that their cars look good and keep running. They don't care how they were made. Further, they want to clean with

What is the real product?

detergent, not analyze it. And when they order something, they don't really care how much out of the way the driver had to go or where he has been. They just want their package.

Similarly, when producers and middlemen buy products, they are interested in the profit they will make from their purchase—through its use and resale—not how the products were made.

The idea of product as potential customer satisfactions or benefits is very important. Many business managers—trained in the production side of business—get wrapped up in the number of nuts and bolts, the tightness of the nuts, the fertilizer application per acre, and other technical problems. Middlemen, too, are often concerned with technical details. But while these are important to them, they have little effect on the way most customers view the product. What matters to customers is how *they* see what is being offered. And these two views may be far apart.

Total product is more than just a physical thing

The "total product" is more than just a physical product with its related features. It includes accessories, installation, instruction on use, the package, perhaps a brand name which fills some psychological needs, a warranty, and confidence that service will be available after the purchase.

Product may only be a service

The total product may not include a physical product at all! The product of a barber or hair stylist is the trimming or styling of your hair. A medical doctor may just look at you—neither taking anything away nor giving you any physical product. Nevertheless, each satisfies needs—and provides a product in the sense we will use "product" in this book.

Need satisfaction comes from the total product

This bigger view of a product must be understood completely—it's too easy to slip into a *physical product* point of view. In fact, marketing has usually focused on physical goods—almost ignoring services. Actually,

"Hey! Isn't installation included, too?"

however, services are a very important and growing share of total national income. We certainly can't ignore services. But we don't want to just focus on services either.

Instead, we want to think of a product in terms of the *needs it satisfies.* Customer needs are satisfied not only by physical products but also by services. Indeed, one author has suggested that there are very few pure physical goods or pure services. Most products are a combination of the two.[1] If the objective of the firm is to satisfy customer needs, it must see that service is part of or may be *the* product—and has to be provided as part of the marketing mix. An automobile without any repair service, for example, is not a very useful product.

Whole product lines must be developed, too

We have been talking about a single total product. But customer needs cannot always be satisfied by one product. Manufacturers and wholesalers may have to offer complete lines of products to satisfy their customers. Retailers also have to offer a wide assortment. This makes the job of product planning harder. But if this is what customers want, then complete lines have to be offered.

For convenience, we will focus mainly on developing one marketing strategy at a time. But you should remember that several physical products and/or services might have to be planned to develop an effective marketing program for a whole company.

GOODS CLASSES AFFECT MARKETING STRATEGY PLANNING

To avoid trying to treat *every* product as unique when planning strategies, it would help to have some goods classes which are related to marketing mixes. Luckily, products can be classified this way. These goods classes will be a useful starting point for developing marketing mixes for new products and evaluating present mixes.

Goods class depends on who wil use the product

Whether a product should be treated as a consumer or industrial good depends on who will use it. **Consumer goods** are those products meant for the final consumer. **Industrial goods** are products meant for use in producing other products. All goods fit into one of these two groups. Customer research supports the idea that these goods classes are useful in marketing mix planning.[2]

CONSUMER GOODS CLASSES

Based on customer buying behavior

Workable consumer goods classes are based on the way people buy products. Since the aim of marketing is to satisfy consumers' needs, basing goods classes on consumer buying behavior makes sense. It also follows from our discussion—in Chapter 5—of the consumer as a problem solver. Consumer goods can be divided into four groups: (1) convenience goods, (2) shopping goods, (3) specialty goods, and (4) unsought goods. See

Figure 8–1

Consumer goods classes and marketing mix planning

1. *Convenience goods.*
   a. *Staples*—need maximum exposure—need widespread distribution at low cost.
   b. *Impulse goods*—need maximum exposure—need widespread distribution but with assurance of preferred display or counter position.
   c. *Emergency goods*—need widespread distribution near probable point of use.
2. *Shopping goods.*
   a. *Homogeneous*—need enough exposure to facilitate price comparison.
   b. *Heterogeneous*—need adequate representation in major shopping districts or large shopping centers near other, similar shopping goods.
3. *Specialty goods*—can have limited availability, but in general should be treated as a convenience or shopping good (in whichever category product would normally be included), to reach persons not yet sold on its specialty-goods status.
4. *Unsought goods*—need attention directed to product and aggressive promotion in outlets, or must be available in places where similar products would be sought.

Figure 8–1 for a summary of how these goods classes are related to a marketing mix.

CONVENIENCE GOODS—USUALLY PURCHASED QUICKLY

Convenience goods are products the customer needs but isn't willing to spend much time shopping for. Examples are: cigarettes, soap, drugs, newspapers, magazines, chewing gum, candy, and most grocery products. These products are bought often, require little service or selling, don't cost much, and may even be bought by habit.

Convenience goods are of three types—staples, impulse goods, and emergency goods—again based on *how customers think about products—not* the features of the products themselves.

Staples—purchased and used regularly

Staples are goods which are bought often and routinely without much thought. Examples include food and drug items used regularly in every household. Here, branding can become important to help customers cut shopping effort.

Staples are sold in convenient places like food stores, drug stores, discount and hardware stores, and vending machines. Some customers want convenience so much that they have milk, bread, and newspapers delivered directly to their homes.

Shopping for staples may not even be planned. Many shoppers plan meals in the store and modern supermarkets are laid out to make this

Impulse goods must be available at the right time and place.

easier. "Go-togethers" like strawberries and sponge cake or ice cream and chocolate sauce are placed next to each other to encourage unplanned buying.

Impulse goods—bought immediately on sight

Impulse goods are goods which are bought as unplanned purchases but customers don't shop for them at all. True impulse goods are items that the customer decides to buy on sight, may have bought the same way many times before, and wants "right now."

If a shopper passes a street corner vendor, for example, and gets a sudden urge for ice cream, that ice cream bar is an impulse good. But if the same shopper bought a box of ice cream bars in the supermarket as a family desert, the bars would be staples because the shopper was looking for a dessert.

There is an important difference between buying something to satisfy a current need and buying for later use. If the customer doesn't buy an impulse good immediately, the need may disappear and no purchase will be made. But if the customer needs a dessert, a purchase probably will be made eventually.

This difference is important because it affects Place and the whole marketing mix. Place is very important for impulse goods. If the buyer doesn't see them at the "right" time, the sale may be lost. As a result, special methods are developed for selling impulse goods. They are put where they'll be seen and bought—near front doors, near the checkout counters, or on display shelves in front of the store.

Emergency goods— purchased only when urgently needed

Emergency goods are goods which are purchased only when the need is great. Little shopping may be done. The customer needs the product immediately. Price isn't important. Examples are ambulance services, umbrellas or raincoats during a rainstorm, and tire chains during a snowstorm.

178

Emergency goods are purchased only when need is great.

Some retailers carry emergency goods to meet such needs. They know that many potential customers will face certain kinds of emergencies. And they set up their operations to serve them. Small gasoline stations in rural areas and service stations on toll-roads and thruways carry tires to meet emergency needs. The buyer probably could get a tire at a lower price back home—but with a blowout, any price is right.

Some small, neighborhood grocery stores meet the "fill-in" needs of customers who need a few items between weekly supermarket trips. Usually these stores charge higher prices. But customers will pay it because they think of these goods as "emergencies." One study found that almost 80 percent of households use such a "fill-in" store.[3] In the last 20 years, chains of such convenience food stores have been spreading. They provide "emergency" service—staying open "7 till 11" and stocking items that are needed in a hurry.

SHOPPING GOODS

Shopping goods are those products that a customer feels are worth the time and effort to compare with competing products.

Shopping goods can be divided into two types—depending on what customers are comparing: (1) homogeneous and (2) heterogeneous shopping goods.

Homogeneous shopping goods—the price must be right

Homogeneous shopping goods are shopping goods that the customer sees as basically the same and wants at the lowest price. Some consumers feel that certain sizes and types of refrigerators, television sets, washing machines, and even automobiles are basically similar. They are shopping for the best price.

In one study of automobile purchasing behavior, about half of the people wanted the "best price" or "best deal" and did shop at more than one dealership.[4] Three out of four supermarket shoppers shop for advertised specials every week.[5]

This buyer interest in price helps explain why some retailers emphasize "low prices" and "price cuts."

LOW-PRICE ITEMS ARE SEEN THIS WAY, TOO

Even some inexpensive items like butter, coffee, and other food items may be thought of as homogeneous shopping goods. Some customers carefully read food store advertising for the lowest prices. Then they go from store to store getting the items. (This is called "cherry picking" in the food business.)

Heterogeneous shopping goods—the product must be right

Heterogeneous shopping goods are shopping goods that the customer sees as different and wants to inspect for quality and suitability. Examples are furniture, dishes, some cameras, and clothing. Style is important—price is less important.

Even if an item costs only $5 or $10, consumers may look in three or four stores to be sure they have done a good job of shopping.

Price isn't ignored. But for nonstandardized goods, it is harder to compare price. Once the customer has found the right product, price may not matter—providing it is reasonable.

Branding may be less important for heterogeneous shopping goods. The more consumers want to make their own comparisons, the less they depend on brand names and labels.

Often the buyer of heterogeneous shopping goods not only wants but expects some kind of help in buying. And, if the product is expensive, the buyer may want extra service—such as alteration of clothing or installation of appliances.

SPECIALTY GOODS

Specialty goods are consumer goods that the customer really wants and will make a special effort to buy. Shopping for a specialty good doesn't mean comparing—the buyer wants that special product and is willing to search for it. It is not the extent of searching, but the customer's *willingness* to search that makes it a specialty good.

Specialty goods usually are specific branded products—not broad product categories

Don't want substitutes!

Specialty goods don't have to be expensive, once-in-a-lifetime purchases. *Any* branded item that develops a strong customer franchise may win specialty goods status. Consumers have been observed asking for a drug product by its brand name and—when offered a chemically identical substitute—actually leaving the store in anger.

UNSOUGHT GOODS

Unsought goods are goods that potential customers do not yet want or know they can buy. Therefore, they don't search for them at all. In fact, consumers probably wouldn't buy these goods if they saw them—unless Promotion could show their value.

There are two types of unsought goods: new unsought and regularly unsought.

New unsought goods are products offering really new ideas that potential customers don't know about yet. Informative promotion can help convince consumers to accept or even seek out the products—ending their unsought status.

Regularly unsought goods are products—like gravestones, life insurance, and encyclopedias—that may stay unsought but not unbought forever. These products may become some of the biggest purchases a family every makes—but few people would even drive around the block to find them. There may be a need—but the potential customers are not motivated to satisfy it. And there probably is little hope that they will move out of the unsought category for most consumers. For this kind of product, Promotion is very important.

ONE PRODUCT MAY BE SEEN AS SEVERAL CONSUMER GOODS

We have been looking at one good at a time. But the same product might be seen in different ways by different target markets *at the same time.*

The marketing manager might find that the market consists of several groups of people—each of whom has similar attitudes toward the product. This is shown in Figure 8–2. This diagram groups people in terms of their willingness to shop and brand familiarity. It is a simple way of summarizing our discussion of consumer goods. Each of these groups might need a different marketing mix.

A tale of four motels

Motels are a good example of a service that can be seen as *four different* kinds of goods. Some tired motorists are satisfied with the first motel they come to—a convenience good. Other travelers shop for the kind of facilities they want at a fair price—a heterogeneous shopping good. Others shop for just basic facilities at the lowest price—a homogeneous shopping good. And others study tourist guides, talk with traveling friends, and phone ahead to reserve a place in a recommended motel—a specialty good.

Perhaps one motel could satisfy all potential customers. But it would be hard to produce a marketing mix attractive to everyone—easy access for convenience, good facilities at the right price for shopping goods buyers, and qualities special enough to attract the specialty goods travelers.

Figure 8–2
How potential customers might view some product[6]

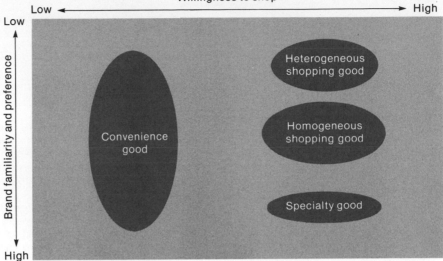

*The number of people holding each view is indicated roughly by the size of the cluster.

As a result, we see very different kinds of motels—seemingly (but not really) competing with each other.

Anyone planning new strategies can improve their understanding of what is needed by studying potential target markets in terms of these goods classes. Of course, strategy planners would like to know more about potential customers than the consumer goods classes can tell them. But they at least give a beginning which can help in later planning.

INDUSTRIAL GOODS CLASSES

Industrial goods buyers do little shopping—especially compared to consumer goods buyers. Usually the seller comes to the buyer. This means that product classes based on shopping behavior are not useful.

Industrial goods classes are based on how buyers see products and how the products are to be used. Expensive and/or long-lasting products are treated differently than inexpensive items. Products that become a part of a firm's own product are seen differently from those which only aid production. Finally, the size of a particular purchase can make a difference. An air compressor may not be very important to a buyer for General Motors, but it might be very important for a small garage owner.

The classes of industrial goods are: (1) installations, (2) accessory equipment, (3) raw materials, (4) component parts and materials, (5) supplies, and (6) services. See Figure 8–3 for a summary of how these goods classes are related to what is needed in a marketing mix.

Figure 8–3
Industrial goods and marketing mix planning

KNOW

INDUSTRIAL
1) INSTALLATIONS
2) ACCESSORY
3) RAW MATERIALS
4) COMPONENT PART
5) SUPPLIES
6) SERVICE

1. *Installations.*
   a. *Buildings (used) and land rights*—need widespread and/or knowledgeable contacts, depending upon specialized nature of product.
   b. *Buildings (new)*—need technical and experienced personal contact, probably at top-management level (multiple buying influence).
   c. *Major equipment.*
      i. *Custom-made*—need technical (design) contacts by person able to visualize and design applications, and present to high-level and technical management.
      ii. *Standard*—need experienced (not necessarily highly technical) contacts by person able to visualize applications and present to high-level and technical management.
2. *Accessory equipment*—need fairly widespread and numerous contacts by experienced and sometimes technically trained personnel.
3. *Raw materials.*
   a. *Farm products*—need contacts with many small farmer producers and fairly widespread contact with users.
   b. *Natural products*—need fairly widespread contacts with users.
4. *Component parts and materials*—need technical contacts to determine specifications required—widespread contacts usually not necessary.
5. *Supplies.*
   a. *Maintenance*—need very widespread distribution for prompt delivery.
   b. *Repairs*—need widespread distribution for some, and prompt service from factory for others (depends on customers' preferences).
   c. *Operating supplies*—need fair to widespread distribution for prompt delivery.
6. *Services*—most need very widespread availability.

INSTALLATIONS—MAJOR CAPITAL ITEMS

Installations are important long-lasting capital goods. They include buildings and land rights, custom-made equipment, and standard equipment. Buildings and custom-made equipment generally require special negotiations for each individual product because they are one-of-a-kind. Standard major equipment is more homogeneous and can be treated more routinely. All installations, however, are important enough to require high-level and even top-management consideration.

Size of market small at any time

Installations are long-lasting goods—so they are not bought very often. The number of potential buyers at any particular time usually is small. For custom-made machines, there may be only a half-dozen potential customers—compared to a thousand or more potential buyers for standard machines of similar type.

Potential customers are generally in the same industry. Their plants are likely to be near to each other—which makes Promotion easier. The automobile industry, for example, is heavily concentrated in and around

Michigan. The tire industry is in Ohio. Copper mining is in the western states. And the aircraft industry—from a world view—is in the United States.

Buying needs basically economic

Buying needs are basically economic and concerned with the performance of the installation over its expected life. After comparing expected performance to present costs and figuring interest, the expected return on capital can be determined. Yet emotional needs—such as a desire for industry leadership and status—also may be involved.

Installations may have to be leased or rented

Since installations are expensive, the producer often will lease or rent the product rather than sell it outright. Examples are buildings and land rights and some special equipment—including computers.

Specialized services are needed as part of the product

Since the expected return on an installation is based on efficient operation, the sales contract may require regular service visits. Service people may even be permanently attached to the company. Computer manufacturers sometimes station service people with the machines. The cost is included in the price or rent.

ACCESSORY EQUIPMENT—IMPORTANT BUT SHORT-LIVED CAPITAL ITEMS

Accessory equipment are less expensive, short-lived capital goods. They are the tools and equipment used in production or office activities. Examples include portable drills, sanding machines, electric lift trucks, typewriters, filing cases, accounting machines, wheelbarrows, hand trucks, and small lathes.

Since these products cost less and last a shorter time than installations, the multiple buying influence is less important. Operating people and purchasing agents—rather than top-level managers—may do the buying.

More target markets requiring different marketing mixes

Accessories are more standardized than installations. And they are usually needed by more customers! A large, special-purpose belt sanding machine, for example, might be produced as a custom-made installation

Accessory equipment includes tools and equipment used in production and office activities.

for woodworking firms. But small portable sanding machines would be considered accessory equipment. Since there are many more possible customers and less geographic concentration, different marketing mixes would be needed for accessory equipment than for installations.

Might prefer to lease or rent

Leasing or renting accessories is attractive to some target markets because the costs can be treated as expenses. A manufacturer of electric lift trucks, for instance, was able to expand its sales by selling the basic truck outright, but charging for the expensive battery system by the amount of time it was used. This increased sales because, as one of the company managers said: "Nobody worries about costs which are buried as an operating expense."[7]

RAW MATERIALS—FARM PRODUCTS AND NATURAL PRODUCTS ARE EXPENSE ITEMS

Become part of a physical product

Raw materials are basic goods—such as logs, iron ore, sand, and freshly caught fish—that are processed only as much as needed to move them to the next step in the production process. Unlike installations and accessories, raw materials become part of a physical product and are expense items.

We can break raw materials into two categories: (1) farm products and (2) natural products. **Farm products** are grown by farmers—examples are cotton, wheat, strawberries, sugar cane, cattle, hogs, poultry, eggs, and milk. **Natural products** are products which occur in nature—such as fish and game, lumber and maple syrup, and copper, zinc, iron ore, oil, and coal.

FARM PRODUCTS ARE VARIABLE IN QUALITY AND QUANTITY

Involve grading, storage, and/or transportation

The need for grading is one of the important differences between farm products and other industrial goods. Nature produces what it will, and someone must sort and grade farm products to satisfy various market segments. Some of the top grades of fruits and vegetables find their way into the consumer goods market. The lower grades are treated as industrial goods and used in juices, sauces, and frozen pies.

Most farm products are produced seasonally—yet the demand for them is fairly constant all year. As a result, storage and transportation are important in their marketing process.

As noted, buyers of industrial goods usually don't seek suppliers. This complicates the marketing of farm products. The many small farms usually are widely scattered—sometimes far from potential buyers. Selling direct to final users would be difficult. So Place and Promotion are important in marketing mixes for these products.

NATURAL PRODUCTS—QUANTITIES ARE MORE ADJUSTABLE

In contrast to the farm products market with its many producers, natural products are produced by fewer and larger companies. There are some exceptions—such as the coal and lumber industries—but oligopoly conditions are common.

Typically, the total supply of natural products is limited and can't be expanded easily. But the supply harvested or mined in any one year is adjustable.

Most of the products are bulky and have transportation problems. But storage is less important, since few are perishable. And some can be produced year-round. Major exceptions are fish and game, which have "runs" or seasons are more like farm products than forest or mineral products in their marketing patterns.

As with farm products, buyers of natural products usually need specific grades and dependable supply sources to be sure of continued production in their own plants. Large buyers, therefore, often try to buy—or at least control—their sources of supply. This is easier than with farm products because fewer and larger production facilities are involved.

One way to control supply sources is **vertical integration**—here meaning ownership of the natural product source by the user. Examples are paper manufacturers who control timber resources, oil refiners who control crude oil sources, and tire manufacturers who control rubber plantations.

Sellers who do not integrate with users usually find that their customers want to be sure of dependable sources of supply. This is often done through contracts—perhaps negotiated by top-level managers—using standard grades or specifications.

COMPONENT PARTS AND MATERIALS—IMPORTANT EXPENSE ITEMS

The sum is no better than . . .

Component parts and materials are expense items which have had more processing than raw materials. They require different marketing mixes than raw materials—even though they both become part of a finished product.

Component *parts* include those items that are (1) finished and ready for assembly or (2) nearly finished—requiring only minor processing (such as grinding or polishing) before being assembled into the final product. Examples are automobile batteries, small motors, and tires—all of which go directly into a finshed product.

Component *materials* are items such as wire, paper, textiles, or cement. They have already been processed but must be processed further before becoming part of the final product.

Multiple buying influences

Component parts are often custom-made. Much negotiation may be necessary between the engineering staffs of both buyer and seller to arrive

Oil filters are a component part for auto manufacturing.

at the proper specifications. If the price of the item is high—or if it is extremely important in the final product—top-level managers may become involved.

Other component parts and materials are produced to commonly accepted standards or specifications—and produced in quantity. Production people in the buying firm may specify quality—but the purchasing agent will do the buying. And he will want several dependable sources of supply.

Since components go into the firm's own product, quality is important. The buyer's own name and whole marketing mix are at stake. Quality may be less important for component parts that are well branded (such as a tire or spark plug). The blame for a defective product can fall upon the component supplier. Generally, however, a buyer will try to buy from component sources that help guarantee a good product.

SUPPLIES—EVERYBODY WANTS THESE EXPENSE ITEMS, BUT HOW MUCH?

Supplies are expense items that do not become a part of the final product. They may be treated less seriously by buyers.

They are called MRO items

Supplies can be divided into three categories: (1) maintenance, (2) repair, and (3) operating supplies—giving them their common name: "MRO items."

Maintenance items include such things as paint, nails, light bulbs, sweeping compounds, brooms, and window-cleaning equipment. Repair items are nuts and bolts or parts needed to repair existing equipment. Operating supplies include lubricating oils and greases, grinding compounds, coal, typing paper, ink, pencils, and paper clips.

Some operating supplies are needed regularly and in large amounts. They receive special treatment from buyers. Some companies buy coal and fuel oil in carload quantities. Usually there are several sources for such homogeneous products—and large volumes may be purchased in highly competitive markets. Or contracts may be negotiated, perhaps by high-level managers.

Maintenance and most operating supplies

These items are like convenience goods. They are so numerous that a purchasing agent can't possibly be an expert in buying all of them.

Each requisition for maintenance and small operating supplies may be for a relatively few items. The purchase requisitions can amount to only $1 to $2. Although the cost of handling a purchase order may be from $5 to $10, the item will be ordered because it is needed. But not much time will be spent on it.

Branding can become important for such products. It makes product identification and buying easier for such "nuisance" items.

A new company offering only one supply item might have trouble entering this market. The job of buying these many small items is hard enough—buyers usually don't have time to review the small advantages of each new product or supplier. The width of assortment and the dependability a seller could offer are more important when buying supply items. Middlemen usually handle the many supply items.

Repair items

The original supplier of installations or accessory equipment may be the only source of supply for repairs and parts. The cost of repairs in relation to the cost of a production break-down may be so small that buyers are willing to pay the price charged—whatever it is.

SERVICES—YOU EXPENSE THEM

Services are expense items which support the operations of a firm. Engineering or management consulting services can improve the plant layout or the operation of the company. Design services can supply designs for the physical plant, products, and graphic materials. Maintenance services can handle window-cleaning, painting, or general housekeeping. Other companies can supply in-plant lunches and piped-in music to improve employee morale and production.

The cost of buying services outside the firm is compared with the cost of having company people do them. For special skills needed only occasionally, an outsider can be the best source. And service specialists are growing in number in our complex economy.

PRODUCTS HAVE LIFE CYCLES

Industry sales and profits don't move together

Products—like consumers—have life cycles. So it is important that a company do product and marketing mix planning. Competitors are always developing and copying ideas and products—making existing products out-of-date more quickly than ever.

The **product life cycle** is the stages a new product goes through from

KNOW GRAPH
AND STAGES

Figure 8–4
Life cycle of a typical product

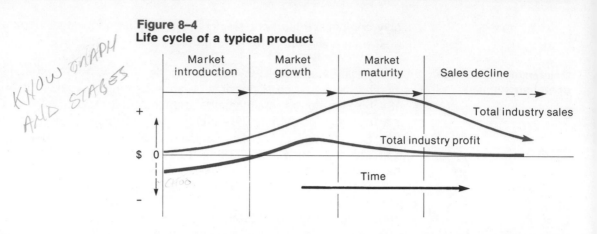

beginning to end. It is divided into four major stages: market introduction, market growth, market maturity, and sales decline. A particular firm's marketing mix for a product should change during these stages for several reasons. Customers' attitudes and needs may change through the course of the product's life cycle. Entirely different target markets may be appealed to at different stages in the life cycle. The nature of competition moves toward pure competition or oligopoly.

Further, the total sales of the product—by all competitors in the industry—varies in each of its four stages. And more importantly, the profit picture changes. It is important to see that the two do not move together. Profits decline while sales are still rising. Their general relationships can be seen in Figure 8–4.

Market introduction— investing in the future

The **market introduction** stage is while a new idea is being introduced to a market. Customers aren't looking for the product. They don't even know about it. Promotion is needed to tell potential customers about the new product—its advantages and uses.

Even though a firm promotes its new product, it takes time for customers to learn that the product is available. The introductory stage usually is marked by losses—with much money spent for promotion and product and place development. Money is being invested in the hope of future profits.

Market growth—many competing products and best profits

The **market growth** stage occurs when industry sales start growing fast. The innovator begins to make big profits. Competitors start coming into the market—each tries to develop a better product design. There is much product variety. But some competitors copy the most successful products. Monopolistic competition with downsloping demand curves is typical of the market growth stage.

During this stage, the sales of the industry are rising fairly fast as more and more customers buy. This second stage may last from several days

Our electronic calculators will cause history to repeat itself in the 70's.

A lot of people may never know that Texas Instruments designed and developed the first transistor radio. The reason? We never marketed it. Instead, we chose to supply components for other manufacturers. And the rest is history. The transistor radio became one of the most exciting and profitable retail items ever. And TI became the world's largest manufacturer of solid-state components.

In the 70's, we will again play a major role in a rapidly developing new market. Electronic calculators.

This time the key element Texas Instruments developed was the integrated circuit. The part which makes it possible to produce small size electronic calculators at an economical price.

And we have entered this market with our own line of TI electronic calculators. Calculators built with the same dedication to quality that has made TI famous. And that means part-by-part quality checks. Every step of the way. Quality assurance like that makes a difference to your customers.

TI's 3-to-1 Test Market Preference

In a recent test market, our portable TI-2500 model outsold all other electronic calculators in its class (under $200). And outsold them 3-to-1.

The Quality Line of TI Calculators
The TI-2500
- Fully Portable
- Built-in rechargeable batteries
- Weighs less than 12 ounces
- Full four function capability
- Bright 8-digit readout
- Full floating decimal
- Chain/Constant operation
- Comes with AC adapter/charger, carrying case

The TI-3000
- Attractive, compact desk model
- Weighs only 30 ounces
- Full four function capability
- Bright 8-digit readout
- Full floating decimal
- Complete with dust cover

The TI-3500
- Increased capability desk model
- Bright 10-digit readout
- Weighs just 30 ounces
- Chain/Constant operation
- 2, 4, and floating decimal selection
- Complete with dust cover

TI Provides Marketing Assistance

TI offers one of the best co-op advertising plans around. Plus, we supply a comprehensive Admaker kit with headline suggestions. Copy points. 30- and 60-second radio scripts. A 30-second television commercial with 5 seconds at the end for your store identification. And a variety of photographs and other

reproducible art. All in all, over 92 separate elements for your use. Including counter displays, brochures, and statement stuffers to reach your present customers.

Free In-Store Sales Training for Your Employees

To help your salespeople gain a thorough knowledge of our product, we offer a complete training program. A program which will enable them to effectively demonstrate calculators, and confidently answer any question a customer may ask. Audio-visual training material is available for your use at no charge.

Talk to a TI Representative Soon

He can tell you about your price protection in the event our prices change. He can tell you how TI manufactures every critical component for every TI calculator—and checks the quality every step of the way. And because of these quality controls, he will tell you that TI guarantees the finished product.

The Difference in Electronic Calculators Is Texas Instruments

We've come a long way since the first transistor radio. Always keeping one important thing in mind. Quality. It's the thing that sets the TI electronic calculator apart from the crowd. And makes us confident that history will repeat itself.

The TI-3000

The TI-2500

That means consumer acceptance of the TI calculator has already been established. And it's this kind of recognizable quality, at a reasonable price, that makes TI the line of calculators that every other entry in the field will be compared to.

The TI-3500

For the name of your nearest TI representative, Write: Texas Instruments Incorporated
P.O. Box 5012
M/S 84
Dallas, Texas 75222

TEXAS INSTRUMENTS
INCORPORATED

Small electric calculators began their product life cycle in the 1970s.

to several years—depending on whether the product is hula hoops, credit card service, or color television sets. This is the time of biggest profits— for the industry. *But* it is *also the beginning of the decline of industry profits.*

Market maturity— competition up, profits down

The **market maturity** stage occurs when industry sales level out and competition gets tougher. Many competitors have entered the race for profits—unless oligopoly conditions prevail. In either case, competition becomes more aggressive. Industry profits go down throughout the market maturity stage because promotion costs climb. Some competitors begin to cut prices to attract business. Even in oligopoly situations, there is a long-run downward pressure on prices.

New firms may enter the market at this stage—increasing competition even more. Note that late entries do skip the early stages—including the profitable market growth stage!

Promotion becomes more important during the market maturity stage. Products differ only slightly—if at all. Most competitors have discovered the most effective appeals—or copied the leaders.

In monopolistic competition, we see increasing competition on product, price, and promotion. Although each firm may still have its own demand curve, the curves are becoming increasingly elastic as the various products become almost the same in the minds of potential consumers.

In the United States, the markets for most automobiles, boats, many household appliances, most groceries, television sets, and tobacco products are in the market maturity stage.[8] This period may continue for many years until a basically new product idea comes along. This is true although different brands or models may come and go. Gasoline-powered automobiles, for example, replaced horse-drawn carriages. Eventually they may be replaced by some other method of transportation, such as electric autos and high-speed mass transit.

Sales decline—a period of replacement

The **sales decline** stage occurs when new products replace the old. Price competition from dying products may become more vigorous—but products with strong customer franchises may make profits almost till the end. These firms will have downsloping demand curves because they have successfully differentiated their products.

As the new products go through their introductory stage, the old ones may keep some sales by appealing to the most loyal target customers.

Our earlier discussion of customer buying behavior showed that some customers accept new ideas more easily than others. The former would "discover" the new product. More conservative buyers might switch later—smoothing the sales decline.

Product life cycles are getting shorter

The total length of the cycle may vary from 90 days—in the case of hula hoops—to possibly 90 years for automobiles. In general, however, product life cycles are shortening.

In the highly competitive grocery products industry, they are down to 12–18 months for really new ideas. Simple variations of such a new idea

"What do you mean, we're going into a sales decline? Our product hasn't even been introduced yet!"

may have even shorter life cycles. Competitors may copy flavor or packaging changes in a matter of weeks or months.

Large manufacturers—even in the industrial goods area—face product life cycles. A top Du Pont executive said: "Lead time is gone . . . there's no company so outstanding technically today that it can expect a long lead time in a new discovery."[9] Du Pont had nylon to itself for 15 years. But in just 2 years a major competitor, Celanese Corp. came out with something very competitive to Delrin—another synthetic fiber discovery that Du Pont hoped would be as important as nylon. Similarly, six months after U.S. Steel came out with a new "thin tin" plate, competitors were out with even better products.

Even copying products is not uncommon. And this speeds up the cycle. Westinghouse found a company copying its new hair dryer and instruction book almost exactly.[10] And patents may not be much protection. The product's life may be over before a case would get through the courts. The copier might be out of business by then.

The early bird makes the profits

The increasing speed of the product life cycle means that the modern firm must be developing new products all the time. It must try to have marketing mixes that will make the most of the market growth stage—when profits are highest.

Length of cycle affects strategy planning

The probable length of the cycle affects strategy planning—realistic plans must be made for the later stages. In fact, where a product is in its life cycle—and how fast it's moving to the next stage—should affect strategy planning. Figure 8–5 shows the relation of the product life cycle to various marketing variables. The "technical" terms in this figure are discussed later in the book.

Product life cycles keep moving, but a company does not have to sit by and watch its products go through a complete product life cycle. It has choices. It can improve the product—for the same or a different market—and let it start off on a new cycle. Or it can withdraw it before it completes the cycle. These two choices are shown in Figure 8–6.

Product life cycles can be extended

When a product wins a customer franchise, its life may last as long as it continues to meet the needs of those customers. If the needs change, the product may have to change, but the consumers will continue to buy if it does meet their needs. An outstanding example is Procter & Gamble's *Tide.* Introduced in 1947, this synthetic detergent gave consumers a cleaner wash than they were able to get before—because it eliminated the soap film which was common with the soaps made from animal fats. *Tide* led to a whole new generation of laundry products and made the modern automatic washing machine possible—it produced better cleaning with fewer suds. Since 1947, washing machines and fabrics have changed, so the *Tide* sold today is much different than the one sold in 1947. In fact, there were 55 technical changes during its first 29 years of life. But

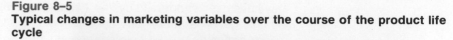

Figure 8–5
Typical changes in marketing variables over the course of the product life cycle

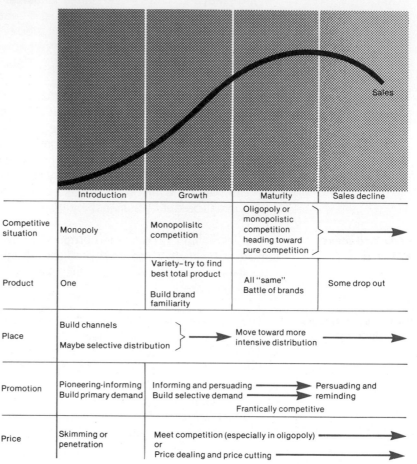

	Introduction	Growth	Maturity	Sales decline
Competitive situation	Monopoly	Monopolisitc competition	Oligopoly or monopolistic competition heading toward pure competition →	
Product	One	Variety–try to find best total product / Build brand familiarity	All "same" Battle of brands	Some drop out
Place	Build channels / Maybe selective distribution →		Move toward more intensive distribution →	
Promotion	Pioneering-informing Build primary demand	Informing and persuading → Persuading and Build selective demand → reminding / Frantically competitive		
Price	Skimming or penetration	Meet competition (especially in oligopoly) → or Price dealing and price cutting →		

the product continues to sell well—because it continues to meet consumers' needs.[11]

Do the kinds of product changes made on *Tide* create a new product which should have its own product life cycle, or are they just adjustments of the original product concept? We will take the second position—focusing on the idea of "product as need satisfier." Detergents did permit a new standard of cleaning. And people who wanted cleanliness did shift quite rapidly to detergent products—causing sales decline for the traditional soaps. As detergents were gaining acceptance, they went through the early stages of the product life cycle. Now they will continue, in market maturity—with various technical changes—until a new idea—perhaps, ultrasonic cleaning—comes along.

Figure 8–6
Significantly improved product starts a new cycle, but maybe with short introductory stage

Profit-oriented firm dropping out of market during market maturity stage

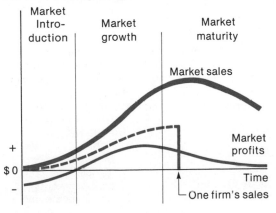

Conclusion

In this chapter, we looked at Product very broadly. A Product may not be a physical product at all. It may be a service. Or it may be some combination—like a meal at a restaurant.

A firm's total product is what satisfies the needs of its target market. This *may* be a physical product, but also could include a package, brand, installation, repair service, and so on—whatever is needed to satisfy target customers.

Consumer goods and industrial goods classes were introduced to simplify your study of marketing and help in planning marketing mixes. The consumer goods classes are based on consumers' buying behavior. Industrial goods classes are based on the products themselves and how they are used.

Knowing these goods classes and learning how marketers handle specific products within these classes will speed the development of your "marketing sense."

The fact that different people may view the same product as different goods helps explain why firms may use very different marketing mixes—quite successfully.

The product life cycle is also very important to understanding markets and planning strategies. It shows that different marketing mixes—and even strategies—are needed as a product moves through its cycle. You saw that profits change during the cycle—with the biggest profits being earned in the market growth stage.

Questions for discussion

1 Define, in your own words, what a product is.

2 Explain how the addition of guarantees, service, and credit can improve a "total product." Cite a specific case where this has been done and explain how customers viewed this new total product.

3 What "products" are being offered by an exclusive men's shop? By a nightclub? By a soda fountain? By a supermarket?

4 Discuss the social value of encouraging people to throw away products that are not "all worn out." Is this an economic waste? How worn out is "all worn out"? Must a shirt have holes in it? How big?

5 After ten years of selling Pringles as a "new concept in potato chips"—involving uniform shape in a canister package—Procter & Gamble began offering a completely revamped "all natural" Pringles in 1978. The "new" product contained no preservatives and used no artificial ingredients. Why do you think it made this switch? Is this likely to increase sales of Pringles, which are considered by some to be one of the biggest "bombs" of the 1970s?

6 What kinds of consumer goods are the following: *(a)* fountain pens, *(b)* men's shirts, *(c)* cosmetics? Explain your reasoning.

7 Some goods seem to be treated perpetually as unsought goods by their producers. Give an example and explain why.

8 How would the marketing mix for a staple convenience good differ from one for a homogeneous shopping good? How would the mix for a specialty good differ from the mix for a heterogeneous shopping good? Use examples.

9 Would the marketing mix for all convenience goods be essentially the same? Discuss, using an example for each type of convenience good.

10 In what types of stores would you expect to find: *(a)* convenience goods, *(b)* shopping goods, *(c)* specialty goods, and *(d)* unsought goods?

11 Would you expect to find any wholesalers selling the various types of industrial goods? Are retail stores required (or something like retail stores)?

12 What kinds of industrial goods are the following?
a. Nails and screws.
b. Paint.
c. Dust-collecting and ventilating systems.
d. An electric lift truck.
Explain your reasoning.

13 How do farm product raw materials differ from other raw materials or other industrial goods? Do the differences have any impact on their marketing mixes? If so, what, specifically?

14 For the kinds of industrial goods described in this chapter, complete the following table (use one or a few *well-chosen* words.)

Goods	*1*	*2*	*3*
Installations			
Buildings and land rights			
Major equipment			
Standard			
Custom made			
Accessory equipment			
Raw materials			
Farm products			
Natural products			
Components			
Parts			
Materials			
Supplies			
Operating supplies			
Maintenance and small operating supplies			
Services			

1—Kind of distribution facility(ies) needed and functions they will provide.
2—Caliber of sales people required.
3—Kind of advertising required.

15 Explain how market sales and market profits behave over the product life cycle.

16 Cite two examples of products that you feel are currently in each of the product life-cycle stages.

17 Explain how different conclusions might be reached with respect to the correct product life-cycle stage(s) in the automobile market, especially if different views of the market are held.

18 Can product life cycles be extended? Illustrate your answer for a specific product.

19 Discuss the life cycle of a product in terms of its probable impact on a manufacturer's marketing mix. Illustrate, using battery-operated toothbrushes.

Suggested cases

9 Betty's Shop

10 Block Pharmaceutical Company

18 Sports Sales Company

Includes...

* **Cake Mix**
* **Ready-to-Spread Frosting**
* **5"x 7" Foil-lined Pan**

Lemon / Lemon
CAKE MIX / FROSTING

NET WT 13.5 OZ

When you finish this chapter you should:

1 Know what is involved in designing new products and what "new products" really are.
2 Understand the strategic importance of packaging.
3 Understand what branding is and why it developed.
4 Understand new product development as a total company effort.
5 Understand the need for product or brand managers.
6 Recognize the important new terms shown in red.

NEW PRODUCT PLANNING AND POLICIES

A modern firm has to develop new products just to survive. If the new offering is a physical product, it probably will need packaging. Both physical products *and* services should be branded. A successful marketer wants to be sure that satisfied customers will know what to ask for the next time.

There is much more to packaging and branding than just buying a cardboard box and sticking on the company's name. Sometimes, the packaging and branding decisions may be more important than physical product decisions.

In this chapter, we will talk about the strategic decisions of manufacturers or middlemen who must take these new product, packaging, and branding decisions. The strategic decisions we are concerned about are shown in Figure 9–1.

DESIGNING NEW PRODUCTS

What is a new product—lemons?

A **new product** is one that is new *in any way* for the company concerned. A "new product" can become "new" in many ways. A new idea can be turned into a new item or service. Small changes in an existing product also can make it "new." Or an existing product may be offered to new markets as a "new" product. Lemons are a good example.

In the marketing of lemons by one company, no physical changes were made—but much promotion created many "new" products. The same

197

Figure 9–1
Strategy planning for Product

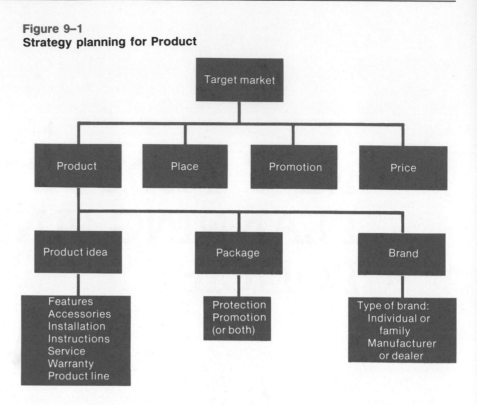

old lemons were promoted successfully for lemonade, mixed drinks, diet supplements, cold remedies, lemon cream pies, a salad dressing, sauce for fish, and many other uses. For each of these markets, the product had to go through the early stages of the product life cycle.[1]

A product can be called "new" for only a limited time. Six months is the longest time that a product should be called new—according to the **Federal Trade Commission (FTC)**—the federal government agency which polices anti-monopoly laws. To be called new—says the FTC—a product must be entirely new or changed in "a functionally significant or substantial respect."[2] While six months may seem a very short time for production-oriented managers, it may be reasonable given the length of product life cycles.

Find out what the customers and middlemen want

Everyone who handles, sells, or uses a product must be considered when developing a new product. Of course, the product should reflect the needs and attitudes of the target customers. But the product designers must not only think about final customers—but intermediate customers too. There may be special packaging or handling needs. The shelf height in supermarkets, for example, might limit package size. Shipping or handling problems in the warehouse or on carriers might call for different types of packaging or package sizes—to keep damage down or make the package easier to handle.

More, perhaps, than you care   to know about Sunkist lemons.

A simple product can be aimed at many different markets.

Design long-term "goodness" into products if possible

Socially responsible firms are becoming aware that they should consider consumers' long-term interests when designing products. Consumer groups are helping to force this awareness on more firms.

The firm's final choice in product design should fit with the company's overall objectives and make good use of the firm's resources. But it would also be desirable to create a need-satisfying product which will appeal to consumers—not only in the short run but also in the long run. These kinds of new product opportunities are shown in Figure 9–2. Obviously, a socially responsible firm would try to find "desirable" opportunities rather than "deficient" ones. This may not be as easy as it sounds, however. Consumers may want "pleasing products" instead of "desirable products." And some competitors may be very willing to offer what consumers want. Being "socially responsible" will challenge new-product planners.

Safety should also be considered in product design

Real acceptance of the marketing concept would certainly lead to the design of safety into products. But the Consumer Product Safety Act of 1972 demands more awareness of safety in product design, and better

Figure 9–2
Types of new-product opportunities[3]

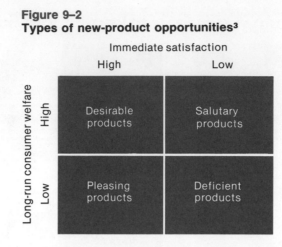

quality control. The Consumer Product Safety Commission can order expensive repairs or returns of "unsafe products." And it can back up its orders with fines and jail sentences. The Food and Drug Administration has similar powers for foods and drugs.

PRODUCT LIABILITY MUST BE TAKEN SERIOUSLY

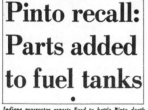

Indiana prosecutor expects Ford to battle Pinto death indictments. Page 13A.

Something new has been added recently regarding safety—large product liability settlements and claims for injury or death. Businesses are responsible for what they sell and so they usually buy insurance to protect against large claims. Now some firms are finding their product liability insurance costs rising rapidly, to the point where they have to "self-insure"—take the risk themselves—or go out of business. And the potential for more suits is great. Recently, a paper-making machinery manufacturer was notified of claims by users of two of its presses for damages due to industrial accidents. One of the presses was built in 1895, and the other in 1897![4]

The uncontrollable environment has changed—especially where safety is concerned. Safety is one of the four basic needs—and people feel strongly about it. So it is more important than ever to take product planning—and especially product safety—seriously. Production-oriented managers will have to become more market-oriented—or they may be forced out of business.

Warranty should mean something

Common law says that producers should stand behind—i.e., provide a warranty for—their products. A **warranty** explains what the seller guarantees about its product. FTC guidelines try to make sure that warranties are not "deceptive" or "unfair." Basically, the FTC wants to be sure the warranty is clear and definite. Some firms used to say their products were "fully warranted" or "absolutely guaranteed." The time period was not stated. And the meaning of the guarantee was not spelled out.

Now the company has to make clear what it's offering. Some firms

LIMITED WARRANTY
SHEPARD'S SHOES, INC. GUARANTEE

Except as specifically otherwise provided below, we will repair or replace for no charge any part of any leather shoe that wears out during the guarantee period according to the following schedule:

Children: (age 15 or under) — 3 months from date of purchase.
Women: (age 16 and over) — 4 months from date of purchase.
Men: (age 16 and over) — 6 months from date of purchase.

SPECIFICALLY EXCLUDED FROM THIS GUARANTEE OF REPAIR OR REPLACEMENT ARE THE FOLLOWING:

1. This guarantee does not cover any part of a patent leather shoe.
2. This guarantee does not cover any damage caused by water.
3. This guarantee does not cover more than a single repair or replacement to each part of a leather shoe.

This guarantee will be honored in all cases where the condition of the shoe is such that repair or replacement of any part is required in order to render it fit for the normal use required of it.

To receive the free repair or replacement, this guarantee must be presented at any Shepard's Shoes location before expiration of the guarantee period. Shepard's Shoe Stores are located at 326 South Washington Square, Lansing, Michigan and 317 East Grand River Avenue, East Lansing, Michigan.

Category _Women's Bass_   Authorization _Bill Shepard_

Stock No. _2501_   Size _8½M_   _Jane P. Doe_
                                          Name

Date _9/20/78_   _000 Anywhere_
                                          Address

Jane P. Doe   _St. Louis_
        Signature   City

A warranty explains what the seller guarantees about the product.

just guarantee their products against "defects of material or workmanship" for 30 to 90 days. Others are trying to design more quality into their products—they offer longer and stronger warranties. Some companies—for example, Sears Roebuck—have gone even further by providing a one-year replacement—not just repair—guarantee on some small appliances.

Customers might like a strong warranty, but it can be very expensive. It might even be economically impossible for small producers. Some customers abuse products and demand a lot of service on warranties. Backing up warranties can be a problem too. Although manufacturers may be responsible, they may have to depend upon reluctant middlemen to do the job—or set up their own service companies. This can make it hard for a small firm to compete with larger firms that have many service centers. Foreign auto producers and small U.S. auto producers, for example, can't match the number of Chevrolet or Ford service locations.

Product positioning may see new possibilities

A new aid to product planning—**product positioning**—shows where proposed and/or present brands are located in a market. It requires some formal marketing research. The results are usually plotted on graphs to help see where the products are "positioned" in relation to competitors. Usually, the products' positions are related to two product features which are important to the target customers.

Product positioning techniques are beyond the scope of this text. But the results of one such analysis—for the beer industry—shows the possibili-

Figure 9–3
Product space for the Chicago beer market[5]

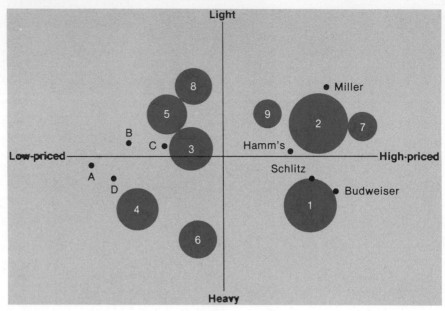

ties. In this case—besides plotting the customers' view of several beers in relation to two product features—the respondents were also asked about their "ideal" beer.

Figure 9–3 shows the product space for various beers using two dimensions—price and lightness. This data was obtained by asking beer drinkers to rate several beers. Then computer routines analyzed these ratings and plotted the results as shown. Note that the "name" brands are seen as high priced—as the "premium" beers. But not all the premium beers are direct competitors with respect to lightness.

The circles on Figure 9–3 show consumers clustered near their "ideal" beer preferences. These clusters were obtained by asking the consumers to rate their ideal beer, plotting the results, and then drawing circles around concentrations of consumers.

Note that there are several ideal clusters which aren't near any of the present brands. This might be an opportunity for introducing new products—both heavier and lighter beers at lower prices. You can see that product positioning can help one learn how customers see markets.

THE STRATEGIC IMPORTANCE OF PACKAGING

**May improve or create a
"new" product**

A new package can make *the* important difference in a new marketing strategy—by improving the total product. A better box, wrapper, can, or

bottle may even let a relatively small, unknown firm compete successfully with the established competitors. Carter Products Co.—new to the men's toiletries field—introduced its first product, Rise shaving cream, in aerosol cans and was able to compete effectively. The usual tube and carton might not have been so successful.

A package change often creates a "new" product by giving customers a more desirable quantity. Packaging frozen vegetables in 1-pound packages instead of 10-ounce packages served larger families better. The smaller packages held too little for them—while two packages held too much.

Multiple packs can be the basis of a new marketing strategy, too. Consumer surveys showed that some customers were buying several units at a time of products like soft drinks, beer, and frozen orange juice. This suggested a "new" market. Manufacturers tried packaging in 4-, 6-, and 8-packs and have been very successful.

May lower total distribution costs

Better protective packaging is especially important to manufacturers and wholesalers. They often have to pay the cost of goods damaged in shipment. There are also costs for settling such claims—and getting them settled is a nuisance. Goods damaged in shipment also may delay production or cause lost sales.

Retailers need good packaging too. Packaging which provides better protection can reduce store costs by cutting breakage, preventing discoloration, and stopping theft. Packages that are easier to handle can cut costs by speeding price marking, improving handling and display, and saving space.

MAY BE "BETTER" THAN ADVERTISING

Packaged goods are regularly seen in retail stores. They may actually be seen by many more potential customers than the company's advertising. A good package sometimes gives a firm more promotion effect than it could possibly afford with advertising.

Promotion-oriented packaging also may reduce total distribution costs. An attractive package may speed turnover so much that total costs will decline as a percentage of sales. Rapid turnover is one of the reasons for the success of self-service retailing. Without packages that "sell themselves," self-service retailing would not be possible.

Or . . . may raise total costs

In other cases, total distribution costs may rise because of packaging. But customers may be satisfied because the packaging improves the total product—perhaps by offering much greater convenience or reducing waste.

Packaging costs as a percentage of a manufacturer's selling price vary widely—ranging from 1 to 70 percent. Let's look at sugar as an example. In 100-pound bags, the cost of packaging sugar is only 1 percent of the selling price. In 2- to 5-pound cartons, it is 25–30 percent. And for individual serving packages, it is 50 percent. Most customers don't want to haul a 100-pound bag home and are quite willing to pay for more convenient packages. Restaurants use one-serving envelopes of sugar—finding that they reduce the cost of filling and washing sugar bowls and that customers prefer the more sanitary little packages. In both cases, packaging adds value to the total product. More accurately, it creates new products and new marketing strategies.

The right packaging is just enough packaging

Experience shows that a specific package must be designed for each product. The package must safely transport its contents, serve in a specific climate (especially if the product is to be exported), and last for a specific time. To provide such packaging, the manufacturer must know the product, the target customers, and how the product will be delivered to them. Under-packaging costs money for damage claims or poor sales. But overpackaging also costs money because dollars are spent for no benefit. Glassware, for example, needs to be protected from even relatively light blows that might smash it. Heavy-duty machinery doesn't need protection from blows but may need protection from moisture.

WHAT IS SOCIALLY RESPONSIBLE PACKAGING?

In spite of the time and money spent on packaging, there is still need for improvement. In one survey, 85 percent of the homemakers told of having been hurt when opening a package. They were especially annoyed about having to use knives to open containers of frozen strawberries. Complaints were common about bottles that break and metal containers with sharp edges. The result—unsatisfied target markets.

Critics of business say that some package designs are misleading— perhaps on purpose. They feel that the great variety of package designs makes it hard for consumers to compare values.

Federal law tries to help

Consumer criticism finally led to the passage of another law. The Federal Fair Packaging and Labeling Act of 1966 requires that consumer products be clearly labeled in understandable terms. The aim is to give the customer more information. The law asks government agencies and industry to try to reduce the number of package sizes and to make the labels more meaningful.[6]

```
        NUTRITION INFORMATION PER SERVING
SERVING SIZE . . . . . . . . . . . . . . . . . . . . . . 1 LEVEL TSP.
SERVINGS PER CONTAINER . . . . . . . . . . . . . . . . . . . .311
CALORIES . . . . . . . . . . . . . . . . . . . . . . . . . . . . . . . . . . . .10
PROTEIN . . . . . . . . . . . . . . . . . . . . . . . . . . . . . . . . . . . . . 0g
CARBOHYDRATE . . . . . . . . . . . . . . . . . . . . . . . . . . . . . . 1g
FAT . . . . . . . . . . . . . . . . . . . . . . . . . . . . . . . . . . . . . . . . . 1g
         PERCENTAGE OF U.S. RECOMMENDED
           DAILY ALLOWANCES (U.S. RDA)

CONTAINS LESS THAN 2 PERCENT OF THE U.S. RDA OF
PROTEIN, VITAMIN A, VITAMIN C, THIAMINE, RIBO-
FLAVIN, NIACIN, CALCIUM, AND IRON.

INGREDIENTS: CORN SYRUP SOLIDS, HYDROGEN-
ATED COCONUT OIL, LACTOSE, SODIUM CASEIN-
ATE, DIPOTASSIUM PHOSPHATE, MONO AND DIGLY-
CERIDES, SODIUM SILICOALUMINATE, ARTIFICIAL
COLORS, LECITHIN, ARTIFICIAL FLAVOR.
```

Food products must now list nutrition information, as well as weight or volume. But there is some question whether many consumers under-stand this information—or know what to do with it—or even whether this is the information they want. At the same time, it may be difficult or impossi-ble to provide the kind of information they do want—for example, regarding taste, color, and texture.[7]

Unit-pricing—a possible help

There is growing interest in unit-pricing, which aids comparison shop-ping—using weight and volume. **Unit-pricing** involves placing the price per ounce (or some other standard measure) on or near the product. Some supermarket chains offer unit-pricing. And many consumers do appreciate this service.[8]

Universal product codes may lead to less price information

Figure 9–4
An illustration of a universal product code for a ballpoint pen

To "automate" the handling of foods and drugs, government and industry representatives have developed a **universal product code**—which identifies each product with marks that can be "read" by electronic scanners and related to prices by computers. Figure 9–4 shows a universal product code mark.

Large supermarket chains have been eager to use these codes. They would speed the checkout process and get rid of the need for marking the price on every item in the store. Prices would still be shown near the product—but not on each individual item.

Some consumers don't like the codes, however, because they can't compare prices later—either in the store or at home. These complaints have made the code idea less attractive. But it is likely that more electronic checkout systems will be installed—whether the prices are marked on each item or not—because it does speed the checkout process and also improves inventory control.

BRANDING—WHY IT DEVELOPED

Brands meet needs

There are so many brands—and we're so used to seeing them—that we take them for granted. In the grocery products area alone, there are about 38,000 brands.

Branding started during the Middle Ages when craft guilds (similar to labor unions) and merchant guilds formed to control the quantity and quality of production. Each producer had to mark his goods so output could be cut back when necessary. This also meant that poor quality—which might reflect unfavorably on other guild products and discourage future trade—could be traced back to the guilty producer. Early trademarks were also a protection to the buyer—who could now know the source of the product.

Not restriction but identification

More recently, brands have been used mainly for identification.

The earliest and most aggressive brand promoters in America were the patent medicine companies. They were joined by the food manufacturers—who grew in size after the Civil War. Some of the brands started in the 1860s and 1870s (and still going strong) are Dr. Lyon's Tooth Powder, Borden's Condensed Milk, Quaker Oats, Vaseline, Pillsbury's Best Flour, and Ivory Soap.[9]

Customers are willing to buy by brand without inspection when they can be sure of quality. In many countries, however, the consumer doesn't feel so sure. In India, for example, inspecting the product is common because there is little faith in packaged goods and brands. There is good reason for this. Foods are often mixed with sawdust, husks, and colored earth—which may be 10–50 percent of the weight of packaged or prepared foods. And an Indian car battery manufacturer has had great success with its brand by correctly advertising "the battery you don't have to test."

CONDITIONS FAVORABLE TO BRANDING

Most marketing managers accept branding and are concerned with seeing that their brand succeeds.

The following conditions would be favorable to successful branding:

1. The demand for the general product class should be large.
2. The demand should be strong enough so that the market price can be high enough to make the effort profitable.
3. There should be economies of size. If the branding were really successful, the cost of production would drop and profits would increase.
4. The product quality should be the best for the price. And the quality should be easily maintained.
5. The product should be easy to identify by brand or trademark.
6. Dependable and widespread availability should be possible. When customers start using a brand, they want to be able to continue finding it in their stores.
7. Favorable positioning in stores will help.

ACHIEVING BRAND FAMILIARITY IS NOT EASY

Brand acceptance must be earned with a good product and regular promotion. **Brand familiarity** means how well customers recognize and accept a company's brand.

There are five levels of brand familiarity

Five levels of brand familiarity are useful for strategic planning: (1) rejection, (2) non-recognition, (3) recognition, (4) preference, and (5) insistence.

"Well, honey, I'd *never* buy this stuff; never heard of this one; saw this on TV; I like this a whole bunch; and *this* I'd just go anywhere for . . . am I on TV?"

(Note the five different levels of brand familiarity.)

The brand familiarity earned by the brander (and competitors) obviously affects the planning for the rest of the marketing mix—especially where the product should be offered and what promotion is needed.

REJECTION OF BRAND

Some brands have been tried and found wanting. **Rejection** means the potential customers won't buy a brand—unless its current image is changed. Rejection may suggest a change in the product—or perhaps only a shift to target customers who have a better image of the brand. Overcoming negative images is difficult and can be very expensive.

NON-RECOGNITION OF BRAND

Some products are seen as basically the same. **Non-recognition** means a brand is not recognized by final consumers at all—even though middlemen may use the brand name for identification and inventory control. Examples here are: school supplies, novelties, inexpensive dinnerware, and similar goods found in discount stores.

BRAND RECOGNITION

Brand recognition means that customers remember the brand. This can be a big advantage if there are many "nothing" brands on the market.

BRAND PREFERENCE

Most branders would like to win **brand preference**—which means target customers will choose the brand out of habit or past experience.

BRAND INSISTENCE

Brand insistence means customers insist upon a product and would be willing to search for it. This is the goal of many target marketers.

Knowing how well you're known may take research

While the level of brand familiarity will affect the development of a marketing mix, marketing research may be needed to find out exactly how well the firm is known—and in which target markets. Sometimes, managers feel their products have a higher level of brand familiarity than they really do—and they develop their marketing mixes accordingly. This mistake puts too much stress on the other Ps in their marketing mixes. Studies show that some brands don't reach even the brand recognition level. One study, for example, showed that two out of every five homemakers couldn't name the brand of furniture they owned.[10]

CHOOSING A BRAND NAME

Brand name selection is still an art. It's hard to say what is a good brand name. Some successful brand names seem to break all the rules. Many of these names, however, got started when there was less competition.

A good brand name can make a difference—helping to tell something

---

Figure 9–5
Characteristics of a good brand name

Short and simple.
Easy to spell and read.
Easy to recognize and remember.
Pleasing when read and easy to pronounce.
Pronounceable in only one way.
Always timely (does not get out of date).
Adaptable to packaging or labeling needs.
Available for use (not in use by another firm).
Pronounceable in all languages (for goods to be exported).
Not offensive, obscene, or negative.
A selling suggestion.
Adaptable to any advertising medium (especially billboards and television).

---

important about the company or its product. Just using the company's name or a family member's name is no longer enough. See Figure 9–5 for the characteristics of a good brand name.

WHAT IS A BRAND?

We have used the words branding, brand name, and trademark interchangeably so far. Now we have to describe their differences.

Branding means the use of a name, term, symbol, or design—or a combination of these—to identify a product. It includes the use of brand names, trademarks, and practically all other means of product identification.

Brand name has a narrower meaning. A **brand name** is a word, letter, or a group of words or letters.

Trademark is a legal term. A **trademark** includes only those words, symbols, or marks that the law says are trademarks.

The word Buick can be used to explain these differences. The Buick car is *branded* under the *brand name* "Buick" (whether it is spoken or printed in any manner). When "Buick" is printed in a certain kind of script, however, it becomes a *trademark.* A trademark need not be attached to the product. It need not even be a word. A symbol can be used.

These differences may seem technical. But they are very important to business firms that spend much money to protect their brands.

PROTECTING BRAND NAMES AND TRADEMARKS

Common law protects the rights of the owners of trademarks and brand names. And the *Lanham Act* of 1946 spells out the exact method for protecting trademarks and what types of marks (including brand names) can be protected. The law applies to goods shipped in interstate or foreign commerce.

Registering for foreign trade

The Lanham Act does not force registration.

A good reason for registering under the Lanham Act is to protect a trademark to be used in foreign markets. Before a trademark can be protected in a foreign country, some nations require that it be registered in its home country.

A trademark can be a real asset to a company. So each firm should try to see that it doesn't become a common descriptive term for its kind of product. When this happens, the brand name or trademark becomes public property—the owner loses all rights to it. This happened with the names cellophane, aspirin, shredded wheat, and kerosene. There was concern that "Teflon" and "Scotch Tape" might become public property—and Miller Brewing Co. tried to protect its "Lite" beer by suing brewers that wanted to use the word "light."[11]

WHAT KIND OF BRAND TO USE?

Keep it in the family

Branders who manufacture or handle more than one item must decide whether they are going to use a **family brand**—the same brand name for several products—or individual brands for each product.

The use of the same brand for many products makes sense if all are about the same in nature and quality. The goodwill attached to one or two products may help the others. This cuts promotion costs. It tends to build a customer franchise for the family brand and makes it easier to introduce new products.

Examples of family brands are the Heinz "57" food products, and three A&P brands (Ann Page, Sultana, and Iona) and Sears' "Craftsman" tools and "Kenmore" appliances.

Individual brands for outside and inside competition

Individual brands are used by a manufacturer when its products are of varying quality or type. If the products are distinctly different—such as meat products and glue—individual brands are better.

Sometimes firms use individual brands to encourage competition within the organization. Each brand is the responsibility of a different group. Management feels that internal competition keeps everyone alert. The theory is that—if anyone is going to take business away from them—it ought to be their own brand. This kind of competition is found among General Motors' brands. Chevrolet, Pontiac, Oldsmobile, Buick, and even Cadillac compete with each other in some markets.

WHO SHOULD DO THE BRANDING?

Manufacturer brands versus dealer brands

Manufacturer brands are brands which are created by manufacturers. These are sometimes called "national brands" because manufacturers often promote these brands all across the country or in large regions.

Such brands include Kellogg's, Stokely, Whirlpool, International Harvester, and IBM.

Dealer brands are brands created by middlemen. These are sometimes called "private brands." Examples of dealer brands include the brands of Kroger, A&P, Sears Roebuck, and Montgomery Ward. Some of these are advertised and distributed more widely than many "national brands."

Middlemen have been moving into branding their own products. They see the big sales volumes involved. And they see the profit possibilities of controlling their own brands—especially when they know that they control the end of the distribution channel.

THE BATTLE OF THE BRANDS—WHO'S WINNING?

The **battle of the brands** is the competition between dealer brands and manufacturer brands. The "battle" is just a question of whose brands are to be more popular and who is to be in control.

Some research suggested (for food products at least) that manufacturers' brands may be losing the fight. In 1951, manufacturers' brands were preferred by 2 or 3 to 1. Even higher prices were accepted. This strong preference has continued to go down. By 1970, almost half of the consumers had shifted to dealer brands. Younger households may be leading here.[12]

One of the reasons for this shift is that some of the manufacturers' brands have come to be thought of as luxuries—while the dealer-branded chain store products are seen as necessities.[13] Then, too, the chains' dealer-branded products are more likely to be in stock—because the chains control the channel of distribution.

Another reason for the growth of dealer branding is that established stores needed a competitive weapon against retail price cutters—who promoted "discounts" on well-known manufacturer brands. Department stores, supermarkets, service stations, clothing stores, appliance dealers, and drugstores are all doing more dealer branding.

Manufacturers may become only manufacturers

The battle of the brands certainly isn't over. But the former dominance of manufacturers' brands may have ended. If the trend continues, manufacturers could become just that—only production departments for middlemen. Retailers and wholesalers might become the leaders in marketing. Certainly, they are closer to final consumers and can have more control of the final sale.[14]

NEW-PRODUCT DEVELOPMENT: A TOTAL COMPANY EFFORT

Some organization helps

A new-product development group helps make sure that new ideas for products are carefully studied—and good ones marketed profitably. Delays can lead to late introductions and give competition a head start in the product life cycle. A delay of even six months may make the difference between a product's success or failure in a competitive market.

A well-organized development procedure might even help a firm copy good ideas quickly and profitably. This shouldn't be overlooked. No one company can hope to be first always—with the best.[15]

Top-level support is needed

New-product development must have the support of top management. New products tend to upset the old routines. So someone has to be responsible for new-product development. The organization arrangement may not be too important—as long as new-product development has top-level support.[16]

A total company effort is needed

Developing new products should be a total company effort—as Figure 9–6 shows. Here, we see that the whole process involves people in management, research, production, promotion, packaging, and branding. The process moves from exploration of ideas to development of the product and product-related ideas. Technical development of the product itself is *not* the first step in new-product development. Evaluating the idea comes first. Many "odd-ball" items can be produced—but who wants them?

After the product has been developed, the total marketing mix is developed and matched against the company's resources to see whether the product looks profitable.

Figure 9–6
New-product market development sequence[17]

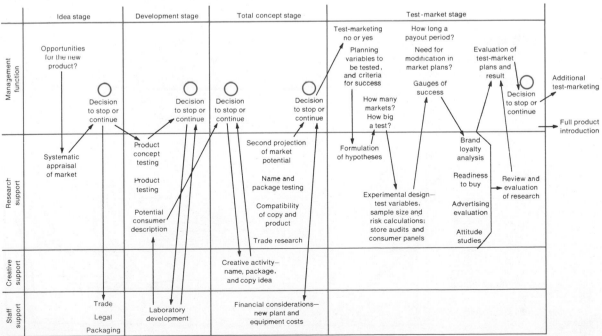

If the answer is yes, then management must make another decision: Does it want to test-market before the real market introduction? This is an important decision. Although test marketing can check ideas, it also alerts competitors. After seeing the speed of product life cycles, you can see why some firms avoid test marketing.

Rejection and failure rates are high

The role of marketing management and top management in product development is shown in Figure 9–6. Management has the power to push or reject development. Developing new ideas costs money. As a result, the rejection rate for new ideas during this process is high. One study of 80 companies found that only 1 out of 40 new ideas survive this kind of organized development process.[18]

As the development process moves along, the decisions become more difficult. The costs and risks increase. And managers know that even with careful work, more than half of new products do fail.[19]

NEED FOR PRODUCT MANAGERS

Product variety leads to product managers

When a company has only one or a few related products, the whole firm is interested in them. But when *new* products are being developed, someone should be in charge of new product planning—to be sure it isn't neglected. Also, when a firm has several different kinds of products, it may decide to put someone in charge of each one (or even each brand) to be sure they are not lost in the rush of business. **Product managers** or **brand managers** manage specific products—often taking over the jobs formerly handled by an advertising manager.

Experience is vital

Product managers are common in large companies that produce many kinds of products. There may be several product managers working under

"I *love* deciding on new product ideas–it gets me in shape for basketball!"

(Only 1 in 40 new product ideas makes it.)

a marketing manager. Sometimes a product manager is responsible for the profitable operation of the whole marketing effort for a particular product. In other situations, he may be basically a "product champion"—concerned with planning and getting the promotion effort done.

The activities of product managers vary considerably, depending on their experience and aggressiveness. But now more emphasis is being placed on marketing experience—as it becomes clear that this important job takes more than academic training and enthusiasm.[20]

Conclusion

Product planning is an increasingly important activity. It is no longer very profitable to sell just "commodities." Product positioning was introduced as an aid to product planning. And the importance of designing safe products was stressed.

Packaging and branding can create a new total product. Variations in packaging can make a product saleable in various target markets. A specific package must be developed for each product. Both underpackaging and overpackaging can be expensive.

To customers, the main value of brands is as a guarantee of quality. This leads to repeat purchasing. For marketers, such "routine" buying means lower promotion costs and higher sales.

Should brands be stressed? The decision depends on whether the costs of brand promotion and honoring the brand guarantee can be more than covered by a higher price or more rapid turnover—or both. The cost of branding may reduce other costs—by reducing pressure on the other three Ps.

In recent years, the strength of manufacturers' brands has declined and dealer brands have become more important. The dealer-labeled products may win in the battle of the brands—because dealers are closer to customers and can emphasize their own brands.

Branding gives marketing managers choice. They can add brands and use individual or family brands. In the end, however, customers express their approval or disapproval of the total product (including the brand). The degree of brand familiarity is a measure of management's ability to carve out a separate market—and affects Place, Price, and Promotion decisions.

New products are so important to the survival of firms in our competitive economy that some organized method for developing them is needed. A general approach was discussed. But it is obvious that it must be a total company effort to be successful.

The failure rate of new products in high, but it is lower for better-managed firms that have recognized the importance of product planning. It is so important that some firms have product managers to manage individual products. And some have new-product committees to assure that the process is carried out successfully.

Questions for discussion

1 What is a new product? Illustrate your answer.

2 Explain how product positioning differs from segmenting markets. Is target marketing involved in product positioning?

3 Explain the increasing interest in packaging, not only for consumer goods but also for industrial goods. Is this likely to continue?

4 Suggest an example where packaging costs probably: *(a)* lower total distribution costs, and *(b)* raise total distribution costs.

5 Is there any difference between a brand name and a trademark? If so, why is this difference important?

6 Is a well-known brand valuable to only the owner of the brand?

7 Would it be profitable for a firm to spend large sums of money to establish a brand for any type of product in any competitive situation? Why, or why not? If the answer is no, suggest examples.

8 Evaluate the suitability of the following brand names: *(a)* Star (sausage), *(b)* Pleasing (books), *(c)* Rugged (shoes), *(d)* Shiny (shoe polish), *(e)* Lord Jim (ties).

9 Explain family brands. Sears Roebuck and A&P use family brands but they have several different family brands. If the idea is a good one, why don't they have just one brand?

10 What is the "battle of the brands"? Who do you think will win and why?

11 What does the degree of brand familiarity imply about previous promotion efforts and the future promotional task? Also, how does the degree of brand familiarity affect the Place and Price variables?

12 Explain the importance of an organized new-product development process and illustrate how it might be used for: *(a)* an improved phonograph, *(b)* new frozen-food items, *(c)* a new children's toy.

13 You have been operating a small supermarket with emphasis on manufacturers' brands and have been barely breaking even. Now you have been approached by a large wholesaler who offers a full line of dealer-branded groceries at substantially lower prices than are now available to you from your regular wholesalers—for nationally advertised manufacturers' brands. The new wholesaler would like you to emphasize his own brands, filling in with a few strongly demanded manufacturers' brands, which he would supply at competitive prices. To help you get his brands established, he will supply some promotion materials free and "price specials" for the first three months after the switch. How would you evaluate this proposal? Specify any assumptions necessary to obtain a definite answer.

Suggested cases

11 Low Corporation
12 Alpine Sports Shop

When you finish this chapter, you should:

1 Understand how and why marketing specialists adjust discrepancies of quantity and assortment.
2 Know why physical distribution is such an important part of Place *and* marketing.
3 Know about the transporting and storing possibilities a marketing manager can use.
4 Know about the different kinds of channel systems.
5 Understand how much market exposure would be "ideal."
6 Recognize the important new terms shown in red.

PLACE AND PHYSICAL DISTRIBUTION

In the next three chapters, we will look at some of the activities and specialists needed to provide "Place" and build channels of distribution. **Place** is concerned with the selection and use of marketing specialists—middlemen and transportation and storage agencies—to provide target customers with time, place, and possession utilities. A marketing manager's decisions on Place have long-range effects. They are harder to change than Product, Price, and Promotion decisions. It's hard to move retail stores and wholesale facilities. And good working arrangements among middlemen may take several years and a good deal of money to develop.

Place decisions are important strategic decisions. See Figure 10–1 for a "picture" of the strategic areas we will discuss in the next three chapters.

SPECIALISTS AND CHANNEL SYSTEMS DEVELOP TO ADJUST DISCREPANCIES

Direct channel systems may be desirable, sometimes

Many producers like to handle the whole distribution job themselves. There are advantages in selling directly to the final user or consumer. Marketing research is easier, because the producer's sales reps are in direct contact with the target customers. If any special selling effort or technical services are needed, the marketing manager can be sure that the sales force will receive the necessary training and motivation.

It is important to see that a direct-to-user channel is not uncommon. It is not *always* necessary to use middlemen. On the other hand, it is not necessarily cheaper or more efficient to do without middlemen!

217

Figure 10–1
Strategy planning for Place

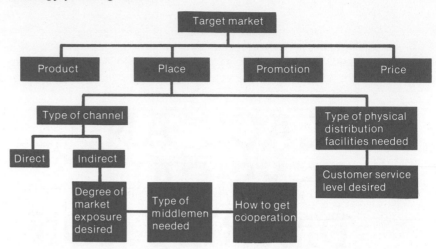

Discrepancies require channel specialists

All producers want to be sure that their products reach the final customer. But the assortment and quantity of goods wanted by customers may be different than the assortment and quantity of goods normally produced. Specialists have developed to adjust these discrepancies.

Discrepancy of quantity means the difference between the quantity of goods it is economical for a producer to make, and the quantity normally wanted by final users or consumers. For example, most manufacturers of golf balls produce large quantities—such as 200,000 to 500,000 in a given time period. The average golfer, however, wants only a few balls at a time. Adjusting for this discrepancy usually requires middlemen—wholesalers and retailers.

Producers typically specialize by product, and therefore another discrepancy develops. **Discrepancy of assortment** means the difference between the lines the typical producer makes and the assortment wanted by final consumers or users. Most golfers, for example, need more than golf balls. They want golf shoes, gloves, clubs, a bag, and so forth. And probably they would prefer not to shop around for each item. So again there is a need for middlemen to adjust these discrepancies.

Channel specialists adjust discrepancies with regrouping activities

Regrouping activities involve adjusting the quantities and/or assortments of goods handled at each level in a channel of distribution.

There are four regrouping activities: accumulation, allocation, sorting-out, and assorting. When one or more of these activities is required, a marketing specialist might develop to fill this need.

ADJUSTING QUANTITY DISCREPANCIES BY ACCUMULATING AND ALLOCATING

The **accumulation process** involves collecting products from many small producers. This is common for agricultural products. It is a way of obtaining the lowest transportation rate—by putting together small quantities which then can be shipped in truckload or carload quantities.

The **allocation process** involves breaking bulk—breaking up the carload or truckload shipments into smaller quantities as the goods get closer to the final market. This may involve several middlemen. Wholesalers may sell smaller quantities to other wholesalers or directly to retailers. Retailers continue the allocation process as they "break bulk" to their customers.

ADJUSTING ASSORTMENT DISCREPANCIES BY SORTING-OUT AND ASSORTING

Different types of specialists are needed to adjust assortment discrepancies. Two types of regrouping activities may be needed: sorting-out and assorting.

The **sorting-out process** means grading or sorting products. This is a common process for agricultural products. Nature produces what it wants and these products must be sorted into the grades and qualities desired by different target markets.

The **assorting process** means putting together a variety of products to give a target market what it wants. Here, instead of nature producing a mixed assortment which must be sorted out, marketing specialists put together an assortment to satisfy some target market. This usually is done by those close to the final consumer or user—retailers or wholesalers who try to supply a wide assortment of products for the convenience of their customers. An electrical goods wholesaler, for example, may take on a line of lawnmowers or garden products for the convenience of hardware retailer-customers.

Channel systems can be complex

Adjusting discrepancies can lead to complex channels of distribution. The possibility for competition between different channels is illustrated in

"Y'know, if you ever get past accumulation and on to allocation, you'll be a great little middleman!"

Figure 10–2
Sales of fuses are made through many kinds of wholesalers[1]

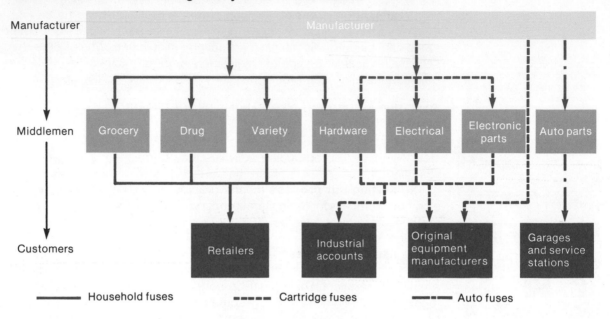

Figure 10–2. This figure shows the many channels used by manufacturers of household, cartridge, and auto fuses. These can be both consumer goods and industrial goods. This helps explain why some channels would develop. But note that the household fuses alone go through grocery, drug, variety and hardware wholesalers. This can cause problems, because these wholesalers supply retailers who are used to different markups. Among such channels, there is a lot of competition—including price competition. And the different markups may lead to open price wars, especially on well-known and branded products.

Dual distribution occurs when a manufacturer uses several competing channels to reach the same target market—perhaps using several middlemen and selling directly himself. This is resented by some established middlemen because they do not appreciate *any* competition—especially competition set up by their own suppliers. But manufacturers often are forced to use dual distribution because their present channels are doing a poor job or aren't reaching some potential customers.

SOMETIMES THERE'S NOT MUCH CHOICE

The fuse example seems to suggest that there are plenty of middlemen around to form almost any kind of channel system. But this isn't true. Sometimes there is only one key middleman serving a market. To reach this market, producers may have no choice but to use this one middleman. In other cases, there are no middlemen at all! Then a producer may

Physical distribution involves
transporting and storing.

try to go directly to target customers. If this isn't possible, the product
may die because it can't be economically distributed. Some products are
not wanted in big enough volume and/or at high enough prices to justify
any middlemen providing the regrouping activities needed to reach the
potential customers.

PHYSICAL DISTRIBUTION IS AN IMPORTANT PART OF PLACE PLANNING

Physical distribution (PD) is the transporting and storing of physical
goods within individual firms and along channel systems. Nearly half of
the costs of marketing are spent on physical distribution. These PD activities
are very important to a firm and the macro-marketing system. Goods that
remain in the factory or on the farm really have no "use" at all. And
possession utility is not possible until time and place utility have been
provided. This requires the transporting and storing functions that are a
part of physical distribution.

A marketing manager must decide how the transporting and storing
functions should be divided within a channel. Physical distribution can
be varied endlessly in a marketing mix and in a channel system. But
these decisions will affect the other three Ps—especially Price.

THE TRANSPORTING FUNCTION

Modern transportation facilities—including railroads, pipe lines, trucks,
barges and ships, and airplanes—have changed marketing. Without these
transportation facilities, there could be no mass distribution with its regrouping activities or any urban life as we know it today. Producers in small
towns and rural areas can now reach customers all over the world.

Seventy-five percent of all U.S. freight moves by trucks—at least part
of the way. Railroads carry goods for long distances, but trucks have
the bulk of the short-haul business. The trucking industry slogan, "If you

have it, it came by truck," is true for consumer goods. However, many industrial goods are still delivered by railroads or by other kinds of transportation. See Table 10–1.

Can you afford to hit the target?

The cost of shipping an average product by rail is about 5 percent of wholesale cost.[2] For many bulky and low-value products, however, the percentage is much higher. Transporting sand and gravel, for example, costs about 55 percent of its value. At the other extreme, lighter or more valuable commodities such as copper or office machines are transported for less than 1 percent of wholesale cost.[3]

Different transporters charge different rates

Common carriers—such as the railroads and major truck lines—must maintain regular schedules and accept goods from any shipper. They charge rates which are fixed for all users by government regulators. **Contract carriers** can work for anyone for an agreed sum and for any length of time. They are less strictly regulated.

Common carriers provide a dependable transportation service for the many producers and middlemen who make small shipments in various directions. Contract carriers, on the other hand, are a more freewheeling group—going wherever goods have to be moved.

Marketing manager can affect rates

There is nothing final about the present common carrier rate structure. Carriers can and do propose changes—and if no one objects—the new rates usually go into effect. Rate changes can be made relatively quickly (1 to 30 days) and easily. Each year, about 150,000 changes are made in rail rates alone.

Creative marketing managers—by bargaining for rate changes—can help their channel system members with the transporting function. In fact, some manufacturers and middlemen maintain traffic departments to deal with carriers. These departments can be a great help not only to their own firms but also to their suppliers and customers—finding the best route at the lowest rates.

Table 10–1
Intercity freight movement in the United States

	Ton-miles carried (in billions)	Percent of total
Railways	757	36.4
Pipelines	488	23.5
Motor vehicles	488	23.5
Inland waterways	343	16.5
Airways	4	0.2
Total	2,080	100.0

Source: *Statistical Abstract of the United States, 1977*, p. 627.

Which transportation
alternative is best?

The best transportation choice should not only be as low in cost as possible, but also provide the level of service (e.g., speed and dependability) required. Sometimes this would mean using one of the special services offered by railroads. In other cases, air freight might be the best choice.

RAILROADS

The railroads have been the workhorses of U.S. transportation—carrying heavy, bulky freight such as coal, sand, and steel. By handling large quantities of such goods, the railroads are able to charge relatively low rates. But railroads have had profit difficulties in recent years, in part because trucks have set their rates low enough to get some of the more profitable business that railroads were counting on to make up for the low rates on the bulky products.

Truck competition has forced the railroads to offer faster and more flexible services. A "fast freight" service for perishable or high-value items, for example, can be competitive with trucks if the shippers and receivers are located near rail lines. And a **piggy-back service** loads truck trailers on rail cars and can provide both speed and flexibility. On some routes it may even cost less. A loaded truck trailer can be shipped piggy-back from the Midwest to the West Coast for about half the cost of sending it over the highways.

TRUCKS

The flexibility of trucks makes them especially good for moving small loads for short distances. They can travel on almost any road. They can give extremely fast service. Also, trucks cause less breakage and handling than rails—an important factor because it may permit a reduction in packaging cost. For short distances and for higher-value products, trucks may charge rates that are the same as (or lower than) railroad rates—yet provide much faster service.

Fishy-back service improves the speed and flexibility of water transportation.

SHIPS AND BARGES

Water transportation is the lowest-cost method—but it is also the slowest. Where speed is not as important, however, barges or ships are important methods of transportation. Barges on internal waterways are used for bulky, nonperishable products such as iron ore, grain, steel, petroleum, cement, gravel, sand, coal, and coke. By a combination of rivers, canals, and locks, it is possible to ship goods from the industrial and agricultural regions of inland United States all over the world. Foreign ships regularly move on the Great Lakes. Ocean-going barges can reach as far north as Minneapolis–St. Paul, and deep into Arkansas.

More manufactured goods are being shipped by water as large standard-sized containers are being loaded at factories and then shipped as a unit all the way to their destination. Now, ships combined with trucks offer a **fishy-back service** similar to rail piggy back. Door-to-door service is now offered between the United States and European cities!

AIRPLANES

The most expensive means of cargo transportation is air freight—but it also is fast! Air freight rates normally are at least twice as high as trucking rates—but the greater speed may be worth the added cost. Most air freight so far has been fashions, perishable commodities, and high-value industrial parts for the electronics and metal-working industries. California's strawberries, for example, are flown to the Midwest and East all through the year.

A big advantage of air transport is that the cost of packing, unpacking, and preparing the goods for sale may be reduced or eliminated when the goods are shipped by air. Some women's fashions are shipped on racks which eventually are moved right into the store!

Air freight can help a producer reduce inventory costs by eliminating outlying warehouses. The greater speed may also reduce spoilage, theft, and damage. So, although the *transportation cost* may be higher, the *total cost of distribution* for a firm using air freight may be lower.

STORING MAY BE NEEDED IN SOME CHANNELS

Storing is the marketing function of holding goods. It provides time utility. Storing is necessary because production does not always match consumption. Some products, such as farm produce, are produced seasonally although they are in demand year-round. And some products, such as antifreeze, have a big demand for short periods.

Storing can be done by both manufacturers and middlemen. It can balance supply and demand—keeping stocks at convenient locations, ready to meet customers' needs. Storing is one of the major activities of some middlemen.

Specialized storage facilities can be very helpful

Private warehouses are storing facilities owned by companies for their own use. Most manufacturers, wholesalers, and retailers have some storage facilities in their own main buildings or in a warehouse district.

Private warehouses are used when a large volume of goods must be stored regularly. Owning warehouse space can be expensive, however. If the need changes, the extra space may be hard—or impossible—to rent to others.

Public warehouses are independent storing facilities that provide all the services that could be obtained in a company's own warehouse. A company might choose to use a public warehouse if it did not have a regular need for warehouse space. With a public warehouse, the customer pays only for space used and may purchase a variety of additional services. Public warehouses are useful to manufacturers who must maintain stocks in many locations, including foreign countries. Public warehouses are found in all major urban areas and many smaller cities. Rural towns also have public warehouses for locally produced agricultural commodities.

General merchandise warehouses store almost any kind of manufactured goods. **Bonded warehouses** specialize in imported goods or other goods (such as liquors or cigarettes) on which a tax must be paid before the goods are released for sale. There are **commodity warehouses** and **cold-storage warehouses** that are designed specifically for storing perishable products such as grain, apples, butter, and furs. Grain is stored in big elevators which move the grain around to keep it cool.

MODERNIZED WAREHOUSING FACILITIES HAVE DEVELOPED

The cost of physical handling is a major storage cost. The goods must be handled once when put into storage and again when removed to be sold. Further, in the typical old "downtown" warehouse districts, traffic

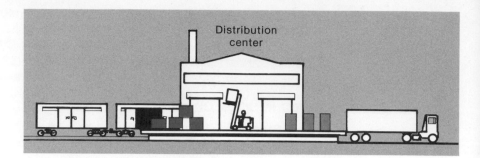

Distribution center

congestion, crowded storage areas, and slow freight elevators slow the process. This increases the cost.

Today, modern one-story structures are replacing the old multistoried buildings. They are located away from downtown traffic. These single-level designs use power-operated lift trucks, battery-operated motor scooters, roller-skating order-pickers, electric hoists for heavy items, and hydraulic ramps to aid loading and unloading.

Distribution center is a different kind of warehouse

A **distribution center** is a special kind of warehouse designed to speed the flow of goods and avoid unnecessary storage. Basically, it is a breaking-bulk operation. Turnover is increased, and the cost of carrying inventory is reduced. This is important because these costs may run as high as 35 percent a year of the value of the average inventory.

The idea behind the distribution center is that reducing costs and increasing turnover will lead to bigger profits. Storing is sensible only if it helps achieve time utility.

Some large food manufacturers and supermarket operators run their own distribution centers. For example, Pillsbury Co.—a large manufacturer of baking mixes and flour—ships products in rail carloads from its various manufacturing plants (which each specialize in a few product lines) directly to distribution centers. Almost no goods are stored at the factories. These distribution centers are able to quickly ship any combination of goods by the most economical transportation route. This lets Pillsbury offer faster service at lower cost.

PHYSICAL DISTRIBUTION CONCEPT FOCUSES ON WHOLE DISTRIBUTION SYSTEM

We have been looking at the transporting and storing functions as separate activities—partly because this simplifies discussion but also because it is the usual approach. Recently, however, attention has turned to the *whole* physical distribution function—not just warehousing and transportation. Focusing only on one function at a time may actually increase a firm's and channel's total distribution costs. "Physical distribution" people usually study the total cost of possible PD systems because there may be attractive "trade-offs." For example, higher transportation costs may be more than offset by lower storage costs—as with air freight.

Total cost approach helps

The **total cost approach**—to selecting a PD system—evaluates *all* the costs of possible PD systems. This means that all costs—including some which are sometimes ignored—should be considered. Inventory costs for example, are often ignored in marketing decisions because these costs are buried in "overhead costs." But inventory costs may be very high. In fact, including them may lead to a different decision. See Figure 10–3 for a picture of the typical relation of physical distribution costs.

Physical distribution not just cost-oriented

Early physical distribution efforts focused attention on lowering costs. Now, there is more emphasis on making physical distribution planning a part of the company's strategy planning. Sometimes, by increasing physical distribution cost somewhat, the customer service level can be increased so much that, in effect, a new and better marketing mix is created.

Customer service level means the percent of customers served within some time period. Figure 10–3 shows the typical relation between physical distribution costs and customer service level. When a firm decides to minimize total cost, it may also be settling for a lower customer service level. By increasing the number of distribution points, the firm might be able to serve more customers within a specified time period. Transportation costs would be reduced but warehousing and inventory costs would be increased. The higher service level, however, might greatly improve the company's strategy. Increased sales might more than make up for increased costs. Clearly, the marketing manager has a strategic decision

Figure 10–3
Higher customer service levels are obtalned at a cost

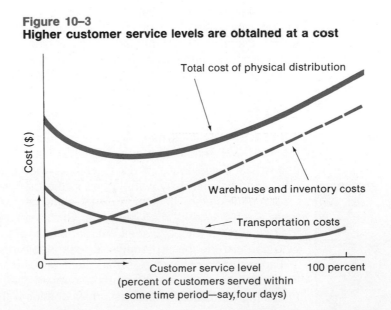

A channel captain helps direct the activities of a whole channel.

about what service level to offer. Minimizing cost is not always the right answer.

CHANNEL CAPTAIN NEEDED TO GUIDE CHANNEL PLANNING

Until now, we have considered an individual marketing manager as the strategy planner. But now we see that there may be several firms and managers in a single distribution channel. It is logical that each channel have a **channel captain**—a manager who would help direct the activities of the whole channel. The question is: which marketing manager should be the captain?

The idea of a single channel captain makes sense, but some channels may not have such a captain. The various firms may not be acting as a system because of lack of leadership. Or, the members of a system may not understand that they are part of a channel.

But, even if they don't know it, firms *are* connected by their policies. It makes sense to try to avoid channel conflicts by planning for channel relations.

Manufacturer or middlemen?

In the United States, manufacturers frequently are the leaders in channel relations. Middlemen wait and see what the manufacturer intends to do and what it wants done. Then they decide whether their roles will be profitable—and whether they want to join in the manufacturer's plans.

Some middlemen do take the lead, especially in foreign markets where there are fewer large manufacturers. Such middlemen may decide what their customers want and seek out manufacturers—perhaps small ones—who can provide these products at reasonable prices.

Large middlemen are closer to the final user or consumer and in an ideal position to assume the channel captain role. It is even possible that middlemen—especially retailers—may dominate the marketing system of the future.

Our captain the producer—for convenience only

For convenience, let's assume that the channel captain is a producer. (Remember, though, that a middleman may play this role too.)[4]

The job of the channel captain is to arrange for the necessary marketing activities in the best way. This might be done as shown in Figure 10–4 in a manufacturer-dominated channel system. Here, the manufacturer has selected a target market and developed a product, set the price structure, done some promotion, and developed the place setup. Middlemen are then expected to finsih the promotion job at their own places.

If a middleman is the channel captain, we would see quite a different diagram. In the extreme, in a channel like that dominated by Sears Roebuck, the middleman circle would be almost completely shaded for some products. Manufacturers would be mainly concerned with manufacturing the product to meet Sears' requirements.

A coordinated channel system may help everyone

A channel system in which the members have accepted the leadership of a channel captain can work very well—even though not everyone in the channel system is strongly market-oriented. As long as the channel captain is market-conscious, it should be possible to win the confidence and support of production-oriented firms and make the whole channel work well. Small production-oriented producers in Japan or Hong Kong, for example, may become part of an effective channel reaching the U. S. market if there is a middleman who correctly understands market needs and explains them clearly to the producers. The producers may not even know where their products are going, but the system still can compete with other systems and be profitable for the members.

Vertical marketing systems—new wave in the marketplace

The advantages of a coordinated channel system have been understood by progressive marketers. Some corporations integrate vertically to link production with wholesaling and/or retailing. Others are simply developing contractual or informal (administered) relationships with others in their

Figure 10–4
How channel strategy might be handled in a manufacturer-dominated system[5]

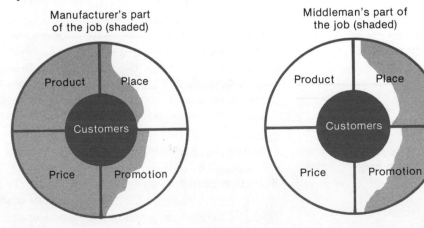

Manufacturer's part of the job (shaded)   Middleman's part of the job (shaded)

Figure 10–5
Types of channel systems

	Traditional	Vertical marketing systems		
		Administered	Contractual	Corporate
Amount of cooperation	Little or none	Some to good	Fairly good to good	Complete
Control maintained by	None	Economic power and leadership	Contracts	Ownership by one company
Examples	Typical channel of "independents"	General Electric, Miller's Beer, O. M. Scott & Sons (lawn products)	McDonald's, Holiday Inn, IGA, Ace Hardware, Super Valu, Coca-Cola, Chevrolet	Florsheim Shoes, Firestone Tire

channel system. See Figure 10–5. These more smoothly operating channel systems appear to be competively better than the traditional channel systems which do not cooperate.

In the consumer goods field, corporate chains that are at least partially vertically integrated have about 26 percent of total retail sales. And firms which are linked to various contractual and administered systems have an additional 37.5 percent. This gives vertical marketing systems selling consumer goods much more than half of retail sales. Importantly, it appears that such systems will continue to increase their share in the future. Vertical marketing systems are becoming the key units in the U.S. distribution system.[6]

THE BEST CHANNEL SYSTEM SHOULD ACHEIVE IDEAL MARKET EXPOSURE

The best channel system does not just happen. Someone must plan the system. And someone must make specific decisions about how much market exposure will be needed in each geographic area. Although it might seem that all marketing managers would want their products to have maximum exposure to potential customers, this is not the case. Some products require much less market exposure than others.

The **ideal market exposure** should make a product widely enough available to satisfy target customers' needs—but not exceed them. Too much exposure would only increase the total marketing cost.

Three degrees of market exposure may be ideal

Intensive distribution is selling a product through any responsible and suitable wholesaler or retailer who will stock and/or sell the product. **Selective distribution** is selling through only those middlemen who will do a good job with the product. **Exclusive distribution** is selling through only one middleman in each particular geographic area.

Firestone
PLANTATIONS COMPANY
HARBEL LIBERIA

The beginning of the Firestone vertical marketing system.

In practice, this means that cigarettes are handled—through intensive distribution—by at least a million U.S. outlets, while Rolls Royces are handled—through exclusive distribution— by only a limited number of middlemen across the country.

Intensive distribution— sell it where they buy it

Intensive distribution is commonly needed for convenience goods and for industrial supplies (such as pencils, paper clips, and typing paper) used by all plants or offices. Customers want such goods near by.

The seller's *intent* is important here. Intensive distribution refers to the *desire* to sell through all responsible and suitable outlets. What this means depends on customer habits and preferences. If the target customers normally buy a certain product in a certain type of outlet, then ideally we would specify this type of outlet in our Place policy. If customers prefer to buy hardware items only at hardware stores, for example, then an intensive distribution policy would mean selling through all hardware stores. If, however, as it seems today, many customers will buy certain hardware items at any convenient outlet, including drug stores and food stores, then an intensive distribution policy would require use of these outlets— and probably more than one channel of distribution.

Selective distribution— sell it where it sells best

Selective distribution covers the area between intensive and exclusive distribution. It can be suitable for any kind of product. Only the better middlemen are used here. The usual purpose is to get some of the advantages of exclusive distribution while still getting fairly widespread coverage.

A selective distribution policy might be used to avoid selling to wholesalers or retailers who: (1) have a poor credit rating, (2) have a reputation for making too many returns or requesting too much service, (3) place orders that are too small to justify making calls or providing service, or (4) are not in a position, for any other reason, to do a satisfactory marketing job.

Selective distribution is growing in popularity as marketers decide it is not necessary to get 100 percent coverage of a market. Some perfume manufacturers, for example, use selective distribution because they want good display and sales help for their products.

Exclusive distribution sometimes makes sense

Exclusive distribution means that one (only) middleman is selected in each geographic area. Besides the various advantages of selective distribution, manufacturers might want to use exclusive distribution to help control prices and the service offered in a channel.

But is limiting market exposure legal?

Exclusive distribution is not specifically illegal in the antimonopoly laws. But current interpretation of these laws by the courts gives the impression that almost any exclusive distribution arrangement *could be* interpreted as an injury to some competitor somewhere.

HORIZONTAL ARRANGEMENTS ARE PROBABLY ILLEGAL

The Supreme Court has consistently ruled that horizontal arrangements—agreements among competitors—to limit sales by customer or territory are illegal.

VERTICAL ARRANGEMENTS MAY BE LEGAL

The legality of vertical arrangements—agreements between producers and middlemen—is not as clear. A 1977 Supreme Court decision reversed its 1967 ruling that vertical relationships that would limit territories were automatically illegal. Now, possible good effects to the consumer can be weighed against possible restrictions on competition. Under the previous rule, the price-cutting "maverick" who came in after the introductory work had been done could not be controlled. Now it may be legal to control vertical relations (including price-cutting) as long as some good reasons can be shown for limiting distribution. Such reasons might include building stronger retailers who can and will offer advertising and sales support and better repair services for customers.[7]

CAUTION IS SUGGESTED

In spite of the recent Supreme Court ruling, firms should be very careful about entering into any exclusive distribution arrangements. The antimonopoly rules still apply. The courts can force a change in expensively developed relationships. And, perhaps even worse, triple damages might be imposed if the courts rule that competition has been hurt. Apparently the law will allow some exclusive arrangements to permit the introduction of a new product or to let a new company enter a market. But these arrangements probably should be short term.

The same cautions probably apply to selective distribution. Here, however, less formal and binding arrangements are typical. And the possible impact on competition is harder to prove. It now may be more acceptable to carefully select channel members when building a channel system. Refusing to sell to some middlemen, however, should be a part of a logical plan which has longer-term benefits.

PUSHING OR PULLING THROUGH AN INDIRECT CHANNEL SYSTEM

A producer has a special challenge with respect to channel systems: How to win channel cooperation to make sure that the product reaches the target market.

The two basic methods of achieving channel cooperation are pushing and pulling.

Pushing policy—get a hand from the firm in the channel

Pushing a product through the channels means using normal promotion effort—personal selling and advertising—to help sell the whole marketing mix to possible channel members. This approach emphasizes the importance of building a channel and getting the cooperation of channel members. The producer, in effect, tries to develop a team that will work well to get the product to the user.

Pulling policy—make them reach for it out there

By contrast, **pulling** means getting consumers to ask middlemen for the product. This usually involves very aggressive promotion to final consumers—perhaps using coupons or samples. If the promotion works, the middlemen are forced to carry the product to satisfy their customers. Of course, the middlemen should be told about the promotion so they can be ready if it is successful.

This method—common in the soap industry—may be necessary if many products are already competing in all desired outlets.

Sell the whole mix to channel members

However channel cooperation is won, potential channel members must be convinced that the producer knows what he's trying to do and why. The marketing manager's sales reps must be able to tell prospective channel members what is expected of them and how much competition they

"All of a sudden I feel I should be more careful about channels."

may get from other channels. It may be a good idea to spell out how the firm and channels will react to probable competitive marketing mixes. In other words, Place policies must be tied in with the rest of the marketing mix if the whole mix is going to work.

Conclusion

This chapter has discussed the role of Place and noted that Place decisions are especially important because they may be difficult to change.

Marketing specialists and channel systems develop to adjust discrepancies of quantity and assortment. Their regrouping activities are basic in any economic system, and adjusting discrepancies provides opportunities for creative marketers.

Physical distribution functions—basically transporting and storing—were discussed. These activities are needed to provide time, place, and possession utility. And by using the total cost approach, the lowest cost PD alternative or the cost of various customer service levels can be found.

The importance of planning channel systems was discussed—along with the role of a channel captain. It was stressed that channel systems compete with each other and that smoothly operating vertical marketing systems seem to be winning out in the marketplace.

Channel planning also requires deciding on the degree of market exposure desired. The legality of limiting market exposures should also be considered—to avoid jail or having to undo an expensively developed channel system.

Finally, it was emphasized that producers aren't necessarily channel captains. Often, middlemen control or even dominate channels of distribution. The degree of this control must be considered by producers when they decide whether they should try to push or pull their product through a channel system.

Questions for discussion

1 Explain "discrepancies of quantity and assortment" using the clothing business as an example. How does the application of the concept of discrepancies change when coal for sale to the steel industry is considered rather than clothing? What impact does this have on the number and kinds of marketing specialists required?

2 Explain the four steps in the regrouping process with an example from the building supply industry (nails, paint, flooring, plumbing fixtures, etc.). Would you expect many specialists to develop in this industry or would the manufacturers handle the job themselves? What kind of marketing channels would you expect to find in this industry and what functions would be provided by various channel members?

3 If a manufacturer has five different markets to reach, how many channels is he likely to use? If only one, why? If more than one, what sort of problems will this raise?

4 Discuss the relative advantages and disadvantages of railroads, trucks, and airlines as transporting methods.

5 Distinguish between common carriers and contract carriers. What role do the contract carriers play in our economic system? How would our economy be different if there were no common carriers?

6 Explain which transportation method would probably be most suitable for shipment of goods to a large Chicago department store:
a. A 10,000-lb. shipment of dishes from Japan.
b. 15 lbs. of screwdrivers from New York.
c. Three couches from High Point, N.C.
d. 500 high-fashion dresses from the garment district in New York City.
e. 300 lbs. of Maine lobsters.
f. 60,000 lbs. of various appliances from Evansville, Indiana.
How would your answers change if this department store were the only one in a large factory town in Ohio?

7 Indicate the nearest location where you would expect to find substantial storage facilities. What kinds of products would be stored there, and why are they stored there instead of some other place?

8 Indicate when a producer or middleman would find it desirable to use a public warehouse rather than a private warehouse. Illustrate, using a specific product or situation.

9 Discuss the distribution center concept. Is this likely to eliminate the storing function of conventional wholesalers? Is it applicable to all products? If not, cite several examples.

10 Clearly differentiate between a warehouse and a distribution center. Explain how a specific product would be handled differently by these marketing institutions.

11 Explain total cost approach and customer service level in your own words. Explain why raising customer service levels might increase the total cost.

12 Explain how a "channel captain" could help independent firms compete with integrated ones.

13 Relate the nature of the product to the degree of market exposure desired.

14 Why would middlemen seek to be exclusive distributors for a product? Why would producers seek exclusive distributors? Would middlemen be equally anxious to obtain exclusive distribution for any type of product? Why or why not? Explain with reference to the following products: cornflakes, razor blades, golf clubs, golf balls, steak knives, hi-fi equipment, and industrial woodworking machinery.

15 Explain the present legal status of exclusive distribution.

16 Discuss the promotion a grocery products manufacturer would need in order to develop appropriate channels and move goods through these channels. Would the nature of this job change at all for a dress manufacturer? How about for a small producer of installations?

17 Discuss the advantages and disadvantages of either a pushing or pulling policy for a very small manufacturer who is just getting into the candy business with a line of inexpensive candy bars. Which policy would probably be most appropriate? State any assumptions you need to obtain a definite answer.

Suggested cases

14 Mead Company

15 Miller Sales Company

When you finish this chapter, you should:

1 Recognize that retailers must plan their own marketing strategies.
2 Know about the many kinds of retailers which might become members of producers' or wholesalers' channel systems.
3 Understand the differences between conventional retailers and those who have accepted the mass merchandising concept.
4 Understand scrambled merchandising and the "wheel of retailing."
5 Recognize the important new terms shown in red.

11

RETAILING

Retailing is a very important activity. It is concerned with satisfying *final* consumers. It is *not* concerned with industrial goods—or the sale of consumer goods in the channels.

Retailing covers all of the activities involved in the sale of goods and/or services to final consumers for their own use. The retailer must (1) put together an assortment of products to satisfy some target market, (2) make these products available at a reasonable price, and (3) convince customers that these products will satisfy their needs. The term "merchandising" is often used to cover all these activities.

RETAILERS MUST PLAN MARKETING STRATEGIES, TOO

A retailer should plan a marketing strategy just like any other marketing manager. In fact, retailers are so close to final consumers that their strategy *has* to work if they are to survive. Unlike some manufacturers or wholesalers, they can't "unload" their mistakes on middlemen. Because they are so aware that they must satisfy consumers, retailers make *buying* an important activity. Successful retailers are well aware of an old rule: "Goods well bought are half sold."

It's important to see that a particular retailer may appeal to more than one target market at the same time. Further, they usually sell whole *assortments* (or combinations) of goods and services—not just individual products. So, it is useful to think of a retailer's whole offering as a "prod-

237

uct." Then, most of what we said in the Product area can be applied here, too.

Goods classes help understand store types

Retail strategy planning can be simplified by recalling our earlier discussion of consumer behavior and the consumer goods classes—convenience goods, shopping goods, and specialty goods.

We can define three types of stores: *convenience* stores, *shopping* stores, and *specialty* stores. But it is very important to see that these classifications refer to the *customer's* image of the store.

A **convenience store** is a convenient place to shop—either centrally located "downtown" or "in the neighborhood." Such stores attract many customers because they are so handy.

Shopping stores attract customers from greater distances because of the width and depth of their assortments. Stores selling clothing, furniture, or household appliances are usually thought of as shopping stores.

Specialty stores are those for which customers have developed a strong attraction. For whatever reasons—service, selection, or reputation—some customers will consistently buy convenience, shopping, and specialty goods at these stores.

Store type sets strategy guidelines

A retailer's strategy planning should consider potential customers' attitudes toward both the product and the store. Classifying stores by type of goods—as shown in Figure 11–1—helps you understand a retailer's possibilities. By identifying which competitors are satisfying various market segments, a retailer may see new opportunities. In some cases, the manager may find that he and his competitors are all concentrating on only certain customers and completely missing others. Or he may see an opportunity for building a new strategy—as Liz Gray did.

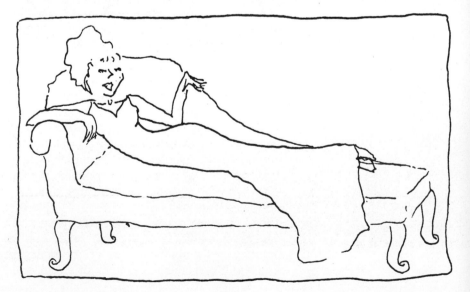

"Dahling, Breckman's is the *only* place I'd ever shop."

(Specialty stores have loyal customers.)

Figure 11–1
How customers view store-product combinations[1]

Store type / Product type	Convenience	Shopping	Specialty
Convenience	Will buy any brand at most accessible store.	Shop around to find better service and/or lower prices.	Prefer store. Brand may be important.
Shopping	Want some selection but will settle for assortment at most accessible store.	Want to compare both products and store mixes.	Prefer store but insist on adequate assortment.
Specialty	Prefer particular product but like place convenience, too.	Prefer particular product but still seeking best total product and mix.	Prefer both store and product.

LIZ GRAY OPENS A CONVENIENCE STORE FOR SHOPPING GOODS

Liz Gray—a buyer in a local department store—is considering opening her own women's clothing shop. She knows that most of her competitors are shopping or specialty stores—carrying the kinds of shopping goods Liz would like to offer. Checking further, she finds that the convenience store-shopping goods market has been overlooked by her competitors. Liz rents a store in a small shopping center where no competitors are located. She decides to avoid competing directly in the other markets. Instead, Liz plans to offer a reasonable selection of *shopping* goods items at her *convenient* location. She knows prices will have to be reasonable because customers do shop around. But since she will have no direct competition, a "sale" atmosphere won't be necessary. And, she won't have to carry deep assortments of high-fashion items. Liz feels that a selection of smart but not "faddy" blouses, skirts, sweaters, and accessories will meet the needs of this market segment. Of course, she plans to study the special needs and attitudes of the people in the nearby area when selecting her stock, but the store-goods classification helped Liz set the guidelines for her strategy.

NUMBER AND SIZE OF RETAIL FACILITIES ALREADY COMPETING

Lots of small retailers, but . . .

There are lots of retailers—almost two million—partly because it's so easy to enter retailing. You can open and close a lemonade stand in one day. And a more serious retailer can rent an empty store and be in business without putting up much money (capital).

Table 11–1
Retail trade, sales by size of establishment (United States)

Sales size of establishments	Establishments			Sales volume		
	Number (000)	Per-cent	Cumula-tive percent	Sales ($000,000)	Per-cent	Cumula-tive percent
Total, all establishments	1,913			459,040		
Total, establishments operated for the entire year	1,710	100.0		427,640	100.0	
Annual sales of:						
$5,000,000 or more	9	0.5	0.5	89,705	21.0	21.0
$2,000,000 to $4,999,999	27	1.6	2.1	81,128	19.0	40.0
$1,000,000 to $1,999,999	38	2.2	4.3	53,764	12.6	52.6
$ 500,000 to $ 999,999	71	4.1	8.4	48,823	11.4	64.0
$ 300,000 to $ 499,999	106	6.2	14.6	40,497	9.4	73.4
$ 100,000 to $ 299,999	450	26.3	40.9	77,724	18.2	91.6
$ 50,000 to $ 99,999	304	18.0	58.9	21,972	5.1	96.7
$ 30,000 to $ 49,999	188	11.0	69.9	7,354	1.7	98.4
$ 20,000 to $ 29,999	127	7.4	77.3	3,101	0.7	99.1
$ 10,000 to $ 19,999	171	10.0	87.3	2,408	0.6	99.7
Less than $10,000	217	12.7	100.0	1,165	0.3	100.0

Source: *1972 Census of Retail Trade,* Table 1a, p. 1–8.

The large number of retailers might suggest that the field of retailing is made up of small businesses. To an extent, this is true. But as Table 11–1 shows, more than half the nation's retailers account for less than 10 percent of total retail sales and sell less than $100,000 annually.

But retailing is big business. And the larger retail stores—those selling more than $1 million in goods or services annually—do most of the business. Only 4.3 percent of the retail stores sell such large amounts, yet they account for more than half of all retail sales.

EVOLUTION OF CONVENTIONAL RETAILERS

Many different kinds of retailers have developed over the years to meet changing customer needs. In the following sections, you will learn why these retailers have developed and why there are so many stores—especially so many small stores.

Actually, there is constant change in the retailing area. So a good understanding of the *why* of various kinds of retailing facilities will help you plan better marketing strategies now—and in the future.

Figure 11–2 shows some types of retailers which have survived by finding a place in a very competitive market.

Conventional retailers have been around for a long time. It is clear that they satisfy some consumers' needs. Usually conventional retailers start with one person or family running the store. Their assortment is limited by how much money (capital) they have and how well they can manage the whole operation by themselves. They may handle a single or limited line of merchandise—so they can carry the minimum assortment which will satisfy their potential customers. If they face much competition, however, they may increase their assortment or specialize further. At the same time, they try to keep costs down and prices up by avoiding competition on the same products. Let's take a closer look at these conventional retailers.

Door-to-door retailers— effective for "unsought goods"

Door-to-door selling means going directly to the consumer's home. This can be a good method for introducing a new product or for selling unsought goods. But it is an expensive method—markups range from 30 to 50 percent, and often higher.

Door-to-door selling can be very successful, although it accounts for less than 1 percent of retail sales. Electrolux sells vacuum cleaners this way and claims the top position in the vacuum cleaner business—selling all its cleaners at list price! Fuller Brush, Avon, and most encyclopedia companies also use this approach successfully.

General stores were popular

General stores sell anything the local consumers will buy in enough volume to justify carrying it. In the early days of our country, they were the main type of retail outlet. And they served as more than just a retail store. They were also a social center, perhaps the post office, and a collecting point for agricultural products.

Figure 11–2
Types of retailers and the nature of their offerings

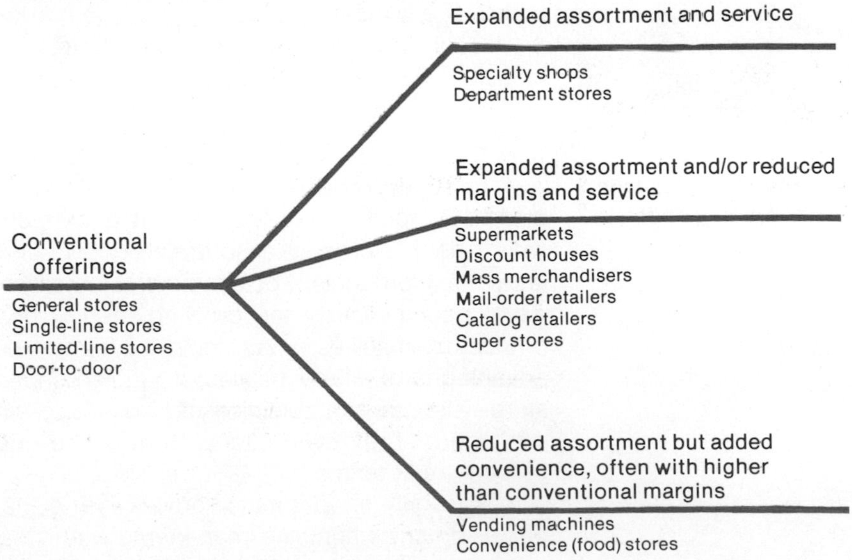

Expanded assortment and service
Specialty shops
Department stores

Expanded assortment and/or reduced margins and service
Supermarkets
Discount houses
Mass merchandisers
Mail-order retailers
Catalog retailers
Super stores

Conventional offerings
General stores
Single-line stores
Limited-line stores
Door-to-door

Reduced assortment but added convenience, often with higher than conventional margins
Vending machines
Convenience (food) stores

Such stores—carrying mostly food and other convenience goods—are still found at rural crossroads and in some small towns. But there are so few now that the U.S. Bureau of Census no longer reports them as a separate category.

Single-line, limited-line stores are being squeezed

Single-line or limited-line stores specialize in certain lines rather than the broad assortment carried by general stores. These kinds of stores became common after the U.S. Civil War. The increasing output and variety of consumer goods made it impossible for the general store to carry large assortments in all its traditional lines. Some stores began specializing in clothing, furniture, or groceries. Some specialized even within a single line—like butcher shops, bakeries, or fish stores.

Most conventional retailers are single-line or limited-line stores. And this probably will be true as long as customers demand a wide choice of products. These stores can satisfy *some* target markets very well. Their major disadvantage is that they are usually small and their expenses are high in relation to sales. This leads them to adopt the conventional retailer's philosophy of "buy low and sell high." It is this attitude which is causing some of them to be squeezed out by newer types of retailers.

Convenience stores must have the right assortment

Convenience (food) stores are a variation of the conventional limited-line food stores. Instead of carrying a big variety, they limit their stock to "fill-in" items like bread, milk, ice cream or beer. Stores such as 7–11 or Majik Markets fill needs between major shopping trips. They are offering *convenience*—not assortment—and often charge prices 10–20 percent higher than at nearby supermarkets.

The number of these stores has been growing rapidly in recent years. Their higher margins together with fast turnover of a narrow assortment makes them more profitable than supermarkets. They net approximately 4 percent on sales while the supermarkets net less than 1 percent! This helps explain why their number has increased from 2,500 in 1960 to 27,500 in 1977.[2]

Specialty shops usually sell shopping goods

A **specialty shop**—a type of limited-line store—usually is small, with a distinct "personality." It aims at a carefully defined market segment with a unique product assortment, good service, and sales people who know their products. For example, a small chain of specialty shops has developed to satisfy the growing market of "joggers." The clerks are runners themselves. They know the sport and are eager to explain the advantages of different styles of running shoes to their customers. These stores also carry a selection of books on running, as well as clothes for the jogger. They even offer a discount to customers who are members of local track teams.

A specialty shop's major advantage is that it caters to certain types of customers whom the management and sales people come to know

A specialty shop aims at a carefully defined market with a unique product assortment and knowledgable sales people.

well. This is important because specialty shops usually offer special types of shopping goods. Knowing their customers simplifies buying, speeds turnover, and cuts cost.

Specialty shops probably will continue to be a part of the retailing scene as long as customers have varied tastes and the money to satisfy them.

Do not confuse specialty *shops* with specialty *stores*. A specialty *store* is a store that for some reason (service, quality, etc.) has become THE store for some customers. For example, a large number of customers buy all their appliances, tools, hardware, and paint supplies at Sears. For this group of consumers, Sears is a specialty store *for those items*. They do not plan to "shop around" in other stores first—they always "shop Sears."

Department stores are many limited-line stores and specialty shops

Department stores are larger stores—organized into separate departments. Each of these departments is really a limited-line store or specialty shop. In this way, the department store can get some economies of size. Department stores handle a wide variety of goods—such as women's ready-to-wear accessories, men's and boy's wear, fabrics, housewares, and house furnishings.

Department stores usually try to serve customers seeking *shopping goods* and probably would be thought of as shopping *stores* by most people. Some department stores, however, have earned the specialty store status. They have a strong grip on their market.

In fact, department stores are often looked to as the retailing leaders in a community. Leaders, first, because of generous customer services—

including credit, merchandise return, delivery, fashion shows, and Christmas displays—and leaders also because of their size. The annual sales volume of U.S. department stores averages more than $5 million compared to about $240,000 for the average retail store. The biggest—Macy's, Marshall Fields, and Dayton-Hudson's—each top $500 million in sales annually! Although department stores make up less than 1 percent (7,742) of the total number of retail stores, they account for over 10 percent of total retail sales!

The original department stores in the United States were formed in the 1800s. They were located in downtown districts—close to other department stores and convenient to many potential customers. Since the 1940s, many of these customers have moved to the suburbs. Some downtown department stores have opened surburban branches to serve these consumers. These changes have hurt the downtown stores. Many downtown locations have closed.

The building of downtown apartment buildings, urban redevelopment, and improved mass transit may save some of the big downtown stores.[3] But others may disappear from the scene. They have not changed to compete with the many new forms of retailing.

Mail-order retailing reaches out

Mail-order retailing allows customers to "shop by mail"—using the mail-order retailers' catalogs to "see" the offerings. The customer's purchases are delivered by mail or truck. This method can be very useful for reaching widely scattered markets. Some mail-order houses aim at narrow target markets—selling only electronic components, phonograph records, or health foods. Large mail-order houses like Sears and Montgomery Ward offer both convenience goods and shopping goods.

Mail-order houses have continued to grow with the U.S. economy—numbering almost 8,000. Yet they have never sold more than 1.3 percent of total U.S. sales, and now they are down to about 1 percent.

The early mail-order houses were extremely successful—because of their low prices and wide variety. But today, mail-order selling isn't what it used to be. The emphasis isn't only on low price anymore. Many mail-order retailers now offer high fashion clothes and luxury gift items. Some companies have catalog stores, telephone service, convenient pick-up stations—even delivery service—to make it easier to buy from their catalogs. Even some deparment stores and limited-line stores are selling by mail.

Vending machines are convenient

Automatic vending is selling and delivering goods with vending machines. Vending machine sales have increased—but still represent less than 1 percent of total U.S. retail sales. In some lines, however, vending machines are very important—16 percent of all cigarettes, 20 percent of candy bars, and 25 percent of packaged soft drinks are sold through machines.[4]

The major problem with automatic vending is the high cost. Marketers of similar, nonvended products can operate profitably on a margin of about 20 percent—while the vending industry requires about 41 percent. So they must charge higher prices.[5] But where consumers want convenience, vending machines can be *the* right method for delivering the goods.

Planned shopping centers—not just a group of stores

Planned shopping centers consist of a group of stores planned as a unit—to satisfy some market needs. Usually, free parking facilities are provided. Many centers are enclosed to make shopping more pleasant. The centers are made up of several independent merchants who sometimes act together for Promotion purposes.

Neighborhood shopping centers are made up of several convenience stores. These centers usually include a supermarket, drug store, hardware store, beauty shop, laundry, dry cleaner, gas station, and perhaps others, such as a bakery or appliance shop. They normally must serve 7,500 to 40,000 people living within 6 to 10 minutes driving distance.

Community shopping centers are larger and offer some shopping stores as well as the convenience stores found in neighborhood shopping centers. They usually include a small department store which carries shopping goods (clothing and home furnishings). But the bulk of sales in these centers are convenience goods. These centers must serve 40,000 to 150,000 people within a radius of 3–4 miles.

Regional shopping centers are much larger and emphasize shopping stores and shopping goods. They include one or two large department stores and as many as 200 smaller stores. Stores that feature convenience goods are often placed at the edge of the center—so they won't get in the way of customers primarily interested in shopping.

Regional centers must serve 150,000 or more persons within a radius of 5–6 miles. They are like downtown shopping districts of larger cities. Regional centers usually are found near suburban areas.

Regional shopping centers may have as many as 200 stores.

EVOLUTION OF MASS MERCHANDISING

Mass merchandising is different than conventional retailing

So far we have been describing retailers mainly in terms of the *number of lines carried* and their *physical facilities*. This is the conventional way to think about retailing. We could talk about supermarkets and discount houses in these terms, too. But then we would miss an important difference. Many conventional retailers made that mistake when supermarkets and discount houses first appeared.

Conventional retailers follow a policy of "buy low and sell high." Some modern retailers, however, have accepted the **mass merchandising concept**—which says that retailers should offer low prices to get faster turnover and greater sales—by appealing to larger markets. To better understand what mass merchandising is, let's look at the way it has developed from supermarkets and discount houses to the modern mass merchandisers like K mart.

Supermarkets started the move to mass merchandising

A **supermarket** is a large store specializing in groceries—with self-service and wide assortments. As late as 1930, most food stores were small single-line or limited-line stores. In the early depression years, some creative people felt that they could increase their sales by charging lower prices. Their early experiments—in large warehouses—were an instant success. Independent and chain foodstores quickly copied this new idea—emphasizing low prices and self-service.

According to the Food Marketing Institute, $1 million is the minimum annual sales volume for a store to be called a supermarket. In 1975, there were 18,890 supermarkets—about 14 percent of all grocery stores—and they handled about 67 percent of total grocery sales. Today, there are almost too many supermarkets, yet new ones still do well when they are well located.[6]

"Get me more fast-selling items like those and I'll give you more shelf space."

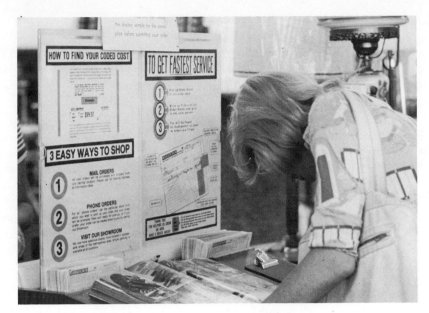

Catalog retailers offer savings on a wide variety of goods.

Supermarkets sell convenience goods, but in *quantity*. These stores are planned so goods can easily be loaded on the shelves. The store layout makes it easy for customers to shop quickly. Some stores carefully study the sales and profits of each item—and allow more shelf space for the faster moving and higher profit items. This approach helps sell more in less time, reduces the investment in inventory, makes stocking easier, and lowers the cost of handling goods. Such efficiency is very important because there is so much competition. Net profits in grocery supermarkets usually run a thin 1 percent of sales *or less*.

Catalog retailers preceded discount houses

Catalog retailers sell several lines out of a catalog and display showroom with backup inventories. Before 1940, these retailers were usually wholesalers who also sold at retail to friends and members of groups—such as labor unions or church groups. In the 1970s, however, these operations expanded rapidly—offering significant price savings on jewelry, gifts, luggage, and small appliances.

The conventional retailers weren't worried about the early catalog retailers. They were not well publicized and accounted for only a small part of total retail sales. If these pioneer catalog retailers had moved ahead aggressively—as the current catalog retailers are doing—the retailing scene might be quite different. But instead, discount houses developed.

Discount houses upset some conventional retailers

Right after World War II, some retailers moved beyond offering discounts to "selected customers." These **discount houses** offered "hard goods" (cameras, TVs, appliances) at substantial price cuts—to customers who would go to the discounter's low-rent store, pay cash, and take care of any service or repair problems. They cut prices to obtain fast turnover. And when, in the early 1950s, well-known brands became more plentiful, discount houses began to offer full assortments. They also tried to improve their image by moving to better locations and offering more services and guarantees. They began to act more like conventional retailers—but still kept their prices lower to keep turnover high.

Mass merchandisers are more than discounters

The **mass merchandisers** are large self-service stores with many departments which tend to emphasize "soft goods" (housewares, clothing, and fabrics) but still follow the discount house's emphasis on lower margins to get faster turnover. Mass merchandisers—for example, K mart and Woolco—have checkout counters in the front of the store and little or no sales help on the floor. This is in contrast to more conventional retailers—such as Sears and Penney's—who still offer some service and have sales stations and cash registers in each department.

Recently, some of the mass merchandisers have moved into groceries. These "discount" stores are a real threat to their competitors. They are selling more food—among other things—per store than the chain supermarkets!

In 1975, there were about 5,000 mass merchandisers. The average one has nearly 60,000 square feet of floor space. This is 3–4 times the size of the average supermarket.[7]

The mass merchandisers may have reached the market maturity stage of their life cycle. Profits are declining and some have gone bankrupt. The number of stores grew so rapidly in some areas that they were no longer taking customers from conventional retailers, but from each other.[8]

Seeing fewer opportunities in big cities, K mart has started moving into small towns with a slightly smaller K mart. This has really upset some small-town merchants who felt they were safe from this kind of competition.

Super-stores meet all routine needs

Super-stores are very large stores that try to carry not only foods, but all goods and services which the consumer purchases *routinely*. Such a store may *look* like a mass merchandiser, but it is different. The super-store is attempting to meet *all* the customer's routine needs—at a low price.

Some supermarkets and mass merchandisers have moved toward becoming super-stores—but the super-store idea is big. It requires the firm to carry not only foods, but also personal care products, alcoholic beverages, some apparel products, some lawn and garden products, gasoline, and household services such as laundry, dry cleaning, shoe repair, check cashing, and bill paying. If the trend to super-stores continues, the "groceries-only" supermarkets may suffer badly. Their present buildings and parking lots are not large enough to become super-stores. Super-stores could put 50 percent of the existing supermarkets out of business in the near future.[9]

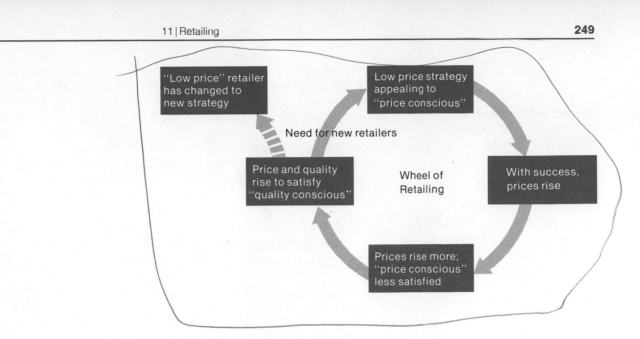

WILL SCRAMBLED MERCHANDISING CONTINUE?

Who's selling what to whom?

Conventional retailers tend to specialize by product line. But current retailing can be called **scrambled merchandising.** This means that retailers are carrying *any* product lines which they feel they can sell profitably. Mass merchandisers are selling groceries—while supermarkets are selling anything they can move in volume.

The wheel of retailing keeps rolling

What is behind this scrambled merchandising? The **wheel of retailing** theory says that new retailers enter the market as low-status, low-margin, low-price operators and then—if they are successful—evolve into more conventional stores, offering more services at higher prices. Then they must compete with new low-status, low-margin, low-price outlets—and the wheel turns again.

Early department stores began this way. Then they became higher priced and built basement departments to serve the more cost-conscious customers. The mail-order house was developed on a price basis. So were the food chains, economy apparel chains, drug chains, and the automobile accessory chains which developed during the 1920s.

Some innovators start with high margins

The wheel of retailing theory, however, does not explain all major retailing developments. Vending machines entered retailing as high-cost, high-margin operations. Convenience food stores are high priced. The development of suburban shopping centers has not had a low-price emphasis.

The probable cause of these exceptions has been summarized very well by Hollander:

. . . retailers are constantly probing the empty sectors of competitive strategy with many failures until someone uses exactly the right technique at the right time. In at least a few cases, the merchant prince's skill may have been in judging opportunities rather than in originating techniques.[10]

Customers' needs and preferences help explain scrambled retailing

A clear view of current retailing can be seen in Figure 11–3—which gives a simplified view of the consumer market. It suggests that three consumer-oriented dimensions affect the types of retailers customers choose. These dimensions are: (1) width of assortment desired; (2) depth of assortment desired; and (3) price/service combination desired. It is possible to position most current retailers within this three-dimensional market.

Figure 11–3, for example, suggest the *why* of vending machines. Some people—in the front upper left-hand corner—have an urgent need for a specific item and are not interested in width of assortment, depth of assortment, *or* price.

Some customers, however, have very specific needs and want the choice of a deep assortment *and* a range of prices. Various kinds of specialty shops have developed to fill these needs. This market can be seen in the lower left front corner of Figure 11–3.

PRODUCT LIFE-CYCLE CONCEPT HELPS, TOO

People's needs help explain why the various kinds of retailers developed. But we need to apply the product life-cycle concept to understand

Figure 11–3
A three-dimensional view of the market for retail facilities and the probable position of some present offerings

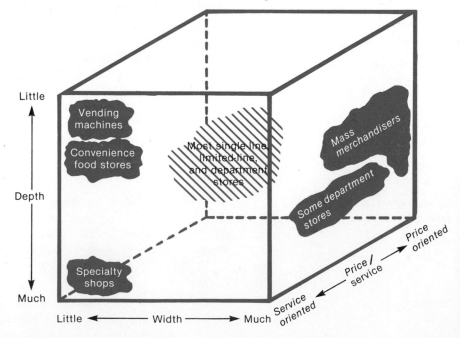

this evolutionary process better. A "merchant prince" may take big profits on a new idea—for a while—but if it's really a good idea, he can count on fairly speedy imitation and a squeeze on his profits.

Some conventional retailers are far along in their cycle. And some have already declined, while current innovators are still in the market growth stage. Some retailers are confused by the scrambling going on around them. They don't see this evolutionary process. They don't understand that some of their more successful competitors are aiming at the needs of different market segments—instead of just selling products.

It is not surprising to find that some modern success stories in retailing are among firms which moved into a new market and started another "product life cycle"—by aiming at needs along the edges of the market shown in Figure 11–3. The convenience food store chains, for example, don't just sell food. They deliberately sell a particular assortment-service combination to meet a different need. This is also true of specialty shops—and some of the mass merchandisers and department store chains.[11]

GAINING ECONOMIES OF SIZE IN RETAILING

Some retailers have expanded to try to achieve economies of size. Let's see why such growth may be desirable.

Small size may be expensive

A small independent retailer may satisfy some emotional needs by being his own boss. Also, he can be very helpful to some target customers because of his flexibility. But the store may only *seem* profitable because some of the costs of doing business are ignored. The owner may not be allowing for depreciation—or for family members clerking or keeping books without pay. Sometimes he can keep the doors open only because he has a full-time job elsewhere. About 700,000 retailers sell less than $50,000 in sales annually. After expenses, this leaves hardly enough to support one person.

Even the average retail store is too small to gain economies of size. Annual sales for the average store of only $240,000 is not very impressive, especially considering that net profits as a percentage of sales range from 1 to 5 percent. To get a better idea about size, remember that a supermarket sells more than $1 million per year!

The disadvantage of small size may even apply to the many departments within a large department store. It consists of many small-scale specialty shops and limited-line stores which may not be any larger than independent limited-line stores. So there may be little or no possibility for volume buying.

Being in a chain may help

The disadvantages of small size—even in department stores—has led to the growth of chains—to achieve the benefits of large-scale operations. A **chain store** is a member of a group which works together to operate more efficiently. Chains grew slowly until after World War I, then spurted ahead during the 1920s. In 1975, about 31 percent of the country's retail sales were made by chain stores. In some lines, chain stores are dominant. Variety chain stores—such as Woolworth's—have 81 percent of sales in that field. Department store chains have 89 percent of that business. Sears, Montgomery Ward, and J. C. Penney are in this category. And supermarket chains have 56 percent of grocery sales.

Independents form chains, too

ASSOCIATED GROCERS, CO.

The growth of corporate chains has encouraged the development of both cooperative chains and voluntary chains.

Cooperative chains are retailer-sponsored groups—formed by independent retailers—to run their own buying organization. Sales of cooperative chains have been rising as they have learned how to meet the corporate chain competition. Examples include Associated Grocers and Certified Grocers.

Voluntary chains are wholesaler-sponsored groups which work with "independent" retailers. Some are linked by contracts stating common operating procedures—and the use of common store front designs, store name, and joint promotion efforts. Examples include IGA and Super Valu in groceries, ACE in hardware, and Western Auto in auto supplies.

Franchising is similar

Franchise operations are like voluntary chains in that the franchiser has developed a good marketing strategy and the franchise holders carry out the strategy in their own units. Examples include McDonald's, Burger King, Wendy's, and automobile (new) dealerships. The voluntary chains have tended to work with existing retailers, while some franchisers like to work with newcomers—whom they train and get started. Sometimes they will locate the site, as well as supervise building and the initial promotion and opening.[12]

Co-ops try—but usually in vain

Cooperative and voluntary chains should not be confused with **consumer cooperatives**—which are groups of *consumers* who buy together. These groups usually operate on a nonprofit basis with voluntary or poorly paid management. Consumer cooperatives have never made much of an impact in the United States. Their high point was 1 percent of retail sales in 1954.

Consumer cooperatives have been more successful in Europe—where most retailers have been high priced and inefficient. Most U.S. markets, on the other hand, have been so competitive that customers have not been willing to go to the typically out-of-the-way location for the (sometimes) unknown or co-op dealer brand which may or may not be offered at lower prices.

FUTURE POSSIBILITIES IN RETAILING

Retailing has changed rapidly in the last 30 years. Scrambled merchandising may become more scrambled. Some people are forecasting larger

Electronic developments offer
marketers new opportunities.

stores. Others are predicting smaller ones. What is behind these different
predictions?

**More customer-oriented
retailing may be coming**

Forecasting trends is risky, but our three dimensional picture of the
retailing market (Figure 11–3) can be helpful. Those who suggest larger
stores may be primarily concerned with the mass market. Those who
expect more small stores and specialty shops may be anticipating more
small but increasingly wealthy target markets able to afford higher prices
for different products.

To serve small but wealthy markets, convenience food stores continue
to spread. Sales by vending machines—even with their higher operating
costs and prices—may grow. Certainly, some customers are getting tired
of the large supermarkets that take so much of their time. Logically, convenience goods should be offered at the customer's, rather than the retailer's
convenience. Some retailers still fight night and weekend hours, for example, although it is convenient for most working people to shop then.

Telephone shopping may become more popular also. The catalog
houses and department stores already find phone business attractive. Telephone supermarkets—now a reality—sell only by phone and deliver all
orders. Linking the phone to closed-circuit TV would let the customer see
the goods at home while hearing well-prepared sales presentations. The
customer could place an order through a small computer system which
would also handle the billing and delivery.

We now have far greater electronic capabilities than we are using. There
seems to be no reason why the customer couldn't shop in the home—
saving time and gasoline. Such automated retailing could take over a

large share of the convenience goods and homogeneous shopping goods business.

Retailers becoming manufacturers and vice versa

We also may see more horizontally and vertically administered channel systems. This would have a major impact on present manufacturers. Some retailers are developing their own brands and using manufacturers mainly as production arms.

The large manufacturers themselves may go into retailing—for self-protection. Various drug, paint, tire, and shoe manufacturers already control their own retail outlets.

Retailing certainly will continue to be needed. But the role of individual retailers—and even the concept of a retail store—may have to change. Customers will always have needs and they will probably want to satisfy those needs with combinations of goods and services. But retail stores may not be the only way of doing this.

Retailers must face the challenge

One thing is certain—retailing will change. For years, traditional retailers' profits have gone down. Even some of the newer discounters and shopping centers haven't done well. Department stores and food and drug chains have had profit declines. The old variety stores are even worse. Some are shifting into mass merchandising, and—as we saw—even some mass merchandisers are in trouble too.

A few firms—among them Sears, K mart, and Penney's—have avoided this general profit squeeze. But the future looks grim for retailers who can't change their old ways.

In fact, it seems that there isn't an easy way to big profits any more. Instead, careful strategy planning and great care in carrying out the plan will be needed for success in the future. This means more careful market segmenting to find unsatisfied needs which (1) have a long life expectancy and (2) can be satisfied with low levels of investment. This won't be easy. But you can be sure that the imaginative marketing planner will find more profitable opportunities than a conventional retailer—who doesn't know that a product life cycle is moving along and is just "hoping for the best."[13]

Conclusion

Modern retailing is scrambled. And we will probably see more changes in the future. A producer's marketing manager must choose among the available retailers very carefully. Retailers must plan the kind of store they are going to run with their target customers' needs in mind.

We described a wide variety of retailers and saw that each has its advantages—and disadvantages. We also saw that some modern retailers have left conventional ways behind. The old "buy low and sell high" idea is no longer an effective rule. Faster turnover with lower margins is the new idea—as retailers move from discounting into mass merchandising. Even this is no guarantee of success as retailers' product life cycles move on.

Scrambled merchandising will probably continue as the Wheel of Retailing continues to roll. But important breakthroughs are possible, because consumers may want different retail facilities. Convenience goods, for example, may be made more easily available by some combination of electronic ordering and home delivery or vending. Our society needs a retailing function, but it is not clear that *all* the present facilities are needed. The future retail scene will offer the marketing manager new challenges and opportunities.

Questions for discussion

1   Identify a specialty store selling convenience goods in your city. Explain why you feel it is that kind of a store and why an awareness of this status would be important to a manufacturer. Does it give the retailer any particular advantage? If so, with whom?

2   What sort of a "product" are specialty shops offering? What are the prospects for organizing a chain of specialty shops?

3   A department store consists of many departments. Is this horizontal integration? Are all of the advantages of horizontal integration achieved in a department store operation?

4   Many department stores have a bargain basement. Does the basement represent just another department; like the hat department or the luggage department, for example, or is some whole new concept involved?

5   Distinguish among discount houses, discount selling, and mass merchandising. Forecast the future of low-price selling in food, clothing, and appliances.

6   Suggest what the supermarket or scrambled merchandising outlet of the future may be like.

7   List five products that seem suitable for automatic vending and yet are not normally sold in this manner. Generally, what characteristics are required?

8   Apply the "Wheel of Retailing" theory to your local community. What changes seem likely? Does it seem likely that established retailers will see the need for change, or will entirely new firms have to develop?

9   Discuss the kinds of markets served by the three types of shopping centers. Are they directly competitive? Do they contain the same kinds of stores? Is the long-run outlook for all of them similar?

10   Explain the growth and decline of various types of retailers and shopping centers in your own community, using the text's market grid (Figure 11–3) and the product life-cycle concept and treating the retailers' total offering as a "product."

11   Many retailers are expanding their operations by selling by mail. Some catalogs cost from $1.00 to $2.50 each, and they go out by the millions. Department stores have also become more interested in this method of selling. Most have found that there are no really "hot" items. But sales have been good for food processors, microwave oven cookware, soft-sided luggage, and "cold weather–oriented" articles like shawls, warm sleepwear, and electric blankets. Although there have been no outstanding winners, it is clear that the department stores are avoiding some items, such as children's clothing, toys, and "brown" goods—like television sets, because they do not view them as department-store items. Instead, the department stores seem to be concentrating on softer-looking clothing, accessories for both men and women, and currently popular home goods such as linens, glassware, and small appliances. As more department stores enter the competition, the costs are rising; so are the costs of errors. Evaluate the department stores' current product offerings. Suggest what you would offer and explain why.

Suggested cases:

13   Photo Supply, Inc.

16   The Neil Company

When you finish this chapter you should:

1 Understand what wholesalers are and the wholesaling functions they *may* provide for others in channel systems.
2 Understand when and where the various kinds of merchant wholesalers and agent middlemen would be most useful to channel planners.
3 Understand why wholesalers have lasted.
4 Recognize the important new terms shown in red.

12

WHOLESALING

Wholesaling is an important activity in the marketing process. To understand the wholesalers' role better, think of them as members of channels of distribution. Although they are individual firms, they help link many producers and final consumers.

WHAT IS A WHOLESALER?

It is not easy to define what a wholesaler is because there are so many different kinds of wholesalers doing different jobs. Some of their activities may even seem like manufacturing. As a result, we find some "wholesalers" calling themselves "manufacturer and dealer." Others like to identify themselves with such general terms as merchant, dealer, or distributor—because they do various jobs. Others just use the name which is commonly used in their trade—without really thinking about what it means.

To avoid a long technical discussion of the nature of wholesaling, we will use the U.S. Bureau of Census definition. This is basically:

> **Wholesaling** is concerned with the activities of those persons or establishments which sell to retailers and other merchants and/or to industrial, institutional, and commercial users, but who do not sell in large amounts to final consumers.

Wholesalers are firms whose main function is providing wholesaling activities.

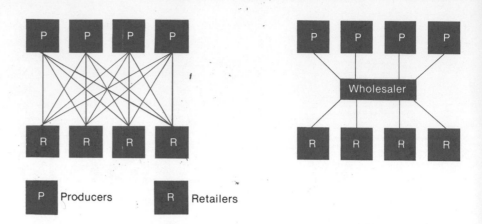

It is important to see that producers who take over wholesaling functions are *not* wholesalers. However, if separate "middlemen facilities"—such as branch warehouses—are set up by producers, then the U.S. Census counts these as wholesalers.

Wholesaling must be understood as a middleman activity. Let's look at these wholesaling functions.

POSSIBLE WHOLESALING FUNCTIONS

Wholesalers *may* perform certain functions for both their own customers and their suppliers. Remember—these functions are provided by *some,* but *not all,* wholesalers.

What a wholesaler might do for customers

1. *Anticipate needs*—forecast customers' demands and buy for them.
2. *Regroup goods*—provide the assortment wanted by customers at the lowest possible cost.
3. *Carry stocks*—carry inventory so customers don't have to store a large inventory.
4. *Deliver goods*—provide prompt delivery at low cost.
5. *Grant credit*—give credit to customers, perhaps supplying their working capital. Note: This financing function may be very important to small customers and is sometimes the major reason why they use wholesalers rather than buying directly from manufacturers.
6. *Provide information and advisory service*—supply price and technical information as well as suggestions on how to install and sell products. Note: The wholesaler's sales force may be experts in the products they sell.
7. *Provide part of buying function*—offer products to potential customers so they do not have to hunt for supply sources.
8. *Own and transfer title to goods*—to permit completing a sale without the need for other middlemen—speeding the whole buying and selling process.

What a wholesaler might do for producer-suppliers	1. *Provide part of producer's selling function*—by going to producer-suppliers, instead of waiting for their sales reps to call.
	2. *Store inventory*—this reduces a producer's need to carry large stocks—and cuts his warehousing expenses.
	3. *Supply capital*—producer's need for working capital is reduced by buying his output and carrying it in inventory until it is sold.
	4. *Reduce credit risks*—by selling to customers the wholesaler knows and taking the loss if these customers do not pay.
	5. *Provide market information*—as an informed buyer and seller closer to the market, the wholesaler reduces the producer's need for market research.

KINDS AND COSTS OF AVAILABLE WHOLESALERS

Table 12–1 lists the types, numbers, sales volume, and operating expenses of wholesalers. The differences in operating expenses show that each of these wholesaler types performs different wholesaling functions. But which ones and why?

Why, for example, do manufacturers use merchant wholesalers costing 13.9 percent of sales when manufacturers' branches with stock cost only 11.0 percent?

Table 12–1
Wholesale trade by type of operation (United States)

Type of operation	Number of establish-ments	Sales ($000)	Operating expenses (including payroll) percent of sales
United States, total	369,791	$695,223,644	10.2%
Merchant wholesalers, total	289,974	353,918,969	13.9
Wholesale merchants and distributors	274,727	305,065,300	14.9
Importers	6,811	23,092,407	10.5
Exporters	2,650	14,320,613	4.5
Terminal grain elevators	5,811	11,440,699	6.0
Manufacturers' sales offices and branches, total	47,197	255,678,995	7.2
Manufacturers' sales branches (with stock)	32,611	124,458,472	11.0
Manufacturers' sales offices (without stock)	14,586	131,220,523	4.1
Merchandise agents and brokers, total	32,620	85,625,680	4.2
Auction companies	1,769	8,060,207	2.5
Merchandise brokers	4,770	20,397,799	3.2
Commission merchants	6,940	18,970,904	3.8
Import agents	265	2,899,576	1.3
Export agents	440	4,694,104	1.9
Manufacturers' agents	16,529	23,344,579	7.1
Selling agents	1,722	6,493,714	3.2
Purchasing agents and resident buyers	185	764,797	3.9

Source: *1972 Census of Wholesale Trade*, vol. I, p. 8.

Figure 12–1
Types of wholesalers

Merchant wholesalers (Own the goods)		Agent middlemen (Don't own the goods, emphasize selling)
Service (All the functions)	Limited function (Some of the functions)	
General merchandise wholesalers (or mill supply houses)	Cash-and-carry wholesalers	Auction companies
	Drop-shippers	Brokers
	Truck wholesalers	Commission merchants
Single-line or general-line wholesalers	Mail-order wholesalers	Manufacturers' agents
	Producers' cooperatives	Food brokers
	Rack jobbers	Selling agents
Specialty wholesalers		

Why use either when brokers cost only 3.2 percent?

To answer these questions we must understand what these wholesalers do—and do not do. Figure 12–1 gives a big-picture view of the wholesalers described in more detail below. Note that a major difference is whether they *own* the goods they sell.

MERCHANT WHOLESALERS ARE THE MOST NUMEROUS

Merchant wholesalers own (take title to) the goods they sell. They also provide some—or all—of the wholesaling functions. There are two basic kinds of merchant wholesalers: (1) service—sometimes called full-service—wholesalers, and (2) limited-function or limited-service wholesalers. Their names explain their difference.

More than three-fourths of all wholesaling establishments are merchant wholesalers, but they handle only about half of wholesale sales. Why?

Service wholesalers provide all the functions

Service wholesalers provide all the wholesaling functions. Within this basic group are three subtypes: (1) general merchandise, (2) single-line, and (3) specialty.

General merchandise wholesalers carry a wide variety of nonperishable staple items such as hardware, electrical supplies, plumbing, furniture, drugs, cosmetics, and automobile equipment. With this broad line of convenience and shopping goods, they can serve many kinds of retail stores. In the industrial goods field, the "mill supply house" operates in the same way. Somewhat like a retail hardware store, the mill supply house carries a wide variety of accessories and supplies for industrial customers.

Single-line or general-line wholesalers carry a narrower line of merchandise than general merchandise wholesalers. For example, they might carry only groceries, or wearing apparel, or paint, or certain types of industrial accessories or supplies.

Specialty wholesalers carry a very narrow range of products. A *consumer goods* specialty wholesaler might carry only health foods or Oriental foods—instead of a full line of groceries. For industrial goods, a specialty wholesaler might limit itself to fields requiring technical knowledge or service—perhaps electronics or plastics.

The specialty wholesaler tries to become an expert in selling the product lines it carries. Where there is need for this kind of technical service, the specialty wholesaler's sales people usually have little difficulty taking business away from less specialized wholesalers.

The Cadillac Plastic & Chemical Co. in Detroit, for example, became a specialty wholesaler serving the needs of plastics makers *and* users. Neither the large plastics manufacturers, nor the merchant wholesalers with wide lines were able to give individual advice to the many users (who often could not judge which product would be best for them). Cadillac carries 10,000 items and sells to 25,000 customers—ranging in size from very small firms to General Motors.

Limited-function wholesalers provide certain functions

Limited-function wholesalers provide only *some* wholesaling functions. Table 12–2 shows the functions typically provided and not provided. In the following paragraphs, the main features of these wholesalers will be discussed. Some are not very numerous. In fact, they are not counted separately by the U.S. Census Bureau. Nevertheless, these wholesalers are very important for some products.

CASH-AND-CARRY WHOLESALER WANTS CASH

A **cash-and-carry wholesaler** operates like a service wholesaler—except that the customer must pay cash. Many small retailers, especially

General merchandise wholesalers carry a wide variety of items.

Table 12–2
Functions provided by limited-function merchant wholesalers

Functions	Cash-and-carry	Drop-shipper	Truck	Mail-order	Coopera-tives	Rack jobbers
For customer:						
Anticipates needs	X		X	X	X	X
"Regroups" goods (one or more of four steps)	X		X	X	X	X
Carries stocks	X		X	X	X	X
Delivers goods			X		X	X
Grants credit		X	Maybe	Maybe	Maybe	Consignment (in some cases)
Provides information and advisory services		X	Some	Some	X	
Provides buying function		X	X	X	Some	X
Owns and transfers title to goods	X	X	X	X	X	X
For producers:						
Provides producer's selling function	X	X	X	X	X	X
Stores inventory	X		X	X	X	X
Helps finance by owning stocks	X		X	X	X	X
Reduces credit risk	X	X	X	X	X	X
Provides market information	X	X	Some	X	X	Some

small grocers and garages, are too small to be served profitably by a service wholesaler. To handle these markets, service wholesalers often set up cash-and-carry operations—to serve these small retailers for cash on the counter. The cash-and-carry wholesaler can operate at lower cost because the retailer takes over many wholesaling functions.

DROP-SHIPPER DOES NOT HANDLE THE GOODS

Drop-shippers own the goods they sell—but do not actually handle, stock, or deliver them. These wholesalers are mainly involved in selling. They get orders—from wholesalers, retailers, or industrial users—and pass these orders on to producers. Then the orders are shipped directly to the customers. Because drop-shippers do not have to handle the goods, their operating costs are lower.

Drop-shippers commonly sell products which are so bulky that additional handling would be expensive and possibly damaging. Also, the quantities they usually sell are so large that there is little need for regrouping—for example, rail carload shipments of coal, lumber, oil, or chemical products.

TRUCK WHOLESALERS DELIVER—AT A COST

Truck wholesalers specialize in delivering goods which they stock in their own trucks. Handling perishable products in general demand—tobacco, candy, potato chips, and salad dressings—truck wholesalers may provide almost the same functions as full-service wholesalers. Their big advantage is that they deliver perishable products that regular wholesalers prefer not to carry. Also, they may call on many small service stations and "back-alley" garages—providing local delivery of the many small items these customers often forget to pick up from a service wholesaler. Truck wholesalers' operating costs are relatively high—because they provide a lot of service for the little they sell.

MAIL-ORDER WHOLESALERS REACH OUTLYING STORES

A **mail-order wholesaler** sells out of a catalog which may be distributed widely to industrial customers or retailers. These wholesalers operate in the hardware, jewelry, sporting goods, and general merchandise lines. Their markets are often small industrial or retailer customers who might not be called on by other middlemen.

PRODUCERS' COOPERATIVE DOES SORTING-OUT

a peeling experience

the orange without seeds

Sunkist navel oranges

Producers' cooperatives operate almost as full service wholesalers—with the "profits" going to the cooperative's customer-members—but some of the wholesaling functions may be cut out because the producers don't want them.

The successful producers' cooperatives have emphasized the sorting-out process—to improve the quality of farm products offered to the market. Some have also branded their products and promoted these brands. Farmers' cooperatives have sometimes had success limiting production and then increasing price—by taking advantage of the normal inelastic demand for agricultural goods.

Examples of producers cooperatives are the California Fruit Growers Exchange (citrus fruits), Sunmaid Raisin Growers Association, the California Almond Exchange, and Land-O-Lakes Creameries, Inc.

RACK-JOBBER SELLS HARD-TO-HANDLE ASSORTMENTS

A **rack-jobber** specializes in nonfood items which are sold through grocery stores and supermarkets—and often displays them on his own wire racks. Many grocers don't want to bother with nonfood items (housewares, hardware items, and health and beauty aids) because they sell small quantities of so many different kinds of goods. So the rack-jobber specializes in these items.

Rack-jobbers are almost service wholesalers, except that they usually are paid cash for the stock sold or delivered. This is a relatively expensive service—with operating costs of about 18 percent of sales. The large volume of nonfood sales from these racks has encouraged some large food chains to try to handle these items themselves. But they often find

IBM sales branch.

that rack-jobbers can provide this service as well as—or better than—they can.

MANUFACTURERS' SALES BRANCHES PROVIDE WHOLESALING FUNCTIONS, TOO

Manufacturers' sales branches are separate businesses which manufacturers set up away from their factories. For example, computer manufacturers like IBM set up local branches to provide service, display equipment, and handle sales. About 15 percent of wholesale businesses are owned by manufacturers—but they handle 37 percent of total wholesale sales. One reason the sales per branch are so high is that they are usually placed in the best market areas. This also helps explain why their operating costs are often lower. But cost comparisons between various channels can be misleading, since sometimes the cost of selling is not charged to the branch. If all their expenses were charged to the manufacturers' sales branches, they probably would turn out to be more costly than they seem now.

AGENT MIDDLEMEN ARE STRONG ON SELLING

They don't own the goods

Agent middlemen *do not* own the goods they sell. Their main purpose is to help in buying and selling. They usually provide even fewer functions than the limited-function wholesalers. In certain trades, however, they are extremely valuable. They may operate at relatively low cost too—sometimes 2–6 percent of selling price.

In the following paragraphs, only the most important points about each type will be mentioned. See Table 12–3 for details on the functions provided by each. It is obvious from the number of empty spaces in Table 12–3 that agent middlemen provide fewer functions than merchant wholesalers.

**Auction companies—
display the goods**

Auction companies provide a place where buyers and sellers can come together and complete a transaction. There aren't many of these middlemen (see Table 12–3) but they are very important in certain lines—such as fruit, livestock, fur, tobacco, and used cars. For these products, demand and supply conditions change rapidly. Also, these goods must be looked at. The auction company allows buyers and sellers to come together and set the price while the goods are being inspected.

Facilities can be simple—keeping overhead low. Often, auction companies are close to transportation so that the products can be reshipped quickly. The auction company just charges a set fee or commission for the use of its facilities and services.

**Brokers—provide
information**

Brokers bring buyers and sellers together. Unlike the auction company, a broker does not need any physical facilities. Brokers may not even have a separate office. They may work out of their homes—perhaps with the aid of an answering service. Their "product" is information about what buyers need and what supplies are available. They aid in buyer-seller negotiations. When a deal is completed, they earn a commission from whoever hired them.

Brokers are especially useful for selling seasonal products—like fruits and vegetables. They also sell used machinery, real estate, and even

**Table 12–3
Functions provided by agent middlemen**

Functions	Auction companies	Brokers	Commission merchants	Manufacturers' agents and food brokers	Selling agents
For customers:					
Anticipates needs		Some		Sometimes	
"Regroups" goods (one or more of four steps)	X		X	Some	
Carries stocks	Sometimes		X	Sometimes	
Delivers goods			X	Sometimes	
Grants credit	Some		Sometimes		X
Provides information and advisory services		X	X	X	X
Provides buying function	X	Some	X	X	X
Owns and transfers title to goods	Transfers only		Transfers only		
For producer:					
Provides selling function	X	Some	X	X	X
Stores inventory	X		X	Sometimes	
Helps finance by owning stocks					
Reduces credit risk	Some				X
Provides market information		X	X	X	X

J.D. SMITH BROKERS

"Well, I can't get you strawberries, but if you'd like a battleship, I've got a beauty!"

ships. These products are not similar but the needed marketing functions *are.* In each case, buyers don't come into the market often. Someone with knowledge of the available products is needed to help both buyers and sellers complete the sale quickly and at a reasonable cost.

Commission merchants handle and sell the goods in distant markets

Commission merchants handle goods shipped to them by sellers, complete the sale, and send the money—minus their commission—to each seller.

Commission merchants are common in agricultural markets where farmers must ship to big-city central markets. They need someone to handle the goods there as well as to sell them—since the farmer cannot go with each shipment. Although commission merchants do not own the goods, they generally are allowed to sell them at the market price or the best price above some stated minimum. Prices in these markets usually are published in newspapers, so the producer-seller has a check on the commission merchant. Usually costs are low because commission merchants handle large volumes of goods and buyers usually come to them.

Commission merchants are sometimes used in other trades, too—such as textiles. Here, many small producers wish to reach buyers in a central market without having to maintain their own sales forces.

Manufacturers' agents— free-wheeling sales reps

A **manufacturers' agent** sells similar products for several noncompeting manufacturers—for a commission on what is actually sold. Such agents work almost as members of each company's sales force—but they are really independent middlemen. They may cover one city or several states.

Their big "plus" is that they already call on a group of customers and can add another product line at relatively low cost. If the sales potential in an area is low, a manufacturers' agent may be used instead of a company's own sales rep because he can do the job at lower cost. A small producer often has to use agents because its sales volume is too small to support a sales force anywhere.

Manufacturers' agents are very useful in fields where there are many small manufacturers who need to call on customers. These agents are often used in the sale of machinery and equipment, electrical goods, automobile products, clothing and apparel accessories, and some food products.

The agent's main job is selling. The agent, or his customer, sends the orders to the producer. The agent, of course, gets credit for the sale. Agents seldom have any part in setting prices or deciding on the producer's policies. Basically, they are independent, aggressive sales people.

Agents can be especially useful in introducing new products. For this service, they may earn 10 to 15 percent commission. (By contrast, their commission on large-volume established goods may be quite low—perhaps only 2 percent.) The higher rates for new products often come to be the agent's major disadvantage for the manufacturer. The 10 to 15 percent commission rate may have seemed small when the product was new and sales volume was low. Once the product is selling well, the rate seems high. At about this time, the producer often begins using its own sales reps and the manufacturers' agents must look for other new products to develop. Agents are well aware of this possibility, and try to work for many manufacturers so they are not dependent on only one or a few lines.

Food brokers—fill a gap

Food brokers are manufacturers' agents who specialize in grocery distribution. More than half of the processed goods handled by grocery stores is sold by these brokers.

Food brokers call on grocery wholesalers and large retailers for their manufacturer clients. Because they know their own territory so well, some aggressive food brokers have become involved with their client's strategy planning. They may even work closely with the producer's advertising agency.[1]

For the usual commission of 5 percent of sales, food brokers may take over the entire selling function for a manufacturer. Some even suggest what prices and advertising allowances should be offered to particular retailers. For a small manufacturer—or even large firms with many small divisions—food brokers can be a great help.

Food brokers specialize by geographic area. A manufacturer could achieve national distribution with 70 to 100 food brokers.

The food broker fills a need for manufacturers. Brokers hire very capable sales people—and pay them well. So their sales reps stay on the job longer—and they develop greater understanding of their markets. In con-

"Get me a selling agent!"

(A selling agent takes over the whole marketing job for a manufacturer.)

trast, manufacturers often use their sales territories as training grounds. They move good sales people to larger territories or home offices as soon as—and sometimes before—they have really become effective in their sales areas.

Selling agents—almost marketing managers

A **selling agent** takes over the whole marketing job of a manufacturer—not just the selling function. A selling agent may handle the entire output of one or more producers—even competing producers—with almost complete control of pricing, selling, and advertising. In effect, the agent becomes each producer's marketing manager.

Financial trouble is the main reason a producer calls in a selling agent. The selling agent may provide working captial—while taking over the affairs of the business.

Selling agents have been common in highly competitive fields like fabrics or coal. They also have been used for marketing lumber and some food, clothing, and metal products. In these industries, marketing is much more important than production for survival. The selling agent provides the necessary financial assistance and marketing know-how.

International marketing is not so different

We find agent middlemen in international trade, too. Most operate much like the ones we just discussed. **Export or import agents** are basically manufacturers' agents. **Export or import commission houses** and **export or import brokers** are really brokers. A **combination export manager** is a blend of a manufacturers' agent and a selling agent—handling the entire export function for several manufacturers of noncompeting lines.

Agent middlemen are more common in international trade because financing is usually needed and yet many markets include only a few well-financed merchant wholesalers. The best that many manufacturers can do is obtain local representation through agent middlemen and arrange financing through banks which specialize in international trade.

WHOLESALERS TEND TO CONCENTRATE TOGETHER

Different wholesalers are found in different places

Some wholesalers—such as grain elevator operators—are located close to producers. But most wholesaling is done in or near large cities. Almost half of all wholesale sales are made in the 15 largest Standard Metropolitan Statistical Areas.

This heavy concentration of wholesale sales in large cities is because many large wholesalers and industrial buyers are there. Some large manufacturers buy for all their plants through one purchasing department located in these large cities. Further, merchant wholesalers need the transporting, warehousing, and financing facilities available in these big cities.

The dominant role played by the New York area should be noted—13 percent of all wholesale sales. This is partly because of the concentration of much of the U.S. wholesale clothing and jewelry industries in this one market. But it emphasizes the important role played by large cities. This is true not only in the United States—but also in world markets.

COMEBACK AND FUTURE OF WHOLESALERS

Necessary—and lasting

In the 1800s in the United States—and even today in some international markets—wholesalers dominated marketing. The many small producers and retailers needed their services. But as producers became larger, some bypassed the wholesalers. When retailers also began to grow larger—especially during the 1920s when the chain stores began to spread rapidly—many predicted the end of wholesalers. Some people felt this would be desirable because many wholesalers apparently had grown "fat and lazy"—contributing little more than breaking bulk. Their sales people often were only order-takers. The selling function was neglected. High-quality management was not attracted to wholesaling.

We have seen, however, that wholesaling functions are necessary. And wholesalers have not disappeared. Although their sales volume declined in the 1930s, by 1954 they had returned to the same importance they had in 1929. And they have continued to hold their own.[2]

Producing profits, not chasing orders

Wholesalers have lasted, in part, because of new management and new techniques. Many are still operating in the old ways. But progressive wholesalers have become more concerned with their customers and with channel systems. Some are offering more services. Others are developing voluntary chains that bind them more closely to their customers. Some of this ordering is done routinely by mail, telephone, or directly by telephone to computer.

Some modern wholesalers no longer make all customers pay for services simply because some customers use them. This traditional practice had the effect of encouraging limited-function wholesalers and direct channels. Now, some wholesalers are making a basic service available at a minimum cost—then charging additional fees for any special services required. In the grocery field, for instance, the basic servicing of a store might cost 3 to 4 percent of wholesale sales. Promotion assistance and other aids are offered at extra cost.

Modern wholesalers also are becoming more selective in picking customers—as cost analysis shows that many of their small customers are unprofitable. By cutting out these customers, wholesalers can give more attention to their better customers. In this way, they are helping to promote healthy retailers who are able to compete in any market.

Today's *progressive* wholesaler is no longer just an order-taker. Some wholesalers have renamed their sales people "store advisors" or "supervisors" to reflect their new roles. They may provide management advisory services, including site selection and store design. They may offer legal assistance on new leases or adjustment in old leases. They may even provide store-opening services, sales training and merchandising assistance, and advertising help.

Some wholesalers are using electronic data processing systems to control inventory. Others are modernizing their warehouses and physical handling facilities, and offering central bookkeeping facilities. Modern wholesalers realize that their own survival is tied to their customers' survival. Now, instead of overloading their retailer's shelves, they try to clear the merchandise *off* the retailer's shelves. They know the old line is true: "Nothing is really sold until it is sold at retail."[3]

Good-bye to some

Not all wholesalers are progressive, however. Some of the smaller, less efficient ones may fail. While the average operating expense ratio is 13.9 percent for merchant wholesalers, some small wholesalers have expense ratios of 20–30 percent.

Low cost, however, is not the only thing required for success. The higher operating expenses of some wholesalers may be caused by the special services they offer to *some* customers. Truck wholesalers, for example, are usually small and have high operating expenses—yet *some* customers are willing to pay the higher cost of this service. And although full-service wholesalers can seem expensive, some probably will continue operating because they offer the wholesale functions and sales contacts needed by *some* small manufacturers.

It is clear that if they are going to survive, wholesalers must each carve out a specific market. Profit margins are not large in wholesaling—typically ranging from less than 1 percent to 2 percent—and they have been declining in recent years as the competitive squeeze has tightened.

The function of wholesaling certainly will last, but weaker, less aggressive wholesalers may not.

Conclusion

Wholesalers can provide wholesaling functions for those both above and below them in a channel of distribution. These functions are closely related to the basic marketing functions.

There are many types of wholesalers. Some provide all the wholesaling functions, while others specialize in only a few. Eliminating wholesalers would not eliminate the need for the functions they provide. And we cannot assume that direct channels will be more efficient.

Merchant wholesalers are the most numerous, and account for just over half of wholesale sales. They take title to—and often possession of—goods. Agent middlemen, on the other hand, act more like sales representatives. And usually they *do not* take title or possession.

Despite predictions of the end of wholesalers, they're still around. The more progressive ones have adapted to a changing environment. No such revolutions as we saw in retailing have yet taken place in wholesaling and none seems likely. But it is probable that some smaller and less progressive wholesalers will fail in the future.

Questions for discussion

1 Discuss the evolution of wholesaling in relation to the evolution of retailing.

2 What risks do merchant wholesalers assume by taking title to goods? Is the size of this risk about constant for all merchant wholesalers?

3 Why would a manufacturer set up its own sales branches if established wholesalers were already available?

4 What is an agent middleman's marketing mix? Why don't manufacturers use their own sales people instead of agent middlemen?

5 Discuss the future growth and nature of wholesaling if low-margin retailing and scrambled merchandising become more important. How will wholesalers have to adjust their mixes if retail establishments become larger and the retail managers more professional? Might the wholesalers be eliminated? If not, what wholesaling functions would be most important? Are there any particular lines of trade where wholesalers may have increasing difficulty?

6 Which types of wholesalers would be most appropriate for the following products? If more than one type of wholesaler could be used, provide the specifications for the situation in each case. For example, if size or financial strength of a company has a bearing, then so indicate. If several wholesalers could be used in this same channel, explain this also.

a. Fresh tomatoes.

b. Paper-stapling machines.

c. Auto mechanics' tools.

d. Canned tomatoes.

e. Men's shoes.

f. An industrial accessory machine.

g. Ballpoint pens.

h. Shoelaces.

7 Would a drop-shipper be desirable for the following products: coal, lumber, iron ore, sand and gravel, steel, furniture, tractors? Why, or why not? What channels might be used for each of these products if drop-shippers were not used?

8 Which types of wholesalers are likely to become more important in the next 25 years? Why?

Suggested cases

14 Mead Company

15 Miller Sales Company

25 Riverside Processing Company

When you finish this chapter, you should:

1. Know the advantages and disadvantages of the promotion methods which a marketing manager can use in strategy planning.
2. Understand the importance of promotion objectives.
3. Know how the communication process should affect promotion planning.
4. Understand how promotion blends may have to change along the adoption curve.
5. Recognize the important new terms shown in red.

13

PROMOTION-INTRODUCTION

Promotion is communicating information between seller and buyer—to change attitudes and behavior. The marketing manager's promotion job is to tell target customers that the right Product is available at the right Place at the right Price.

What the marketing manager communicates is pretty well set when the target customers' needs and attitudes are known.

How the messages are delivered depends on what promotion methods are chosen.

SEVERAL PROMOTION METHODS ARE AVAILABLE

The marketing manager can choose from three promotion methods. These are personal selling, mass selling, and sales promotion. See Figure 13–1.

Personal selling—flexibility is its biggest asset

Personal selling involves direct face-to-face communication between sellers and potential customers. It lets the salesperson see the customer's reactions immediately. This allows the sales people to adapt the company's marketing mix to the needs of each target market.

Sales people are included in most marketing mixes. Personal selling can be very expensive, however. It is often necessary to combine personal selling with mass selling and sales promotion.

Mass selling—reaches millions at a price or even free

Mass selling is communicating with large numbers of customers at the same time. It is less flexible than personal selling. But when the target market is large and spread out, mass selling may be less expensive.

273

Figure 13–1
Basic promotion methods and strategy planning

Advertising is the main form of mass selling. **Advertising** is any *paid* form of nonpersonal presentation of ideas, goods, or services by an identified sponsor. It uses such media as magazines, newspapers, radio and TV, signs, and direct mail. While advertising must be paid for, another form of mass selling—publicity—is "free."

PUBLICITY IS "FREE"

Publicity is any *unpaid* form of nonpersonal presentation of ideas, goods, or services. Although, of course, publicity people get paid, they try to attract attention to the firm and its offerings *without having to pay media costs.*

If the firm has a "new" message, publicity may be more effective than advertising. Trade magazines, for example, may carry articles featuring the newsworthy products of regular advertisers—in part because they *are* regular advertisers. This publicity may raise more interest than the company's paid advertising. The publicity people probably would write the basic copy, and then "sell" its use to the magazine editors.

Large firms have specialists to handle this job. Usually though, it is treated as just another kind of advertising. And often it isn't used as effectively as it could be. Much more attention needs to be paid to publicity in the future.[1]

Sales promotion tries to complement

Sales promotion refers to those promotion activities—other than personal selling and mass selling—that encourage customers to buy. Sales promotion tries to complement the firm's personal selling and mass selling efforts. It may use displays, shows and exhibitions, or demonstrations.

Sales promotion people develop—and may install—point-of-purchase

materials. They may invent contests. They may also prepare training materials for the company's own sales force. They may even design the sales materials for the company's own sales force to use during sales calls.

Sales promotion—like publicity—is a weak spot in marketing. Sales promotion involves a wide variety of activities—each of which may be custom-designed and used only once. Few companies develop their own "experts" in sales promotion. Many companies, even large ones, do not have a separate budget for sales promotion. Few even know what it costs in total. This neglect of the sales promotion area is a mistake because the total sales promotion cost may be greater than total advertising costs![2]

The spending on sales promotion is large and growing. This growth is due to a number of reasons. First, sales promotion activities are becoming more accepted as they prove successful in competitive markets. Also, product managers in larger companies have made greater use of sales promotion because they need to get results fast. Sales promotion activities can usually be started quickly and may produce results sooner then advertising. They also may help the product manager win support from an overworked sales force. Sales people welcome sales promotion—including promotion in the channels—because it makes their jobs easier.[3]

Sales promotion work is not a side line for amateurs. It is not something that should be turned over to a sales trainee. In fact, specialists in sales promotion have developed—both inside firms and as outside consultants. Some are very creative and might be willing to take over the whole promotion job. But it's the marketing manager who must set promotion objectives and the policies which will fit in with the rest of the marketing strategy.[4]

WHICH METHOD TO USE DEPENDS ON PROMOTION OBJECTIVES

Marketers want to affect buying decisions

Good marketers don't want to just "communicate." They want to communicate information so that target customers choose their product. There-

Sales promotion people set up product demonstrations.

fore, they are interested in (1) reinforcing present attitudes that can lead to favorable behavior, and (2) actually changing the attitudes and behavior of the firm's target market.

Informing, persuading, and reminding are promotion objectives

For a firm's promotion to work, it's necessary to clearly define the firm's promotion objectives. This is because the right promotion blend depends on what the firm wants to accomplish.

The three general **promotion objectives** are to *inform, persuade,* and *remind* target customers about the company and its marketing mix. All three aim at providing more information.

A specific set of promotion objectives—that states exactly *who* the firm would want to inform, persuade, or remind to do *what*—would be desirable in a specific case. But this is unique to each company strategy and too detailed to discuss here. Instead, we will focus on these three general promotion objectives—and how we might reach them.

INFORMING IS EDUCATING

An informing objective would be used when the manager just wants to tell customers about a firm's product. Potential customers have to know about product offerings before they buy at all.

PERSUADING USUALLY NECESSARY

A persuading objective would be necessary when competitors are offering similar products. The firm must not only inform target customers that its products are available—it must also persuade them to buy. The company might try to develop or reinforce a favorable set of attitudes—hoping to affect buying behavior. Here, comparative information could be supplied.

REMINDING MAY BE ENOUGH, SOMETIMES

A reminding objective might be used if the firm's target customers already have positive attitudes about the firm's offering. This objective can be extremely important. Even though customers had been attracted and sold once, they are still targets for competitors' promotion. Reminding them of their past satisfaction may keep them from shifting to a competitor.

PROMOTION REQUIRES EFFECTIVE COMMUNICATION

Promotion obviously must get the attention of the target market or it is wasted. What is obvious, however, isn't always easy to do. Much promotion doesn't really communicate. Behavioral science studies show that the communication process may be more complicated than we thought.

The same message may be interpreted differently

Different people see the same message in different ways. They may interpret the same words differently. Such differences are common in international marketing where translation is a problem. Parker Pen Co., for example, once blanketed Latin America with an ad campaign that, unfortu-

Noise in the channel can block the communication process.

nately, suggested that its new ink would help prevent unwanted pregnancies. General Motors had trouble in Puerto Rico with its Nova automobile. Then it was discovered that while Nova means "star" in Spanish, when it is spoken it sounds like "no va," which means "it doesn't go." The company quickly changed the car's name to "Caribe" and it sold well.[5]

Such problems in the same language may not be so obvious. But they must be recognized and solved to avoid offending customers. This is an especially sensitive matter now—to make sure that advertising does not offend any minority groups. Blacks and women have been especially vocal, but other minorities are becoming more sensitive. These may seem like small differences, but they can make a target market tune out a message—wasting the whole promotion effort.

The communication process needs feedback

The **communication process** shows how a source tries to reach a receiver with a message. Figure 13–2 illustrates this. Here we see that a

Figure 13–2
The communication process

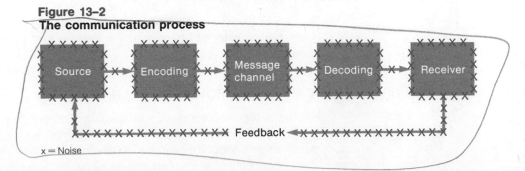

Source → Encoding → Message channel → Decoding → Receiver

Feedback

x = Noise

source—the sender of a message—is trying to deliver a message to a **receiver**—a potential customer. A source can deliver a message by many message channels. The personal salesperson does it with voice and actions. Advertising must do it with mass media—such as magazines, newspapers, radio, and TV.

A major advantage of personal selling is that the source—the seller—can receive immediate feedback from the receiver. The source can judge how the message is being received and change it if necessary. This is a real advantage to personal selling. Mass sellers must depend on marketing research or total sales figures to measure success.

The **noise**—shown in Figure 13–2—is any factor which reduces the effectiveness of the communication process. Perhaps the source can't agree on what should be said and how—and settles for a general message. Or the receiver—perhaps a parent—may be distracted by children when the message comes out of the radio. Or other advertisers or sales people may be saying the same things, and the receiver may become confused and ignore everyone.

Encoding and decoding depend on common frames of reference

Figure 13–3

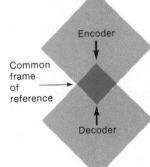

The basic difficulty in the communication process occurs during encoding and decoding. **Encoding** is the source deciding what it wants to say and translating it into words that will have the same meaning to the receiver. **Decoding** is the receiver translating the message. The whole process can be very tricky because the meanings of various words and symbols may differ depending on the attitudes and experiences of the two groups. This can be seen in Figure 13–3.

Average car drivers, for example, might think of the Ford Mustang as a sports car. If they are the target market, they want to hear about ease of handling, acceleration, and racing symbols—such as wide tires. Auto engineers and sports car fanatics, however, don't consider the Mustang a real sports car. So, if they were writing, or approving copy, they might encode the message in regular ''small-car'' terms.

MESSAGE CHANNEL IS IMPORTANT, TOO

The communication process is complicated even more because the receiver is aware that the message is not only coming from a source but also coming through some **message channel**—the carrier of the message. The receiver may attach more value to a product if its message comes in a well-respected newspaper or magazine. Similarly, information from the president of a company might be more impressive than from a junior sales representative.

ADOPTION PROCESSES CAN GUIDE PROMOTION PLANNING

The adoption process discussed in Chapter 5 is related to effective communication and promotion planning. You learned that there were six steps in that adoption process: awareness, interest, evaluation, trial, decision, and confirmation. Further, in Chapter 5 we saw consumer buying

Figure 13–4
Relation of promotion objectives, adoption process, and AIDA model

Promotion objectives	Adoption process (Chapter 5)	AIDA model
Informing	Awareness	Attention
	Interest	Interest
Persuading	Evaluation }	Desire
	Trial	
	Decision }	Action
Reminding	Confirmation	

as a problem-solving process in which buyers go through these several steps on the way to adopting (or rejecting) an idea or product. Now we will see that the basic promotion objectives can be related to these various steps—to show what is needed to achieve the objectives. See Figure 13–4.

Informing and persuading may be needed to affect the potential customer's knowledge and attitudes about a product—and then bring about its adoption. Later, promotion can simply remind the customer about that favorable experience—aiming to confirm the adoption decision.

The AIDA model is a practical approach

The basic adoption process fits very neatly with another action-oriented model—called AIDA—which we will use in this and the next two chapters to guide some of our discussion.

The **AIDA model** consists of four promotion jobs which have guided promotion specialists for years: (1) to get *Attention* (2) to hold *Interest*, (3) to arouse *Desire,* and (4) to obtain *Action*[6] (As a memory aid, note that the first letters of the four key words spell AIDA—the well-known opera.)

The relationship of the adoption process to the AIDA tasks can be seen in Figure 13–4.

Getting attention is necessary if the potential customer is to become aware of the company's offering. Holding interest gives the communication a chance to really build the prospect's interest in the product. Arousing desire affects the evaluation process, perhaps building preference. And obtaining action includes obtaining trial which then may lead to a purchase decision. Continuing promotion is needed to confirm the decision and encourage continuing action.

GOOD COMMUNICATION VARIES PROMOTION BLENDS ALONG ADOPTION CURVE

The communication and adoption processes discussed above look at individuals. This emphasis on individuals helps us understand how people

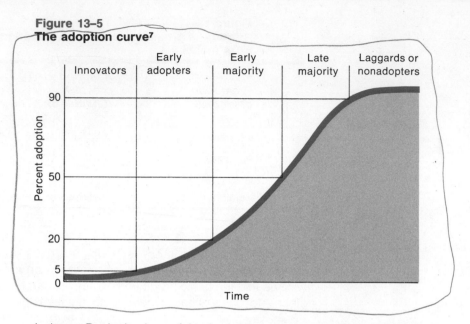

Figure 13–5
The adoption curve[7]

behave. But it also is useful to look at markets as a whole. Different customers within a market may behave differently—with some taking the lead in accepting products and, in turn, influencing others.

Adoption curve focuses on market segments, not individuals

Research on how markets accept new ideas has led to the adoption-curve concept. The **adoption curve** shows when different groups accept ideas. It shows the need to change the promotion effort as time passes. It also emphasizes the relations among groups. It shows that some groups act as leaders in accepting a new idea.

Promotion for innovators leaves laggards behind

The adoption curve for a typical successful product is shown in Figure 13–5. Some of the important characteristics of each of these customer groups are discussed below. Which one are you?

INNOVATORS—3 TO 5 PERCENT OF THE MARKET

The **innovators** are the first to adopt. They tend to be young and—at the same time—high in social and economic status. They have many contacts outside their own social group and community. They are also mobile and creative.

An important characteristic of innovators is that they rely on impersonal and scientific information sources or other innovators—instead of personal sales people. They often read articles in technical publications or informative advertisements in "respectable" publications.

EARLY ADOPTERS—10 TO 15 PERCENT OF THE MARKET

Early adopters are relatively high in social status—and probably opinion leaders. They are younger, more mobile, and more creative than later

Early adopters are younger, more mobile, and more creative than later adopters.

adopters. But they have few contacts outside their own social group or community. Of all the groups, this one tends to have the greatest contact with sales people. Mass media are important information sources, too.

EARLY MAJORITY—ABOUT 34 PERCENT OF THE MARKET

The **early majority** are those with above average social status. They usually will not consider a new idea until many early adopters have tried it. There may be a long time between trial and adoption.

The early majority have a lot of contact with mass media, sales people, and early adopters.

LATE MAJORITY—34 PERCENT OF THE MARKET

The **late majority** tend to be below average in social status and income. They are less likely to follow opinion leaders and early adopters. In fact, some social pressure from their own group may be needed before they try the product. Then adoption may follow quickly.

The late majority make little use of mass media or sales people. They are influenced more by other late adopters than by outside sources of information.

LAGGARDS OR NONADOPTERS—5 TO 16 PERCENT OF THE MARKET

The **laggards** or **nonadopters** have the lowest social status and income. They tend to stay with their traditional ideas.

The main source of information for laggards is other laggards. This certainly is bad news for marketers who want to reach a whole market quickly or use only one promotion method. In fact, it may not pay to bother with this group![8]

Opinion leaders get the web of word-of-mouth going.

Opinion leaders help spread the word

Adoption curve research supports our earlier discussion (in Chapter 5) on opinion leaders. It shows the importance of the early adopters. They influence the early majority—and help spread the word to many others.

Marketers recognize the importance of these personal conversations and recommendations by opinion leaders. If early groups reject the product, it may never get off the ground. But if the early groups accept it, then what the opinion leaders in each social group say about it may be very important. The "web of word-of-mouth" may do the real selling job long before the customer ever walks into the retail store. This shows the importance of trying to reach the opinion leaders in various social groups. But because they are hard to identify—recall from Chapter 5 that different kinds of people may be opinion leaders for different products—mass media can play an important role in getting the message to them.

MAY NEED A DIFFERENT BLEND FOR EACH MARKET SEGMENT

Each market segment needs a separate marketing mix—and each may require a different promotion blend. This is mentioned here because some mass selling specialists have missed this point. They think mainly in "mass marketing"—rather than target marketing—terms. Aiming at large markets may be all right in some situations, but unfortunately, promotion aimed at everyone can end up hitting no one. In the promotion area, we should be especially careful about using a "shotgun" approach when what is really needed is a "rifle" approach—with careful aiming.

SUCCESSFUL PROMOTION MAY BE AN ECONOMICAL BLEND

Once promotion objectives have been set, a marketing manager may decide to use a blend of promotion methods. Certain jobs can be done more cheaply one way than another. This can be seen most clearly in the industrial goods market.

A personal sales call can be expensive

While personal selling dominates most industrial goods promotion budgets, mass selling is necessary, too. Personal sales people nearly always have to complete the sale. But it is usually too expensive for them to do the whole promotion job. The direct cost (not counting supervisors or overhead) of a sales call can easily be $15–$30.[9] This relatively high cost comes from the fact that sales people have only limited time during the "business day" and much of that time is spent on nonselling activities—traveling, paper work, sales meetings, and service calls. Only 42 percent of their time is available for face-to-face selling.

The job of reaching all the possible customers is made more costly and difficult by the constant turnover of buyers and influencers. An industrial salesperson may be responsible for several hundred customers and prospects—with about four "buying influencers" per company. They don't have enough time to get the company's whole message across to every possible contact. The problem is shown in the classic McGraw-Hill advertisement in Figure 13–6. As the ad suggests, too much has been invested in a salesperson to use his time and skill to answer questions that could be handled better by mass selling. Mass selling can do the general ground work. The salesperson should concentrate on answering specific questions and closing the sale. These mass selling "sales calls" can be made at a small fraction of the cost of a personal call. One McGraw-Hill study found a mass selling "call" costing 1/645th the cost of a personal call.[10]

HOW TYPICAL PROMOTION BUDGETS ARE BLENDED

There is no one right blend

There is no one right promotion blend. Each must be developed as part of a marketing mix. But to sum up our discussion of promotion blends, we can make some general statements about how manufacturers have divided their promotion budgets. They do vary a lot. Retailers' blends also vary widely. Wholesalers' blends, on the other hand, use personal selling almost exclusively.

Figure 13–7 shows how manufacturers have divided their promotion budgets. It shows the relationship of advertising expenditures to personal selling which might be expected in various situations.

Figure 13–7 shows that manufacturers of well-branded consumer goods —such as cars, breakfast cereals, and nonprescription drugs—tend to favor advertising. This is especially true of those trying to build brand familiarity. And the emphasis on advertising might be even stronger if the firm had already established its channel relationships.

At the other extreme, smaller companies with new consumer goods would tend to use more personal selling. The same thing applies for most industrial goods. Because buyers want several sources of supply, personal selling is quite important—to be sure that the seller continues to satisfy and remain on the supplier list.[11]

Figure 13–6

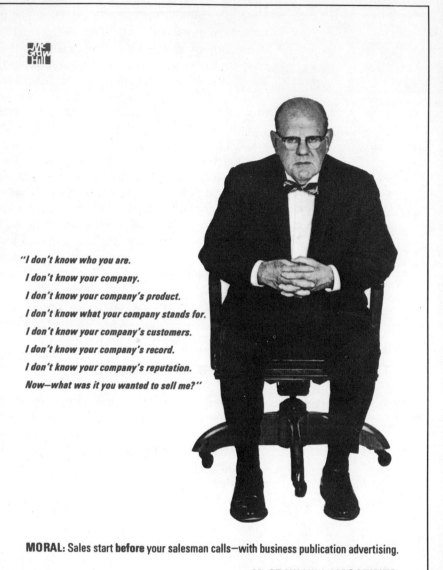

"I don't know who you are.
I don't know your company.
I don't know your company's product.
I don't know what your company stands for.
I don't know your company's customers.
I don't know your company's record.
I don't know your company's reputation.
Now—what was it you wanted to sell me?"

MORAL: Sales start **before** your salesman calls—with business publication advertising.

McGRAW-HILL MAGAZINES
BUSINESS•PROFESSIONAL•TECHNICAL

Figure 13–7
Typical promotion blends of manufacturers (ratio of advertising to personal selling)

10:1	5:1	1:1	1:5	1:10
◄────── Advertising emphasis ──────►		◄────── Personal selling emphasis ──────►		
	Firms with well-branded consumer goods (with established channels)	Blend of consumer and industrial goods	Smaller companies and any firms offering relatively undifferentiated consumer goods or industrial goods	

Personal selling usually is dominant

The relatively heavier emphasis on personal selling which you might have assumed from the figure is correct. The many advertisements you see in magazines and newspapers and on television are impressive and expensive. But this shouldn't make you forget that most retail sales are completed by sales clerks. Further—behind the scenes—much personal selling is going on in the channels.

PROMOTION BLEND—SOMEONE HAS TO PLAN IT—AND MAKE IT WORK

Good blending calls for a marketing manager

Choosing a promotion blend is a difficult strategic decision which should fit in with the rest of the marketing strategy.

Deciding on the right promotion blend is a job for the marketing manager.

Sales managers are concerned with managing personal selling. The sales manager may also be responsible for building good distribution channels.

Advertising managers are concerned with managing a company's mass selling effort—in television, newspapers, magazines, and other media. Their job is choosing the right media for each purpose, and developing the ads. They may use an advertising department within their own firms—especially if they are in retailing—or work through outside advertising agencies. They may also handle publicity.

Sales promotion managers fill the gaps between the sales and advertising managers—increasing their effectiveness. Nearly everything the sales promotion department does *could* be done by the sales or advertising departments. But sales promotion activities are so varied that specialists often develop. In some companies, the sales promotion managers work for the sales managers. In others, they report directly to the marketing manager.

Marketing manager puts the parts together

Because of differences in outlook and experience, the advertising, sales, and sales promotion managers may have a hard time working together.

Personal selling dominates
most promotion blends.

It is the marketing manager's job to decide the value of the various approaches. Then he has to develop an effective promotion blend—fitting the various departments and personalities into it and tying their efforts together.

Conclusion

Promotion is an important part of any marketing mix. Most consumers and intermediate customers can choose from among many products. To be successful, a producer must do more than offer a good product at a reasonable price. It must also tell potential customers about the product and where they can buy it. Producers must also tell wholesalers and retailers in the channel about their product and their marketing mix. These middlemen, in turn, must use promotion to reach *their* customers.

The promotion effort should fit into the strategy which is being developed to satisfy the needs of some target market. *What* should be communicated to them and *how* should be stated as part of the strategy planning.

Basically, promotion is concerned with affecting buying behavior. But three general promotion objectives were discussed—informing, persuading, and reminding.

Various promotion methods can be used to reach these objectives. How the promotion methods are combined for successful communication can be guided by behavioral science findings. In particular, we know something about the communications process—how individuals adopt new ideas—and the adoption curve—how groups react.

An action-oriented framework—called AIDA—will help guide strategic planning of promotion blends. But finally, the marketing manager is responsible for blending the alternative promotion methods into one promotion effort—for each marketing mix.

Questions for discussion

1. Briefly explain the nature of the three basic promotion methods which are available to a marketing manager. Explain why sales promotion is currently a "weak spot" in marketing and suggest what might be done about it.

2. Relate the three basic promotion objectives to the four tasks (AIDA) of the promotion job, using a specific example.

3. Discuss the communication process in relation to a manufacturer's promotion of an accessory good, say, a portable air hammer used for breaking up concrete pavement.

4. Explain how an understanding of the way individuals adopt new ideas or products (the adoption process) would be helpful in developing a promotion blend. In particular, explain how it might be desirable to change a promotion blend during the course of the adoption process. To make this more concrete, discuss it in relation to the acceptance of a new men's sportcoat style.

5. Discuss how our understanding of the adoption curve should be applied to planning the promotion blend(s) for a new, small (personal) electric car.

6. Discuss the nature of the promotion job in relation to the life cycle of a product. Illustrate, using household dishwashing machines.

7. Promotion has been the target of considerable criticism. What specific types of promotion are probably the object of this criticism?

8. Might promotion be successful in expanding the general demand for: *(a)* oranges, *(b)* automobiles, *(c)* tennis rackets, *(d)* cashmere sweaters, *(e)* iron ore, *(f)* steel, *(g)* cement? Explain why or why not in each case.

9. Indicate the promotion blend that might be most appropriate for manufacturers of the following established products (assume average- to large-sized firms in each case) and support your answer:

a. Candy bars
b. Men's T-shirts.
c. Castings for automobile engines.
d. Car batteries.
e. Industrial fire insurance.
f. Inexpensive plastic raincoats.
g. A camera that has achieved a specialty-goods status.

10. Discuss the potential conflict among the various promotion managers. How might this be reduced?

Suggested cases

17 Arrow National Bank
18 Sports Sales Company

When you finish this chapter, you should:

1. Understand the importance and nature of personal selling.
2. Know the three basic sales tasks and what the various kinds of sales people can be expected to do.
3. Understand when and where the three types of sales presentations should be used.
4. Know what a sales manager must do to carry out the job assigned to personal selling.
5. Recognize the important new terms shown in red.

PERSONAL SELLING

A seller needs to communicate with possible customers. Personal selling is often the best way to do it.

Sales managers and marketing managers must decide how much and what kind of personal selling effort are needed in each marketing mix. As part of their strategy planning, they must decide: (1) how many sales people will be needed, (2) what kind of sales people are needed, (3) what kind of sales presentation is desired, (4) how sales people should be selected, and (5) how they should be motivated. These strategic decisions can be seen more clearly in Figure 14–1.

In this chapter, we'll talk about the importance and nature of personal selling—so you will be able to understand the strategic decisions which face sales managers and marketing managers.

THE IMPORTANCE OF PERSONAL SELLING

Our economy needs and uses many sales people. U.S. Census Bureau statistics show that almost 10 percent of the total U.S. labor force is in sales work. That's over 8 million people in personal selling! (In contrast, there are less than half a million people working in advertising.) Any activity that employs so many people and is so important to the economy deserves study.

Death of a salesman?   In spite of its importance, personal selling is often criticized. The too-aggressive and sometimes dishonest practices of some sales people—

Figure 14–1
Strategy planning for personal selling

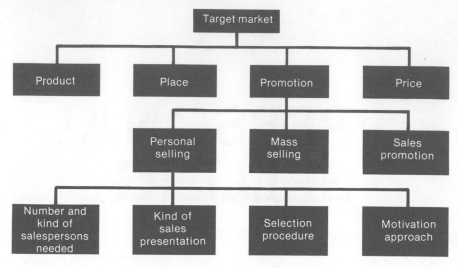

especially door-to-door peddlers and the "hucksters" involved in county or street fairs—have discouraged some from entering the sales field. There also have been doubts about the effectiveness of personal selling—especially at the retail level. Everyone has had experiences with indifferent retail clerks who couldn't care less about customers or their needs.

The poor image of personal selling—along with the incompetence of many sales people—led some to predict that personal selling would die out. This *has* happened in some parts of retailing—resulting in more self-service stores.

Rebirth of sales people

Personal sales people are far from "dead." Their role is just being redefined and upgraded—as different types of sales jobs are needed. Modern sales and marketing management have gone far in redefining what needs to be done—then selecting, training, and motivating sales people to perform effectively—while also providing them with personal satisfaction. In some cases, selling is becoming a profession. Most high-level sales people believe in the importance and value of personal selling. Some follow codes of ethics.

It's more than "get rid of the product"

While discussing selling—within marketing strategy planning—we will assume that the product the sales people are to sell is reasonably good. But in fairness to sales people, this is not always the case. Production-oriented managers often feel that it is the salesperson's job to "get rid of the product," whether it's any good or not. If the sales people know that they don't have much to sell, you can see why their morale would slip—and the whole promotion job might suffer.

Helping to buy is good selling

Increasingly, good sales people don't try to "sell" the customer. Rather, they try to help him buy by presenting both the advantages and disadvantages of their product and showing how it will satisfy needs. They find that this helpfulness results in satisfied customers and long-term relationships.

The old-time salesman with the funny story and the big smile is being replaced by sales people who have something real to contribute. The smiling "bag of wind" with the big expense account is on the way out.

Sales people represent the whole company

Increasingly, the salesperson is recognized as a representative of the whole company—responsible for explaining its total effort to target customers—rather than just moving products. As evidence of this change in thinking, some companies now give their sales people such titles as field manager, market specialist, sales representative, or sales engineer.

A SALESPERSON IS BOTH TRANSMITTER AND RECEIVER

A salesperson is expected to do much more than just bring in new business—though this certainly is an important part of the job. At the same time, the salesperson should gather feedback to help the company to do a better job in its future planning.

The modern salesperson, in other words, not only communicates the company's story to customers, but also feeds back customer reaction to the company. He is an important link in both the communication and marketing processes.

Sales people can be strategy planners, too

Some sales representatives are expected to be marketing managers in their geographic territories. Some may become marketing managers

"You're a salesman—sell *them!*"

Helping to buy is good selling.

by default because their own managers have not provided clear guidelines. In this case, the salesperson must develop his own marketing mix or even his own strategy. He may be given a geographic territory, but it may be unclear exactly who his customers are. He may have to start from scratch in his strategy planning. The only restrictions may be the product line he is expected to sell and probably a price structure. He may have his own choice about (1) who he aims at, (2) which particular products in the line he will push aggressively, (3) which middlemen he will try to work with, (4) how he will spend any promotion money that he controls, and (5) how he will adjust prices within company limits.

A salesperson who can put together profitable strategies and make them work can rise very rapidly. If a strategy will work in his territory, it may work elsewhere. And it is very likely that he will become responsible for larger territories. The opportunity is there for those who are prepared and willing to work.

And even the starting selling job may offer great opportunities. Some beginning sales people—especially those working for manufacturers or wholesalers—are responsible for larger sales volumes than are achieved by average or even large-sized retail stores. This is a responsibility which must be taken seriously and should be planned for.

Further, the sales job is often used as an entry-level position—to find out what a new employee can do. Success in this job can lead to rapid promotion to higher-level sales and marketing jobs and, of course, more money and security.

BASIC SALES TASKS MAY BE SPLIT

One of the difficulties of discussing selling is that every sales job is different. While the engineer or accountant can look forward to fairly specific duties, the salesperson's job is constantly changing.

Selling is divided into three parts

There are three basic sales tasks which a sales representative might have to perform. These tasks are (1) order getting, (2) order taking, and (3) supporting. For convenience, we will describe sales people by these terms—referring to their main task—although one person might have to do all three jobs in some situations.

As the names imply, order getters and order takers are interested in obtaining orders for their companies. In contrast, supporting sales people are not directly interested in orders. Their job is to help the order-oriented sales people. With this variety, you can see that there is a place in personal selling for almost everyone.

Order getters develop new business

Order getters are concerned with developing new business. **Order getting** means aggressively seeking out possible buyers with a well-organized sales presentation designed to sell a product, service, or idea.

Order-getting sales people work for manufacturers, wholesalers, and retailers. They normally are well paid—many earning more than $25,000 per year.

Manufacturers' order getters—find new opportunities

Manufacturers of all kinds of goods—but especially industrial goods—have a great need for order getters. They are needed to locate new prospects, open new accounts, see new opportunities, and help establish and build channel relationships.

Industrial goods order getters need the "know-how" to help solve their customers' problems. To be sure of technically competent order getters, producers often give special training to business-trained college graduates. Such sales people are a real help to their customers. In fact, they may be more technically able—in their narrow specialty—than anyone in the customer's firm, and can provide a unique service.

Wholesalers' order getters—hand it to the customer, almost

Progressive wholesalers are developing into counselors and store advisors—rather than just order takers. Such order getters are almost "partners" of retailers in the job of moving goods from the wholesale warehouse

Firms often give special sales training to college graduates.

through the retail store to consumers. These order getters practically become a part of the retailer's staff—helping to check stock, write orders, conduct demonstrations, and plan advertising, special promotions, and other retailing activities.

Retail order getters— visionaries at the storm window

Order getters are necessary for unsought goods and desirable for some shopping goods.

UNSOUGHT GOODS NEED ORDER GETTERS

Convincing customers of the value of products they have not seriously considered takes a high degree of personal sales ability. Order getters have to be able to see how a new product might satisfy needs now being filled by something else. Early order getters for aluminum storm windows and other aluminum and plastic home improvements faced a difficult task— convincing skeptical customers that these materials were not only durable but also would save money and require less maintenance in the long run. Similar problems were faced by early refrigerator sales people in the 1920s and air-conditioning sales people in the 1930s.

Without order getters, many of the products we now accept as part of our standard of living—such as refrigerators and window air-conditioners—might have died in the introductory stage. It is the order getter who sells enough customers to get the web-of-word-of-mouth going. Without sales and profits in the early stages, the product may fail and never be offered again.

THEY HELP SELL SHOPPING GOODS

Order getters are desirable for selling heterogeneous shopping goods. Consumers shop for many of these items on the basis of price and quality. They welcome useful information. Automobiles, furniture and furnishings, cameras and photographic supplies, and fashion items can be sold effectively by an order getter. Helpful advice—based on knowledge of the product and its alternatives—may help consumers make a choice and bring profits to the salesperson and the retailers.

Order takers—keep the business coming

Order takers are concerned with selling the regular or typical customers. Order takers complete most sales transactions. After the customer becomes interested in the products of a specific firm—from an order getter or a supporting salesperson or through advertising or sales promotion— an order taker usually is necessary to answer any final questions and complete the sale. **Order taking** is defined as the routine completion of sales made regularly to the target customers.

Sometimes sales managers or customers will use the term "order taker" as a "put down" when referring to unaggressive sales people. While a particular salesperson may perform so poorly that criticism of him is justified, it is a mistake to downgrade the function of order taking. Order taking is extremely important—whether handled by human hands or machines.

Order takers have to be energetic, persistent, and friendly to make their many calls.

Manufacturers' order takers—train and explain

After order getters open up industrial, wholesale, or retail accounts, regular follow-up is necessary. Someone has to explain details, make adjustments, handle complaints, and keep customers informed about new developments. The customers' employees may need training to use machines or products. In sales to middlemen, it may be necessary to train the wholesalers' or retailers' sales people. These activities are part of the order taker's job.

Usually these sales people have a regular route with many calls. To handle these calls well, they must have physical energy, persistence, enthusiasm, and a friendly personality.

Sometimes jobs that are basically order taking are used to train potential order getters and managers—since they may offer some order-getting possibilities. This can be seen in the following description of his job by a young Colgate salesman—who moved rapidly into the ranks of sales management.

Over many months, I worked carefully with Gromer's Super Market. It was an aggressive young store. After a few calls, I felt I had built up a warm friendship with the store personnel. They came to trust me and, more frequently than not, after I straightened shelves, checked out-of-stocks, and did the usual dusting and rearranging, I gave them an order blank already filled in.

It got to be a joke with big, husky Paul Gromer, the owner, and his hard-working manager-brother. They kept asking, "Well, what did we buy today?" and they signed the order book without checking.

Naturally, I worked at the order like it was my own business, making certain that they were never stuck with dead stock or over-orders. They were making continual progress, though nothing sensational.

Finally, Colgate came out with a good deal. I knew it was right for Gromer's and I thought the store ought to double its weekly order to 400 cases. I talked to Paul Gromer about it and, without any reason that I'm able to think of today, I said, "Paul, this is a hot deal and I think you're ready for a carload order."

He looked at me for just a moment. I braced myself for an argument. Then he said, "Sure, why not? You've always been right before. Just ship it."

It was the biggest order of soap Gromer's had ever taken—and the store soon became a regular carload buyer.[1]

Wholesaler's order takers—not getting orders but keeping them

While manufacturers' order takers handle relatively few items and sometimes even a single item, wholesalers' order takers may handle 125,000 items or more. Most of these order takers just sell out of their catalog. They have so many items that they can't possibly give aggressive sales effort to many—except perhaps the newer or more profitable items. The strength of this type of order taker is his wide assortment rather than detailed knowledge of individual products.

The wholesale order taker's main function is to keep in close contact with his customers—perhaps once a week—and fill any needs that have developed. Some retailers let him take inventory and write up his own order. Obviously, this position of trust can't be abused. After writing up the order, the order taker normally checks to be sure his company fills the order promptly and accurately. He also handles any adjustments or complaints, and generally acts as a link between his company and customers.

Such sales people are usually of the low-pressure type, friendly and easy going. Usually these jobs are not as high paying as the order-getting ones, but are attractive to many because they aren't as demanding. Relatively little traveling is required. And there is little or no pressure to develop new accounts.

Retail order takers— often they are poor sales clerks

Order taking may be almost mechanical at the retail level—say at the supermarket checkout counter. Sometimes, retail clerks seem to be annoyed by having to complete sales. This is too bad because order taking is important. They may be poor order takers, however, because they are not paid very well—often at the minimum wage. But they may be paid little because they do little. In any case, order taking at the retail level appears to be declining in quality. Probably there will be far fewer such jobs in the future as more and more marketers turn to self-service selling.

Supporting sales force—informs and promotes in the channel

Supporting sales people help the order-oriented sales people—but don't try to get orders themselves. Their activities are directed toward obtaining sales in the long run. For the short run, however, they are ambassadors of goodwill who provide specialized services. Almost all supporting sales people work for manufacturers or middlemen who do this supporting work for manufacturers. There are two types of supporting sales people: missionary sales people and technical specialists.

Missionary sales people develop goodwill and stimulate demand.

MISSIONARY SALES PEOPLE

Missionary sales people are employed by a manufacturer to work with its middlemen and their customers. The usual purposes are to develop goodwill and stimulate demand, help the middlemen train their sales people, and often take orders for delivery by the middlemen.

Missionary sales people are sometimes called *merchandisers* or *detailers*.[2] They may be absolutely vital if a manufacturer uses the typical merchant wholesalers to obtain widespread distribution—but knows that the retailers will need promotion help which won't come from the merchant wholesalers. Merchandisers or detailers may be able to give an occasional "shot in the arm" to the company's regular wholesalers and retailers. Or, they may work regularly with these middlemen, setting up displays, arranging promotions, and, in general, supplying what the company's sales promotion specialists have developed.

TECHNICAL SPECIALISTS

Technical specialists provide technical assistance to order-oriented sales people. They are usually scientists or engineers who have little interest in sales. Instead, they have technical know-how—plus the ability to explain the advantages of the company's product. Since they usually talk to the customer's technical people, there is little need for much sales ability. Before the specialist's visit, an order getter probably has stimulated interest. The technical specialist provides the details. Some of these technical specialists eventually become fine order getters. But most are more

"Den you put dis 'ting here an' dat 'ting dere an' . . . EUREKA!"

(Most technical specialists are more interested in proving technical excellence than in getting sales.)

interested in proving the technical excellence of their product than in actual sales work.

Most selling requires a blend of all three sales tasks

We have described three sales tasks—order getting, order taking, and supporting. Remember, however, that a particular salesperson might have to do any or all of these jobs. Ten percent of a particular job may be order getting, 80 percent order taking, and the additional 10 percent supporting.

The kind of person needed for a given sales position—and the level of compensation—will depend largely on which sales tasks are required and in what combination. This is why job descriptions are so important.

JOB DESCRIPTIONS ARE NEEDED

A **job description** shows what a salesperson is expected to do. It might list 10 to 20 specific tasks as well as the routine prospecting and sales report writing. Each company must write its own job specifications—but when they are written, they should provide clear guidelines to what kind of sales people should be selected and how they should be motivated. These strategic matters are discussed later in the chapter.

NATURE OF THE PERSONAL SELLING JOB

Good sales people are taught, not born

The idea that good sales people are born has some truth in it, but it is far from the whole story. Experiments have shown that it is possible to train any alert person to be a good salesperson. This training includes

Figure 14–2
Personal selling is a communication process

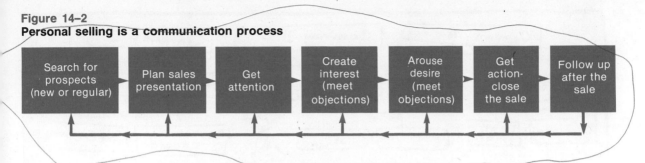

basic steps which each salesperson should follow. These include: prospecting, planning sales presentations, making sales presentations, and following up after the sale. See Figure 14–2 for a diagram which shows that a personal salesperson is just carrying out the communications process discussed in the last chapter.

While these basic steps may seem logical, managers don't always follow them. New sales people often are hired and sent out on the road or retail selling floor with no training in the basic steps and no information about the product or the customer—just a price list and a pat on the back. This isn't enough!

It is up to sales and marketing management to be sure that the sales people know what they are supposed to do and how to do it.

Finding prospects—the big buyer who wasn't there

Finding "live" prospects is not as easy as it sounds. Although the marketing strategy should specify the target market, we have already seen that some people within a target market may be very interested in change, while others are late adopters.

Basically, **prospecting** involves following down all the "leads" in the target market. But which ones are currently "live" and will help make the buying decision? In the industrial goods area, for example about two thirds of industrial calls are made on the wrong person because of multiple buying influences and the fact that companies often change their organizational structures and buying responsibilities. This means that constant and detailed customer analysis is needed. This requires lots of personal calls and telephone calls.

HOW LONG TO SPEND WITH WHOM?

Another part of prospecting is deciding how much time to spend developing each prospect. Here, the potential sales volume as well as the probability of actually making a sale must be considered. This obviously requires judgment. But well-organized sales people usually develop some system to guide prospecting—because most of them have too many potential customers. They can't afford to "wine and dine" all of them. Some prospects deserve only a phone call—taking them to lunch would be a waste of the salesperson's time. There are only a few hours in each business day for personal sales calls. This time must be used carefully if the salesper-

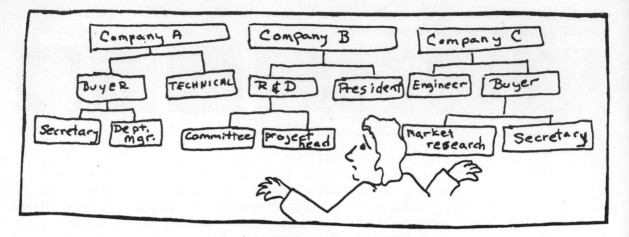

Careful customer analysis is needed to find the best prospects.

son is to succeed. So it is clear that effective prospecting is important to success. In fact, it may be more important than making a good sales presentation—especially if the company's marketing mix is basically strong.

Three kinds of sales presentations may be useful

Once a promising prospect has been found, it is necessary to make a **sales presentation**—a salesperson's effort to make a sale. Someone has to plan what kind of sales presentation is to be made. This is a strategic matter. The kind of presentation should be set *before* the salesperson is sent prospecting. Or, in situations where the customer comes to the salesperson—for example, in a retail store—the planners have to make sure that prospects are brought together with sales people. Then, the planned sales presentation must be made.

The marketing manager can choose among three basically different sales presentations: the black box approach, the selling formula approach, and the need-satisfaction approach. Each of these has its place.

The black box approach

The **black box approach** uses a "canned" or prepared sales presentation—building on the black box (stimulus-response) model discussed in Chapter 5. This model says that a customer faced with a particular stimulus will give the desired response—say, a "yes" answer to the salesperson's request for an order.

The use of these prepared sales presentations is shown in Figure 14–3. Basically, the salesperson does most of the talking—see the shaded area in Figure 14–3—only occasionally letting the customer talk when the salesperson attempts to close. If one closing attempt does not work, he goes on until he makes another try at closing. This procedure can go on until either the salesperson runs out of material or the customer buys or decides to leave.

"Would you like to try it on?"

This approach can be effective and practical when the possible sale is low in value and the time that can be spent on selling is short. This is true, for example, for many convenience goods in food stores, drug stores, and department stores. The presentation might be as simple as: "That's very nice, should I wrap it up?" or "Would you like to try it on?" or "Would you like a carton instead of a package?" or "Should I fill'er up?"

The black box approach treats all potential customers the same. It may work for some and not for others—and the sales people probably won't know why. They don't improve their performance as a result of this experience, because they are just mechanically trying a standardized presentation. This method can be suitable for simple order taking. It is no longer considered good selling for complicated situations.

Selling formula approach

The **selling formula approach** uses a prepared outline—also building on the black box (stimulus-response) model—taking the customers through some logical steps to a final close. The steps are logical because we assume that we know something about the target customers' needs and attitudes.

The selling formula approach is illustrated in Figure 14–4. A salesperson does most of the talking at the beginning of the presentation, because he knows exactly what he wants to say—it even may have been prepared as part of the marketing strategy. Then he brings the customer into the discussion to see what special needs this customer has. Next, the salesperson tries to show how his product satisfies those needs. Finally, he goes on to close the sale.

This approach can be useful for both order-getting and order-taking situations—where potential customers are similar and relatively untrained sales people must be used. This is a little like using mass selling—where only one general presentation must be tailored to a large audience—only here several preplanned presentations are possible. Some of the office

Figure 14–3
Black box approach to sales presentations[3]

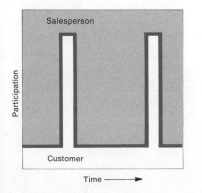

Figure 14–4
Selling formula approach to sales presentations[4]

Figure 14–5
Need-satisfaction approach to sales presentations[5]

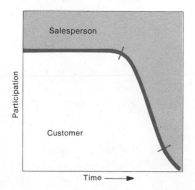

"What exactly are you looking for in a car?"

(The needs satisfaction approach tries to find the customer's real needs.)

equipment and computer manufacturers, for example, have used this approach. They know the kinds of situations that their sales people will meet and roughly what they want them to say. Using the selling formula approach speeds the training process and makes the sales force productive sooner.

Need-satisfaction approach

The **need-satisfaction approach** involves developing a good understanding of the prospective customer's needs before trying to close the sale. Here, the salesperson leads the customer to do most of the talking at first—to help the salesperson pinpoint the customer's needs. See Figure 14–5. When he feels that he understands the customer's needs, the sales rep begins to do more in the sales presentation—trying to help the customer understand his own needs better. Once they agree, the seller tries to show how his product fills the customer's special needs and then close the sale.

The need-satisfaction approach can be useful if there are many differences among the various customers in a target market. The salesperson has to discover which of the many potentially relevant dimensions describe a particular person—and then to help that customer understand what his needs are. This kind of sales presentation obviously takes more skill and also more time. This approach is more practical when the sale is large.

With this approach, the salesperson is much more on his own. He should have a good understanding of the company's products and policies. Some knowledge of the behavioral science theories we have discussed would also be useful—especially a good understanding of the "hierarchy of needs."

Using AIDA to plan sales presentations

AIDA—Attention, Interest, Desire, Action. Each presentation—except some simple black box types—follows this AIDA sequence. The "how-to-do-it" might even be spelled out as part of the marketing strategy.

Attention   Interest   Desire   Action

The time spent with each of the steps might vary depending on the situation and the selling approach being applied. But it is still necessary to begin a presentation by getting the prospect's attention and, hopefully, moving him to action at the close. The ways in which these steps might work are discussed in the following paragraphs.

ATTENTION

There is no sure way to get a prospect's attention. Much depends on the salesperson's instincts and originality—as well as knowledge of his customers. If a salesperson calls on the same people frequently, he will want to use a new approach each time. If each call is on a new prospect, a few successful attention getters will do.

At the first stage of a meeting with a customer, the salesperson's main purpose is to distract the potential customer from his current thoughts and begin a conversation. The seller might do this by just introducing himself or saying, "Hello, can I help you?" as a retail clerk might. Or a statement about the plans of the prospect's competitors might get attention.

Whatever method is used, the attention getter should be casual, so that the presentation can move quickly, naturally, and logically into the next step—creating interest.

INTEREST

Creating interest takes more time. The best way is to look for the prospect's basic needs or problems—especially those which the salesperson might be able to solve. A furniture store sales clerk should not make a prepared speech about rugs every time a customer comes in—some might want lamps, chairs, and so on. Getting the customer to talk helps the salesperson get the all-important feedback which guides further effort. Of course, the sales rep should understand his target market. By choosing prospects from this group, he can know roughly what they want and have a marketing mix that has been designed specifically for them.

DESIRE

Arousing desire requires an even more persuasive effort. At this stage, the salesperson definitely has to determine exactly what the prospect's specific needs are. This lets the seller show how his product fits the needs, answer objections, and prepare to close the sale. This feedback is vital to the sales presentation and is an important "plus" of personal selling.

ACTION

Finally, the salesperson will try to summarize the important points, suiting arguments to the customer's needs and attitudes, and try to close the sale—i.e., affect the prospect's behavior. It is interesting to note that one of the most frequent reasons for losing a sale is that the salesperson *never asks for the order!* Perhaps this is because he's afraid that a direct request for the order is too easily answered with a "no."

The experienced salesperson knows how to avoid this awful word. Without asking for a direct "yes" or "no," he may just assume that "of course" the customer will buy. He may begin to write up the order or ask which of various delivery dates would be better. He may ask what quantity the customer would like to try in a new display. This may lead the customer into taking action without consciously having to make a direct decision—a difficult step for some people.

SALES MANAGEMENT MUST BE PLANNED, TOO

Marketing strategy planning must include some guidelines about how the personal selling job will be carried out—including how the jobs of selecting and motivating sales people will be handled.

Besides helping the marketing manager set these guidelines, the sales manager must (1) organize and train a sales force, (2) assign territories, (3) set quotas, and (4) evaluate and control the whole process. We can't cover all the details of sales management here, but it is important to see that they are done within the guidelines set by the marketing strategy. The more that is known about the needs and attitudes of the target market, the easier it will be for the sales manager to set his own plan.

Selecting good sales people takes judgment, plus

It is very important to obtain good, competent sales people. A careful job description—related to the whole marketing strategy—should be the basis for choosing a sales force.

Unfortunately, the selection of sales people in most companies is a hit-or-miss affair. They are often hired without any job description or serious thought about exactly what kind of person is needed. This approach has led to poor sales and high personnel turnover for many companies.

Progressive companies have tried to use more scientific procedures in hiring—including interviews with various managers and psychological tests. Unfortunately, these techniques do not guarantee success. But experiments have shown that using *some* kind of selection method brings in better people than using no selection aids at all.

Compensating and motivating

While it is true that public recognition, sales contests, or just personal recognition for a job well done may be effective in stimulating greater sales effort, most companies also use cash incentives to encourage sales people. Let's take a look at some ways this can be done.

Two basic decisions must be made in developing a compensation plan: (1) the level of compensation and (2) the method of payment.

LEVEL OF COMPENSATION

To attract and keep good people, most companies must at least pay the going market level for the different kinds of sales people. Order getters are paid more than order takers, for example.

The job description explains the salesperson's role in the marketing mix. It should show whether any special skills or responsibilities are required—perhaps suggesting higher pay levels. To make sure that it can afford a given type of salesperson, the company should estimate—at the time this description is being written—how valuable such a salesperson will be. A good order getter might be worth over $50,000 a year to one company, but only $5,000 to another—simply because the second one doesn't have enough to sell. In such a case, the second company will have to rethink its job specification or completely change its promotion plans, because the "going rate" for good order getters is much higher than $5,000 a year.

"I'll give you 2¢ for everyone you send here."

(Order getters can be expensive.)

If a job will require a lot of traveling, aggressive pioneering, or contacts with difficult customers, the pay may have to be increased. The salespersons' compensation level should compare at least roughly with the pay scale of the rest of the firm. They are normally paid more than the office or production force, but usually less than the managers who supervise them.

METHOD OF PAYMENT

Once the general level of compensation has been determined, then the method of payment must be set. There are three basic methods of payment: (1) straight salary, (2) straight commission, or (3) a combination plan.

Straight salary supplies the most security for the salesperson, and straight commission, the most incentive. Most companies want to offer some balance between incentive and security. Therefore, the most popular method of payment is a combination plan—which includes some salary and some commission. Bonuses and other goal-directed incentives are becoming more popular, too. Pensions, insurance, and other fringe benefits may be included, but salary and/or commission are basic to most combinations plans.

A sales manager's control over a sales rep depends on the compensation plan. The straight salary plan permits the greatest amount of supervision. The person on commission tends to be his own boss.

The marketing manager should probably try to avoid very complicated compensation plans or plans that change frequently. Complicated plans are hard for sales people to understand—and costly for the accounting department to handle. Also, low morale may result if sales people can't see a direct relationship between their effort and their income.

Simplicity is probably best achieved with straight commission. But, in practice, it is usually better to give up some simplicity to have some control over sales people—while still providing flexibility and incentive.[6]

Sales management must work with marketing management

There are, unfortunately, no easy answers to the compensation problem. It is up to the sales manager—working with the marketing manager—to develop a good compensation plan. The sales manager's efforts have to be part of the whole marketing plan, because he can't accomplish his goals if enough funds aren't included for this job.

It is the marketing manager's job to balance the promotion blend. The expected cost and performance of the sales force are only two things he must consider. To make these judgments, the marketing manager must know what kind of sales force is needed, what its goals should be, and how much it will cost.

When the marketing manager has OK'd the sales manager's basic plan and budget, the sales manager must carry out the plan. This includes directing and controlling the sales force, determining and assigning sales territories, and evaluating performance. You can see that a sales manager is really concerned with the basic management tasks of planning and control—as well as implementing the personal selling effort.

Conclusion

In this chapter, we have discussed the importance and nature of personal selling. Selling is much more than just "getting rid of the product." In fact, a salesperson who is not provided with strategic guidelines may have to become his own strategic planner. Ideally, however, the sales manager and marketing manager should work together to decide some strategic matters: the number and kind of salespersons needed, the kind of sales presentations, and salesperson selection and motivation approaches.

Three basic kinds of sales tasks were described: (1) order getting, (2) order taking, and (3) supporting. Most sales jobs are a combination of at least two of these three tasks. The level and method of compensation depend, in large part, on the blend of these tasks. A job description should be developed for each sales job. This provides the guidelines for selecting and compensating sales people.

Three kinds of sales presentations were discussed. Each has its place, but the need-satisfaction approach seems best for higher-level sales jobs. It is in these kinds of jobs that personal selling is achieving a new, professional status—because of the ability and amount of personal responsibility needed by the salesperson. The grinning glad-hander is being replaced by the specialist who is creative, hard-working, persuasive, highly trained, and therefore able to help the buyer. This type of salesperson probably will always be in short supply. Now, the demand for such high-caliber sales people is growing.

Questions for discussion

1 Identify the strategic planning decisions needed in the personal selling area and explain why they should be treated as strategic decisions to be made by the marketing manager.

2 What kind of salesperson (or what blend of the basic sales tasks) is required to sell the following products? If there are several selling jobs in the channel for each product, then indicate the kinds of sales people required. (Specify any assumptions necessary to give definite answers.)
a. Soya bean oil.
b. Costume jewelry.
c. Nuts and bolts.
d. Handkerchiefs.
e. Mattresses.
f. Corn.
g. Cigarettes.

3 Distinguish among the jobs of manufacturers', wholesalers', and retailers' order-getting sales people. If one order getter is needed, must all the sales people in a channel be order getters? Illustrate.

4 Discuss the role of the manufacturers' agent in the marketing manager's promotion plans. What kind of salesperson is he?

5 Discuss the future of the specialty shop if manufacturers place greater emphasis on mass selling because of the inadequacy of retail order taking.

6 Explain the sequential nature of the personal selling job.

7 Cite an actual local example of each of the three kinds of sales presentations discussed in the chapter. Explain for each situation whether a different type of presentation would have been better.

8 Describe a need-satisfaction sales presentation which you have experienced recently and explain how it might have been improved by fuller use of the AIDA framework.

9 Explain how a straight commission system might provide flexibility in the sale of a line of women's clothing products which continually vary in profitability.

10 Explain how a compensation system could be developed to provide incentives for older sales people and yet make some provision for trainees who have not yet learned their job.

11 Describe the operation of our economy if personal sales people were outlawed. Could the economy work? If so, how; if not, what is the minimum personal selling effort necessary? Could this minimum personal selling effort be controlled effectively by law?

Suggested cases

19 Cabco Corporation
20 Bishop Furniture Company
27 The Ross Tool Company

When you finish this chapter, you should:

1 Understand when the various kinds of advertising are needed.
2 Understand how to go about choosing the "best" medium.
3 Understand how to plan the "best" message—i.e., the copy thrust.
5 Understand what advertising agencies do and how they are paid.
5 Understand how to advertise legally.
6 Recognize the important new terms shown in red.

MASS SELLING

To reach a lot of people quickly and cheaply, mass selling may be the answer.

Mass selling makes widespread distribution easier. Although a marketing manager might prefer to use only personal selling, it is very expensive. Mass selling can be much cheaper. It is not as flexible as personal selling, but it can reach large numbers of potential customers at the same time. Today, most promotion blends contain both personal selling and mass selling.

Marketing managers have strategic decisions to make about mass selling. Working with advertising managers, they must decide: (1) who is the target, (2) what kind of advertising to use, (3) how customers are to be reached (through which types of media), (4) what is to be said to them (the copy thrust), and (5) by whom (i.e., the firm's own advertising department or outside advertising agencies. (See Figure 15–1).

THE IMPORTANCE OF ADVERTISING

$50 billion in ads by 1980
Advertising can get results in a promotion blend. Good results are obtained at a cost, of course. The amount spent in the United States for advertising has been growing continuously since World War II. And more growth is expected. In 1946, it was slightly more than $3 billion. By 1977, it topped $37 billion. And by 1980 the total annual advertising expenditure may be $50 billion.

Figure 15–1
Strategy planning for advertising

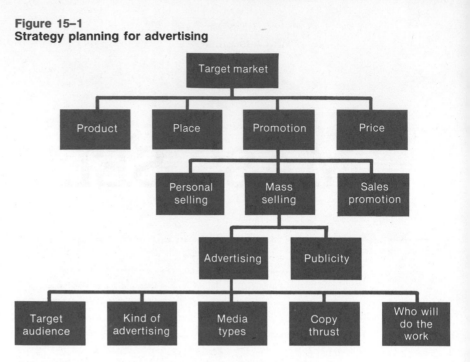

It's all done by less than half a million people

While total advertising expenditures are large, the advertising industry itself employs relatively few people. The major expense is for media time and space. And in the United States, the largest share of this—30 percent—goes for newspaper space. Television takes about 20 percent of the total. Direct mail takes about 14 percent.[1]

Fewer than 500,000 people work directly in the U.S. advertising industry. This includes all people who help create or sell advertising for advertising media (such as radio and television stations, newspapers, and magazines), those in advertising agencies, and those working on advertising for retailers, wholesalers, and manufacturers. The sometimes glamorous and often criticized 4,800 U.S. ad agencies employ only 200,000 persons. Most of these agencies are small—employing fewer than ten persons. Many of these agencies are located in New York and Chicago.[2]

Advertisers aren't really spending that much

U.S. corporations spend only about 1.5 percent of their sales dollar on advertising. This is relatively small compared to the total cost of marketing—which is about 50 percent of the consumer's dollar.

Some spend more than others

Some industries spend a much larger percentage of sales for advertising than the average of 1.5 percent. One study showed that soap and related products manufacturers spent 14.2 percent; drug manufacturers, 11.05 percent; and tobacco manufacturers, 6.06 percent. At the other extreme, coal mining companies spent only 0.09 percent; construction companies,

0.10 percent; men's and boys' clothing, 0.11 percent; and wholesalers and retailers in total, 1.05 percent.[3]

You can see that advertising is important in certain markets—especially the consumer goods markets. But remember that—in total—it costs much less than personal selling.

ADVERTISING TASKS ARE SET BY MARKETING STRATEGY

Every advertisement and every advertising campaign should have clearly defined objectives. These should flow from the overall marketing strategy and the job assigned to advertising. But it is not enough for the marketing manager to just say, "Promote the product."

If you want half the market, say so!

A marketing manager should spell out exactly what is wanted. A general objective: "To assist in the expansion of market share," could be stated more specifically: "To increase traffic in our cooperating retail outlets by 25 percent during the next three months."

Such specific objectives would obviously affect promotion methods. Advertising that might be right for building a good image among opinion leaders might be all wrong for getting customers into the retailers' stores.

Advertising objectives should be very specific—much more so than personal selling objectives. One of the advantages of personal selling is that the sales people can change their presentations to meet customers'

"Gee, sir, I know we asked for specific advertising objectives, but I think your getting elected president within 30 days is more than we can handle."

needs. Each advertisement, however, is a specific communication that must be effective—not just for one customer—but for thousands or millions of target customers. This means that definite objectives should be set for each advertisement—as well as a whole advertising campaign. If this isn't done, a "creative" advertising staff may just set some general objective like "selling the product." Then it will plan ads that will win artistic awards within the advertising industry—but may fail to do the advertising job management expected.

OBJECTIVES DETERMINE THE KINDS OF ADVERTISING NEEDED

The advertising objectives will determine which of two basic types of advertising to use—product or institutional.

Product advertising tries to sell a product. It may be aimed at final users or channel members.

Institutional advertising tries to develop goodwill for a company or even an industry, instead of a specific product.

Product advertising— meet us, like us, remember us

PIONEERING ADVERTISING—BUILDS PRIMARY DEMAND

Pioneering advertising tries to develop **primary demand**—demand for a product type rather than a specific brand. Its basic job is to inform—not persuade. It is needed in the early stages of the adoption process—to inform potential customers about a new product. It is also needed in the introductory stage of the product life cycle.

Pioneering advertising doesn't have to mention a brand or specific company at all. The California olive industry promoted olives as olives—not certain brands. This was so successful that after only five years of promotion, the industry's surpluses became shortages. Then it shifted promotion funds to product research—to increase production.

COMPETITIVE ADVERTISING—EMPHASIZES SELECTIVE DEMAND

Competitive advertising tries to develop **selective demand**—demand for a specific brand rather than a product category. A firm can be forced into competitive advertising—as the product life cycle moves along—to hold its own against competitors. The United Fruit Company gave up a 20-year pioneering effort to promote bananas in favor of advertising its own "Chiquita" brand. The reason was simple. While United Fruit was promoting "bananas," it slowly lost market share to competitors. The competitive advertising campaign tried to stop these losses.

Competitive advertising may be either direct or indirect The **direct type** aims for immediate buying action. The **indirect type** points out product advantages—to affect future buying decisions.

Airline advertising uses both types of competitive advertising. Direct-action ads use prices, timetables, and phone numbers to call for reservations. Indirect-action ads suggest that you mention the airline name when talking to your travel agent.

While this side is showing your favorite Monday night 9 o'clock show, this side is videotaping your other favorite Monday night 9 o'clock show.

We've all been in the situation where there are two TV programs on opposite each other and we'd give anything to be able to see both of them.

Well, now you can see both of them.

Sony's revolutionary new Betamax can actually videotape something off one channel while you're watching another channel.

Then, whenever you're ready, all you do is push a

ACTUAL CLOSED-CIRCUIT PICTURE

button and presto! You see what you just missed.

Let's take another situation.

It's the one night a year you have dinner at your in-laws' and there's something on TV you'd give your right arm to see.

Well, believe it or not, Sony's Betamax has an automatic timer that you can set to actually tape up to one hour while you're not there.

When you come home, just press that magic button again—and you can see what went on at 9 o'clock at 12 o'clock.

Of course, the tapes are reusable—just record over them, and use them over and over again. Also, there are a number of pre-recorded telecourses available from Time-Life Video.

Best of all, everything you see on Betamax you see on our 19" (diagonal) Trinitron® screen—the same sharp, crisp color that everyone marvels at on our smaller sets.

Sony's revolutionary new Betamax. Now you can have your cake and eat it, too.

INTRODUCING BETAMAX®

"IT'S A SONY."

Comparative advertising is even rougher. **Comparative advertising** means making specific brand comparisons—using actual product names. Although the Federal Trade Commission has encouraged this kind of advertising, some ad agencies are backing away from it. They feel this approach has raised legal as well as ethical problems. Research is supposed to support superiority claims, but the rules aren't clear. Some firms just keep running small tests until they get the results they want. Others focus on minor differences that do not reflect the overall benefits of a product. This may make consumers less—rather than more—informed. Some comparative ads leave consumers confused—or even angry if the product they are using has been criticized. And, in at least one instance, comparative ads seem to have helped the competitive product (Tylenol) more than the advertisers' products (Datril, Anacin, and Bayer aspirin).[4]

Many advertisers don't like comparative advertising. But it is likely that the approach will be continued by some advertisers and encouraged by the government as long as the ad copy is not obviously false.[5]

REMINDER ADVERTISING—REINFORCES EARLY PROMOTION

Reminder advertising tries to keep the product's name before the public. The advertiser may use "soft-sell" ads that just mention the name—as a reminder. Much Coca-Cola advertising has been of this type. Reminder advertising may be useful when the product has achieved brand preference or insistence—perhaps in the market maturity or sales decline stages of the product life cycle.

Institutional advertising—remember our name in Dallas, Seattle, Boston

Institutional advertising emphasizes the name and prestige of a company or industry. It tries to inform, persuade, or remind. General Motors Corp., for example, does institutional advertising of the GM name—emphasizing the quality and research behind all GM products. These are often keyed to GM's "Mark of Excellence." See Figure 15–2.

Sometimes an advertising campaign may have both product and institutional aspects because the federal government has limited tax deductions on institutional advertising. Defense contractors are specifically prevented from including advertising expenditures as a cost of doing business with the government.[6]

COOPERATIVE ADVERTISING MAY BUY MORE

Vertical cooperation—advertising allowances, cooperative advertising

The discussion above might suggest that only producers do advertising. This isn't true, of course. But producers can affect the advertising done by others. Sometimes a manufacturer knows what he wants advertising to do, but finds that it can be done better or cheaper by someone further along in the channel. In this case, he may offer **advertising allowances**—price reductions to firms further along in the channel to encourage them to advertise or otherwise promote goods locally.

In fact, Ban Roll-On is more effective at stopping wetness than all leading aerosols.

Figure 15–2
An example of institutional advertising

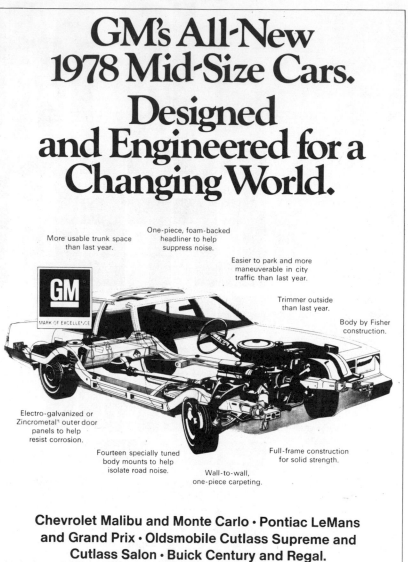

GM's All-New 1978 Mid-Size Cars. Designed and Engineered for a Changing World.

More usable trunk space than last year.

One-piece, foam-backed headliner to help suppress noise.

Easier to park and more maneuverable in city traffic than last year.

Trimmer outside than last year.

Body by Fisher construction.

GM
MARK OF EXCELLENCE

Electro-galvanized or Zincrometal® outer door panels to help resist corrosion.

Fourteen specially tuned body mounts to help isolate road noise.

Wall-to-wall, one-piece carpeting.

Full-frame construction for solid strength.

Chevrolet Malibu and Monte Carlo • Pontiac LeMans and Grand Prix • Oldsmobile Cutlass Supreme and Cutlass Salon • Buick Century and Regal.

COOPERATIVE ADVERTISING MAY GET MORE COOPERATION

Cooperative advertising involves middlemen and producers sharing in the cost of ads.

It helps a manufacturer get more promotion for the advertising dollar. Media rate structures usually give local advertisers lower rates than national firms. Also, a retailer is more likely to follow through when he is paying part of the cost.

Cooperative advertising and advertising allowances can be abused. Allowances can be given to retailers without really expecting that they will be used for ad purposes. This may become a hidden price cut—and even price discrimination. The Federal Trade Commission has become more interested in this problem. Some manufacturers have pulled back from cooperative advertising. To avoid legal problems, wise producers insist on proof of use from retailers.

CHOOSING THE "BEST" MEDIUM—HOW TO DELIVER THE MESSAGE

For effective promotion, ads have to reach specific target customers. Unfortunately, not all potential customers read all newspapers or magazines—or listen to every radio and television program. So not all media are equally effective.

There is no simple answer to the question: What is the best medium? Effectiveness depends on how well it fits with the rest of a particular marketing strategy. It depends on (1) your promotion objectives, (2) your target markets, (3) the funds available for advertising, and (4) the nature of the media—including life of message, visual possibilities, and cost.

Specify promotion objectives

Before a firm can choose the best medium, it must decide on its promotion objectives. They can affect which media are practical. For example, if the objective is to inform—telling a long story with a lot of detail and pictures—then magazines or newspapers may be best. Jockey switched its annual budget of more than $1 million from TV to magazines when it decided to show the variety of colors, patterns, and styles that Jockey briefs offer. They felt that it was too hard to show this in a 30-second TV spot. Jockey ads were run in men's magazines such as *Sports Illustrated, Outdoor Life, Field and Stream, Esquire,* and *Playboy.* But, aware that women buy over 80 percent of men's ordinary underwear and 50 percent of fashion styles, they also placed ads in *TV Guide, New Yorker, People, Money, Time,* and *Newsweek.* And a page of scantily clad males was run in *Cosmopolitan.*[7]

Specify target markets and match with media

To guarantee good media selection, the advertiser must specify its target market—a step necessary for all marketing strategy planning. Then, media can be chosen that will reach these target customers.

Matching target customers and media is the hardest part of effective media selection. It's hard to be sure who sees or hears what. Most of the major media use marketing research to develop profiles of the people who buy their publications or live in their broadcasting area. But they can't be as definite about who actually reads each page or sees or hears each show.

The difficulty of evaluating alternative media has led some media buyers to select media based on the lowest "cost per 1,000 people" figures. This concern with "bodies" can lead to ignoring the target market's dimen-

"I know it has good cost per thousand, but not many *Popular Mechanics* readers are interested in cake decorating kits."

sions and slipping into "mass marketing." The media buyer may look only at the relatively low cost (per 1,000 persons) "mass media" such as national network radio or TV, when a more specialized medium—aimed at the buyer's target market—might be a much better buy.

SPECIALIZED MEDIA HELP ZERO IN ON TARGET MARKETS

Media are now trying to reach smaller, more defined target markets. National media may offer regional editions. *Time* magazine, for example, offers not only several regional editions, but also special editions for college students, educators, doctors, and business managers.

Many magazines serve only special-interest groups, such as fishermen, radio and television enthusiasts, homemakers, religious groups, and professional groups. In fact, the most profitable magazines seem to be the ones aiming at clearly defined markets—while the mass magazines are experiencing difficulties. *Life* and *Look* went out of business, while magazines such as *Playboy, Car Craft, Skiing, Bride's Magazine,* and *Southern Living* have been doing well.

Radio was hit hard at first by TV competition. But now—like some magazines and newspapers—it has become more specialized. Some stations aim at particular nationality, racial, and religious groups (such as Puerto Ricans, blacks, and Catholics) while others feature country, rock, or classical music.

Perhaps the most specific medium is **direct-mail advertising**—selling directly to the customer via his mailbox. The method is to send a specific message to a carefully selected list of names. Some firms specialize in providing mailing lists—ranging in number from hundreds to millions of names. The variety of these lists is shown in Table 15–1 and again shows the importance of knowing the firm's target market.[8]

Table 15–1
Examples of available mailing lists

Quantity of names	Name of list
425	Small Business Advisors
40,000	Social Register of Canada
5,000	Society of American Bacteriologists
500	South Carolina Engineering Society
2,000	South Dakota State Pharmaceutical Association
250	Southern California Academy of Science
12,000	Texas Manufacturing Executives
720	Trailer Coach Association
1,200	United Community Funds of America
50,000	University of Utah Alumni
19,000	Veterinarians

"Must buys" may use up available money

Selecting which media to use is still pretty much an art. The media buyer may start with a budgeted amount and attempt to buy the best blend to reach the target audience. There may be some media that are obvious "must buys"—for example, the only local newspaper for a retailer in a small town. Such "must buys" may use all the available money. If not, then the media buyer must think of the advantages and disadvantages of the possible alternatives.

The buyer might want to select a media blend which combines some "expensive" media—such as TV—with cheaper ones which might reach additional customers.

PLANNING THE "BEST" MESSAGE—WHAT IS TO BE COMMUNICATED

Specifying the copy thrust

Once it has been decided how the messages are to reach the target audience, then it is necessary to decide on the copy thrust. The **copy thrust** is *what* is to be communicated by the written copy and illustrations. This should flow from the promotion objectives and the specific tasks assigned to advertising.

Carrying out the copy thrust is the job of advertising specialists. But the advertising manager and the marketing manager should have an understanding of the process—to be sure that the job is done well.

Let AIDA help guide message planning

There are few tried-and-true rules in message planning. It is clear that the overall marketing strategy should determine *what* should be said in the message. Then management judgment—with the help of marketing research—can decide how this message can be encoded so it will be decoded as intended.

As a guide to message planning, we can make use of the communication process and the AIDA concept: getting Attention, holding Interest, arousing Desire, and obtaining Action.

GETTING ATTENTION

Getting attention is the first job of an advertisement. If this is not done, the whole effort is wasted. Many readers page through magazines or newspapers without paying attention to any of the advertisements. Many listeners or viewers run errands or get snacks during commericals on radio and TV.

There are many ways to catch the customer's attention. A large headline, newsy or shocking statements, pictures of pretty girls, babies, cartoon characters—anything that is "different" or eye catching—may work. But . . . the attention-getting device must not take away from the next step—holding interest.

HOLDING INTEREST

Holding interest is another matter. A pretty girl may get attention. But once you've seen her, then what? A man will pause to appreciate her. Women will evaluate her. But if there is no relation between the girl and the product, observers of both sexes will ignore the ad.

More is known about holding interest than getting attention. The tone and language of the advertisement must fit in with the experience and attitudes of target customers. A food advertisement featuring fox hunters in riding costumes, for example, might not communicate with many potential customers who do not "ride to the hounds."

Further, the advertising layouts should look right to the customer. Print illustrations and copy should be arranged so that the reader's eye is encouraged to move smoothly through the ad.

AROUSING DESIRE

Arousing desire for a particular product is one of the most difficult jobs. It requires that the advertiser communicate effectively with the target customers. This means that the advertiser should understand how these customers think, behave, and make decisions—and then give them a reason to buy.

To be successful, an advertisement must convince customers that the product can meet their needs. Pioneering advertising may be useful to develop primary demand for the whole product class. Later—in the market growth and market maturity stages—competitive advertising can show how a particular brand satisfies particular wants.

OBTAINING ACTION

Getting action is the final requirement. It is not easy. The potential customer should be encouraged to try the product. He should go beyond considering how the product might fit into his life to actually trying it—or letting the company's sales rep come in and show how it works.

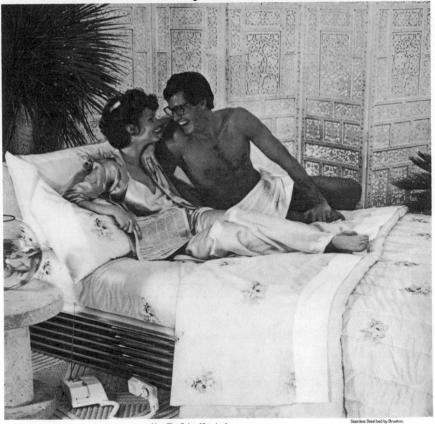

It's one third of your life. Live a little.

Now. The Calvin Klein bed.
Good news! Life is just a bed of roses. Indulge yourself in Wamsutta sheets.
Calvin Klein has designed "Checkered Rose" just for the occasion.
Crisp tattersall combined with a touch of femininity make this the freshest look for a bed today.
The feeling is rich. Because these sheets are a soft no-iron blend of cotton and Fortrel® polyester.
And the quality is distinctly Wamsutta. But then it's to be expected. Over 130 years of crafting bed linens has taught us a thing or two.
Besides, we're involved in one third of your life.
We want it to be sensational. **Wamsutta**
Div. M. Lowenstein & Sons, 111 West 40th St., N.Y.

Stainless Steel bed by Brueton.

Getting attention is the first job of advertising.

Strongly felt customer needs might be featured in the ads—to communicate better. Careful research on the attitudes in the target market may help uncover such strongly felt but unsatisfied needs.

Appealing to these needs can get more action and also provide the kind of information the buyer needs to confirm his decision. Postpurchase doubts may set in after the purchase. So providing reassurance may be one of the important roles of advertising. Some customers seem to read more advertising *after* the purchase than before. What is communicated to them may be very important if satisfied customers are to start or keep the web-of-word-of-mouth going. The ad may reassure them about the correctness of their decision. It may also supply the words they use to tell others about the product.

Glad trash bags help consumers solve an annoying problem—trash bags breaking.

ADVERTISING MANAGER DIRECTS MASS SELLING

An advertising manager manages a company's mass selling effort. Many advertising managers—especially those working for retailers—have their own advertising departments that plan the specific advertising campaigns and carry out the details. Others use advertising agencies.

ADVERTISING AGENCIES OFTEN DO THE WORK

Ad agencies are specialists

Advertising agencies are specialists in planning and handling mass selling details for advertisers. Agencies play a useful role because they are independent of the advertiser and have an outside viewpoint. They bring experience to the individual client's problems because they work for many other clients. Further, as specialists they often can do the job more economically than a company's own department.

Are they paid too much?

The major users of advertising agencies are manufacturers or national middlemen—because of the media rate structure. Normally, media have two prices: one for national advertisers and a lower rate for local advertisers, such as retailers. The advertising agency gets a 15 percent discount only on national rates. This makes it worthwhile for national advertisers to use agencies. The national firm would have to pay the higher media rate, anyway. So it makes sense to let the agency experts do the work—and earn their discount. Local retailers—allowed the lower media rate—seldom use agencies.

There is a growing resistance to the traditional method of paying agencies. The chief complaints are (1) that the agencies receive the flat 15 percent commission, regardless of work performed, and (2) that the commission system makes it hard for the agencies to be completely objective about low-cost media or promotion campaigns that use little space or time.

Not all agencies are satisfied with the present arrangement either. Some would like to charge additional fees—as they see costs rising and advertisers demanding more services.

The fixed commission system is most favored by accounts—such as producers of industrial goods—that need a lot of service but buy relatively little advertising. These are the firms the agencies would like to—and sometimes do—charge additional fees.

The fixed commission system is generally opposed by very large consumer goods advertisers who do much of their own advertising research and planning. They need only basic services from their agencies. Some of these accounts can be very profitable for agencies. Naturally, these agencies would prefer the fixed-commission system.

FIFTEEN PERCENT IS NOT REQUIRED

The Federal Trade Commission worked for many years to change the method of advertising agency compensation. Finally, in 1956, the American Association of Advertising Agencies agreed they would no longer require the 15 percent commission system. This opened the way to discounts and fee increases. Du Pont, for example, recently reported that it was paying agencies an average of 21 percent on billings on industrial products and 14 percent on consumer goods. Other companies report very different arrangements with their agencies, but most seem to take off from the 15 percent base.[9]

MEASURING ADVERTISING EFFECTIVENESS IS NOT EASY

Success depends on the total marketing mix

It would be convenient if we could measure advertising results by a simple analysis of sales. Unfortunately, this isn't possible—although the advertising literature is filled with success stories that "prove" advertising has increased sales. The total marketing mix—not just promotion—is responsible for the sales result. The one exception to this rule is direct-mail advertising. If it doesn't produce immediate results, it is considered a failure.

Research and testing can improve the odds

Ideally, advertisers should test advertising. They shouldn't depend only on the judgment of creative people or advertising "experts."

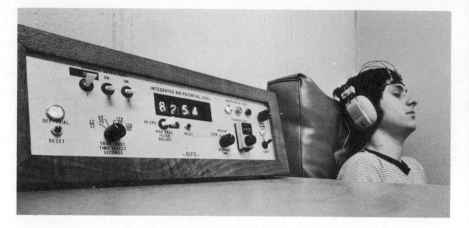

Some advertisers use laboratory tests to evaluate ads.

Some progressive advertisers now demand laboratory or market tests to evaluate the effectiveness of ads. Sometimes, opinion and attitude research is used before ads are run generally. Or researchers may try to evaluate consumers' reactions to particular advertisements with devices which measure skin moisture or eye reaction.

While advertising research techniques are far from foolproof, they are probably much better than depending only on the judgment of advertising "experts." Until better advertising research tools are developed, the present methods seem safest. This means carefully defining specific advertising objectives, choosing media messages to accomplish these objectives, testing plans, and then evaluating the results of actual advertisements.

HOW TO ADVERTISE LEGALLY

FTC is getting tougher about unfair practices

The Federal Trade Commission now has the power to control unfair or deceptive business practices—including "deceptive advertising." Both advertising agencies and advertisers must share equal blame for false, misleading, or unfair ads. The possibility of large fines and/or the need to pay for new ads—to correct past "mistakes"—has caused more agencies and advertisers to stay well within the law.

The FTC may begin to move more aggressively against what it feels may be "unfair" practices. It is considering, for example, whether it is unfair to aim ads at children. The Federal Trade Commission is also concerned about the effective use of energy. An FTC lawyer recently created a stir by criticizing electric hair dryers. His feeling was "that if you wait 15 minutes, your hair gets dry anyway." There is also some question whether food and drug advertising should be controlled to protect "vulnerable" groups such as the aged, poor, non–English-speaking, and less-educated adults. For example, a question was raised as to whether obesity among low-income women might be caused by ads for high-calorie foods.[10]

What is unfair or deceptive is changing

What is unfair and deceptive is a difficult topic—which marketing managers will have to deal with for years. Obviously, the social and political environment has changed. Practices considered acceptable in the past are now questioned or actually considered deceptive.

This is a serious matter. If the FTC decides that a particular practice is unfair or deceptive, it has the power to require **corrective advertising**—ads to correct deceptive advertising—or "affirmative disclosures"—such as the health warnings on cigarettes. Industry groups have made some efforts at self-regulation. But the offenders usually aren't members of such groups. So the need for some government regulation will probably continue.

In the long run, however, the safest way to avoid "unfair" and "deceptive" criticisms will be to stop trying to sell "me-too" products as really new or better offerings. Some advertising agencies are already reluctant to take on such assignments.

Conclusion

It may seem simple to develop a mass selling effort. Simply pick the media and develop a message. It's not that easy. Effectiveness depends upon using the "best" medium and the "best" message, considering: (1) promotion objectives, (2) the target market, and (3) the funds available for advertising.

Specific advertising objectives will determine what kind of advertising to use—product or institutional. If product advertising is needed, then the particular type must be decided—pioneering, competitive (direct or indirect action), or reminder. And advertising allowances and cooperative advertising may be helpful.

There are many technical details involved in mass selling. Specialists—advertising agencies—have evolved to handle some of these tasks. But they need to have specific objectives set for them. Or their advertising may have little direction and be almost impossible to evaluate.

Effective advertising should affect sales. But the whole marketing mix affects sales. The results of advertising cannot be measured by sales changes alone. Advertising is only a part of promotion. And promotion is only a part of the total marketing mix that the marketing manager must develop to satisfy target customers.

Questions for discussion

1 Identify the strategic decisions a marketing manager must make about mass selling.

2 Discuss the relation of advertising objectives to marketing strategy planning and the kinds of advertising actually needed. Illustrate.

3 Present three examples where advertising to middlemen might be necessary. What would be the objective(s) of such moves?

4 What does it mean to say that "money is invested in advertising"? Is all advertising an investment? Illustrate.

5 Find advertisements to final consumers which illustrate the following types of advertising: *(a)* institutional, *(b)* pioneering, *(c)* competitive, *(d)* reminder. What objective(s) does each of these ads have? List the needs utilized in each of these advertisements.

6 Describe the type of media that might be most suitable for promoting: *(a)* tomato soup, *(b)* greeting cards, *(c)* an industrial component material, *(d)* playground equipment. Specify any assumptions necessary to obtain a definite answer.

7 Discuss the use of testimonials in advertising. Which of the four AIDA steps might testimonials accomplish? Would they be suitable for all types of products? If not, for which types would they be most suitable?

8 Find an advertisement that seeks to accomplish all four AIDA steps and explain how you feel this advertisement is accomplishing each of these steps.

9 Discuss the future of independent advertising agencies now that the 15 percent commission system is not required.

10 How would retailing promotion be affected if all local advertising via mass media such as radio, television, and newspapers were prohibited? Would there be any impact on total sales? If so, would it probably affect all goods and stores equally?

11 Is it "unfair" to advertise to children? Is it "unfair" to advertise to less educated or less experienced people of any age? Is it "unfair" to advertise for "unnecessary" products?

Suggested cases

17 Arrow National Bank

18 Sports Sales Company

appendix B

MARKETING ARITHMETIC

When you finish this appendix, you should:

1 Understand the components of an operating statement (profit and loss statement).
2 Know how to compute the stockturn rate.
3 Understand how operating ratios can help analyze a business.
4 Understand how to calculate markups and markdowns.
5 Recognize the important new terms shown in red.

A beginning business student ought to know the basics of the "language of business." Business people commonly use accounting terms when discussing costs, prices, and profit. It is important for you to understand these terms—if the use of accounting data is to be a practical tool in analyzing marketing problems.

The following discussion introduces the operating statement, stockturn rates, operating ratios, markups, and the markdown ratio.

THE OPERATING STATEMENT

An operating statement—commonly referred to as a profit and loss statement—is shown in Figure B–1 for a wholesale or retail business. A complete and detailed statement is shown so you will see the framework during our discussion. But the amount of detail on an operating statement is not fixed. Many companies use a much less detailed statement. They emphasize readability—rather than detail. To really understand an operating statement, however, you must know about its parts.

An **operating statement** is a simple summary of the financial results of the operation of a company over a specified period of time. Some beginning students may feel the operating statement is not simple—but, as we shall see—this isn't true. The main purpose of an operating statement is to determine the net profit figure—and show data to support that figure.

Figure B–1

XYZ COMPANY
Operating Statement
For the Year Ended December 31, 197X

Gross sales			$54,000
Less: Returns and allowances			4,000
Net sales			$50,000
Cost of goods sold			
Beginning inventory at cost		$ 8,000	
Purchases at billed cost	$31,000		
Less: Purchase discounts	4,000		
Purchases at net cost	$27,000		
Plus freight-in	2,000		
Net cost of delivered purchases		29,000	
Cost of goods available for sale		$37,000	
Less: Ending inventory at cost		7,000	
Cost of goods sold			30,000
Gross margin (gross profit)			$20,000
Expenses			
Selling expenses			
Sales salaries	$ 6,000		
Advertising expense	2,000		
Delivery expense	2,000		
Total selling expense		$10,000	
Administrative expense			
Office salaries	$ 3,000		
Office supplies	1,000		
Miscellaneous administrative expense	500		
Total administrative expense		4,500	
General expense			
Rent expense	$ 1,000		
Miscellaneous general expenses	500		
Total general expense		1,500	
Total expenses			16,000
Net profit from operation			$ 4,000

Only three basic components

The basic components of an operating statement are sales—which come from the sale of goods or services; costs—which come from the making and selling process; and the balance (called profit or loss)—which is merely the difference between sales and costs. So there are only three basic components in the statement: *sales, costs,* and *profit.*

Time period covered may vary

There is no one time period which an operating statement covers. Rather, statements are prepared to satisfy the needs of a particular business. This could be at the end of each day or at the end of each week. Usually, however, an operating statement summarizes the results of one month, three months, six months, or a full year. Since this time period does vary with the company preparing the statement, this information is included in the heading of the statement as follows:

XYZ COMPANY
Operating Statement
For the (Period) Ended (Date)

Management uses of operating statements

Before going on to a more detailed discussion of the components of our operating statement, note some of the uses for such a statement. A glance at Figure B–1 shows that a wealth of information is shown in a clear and brief manner. With this information, management can easily figure the relation of its net sales to its cost of goods sold, gross margin, expenses, and net profit. Opening and closing inventory figures are available. So is the amount spent for the purchase of goods for resale. The total expenses are listed to make it easier to compare them with previous statements—to help control these expenses.

All of this information is of vital interest to the management of a company. Assume that a particular company prepared monthly operating statements. By comparing results from one month to the next, management can uncover disappointing trends in the sales, expense, or profit areas of the business—and take the needed action.

A skeleton statement gets down to essential details

Let's refer to Figure B–1 and begin to analyze this seemingly detailed statement. The aim at this point is to get first-hand knowledge of what makes up an operating statement.

As a first step, suppose we take all the items that have dollar amounts extended to the third (right-hand) column. Using these items alone, the operating statement looks like this:

Gross sales	$54,000
Less: Returns and allowances	4,000
Net sales	$50,000
Less: Cost of goods sold	30,000
Gross margin	$20,000
Less: Total expenses	16,000
Net profit (loss)	$ 4,000

Is this a complete operating statement? The answer is yes. The skeleton statement differs from Figure B–1 only in supporting detail. All of the basic components are included. In fact, the only items required to have a complete operating statement are:

Net sales	$50,000
Less: Costs	46,000
Net profit (loss)	$ 4,000

These three items are the heart of an operating statement. All other subdivisions or details are merely helpful additions.

Meaning of "sales"

Now let's define the meaning of the terms that are used in the skeleton statement.

The first item is "sales." What do we mean by sales? The term **gross sales** is the total amount charged to all customers. It is certain, however, that there will be some customer dissatisfaction—or just plain errors in ordering and shipping goods. This results in returns and allowances which reduce gross sales.

A **return** occurs when a customer sends back purchased goods. The company either refunds the purchase price or allows the customer dollar credit on other goods.

An **allowance** occurs when a customer is not satisfied with the purchased goods for some reason. The company gives a price reduction on the original invoice (bill)—but the customer keeps the goods.

These refunds and reductions must be considered when the sales figure for the period is computed. Really, we are only interested in the amount which the company manages to keep. This is **net sales**—the actual sales dollars the company will receive. Therefore, all reductions, refunds, and so forth—made because of returns and allowances—are deducted from the gross sales to get net sales. This is shown below:

Gross sales	$54,000
Less: Returns and allowances	4,000
Net sales	$50,000

Meaning of "cost of goods sold"

The next item in the operating statement—**cost of goods sold**—is the total value (at cost) of all the goods *sold* during the period of the statement. We will discuss its calculation later. Meanwhile, merely note that after the cost of goods sold figure is obtained, it is subtracted from net sales to get the gross margin.

Meaning of "gross margin" and "expenses"

Gross margin (gross profit) is the money left to cover the cost of selling the goods and managing the business—and hopefully, leaving a profit—after subtracting the cost of goods sold.

Selling expense is usually the major expense below the gross margin. Note that in Figure B–1, all **expenses** are subtracted from the gross margin to get the net profit. The expenses in this case are the selling, administrative, and general expenses. (Note that the cost of goods sold is not included in this total expense figure—it was subtracted from net sales earlier to get the gross margin.)

Net profit—at the bottom of the statement—is what the company has earned from its operations during a particular period. It is the amount left after the cost of goods sold and the expenses have been subtracted from net sales.

DETAILED ANALYSIS OF SECTIONS OF THE OPERATING STATEMENT

Cost of goods sold for a wholesale or retail company

The cost of goods sold section includes details which are used to determine the "cost of goods sold" ($30,000 in our example). "Cost of goods sold" means the cost value of goods sold—that is, actually removed from the company's control.

In Figure B–1, it is obvious that beginning and ending inventory, purchases, purchase discounts, and freight-in are all necessary in calculating cost of goods sold. If we take the cost of goods sold section from the operating statement, it appears as follows:

Cost of goods sold
Beginning inventory at cost		$ 8,000
Purchases at billed cost	$31,000	
Less: Purchase discounts	4,000	
Purchases at net cost	$27,000	
Plus: Freight-in	2,000	
Net cost of delivered purchases		29,000
Cost of goods available for sale		$37,000
Less: Ending inventory at cost		7,000
Cost of goods sold		$30,000

The inventory figures merely show the cost of merchandise on hand at the beginning and end of the period the statement covers. These figures may be obtained by an actual count of the merchandise on hand on these dates. Or they may be estimated with inventory records which show the inventory balance at any time.

The net cost of delivered purchases must include freight charges and purchase discounts received. This is because these items affect the cash actually spent to buy the goods and bring them to the place of business. A **purchase discount** is a reduction of the original invoice amount for some business reason. For example, a cash discount can be given for prompt cash payment of the amount due. The total of such discounts is subtracted from the original invoice cost of purchases to find the net cost of purchases. Then we add the freight charges for bringing the goods to the place of business. This gives the net cost of *delivered* purchases. When the net cost of delivered purchases is added to the beginning inventory at cost, we have the total cost of goods available for sale during the period. When we subtract the ending inventory at cost from the cost of the goods available for sale, we finally obtain the cost of goods sold.

Cost of goods sold for a manufacturing company

Figure B–1 shows the way the manager of a wholesale or retail business would arrive at the cost of goods sold. Such a business would buy finished goods and resell them. In a manufacturing firm, the "purchases" section of this operating statement would be replaced by a section called "cost of goods manufactured." This section would include purchases of raw materials and parts, and direct and indirect labor costs. It would also list factory overhead charges (such as heat, light, and power) which are necessary to produce finished goods. The cost of goods manufactured is added to the beginning finished-goods inventory to arrive at the cost of goods available for sale. Frequently, a separate "cost of goods manufactured" statement is prepared, and only the total cost of production is shown in the operating statement. See Figure B–2 for an illustration of the "cost of goods sold" section of an operating statement for a manufacturing company.

Figure B–2
Cost of goods sold section of an operating statement for a manufacturing firm

Cost of goods sold		
Finished goods inventory (beginning)	$ 20,000	
Cost of goods manufactured (Schedule 1)	100,000	
Total cost of finished goods available for sale	$120,000	
Less: Finished goods inventory (ending)	30,000	
Cost of goods sold		$ 90,000

Schedule 1, Schedule of cost of goods manufactured

Beginning work in process inventory			$ 15,000
Raw materials			
Beginning raw materials inventory		$ 10,000	
Net cost of delivered purchases		80,000	
Total cost of materials available for use		$ 90,000	
Less: Ending raw materials inventory		15,000	
Cost of materials placed in production		$ 75,000	
Direct labor		20,000	
Manufacturing expenses			
Indirect labor	$4,000		
Maintenance and repairs	3,000		
Factory supplies	1,000		
Heat, light, and power.............................	2,000		
Total manufacturing expenses		10,000	
Total manufacturing costs			105,000
Total work in process during period			$120,000
Less: Ending work in process inventory			20,000
Cost of goods manufactured			$100,000

Note: The last item, cost of goods manufactured, is used in the operating statement to determine the cost of goods sold, as above.

Expenses

Expenses typically appear below the gross margin. They usually include the costs of selling, and running the business. They do not include the cost of goods—either purchased or produced.

There is no "right" way of classifying the expense accounts or arranging them on an operating statement. They might just as easily have been arranged alphabetically—or according to amount, with the largest placed at the top, and so on down the line. In a business of any size, though, it is desirable to group the expenses in some way and to use subtotals by groups for analysis and control purposes. This was done in Figure B–1.

Summary on operating statements

The operating statement presented in Figure B–1 contains all the basic components in an operating statement—together with a normal amount of supporting detail. Further detail could be added to the statement under any of the headings without changing the nature of the statement. The amount of detail usually depends on how the statement will be used. A stockholder may be presented with a simplified operating statement, while the one prepared for internal company use may include much detail.

We have already seen that leaving out some of the detail in Figure B–1 did not affect the basic components of the statement—net sales, costs, and net profit. Whatever further detail is added to the statement aims to help the reader to see how these three figures have been determined. A very detailed statement might easily run to several single-spaced pages—yet the nature of the operating statement would be the same.

COMPUTING THE STOCKTURN RATE

A detailed operating statement can provide the data needed to determine the **stockturn rate**—a measure of the number of times the average inventory is sold during a year. Note, the stockturn rate is concerned with the turnover *during a year, not* the time covered by a particular operating statement.

The stockturn rate is a very important measure because it shows how fast the firm's inventory is moving. Some lines of trade have slower turnover than others. But a drop in the turnover rate in a particular business can be a warning sign. For one thing, it may mean that the firm's assortment of goods is no longer as attractive as it was. Also, it may mean that more working capital will be needed to handle the same volume of sales. Most businesses pay close attention to the stockturn rate—trying to get faster turnover.

Three methods—all basically similar—can be used to figure the stockturn rate. Which method is used depends on the data which are available. These three methods are shown below and usually give approximately the same results.*

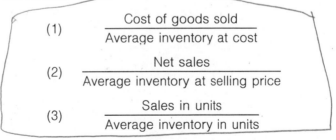

$$(1) \quad \frac{\text{Cost of goods sold}}{\text{Average inventory at cost}}$$

$$(2) \quad \frac{\text{Net sales}}{\text{Average inventory at selling price}}$$

$$(3) \quad \frac{\text{Sales in units}}{\text{Average inventory in units}}$$

Computing the stockturn rate will be illustrated for formula (1)—since all are similar. The only difference is that the cost figures used in formula (1) are changed to a selling price or numerical count basis in formulas (2) and (3). It is necessary—regardless of the method used—to have both items of the formula in the same terms.

Using formula (1), the average inventory at cost is figured by adding the beginning and ending inventories at cost and dividing by 2. This average

---

* Differences will occur because of varied markups and different product assortments. In an assortment of tires, for example, those with high markups might have sold much better than those with small markups, but with formula (3) all tires would be treated equally.

inventory figure is then divided into the cost of goods sold (in cost terms) to get the stockturn rate.

For example, suppose that the cost of goods sold for one year was $100,000. Beginning inventory was $25,000 and ending inventory $15,000. Adding the two inventory figures and dividing by 2, we obtain an average inventory of $20,000. We next divide the cost of goods sold by the average inventory ($100,000 divided by $20,000) and get a stockturn rate of 5.

Further discussion of the use of the stockturn rate is found in Chapter 17.

OPERATING RATIOS HELP ANALYZE THE BUSINESS

The operating statement is also used for a number of other purposes. In particular, many business people calculate **operating ratios**—the ratio of items on the operating statement to net sales—and compare these ratios from one time period to another. They also can compare their own operating ratios with those of competitors. Such competitive data is often available through trade associations. Each firm may report its results to the trade association—then summary results are distributed to the members. These ratios help management control its operations. If some expense ratios are rising, for example, those particular costs are singled out for special attention.

Operating ratios are figured by dividing net sales into the various operating statement items appearing below the net sales level in the statement. Net sales is used as the denominator in the operating ratio, because this figure most concerns a business manager. It is the dollar amount actually received by the business.

We can see the relation of operating ratios to the operating statement if we think of there being another column to the right of the dollar figures in an operating statement. This additional column would list percentage figures—using net sales as 100 percent. This can be seen below:

Gross sales	$540.00	
Less: Returns and allowances	40.00	
Net sales	$500.00	100%
Cost of goods sold	350.00	70
Gross margin	150.00	30%
Expenses	100.00	20
Net profit	$ 50.00	10%

The 30 percent ratio of gross margin to net sales in the above illustration means that 30 percent of the net sales dollar is available to cover sales expenses, run the business, and provide a profit. Note that the ratio of expenses to sales plus the ratio of profit to sales equals the 30 percent gross margin ratio. The net profit ratio of 10 percent shows that 10 percent of the net sales dollar is left for profit.

The usefulness of percentage ratios should be obvious. Percentages are easily figured. And they are much easier to work with than large dollar figures. With net sales as the base figure, they provide a useful means of comparison and control.

Note that because of the relation between these various items and their ratios, only a few pieces of information are necessary and the others can be figured easily. In this case, for example, knowing the gross margin percent and net profit percent makes it possible to figure expense and cost of goods sold percentages. Further, knowing a single dollar amount would let you figure all the other dollar amounts.

MARKUPS

A **markup** is the dollar amount added to the cost of goods to get the selling price. The markup is similar to the gross margin. Gross margin and the idea of markup are related because the amount added onto the unit cost of a product by a retailer (or wholesaler) is expected to cover all the costs of selling and running the business—and to provide a profit.

The markup approach to pricing is discussed in Chapter 17—so it will not be discussed at length here. A simple example will illustrate the idea, however. If a retailer bought an article which cost $1 when delivered to his store, then obviously he must sell it for more than this cost if he hopes to make a profit. He might add 50 cents to the cost of the article to cover his selling and other costs and, hopefully, to provide a profit. The 50 cents would be the "markup."

It would also be the gross margin (or gross profit) on that item if it is sold. But note that it is *not* the net profit. His selling expenses might amount to 35 cents, 45 cents, or even 55 cents. In other words, there is no guarantee that the markup will cover his costs. Also, there is no guarantee that the customers will buy at the marked-up price. This may require markdowns. They are discussed later in this appendix.

Markup conversions

Sometimes it is convenient to talk in terms of *markups on cost,* while at other times *markups on selling prices* are useful. To have some agreement, **markup** (without any explanation) will mean percentage of selling price. By this definition, the 50-cent markup part of the $1.50 selling price is a markup of 33⅓ percent [i.e., (50/1.50) x 100 = 33⅓].

Some retailers and wholesalers have developed markup conversion tables so they can easily convert from cost to selling price—depending on the markup they want. To see the interrelation, look at the two formulas below. They can be used to convert either type of markup to the other.

$$(4) \quad \frac{\text{Percentage markup}}{\text{on selling price}} = \frac{\text{Percentage markup on cost}}{100\% + \text{Percentage markup on cost}}$$

$$(5) \quad \frac{\text{Percentage markup}}{\text{on cost}} = \frac{\text{Percentage markup on selling price}}{100\% - \text{Percentage markup on selling price}}$$

In the previous example, we had a cost of $1, a markup of 50 cents, and a selling price of $1.50. We saw that the markup on selling price was 33⅓ percent. On cost, it was 50 percent. Let us substitute these percentage figures into formulas (4) and (5) to see how to convert markups from one basis to another. First, assume that we only know the markup on selling price and want to convert to markup on cost. Using formula (5) we have:

$$\text{Percentage markup on cost} = \frac{33\ 1/3\%}{100\% - 33\ 1/3\%} = \frac{33\ 1/3\%}{66\ 2/3\%} = 50\%$$

If we know, on the other hand, only the percentage markup on cost, we could convert to markup on selling price as follows:

$$\text{Percentage markup on selling price} = \frac{50\%}{100\% + 50\%} = \frac{50\%}{150\%} = 33\ 1/3\%$$

These results can be proved and summarized as follows:

Markup	$0.50 =	50% of cost or 33 1/3% of selling price
plus Cost	$1.00 =	100% of cost or 66 2/3% of selling price
Selling price	$1.50 =	150% of cost or 100% of selling price

It is important to see that only the percentage figures changed—while the money amounts for cost, markup, and selling price stayed the same. Notice, too, that when the selling price is used as the base figure (100 percent), then the cost percentage plus the markup percentage equals 100 percent. But when the cost of the product is used as the base figure (100 percent), it is obvious that the selling price percentage must exceed 100 percent—by the markup on cost.

MARKDOWN RATIOS HELP CONTROL RETAIL OPERATIONS

The ratios we discussed above were concerned with numbers on the operating statement. Another important ratio—the **markdown ratio**—is a tool used by many retailers to measure the efficiency of various departments and their whole business. But note—it is not related to the operating statement. It requires special calculations.

A **markdown** is a retail price reduction which is required because the customers will not buy some item at the originally marked-up price. This refusal to buy may be due to a variety of "business errors"—soiling, style changes, fading, damage caused by handling—or an original markup which was too high. To get rid of these goods, the retailer offers them at a lower price.

Markdowns are similar to allowances because price reductions are made. So, in computing a markdown ratio, markdowns and allowances are added together and then divided by net sales. This markdown ratio is computed as follows:

BEFORE PURCHASE   AFTER PURCHASE

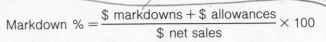

$$\text{Markdown \%} = \frac{\$ \text{ markdowns} + \$ \text{ allowances}}{\$ \text{ net sales}} \times 100$$

The 100 is multiplied by the fraction to get rid of decimal points.

Returns are not included when figuring the markdown ratio. Returns are considered as "consumer errors"—not "business errors"—and therefore are not included in this measure of business efficiency.

Retailers who use markdown ratios keep a record of the amount of markdowns and allowances in each department and then divide the total by the net sales in each department. Over a period of time, these ratios give management a measure of the efficiency of the buyers and salespersons in the various departments.

It should be stressed again that the markdown ratio has nothing to do with the operating statement. It is not figured directly from data on the operating statement—since the markdowns take place before the goods are sold. In fact, some goods may be marked down and still not sold. Even if the marked-down items are not sold, the markdowns are included in the calculations in the time period when they are taken.

The markdown ratio would be calculated for a whole department (or profit center)—not individual items. What we want is a measure of the effectiveness of a whole department—not how well the department did on individual items.

Questions for discussion

1 Distinguish between the following pairs of items which appear on operating statements:
a. Gross sales and net sales.
b. Purchases at billed cost and purchases at net cost.
c. Cost of goods available for sale and cost of goods sold.

2 How does gross margin differ from gross profit? From net profit?

3 Explain the similarity between markups and gross margin. What connection do markdowns have with the operating statement?

4 Compute the net profit for a company with the following data:

Beginning inventory (cost)	$ 15,000
Purchases at billed cost	33,000
Sales returns and allowances	25,000
Rent	6,000
Salaries	40,000
Heat and light	18,000
Ending inventory (cost)	25,000
Freight cost (inbound)	9,000
Gross sales	130,000

5 Construct an operating statement from the following data:

Returns and allowances	$ 15,000
Expenses	20%
Closing inventory at cost	60,000
Markdowns	2%
Inward transportation	3,000
Purchases	100,000
Net profit (5%)	30,000

6 Data given:

Markdowns	$ 10,000
Gross sales	100,000
Returns	8,000
Allowances	12,000

Compute net sales and percent of markdowns.

7 (a) What percentage markups on cost are equivalent to the following percentage markups on selling price: 20, 37½, 50, and 66⅔? (b) What percentage markups on selling price are equivalent to the following percentage markups on cost: 33⅓, 20, 40, and 50?

8 What net sales volume is required to secure a stockturn rate of 20 times a year on an average inventory at cost of $100,000, with a gross margin of 30 percent?

9 Explain how the general manager of a department store might use the markdown ratios computed for his various departments? Would this be a fair measure? Of what?

When you finish this chapter, you should:

1 Understand how pricing objectives should affect pricing.
2 Understand the choices the marketing manager must make about—price flexibility, price level, and pricing over the product life cycle.
3 Understand the legality of price level and price flexibility policies.
4 Understand the many possible variables of a price structure.
5 Recognize the important new terms shown in red.

PLACE
PRICE
PRODUCT
PROMOTION

PRICING POLICIES

Price is one of the four major variables that the marketing manager controls. Price decisions affect both the firm's sales and profits. So they must be taken seriously.

Guided by the company's objectives, marketing managers must develop a set of pricing objectives and then pricing policies. These policies should state: (1) how flexible prices will be, (2) what price level will be set, (3) how pricing will be handled during the course of the product life cycle, (4) how transportation costs will be handled, and (5) to whom and when discounts and allowances will be given. These pricing decision areas are illustrated in Figure 16–1.

PRICING OBJECTIVES SHOULD GUIDE PRICING

Pricing objectives should flow from company-level objectives. They should be clearly stated because they have a direct effect on pricing policies and the price setting method used.

Possible pricing objectives are shown in Figure 16–2

Profit-oriented objectives

TARGET RETURNS PROVIDE SPECIFIC GUIDELINES

A **target return objective** sets a specific profit-related goal. Seeking a target return is a common profit-oriented objective. The firm's "target" may be a certain percentage return on sales—perhaps a 1 percent return on sales, as in the supermarket industry. Or a large producer might aim

Figure 16–1
Strategy planning for Price

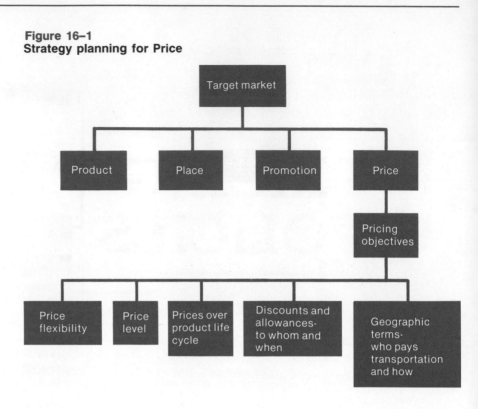

for a 25 percent return on investment. Or a small family-run firm might want a fixed dollar amount of profit to cover living expenses.

A target return objective has advantages for a large company. It makes it easier for everyone to know what they are supposed to do. And it makes it easier to control the various divisions. Some companies will cut out divisions or drop products that don't earn a target return on investment. Naturally, therefore, managers try to hit this target.

PROFIT MAXIMIZATION CAN BE SOCIALLY RESPONSIBLE

A **profit maximization objective** states that the firm seeks to get as much profit as it can. It might be stated as a desire for a rapid return on investment. Or—more bluntly—to earn "all the traffic will bear."

Profit maximization objectives seem to be more common among small firms—small retailers and manufacturers—who are out of the public eye.[1] Large firms, on the other hand, might avoid a profit maximization objective.

The public—and many business executives—link a profit maximization objective with high prices and monopolies. They feel that anyone trying to maximize profits is not operating in the public interest.

Economic theory does not support this idea. Profit maximization doesn't always lead to high prices. True, demand and supply *may* bring extremely high prices if competition can't offer good substitutes. But this happens

Figure 16–2
Possible pricing objectives

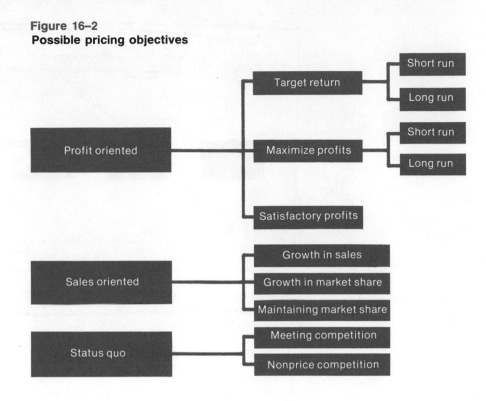

if and only if demand is highly inelastic. If demand is very elastic, it might be in a monopolist's interest to charge relatively low prices so sales will increase.

SOME JUST WANT SATISFACTORY PROFITS

Some businesses aim for only "satisfactory" profits. They may work for profits, but they aren't nearly as aggressive as they might be if they were trying to maximize profits. They want to convince stockholders of their competence. And they also want to be sure of the firm's survival. As long as profits are "good enough," they feel that they have reached their objective.[2]

Sales-oriented objectives

SALES GROWTH DOES NOT MEAN BIG PROFITS

Some business managers seem more concerned about sales growth than profits. This is probably because many feel sales growth always means big profits. This belief is dying, however. Major corporations have faced a continuing profit squeeze over the last 20 years while sales have grown. More attention is now being paid to profits—along with sales.[3]

Another reason for the popularity of sales growth-oriented objectives is that a manager's salary may be more closely tied to sales than to profits.[4] Here, compensation systems may have affected the selection of objectives—rather than vice versa!

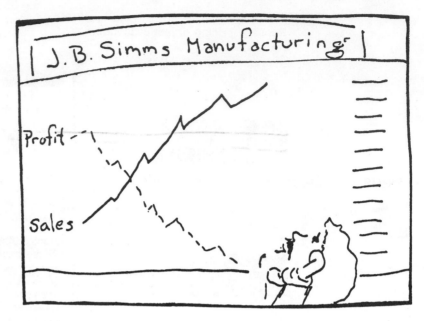

"J. B., sales are great–fan-tas-tic! Profit? . . . Sales are fan-tas-tic!"

(Big sales don't always mean big profits.)

MAINTAINING MARKET SHARE MAY BE ENOUGH

Just maintaining market share—the percentage of the market you are "entitled" to because of your size and reputation—seems to be very important to some managers. This is partly because market share is easier to measure than whether profits are being maximized. It is fairly easy to measure whether a company has maintained its percentage of a market. So, as long as some profit is earned, the managers may prefer stressing market share instead—especially if job promotions are based on market share.

HOW ABOUT INCREASING MARKET SHARE?

Aggressive companies often aim to increase market share or even to control a market. In some businesses, economies of size logically encourage a firm to seek increased market share—and probably greater profits. Sometimes, however, firms blindly follow the market growth goal. This leads to pricing almost at cost to get more of the market. Sales growth objectives sometimes lead to profitless prosperity—where slight errors lead to bankruptcy.

Status quo objectives

DON'T ROCK THE BOAT OBJECTIVES

Status quo objectives are "don't-rock-the-*pricing*-boat" objectives—and are fairly common. They may be stated as "meeting competition" or "avoiding competition" or "stabilizing prices."

Often a status quo objective is held by conservative managers who want to reduce the risk of loss. They prefer instead a comfortable way of life and some assurance of profit. Maintaining stable prices may discourage price competition and remove the need for hard decisions. The managers may have more time for golf!

OR STRESS NONPRICE COMPETITION INSTEAD

On the other hand, a status quo *pricing* objective can be part of an extremely aggressive marketing strategy. The pricing objective may seem conservative, but the aim could be to avoid price competition in favor of **nonprice competition**—aggressive action on one or more of the Ps other than Price.

MOST FIRMS SET SPECIFIC PRICING POLICIES

Specific pricing policies are important for any firm. Otherwise, the marketing manager must rethink his strategy every time a customer asks for a price.

Price policies usually lead to **administered prices**—consciously set prices. In other words, instead of letting daily market forces decide their prices, most firms set their own prices. Some firms do their pricing mechanically and without much thought—just "meeting competition." Actually, however, they do have many choices. And they should consider price setting carefully. If the customers won't pay the price—the whole marketing mix fails. In the rest of this chapter, we will talk about the pricing policies a marketing manager must set to do an effective job of administering Price.

PRICE FLEXIBILITY POLICIES

One of the first decisions any marketing manager has to make is about price flexibility. Shall he have a one-price or a flexible-price policy.

One-price policy—the same price for everyone

A **one-price policy** means offering the same price to all customers who buy goods under basically the same conditions and in the same quantities. Most U.S. firms use a one-price policy. This is mainly for convenience and to maintain goodwill among customers.

A one-price policy makes pricing easier, but the marketing manager must be careful not to be inflexible about it. This could amount to broadcasting a price which competitors could undercut—especially if the price is somewhat high. One reason for the growth of discount houses is that conventional retailers used traditional margins and stuck to them.

Flexible-price policy—different prices for different customers

A **flexible-price policy** means the same products and quantities are offered to different customers at different prices.[5]

Flexible pricing was most common when businesses were small, products were not standardized, and bargaining was expected. These conditions still exist in most foreign countries.

Flexible pricing does have advantages, however, and is often used in the channels, in direct sales of industrial goods, and at retail for more

 344

A one-price policy means charging everyone the same price.

expensive items. It allows a sales rep to make adjustments for market conditions—instead of having to turn down an order.

It has disadvantages, too. If customers know that prices are flexible, they may want to bargain. The cost of selling may rise as buyers become aware that bargaining could save them money. Also, some sales reps may let price cutting become a habit. This could make price useless as a competitive tool and lead, instead, to a lower price level.

PRICE-LEVEL POLICIES

When marketing managers administer prices—as most do—they must decide on a price-level policy: Will the price be set below the market, at the same level as competition, or above the market?

Is it below, at, or above the market?

Some firms seem to emphasize below-the-market prices in their marketing mixes. Retail discounters and mass merchandisers offer goods below the prices charged by conventional retailers. And some manufacturers, such as Honda, regularly sell products which appear to be offered below the market. At the other extreme, manufacturers such as Zenith Radio Corporation proudly claimed that their prices started well above those of competing models. They felt that one of the reasons for many successful sales years was that Zenith regularly maintained high quality—and prices—while other companies cut prices and skimped on quality.

The question is: Do these various strategies contain prices which are above or below the market? Or are they just different prices in different markets? Perhaps some target customers do see important differences in the physical product or in the whole marketing mix. Then what we are really talking about are different marketing strategies—not different price levels. Lower prices are just *part* of different marketing strategies. The retail discounters, for example, may have lower prices than conventional retailers, but they may not be direct competitors for some customers. Economic shoppers may be comparing prices only between discounters—a fact which some discounters are beginning to discover to their dismay!

Obviously, target marketing applies here. If some market segment was not previously satisfied, a more attractive marketing mix might be offered with a higher price. That price should not be thought of as "above the market," but as a new price which is part of a new marketing mix. Similarly, a "lower" price may not automatically cause the firm to be "below the market." It may be the price needed to make a good mix and compete with similar "low-price" mixes—i.e., it is "at the market" against these mixes.[6]

MEETING COMPETITION MAY BE BEST IN OLIGOPOLY

In highly competitive markets, and especially in oligopoly situations, pricing "at the market"—i.e., meeting competition—may be the only sensible policy. To raise prices might lead to a substantial loss in sales. And cutting the price would probably cause competitors to cut price too. This can only lead to a drop in total revenue for the industry and probably for each firm. Therefore, a meeting-competition policy may make sense for each firm. And price stability may develop without any price fixing in the industry.

PRICING OVER THE PRODUCT LIFE CYCLE

When the original price level for a new product is set, the product life cycle should be considered. The price will affect how fast the product moves through the cycle. A high price, for example, may lead to attractive profits but also to competition and a faster cycle. With this in mind, should a firm's original price be a skimming or a penetration price?

Skimming pricing—feeling out demand at a good price

A **skimming pricing policy** tries to get the "cream" of a market (the top of a demand curve) at a high price before aiming at the more price-sensitive segments of that market.

Skimming is useful for feeling out demand—for getting a better understanding of the shape of the demand curve. It is easier to start with a high price and lower it, than to start with a low price and then try to raise it.

Penetration pricing—get the business at a low price

A **penetration pricing policy** tries to sell the whole market at one low price. This policy might be used where there is no "elite" market—where the whole demand curve is fairly elastic—even in the early stages of the product life cycle.

A penetration policy will be even more attractive if—as volume expands—economies of size reduce costs. And it may be wise if the firm expects strong competition very soon after introduction. A *low* penetration price is a "stay-out" price. It is intended to discourage competitors from entering the market.

Introductory price dealing—temporary price cuts

Price cuts do attract customers. Therefore, marketers often use **introductory price dealing**—temporary price cuts—to speed new products into a market. These temporary price cuts should not be confused with low penetration prices, however. The plan here is to raise prices as soon as the introductory offer is over.

Established competitors often choose not to meet introductory price dealing—as long as the introductory period is not too long or too successful.[7]

LEGALITY OF PRICE FLEXIBILITY AND PRICE LEVEL POLICIES

Even very high prices may be ok—if they are not fixed

From our general discussion of legislation in Chapter 3, you might think that companies have little freedom in pricing or may even need government approval for their prices. Generally speaking, this is not true. They can charge what they want—even "outrageously high" prices—if they are not fixed with competitors.

BUT THEY SHOULD BE LEGAL—TO AVOID FINES OR JAIL

There are some restrictions on pricing, however. Difficulties with pricing—and perhaps violation of price legislation—usually occur only when competing marketing mixes are quite similar. When the success of an entire marketing strategy depends upon price, there is pressure (and temptation) to make agreements with competitors (conspire). And **price fixing**—competitors getting together to set higher than competitive prices—is common and relatively easy. But it is also completely illegal. It is a "conspiracy" under the antimonopoly laws. And fixing prices can be dangerous. Some business managers have already gone to jail! And governments are getting tougher on price fixing—especially by smaller companies.

"Honest, Judge, we were just *discussing* prices over lunch—we weren't *fixing* them!"

The first step to understanding pricing legislation is to know the thinking of legislators and the courts. Ideally, they try to help the economy perform more effectively in the consumers' interest. In practice, this doesn't always work out as neatly as planned. But generally their intentions are good. And if we take this view, we get a better idea of the "why" of legislation. This helps us to anticipate future rulings. We will look at U.S. legislation here, but other countries have similar laws on pricing.[8]

Unfair trade practice acts control some minimum prices

The **unfair trade practice acts**— passed in more than half the states— put a floor under prices, especially at the wholesale and retail levels. Selling below cost in these states is illegal. Wholesalers and retailers are usually required to take a certain minimum percentage markup over their merchandise-plus-transportation costs. The most common markup figures are 6 percent at retail and 2 percent at wholesale.

Most retailers know enough about their costs to set larger markups than these minimums. The practical effect of these laws is to protect certain limited-line food retailers—such as dairy stores—from the kind of "ruinous" competition that full-line stores might offer if they sold milk as a "leader"— offering it below cost—for a long time.

Antimonopoly legislation bans price discrimination unless . . .

Price level and price flexibility policies can lead to price discrimination. The **Robinson-Patman Act** of 1936 makes illegal any **price discrimination**—selling the same goods to different buyers at different prices. This law does permit some price differences—but they must be based on cost differences or the need to meet competition. Both buyers and sellers are guilty if they know they are entering into discriminatory agreements. This is a serious matter and price discrimination suits are common.

WHAT DOES "LIKE GRADE AND QUALITY" MEAN?

The Robinson-Patman Act lets a marketing manager charge different prices for *similar* products if they are not of "like grade and quality." But how *similar* can they be? The FTC position is that if the physical characteristics of a product are similar, then they are of like grade and quality. The FTC's view was upheld in a 1966 U.S. Supreme Court ruling against the Borden Company. The court ruled that a well-known label alone does not make a product different from the one with an unknown label. The issue was clear-cut in the Borden case because the company admitted that the physical characteristics of the canned milk it sold at different prices under different labels were basically the same.

The FTC's "victory" in the Borden case was not complete, however. Although the U.S. Supreme Court agreed with the FTC in the Borden case with respect to like grade and quality, it sent the case back to the U.S. Court of Appeals to determine whether the price difference actually injured competition—which is also required by the law. In 1967, this court found no injury unless Borden's price difference was more than the "recog-

Many of Borden's products have "recognized consumer appeal."

nized consumer appeal of the Borden label." How "consumer appeal" is to be measured was not spelled out and may lead to more court cases.[9]

Eventually, what the consumer thinks about the product may be the deciding factor. For now, however, it would be safer for producers who want to sell several brands at lower prices than their main brand to offer actual physical differences—and differences that are useful, not just decorative.[10]

CAN COST ANALYSIS JUSTIFY PRICE DIFFERENTIALS?

The Robinson-Patman Act allows price differences if there are cost differences. Justifying cost differences is difficult, however. Costs usually must be charged to several products using rather arbitrary methods. It is easy, then, for the FTC to object to whatever method is used. Such objections are often raised because the FTC has been concerned about the impact of price differences on competition—but especially on small competitors.[11]

CAN YOU LEGALLY MEET PRICE CUTS?

Meeting competition is allowed as a defense in price discrimination situations—although the FTC normally has taken a negative view of this argument.

A major aim of antimonopoly legislation is to protect competition, not competitors—and "meeting competition" in "good faith" still seems to be legal.

SPECIAL PROMOTION ALLOWANCES MIGHT NOT BE ALLOWED

Some firms have violated the Robinson-Patman Act by giving promotion allowances to some customers and not others. The act bans such allowances unless they are made available to all customers on ''proportionately equal'' terms. No proof of injury to competition is necessary. The FTC has been fairly successful in prosecuting such cases.

The need for such a rule is clear—once price regulation begins. Allowances for promotion could be granted to retailers or wholesalers without expecting that any promotion would be done. This plainly would be price discrimination in disguise.

HOW TO AVOID DISCRIMINATING

One way to avoid discriminating is to avoid price differences. Until this powerful but confusing legislation is made clearer, many business managers will continue to play down Price as a marketing variable. They have decided that it is safer to offer the same cost-based prices to all customers.

A PRICE STRUCTURE HAS MANY DIMENSIONS

While economists casually refer to ''market price,'' it is not so easy to define price in real-life situations. Price has many dimensions. For example, if you were offered a current-model Ford station wagon for $1,000, would this be a good price for a car that normally sells for over $3,000? Or, if you were offered a 21-inch television set for $100 that normally sells for $200, would this be a good buy?

In each case, the first reaction might be an eager ''Yes.'' But wait a minute! It might be wise to look further. The $1,000 for the Ford station wagon might be the price of a wreck worth only a few hundred dollars at the junk yard. And the $100 for the TV set might be a reasonable price for all its components in parts bins at the factory. If you wanted these assembled, you would have to pay $25 extra. If you wanted a cabinet, it might be an additional $25. And if you wanted a quality guarantee, there might be an added charge of $50.

The price equation: Price equals Something

These examples show that a price should be related to some assortment of goods and/or services. Any business transaction can be thought of as an exchange of money—the money being the price—for Something.

This Something can be a physical product in various stages of completion—with or without the services usually provided, with or without quality guarantees, and so on. And, this ''product'' may or may not be conveniently available.

How much money is charged for this Something will depend on what is included. Some consumers may pay list price, while others may get discounts or allowances because some service is not included. The possible variations are shown in Figure 16–3 for consumers or users and in Figure 16–4 for channel members. Some of these variations will be dis-

Figure 16–3
Price as seen by consumers or users

Price	equals	Something

List price
Less: *Discounts:*
    Quantity
    Seasonal
    Cash
Less: *Allowances:*
    Trade-ins
    Damaged goods
	equals	*Product:*
		  Physical product
		  Service
		  Assurance of quality
		  Repair facilities
		  Packaging
		  Credit
		  Trading stamps or coupons
		Place of delivery or availability

cussed more fully below—but here it should be clear that price has many dimensions.

Prices start with a list price

Most price structures are built around list prices. How these list prices are set is discussed in the next chapter. For now, however, we must see that there may be several list prices. Then, we will go on to see the many variations from list.

BASIC LIST PRICES—ARE "LIST PRICES"

Basic list prices are the prices that final consumers or users are normally asked to pay for goods. Unless noted otherwise, "list price" refers to "basic list price" in this book.

Figure 16–4
Price as seen by channel members

Price	equals	Something

List price
Less: *Discounts:*
    Quantity
    Seasonal
    Cash
    Trade or functional
Less: *Allowances:*
    Damaged goods
    Advertising
    Push money
	equals	*Product:*
		  Branded—well known
		  Guaranteed
		  Warranted
		  Service—repair facilities
		  Convenient packaging for
		    handling
		Place:
		  Availability—when and where
		Price:
		  Price-level guarantee
		  Sufficient margin to allow
		    chance for profit
		Promotion:
		  Promotion aimed at customers

Model	Model Code	MSRP a	Dest. Chg.	Total	Local Price	Model	Model Code	MSRP a	Dest. Chg.	Total	Local Price
STARFIRE											
Coupe	T07	$3964.36				**CUTLASS SUPREME**					
SX Coupe	D07	$4171.68				Coupe	R47	$4872.54			
OMEGA											
Hatchback Coupe	B17	$4173.60									
Coupe	B27	$4009.30				**CUTLASS CALAIS**					
Sedan	B69	$4094.30				Coupe	K47	$5230.54			
OMEGA BROUGHAM											
Coupe	E27	$4215.30				**CUTLASS SUPREME BROUGHAM**					
Sedan	E69	$4300.30				Coupe	M47	$5281.54			
CUTLASS SALON											
Sedan	G09	$4543.22									
Coupe	G87	$4433.22				**CUTLASS CRUISER**					
CUTLASS SALON BROUGHAM						2-Seat Wagon	H35	$5286.78			
Sedan	J09	$4827.78									
Coupe	J87	$4717.78									

MODEL PRICES ... Compact and Mid-Size Models

a—Manufacturer's Suggested Retail Prices. Includes reimbursement for New Vehicle Preparation Charges. *PRICES EFFECTIVE May 1, 1978

Oldsmobile suggests list prices from which adjustments are made.

UNCHANGING LIST PRICES—AN ADMINISTRATIVE CONVENIENCE

Unchanging list prices are published prices that remain the same for long periods of time—perhaps years—but the actual price is adjusted upward or downward by "add-ons" or discounts. This method of changing prices is often used where frequent price changes are necessary. It avoids many catalog price revisions. Rather than printing a complete new catalog, the seller can just publish a new list of add-ons or discounts.

PHONY LIST PRICES FOR "BARGAIN HUNTERS"

Phony list prices are prices that customers can be shown to suggest that the price they are to pay has been discounted from "list." Some customers, in fact, seem more interested in the size of the supposed discount that the list price itself. And they can end up paying more than the competitive market price.

Most businesses, Better Business Bureaus, and government agencies frown on phony prices. And the FTC tries to stop such pricing—using the **Wheeler-Lea Amendment**—which bans "unfair or deceptive acts in commerce."

The FTC says that firms "must in every case act honestly and in good faith on advertising a list price, and not with the intention of establishing a basis . . . for a deceptive comparison in any local . . . trade area."[12]

The FTC has had some court success. But deception is difficult to define. Sometimes "two-for-one" and "1-cent" sales are real offers appealing to the price conscious.[13]

There is also some question whether customers are really deceived by "high" list prices from which they bargain. Do the list prices from which "discounts" are offered on cars fool anyone? The FTC thinks so. But auto industry executives feel that consumers understand the meaning of the sticker price—as a starting point from which to begin bargaining. What do you think?

SOME CUSTOMERS GET DISCOUNTS OFF LIST

Discounts are reductions from list price that are given by a seller to a buyer who either gives up some marketing function or provides the function for himself. Discounts can be useful tools in marketing strategy planning.

In the following discussion, think about what function the buyers are giving up or providing when they get each of these discounts.

Quantity discounts encourage volume buying

Quantity discounts are offered to encourage customers to buy in larger quantities. This lets the seller get more of a buyer's business, shifts some of the storing function to the buyer, reduces shipping and selling costs—or all of these. These discounts are of two kinds: cumulative and noncumulative.

Cumulative quantity discounts apply to purchases over a given period—such as a year—and normally increase as the quantity purchased increases. Cumulative discounts are intended to encourage buying from a single company by reducing the price for additional purchases.

Noncumulative quantity discounts apply only to individual orders. Such discounts encourage larger orders, but do not tie a buyer to the seller after that one purchase.

Quantity discounts may be based on the dollar value of the entire order, or on the number of units purchased, or on the size of the package purchased. While quantity discounts are usually given as price cuts, sometimes they are given as "free" or "bonus" goods. Customers may receive one or more units "free" with the purchase of some quantity.

Quantity discounts can be a very useful tool for the marketing manager. Some customers are eager to get them. But marketing managers must use quantity discounts carefully to avoid price discrimination.

Seasonal discounts— buy sooner and store

Seasonal discounts are offered to encourage buyers to stock earlier than present demand requires. If used by producers, this discount tends to shift the storing function further along in the channel. It also tends to smooth out sales during the year and, therefore, permit year-round operation. If seasonal discounts are large, channel members may pass them along to their customers. In coal sales, for example, seasonal discounts are given in the spring and summer all the way through the channel to final consumers and users.

Payment terms and cash discounts set payment dates

Most sales to channel members and final users are made on credit. The seller issues a bill (invoice), and the buyer sends it through the accounting department for payment. Many channel members come to depend on other members for temporary working capital. Therefore, it is very important for both sides to clearly state the terms of payment—including the availability of cash discounts. The following terms of payment commonly are used.

Net means that payment for the face value of the invoice is due immediately. These terms are sometimes changed to "net 10" or "net 30"—which mean payment is due within 10 or 30 days of the date on the invoice.

1/10 net 30 means that a 1 percent discount off the face value of the invoice is allowed if the invoice is paid within 10 days. Otherwise, the full face value is due within 30 days. And it usually is understood that an interest charge will be made after the 30-day free credit period.

WHY CASH DISCOUNTS ARE GIVEN AND SHOULD BE TAKEN

Cash discounts are reductions in the price to encourage buyers to pay their bills promptly. Smart buyers take advantage of them. A discount

Quantity discounts encourage volume buying.

An invoice shows the terms of the sale.

of say 2/10, net 30 may not look like very much, but any company that passes it up is missing a good chance to save money. In this case, a 2 percent discount would be earned just for paying 20 days before the full amount is due anyway. This would amount to an annual interest rate of about 36 percent. The company would be better off to borrow at a bank— if necessary—to pay such invoices on time.

While the marketing manager can often use cash discounts as a marketing variable, a specific cash discount may be so firmly established in his industry that he can't change it. He must give the usual terms—even if he has no need for cash. Purchasing agents are aware of the value of cash discounts and will insist that the marketing manager offer the same terms offered by competitors. In fact, some buyers automatically deduct the accepted cash discount from their invoices—regardless of the seller's invoice terms.

Trade discounts often are set by tradition

A **trade (functional) discount** is a list price reduction given to channel members for the job they are going to do.

A manufacturer, for example, might allow retailers a 30 percent trade discount from the suggested retail list price—to cover the cost of the retailing function and their profit. Similarly, the manufacturer might allow wholesalers a chain discount of 30 percent and 10 percent off the retail price. In this case, the wholesalers would be expected to pass the 30 percent discount on to retailers.

Trade discounts might seem to offer a manufacturer's or wholesaler's marketing manager great flexibility in varying a marketing mix. In fact, they may limit him greatly. The customary trade discount can be so well established that he has to accept it in setting his prices.

SOME CUSTOMERS GET ALLOWANCES OFF LIST

Allowances—like discounts—are given to final consumers, customers, or channel members for doing "something" or accepting less of "something."

Bring in the old, ring up the new—with trade-ins

A **trade-in allowance** is a price reduction given for used goods when similar new goods are bought.

Trade-ins give the marketing manager an easy way to lower the price without reducing list price. Proper handling of trade-ins is important when selling durable goods. Customers buying machinery or buildings, for example, buy long-term satisfaction in terms of more manufacturing capacity. If the list price less the trade-in allowance does not offer greater satisfaction—as the customer sees it—then no sales will be made.

Many firms replace machinery slowly—perhaps too slowly—because they value their old equipment above market value. This also applies to new cars. Customers want higher trade-ins for their old cars than the current market value. This encourages the use of high, perhaps "phony," list prices so that high trade-in allowances can be given.

Advertising allowances—something for something

Advertising allowances are price reductions given to firms further along in a channel to encourage them to advertise or otherwise promote goods locally. Channel system thinking is involved here. General Electric has given a 1.5 percent allowance to its wholesalers of housewares and radios. They, in turn, are expected to provide something—in this case, local advertising.

P.M.s—push for cash

Push Money (or Prize Money) allowances are given to retailers by manufacturers or wholesalers to pass on to the retailers' sales clerks—for aggressively selling particular items. P.M. allowances are used for new merchandise, slower moving items, or higher margin items. They are especially common in the furniture and clothing industries. A sales clerk, for example, might earn an additional $5 for each mattress of a new type sold.

SOME CUSTOMERS GET EXTRA SOMETHINGS

Trading stamps— something for nothing?

Trading stamps are free stamps (like "Green Stamps") given by some retailers with every purchase.

Retailers can buy trading stamps from trading-stamp companies or set up their own plans. In either case, customers can trade stamps for merchandise premiums or cash or goods at the merchant's own store or at stamp redemption centers.

Some retailers offer trading stamps to their customers to differentiate their offering. Some customers seem to be attracted by trading stamps.

They feel they are getting something for nothing. And, sometimes they are—if competitive pressures don't allow the retailers to pass the cost of the stamps (2 to 3 percent of sales) along to customers. Also, lower promotion costs or a large increase in sales may make up for the increased cost of the stamps.[14]

The early users of stamps in a community seem to gain a competitive advantage. But when competitors start offering stamps, the advantage can disappear. This is similar to competition in the product life cycle—where new ideas are copied and profits are squeezed.

There was much interest in trading stamps in the 1950s and 1960s. Then their use declined—especially in grocery retailing. There, food discounters cut into the attractiveness of seemingly "higher cost" stamp givers. Now that some of the enthusiasm for stamp plans is dying down, perhaps they can be seen for what they really are. They are a potential addition to a marketing mix—perhaps instead of a price reduction. In some situations, stamp plans may be very effective—especially if half of a market wants stamps.[15] So we may see them used more in the future.

Clipping coupons brings other extras

Many manufacturers and retailers are offering discounts or free items through the use of coupons found in packages, mailings, newspapers and magazine advertising—or at the store. By presenting a coupon to a retailer, the consumer is given "10 cents off" or may be given the product at no charge. This plan is especially effective in the food business. Supermarkets are filled with customers clutching handfuls of coupons.[16]

LIST PRICE DEPENDS ON WHO PAYS TRANSPORTATION COSTS

Retail list prices often include free delivery—because the cost may be small. But producers and middlemen must take the matter of who pays for transportation more seriously. Much more money may be involved. Usually, purchase orders spell out these matters because transportation cost might be as much as half of the delivered cost of goods! There are many possible variations here for a creative marketing manager. Some special terms have developed. A few are discussed in the following paragraphs.

F.O.B. pricing is easy

A commonly used transportation term is F.O.B. **F.O.B.** means "free on board" some vehicle at some place. Typically, it is used with the place named, that is, the location of the seller's factory or warehouse—as in "F.O.B. Detroit," "F.O.B. Houston," or "F.O.B. mill." It means that the seller pays the cost of loading the merchandise onto some vehicle—usually a common carrier such as a truck, railroad car, or ship. At the point of loading, title to the goods passes to the buyer. Then the buyer pays the freight and takes responsibility for damage in transit—except as covered by the transportation company.

Variations are made easily—by changing the place part of the term. If the marketing manager wanted to pay the freight for the convenience of customers, he could use: "F.O.B. delivered" or "F.O.B. buyer's factory" (or warehouse). In this case, title would not pass until the goods were delivered. If he did want title to pass immediately—but still wanted to pay the freight (and then include it in the invoice)—he could use "F.O.B. seller's factory-freight prepaid."

F.O.B. "shipping point" pricing simplifies the seller's pricing—but it may narrow his market. Since the delivered cost of goods will vary depending on the buyer's location, a customer located farther from the seller must pay more and might buy from closer suppliers.

Zone pricing smoothes delivered prices

Zone pricing means making an average freight charge to all buyers within specified geographic areas. The seller pays the actual freight charges and then bills the customer for an average charge. The United States might be divided into five zones, for example, and all buyers within each zone would pay the same freight charge.

Zone pricing reduces the wide variation in delivered prices which result from an F.O.B. shipping point pricing policy. It also simplifies charging for transportation.

This approach often is used by manufacturers of hardware and food items—both to lower the possibility of price competition in the channels and to simplify figuring transportation charges for the thousands of wholesalers and retailers they serve.

Uniform deliverd pricing—one price to all

Uniform delivered pricing means making an average freight charge to all buyers. It is an extension of zone pricing. An entire country may be considered as one zone—and the average cost of delivery is included in the price. It is most often used when transportation costs are relatively low and the seller wishes to sell in all geographic areas at one price—perhaps a nationally advertised price.

Freight-absorption pricing—competing on equal grounds in another territory

When all the firms in an industry use F.O.B. shipping point pricing, a firm usually does well near its shipping point but not so well farther away. As sales reps look for business farther away, delivered prices rise. They find themselves priced out of the market. This problem can be solved with freight absorption.

Freight-absorption pricing means absorbing freight cost so that a firm's delivered price meets the nearest competitor's. This amounts to cutting list price to appeal to new market segments.

With freight absorption pricing, the only limit on the size of a firm's territory is the amount of freight cost it is willing to absorb. These absorbed costs cut net return on each sale, but the new business may raise total profit.

Conclusion

The Price variable offers an alert marketing manager many possibilities for varying marketing mixes. What pricing policies will be used depends on pricing objectives. We looked at profit-oriented, sales-oriented, and status quo-oriented objectives.

A marketing manager must set policies about price flexibility, price level, who will pay the freight, and who will get discounts and allowances. Also, the manager should be aware of pricing legislation affecting these policies.

In most cases, a marketing manager must set prices—that is, administer prices. Starting with a list price, a variety of discounts and allowances may be offered to adjust for the "something" being offered in the marketing mix.

Throughout this chapter, we have assumed that a list price had already been set. We have emphasized what may be included (or specifically excluded) in the "something"—and what objectives a firm might set to guide its pricing policies. Price setting itself was not discussed. We will cover this in the next chapter—showing ways of carrying out the various pricing objectives.

Questions for discussion

1 How should the acceptance of a profit-oriented, a sales-oriented, or a status quo-oriented pricing objective affect the development of a company's marketing strategy? Illustrate for each.

2 Distinguish between one-price and flexible-price policies. Which would be most appropriate for a supermarket? Why?

3 Cite two examples of continuously selling above the market price. Describe the situations.

4 Explain the types of competitive situations that might lead to a "meeting competition" pricing policy.

5 What pricing objective(s) would a skimming pricing policy most likely be implementing? Could the same be true for a penetration pricing policy? Which policy would probably be most appropriate for each of the following products: *(a)* a new type of home lawn-sprinkling system, *(b)* a new low-cost meat substitute, *(c)* a new type of children's toy, *(d)* a faster computer.

6 Discuss unfair trade practices acts. To whom are they "unfair"?

7 Would price discrimination be involved if a large oil company sold gasoline to taxicab associations for resale to individual taxicab operators for 2½ cents a gallon less than charged to retail service stations? What happens if the cab associations resell gasoline not only to taxicab operators but to the general public as well?

8 Indicate what the final consumer really obtains when paying the list price for the following "products": *(a)* an automobile, *(b)* a portable radio, *(c)* a package of frozen peas, and *(d)* a lipstick in a jeweled case.

9 Are seasonal discounts appropriate in agricultural businesses (which are certainly seasonal)?

10 Explain how a marketing manager might change his F.O.B. terms to make his otherwise competitive marketing mix more attractive.

11 What type of geographic pricing policy would seem most appropriate for the following products (specify any assumptions necessary to obtain a definite answer): *(a)* a chemical by-product, *(b)* nationally advertised candy bars, *(c)* rebuilt auto parts, *(d)* tricycles?

12 Explain how banning freight absorption (i.e., requiring F.O.B. factory pricing) might affect a producer with large economies of size when production quantities are increased.

13 In 1978, the Federal Trade Commission (FTC) ruled that five lumber companies had violated the federal antimonopoly laws in their pricing of plywood. The FTC decided that it was illegal for the companies to charge West Coast rail freight rates as part of the price of products shipped from their southern U.S. mills. The companies had regularly sold the plywood on a delivered basis—which was the sum of a base price plus freight charges. The Commission ordered the companies to charge the actual freight rate and to allow customers the option of buying at a "point of origin" price, with the customer to provide transportation. Included in the FTC decision was the observation that it was a "genuinely close and unusual case" because when plywood production spread from the Northwest to the South, it was "consistent with the operation of a competitive market" to sell the southern plywood at a price determined by the price of western plywood. Evaluate the reasoning and correctness of this FTC opinion.

Suggested cases

When you finish this chapter, you should:

1 Understand how most wholesalers and retailers set their prices—using markups.
2 Understand why turnover is so important in pricing.
3 Understand the advantages and disadvantages of average cost pricing.
4 Know how to find the most profitable price and quantity.
5 Know the many ways that price setters use demand estimates in their pricing.
6 Recognize the important new terms shown in red.

PRICE SETTING IN THE REAL WORLD

"How should I price this product?" This is a common problem for marketing managers. In the last chapter, we talked about variations from a list price. Now let's see how the list price might be set in the first place.

Cost-oriented pricing is typical in business. As we will see, however, cost-oriented pricing is not as easy or foolproof as some people think. Ideally, a marketing manager should consider potential customers' demand as well as his own costs when setting prices. We will start, however, by looking at how most firms—including wholesalers and retailers—set cost-oriented prices.

PRICING BY WHOLESALERS AND RETAILERS

Why use traditional markups?

Most retail and wholesale prices are set by using the markups which are commonly used in a particular line of business. The **markup** is the dollar amount added to the cost of goods to get the selling price. For example, retailers usually add a markup to their cost of goods to get their own selling price.

The markup is usually large enough to cover the middleman's cost of doing business and to provide some profit. So these traditional markups are often applied automatically. Some middlemen, in fact, use the same markup for all of their goods. This makes pricing easier for them!

When you think of the large number of items the average retailer and wholesaler carries—and the small sales volume of any one item—this cost-oriented approach makes sense. Spending the time to find the "best"

361

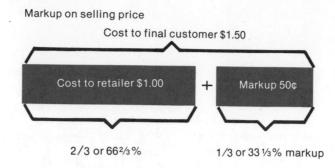

Markup on selling price

Cost to final customer $1.50

| Cost to retailer $1.00 | + | Markup 50¢ |

2/3 or 66⅔%   1/3 or 33⅓% markup

price to charge on every item in stock (day-to-day or week-to-week) probably wouldn't pay.

Should you markup on cost or selling price?

Suppose that a retailer buys an article for $1. To make a profit, the retailer obviously must sell this article for more than $1. If the retailer adds 50 cents to cover operating costs and provide a profit—we say that he is marking up the item 50 cents.

Markups, however, usually are stated as percentages rather than dollar amounts. And this is where the difficulty begins. Is a markup of 50 cents on a cost of $1 a markup of 50 percent? Or should the markup be figured as a percentage of the selling price—$1.50—and therefore be 33 1/3 percent? A clear definition is necessary.

Markup on selling price is a convenient rule

We will use the following definition: Unless otherwise stated: **markup** means "percentage of selling price." So, the 50 cent markup on the $1.50 selling price is a markup of 33 1/3 percent.

Markups are related to selling price for convenience. For one thing, the markup on selling price is roughly equal to the gross margin. Most business managers understand the idea of gross margin because they always see gross margin data on their profit and loss statements. (See Appendix B on Marketing Arithmetic if you are unfamiliar with these ideas.) They know that unless there is a large enough gross margin, there won't be any profit. For this reason, they accept traditional markups that are close to their usual gross margins.

Relating markups to the selling price also agrees with our emphasis on the customer. There is nothing wrong, however, with the idea of markup on cost. The important thing is to state clearly which markup we are using— to avoid confusion.

Retailers often need to change a markup on cost to one based on selling price, or vice versa. Conversion tables are available for this purpose. But they aren't necessary, because the calculations are simple. (See the section on "Markup Conversion" in Appendix B on Marketing Arithmetic.)

Markup chain may be used in channel pricing

A markup chain can set the price structure in a whole channel. A markup is figured on the selling price at each level of the channel. The producer's

Figure 17–1
Example of a markup chain and channel pricing

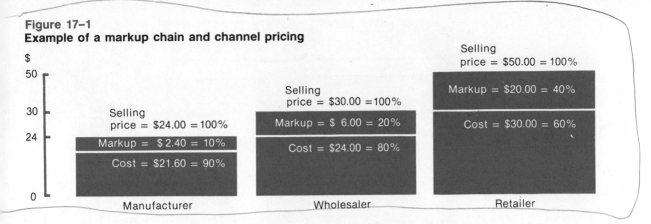

selling price becomes the wholesaler's cost—the wholesaler's selling price becomes the retailer's cost—and this cost plus a retail markup becomes the retail selling price. Each markup should cover the costs of selling, running the business—and leave a profit. Figure 17–1 shows how a markup might be used at each level of a channel system.

Figure 17–1 starts with a production cost (factory cost) of $21.60. In this case, the producer is taking a 10 percent markup and sells the goods for $24. The markup is 10 percent of $24 or $2.40. The producer's selling price now becomes the wholesaler's cost—$24. If the wholesaler is used to taking a 20 percent markup on selling price, the markup is $6—and the selling price becomes $30. The wholesaler's selling price of $30 now becomes the retailer's cost. And if the retailer is used to a 40 percent markup, he adds $20 and the retail selling price becomes $50.

High markups don't always mean big profits

Some people—including many retailers—link high markups with high profits. But this is often not true. Some kinds of business just have high operating costs and need high markups. In other cases, high markups may lower sales and lead to low profits—or even losses.

The problem with trying to get high profits with high markups can be seen by an extreme example. A 90 percent markup on selling price may not be nearly as profitable as a 10 percent markup on selling price! This is easy to understand if we assume that no units are sold at the high markup, but a very large number are sold at the low one. The key is turnover. You can't earn much if you don't sell much—no matter how high your markup. But many retailers and wholesalers seem more concerned with the size of their markup than total profit.

Lower markups can speed turnover—and the stockturn rate

Some retailers and wholesalers, however, are trying to speed turnover to increase profit—even if this means reducing the markup. They see themselves in a business that is running up costs over time. If they can sell a much greater amount in the same time period, they may be able to take a lower markup and still have a higher profit at the end of the period.

Fast-selling items carry a lower markup.

An important idea here is the **stockturn rate**—the number of times the average inventory is sold in a year. Various methods of figuring stockturn rates are used—but they all measure how many times the average inventory is sold in a year. (See the section "Computing the Stockturn Rate" in Appendix B.) If the stockturn rate is low, this may be bad for profits.

At the very least, a low stockturn will increase cost by tying up working capital. If the stockturn were 1 (once per year) instead of 5, selling goods costing $100,000 would require $100,000 rather than $20,000 in working capital—just to carry the necessary inventory.

Whether stockturn is high or low depends on the industry. An annual rate of 1 or 2 might be expected in the retail jewelry industry—while 40 to 50 would be typical for fresh fruits and vegetables.

Grocers run in fast company

Supermarket operators know the importance of fast turnover. They put only small markups on fast-selling items like sugar, shortening, soaps, and detergents, canned milk, soups, desserts, beverages, baby foods, pet foods, bleaches, flour, and canned vegetables. Sugar, for example, may carry a markup of 8 percent; shortening, 9 to 10 percent; soaps and detergents, 10 to 11 percent.

Since supermarket expenses are 16–18 percent of sales, it looks like many of these items are carried at a loss! But since such figures are storewide averages, this need not be true.

Fast-moving goods usually are less expensive to stock and sell. They take up valuable space for shorter periods, are damaged less, and tie up less working capital. Lower markups will cover the costs of these items and make a profit too. With lower markups, the goods may sell even faster—and a small profit per unit will be earned more often.

These fast-moving goods may be more profitable per item—in spite of the low margins—because of the higher turnover. The average turnover in one study was 14 times a year. Yet sugar turned over 31 times, beverages 28 times, shortening 23 times, and soups 21 times.

Note that the high-margin items were not all unprofitable. They simply were not as profitable *per item* as some of the low-margin items.[1]

Discounters are running faster

The modern food discounters and mass merchandisers carry the fast turnover idea of the supermarket even further. By pricing food even lower—and attracting customers from wider areas who purchase in large quantities—they are able to operate profitably on even smaller margins.

PRICING BY PRODUCERS

It's up to the producer to set the list price

Some markups eventually become customary in a trade. Most of the channel members will tend to follow a similar process—adding a certain percentage to the previous price. Who sets price in the first place?

The basic list price usually is decided by the producer and/or brander of the product—a large retailer, a large wholesaler, or most often the producer. From here on, we'll look at the pricing approaches of such firms. For convenience, we will call them "producers."

Figure 17–2
Results of average-cost pricing

Calculation of planned profit *if* 10,000 items are sold		Calculation of actual profit *if* only 5,000 items are sold	
Calculation of costs:		Calculation of costs:	
Fixed overhead expenses	$ 5,000	Fixed overhead expenses	$5,000
Labor and materials	5,000	Labor and materials	2,500
Total costs	$10,000	Total costs	$7,500
"Reasonable" profit	1,000		
Total costs and planned profit	$11,000		

Calculation of "reasonable" price for both possibilities:

$$\frac{\text{Total costs and planned profit}}{\text{Planned number of items to be sold}} = \frac{\$11,000}{10,000} = \$1.10 = \text{"Reasonable" price}$$

Calculation of profit or (loss):		Calculation of profit or (loss):	
Actual unit sales (10,000) times price ($1.10) =	$11,000	Actual unit sales (5,000) times price ($1.10) =	$5,500
Minus: Total costs	10,000	Minus: Total costs	7,500
Profit (loss)	$ 1,000	Profit (loss)	($2,000)
Therefore: Planned ("reasonable") profit of $1,000 is earned if 10,000 items are sold at $1.10 each.		Therefore: Planned ("reasonable") profit of $1,000 is not earned. Instead, $2,000 loss results if 5,000 items are sold at $1.10 each.	

AVERAGE-COST PRICING IS COMMON AND DANGEROUS

Average-cost pricing consists of adding a "reasonable" markup to the average cost of an item. The average cost per unit is usually found by studying past records. The total cost for the last year is divided by all the units produced and sold in that period to get the average cost per unit. If the total cost were $5,000 for labor and materials and $5,000 for fixed overhead expenses—such as selling expenses, rent, and manager salaries—then total cost would be $10,000. If the company produced 10,000 items in that time period, the average cost would be $1 a unit. To get the price, the producer would decide how much profit per unit seems "reasonable." This would be added to the cost per unit. If 10 cents were considered a reasonable profit for each unit, then the new price would be set at $1.10. See Figure 17–2.

It does not make allowances for cost variations as output changes

Figure 17–3
Typical shape of average cost curve

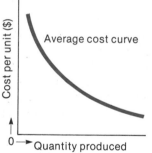

This approach is simple. But it also can be dangerous. It's easy to lose money with average-cost pricing. To see why, let's follow this example further.

If, in the next year only 5,000 units are produced and sold, the firm may be in trouble. Five thousand units sold at $1.10 each would yield a total revenue of $5,500. The overhead would still be fixed at $5,000. And the variable material and labor cost would drop in half to $2,500—for a total of $7,500. This would mean a loss of $2,000 or 40 cents a unit. The method that was supposed to allow a profit of 10 cents a unit actually causes a loss of 40 cents a unit! See Figure 17–2.

The basic problem is that this method did not allow for cost variations at different levels of output. In a typical situation, average costs per unit are high when only a few units are produced. Average costs continually drop as the quantity produced increases. This is shown in Figure 17–3. This typical decline in the average cost curve occurs because of "economies of size." This is why mass production and mass distribution often make sense. And this behavior of cost must be considered when setting prices.

MARKETING MANAGER MUST CONSIDER VARIOUS KINDS OF COST

Average-cost pricing may fail because total cost includes a variety of costs. And each of these costs changes in a different way as output changes. Any pricing method that uses cost must consider these changes. To understand why, however, we need to define six types of costs. Differences among these costs help explain why many companies have problems with pricing.

There are three kinds of total cost

Total fixed cost is the sum of those costs that are fixed in total—no matter how much is produced. Among these fixed costs are rent, depreciation, managers' salaries, property taxes, and insurance. Such costs must be paid even if production stops temporarily.

Total variable cost, on the other hand, is the sum of those changing expenses that are closely related to output—expenses for parts, wages, packaging materials, outgoing freight, and sales commissions.

At zero output, total variable cost is zero. As output increases, so do variable costs. If a dress manufacturer doubles the output of dresses in a year, the total cost of cloth would also roughly double.

Total cost is the sum of total fixed and total variable costs. The growth of total cost depends upon the increase in total variable cost—since total fixed cost is already set.

There are three kinds of average cost

The pricing manager usually is more interested in cost per unit than total cost—because prices are usually quoted per unit. Costs per unit are called "average costs."

Average cost is obtained by dividing total cost by the related quantity (i.e., the total quantity which causes the total costs).

Average fixed cost is obtained by dividing total fixed cost by the related quantity.

Average variable cost is obtained by dividing total variable cost by the related quantity.

An example illustrates cost relations

Table 17–1 shows typical cost data for one firm. Here we assume that average variable cost is the same for each unit. Notice how average fixed cost goes down steadily as the quantity increases. Notice also how total

Table 17–1
Cost structure of a firm

Quantity (Q)	Total fixed costs (TFC)	Average fixed costs (AFC)	Average variable costs (AVC)	Total variable costs (TVC)	Total cost (TC)	Average cost (AC)
0	$30,000	$	$	$ 0	$ 30,000	$
10,000	30,000	3.00	0.80	8,000	38,000	3.80
20,000	30,000	1.50	0.80	16,000	46,000	2.30
30,000	30,000	1.00	0.80	24,000	54,000	1.80
40,000	30,000	0.75	0.80	32,000	62,000	1.51
50,000	30,000	0.60	0.80	40,000	70,000	1.40
60,000	30,000	0.50	0.80	48,000	78,000	1.30
70,000	30,000	0.43	0.80	56,000	86,000	1.23
80,000	30,000	0.38	0.80	64,000	94,000	1.18
90,000	30,000	0.33	0.80	72,000	102,000	1.13
100,000	30,000	0.30	0.80	80,000	110,000	1.10

$$\begin{bmatrix} 110,000 \text{ (TC)} \\ -80,000 \text{ (TVC)} \\ \hline 30,000 \text{ (TFC)} \end{bmatrix} \quad \text{(Q) } 100,000 \overline{\smash{\big)}30,000} \begin{matrix} 0.30 \text{ (AFC)} \\ \text{(TFC)} \end{matrix}$$

$$\text{(Q) } 100,000 \overline{\smash{\big)}80,000} \begin{matrix} 0.80 \text{ (AVC)} \\ \text{(TVC)} \end{matrix}$$

$$\begin{bmatrix} 100,000 \text{ (Q)} \\ \times 0.80 \text{ (AVC)} \\ \hline 80,000 \text{ (TVC)} \end{bmatrix} \quad \begin{bmatrix} 30,000 \text{ (TFC)} \\ +80,000 \text{ (TVC)} \\ \hline 110,000 \text{ (TC)} \end{bmatrix} \quad \text{(Q) } 100,000 \overline{\smash{\big)}110,000} \begin{matrix} 1.10 \text{ (AC)} \\ \text{(TC)} \end{matrix}$$

Figure 17–4
Typical shape of cost (per unit) curves when AVC is assumed constant per unit

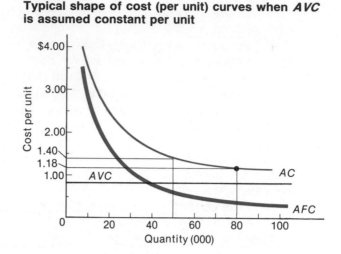

variable cost increases when quantity increases, although the average variable cost remains the same. Average cost decreases continually too. This is because average variable cost is the same and average fixed cost is decreasing. Figure 17–4 graphs the three average-cost curves.

Ignoring demand is major weakness of average-cost pricing

Average-cost pricing works well if the firm actually sells the quantity which was used in setting the average cost price. Losses may result, however, if actual sales are *much lower* than were expected. On the other hand, if sales are much higher than expected, then profits may be very good. But this will only be by accident—because the firm's demand is much larger than expected.

To use average-cost pricing, a marketing manager must make some estimate of the quantity to be sold in the coming period. But unless this quantity is related to price—that is, unless the firm's demand curve is considered—the marketing manager may set a price that doesn't even cover a firm's total cost! This can be seen in a simple illustration for a firm with the cost curves shown in Figure 17–4. This firm's demand curve is shown in Figure 17–5. It is important to see that customers' demands (and their demand curve) are still important—whether management takes time to analyze the demand curve or not.

Figure 17–5
Evaluation of various prices along a firm's demand curve

In this example, whether management sets the price at a high $3 or a low $1.25, it will have a loss. At $3, only 10,000 units will be sold for a total revenue of $30,000. But total costs will be $38,000—for loss of $8,000. At the $1.25 price, 50,000 units will be sold—for a loss of $7,500. If management tried to estimate the demand curve—however roughly— the price probably would be set in the middle of the range, say at $2, where a profit of $6,000 would result. See Figure 17–5.

In short, average-cost pricing is simple in theory, but often fails in practice. In stable situations, prices set by this method may yield profits—but not necessarily maximum profits. And interestingly, such cost-based prices might be higher than a price that would be more profitable for a firm—as shown in Figure 17–5. When demand conditions are changing, average-cost pricing may be even more risky.

FINDING THE MOST PROFITABLE PRICE AND QUANTITY TO PRODUCE

A marketing manager facing the typical downsloping demand curve must pick *one* price (for a time period). His problem is which price to choose. This price, of course, will set the quantity that will be sold.

To maximize profit, the marketing manager should choose the price which will lead to the greatest difference between total revenue and total cost. Finding this best price and quantity requires an estimate of the firm's demand curve. This should be seen as an "iffy" curve—*if* price A is set then quantity A will be sold—*if* price B is set then quantity B will be sold—and so on. By multiplying all these possible prices by their related quantities, you can figure the possible total revenues. Then, by estimating the firm's likely costs it is possible to figure a total cost curve. The difference between these two curves show possible total profits. Clearly, the best price would be the one which has the greatest distance between the total revenue and total cost curves. These ideas are shown in Table 17–2 and in Figure 17–6, where these data are plotted in a graph. In this example, you can see that the best price is $79 and the best quantity is six units.

A profit range is reassuring

Estimating demand curves is not easy. But some estimate of demand is needed to set prices. This is just one of the tough jobs facing marketing managers. Ignoring demand curves does not make them go away! So

Table 17–2
Revenue, cost, and profit for an individual firm

(1) Quantity Q	(2) Price P	(3) Total revenue TR	(4) Total cost TC	(5) Profit TR—TC
0	$150	$ 0	$200	$−200
1	140	140	296	−156
2	130	260	316	− 56
3	117	351	331	+ 20
4	105	420	344	+ 76
5	92	460	355	+105
6	79	474	368	+106
7	66	462	383	+ 79
8	53	424	423	+ 1
9	42	378	507	−129
10	31	310	710	−400

Figure 17–6
Graphic determination of the output giving the greatest total profit for a firm

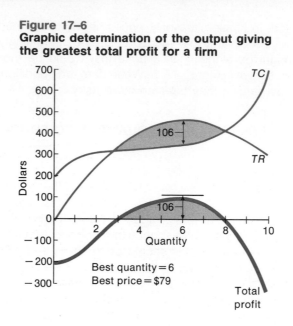

Best quantity = 6
Best price = $79

some estimates must be made. This points up again how important it is to understand the needs and attitudes of your target market.

Notice that the demand estimates do not have to be exact. Figure 17–7 shows that there is a *range* of profitable prices. The firm would be profitable all the way from a price of $53 to $117. $79 is just the "best" price.

The marketing manager probably would want to try to estimate the price which would lead to the middle of the profit range. But a slight "miss" would not mean failure. And at least trying to estimate demand would probably lead to being some place in the profitable range. In contrast, mechanical use of average-cost pricing might lead to much too high or much too low prices—as you saw earlier in the chapter. This is why estimating demand is not only desirable but necessary.

SOME PRICE SETTERS DO ESTIMATE DEMAND

Full use of demand curves is not very common in business. But we do find marketers setting prices as though they believe certain types of demand curves are there. (And pricing research indicates they are.)

The following section discusses various examples of demand-related pricing. Some may be only instinctive adjustments of cost-based prices—but you can see that demand is being considered.

Prestige pricing—make it high and not too low

Prestige pricing involves setting a rather high price to suggest high quality or high status. Some target customers seem to want the "best." If prices are dropped a little below this "high" level, they may see a

Figure 17–7
Range of profitable prices for illustrative data in Table 17–2 and Figure 17–6

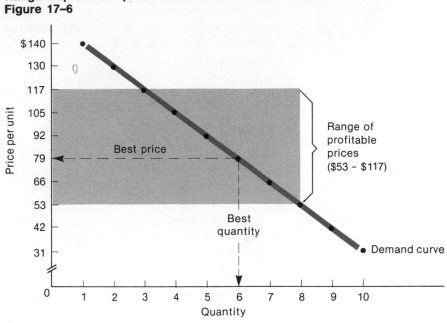

bargain. But if the prices begin to appear ''cheap,'' they may become worried about quality and stop buying.[2]

Target customers who respond to prestige pricing give the marketing manager an unusual demand curve. Instead of a normal downslope, the curve goes down for a while and then bends back to the left again. See Figure 17–8. Marketing managers faced with this kind of demand—such as jewelry and fur retailers and night club owners—typically set high prices.

Leader pricing—make it low to attract customers

Leader pricing is setting some very low prices—real bargains—to get customers into retail stores. Certain products are picked for their promotion value and priced low—but above cost. In food stores, the leader prices are the ''specials'' that are advertised regularly to give an image of low prices.

Leader pricing usually is limited to well-known, widely used items which customers don't stock heavily—milk, butter, eggs, or coffee—but on which they will recognize a real price cut. The idea is to attract customers— not to sell large quantities of the leaders. To avoid hurting the firm's own profits, items may be used that are not directly competitive with major lines—as when bargain-priced cigarettes are sold at a gasoline station.

Bait pricing—offer a ''steal,'' but sell under protest

Bait pricing means setting some very low prices to attract customers— but not to sell goods. It's something like leader pricing. But here the seller *doesn't* plan to sell much at the low price.

This approach is used by some furniture retailers. To attract customers, a store will offer an extremely low price on an item. Once customers are in the store, the sales people are expected to point out the disadvantages of the lower-quality item and sell customers higher-quality, more expensive products instead. Customers can buy the bait items—but only with great difficulty.

This policy tries to attract bargain hunters—or customers on the very low end of the demand curve who are not usually part of the market. If bait pricing is successful, customers may be "traded up"—and the demand for higher-quality products will expand. But extremely aggressive and sometimes dishonest bait-pricing advertising has given this method a bad reputation. The Federal Trade Commission considers bait pricing a deceptive act and has banned its use in interstate commerce. But some retailers who operate only within one state continue to advertise bait prices.

Odd-even pricing

Odd-even pricing means setting prices which end in certain numbers. Some marketers do this because they feel that consumers react better to these prices.

For goods selling under $50, prices ending with 95—such as $5.95, $6.95, and so on—are common. In general, prices ending in nine are most popular, followed by prices ending in five and three. For products selling over $50, prices that are $1 or $2 below the even-dollar figure are the most popular.[3]

Marketers using these prices seem to assume that they have a rather jagged demand curve—that consumers will buy less for a while as prices are lowered and then more as each "magic" price is reached. This kind of demand curve is shown in Figure 17–9.

Odd-even prices were used long ago by some retailers to force their

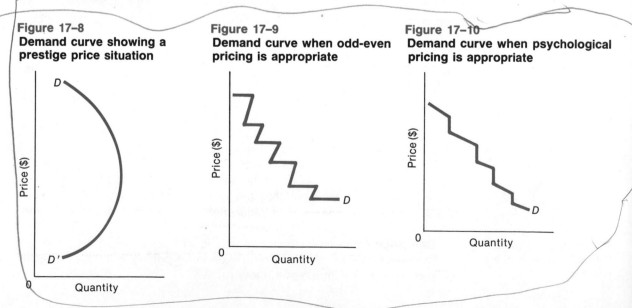

Figure 17–8
Demand curve showing a prestige price situation

Figure 17–9
Demand curve when odd-even pricing is appropriate

Figure 17–10
Demand curve when psychological pricing is appropriate

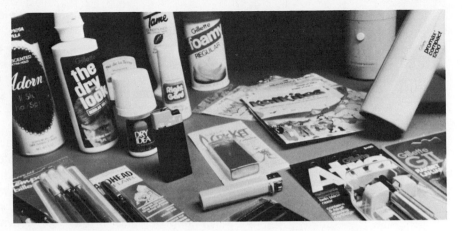

Some of the items in Gillette's product line. [1]

clerks to make change. Then they had to record the sale and could not pocket the money. Today, however, it is not always clear why these prices are used and whether they really work. Perhaps consumers have learned to expect better buys at certain prices and they do work. Or perhaps it is done simply because "everyone else does it."

Psychological pricing—some prices just seem right

Psychological pricing means setting prices which have special appeal to target customers. Some people feel there are whole ranges of prices which potential customers see as the same. Price cuts in these ranges would not increase the quantity sold. But just below this range, customers may buy more. Then, at even lower prices the quantity demanded would stay the same again. And so on.

The kind of demand curve that fits psychological pricing is shown in Figure 17–10. Vertical drops mark the price ranges which customers see as the same. Pricing research shows that there are such demand curves.[4]

PRICING A FULL LINE OR A TOTAL PRODUCT

Our emphasis has been—and will continue to be—on the problem of pricing a single item, mainly because this makes our discussion easier. But most marketing managers are responsible for more than one product. In fact, their "product" may be the whole company line!

Full-line pricing—market or firm oriented?

Full-line pricing means setting a price for a whole line of products. How to do this depends on which of two basic strategies a firm is using. In one case, all products in the company's line are aimed at the same general target market—which makes it important for all prices to be related to one another.

In other cases, the different products in the line are aimed at entirely different target markets. Here, there doesn't have to be any relation between the various prices. A chemical manufacturer of a wide variety of products with several target markets, for example, probably should price each product separately.

Examples of a full line being offered to the same target market are a TV manufacturer selling a whole line to retailers, or a forklift truck producer offering various sizes to large manufacturers, or a grocery retailer with thousands of items. Here the firm has to think of the customers' reaction to its full line of prices.

Cost is not much help in full-line pricing

The marketing manager must try to recover all costs on the whole line—perhaps by pricing quite low on competitive items and much higher on less competitive items. But costs are not much help to the marketing manager in full-line pricing. There is no one "right" way to assign a company's fixed costs to each of the products. And if any method is carried through without considering demand, it may lead to very unrealistic prices. The marketing manager should judge demand for the whole line—as well as demand for each individual product in each target market—to avoid mistakes.

Price lining—a few prices cover the field

Price lining is like full-line pricing, but here the focus is on how prices look at the retail level.

Price lining is the policy of setting a few price levels for given classes of goods and then marking all items at these prices.

Most customers will pay between $2.50 and $10 for a necktie. In price lining, there will not be many prices in this range. There will be only a few. Ties will not be priced at $2.50, $2.65, $2.70, and so on. They might be priced at three levels—$2.50, $5, and $10.

The main advantage of price lining is simplicity—for both clerks and customers. It is less confusing than a big variety of prices. Some customers may consider goods in only one price class. Their big decision then is which items to choose at that price. Price is no longer a question—unless the goods at that price are not satisfactory. Then, perhaps the customer can be "traded up" to the next price level.

For retailers, price lining has several advantages. Sales may increase because (1) they can offer a bigger variety in each price line and (2) it is easier to get customers to make decisions within one price line. Stock planning is simpler, because demand is larger at the relatively few prices. Price lining also can reduce costs because inventory needs are lower even though large stocks are carried in each line. In summary, price lining results in faster turnover, fewer markdowns, quicker sales, and simplified buying.

Demand-backward pricing aids price lining

Demand-backward pricing starts with an acceptable final consumer price and works backward to what a producer can charge. It is commonly used by producers of final consumer goods—especially shopping goods, such as women's and children's clothing and shoes. It is also used for toys or gifts for which customers will spend a specific amount because

"So, you want to sell it for $5. Let's see . . . with the retail markup of 40%, wholesale markup of 20%, and the manufacturer markup of 10% . . . if you can make it for less than $2.16, you're in business."

(An example of demand-backward pricing.)

they are seeking a "five-dollar" or a "ten-dollar" gift. Here, a reverse cost-plus pricing process is used. This method has been called "market-minus" pricing.

The producer starts with the retail price for a particular item and then works backward—subtracting the typical margins which channel members expect. This gives the approximate price that he can charge. Then, he subtracts from this price the average or planned marketing expenses to determine how much can be spent producing the item.

Demand estimates are necessary if demand-backward pricing is to be successful. The quantity which will be demanded affects production costs—i.e., where the firm will be on its average cost curve. Also, since competitors can be expected to make the best product possible, it is important to know customer needs—to set the best amount to be spent on manufacturing costs. By increasing costs a little, the product might be so improved in consumers' eyes that the firm would sell many more units. But if consumers only want novelty—additional quality might not increase the quantity demanded—and shouldn't be offered.

BID PRICING DEPENDS HEAVILY ON COSTS

A new price for every job   **Bid pricing** means offering a specific price for each possible job—rather than developing a price policy that applies for all potential customers. Building contractors, for example, must bid on possible projects. And many companies selling services (like cleaning or data processing) must submit bids for jobs they would like to have.

Even with bid pricing more bargaining may be needed.

The big problem in bid pricing is collecting all the costs that apply to each job. This may sound easy, but thousands of cost components may have to go into a complicated bid. Further, management must include an overhead charge and a charge for profit.

Demand must be considered too

It is when adding in overhead and profit that demand and competition must be considered. Usually, the customer will get several bids and accept the lowest one. So unthinking addition of overhead and profit should be avoided. Some bidders use the same overhead and profit rates on all jobs—regardless of competition—and then are surprised when they don't get some jobs.

Bidding can be expensive. So a firm might want to be selective about which jobs it will bid on—hopefully selecting those where they feel they have the greatest chance of success.[5] Thousands or even millions of dollars have been spent just developing cost-oriented bids for large industrial or government orders.

Sometimes bids are bargained

Some buying situations (including much government buying) require the use of bids, and the purchasing agent must take the lowest bid. In other cases, however, bids may be called for and then the company submitting the most attractive bid—not necessarily the lowest—will be singled out for further bargaining. This may include price adjustments—but it also may be concerned with how additions to the job will be priced, what guarantees will be provided, and the quality of labor and supervisors who will do the job. Some projects—such as construction projects—are hard to define exactly. So it is important that the buyer be satisfied about the whole marketing mix—not just the price. Obviously, effective personal selling can be important here.

Conclusion

In this chapter, we discussed various approaches to price setting. Generally, retailers and wholesalers use traditional markups. Some use the same markups for all their items. Others have found that varying the markups may increase turnover and profit. In other words, demand is considered!

Cost-oriented pricing seems to make sense for middlemen because they handle small quantities of many items. Producers must take price setting more seriously. They are the ones that set the "list price" to which others apply markups.

Producers commonly use average cost curves to help set their prices. But this approach sometimes ignores demand completely. A more realistic approach requires a sales forecast. This may just mean assuming that sales in the next period will be roughly the same as in the last period. This *will* enable the marketing manager to set a price—but this price *may or may not* cover all costs and earn the desired profit.

We discussed how demand could be brought into pricing. This could help a marketing manager maximize profits—if this were his objective. It appears that some marketers do consider demand in their pricing. We saw this with prestige pricing, leader pricing, bait pricing, odd-even pricing, psychological pricing, full-time pricing, and even bid pricing.

We have stressed throughout the book that the customer must be considered before anything is done. This certainly applies to pricing. It means that when managers are setting a price, they have to consider what customers will be willing to pay. This isn't always easy, but it is nice to know that there is a profit range around the "best" price. Therefore, even "guesstimates" about what potential customers will buy at various prices will probably lead to a better price than just mechanical use of traditional markups or cost-oriented formulas.

Questions for discussion

1 Why do department stores seek a markup of about 40 percent when some discount houses operate on a 20 percent markup?

2 A manufacturer of household appliances distributed its products through wholesalers and retailers. The retail selling price was $250, and the manufacturing cost to the company was $100. The retail markup was 40 percent and the wholesale markup 25 percent.

a. What was the cost to the wholesaler? To the retailer?

b. What percentage markup did the manufacturer take?

3 Relate the concept of stock turnover to the rise of discounters. Use a simple example in your answer.

4 If total fixed costs are $100,000 and total variable costs are $200,000 at an output of 10,000 units, what are the probable total fixed costs and total variable costs at an output of 20,000 units? What are the average fixed costs, average variable costs, and the average costs at these two output levels? Determine the price that should be charged. (Make any simplifying assumptions necessary to obtain a definite answer.)

5 Explain how target return pricing differs from average cost pricing.

6 Construct an example showing that mechanical use of a very large or very small markup might still lead to unprofitable operation, while some intermediate price would be profitable.

7 How would a prestige pricing policy fit into a marketing mix? Would exclusive distribution be necessary?

8 Cite a local example of the use of odd-even pricing and then evaluate whether you feel it makes sense.

9 Cite a local example of the use of psychological pricing and then evaluate whether you feel it makes sense.

10 Distinguish between leader pricing and bait pricing. What do they have in common? How can their use affect a marketing mix?

11 Is a full-line pricing policy available only to producers? Cite local examples of full-line pricing. Why is full-line pricing important?

Suggested cases

21 Kennedy Dance Studio

22 Wire Specialties, Inc.

26 Nagel Mfg. Company

When you finish this chapter, you should:

1 Understand the various ways that businesses can get into international marketing.
2 Understand what multinational corporations are.
3 Understand the kinds of opportunities in international markets.
4 Understand the market dimensions which may be useful in segmenting international markets.
5 Recognize the important new terms shown in red.

MARKETING PLANNING FOR INTERNATIONAL MARKETS

Did you know that more spaghetti is bought in Germany than in Italy?

Planning strategies for international markets can be even harder than for domestic markets. Now, cultural differences are more important. Each foreign market must be treated as a separate market—with its own sub-markets. Lumping together all people outside the United States as "foreigners"—or assuming that they are just like U.S. customers—is almost a guarantee of failure.

There has been too much narrow thinking about international marketing. This chapter aims to get rid of some of these ideas—and to suggest how strategy planning has to be changed when a firm enters international markets. We will see that a marketing planner must make several strategic decisions about international marketing: (1) whether the firm even wants to work in international markets, and if so, (2) which markets, and (3) what changes should be made in the firm's methods when it expands outside its own country.

THE IMPORTANCE OF INTERNATIONAL MARKETS TO THE UNITED STATES

As a nation grows, its trade grows

All countries trade to some extent—we live in an interdependent world. But you may be surprised to know that the United States is the largest exporter and importer of goods in the world. Our share of the world's foreign trade is about 12 percent. Even the United Kingdom and Japan—which have built their growth on exports and imports—are below the United

States. Most of the largest traders are highly developed nations. Trade seems to expand as a country grows and industrializes.

But while the United States is the biggest trading nation in the world, foreign trade does not control our economy. This is because of the larger size of our national income. Our foreign trade makes up a relatively small part of our income—less than 10 percent—but the smaller part is still greater in total dollars than in other major trading countries.

EVOLUTION OF CORPORATE INVOLVEMENT IN INTERNATIONAL MARKETING

Opportunities in foreign countries have led many companies into world-wide operations. The marketing concept is less understood in some foreign markets. So there are great opportunities for those who want to apply it abroad—from just exporting, to joint ventures, to investment in foreign operations. Many companies are aggressively pursuing foreign market prospects because they find their foreign operations becoming more profitable than domestic activities.

Exporting often comes first

Some companies get into international marketing by just exporting the products they are now producing. Sometimes this is just a way of "getting rid of" surplus output. Other times, it comes from a real effort to look for new opportunities.

Exporting is selling some of what the firm is producing to foreign markets. Often this is tried without changing the product or even the service or instruction manuals! As a result, some of these early efforts are not very satisfying—to buyers or sellers.

Exporting gets a firm involved in a lot of government "red tape." Beginning exporters may build their own staffs or depend on specialized middlemen to handle these details. Export agents can handle the paper work as the goods are shipped outside the country. Then agents or merchant

Exporters may use international middlemen.

Gerber entered the Japanese baby food market by licensing.

wholesalers can handle the importing details. Even large manufacturers with many foreign operations may use international middlemen for some products or markets. They know how to handle the sometimes confusing formalities and specialized functions. Even a small mistake can tie goods up at national borders for days—or months.

SOME RELATIONSHIPS GET A FIRM MORE INVOLVED

Exporting doesn't have to involve permanent relationships. Of course, channel relationships take time to build and shouldn't be treated lightly. Sales reps' contacts in foreign countries are ''investments.'' Nevertheless, it is relatively easy to cut back on these relationships or even drop them.

Some firms, on the other hand, form more formal and permanent relationships with nationals in foreign countries—including licensing, contract manufacturing, management contracting, and joint venturing.

Licensing is an easy way

Licensing is a relatively easy way to enter foreign markets. **Licensing** means selling the right to use some process, trademark, patent, or other right—for a fee or royalty. The licensee takes most of the risk because it must invest some capital to use the right.

This can be an effective way of entering a market if good partners are available. Gerber entered the Japanese baby food market in this way. But Gerber still exports to other countries.

Contract manufacturing takes care of the production problems

Contract manufacturing means turning over production to others while retaining the marketing process. Sears Roebuck used this approach as it opened stores in Latin America and Spain.

This approach can be especially good where there are difficult labor relations or problems obtaining supplies and ''buying'' government cooperation. Growing nationalistic feelings may make this approach more attractive in the future.

Management contracting sells know-how

Management contracting means the seller provides only management skills—the production facilities are owned by others. Some mines and oil refineries are operated this way—and Hilton operates hotels all over the world for local owners. This is a relatively low-risk approach to international marketing. No commitment is made to fixed facilities which can be taken over or damaged in riots or wars. If conditions get too bad, the key management people can fly off on the next plane and leave the nationals to manage the operation.

Joint venturing is more involved

Joint venturing means a domestic firm entering into a partnership with a foreign firm. As with any partnership, there can be honest disagreements over objectives—for example, about how much profit is desired and how fast is should be paid out—and operating policies. Where a close working relationship can be developed—perhaps based on a U.S. firm's technical and marketing know-how, and the foreign partner's knowledge of the market and political connections—this approach can be very attractive to both parties. At its worst, it can be a nightmare and cause the U.S. firm to want to go into a wholly owned operation. But the terms of the joint venture may block this for years. Or the foreign partners may acquire enough know-how to be tough competitors.

Wholly owned subsidiaries give more control

When a firm feels that a foreign market looks really promising, it may want to go the final step. A **wholly owned subsidiary** is a separate firm, owned by a parent company. This gives complete control and helps a foreign branch work more easily with the rest of the company.

Some multinational companies have gone this way. It gives them a great deal of freedom to move goods from one country to another. If it has too much capacity in a country with low production costs, for example, some production may be moved there from other plants—and then exported to countries with higher production costs. This is the same way that large firms in the United States ship goods from one area to another—depending on costs and local needs.

MULTINATIONAL CORPORATIONS EVOLVE TO MEET INTERNATIONAL CHALLENGE

Multinational corporations have a direct investment in several countries and run their businesses depending on the choices available anywhere in the world. Well known U.S.-based multinational firms include Eastman Kodak, Warner-Lambert, Pfizer, Anaconda, Goodyear, Ford, IBM, ITT, Corn Products, 3M, National Cash Register, H. J. Heinz, and Gillette. They regularly earn over 30 percent of their total sales or profits abroad. And Coca-Cola recently moved past the half-way point—more than half of its profits come from international operations! Coca-Cola sees the day coming when as much as 75 percent of its earnings will be from abroad—because there will be more young people with money there than in aging America.[1]

Most multinational companies are American. But there are some well-known foreign-based companies such as Nestle's, Shell (Royal Dutile Shell), and Lever Brothers (Unilever). They have well-accepted "foreign"

Japanese companies make products in the United States.

brands—not only in the United States, but around the world. And Japanese firms producing Sony, Honda, Panasonic, and other well-known brands are operating around the globe.

Multinational operations make sense to more firms

As firms move more deeply into international marketing, some reach the point where the firm sees itself as a worldwide business. As a chief executive of Abbott Laboratories—a pharmaceutical company with plants in 22 countries—said, "We are no longer just a U.S. company with interests abroad. Abbott is a worldwide enterprise and many major fundamental decisions must be made on a global basis."

A Texas Instruments executive had a similar view: "When we consider new opportunities and one is abroad and the other domestic, we can't afford to look upon the alternative here as an inherently superior business opportunity simply because it is in the United States. We view an overseas market just as we do our market, say, in Arizona, as one more market in the world."

A General Motors executive sees this trend as ". . . the emergence of the modern industrial corporation as an institution that is transcending national boundaries."[2]

Much of the multinational activity of the 1960s and early 1970s was U.S.-based firms expanding to other countries. As these opportunities became less attractive in the mid-1970s—due to the energy crisis, inflation, currency devaluations, labor unrest, and unstable governments—foreign multinational companies have been moving into the United States. The United States is, after all, one of the richest markets in the world.

Foreign firms are beginning to see that it may be attractive to operate in this large—if competitive—market. The Japanese "invasion" with all kinds of electronic products is well known. And they are building plants, too. For example, Sony has a TV assembly plant and a TV tube plant in southern California. And French firms (including the producers of Michelin tires) are setting up or buying facilities in the United States.[3]

Multinational companies overcome national boundaries

From an international view, multinational firms do—as the GM executive said—"transcend national boundaries." They see world market opportunities and locate their production and distribution facilities for greatest effectiveness. This has upset some nationalistic business managers and politicians. But these multinational operations may be difficult to stop. They are no longer just exporting or importing. They hire local residents and build plants. And they have business relationships with local business managers and politicians. These are powerful organizations which have learned to deal with nationalistic feelings and typical border barriers—treating them simply as uncontrollable variables.

We do not have "one world" politically as yet—but business is moving in that direction. We may have to develop new kinds of corporations and laws to govern multinational operations. The limitations of national boundaries on business and politics will make less and less sense in the future.[4]

IDENTIFYING DIFFERENT KINDS OF OPPORTUNITIES

Firms usually start from where they are

A really multinational firm which has accepted the marketing concept will look for opportunities in the same way that we have been discussing throughout the text, i.e., looking for unsatisfied needs that it might be able to satisfy—given its resources and objectives.

The typical approach, however, is to start with the firm's current products and the needs it knows how to satisfy, and try to find new markets— wherever they may be—with the same or similar unsatisfied needs. Next, the firm adapts the product, and perhaps its promotion. Later, the firm may think about developing new products and new promotion policies. Some of these possibilities are shown in Figure 18–1. Here we only look at Product and Promotion—because Place would obviously have to be changed in new markets, and Price adjustments probably would be needed also.

The "Same-Same" box in Figure 18–1 can be illustrated with McDonald's (fast-food chain) entry into European markets. Its Director of International Marketing says, "Ronald McDonald speaks eight languages. Our target audience is the same worldwide—young families with children— and our advertising is designed to appeal to them." The basic promotion messages must be translated, of course, but the same strategy decisions which were made for the U.S. market apply. McDonald's has adapted its Product in Germany, however, by adding beer to appeal to adults who prefer beer over soft drinks. Its efforts have been extremely successful

Figure 18–1
International marketing opportunities as seen by a U.S. firm from the viewpoint of its usual product market in the United States[5]

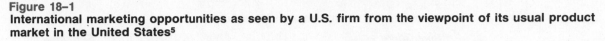

		Product		
		Same	Adaptation	New
Promotion	**Same**	Same needs and use conditions (McDonald's usual strategy)	Basically same needs and use conditions (McDonald's strategy with beer in Germany)	Basically same needs, but different incomes and/or applications (street vendor with low-cost hamburgers)
	Adaptation	Different needs but same use conditions (bicycles)	Different needs and use conditions (clothing)	Different needs and different incomes and/or applications (hand-powered washing machines)

so far. Some stores are selling over $1 million per year—something that took many more years to do in the United States.[6]

McDonald's and other firms expanding into international markets usually move first into markets with good economic potential—such as Western Europe and Japan. But if McDonald's or some other fast-food company wanted to move into much lower-income areas, it might have to develop a whole new Product—perhaps a traveling street vendor with "hamburgers" made out of soy products. This kind of opportunity is in the upper right-hand corner of Figure 18–1.

The lower left-hand box in this figure is illustrated by the different kind of promotion that is needed for just a simple bicycle. In some parts of the world, a bicycle provides basic transportation—while in the United States it is mainly a recreation vehicle. So a different promotion emphasis is needed in these different target markets.

Both product and promotion changes will be needed as one moves to the right along the bottom row of Figure 18–1. Such moves would obviously require more market knowledge—and may increase the risk.

The risk of opportunities varies by environmental sensitivity

International marketing means going into unfamiliar markets. This can increase risks. The farther one is from familiar territory, the greater the likelihood of making big mistakes. But not all products offer the same risk. It is useful to think of the risks running along a "continuum of environmental sensitivity." See Figure 18–2. Some products are relatively insensitive to the economic or cultural environment in which they are placed. These products may be accepted as it. Or they may require relatively

Figure 18–2
Continuum of environmental sensitivity

Insensitive | *Sensitive*

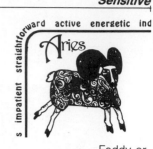

Industrial
goods

Basic
commodity-type
consumer
goods

Faddy or
high-style
consumer
goods

little adaption to make them suitable for local use. Most industrial goods would tend to be near the insensitive end of this continuum.

At the other end of the continuum, we find highly sensitive products which may be difficult or impossible to adapt to all international situations. At this end we would find faddy or high-style consumer goods. It is sometimes difficult to understand why a particular product is well accepted in a home market—so this makes it even more difficult to know how it might be received in a different environment.

This continuum helps explain why many of the early successes in international marketing involved basic commodities such as gasoline, soap, transportation vehicles, mining equipment, and agricultural machinery. It also suggests that firms producing and/or selling highly sensitive products should carefully analyze how their products will be seen and used in the new environment.[7]

Evaluating opportunities in alternative international markets

Judging opportunities in international markets uses the same principles we have been discussing. Basically, each opportunity must be evaluated within the uncontrollable variables. But there may be more of these and they may be more difficult to evaluate in international markets. Estimating the risk involved in particular opportunities may be very difficult. Some countries are not as stable politically as the United States. Their governments and constitutions come and go. An investment that was safe under one government might become the target for a take-over under another. Further, the possibility of foreign exchange controls and tax rate changes can reduce the chance of getting profits and capital back to the home country.

Because the risks are hard to judge, it may be wise to enter international marketing by exporting first—building know-how and confidence over time. Experience and judgment are needed even more in unfamiliar areas. Allowing time to develop these skills among a firm's top management—as well as its international managers—makes sense. Then the firm will be in a better position to estimate the prospects and risks of going further into international markets.

INTERNATIONAL MARKETING REQUIRES EVEN MORE SEGMENTING

Success in international marketing requires even more attention to segmenting. There are over 140 nations with their own unique differences! There can be big differences in language, customs, beliefs, religion, race, and even income distribution patterns from one country to another. This obviously complicates the segmenting process. But what makes it even worse is that there is less good data as one moves into international markets. While the number of variables increases, the quantity and quality of data go down. This is one reason why some multinational firms insist that local operations be handled by natives. They at least have a "feel" for their markets.

There are more dimensions—but there is a way

Segmenting international markets may require more dimensions. But a practical method adds just one step before the seven-step approach discussed in Chapter 7. See Figure 18–3. First, segment by country or region, looking at demographic, cultural, and other characteristics—including stage of economic development. This may help find reasonably similar subsets. Then, depending upon whether the firm is aiming at final consumers or intermediate customers, it could apply the seven-step approach discussed earlier.

Most of the discussion in the rest of this chapter will emphasize final consumer differences because they are likely to be greater than intermediate customer differences. Also, we will consider regional groupings and stages of economic development which can aid your segmentation efforts. Basically, our objective is to broaden your view of international markets.

Figure 18–3
Segmenting in international markets

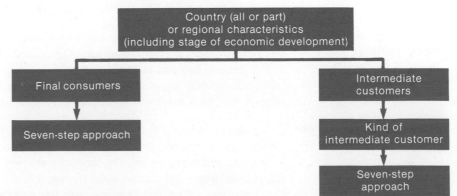

REGIONAL GROUPINGS MAY MEAN MORE THAN NATIONAL BOUNDARIES

While national boundaries are a common and logical dimension for segmenting markets, sometimes it makes more sense to treat several nearby countries with similar cultures as one region. Or, if several nations have banded together to have common economic boundaries, then these nations may be treated as a unit. The outstanding example is the European Economic Community (EEC). They have dared to abandon old ideas and nationalistic prejudices—in favor of cooperative efforts to reduce tariffs and other controls commonly applied at national boundaries.

These cooperative arrangements are very important because the taxes and restrictions at national borders can be not only annoying but may greatly reduce marketing opportunities. **Tariffs**—taxes on incoming goods—vary depending on whether the country is trying to raise revenue or limit trade. Restrictive tariffs often block all movement. But even revenue-producing tariffs cause red-tape and discourage free movement of goods. Quotas act like restrictive tariffs. **Quotas** set the specific quantities of goods which can move in or out of a country. There might be great market opportunities in a country, but import quotas (or export controls applied against a specific country) may discourage outsiders from entering. The U.S. government, for example, has controlled Japan's export of TVs to the United States. (Otherwise, we might have had even more Japanese products entering the U.S. market!)

STAGES OF ECONOMIC DEVELOPMENT HELP DEFINE MARKETS

International markets are so varied that we can't make general rules for all of them. Some markets are more advanced and/or growing more rapidly than others. And some countries—or parts of a country—are at different stages of economic development. This means their demands and even their marketing systems will vary.

To get some idea of the many possible differences in potential markets, let's discuss six stages of economic development. These stages are over-simplified, of course. But they are helpful in understanding economic development—and how it affects marketing.

Stage 1—Agricultural self-supporting

In this stage, most people are subsistence farmers. There may be a simple marketing system—perhaps occasional weekly markets—but most of the people are not even in a money economy. Some parts of Africa and New Guinea are in this stage. In a practical marketing sense, these people are not a market—they have no money to buy goods.

Stage 2—Preindustrial or commercial

Some countries in Sub-Sahara Africa and the Middle East are in this second stage. During this stage, we see more market-oriented activity. Raw materials such as oil, tin, and copper are extracted and exported. Agricultural and forest crops such as sugar, rubber, and timber are grown and exported. Often this is done with the help of foreign technical skills

Some parts of Africa and New Guinea are in the agricultural/self-supporting stage.

and capital. A commercial economy may develop along with—but unrelated to—the subsistence economy. These activities may require the beginnings of a transportation system to tie the extracting or growing areas to shipping points. A money economy operates at this stage.

In this stage, there are imports of industrial machinery and equipment. And huge construction projects may need many special supplies. Buying for these needs may be handled by purchasing agents in industrial countries. There is also the need for imports—including luxury goods—to meet the living standards of technical and supervisory people. These may be handled by company stores rather than local retailers.

The relatively few large landowners and those who benefit by this business activity may develop expensive tastes. The few natives employed by these larger firms and the small business managers who serve them may develop into a small, middle-income class. But most of the population are still in the first stage—for practical purposes they are not in the market. This total market may be so small that local importers can easily handle the demand. There is little reason for local manufacturers to try to supply it.

Stage 3—Primary manufacturing

In the third stage, there is some processing of metal ores or the agricultural products that once were shipped out of the country in raw form. Sugar and rubber, for example, are both produced and processed in Indonesia. The same is true for oil on the Persian Gulf. Multinational companies may set up factories to take advantage of low-cost labor. They may export most of the output, but they do stimulate local development. More local labor becomes involved at this stage. A domestic market develops. Small local businesses are starting to handle some of the raw material processing.

Even though the local market expands in this third stage, a large part of the population is still at the subsistence level—almost entirely outside the money economy. There may still be a large foreign population of professionals and technicians needed for the developing agricultural-industrial complex. The demands of this group and of the growing number of wealthy natives are still quite different from the needs of the lower class and the growing middle class. A domestic market among the local people begins to develop. But local manufacturers still may have difficulty finding enough demand to keep them in business.

Stage 4—Nondurable and semidurable consumer goods manufacturing

At this stage, small local manufacturing begins—especially in those lines that need only a small investment to get started. Often, these industries grow out of small firms that developed to supply the primary manufacturers dominating the last stage. For example, plants making sulfuric acid and explosives for extracting mineral resources might expand into soap manufacturing. And recently, multinational firms have speeded development of countries at this stage with investments in promising opportunities.

Paint, drug, food and beverage, and textile industries develop in this stage. The textile industry is usually one of the first to develop. Clothing is a necessity. This early emphasis on the textile industry in developing nations is one reason the world textile market is so competitive.

Some of the small manufacturers become members of the middle- or even upper-income class. They help to expand the demand for imported goods. As this market grows, local businesses begin to see enough volume to operate profitably. So the need for imports to supply nondurable and semidurable goods is less. But consumer durables and capital goods are still imported.

Stage 5—Capital goods and consumer durable goods manufacturing

In this stage, the production of capital goods and consumer durable goods begins. This includes automobiles, refrigerators, and machinery for local industries. Such manufacturing creates other demands—raw materials for the local factories, and food and fibers for clothing for the rural population entering the industrial labor force.

Industrialization has begun. But the economy still depends on exports of raw materials—either wholly unprocessed or slightly processed.

It still may be necessary to import special heavy machinery and equipment at this stage. Imports of consumer durable goods may still compete with local products. The foreign community and the status-conscious wealthy may prefer these imports.

Stage 6—Exporting manufactured products

Countries that have not gone beyond the fifth stage are mainly exporters of raw materials. They import manufactured goods and equipment to build their industrial base. In the sixth stage, exporting manufactured goods becomes most important. The country may specialize in certain types of manufactured goods—such as iron and steel, watches, cameras, electronic equipment, and processed food.

There are many opportunities for importing and exporting at this stage. These countries have grown richer and have needs—and the purchasing power—for a great variety of products. In fact, countries in this stage often carry on a great deal of trade with each other. Each trades those goods in which it has production advantages. In this stage, almost all consumers are in the money economy. And there may be a large middle-income class. The United States, most of the Western European countries, and Japan are at this last stage.[8]

It is important to see that it is not necessary to label a whole country or geographic region as being in one stage. Certainly, different parts of the United States have developed differently and might properly be placed in different stages.

HOW THESE STAGES CAN BE USEFUL IN FINDING MARKET OPPORTUNITIES

A good starting point for estimating present and future market potentials in a country—or part of a country—is to estimate its present stage of economic development and how fast it is moving to another stage. Actually, the speed of movement, if any, and the possibility that stages may be skipped may suggest whether market opportunities are there—or are likely to open. But just naming the present stage can be very useful in deciding what to look at and whether there are prospects for the firm's products.

Fitting the firm to market needs

Manufacturers of automobiles, expensive cameras, or other consumer durable goods, for example, should not plan to set up a mass distribution system in a market that is in the preindustrial (stage 2) or even the primary manufacturing stage (stage 3). One or a few middlemen may be all that's needed. Even the market for U.S. "necessities"—items such as canned foods or drug products—may not yet be large. Large-scale selling of these consumer items requires a large base of cash or credit customers—but as yet too few are part of the money economy.

On the other hand, a market in the nondurable goods manufacturing stage has more potential—especially for durable goods producers. Incomes and the number of potential customers are growing. There is no local competition yet.

Opportunities might still be good for durable goods imports in the fifth stage, even though domestic producers are trying to get started. But more likely, the local government would raise some controls to aid local industry. Then the foreign producer might have to start licensing local producers or building a local plant.

Pursuing that tempting inverted pyramid

Areas or countries in the final stage often are the biggest and most profitable markets. While there may be more competition, there are many more customers with higher incomes. We have already seen how income distribution shifted in the United States from a pyramid to more families with middle and upper incomes. This can be expected during the latter stages—when a "mass market" develops.

OTHER MARKET DIMENSIONS MAY SUGGEST OPPORTUNITIES, TOO

Considering country or regional differences—including stages of economic development—can be useful as a first step in segmenting international markets. After finding some possible areas (and eliminating unattractive ones) we must look at more specific market characteristics.

We discussed many potential dimensions in the U.S. market. It is impossible to cover all possible dimensions in all world markets. But, some of the ideas discussed for the United States certainly apply in other countries. So here, we will just outline some dimensions of international markets and show some examples to emphasize that depending on half-truths about "foreigners" won't work in increasingly competitive international markets.[9]

The number of people in our world is staggering

Although our cities may seem crowded with people, the over 200 million population of the United States is less than 5 percent of the world's population—which is over 4 billion.

NUMBERS ARE IMPORTANT

Instead of a boring breakdown of population statistics, let's look at a. map showing area in proportion to population. Figure 18–4 makes the United States look unimportant because of our small population in relation to land area. This is also true of Latin America and Africa. In contrast, Western Europe is much larger and the Far Eastern countries are even bigger.

Figure 18–4
Map of the world showing area in proportion to population[10]

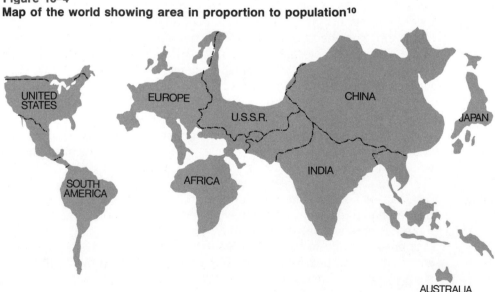

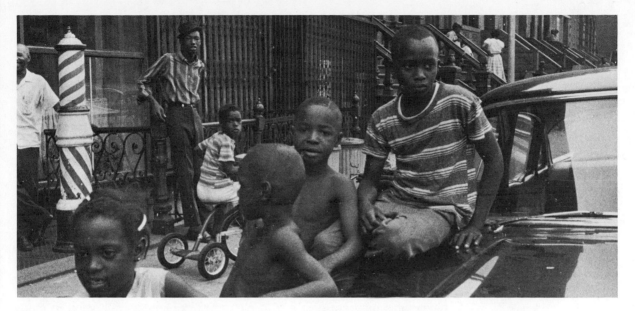

People everywhere are shifting to the cities.

BUT PEOPLE ARE NOT SPREAD OUT EVENLY

People everywhere are moving off the farm and into industrial and urban areas. Shifts in population—combined with already dense populations— have led to extreme crowding in some parts of the world.

Figure 18–5 shows a map of the world emphasizing density of popula-

Figure 18–5
Map of the world emphasizing density of population[11]

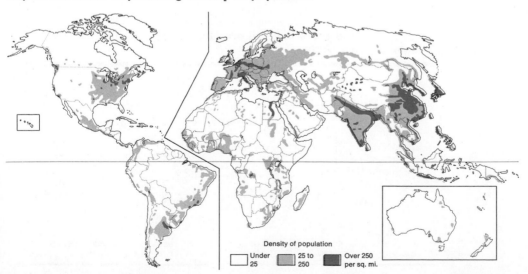

Density of population

Under 25   25 to 250   Over 250 per sq. mi.

tion. The darkest shading shows areas with more than 250 persons per square mile.

The urban areas in the United States show up clearly as densely populated areas. Similar areas are found in Western Europe, along the Nile River Valley in Egypt, and in many parts of Asia. In contrast, many parts of the world (like our western plains and mountain states) have few people.

Population densities are likely to increase in the near future. Birth rates in most parts of the world are high—higher in Africa, Latin America, Asia, and Oceania than in the United States—and death rates are declining as modern medicine is more widely accepted. Generally, population growth is expected in most countries. But the big questions are: How rapidly? and Will output increase faster than population? This is important to marketers because it affects how rapidly some economies move to higher stages of development and become new markets for different kinds of products.

You must sell where the income is

Profitable markets require income as well as people. The best available measure of income in most countries is **gross national product (GNP)**—the total market value of goods and services produced in a year. Unfortunately, this may not give a true picture of consumer well-being in many countries because the methods commonly used for figuring GNP may not be comparable for very different cultures and economies. For instance, do-it-yourself activities, household services, and the growing of produce or meat by family members for their own use are not usually figured as part of GNP. Since the activities of self-sufficient family units are not included, GNP can give a false picture of economic well-being in less-developed countries.

Gross national product, though, is useful and sometimes the only available measure of market potential in many countries. Table 18–1 shows the population and GNP of major regions of the world—except the USSR

Table 18–1
Population and gross national product of major geographic regions of the world

Region	Population (millions)	GNP ($ billions)
North America	237	1,555
Latin America	325	313
Europe*	473	1,445
Africa	401	155
South and East Asia†	1,723	841
Oceania	21	103
Totals	3,180	4,412

* Except USSR.
† Except China.
Source: *Statistical Abstract of the U.S. 1977*, p. 891, and *Yearbook of National Accounts Statistics*, 1976, vol. 2 (New York: United Nations, 1977) pp. 3–9.

and mainland China. You can see that the more developed industrial regions have the biggest share of the world's GNP. This is why so much trade takes place between these countries—and why many companies see them as the more important markets.

Income per person can be more helpful

GNP per person is a commonly available figure—but it can give a mistaken view of market potential. When GNP per person is used for comparison, we assume that the wealth of each country is distributed evenly among all consumers. However, this is seldom true. In an underdeveloped economy, 75 percent of the population may be on farms and receive 25 percent or less of the income.[12] And there may be unequal distribution along class or racial lines. In South Africa, for example, the average family income in 1970 for whites was $5,830; for Asians, $2,352; for mulattos, $1,411; and for blacks, $538.[13]

To provide some examples, the GNP per person for several countries is shown in Table 18–2. The range is wide, from $98 (in U.S. dollars) per person per year in Ethiopia to $6,634 in the United States.

A BUSINESS, AND A HUMAN OPPORTUNITY

You can see that much of the world's population lives in extreme poverty. Many of these countries are in the early stages of economic development. Large parts of their population work on farms and live barely within the money economy.

These people, however, have needs. And many are eager to improve themselves. But they may not be able to raise their living standards without outside help. This presents a challenge and an opportunity to the developed nations—and to their business firms.

Some companies—including American firms—are trying to help the people of less-developed countries. Corporations such as Pillsbury, Corn Products, Monsanto, and Coca-Cola have developed nutritious foods (e.g., Samson) that can be sold cheaply—but still profitably—in poorer countries. One firm sells a milk-based drink—with 10 grams of protein—to the Middle East and the Caribbean areas. Such a drink can make an important addition to diets. Poor people in less-developed lands usually get only 8–12 grams of protein per day in their normal diet. Sixty to 75 grams are considered necessary for an adult.[14]

Reading, writing, and marketing problems

The ability of a country's people to read and write has a direct influence on the development of the economy and on marketing strategy planning. Certainly, the degree of literacy affects the way information is delivered—which in marketing means promotion.

A study of literacy in 136 countries shows that only about half of the world's population can read and write.[15]

Low literacy sometimes causes difficulties with product labels and with instructions—for which we normally use words. In highly illiterate Africa,

Table 18–2
Gross national product per capita for major regions of the world and selected countries (in 1974 U.S. dollars)

	GNP/capita for countries	GNP/capita for regions
North America		$6,634
United States	$6,633	
Canada	6,636	
Latin America		1,040
Argentina	1,988	
Brazil	952	
Haiti	162	
Mexico	1,120	
Europe		4,220
United Kingdom	3,407	
France	5,054	
West Germany	6,216	
Italy	2,754	
Sweden	6,886	
Portugal	1,517	
Near East		1,380
Israel	3,763	
Turkey	769	
Africa		400
Algeria	704	
Egypt	274	
Ethiopia	98	
Kenya	222	
Nigeria	233	
South Africa	1,300	
Rwanda	75	
South and East Asia		560
India	144	
Pakistan	162	
Japan	4,126	
Indonesia	196	
Oceania		4,990
Australia	6,470	
New Zealand	4,401	

Source: *Yearbook of National Accounts Statistics,* 1976, vol. 2 (New York: United Nations, 1977), pp. 3–9.

some manufacturers have found that placing a baby's picture on food packages is unwise. Illiterate natives believe that the product is just that—a ground-up baby! Singer Sewing Machine Co. met this lack of literacy with an instruction book that used no words.[16]

Even in Latin America—which has generally higher literacy rates than Africa or Asia—a large number of people cannot read and write. Marketers have to use symbols, colors, and other nonverbal means of communication if they want to reach the masses.

CAREFUL MARKET ANALYSIS IS BASIC

The opportunities in international marketing are exciting. But market differences present a real challenge to target marketers. Careful market analysis is especially important since there often are fine points that are easy to miss.

What are you drinking?

Tastes do differ across national boundaries. French Burgundy wine going to Belgium must have a higher sugar content than the Burgundy staying in France. Burgundy going to Sweden must have still another sugar content to be sold successfully there.

Milk-drinking habits also differ greatly. Scandinavians consider milk a daily staple—while Latins feel that milk is only for children. A former French premier was able to get his picture on the front page of every Paris newspaper simply by drinking a glass of milk in public.

Who wears the makeup in France?

The great variety in international markets almost demands marketing research to learn the habits and attitudes of the many possible target markets.

The need for research to avoid common stereotypes is emphasized by the following results from a large-scale survey of European Common Market adults:

> The average Frenchman uses almost twice as many cosmetics and beauty aids as his wife.
>
> The Germans and the French buy more spaghetti than the Italians.
>
> French and Italian housewives are not as interested in cooking as their counterparts in Luxembourg and Belgium.[17]

Conclusion

The international market is large and keeps growing in population and income. Many American companies are becoming aware of the enormous opportunities open to alert and aggressive businesses.

The great variations in stages of economic development, income, population, literacy, and other factors, however, mean that foreign markets must be treated as many separate target markets—and studied carefully. Lumping foreign nations together under the common and vague heading of "foreigners"—or, at the other extreme, assuming that they are just like U.S. customers—is almost a guarantee of failure. So is treating them like common Hollywood stereotypes.

Involvement in international marketing usually begins with exporting. Then, a firm may become involved in joint ventures or wholly owned subsidiaries in several countries. Companies that become this involved are called multinational corporations. Some of these corporations have a global outlook and are willing to move across national boundaries as easily as national firms move across state boundaries.

Much of what we have said about strategy planning throughout the text applies directly in international marketing. Sometimes Product adaptions or changes are needed. Promotion messages must be translated into the local languages. And, of course, new Place arrangements and Prices are needed. But blending the four Ps still requires a knowledge of the all-important customer.

The major "roadblock" to success in international marketing is an unwillingness to learn about and adjust to different peoples and cultures. To those who are willing to make these adjustments, the returns can be great.

Questions for discussion

1 Discuss the "typical" evolution of corporate involvement in international marketing. What impact would a wholehearted acceptance of the marketing concept have on this evolutionary process?

2 Distinguish between licensing and contract manufacturing in a foreign country.

3 Distinguish between joint ventures and wholly owned subsidiaries.

4 Discuss the long-run prospects for *(a)* multinational marketing by U.S. firms producing in the United States only, and *(b)* multinational firms willing to operate anywhere.

5 Discuss how a manufacturer interested in finding new international marketing opportunities might organize its search process. What kinds of opportunities would it look for first, second, and so on?

6 Discuss how the approaches to market segmenting (which were described in Chapter 7) might have to be modified when one moves into international markets.

7 Discuss the prospects for a Latin American entrepreneur who is considering building a factory to produce machines that would manufacture cans for the food industry. His country happens to be in stage 4—the nondurable and semidurable consumer goods manufacturing stage. The country's population is approximately 20 million and there is some possibility of establishing sales contacts in a few nearby countries.

8 Discuss the value of gross national product per capita as a measure of market potential. Refer to specific data in your answer.

9 Discuss the possibility of a multinational marketer using essentially the same promotion campaign in the United States and in many international markets.

10 Discuss the kinds of products you feel may become popular in Europe in the near future. Does the material on U.S. consumption behavior, discussed earlier in the text, have any relevance here?

11 Discuss the importance of careful target marketing within the European Common Market.

Suggested cases

29 Phoenix Steel Corporation

12 Alpine Sports Shop

When you finish this chapter, you should:

1 Understand why marketing must be evaluated differently at the micro and macro levels.

2 Understand why the text argues that micro-marketing costs too much.

3 Understand why the text argues that macro-marketing does *not* cost too much.

4 Know some of the challenges facing marketers in the future.

EVALUATION AND CHALLENGE

Does marketing cost too much? This is a basic question. Many people feel strongly that marketing does cost too much—that it is a waste of resources which would be better used elsewhere.

While we have talked about what marketing is, we also have mentioned criticisms of marketing and the possible effects of business practices on consumer welfare. But we have *not* tried to answer the basic question of whether marketing costs too much. We felt you needed background before you could answer that question. Now let's talk about it—and then go on to discuss challenges facing marketers.

Your answer to the basic question is important. Your own business career and the economy in which you will live will be affected by your answer.

MARKETING MUST BE EVALUATED AT TWO LEVELS

As we saw in Chapter 1, it is useful to talk about marketing at two levels: the micro level (how individual firms run) and the macro level (how the whole system works). Some complaints against marketing are aimed at only one of these levels. In other cases, the criticism *seems* to be directed at one level, but actually it is aimed at the other. Some critics of specific ads, for example, probably would not be satisfied with *any* advertising. When evaluating marketing, we have to treat each of these levels separately.

401

HOW SHOULD MARKETING BE EVALUATED?

Different nations have different social and economic objectives. Dictatorships, for example, may be concerned mainly with satisfying the needs of the people at the top. In a socialist state, the objective is to satisy the needs of the people—as defined by social planners.

Therefore, the effectiveness of any nation's marketing system can only be judged in terms of the nation's objectives.

Consumer satisfaction is basic in the United States

The aim of our economic system has been to satisfy consumer needs as they—the consumers—see them. This is no place for a long discussion of the value of this objective. Our democratic political process is where such matters get settled.

Therefore, we will be concerned with evaluating marketing in the American economy where the objective is to satisfy consumer needs—*as consumers see them*. This is the base of our system—and the business firm that ignores this fact is in for trouble.

CAN CONSUMER SATISFACTION BE MEASURED?

Since satisfaction of consumers is our goal, marketing must be measured by how *well* it satisfies them. Unfortunately, however, consumer satisfaction is hard to define and harder to measure.

Measuring macro-marketing isn't easy

Economists believe that consumer satisfaction comes from economic utility—remember form, time, place, and possession utility. However, no practical method of measuring utility has yet been developed. This is in part because satisfaction seems to depend upon each person's own view of things. Further, products that were satisfactory one day may be unsatisfactory the next day and vice versa. Thus, consumer satisfaction is a very personal concept which does not provide a very good standard for evaluating marketing effectiveness. The final measure, probably, is whether the macro-marketing system satisfies eough individual consumer/citizens so that they vote—at the ballot box—to keep it running. So far, we have done so in the United States.

There are ways to measure micro-marketing

Measuring micro-marketing effectiveness is also difficult. But there are ways that individual business firms can measure how well their products satisfy their customers. These methods include attitude studies, analysis of consumer complaints, opinions of middlemen and salespeople, market test results, and profits.[1]

Since every company uses slightly different marketing strategies, it is up to each customer to decide how well individual firms satisfy his or her needs. Generally speaking, customers are willing to pay higher prices to buy more of those goods which satisfy them. So, profits can be used as a rough measure of a firm's success in satisfying customers. In this sense, a firm's own interests and society's interests are the same.

"We must be doing *something* right—profits are up!"

Evaluating marketing effectiveness is difficult—but not impossible

In view of the difficulty of measuring consumer satisfaction—and, therefore, the effectiveness of marketing—it is easy to see why there are different views on the subject. If the objective of the economy is clearly defined, however, the question of marketing effectiveness probably *can* be answered.

In this chapter, we will argue that micro-marketing (how *individual* firms and channels operate) often *does* cost too much. But we will argue too that macro-marketing (how the *whole* marketing system operates) does *not* cost too much, given the present objective of the American economy—consumer satisfaction. In the end, you will have to make your own decision.[2]

MICRO-MARKETING OFTEN DOES COST TOO MUCH

Throughout the text we have talked about what marketing managers could or should do to help their firms do a better job of satisfying customers and achieving company objectives. While many firms carry out very successful marketing programs, many more firms are still too production-oriented and inefficient. It is plain that many consumers are not happy with the marketing efforts of some firms. A recent study showed that "helping consumers get a fair deal when shopping" ranked very high among public concerns. Only inflation, unemployment, government spending, welfare, and taxes were ranked higher.[3]

The failure rate is high

Further evidence that most firms are too production-oriented and not nearly as efficient as they could be is the fact that most new products fail. New and old businesses fail regularly, too. These failures are caused by one or more of three reasons:

FAILURE RATE?

1. Lack of interest in, or understanding of, the customer.
2. Improper blending of the four Ps, because of a lack of a customer orientation.
3. Lack of understanding of, or adjustment to, uncontrollable variables.[4]

The company can get in the way of the customer

Serving the customer should be the goal of business, but some producers seem to feel that customers are eagerly waiting for any product they turn out. They don't understand a business as a "total system" responsible for satisfying customer needs.

Middlemen, too, often get tied up in their own internal problems. Goods may be stocked where it is convenient for the retailer to handle them—rather than for consumers to find them. And fast-moving, hard-to-handle goods may not be stocked at all—because "they are too much trouble" or "we're always running out."

In the same way, accounting or financial departments in all kinds of businesses may try to cut costs by encouraging the production of standardized products—even though this may not be what customers want.

Company objectives may force higher-cost operation

Top management decisions on company objectives may increase the cost of marketing. A decision to aim for growth for growth's sake, for example, might mean too much spending for promotion. Or diversification for diversification's sake could require the development of expensive new Place arrangements.

For these reasons, the marketing manager should take a big part in shaping the firm's objectives. Recognizing the importance of marketing, progressive firms have given marketing management more control in determining company objectives. Unfortunately, though, in many more firms, marketing is still looked upon as the department that "gets rid of" the product.

"I figure everyone else is expanding—so we will, too."

Micro-marketing does cost too much—but things are changing

Marketing *does* cost too much in many firms. The marketing concept has not really been applied in very many places. Sometimes, sales managers are renamed "marketing managers," and vice presidents of sales are called "vice presidents of marketing," but nothing else changes. Marketing mixes are still put together by production-oriented people in the same old ways. The customer is considered last—if at all.

But not all business firms are so old-fashioned. More firms are becoming customer-oriented. And some are paying more attention to strategic planning—to better carry out the marketing concept.

One hopeful sign is the end of the idea that practically anybody can run a business successfully. This never was true. And today the growing complexity of business is drawing more and more professionals into business. This includes not only professional business managers, but psychologists, sociologists, statisticians, and economists.

Managers who adopt the marketing concept as a way of business life do a better job. As more of these professionals enter business, micro-marketing costs will go down.

MACRO-MARKETING DOES *NOT* COST TOO MUCH

Many critics of marketing take aim at the operation of the macro-marketing system. They suggest that advertising—and promotion in general—are socially undesirable. They feel that the macro-marketing system causes a poor distribution of resources, limits income and employment, and leads to an unfair distribution of income. Most of these complaints imply that some micro-marketing activities should not be allowed—and because of them our macro-marketing system does a poor job.

Many of these critics have their own version of the ideal way to run an economy. Some of the most severe critics of our marketing system are economists who use pure competition as their ideal. They would give consumers free choice in the market, but are critical of the way the present market operates. Meanwhile, other critics would scrap our market-directed system and substitute the decisions of central planners for those of individual producers and consumers—reducing freedom of choice in the marketplace. These viewpoints should be kept in mind when evaluating criticisms of marketing.

Is pure competition the ideal?

One criticism of our macro-marketing system is that it permits or even encourages the use of too many resources for marketing activities and that this may actually reduce consumer "welfare." This argument is concerned with how the economy's resources (land, labor, and capital) are used for producing and distributing goods. These critics usually argue that scarce resources should be spent on *producing* goods—not on marketing them. The basis for this view is the idea that marketing activities are unnecessary and don't provide any value. These critics feel that pure competition would result in the greatest consumer benefits.

In pure competition, you remember, we assumed that consumers are "economic men," i.e., that they know all about available offerings and will make "wise" choices. Economic analysis can be made to prove that pure competition will provide greater consumer welfare than monopolistic competition—*if all the conditions of pure competition are met.* But are they?

DIFFERENT PEOPLE WANT DIFFERENT THINGS

First of all, we can say that our present knowledge of consumer behavior and peoples' desire for different products pretty well destroys the economists' "economic man" idea—and therefore, the pure competition ideal.[5] People, in fact, are different and do want different products. With this type of demand (downsloping demand curves), monopoly elements naturally develop. A pioneer in this kind of analysis concluded that "monopoly is necessarily a part of the welfare ideal. . . ."[6]

Once we admit that not all consumers know everything and that they have many different demands, the need for a variety of micro-marketing activities becomes clear.

New ideas help the economy grow

Some critics feel that marketing helps create monopolistic competition, and that this leads to higher prices, limits production, and reduces national income and employment.

It is true that firms in a market-directed economy try to carve out separate markets for themselves with new products. But customers don't have to buy the new product unless they feel it is a better value. The old products are still available. The prices may even be lower on the old products to meet the new competition.

Over several years, the profits of the innovator may rise—but the rising profits also encourage new ideas by competitors. This leads to new investments—which contribute to economic growth—raising the level of national income and employment.

Does marketing make people buy things they don't need?

It would seem that the individual firm's efforts to satisfy consumer needs would lead to a better division of national income. Giving customers what they want, after all, is the purpose of our market-directed economic system. However, some critics feel that most firms, especially large corporations, do not really try to satisfy the consumer. Instead, these critics argue, they use clever ads to persuade consumers to buy whatever the firms want to sell.

Historian Arnold Toynbee, for example, felt that American consumers have been manipulated into buying products which aren't necessary to satisfy "the minimum material requirements of life." Toynbee saw American firms as mainly trying to fulfill *unwanted demand*—demand created by advertising—rather than "genuine wants." He defined *genuine wants* as ". . . wants that we become aware of spontaneously, without having to be told by Madison Avenue that we want something that we should never

"I wish there was no marketing system so that materialism will be wiped out . . ."

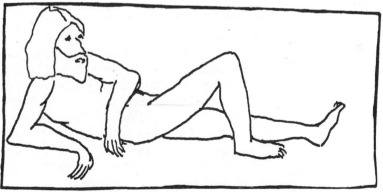

". . . ah . . . Do I get another wish?"

(Marketing delivers a standard of living.)

have thought of wanting if we had been left in peace to find out our wants for ourselves."[7]

WHAT ARE THE MINIMUM REQUIREMENTS OF LIFE?

One problem with this kind of thinking is how to decide what *are* "the minimum material requirements of life." Which products that we use today are unnecessary and should be taken off the market? One writer has suggested, for example, that Americans could and should do without items such as pets, newspaper comic strips, second family automobiles, motor-cycles, snowmobiles, campers, recreational boats and planes, cigarettes, aerosol products, pop and beer cans, and hats.[8] You may agree with some of those, but who should decide "minimum material requirements of life" if not the consumers themselves?

CONSUMERS ARE NOT PUPPETS

The idea that firms can persuade consumers to buy anything the company decides to produce simply isn't true. A consumer who buys a can of soda pop that tastes terrible won't buy another can of that brand no matter how much it's advertised. In fact, *most* new products fail the test of the marketplace. Not even large corporations can be sure of success everytime they market a new product. Consider, for example, the dismal fate of products such as Ford's Edsel, Du Pont's Corfam, Campbell's Red Kettle Soups, the "midi-skirts" that the fashion industry tried to persuade woman to wear back in the 1960s, or more recently, "light whisky."[9]

NEEDS AND WANTS CHANGE

Consumer needs and wants are constantly changing. Few of us would care to live like our grandparents lived, let alone like the pioneers who traveled the rugged journey west in covered wagons. Marketing's job is not to satisfy consumer wants just for today. Rather, marketing must always *keep* looking for new—and better—ways to serve customers.[10]

Does marketing make people materialistic?

There is no doubt that our marketing system caters to materialistic values. But there is a lot of disagreement as to whether marketing creates these values or just appeals to values that are already there.

Anthropologists tell us that—even in the most primitive societies—people decorate themselves with trinkets and want to accumulate possessions. In fact, in some tribal villages social status is measured in terms of how many goats or sheep a person owns. Surely the desire of ancient pharaohs and kings to surround themselves with wealth and treasures can hardly be blamed on the persuasive powers of the advertising agencies!

The idea that marketers create and serve *false tastes*—as defined by individual critics—has been rebutted by a well-known economist, George Stigler, who said:

> The marketplace responds to the tastes of consumers with the goods and services that are salable, whether the tastes are elevated or depraved. It is unfair to criticize the marketplace for fulfilling these desires, when clearly the defects lie in the popular tastes themselves. I consider it a cowardly concession to a false extension of the idea of democracy to make sub rosa attacks on public tastes by denouncing the people who serve them. It is like blaming the waiters in restaurants for obesity.[11]

MARKETING REFLECTS OUR OWN VALUES

The various experts who have studied the issue of materialism seem to agree that—in the short run—marketing reflects social values—while in the long run—it reinforces them. One expert pointed out that consumers vote for what they want in the marketplace *and* in the polling place. To say that what they want is *wrong* is to criticize the basic idea of free choice and democracy![12]

MATERIAL GOODS DO IMPROVE THE QUALITY OF LIFE

More is not always better. The quality of life can't be measured only in terms of quantities of material goods. But when material goods are seen as the means to an end rather than the end itself, we can see that material goods do make it possible to achieve higher-level needs. Modern appliances, for example, have greatly reduced the amount of time and effort that must be spent on household duties—leaving homemakers with more time for other interests.

Consumers ask for it, consumers pay for it

The monopolistic competition typical of our economy is the result of customer demands—not control of markets by business. Monopolistic competition may seem expensive at times—when we look at individual firms—but it seems to work fairly well at the macro level, in serving the many needs and wants of consumers.

All these demands add to the cost of satisfying consumers. Certainly, the total cost is larger than it would be if spartan, undifferentiated products were offered at the factory door on a take-it-or-leave-it basis to long lines of customers.

If the role of the marketing system is to serve the consumer, however, then the cost of whatever services he demands can't be considered too expensive. It is just the cost of serving the consumer the way he wants to be served.[13]

Some people don't feel the need for the more expensive branded products.

MACARONI & CHEESE

MACARONI & CHEESE DINNER   MACARONI & CHEESE DINNER   MACARONI & CHEESE DINNER   MACARONI & CHEESE DINNER

UNBRANDED MACARONI & CHEESE DINNER   23¢

Eberhard   We Want To Be YOUR Food Store

MACARONI & CHEESE

Does macro-marketing cost enough?

The question, "Does marketing cost too much?" has been answered by one well-known financial expert with another question, "Does distribution cost enough?"[14] What he meant was that marketing is such an important part of our economic system that perhaps even more should be spent on it since "distribution is the delivery of a standard of living"—that is, the satisfaction of consumers' basic needs and wants. In this sense, then, macro-marketing does not cost too much. Some of the activities of individual business firms may cost too much. If these micro-level activities are improved, the performance of the macro system probably will improve. But regardless, our macro-marketing system performs a vital role in our economic system—and *does not cost too much.*

CHALLENGES FACING MARKETERS

We have said that our macro-marketing system does *not* cost too much—given the present objective of our economy—while admitting that the performance of many business firms leaves a lot to be desired. This presents a challenge to serious-minded students and marketers. What needs to be done—if anything?

We need better performance at the micro level

Some business managers seem to feel that in a market-directed economy they should be completely "free." They don't understand the idea that our system is a market-directed system and that the needs of consumer/citizens must be met. Instead, they focus on their own internal problems—without satisfying consumers very well.

WE NEED BETTER PLANNING

Most firms are still production-oriented. Some hardly plan at all. Others simply extend this year's plans into next year. Progressive firms are beginning to realize that this doesn't work in our changing marketplaces. Strategy planning is becoming more important in many companies. More attention is being given to the product life cycle—because marketing variables should change through the product's life cycle.[15]

Figure 19–1 shows some of the typical changes in marketing variables which might be needed over the course of a product life cycle. This figure should be a good review, but it also should emphasize why much better planning is needed. As the product life cycle moves on, the marketing manager should *expect* to find more products entering "his" market and pushing the market closer to pure competition or oligopoly. This means that as the cycle moves along, he might want to shift from a selective to an intensive distribution policy *and* move from a skimming to a penetration pricing policy. And the original strategic plan might include these adjustments and the probable timing.

MAY NEED MORE SOCIAL RESPONSIVENESS

A smart business manager would put himself in the consumer's place. This would mean developing more satisfying marketing mixes for specific

Figure 19–1
Typical changes in marketing variables over the course of the product life cycle

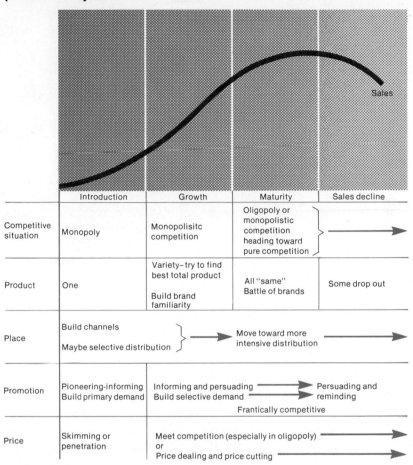

	Introduction	Growth	Maturity	Sales decline
Competitive situation	Monopoly	Monopolisitc competition	Oligopoly or monopolistic competition heading toward pure competition	→
Product	One	Variety–try to find best total product Build brand familiarity	All "same" Battle of brands	Some drop out
Place	Build channels Maybe selective distribution	→	Move toward more intensive distribution	→
Promotion	Pioneering-informing Build primary demand	Informing and persuading → Build selective demand → Frantically competitive	Persuading and reminding	
Price	Skimming or penetration	Meet competition (especially in oligopoly) → or Price dealing and price cutting →		

target markets. This may mean building in more quality or safety. And the consumers' long-run satisfaction should be considered, too. How will the product hold up in use? How will it be kept operating?

It seems doubtful that production-oriented methods will work in the future. Tougher competition and more watchful government agencies may force the typical production-oriented business manager to change. Many of the concerns of the consumerism movement are caused by the failure of businesses to put the marketing concept into practice. This has to change.

MAY NEED MORE ENVIRONMENTAL CONCERN

Besides satisfying consumers' needs, marketers have to be aware of environmental problems. A lack of understanding of uncontrollable vari-

Marketers must be aware of environmental problems.

ables and a failure to recognize new environmental trends could be major causes of marketing failure in the future. Conditions around the world are changing rapidly. Marketing managers must try to anticipate the economic opportunities that every new human problem offers—while at the same time trying to see the social-political problems which are part of every new opportunity.[16] An understanding of new developments may help the firm avoid expensive mistakes and see new opportunities.

We need better performance at the macro level

One of the advantages of a market-directed economic system is that its operation is relatively automatic. But in our version of this system, consumer/citizens provide limits (laws). These laws can be strengthened or modified at any time.

NEED TOUGHER ENFORCEMENT OF PRESENT LAWS

Before piling on too many new laws, however, it probably would be wise to really enforce the ones we have. The anti-monopoly laws, for example, have often been used to protect competitors from each other—when they really were intended to protect competition. Now, however, the FTC seems to be shifting to a consumer-oriented emphasis.[17] Congress and local authorities also are taking stronger stands with respect to product safety, truth-in-lending, and deceptive advertising.

LAWS SHOULD AFFECT TOP MANAGEMENT

The results of strict enforcement of present laws could be far reaching if more price fixers, dishonest advertisers, and others who are obviously breaking the laws were sent to jail or given heavy fines. A quick change in attitudes might occur if top managers—who plan overall business strategy—were prosecuted, rather than the salespersons or advertisers who are expected to "deliver" on weak strategies.

In other words, if the government made it clear that it was serious about improving the performance of our economic system, a lot could be achieved within the present system—without adding new laws or trying to "patch up" the present ones.

NEED BETTER-INFORMED CONSUMERS

We may need some changes to help customers become better informed about the many goods and services on the market. Laws to assure consumers that they will have ways for comparing products—for example, life expectancy of light bulbs and appliances—would be helpful. Consumer education programs designed to teach people how to buy more wisely could be helpful too.

NEED SOCIALLY RESPONSIBLE CONSUMERS

We have been stressing the obligation of producers to act responsibly, but consumers have responsibilities too. Some consumers abuse returned-goods policies, change price tags in self-service stores, expect attractive surroundings and courteous sales and service people, but want discount prices. Others think nothing of "ripping off" businesses.

Americans tend to perform their dual role of consumer/citizens with something of a split personality. We often behave one way as consumers and then take the opposite stand at the ballot box. For example, while our beaches and parks are covered with litter, we call for stiff action to curb pollution. We protest sex and violence in the media and then flock to see *Jaws, The Godfather,* and other R- or X-rated movies. We complain about high energy costs and then purchase low-efficiency appliances.

Consumer advocates have stressed the need for business firms to use social responsibility in the marketplace. They have said almost nothing however, about the need for consumers to behave responsibly.[18]

Some people behave differently as voters than they do as consumers.

"My family likes me better for eliminating our 'energy-gobbling' models, but my stockholders are ready to hang me because we're losing sales."

Let's face it. There is a lot of information already available to improve consumer decision making. The consumerism movement has encouraged nutritional labeling, unit pricing, truth-in-lending, plain language contracts and warranties, and so on. And, government agencies publish many consumer buying guides—as do groups like Consumers Union. But most consumers continue to ignore this information!

We may need to modify our macro-marketing system

Our macro-marketing system is built on the idea that we are trying to satisfy consumers. But with resource shortages and rising energy costs, how far should the marketing concept be allowed to go? Should consumers be treated as kings and queens?

SHOULD MARKETING MANAGERS LIMIT CONSUMERS' FREEDOM OF CHOICE?

A "better" macro-marketing system is certainly a good idea, but an important question is what should marketers do—in their roles as producers? Should they, for example, deliberately refuse to produce "energy-gobbling" appliances or cars that consumers demand? Or should they be expected to install devices which will increase costs and which are very definitely *not* wanted by potential customers—like seat belts with buzzer systems?

CONSUMER/CITIZENS SHOULD VOTE ON THE CHANGES

Marketing managers should be expected to improve and expand the range of goods and services they make available to consumers—always trying to satisfy the needs and wants of potential customers. This is the job which has been assigned to business.

If this objective makes "excessive" demands on scarce resources or causes an "intolerable" level of ecological damage, then consumer/citizens have every right to vote for laws to limit individual firms. These firms can't be expected to fully understand the impact of all their actions. This is the role which we as consumers have assigned to the government—to make sure that the macro-marketing system works effectively.

It is important to see that some critics of marketing are really interested in *basic* changes in our macro-marketing system. And, some basic changes might be accomplished by seemingly minor modifications in our present system. Allowing some government agency (e.g., the FDA or Consumer Product Safety Commission) to ban the sale of products for seemingly good reasons may severely limit our choices in ways we never intended. (Bicycles, for example, are very dangerous consumer products—perhaps they should not be sold!) Clearly, such government actions could seriously reduce consumers' present right to freedom of choice—including "bad" choices.[19]

Consumer/citizens have to be careful to see the difference between changes designed just to modify our system and those designed to change it—perhaps completely. In either case, the consumer/citizen should make the decision (through elected representatives). This decision should not be left in the hands of a few well-placed producers' representatives—even if they are marketing managers—or government planners.

MARKETING PEOPLE MAY BE EVEN MORE NECESSARY IN THE FUTURE

No matter what changes might be voted by consumer/citizens, some kind of a marketing system will be needed. And market-oriented business managers probably would be needed to help define and satisfy any "new needs." In fact, if satisfying more subtle needs—such as the "good life"—becomes the goal, it could be even more necessary to have market-oriented firms. It may be necessary, for example, not only to define individuals' needs, but also society's needs—for a "better neighborhood" or "more enriching social experiences," and so on. As one goes beyond physical goods into more sophisticated need-satisfying blends of goods and services, the trial-and-error approach of the typical production-oriented manager will be even less acceptable.

Conclusion

Macro-marketing does not cost too much. Business firms have been assigned the role—by consumers—of satisfying their needs. Customers find it satisfactory—even desirable—to permit businesses to cater to them. As long as consumers are satisfied, macro-marketing will not cost too much—and business firms will be allowed to continue as profit-making groups.

It must always be remembered that business exists at the consumers' approval. It is only by satisfying the consumer that a particular business firm and our economic system can justify their existence and hope to keep operating.

In carrying out this role granted by consumers, the activities of business firms are not always as effective as they might be. Many business managers do not understand the marketing concept or the role that marketing plays in our way of life. They seem to feel that business has a God-given right to operate as it chooses.

And they proceed in their typical production-oriented ways. Further, many managers have had little or no training in business management and are not as competent as they should be. In this sense, micro-marketing does cost too much. The situation is being improved, however, as training for business expands and as more competent people are attracted to marketing and business generally. Clearly, you have a role to play in improving marketing in the future.

Marketing has new challenges to face in the future. All consumers may have to settle for a lower standard of living. Resource shortages, rising energy costs, and slowing population growth may all combine to reduce income growth. This may force consumers to shift their consumption patterns—and politicians to change some of the rules governing business. Even our present market-directed system may be threatened.

To keep our system working effectively, individual business firms should try to be more efficient and socially responsible as they carry out the marketing concept. At the same time, individual consumers have the responsibility to use goods and services in an intelligent and socially responsible manner. Further, they have the responsibility to vote and make sure that they get the kind of macro-marketing system they want. What kind do you want? What can and should you do to see that fellow consumer/citizens will vote for your system? Is your system likely to satisfy you, personally, as well as another macro-marketing system? You don't have to answer these questions right now, but your answers will affect the future you will live in and how satisfied you will be.

Questions for discussion

1 Explain why marketing must be evaluated at two levels. Also, explain what criteria you feel should be used for evaluating each level of marketing, and defend your answer. Explain why your criteria are "better" than alternative criteria.

2 Discuss the merits of various economic system objectives. Is the objective of the American economic system sensible? Do you feel more consumer satisfaction might be achieved by permitting some sociologists or some public officials to determine how the needs of the lower-income or less-educated members of the society should be satisfied? If you approve of this latter suggestion, what education or income level should be required before an individual is granted free choice by the social planners?

3 Should the goal of our economy be maximum efficiency? If your answer is yes, efficiency in what? If not, what should the goal be?

4 Cite an example of a critic using his own value system when evaluating marketing.

5 Discuss the conflict of interests among production, finance, accounting, and marketing executives. How does this conflict contribute to the operation of an individual business? Of the economic system? Why does this conflict exist?

6 Why does the text indicate that the adoption of the marketing concept will encourage more efficient operation of an individual business? Be specific about the impact of the marketing concept on the various departments of a firm.

7 It appears that competition sometimes leads to inefficiency in the operation of the economic system in the short run. Many people argue for monopoly in order to eliminate this inefficiency. Discuss this solution to the problem of inefficiency.

8 How would officially granted monopolies affect the operation of our economic system? Specifically, consider the effect on allocation of resources, the level of income and employment, and the distribution of income. Is the effect any different than if a monopoly were obtained through winning out in a competitive market?

9 Is there any possibility of a pure-competition economy evolving naturally? Could legislation force a pure-competition economy?

10 Comment on the following statement: "Ultimately, the high cost of marketing is due only to consumers."

11 Should the consumer be king or queen? How should we decide this issue?

12 Should marketing managers, or business managers in general, be expected to refrain from producing profitable products that some target customers want but may not be in their long-run interest? Contrariwise, should firms be expected to produce "good" products that offer a lower rate of profitability than usual? What if only a break-even level were obtainable? What if the products were likely to be unprofitable, but the company was also producing other products which were profitable so that on balance it would still make some profit? What criteria are you using for each of your answers?

13 Should a marketing manager or a business refuse to produce an "energy-gobbling" appliance that some consumers are demanding? Similarly should it install an expensive safety device that does not appear to be desired by potential customers and inevitably will increase costs? Are the same principles involved in both of these questions? Explain.

14 Discuss how much slower economic growth or even no economic growth would affect your college community, and in particular its marketing institutions.

Suggested cases

25 Riverside Processing Company

26 Nagel Mfg. Company

27 The Ross Tool Company

28 "Save-A-Life" Franchise

30 Auto Specialties Manufacturing Company

appendix C

CAREER OPPORTUNITIES IN MARKETING

When you finish this appendix, you should:

1 **Know that there is a job or a career for you in marketing.**
2 **Know that marketing jobs can pay well.**
3 **Understand the difference between "people-oriented" and "thing-oriented" jobs.**
4 **Know about the many different kinds of marketing jobs you can choose from.**

One of the difficult tasks facing most students is choosing a career. It is not the author's role to make this decision for you. You are the best judge of your own goals, interests, and abilities. Only you can decide what career you should pursue. However, you probably owe it to yourself to at least consider the possibility of a career in marketing.

THERE'S A PLACE IN MARKETING FOR YOU

The author is pleased to tell you that there are many opportunities in marketing. Regardless of one's abilities or training, there is a place in marketing for everyone—from a supermarket bagger to a Vice President of Marketing in a large consumer goods company such as Procter & Gamble or General Foods. The opportunities range widely, so it will be helpful to be a little more specific. In the following pages, we will discuss the financial returns in marketing jobs, setting your own goals, and evaluating your interests and abilities, and finally, the kinds of jobs available in marketing.

MARKETING JOBS CAN PAY WELL

The supermarket bagger may get only the minimum wage—but there are many more challenging jobs open to those with marketing training.

418

Appendix C

Table C-1
Average starting salaries of 1977 graduates (with bachelor's degrees) in selected fields

Field	Average starting salary (per month)
Engineering	$1,242
Chemistry	1,108
Accounting	1,067
Sales-marketing	978
Economics-finance	943
Business administration	887
Liberal arts	866

Source: *The Endicott Report—1977.* Evanston, Ill., Northwestern University, The Placement Center, p. 4.

Many marketing jobs do pay well! At the time this text went to press, marketing majors were being offered starting salaries ranging from $10,000 to $13,000 a year. Of course, these figures are only averages. Starting salaries can vary considerably—depending on your background, experience, and location.

As shown in Table C-1, starting salaries in sales-marketing compare favorably with many other fields and are only slightly lower than those for fields such as accounting for which there is currently a very high demand. How far and fast your income rises above the starting level depends on many factors—including your willingness to work, how well you get along with people, and your individual abilities. But most of all it depends on getting results—individually and through other people. And this is where many marketing jobs offer the newcomer great opportunities. It is possible to show initiative, ability, and judgment in marketing jobs. Some young people move up very rapidly in marketing—even ending up at the top in large companies or as owners of their own businesses.

Marketing can be the route to the top

Marketing is where the action is! In the final analysis, the success or failure of a firm depends on the effectiveness of its marketing program. This statement is not meant to put down the importance of other functional areas. It merely reflects the fact that a firm will have little need for accountants, finance people, production managers, and so on—it it can't successfully market its products.

Because marketing is so vital to the survival of a firm, many companies look for people with training and experience in marketing when filling key manager positions. A recent survey of the nation's largest corporations showed that the greatest proportion of top managers had backgrounds in marketing and distribution. See Figure C-1.

Figure C–1
Main career emphasis of corporate chief executive officers*

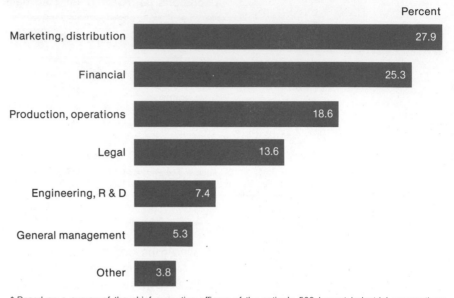

Percent

Marketing, distribution	27.9
Financial	25.3
Production, operations	18.6
Legal	13.6
Engineering, R & D	7.4
General management	5.3
Other	3.8

* Based on a survey of the chief executive officers of the nation's 500 largest industrial corporations and 300 nonindustrial corporations (including commercial banks, life insurance firms, retailers, transportation companies, utilities, and diversified financial enterprises).
Source: Adapted from Charles G. Burck, "A Group Profile of the Fortune 500 Chief Executive," *Fortune*, May 1976, p. 172.

WHAT DO YOU WANT—A JOB OR A CAREER?

Before going on to consider marketing jobs, you really ought to make some tentative decisions about your own goals—what you are seeking out of a job and out of life.

It may be a little early for you to completely define your own objectives—but at least some tentative conclusions are necessary to maximize your return from career hunting. At the very least, you should decide whether you are just looking for a "job" or whether you want to build a "career." And beyond this, do you want the position to be personally satisfying or is the financial return enough? And just how much financial return do you need or are you willing to work for? Some people work only to support themselves and their leisure-time activities. Others work to support themselves and their families. These people seek only financial rewards from their job. They try to find job opportunities that give adequate financial returns, while not being too demanding of time or effort. Other people, however, look first for satisfaction in their job and seek opportunities for career advancement. Financial rewards may be important too, but these may be used simply as measures of success. In the extreme, the career-oriented individual may be willing to sacrifice much—including leisure and social activities—to achieve success in a career.

Once you have tentatively decided on these matters, then it is possible to get more serious about whether you should seek a job or a career in marketing.

WHAT KIND OF A JOB IS RIGHT FOR YOU?

Because of the great variety of marketing jobs, it is difficult to generalize about what aptitudes one should have to pursue a career in marketing. Different jobs attract people with various interests and abilities. Here, we will provide some guidelines about what kinds of interests and abilities marketers should possess. (Note: If you are completely "lost" about your own interests and abilities, you probably should see your campus career counselor and take some vocational aptitude and interests tests. These tests will help you to compare yourself with people who are now working in various career positions. They will not tell you what you should do, but they can help—especially in eliminating things you are less interested in and/or able to do.)

Are you "people-oriented" or "thing-oriented"?

One of the first things you should attempt to decide for yourself is whether you are basically "people-oriented" or "thing-oriented." This is a very important decision. A "people-oriented" person probably would not be very happy in a bookkeeping job, for example, while a "thing-oriented" person might be quite miserable in a personal selling job which involves a lot of customer contact.

Marketing has both "people-oriented" and "thing-oriented" jobs. People-oriented jobs are primarily in the sales area, where company representatives must make contact with potential customers. They may be direct personal selling or customer service activities—for example at complaint desks or repair departments. Thing-oriented jobs focus more on creative activities and analyzing data—as in advertising and marketing research—or on operating warehouses, transportation companies, or the "back-end" of retail stores.

People-oriented jobs tend to pay more, in part because such jobs are more likely to affect sales—the life blood of any business. Thing-oriented jobs, on the other hand, are often seen as "cost-generators" rather than "sales-generators." Taking a big view of the whole company's operations, the thing-oriented jobs are certainly necessary—but without sales no one is needed to do them.

Thing-oriented jobs are usually done at the company's place of business. Further, especially in lower-level jobs, the amount of work that needs to be done and even the nature of the work can be spelled out quite clearly. The time it takes to design questionnaires and tabulate results, for example, can be estimated with reasonable accuracy. Similarly, running a warehouse, totaling inventories, packaging outgoing shipments, and so on are like production operations. They may even be studied by time and motion study people. In any case, it is fairly easy to measure an employee's effectiveness and productivity in a thing-oriented job. At the least, time put in is a measure of the employee's contribution—and many are paid accordingly.

A sales representative, on the other hand, might spend all weekend thinking and planning how to make a half-hour sales presentation on Monday. For what should the sales rep be paid—the half hour presentation, all of the planning and thinking that went into it, or the results? Typically, "outside" sales reps are rewarded according to their sales results—and this helps account for the sometimes extremely high salaries paid to effective order getters. At the same time, some people-oriented jobs can be routinized and are lower paid. For example, sales clerks in some retail stores are paid at or near the minimum wage.

Managers needed for both kinds of jobs

We have oversimplified deliberately to emphasize the differences among types of jobs. Actually, of course, there are many variations between the two extremes. Some sales representatives must do a great deal of analytical work before they make a presentation. Similarly, some marketing researchers must be extremely people-sensitive to get potential customers to reveal their true feelings. But the division is still useful—because it focuses on the basic emphasis in different kinds of jobs and how the people are paid.

Managers are needed for the people in these two kinds of jobs. Managing others generally requires a blend of both people and analytical skills, but the people skills may be the more important of the two. Therefore, we often see people-oriented persons being promoted as managers of either kind of job.

THERE ARE MANY MARKETING JOBS TO CHOOSE FROM

Marketing is such a broad field that it is impossible to describe all the possible jobs. At least one fourth and possibly as much as one third of the U.S. labor force is engaged in some kind of marketing activity. This proportion will probably grow even larger in the future as (1) the service sector of our economy continues to expand and (2) the marketing concept is adopted by more business firms, government agencies, and nonprofit organizations.

Where would you like to work?

Given the wide range of opportunities, it will be helpful if you try to narrow the possibilities. After deciding on your own goals, interests, and abilities, consider where within the marketing system you might like to work. Would you like to work for manufacturers, wholesalers, or retailers? Or doesn't it really matter? And do you want to be involved with consumer goods or industrial goods? By analyzing your feelings about these options, you can begin to focus on the kind of job and the functional area that might interest you most.

What job would you like?   One simple way to get a better idea of the kinds of jobs available in marketing is to review the chapters of this text—this time with an eye for job opportunities rather than new concepts. The following paragraphs contain short descriptions of job areas that are often of interest to marketing students—tied to specific chapters in the text. Some, as noted below, offer good starting opportunities. Others do not. While reading these paragraphs, keep your own goals, interests, and attitudes in mind.

MARKETING MANAGER (CHAPTER 2)

This is usually not an entry-level job—although aggressive students may move quickly into this role in smaller companies.

MARKETING RESEARCH OPPORTUNITIES (CHAPTER 4)

There are entry-level opportunities at all levels in the channel—in large firms where formal marketing research is done—and in advertising agencies and marketing research firms. Quantitative and behavioral science skills are extremely important in marketing research, so many firms prefer to hire statistics or psychology majors rather than marketing majors. Nevertheless, there are many opportunities in marketing research for marketing students. A new employee might begin in a training program—conducting interviews or coding questionnaires—before being promoted to assistant project manager and higher management positions.

CONSUMER RESEARCH (CHAPTERS 5 AND 6)

Opportunities as consumer analysts and market analysts are commonly found in large companies, marketing research organizations, and advertising agencies. Beginners start in "thing-oriented" jobs until their judgment and people-oriented skills have been tested. Because knowledge of statistics and/or behavioral sciences is very important, marketing students will find themselves competing with majors in fields such as psychology, sociology, statistics, and computer science.

PURCHASING AGENT/BUYER (CHAPTER 6)

Opportunities are commonly found in large companies, with beginners starting as trainees or assistant buyers under the supervision of experienced buyers.

MARKET ANALYST (CHAPTER 7)

See Consumer Research.

PRODUCT/BRAND MANAGER (CHAPTER 8)

Many multiproduct firms have brand or product managers handling individual products—in effect, managing each product as a separate business. Some firms hire marketing majors as assistant brand or product managers, although typically only MBAs would be considered. Most firms would prefer that inexperienced beginners spend some time in the field—doing sales work—before moving into brand or product mangement positions.

NEW PRODUCT PLANNER (CHAPTER 9)

This probably would not be an entry-level position. Instead, people with experience on the technical side of the business and/or sales might be moved into new product development as they demonstrate judgment and analytical skills.

PACKAGING SPECIALISTS (CHAPTER 9)

Packaging manufacturers tend to hire and train interested people from various backgrounds—because there is little formal academic training in packaging. There are many sales opportunities in this field, and the manufacturers can train interested people to be specialists fairly quickly in this growing area.

DISTRIBUTION CHANNEL MANAGEMENT (CHAPTER 10)

This work is typically handled or directed by sales managers, and therefore would not be an entry-level position.

PHYSICAL DISTRIBUTION OPPORTUNITIES (CHAPTER 10)

There are many sales opportunities with physical distribution specialists. But there are also many "thing-oriented" jobs—in traffic management, warehousing, and materials handling. Here, training in accounting, finance, and quantitative methods could be quite useful. These kinds of jobs are available at all levels in the channels of distribution—remember that about half of the cost of marketing is caused by physical distribution activities.

RETAILING OPPORTUNITIES (CHAPTER 11)

Most entry-level marketing positions in retailing involve some kind of sales work. Retailing positions tend to offer lower-than-average starting salaries, but frequently provide opportunities for very rapid advancement. Most retailers require new employees to have some selling experience before managing others or buying. A typical marketing major can expect to do some sales work and manage one or several departments before advancing to a store management position or to a staff position which might involve buying, advertising, marketing research, and so on.

WHOLESALING OPPORTUNITIES (CHAPTER 12)

Entry-level marketing opportunities probably would involve sales work, perhaps working with the wholesalers' retailers or other customers—either selling or supporting experienced sales people. The buying side of wholesaling would be available after some sales experience has been gained. Some very large wholesalers, however, do have specialized buyers. See Purchasing Agent/Buyer (Chapter 6).

SALES PROMOTION OPPORTUNITIES (CHAPTER 13)

There will not be many entry-level positions in this area. Creativity and judgment are required—and it is difficult for an inexperienced person to demonstrate these skills. A beginner would probably move from sales or advertising jobs into sales promotion.

PERSONAL SELLING OPPORTUNITIES (CHAPTER 14)

The greatest number of job opportunities—and especially entry-level jobs—involve personal selling. This might be order getting, order taking, or supporting activities. Many students are reluctant to get into personal selling, but this field offers benefits that are hard to match in any other field. These include the opportunity to earn extremely high salaries and commissions—quickly—a chance to develop one's self-confidence and resourcefulness, an opportunity to work with minimal supervision—almost to the point of being one's own boss—and a chance to acquire product and customer knowledge that many firms consider a prerequisite for a successful career in product/brand management, sales management, *and* marketing management. Note, however, that many salespersons spend their entire careers in selling, preferring the freedom and earning potential that go with the job over the headaches—and sometimes lower salaries— of management positions.

SALES MANAGEMENT (CHAPTER 15)

This is a management position which usually is preceded by a variety of sales jobs.

ADVERTISING OPPORTUNITIES (CHAPTER 15)

Job opportunities are plentiful in this area—but highly competitive. And because the ability to communicate and knowledge of the behavioral sciences are important, marketing majors will often find themselves competing with majors from fields such as English, Journalism, Psychology, and Sociology. There are "thing-oriented" jobs such as copywriting, media buying, art, and so on. And there are "people-oriented" positions involving sales— which probably would be of more interest to marketing students. This is a glamorous—but small and extremely competitive—industry where "bright young people" can rise very rapidly, but can also be as easily displaced by new "bright young people."

PRICING OPPORTUNITIES (CHAPTERS 16 AND 17)

Pricing is generally handled by experienced managers, so there are no entry-level opportunities here. In fact, in some companies pricing is not even handled by the sales or marketing people—as explained in the text.

INTERNATIONAL MARKETING OPPORTUNITIES (CHAPTER 18)

Many marketing students are intrigued with the adventure and foreign travel that are a part of international marketing careers. However, very few firms hire recent graduates for positions in international marketing—except some MBA graduates from schools that specialize in international trade. Beginners aspiring to a career in international marketing usually must master the firm's domestic marketing operations before being sent abroad.

CUSTOMER RELATIONS/CONSUMER AFFAIRS OPPORTUNITIES (CHAPTER 19)

Some firms are becoming more concerned about their relations with customers and the general public. Employees for this kind of work, however, will have held various positions with the firm before filling customer relations positions.

START PLANNING YOUR CAREER NOW

You can see that there are many opportunities in marketing. But not all jobs are open to the beginner. Positions such as marketing manager, brand manager, and sales manager are higher rungs on the marketing career ladder. They become available only when one has obtained a few years of experience and shown leadership and judgment.

At the same time, there are many opportunities for someone seeking a career in marketing. If this sounds appealing to you, there is much you can do—and should do—right away to explore the opportunities. Talk to your school's career counselors and placement officers about the kinds of jobs that are being offered to your school's students. Your marketing instructors can help you be more realistic about how you can match your training, abilities, and interests to job opportunities. Read business publications such as *Business Week, Fortune, The Wall Street Journal,* the *Journal of Marketing,* and *Advertising Age.* Don't overlook the business sections of your local newspapers—to keep in touch with marketing developments in your area. Take advantage of any opportunity to talk directly with marketers—ask them what they are doing and what satisfactions they obtain from their jobs. Finally, if your school has a marketing club, join it and participate actively in the club's programs. It will help you meet real marketers and students who have a serious interest in the field. Some may have had very interesting job experiences and will be able to give you leads for part-time jobs or exciting career opportunities.

As you take additional courses in marketing, your understanding of marketing will increase—as will your awareness of possible career opportunities. Once you have decided what you would like to do, you can then apply the marketing concept to marketing an important product—yourself! Meanwhile, now is the time to start planning your marketing strategy. That is, now is the time to start segmenting the market for your services and developing an attractive marketing mix to satisfy the needs and wants of your potential employers. This will make you look more impressive when you begin your job interviews. Remember, while all employers would like to hire a "Superman" or a "Wonder Woman," they are also impressed with candidates who know what they want to do and are aggressively seeking a place where they can fit in and make a contribution.

Whether or not you decide to pursue a marketing career, the author wishes you the best of luck in your search for a challenging and rewarding career—wherever your interests and abilities may take you.

CASES

Guide to the use of these cases

Cases can be used in many ways. And the same case may be fruitfully considered several times for different purposes.

The following cases are organized under several headings to suggest when they might be used *for the first time*. The basic criterion for placement, however, was *not* whether the subject matter of the case fit best there, but rather whether any text principles or technical terminology to be covered later in the text were needed to read the case meaningfully. Some early cases might require some consideration of Price, for example, and might be used twice, say in regard to product planning and, later pricing. But cases listed under Price can be treated more effectively *after* the Price chapters have been covered.

INTRODUCTION TO MARKETING MANAGEMENT

1. Taylor Incorporated

Taylor, Inc., is a 105-year-old Chicago-based food processor. Its multiproduct lines have achieved widespread acceptance under the "Taylor" brand name. The company and subsidiaries engage principally in preparing, canning, packaging, and selling canned and frozen foods. Beginning with beef, the company expanded its operations to include pineapple from Hawaii and other fruits, vegetables, pickles and condiments, Alaskan salmon, and can manufacturing. Operating more than 27 processing plants in the United States, Taylor has become one of the largest U.S. food processors, with annual sales in 1972 of $348,065,000.

Until 1941, Taylor was a subsidiary of a major midwestern meat-packing company, and many of the present executives came up through the meat-packing industry. Taylor's president recently said: "Almeat's [the meat-packing firm] influence is still with us. Taylor has always been run like a meat-packer. As long as new products indicate a potential for an increase in the company's sales volume, they are produced. Traditionally there has been little, if any, attention paid to margins. We are well aware that the profits will come through good products."

In full agreement with the multiproduct-line policy was Howard Keene, a 25-year Taylor employee and now production manager. Keene volunteered, "Volume comes from satisfying needs. We at Taylor will can, pack, or freeze any meat, vegetable, or fruit we think the consumer might want." He also acknowledged that much of the expansion in product lines was dictated by economics. The typical plant facilities in the industry are not fully utilized. By adding new products to use this excess capacity, costs are spread over greater volume. So the production department is regularly looking for new ways to make more effective use of its present facilities.

The wide expansion of product line coupled with Taylor's line-forcing policy has resulted in 85 percent of Taylor's sales coming from supermarket chain stores, such as Kroger and A&P. Smaller stores are generally not willing to accept the Taylor policy, which requires that any store desiring to carry the Taylor brand name must be willing to carry the complete line of 68 varieties of fruits, vegetables, and meats. Keene explains, "We know that only large stores can afford to invest the amount of money in inventory that it would take to be adequately supplied with our products. But, the large stores are the volume! We give the consumers the choice of any Taylor product they want, and the result is maximum sales." Many small retailers have voiced complaints about Taylor's policy, but they have been considered to be too small in potential sales volume per store to be of any significance.

In 1973, a stockholders' revolt concerning low profits (in 1972, they were only $5,769) resulted in Taylor's president and two of its five directors being removed. Thomas Speh, a lawyer previously employed as staff assistant to the chairman of the board, was elected president. One of the first things Speh decided to focus on was the erratic and inadequate level of profits generated by Taylor in the past several years. A comparison of Taylor's results with those of the California Packing Corporation (Calpack) and some other large competitors supports Speh's concern. In the past ten years, Calpack had an average profit return on shareholders' investment of 10.8 percent, H. J. Heinz averaged 9

percent, Hunt Food 6 percent, and Taylor 3.8 percent. Further, Taylor's sales volume, $348,065,000 in 1972, had not increased significantly from the 1956 level of $325 million, while operating costs have soared upward. Profits for Taylor were about $8 million in 1956. The closest they have come since then is about $6 million in 1964.

In his last report to the Taylor board of directors, the outgoing president blamed his failure on an inefficient marketing department. He wrote, "Our marketing department has deteriorated. I can't exactly put my finger on it, but the overall quality of marketing personnel has dropped and morale is bad. The team just didn't perform." When Speh confronted Jerry Brown, the vice president of marketing, with the previous statement, his reply was, "It's not our fault. I think the company made a key mistake after World War II. It expanded horizontally—by increasing its number of product offerings—while competitors like Calpack were expanding vertically, growing their own raw materials and making all of their packing materials. They can control quality and make profits in manufacturing which can be used in marketing. I lost some of my best men from frustration. We just aren't competitive enough to reach the market to the extent we should with a comparable product and price."

In further conversation with Brown, Speh learned more about the nature of Taylor's market. Although all the firms in the food-processing industry advertise extensively to the consumer market, there has been no appreciable increase in the size of the market for processed foods. Further, consumers are not very selective. If they can't find the brand of food they are looking for, they will pick up another brand rather than go without a basic part of their diet. No firm in the industry has much effect on the price at which its products are sold. Chain store buyers are used to paying about the same case rate for any competitor's product and will not exceed it. They will, however, charge any price they wish on a given brand sold at retail. (A 48-can case of sweet peas might be purchased from any supplier for $6.83, no matter whose product it is. Generally, the shelf price for each is no more than a few pennies different, but chain stores occasionally attract customers by placing a well-known brand on "sale.")

At this point Speh is wondering why Taylor is not as profitable as it once was. Also, he is puzzled as to why the competition is putting products on the market with low potential sales volumes. For example, one major competitor recently introduced a small line of dietary fruits and vegetables, with a potential sales volume so small that virtually every nationally known food processor had previously avoided such specialization.

Discuss Taylor's policies and what it might do to improve its present situation.

2. Mike's Home Service

Mike Horn is a 26-year-old ex-Navy frogman and lifelong resident of Traverse City, Michigan, a beautiful summer resort area on Grand Traverse Bay along the eastern shore of Lake Michigan. The permanent population is about 20,000, and this more than triples in the summer months.

Mike spent seven years in the Navy after high school graduation, returning home in June 1974. Mike decided to go into business for himself, after he was unable to find other satisfactory work in the Traverse City area. He established Mike's Home Service. Mike felt that his accumulated savings would enable him to establish the business without borrowing any money. His estimate of required expenditures was: $2,900 for a used panel truck, $425 for a steam-cleaning machine adaptable to carpets and furniture, $270 for a heavy-duty commercial vacuum cleaner, $50 for special brushes and attachments, $75 for the initial supply of cleaning fluids and compounds, and $200 for insurance and other incidental expenses. This total of $3,920 still left Mike with about $2,800 in savings to cover living expenses while getting started.

One of the reasons Mike chose this line of work is his previous work experience. From the time he was 16, Mike had worked part-time for Charles Balcom, who operated the only other successful carpet-cleaning firm in Traverse City. (One other firm operated in Traverse City but was rumored to be near bankruptcy.)

Balcom prided himself on quality work and had gained a loyal clientele. Specializing in residential carpet cleaning, Balcom had been able to build a strong customer franchise. For 35 years, Balcom's major source of new business has been retailer recommendations and satisfied customers who told friends about the quality service received from Balcom. He is so highly thought of that the leading carpet and furniture stores in Traverse City always recommend Balcom's as "preventive maintenance" in quality carpet and furniture care. Often Balcom is entrusted with the keys to Traverse City's finest homes for months at a time when owners are out of town and want Balcom's services. Balcom's customers are so loyal, in fact, that a Vita-Clean national household carpet-cleaning franchise

found it next to impossible to compete with him. Even price cutting was not an effective weapon against him.

Mike Horn felt that he knew the business as well as Balcom, having worked for him many years. Mike was anxious to reach his $20,000-per-year sales goal because he thought this would provide him with a comfortable living in Traverse City. While aware of opportunities for carpet cleaning in businesses, office buildings, motels, and so on, Mike felt that the sales volume available there was only about $7,000, because most businesses maintained their own cleaning staffs. As he saw it, his only opportunity was direct competition with Balcom.

To get started, he allocated $530 to advertise his business in the local newspaper. With this money he was able to purchase two half-page ads and have enough left over to buy daily three-line ads in the classified section, listed under Miscellaneous Residential Services, for 52 weeks. All that was left was to paint a sign on his truck and wait for business to "catch on."

Mike had occasional customers and was able to gross about $100 a week. He had, of course, expected much more. These customers were usually Balcom regulars who, for one reason or another (usually stains, spills, or house guests), weren't able to wait the two weeks required until Balcom could work them in. While these people did admit that Mike's work was of the same quality as Balcom's, they preferred Balcom's "quality care" image. On several occasions Mike did get more work than he could handle. This happened during April and May, when resort owners were preparing for summer openings and owners of summer homes were ready to "open the cottage." The same rush was repeated in September and October as resorts and homes were being closed for the winter. During these months, Mike was able to gross about $100–$120 a day, working ten hours.

Toward the end of his first year in business, Mike Horn began to have thoughts about quitting. While he hated to think of the prospects of having to leave Traverse City, he couldn't see any way of making a living in the carpet and furniture cleaning business in Traverse. Balcom had the whole residential market sewed up, except in the rush seasons and for people who needed fast cleaning.

3. Modern Manufacturing Company

Modern manufacturing Co. is a large manufacturer of basic chemicals and polymer resins, located in Pennsylvania.

Bob Zicuti, a bright young engineer, has been working for Modern as a research engineer in the polymer resins laboratory. His job is to do research on established resins to find new, more profitable applications for resin products.

During the last five years, Bob has been under intense pressure from top management to come up with an idea that would open up new markets for the company's foamed polystyrene.

Two years ago, Bob developed the "spiral dome concept," a method of using the foamed polystyrene to make dome-shaped roofs and other structures. He described the procedure for making domes as follows:

> The construction of a spiral dome involves the use of a specially designed machine which bends, places, and bonds pieces of plastic foam together into a predetermined dome shape. In forming a dome, the machine head is mounted on a boom, which swings around a pivot like the hands of a clock, laying and bonding layer upon layer of foam board in a rising spherical form.

According to Bob, polystyrene foamed boards have several advantages:

1. Foam board is stiff, but capable of controlled deformation and can be bonded to itself by heat alone.
2. Foam board is extremely lightweight and easy to handle. It has good structural rigidity.
3. Foam board has excellent and permanent insulating characteristics. (In fact the major use for foamed board is as an insulator.)
4. Foam board provides an excellent base on which to apply a variety of surface finishes.

With his fine speaking and reasoning abilities, Bob had little trouble convincing top mnagement of the soundness of the idea.

According to a preliminary study carried out by the marketing depai :ment, the following were areas of construction that could be served by the domes:

Why wasn't Mike able to reach his goal of $20,000? Is there any way Mike can stay in business?

1. Bulk storage.
2. Cold storage.
3. Educational construction.
4. Industrial tanks (covers for).
5. Light commercial construction.
6. Planetariums.
7. Recreational construction (such as a golf course starter house).

The study was based on uses for existing dome structures. Most of the existing domes are made out of concrete or some cement base material. It was estimated that considerable savings would be realized by using foam boards, due to the reduction of construction time.

Because of the new technology involved, the company decided to do its own contracting (at least for the first four to five years after starting the sales program). It felt this was necessary to make sure that no mistakes were made by inexperienced contractor crews. For example, if not applied properly, the plastic may burn.

After building a few domes to demonstrate the concept, the company contacted some leading architects across the country. Reactions were as follows:

> It is very interesting, but you know that the Fire Marshal of Detroit will never give his OK.
> Your tests show that foamed domes can be protected against fires, but there are no *good* tests for unconventional building materials as far as I am concerned.
> I like the idea, but foam board does not have the impact resistance of cement.
> We design a lot of recreational facilities and kids will find a way of sawing holes into the foam.
> Building codes around L.A. are written for wood and cement structures. Maybe when the codes change.

After this unexpected reaction, management did not know what to do. Bob still thinks the company should go ahead. He feels that a few reports of well-constructed domes in leading newspapers would go a long way toward selling the idea.

What should Modern do? Why did it get into the present situation?

CUSTOMER BEHAVIOR

4. Recco, Incorporated

William Sloan is the president and only stockholder of Recco, Inc., a small, successful enterprise engaged in the restaurant and recreation business in the small town of Jefferson, the site of the state university (population 7,000 plus 20,000 students). Sloan attended the university in the 1930s, and during his college career paid most of his education and living expenses by selling refreshments at all of the school's athletic events. In a truly enterprising fashion, he expanded his business by hiring local high school students to assist him. The business became so profitable that it was only natural that Sloan stay on in Jefferson after graduation, renting a small building adjacent to the campus and installing a restaurant.

Over the years, his restaurant business prospered and provided Sloan with a $36,000 profit on sales of $1,462,500 in 1975. The restaurant now consists of an attractive 40-table dining room, a large drive-in facility, and free delivery of orders to any point on the campus. The only thing that hasn't substantially changed is Sloan's clientele. He estimates that his restaurant business is still over 90 percent students, and that over three fourths of his sales are made between 6 P.M. and 1 A.M. There are several other restaurants with comparable facilities in the immediate vicinity of the campus, but none of these is as popular with the university students as his "Papa Bill's."

As a result of the restaurant's success with the student market, Sloan has aimed his entire promotional effort in that direction by advertising only through the campus newspaper and over the campus and local "rock" music radio stations. In an attempt to bolster his daytime business, from time to time Sloan has used such devices as coupon mealbooks priced at 85 percent of face value. And he features daily lunch "special" plates. Nevertheless, he concedes that he has been unable to complete with the university cafeterias for daytime business.

In 1972, when Sloan was seeking a new investment opportunity, he contacted a representative of a national manufacturer of bowling equipment and supplies about the feasibility of establishing a bowling lanes operation. Jefferson didn't have such a facility at the time, and Sloan felt that both the local and university communities would provide a receptive market. He already owned a large tract of land which would be suitable for con-struction of the bowling lanes. The land was next to the restaurant, and he felt that such proximity would result in each business stimulating the other.

The decision was made to go ahead with the venture, and to date the results have been nothing short of outstanding. Several local and university groups have formed bowling leagues. The university's men's and women's physical education departments schedule several bowling classes at Sloan's bowling lanes each term. And the casual bowling in the late afternoons and evenings is such that at least 12 of the 16 lanes are almost always in use. Some local radio advertising is done for the bowling lanes, but not much is considered necessary by Sloan. The success of the bowling lanes has prompted the developer of a small shopping center in the "residential" part of town to make tentative plans to include a similar facility in his new development. But Sloan believes that competition won't hurt his business because he has more to offer in his recreation center—a restaurant and bowling.

Overjoyed by the profitability of his latest investment, Sloan decided to expand his recreational center operation even further. He noted the participation of both students and local citizens in his bowling lanes and concluded that the addition of an attractive, modern billiard parlor would also have a common appeal. There were already two "poolrooms" in Jefferson. One was modern, but about two miles from campus. The other one was considered to be a local "hangout" and was avoided by townspeople and students. Sloan decided that distance and atmosphere were the factors that resulted in both operations being only marginally successful. Further, he felt that by offering a billiard parlor operation, he would be able to supply yet another recreational demand of his market. He obtained a loan from a local bank and proceeded to build a third building on the rear portion of his tract of land. The billiard parlor was outfitted with 12 tables, a snack bar, wall-to-wall carpeting, and a soft-music background system.

Today, eight months later, Mr. Sloan is extremely disappointed with the billiard parlor operation. After the first two or three weeks, business steadily dropped off until at the present time only one or two tables are usually in use, even during the evening hours when business at the bowling lanes is at its peak. Promotion for the billiard parlor has been combined with promotions for the other facilities, which are still doing very well.

In an effort to discover what went wrong, Sloan interviewed several of his restaurant and bowling customers. Some typical responses were:

> A coed, "Bowling in a skirt is tricky enough. There's just no way you can gracefully shoot pool in one!"
>
> A fraternity man, "My idea of a good date is dinner at Papa Bill's, then the movies or an evening of bowling. You just can't make a good impression by taking a girl to play pool."

Jefferson citizen, "I've never allowed my children to enter the local pool halls. What's more, as a kid I wasn't allowed either, and thus have never learned the game. It's too late to teach an old dog new tricks!"

Sloan is considering selling the billiard equipment and installing some pinball machines because he has heard they can be very profitable.

Evaluate Sloan's overall position and suggest what should be done.

5. Inland Steel Company

Inland Steel Co. is one of the two major producers of wide-flange beams in the Chicago area. The other major producer in the area is the U.S. Steel Corp. (USS), which is several times larger than Inland as far as production capacity of this particular product is concerned. Bethlehem Steel Co. and USS have eastern plants which produce this product. Also, there are some small competitors in the Chicago area, and foreign competition is sometimes a factor. Generally, however, U.S. Steel and Inland Steel are the major competitors in wide-flange beams in the Chicago area, because typically the mill price charged by all producers is the same and the customer must pay freight from the mill. Therefore, the large eastern mills landed price would not be competitive in the Chicago area.

Wide-flange beams are one of the principal steel products used in construction. They are the "modern" version of what are commonly known as "I-beams." USS rolls a full range of wide flanges from 6 inches to 36 inches. Inland entered the field about 15 years ago when it converted an existing mill for the production of this product. This mill is limited to flanges up to 24 inches, however. At the time of the conversion, it was estimated that customer usage of sizes over 24 inches was likely to be small. In the past few years, however, there has been a very pronounced trend toward the larger and heavier sections.

The beams produced by the various competitors are almost identical, since the customers buy according to standard dimensional and physical property specifications. In the smaller size range, there are a number of competitors, but above 14 inches only USS and Inland compete in the Chicago area. Above 24 inches, USS has not had any competition.

All the steel companies sell these beams through their own sales forces. The customer for these beams is called a "structural fabricator." This fabricator typically buys unshaped beams and other steel products from the mills and shapes them according to the specifications of the customer. The fabricator's customer is the contractor or owner of a particular building or structure which is being built.

The structural fabricator typically sells his product and services on a competitive-bid basis. The bidding is done on the basis of plans and specifications which are prepared by an architectural or structural engineering firm and forwarded to him by the contractor desiring the bid. Although several hundred structural fabricators compete in the Midwest, relatively few account for the majority of wide-flange tonnage. Since the price is the same from all producers, they typically buy beams on the basis of availability (availability to meet production schedules) and performance (reliability in meeting the promised delivery schedule).

Several years ago, Inland production schedulers saw that they were going to have an excess of hot-rolled plate capacity in the near future. At the same time, a new production technique was developed which would enable a steel company to weld three plates together into a section with the same dimensional and physical properties and almost the same cross section as a rolled wide-flange beam. This technical development appeared to offer two advantages to Inland: (1) it would enable Inland to use some of the excess plate capacity, and (2) larger sizes of wide-flange beams could be offered. Cost analysts showed that by using a fully depreciated plate mill and the new welding process it would be possible to produce and sell larger wide-flange beams at "competitive" prices, i.e., at the same price charged by USS.

Inland executives were excited about the possibilities because they thought customers would appreciate having a second source of supply. Also, the new approach would allow the production of up to a 60-inch depth of section and an almost 30-inch width of flange. With a little imagination, these larger sizes could offer a significant breakthrough for the construction industry.

Inland decided to go ahead with the new project. As the production capacity was being converted, the sales people were kept well informed of the progress. They, in turn, promoted this new capability, emphasizing that soon they would be able to offer a full range of beam products. Several general information letters were sent to the trade, but no advertising was used. Moreover, the market development section of the sales department was very busy explaining the new possibilities of the process, particularly to fabricators at engineering trade associations and shows.

When the new line was finally ready to go, the reaction was disappointing. In general, the customers were wary of the new product. The structural fabricators felt they could not use it without the approval of their customers, because it would involve deviating from the specified rolled sections. And, as long as they could still get the rolled section, why make the extra effort for something unfamiliar, especially with no price advantage. The sales people were also plagued with a very common question: How can you take plate that you sell for about $121 per ton and make a product that you can sell for $122? This question came up frequently and tended to divert the whole discussion to the cost of production rather than to the way the new product might be used.

Evaluate Inland's situation. What should it do to gain greater acceptance for its new product?

6. Rocco's Place

Rocco's Place was a fairly large restaurant, covering about 20,000 square feet of floor space, located in the center of a small shopping center which was completed early in 1971. In addition to this restaurant, other businesses in the shopping center included a bakery, a beauty shop, a liquor store, and a meat market. There was room for several cars in front of each of the stores.

The shopping center was located in a residential section of a growing suburb in the East. The center was situated along a heavily traveled major traffic artery. The nearby population was composed largely of middle-income families, and although the ethnic background of the residents was fairly heterogeneous, a large proportion were Italians.

Rocco's Place, which deals primarily in full-course dinners (no bar), is operated by Toni Rocco, a neat-appearing man who was born in the community in 1920, of Italian parentage. He graduated from a local high school and a nearby university and had been living in this town with his wife and two children for many years. He had been in the restaurant business (self-employed) since his graduation from college in 1945. His most recent venture, prior to opening this restaurant, was a large restaurant which he operated successfully with his brother from 1961 to 1967, at which time he sold out because of illness. Following his recovery, he wanted something to do and opened the present restaurant in April 1971.

Toni felt that his plans for the business and his opening were well thought out. He had even designed his very attractive sign three years before. When he was ready to go into this business, he inspected several possible locations before finally deciding on the present one. He said: "I looked everywhere, and this is one of the areas I inspected. I particularly noticed the heavy traffic when I first looked at it. This is the crossroads from north to south for practically every main artery statewise. So obviously the potential is here."

Having decided upon the location, Toni attacked the problem of the new building with vigor. He tiled the floor; put in walls of surfwood; installed new plumbing and electric fixtures, and an extra washroom; and purchased the necessary restaurant equipment, all brand new. All this cost him $32,000—which came from his own cash savings. He then spent an additional $600 for glassware, $1,500 for his initial food stock, and $675 to advertise his opening in the local newspaper. The local newspaper covered quite a large area so the $675 purchased only three quarter-page ads. These expenditures also came from his own personal savings. Next, he hired five waitresses at $50 a week and one chef at $125 a week. Then, with $6,000 cash on hand, he was ready to do business. Reflecting his "sound business sense," Toni realized the necessity of having a substantial cash reserve to fall back on until the business had had time to get on its own feet. He expected this to take about one year. He did not have any expectations about "getting rich overnight."

The business opened in April and by August he had achieved a weekly gross revenue of only $1,200. Toni was a little discouraged with this, but he was still able to meet all his operating expenses without investing any "new money" in the business. However, he was concerned that he might have to do so if business did not pick up in the next couple of months. It had not by September, and Toni did have to invest an additional $1,200 in the business "for survival purposes."

Business had not improved in November, and Toni was still insisting that it would take at least a year to build up a business of this nature. In view of the failure to "catch on rapidly," Toni indicated that he had intensified his advertising to see if this would help the business any. In the last few weeks, he had spent $250 of his own cash for radio advertising—ten late-evening spots. Moreover, he was planning to spend even more during the next several weeks for some newspaper ads.

By February 1972 business had picked up very slightly—about a $50 increase in the average weekly gross.

By April 1972 the situation had begun to improve and by June his weekly gross was up to between $1,700 and $1,800. By March in the following year, the weekly gross had risen to about $2,100. Toni increased the working hours of his staff six to seven hours a week and added another man to handle the increasing number of customers. Toni was more optimistic for the future. He had not put any new money into the business since the summer of 1972 and expected business to continue to rise. He had not yet taken any salary for himself, but indicated that he was in a position to do so if he wished. Instead, he planned to put in an air-conditioning system at a cost of $5,000 and was also planning to use what salary he would have taken for himself to hire two new waitresses to handle his ever-increasing volume of business.

In explaining the successful survival and growth of his business, Toni said: "I had a lot of cash on hand, a well-planned program, and the patience to wait it out."

Evaluate Toni's marketing strategy. How might he have improved his chances for success and achieved more rapid growth?

7. Wallis Properties, Inc.

After several years as a partner responsible for sales in a medium-sized manufacturing concern, Alvin Wallis disposed of his interest in the concern quite profitably. Then, searching for an interesting opportunity that he felt would be less demanding, he spent considerable time researching alternatives. He decided to purchase The Pines, a recently completed 60-room motel at the edge of a small town in a relatively exclusive but rapidly expanding resort area. He saw a strong market potential for public accommodations. The location was also within one-half mile of a new interstate highway which was just being completed. Fifteen miles away in the center of the tourist area were several nationally franchised full-service resort motels suitable for prolonged vacations.

He was able to hire the necessary staff, which initially consisted of four maids and a handyman to care for inside and outside maintenance. Wallis looked after registration and office duties, assisted by his wife. Since he had done a great deal of travel himself and had stayed at many different hotels and motels, he had some definite ideas about what vacationers wanted in the way of accommodations. He felt that a relatively plain but modern room with a comfortable bed, standard bath facilities, and complete air-conditioning would appeal to most patrons.

He did not consider a swimming pool or any other non-revenue-producing additions to be worthwhile, and considered a restaurant to be a greater management problem than the benefits it would offer. However, after many customers commented, he arranged to serve a continental breakfast of coffee and rolls from a service counter in a room next to the registration desk.

During the first year after opening, occupancy began to stabilize at around 50–60 percent of capacity. According to figures which Wallis obtained from the publication *Trends in the Hotel-Motel Business* published by the accounting firm of Harris, Kerr Forster & Company, his occupancy rate ranked considerably below the average of 78 percent for his classification—motels without restaurants.

Examination of these results after two years of operation began to disturb Wallis. He decided to evaluate his operation and search for means of increasing both occupancy rate and profitability. He did not want to sacrifice his independence and was trying not to compete directly with the resort areas offering much more complete services. For advertising and promotion, Wallis had stressed a price appeal in his signs and brochures. He was quite proud of the fact that he had been able to avoid all the "unnecessary" expenses of the resorts and was thus able to offer lodging at a very modest price, much below that of even the lowest-priced resort. He found that the customers who stayed at his motel found the accommodations quite acceptable, but was troubled by what seemed to be a large number of cars driving into his parking lot and looking around but not coming in to register.

Wallis was particularly interested in the results of a recent study conducted by the regional tourist bureau. This study revealed the following information about area vacationers:

1. 68 percent of the visitors to the area are young couples and older couples without children.
2. 40 percent of the visitors plan their vacations and reserve rooms more than 60 days in advance.
3. 66 percent of the visitors stay more than three days in the area and at the same location.
4. 78 percent of the visitors indicated that recreational facilities were important in their choice of accommodations.
5. 13 percent of the visitors had family incomes of less than $7,500 per year.
6. 38 percent of the visitors indicated that it was their first visit to the area.

Evaluate Wallis's strategy. What should he do to improve the profitability of the motel?

8. Polar Ice Palace

Bill Amboy is the manager of the Polar Ice Palace, an ice-skating rink with a conventional hockey rink surface (85 × 200 feet). He has a successful hockey program and is almost breaking even, which is about all that he can expect if he emphasizes hockey. To try to improve his financial condition, Bill is trying to develop a public skating program. If he had such a program, instead of limiting the use of the ice to 12–24 people per hour, it would be possible to have as many as 700 people attending a public session at one time. While the receipts from hockey might be $60 an hour (plus concessions), the receipts from a two-hour public skating session charging $1.50 per person could generate as much as $1,050 for a two-hour period (plus much higher concession revenue). Clearly, the potential revenue from large public skating sessions could add significantly to total receipts and make the Polar Ice Palace a profitable operation.

Bill has put several public skating sessions into his ice schedule, but thus far they have not attracted as many people as he hoped. In fact, on the average, they do not generate any more revenue than if the times were sold for hockey use. And even worse, more staff people are needed to handle a public skating session— guards, a ticket seller, and skate rental and more concession help.

The Sunday afternoon public skating sessions have been the most successful, with an average of 300 people attending during the winter season. Typically, this is a "kid-sitting" session, with more than half of the patrons being young children who have been dropped off by their parents for several hours. There are some family groups. In general, the kids and the families do seem to have a good time, and a fairly loyal group comes back Sunday after Sunday during the winter season. In spring and fall, however, patronage drops about in half, depending on how nice the weather is.

It is the Friday and Saturday evening public sessions that are a big disappointment to Bill. The sessions run from 8:00 until 10:00—a time when he had hoped to attract couples. At $1.50 per person, plus 75 cents for skate rental if necessary, this could be a more economical date than going to the movies. In fact, Bill has seen quite a few young couples; and some keep coming back. But he also sees a surprising number of 8–12-year-olds who have been dropped off by their parents. In other words, there is some similarity to the Sunday afternoon "kid-sitting" session. The younger kids tend to race around the rink, playing tag. This affects the whole atmosphere and makes it less appealing for dating couples.

Bill feels that it should be possible to develop a teenage and young-adult market based on the format used by roller-skating rinks. Their public skating sessions feature a variety of "couples only" and "group games" as well as individuals skating to "danceable" music. This is not the format offered at the usual public ice skating session however. The idea of making them "social" activities has not been common, although there are reports in the industry that a few operators have had success with the roller-skating format.

Bill installed some soft lights to try to change the

evening atmosphere. The music format was designed to encourage couples to skate together. For a few sessions, Bill even tried to have some "couples only" skates, but this was strongly resisted by the young boys who felt that they had paid their money and there was no reason why they should be "kicked off the ice." Bill also tried to attract more young couples by bringing in a local disc jockey to broadcast from the Polar Ice Palace and advertise the public sessions. But all this has had little impact on attendance, which varies from 50 to 100 per two-hour session.

Bill seriously considered the possibility of limiting the evening sessions to people over 13 to try to change the environment. But when he counted the patrons, he realized that this would be risky. More than half of his evening patrons on an average night are 12 or under. This means that he would have to make a serious commitment to building the teenage and young-adult market, but thus far his efforts had not been very successful. He has already invested over $2,000 in lighting changes and several thousand dollars promoting the sessions over the youth-oriented radio station with almost no results.

Some days, Bill feels it is hopeless. Maybe he should just resign himself to the public skating sessions being a "mixed bag." Or maybe he should just sell the time to hockey groups.

What should Bill Amboy do about the evening public skating sessions?

PRODUCT

9. Betty's Shop

Betty's Shop is owned and operated by Bruce and Betty Douglas (a husband and wife team). Offering hundreds of varieties and arrangements of flowers, Betty's also carries small gift items intended to complement a floral arrangement. Mr. Douglas serves primarily as manager and salesclerk, while Mrs. Douglas's artistic talents lend themselves more to the selection and arrangement of appropriate flowers. Since opening in 1965, sales for Betty's have been gratifying. Mr. Douglas, however, is concerned about the failure of a recent addition to the gift line.

The Douglases purchased the present operation in 1965 from Rick Allen, who had been in that location for 20 years. Called Allen's Florists, the shop was then generating about $100,000 a year in business. Bruce and Betty were confident that their previous 12 years' experience owning a smaller floral shop in a tiny (pop. 6,500) resort town less than 20 miles south would enable them to become a success in their new location.

Bruce feels their new store is in an excellent location. Situated in a residential area of a northeast Indiana community of 130,000 population, the new Betty's Shop is somewhat isolated from other neighborhood stores. It is 8 blocks to the nearest store, a drugstore, and 3½ miles to the closest shopping center. But, it is near the intersection of the major north-south and east-west thoroughfares.

Mr. Douglas was keenly aware of his primary customers' characteristics. This perception enabled him to direct his efforts more efficiently. As a result, sales increased steadily from $150,000 at the end of 1965 to $300,000 in 1975. Most of the regular customers were women from medium- to high-income families living in the local middle-class residential areas. Also, Mr. Douglas was pleased to see that some of his "old customers" from the resort town come to Betty's, probably because a strong customer acceptance had been built on friendly service and quality floral arrangements. Those customers who stopped in less frequently were assumed to be similar to the "regulars."

The largest part of the shop's business consists of weddings, funerals, parties, dances, and other big, one-time events which utilize flowers. However, about 25 percent of the purchases are by casual buyers who like to browse and chat with the Douglases. Approximately 60 percent of the sales are telephone orders, while the remaining 40 percent are made in the shop. Almost all of the telephone orders are for special, one-time events, while the walk-in traffic is divided equally between special events and spur-of-the-moment purchases. Virtually no one buys flowers on a daily or regular basis. There is some FTD (Florist Telegraph Delivery) business, but Mr. Douglas considers this to be an added service, and it constitutes only about 5 percent of his volume.

Mr. Douglas feels that flowers are fairly homogeneous, unbranded products. Therefore, he feels that he must charge competitive prices to meet those of his 14 competitors throughout the community.

The shop was remodeled in 1975, and space for

all operations was doubled. To fill in the increased display area, it was decided to add several complementary gift items, such as a famous brand of candies, high-quality flowerpots and vases, a quality line of sheep- and lambskin rugs, pen-and-pencil sets, and candles. All the new lines, except the sheep- and lambskin rugs, have taken hold and have increased in sales each month since they were added. Sales of rugs have been very disappointing. In fact, they haven't paid their way on the basis of display area allotted (about 1/50 of the total display area).

When the busiest store traffic occurs (during a three- to four-day period before traditional flower-giving days), additional help is used. When available, Lisa and Kevin Douglas, the high-school-aged children of the proprietors, fill these jobs. (It was the children who suggested that the market for sheep- and lambskin rugs was growing in their high school during the last school year.) At other times, only one of the proprietors and a full-time salesclerk handle store traffic.

Samples of everything the shop has for sale are on display. The primary activity of the salesclerk is to show customers various selections which could be used for a particular occasion and then ring up the sale. Other than store display, advertising consists only of what is printed on the delivery truck, an ad in the yellow pages of the local telephone directory, and an occasional ad (five or six times per year) in the daily newspaper. None of the advertising mentions anything but flowers, because the proprietors wish to maintain their identity as florists.

Mr. Douglas is wondering if more display area, a lower price, or extra promotion by the salesclerks might increase the movement of the sheep- and lambskin rugs. Further, he is thinking of disposing of the rugs, but isn't sure what should replace them if he did.

Evaluate the present operation and why sheep- and lambskin rugs don't sell. What strategy should the shop follow?

10. Block Pharmaceutical Company

The Block Pharmaceutical Company is a well-known manufacturer of high-quality cosmetics and ointments. A little over a year ago, Mr. Fine, the president of Block, was scanning the operating statements for the last three quarters and did not like what he saw. At the next board meeting he stated that Block should be showing a larger profit. It was generally agreed that the reason for the profit decline was that the firm had not added any new products to its line during the last two years.

Management was directed to investigate this matter and remedy it if possible.

Fine immediately requested a report from the product-planning group and found that it had been working on a new formula for a toothpaste that might be put into production immediately if a new product were needed. Mr. Archer, the head of the research department, assured Fine that the new ingredients in this toothpaste had remarkable qualities. Clinical tests had consistently shown that the new, as yet unnamed, dentifrice cleaned teeth better than the many toothpastes furiously battling for prominence in the market. Based on these tests, Fine concluded that perhaps this product was what was needed and ordered work to proceed quickly to bring it to the market.

The marketing research department was asked to come up with a name that was pleasing, and a tube and carton design. The results were reported back within two months; the product was to be called "Smile" and the package would emphasize eye-pleasing pastels.

The marketing department decided to offer Smile along with its other "prestige" products in the drugstores that were carrying the rest of Block's better-quality, higher-priced products. Block's success had been built on moving quality products through these outlets, and management felt that quality-oriented customers would probably be willing to pay a bit more for a better toothpaste. Block was already well established with the wholesalers selling to these retailers and experienced little difficulty obtaining distribution for Smile.

It is now six months after the introduction of Smile, and the sales results have not been good. The established wholesalers and retailers carried the product, but relatively little was purchased by final consumers. And now many retailers are requesting that Block accept returns on Smile because obviously it is not going to catch on with consumers, despite the extremely large (matching that of competitors) amounts of advertising which have supported Smile.

Fine has requested the marketing research department to analyze the situation and explain the disappointing results thus far. An outside survey agency interviewed several hundred consumers and has tabulated its results. These are pretty well summarized in the following quotes:

"The stuff I'm using now tastes good. Smile tastes terrible!"

"I never saw that brand at the supermarket I shop at."

"I like what I'm using . . . why change?"

"I'm not going to pay that much for any toothpaste . . . it couldn't be *that* much better!"

What recommendation would you make to Fine? Why?

11. Low Corporation

Low Corporation is one of the larger chemical companies in the United States, making a diversified line of organic and inorganic chemicals, plastics, bioproducts, and metals. Research has played a vital role in the company's growth.

Recently, Low's research laboratories developed a new product in the antifreeze line—Lowtherm 209. Much research was devoted to the technical phase, involving various experiments concerned with the quality of the components in the new product.

The antifreeze commonly used now is ethylene glycol. If it leaks into the crankcase oil, it forms a thick pasty sludge that can produce bearing damage, cylinder scoring, or a dozen other costly and time-consuming troubles for both the operator and owner of heavy-duty equipment.

Low Corporation believed that Lowtherm 209 would be very valuable to the owners of heavy-duty diesel and gasoline trucks as well as other heavy-equipment owners. Chemically, Lowtherm 209 consists of methoxy propanol, as distinguished from the conventional glycol and alcohol products. It cannot prevent leakage, but if it does get into the crankcase, it will not cause any problems.

Lowtherm 209 has been proven in the laboratory to prevent seizing of rod and main bearings, pistons, rings, and piston pins, which are common with glycol leakage. The new product will not remain in the engine oil and will cut down on the sludge residue.

At first, Low thought it had two attractive markets for this product: (1) the manufacturers of heavy-duty equipment, and (2) the users of heavy-duty equipment. Low sales reps have made numerous calls and so far neither type of customer has been very interested. The manufacturers are reluctant to show interest in the product until it has been proven in actual use. The buyers for construction companies and other firms using heavy-duty equipment have also been hesitant. Some felt the price was far too high for the advantages offered. Others didn't understand what was wrong with the present antifreeze and dismissed the idea of paying extra for "just another" antifreeze.

The price of Lowtherm 209 is $12.98 per gallon, which is more than twice the price of regular antifreeze. The higher price is a result of higher costs in producing the product and an increment for making a better type of antifreeze.

Explain what has happened so far. What would you do if you were responsible for this product?

12. Alpine Sports Shop

Bill and Mary Schmidt recently graduated from a state university in Colorado. Now, with some family backing, they are planning to open a small ski equipment shop in Aspen, Colorado. They are sure that by offering friendly, personal service they will have something unique and be able to compete with the many other ski shops in town. They are well aware that there are already many competitors, because many skiing enthusiasts choose Aspen as a place to live and then try to find something to do there. By keeping the shop small, however, they hope to be able to manage most of the activities themselves, thereby keeping costs down and also being sure the service is good.

Now they are trying to decide which line or lines of skis they should carry. Almost all the major manufacturers' skis are offered in the competing shops, so Bill and Mary are seriously considering specializing in the Fritzmeier brand, which is not now carried by any local shops. In fact, the Fritzmeier sales rep has assured them that if they are willing to carry the line exclusively, Fritzmeier will not sell its skis to any other retailers in Aspen. This idea has appeal to Bill and Mary because it would give them something unique—a full line of German-made skis which have just been introduced into the American market with supporting full-page ads in skiing magazines. The skis have an injected foam core that is anchored to the glass layers above and below by a patented process which causes the glass fibers to penetrate the foam. This process is used in a full line of skis, so the Schmidts would have a unique story to sell for skis which could satisfy everyones' needs. Further, the suggested retail prices and markups were similar to other manufacturers, so the Alpine Sports Shop could emphasize the unique features of the Fritzmeier skis while feeling confident that their prices were competitive.

Besides the exclusive "fiber-penetrative" construction offered by Fritzmeier for strength and durability, the German company had developed a special recreational ski for women—with the assistance of Olympic triple-medal-winner Rosi Mittermaier. The Schmidts felt that this might be a special selling point for the Fritzmeier line. Many women need and want recreational skis (ones that are easier to use), and a ski designed specifically for them might be appealing and very profitable.

The only thing that worries the Schmidts about committing so completely to the Fritzmeier line is that there are dozens of other manufacturers—both domestic and foreign—which offer full lines and claim to offer unique features. In fact, most ski manufacturers regularly come out with new models and features, and the Schmidts are aware that most consumers are confused about the relative merits of all of the offerings. In the past Bill himself has been reluctant to buy "off-brand" skis, preferring instead to stay with major names such as Hart, Head, K2, and Rossignol. So he is concerned with whether a complete commitment to the Fritzmeier line is wise. On the other hand, the Schmidts want to offer something unique. They are reluctant to simply open "another" ski shop carrying lines that are available "everywhere." The Fritzmeier line is not their only possibility, of course. There are other "off-brands" which are not yet carried in Aspen. But the Schmidts are intrigued with the idea that Fritzmeier is planning to give national promotional support to the skis during the introductory campaign in the U.S. markets. They feel that this might make a big difference in how rapidly the new skis are accepted. And if they provide friendly sales assistance and quick mounting service, perhaps their chances for success will improve. Another reason for committing to the Fritzmeier line is that they like the Fritzmeier sales rep, Bruno Arnold, and they feel he would be of great assistance in their initial stocking and setup efforts. They talked briefly with some other firms' sales people at the major trade shows, but had not gotten along nearly as well with any of them. In fact, most of the sales reps did not seem too interested in helping a newcomer, preferring instead to talk with and entertain buyers from established stores. The major ski shows are over, so any more contacts with manufacturers will require the Schmidts taking the initiative. But from their past experience, this does not sound too appealing to them. Therefore, they seem to be drifting fast toward having the Alpine Sports Shop specialize in selling the Fritzmeier line.

Evaluate the Schmidts' thinking. What would you suggest they do?

PLACE

13. Photo Supply, Inc.

Photo Supply, Inc., is located in a residential area along a major traffic artery about two miles from the downtown of a metropolitan area of 450,000. It is also near a major university. It sells high-quality still and movie cameras, accessories, and projection equipment, including 8 and 16 mm movie projectors, 35 mm slide projectors, opaque and overhead projectors, and a large assortment of projection screens. Most of the sales of the specialized equipment are made to area school boards for classroom use, to industry for use in research and sales, and to the university for use in research and instruction.

Photo Supply offers a wide selection of film and a specialized film-processing service. Rather than processing film on a mass-production basis, each roll of film is given individual attention to accentuate the particular features requested by the customer. This service is used extensively by local industries that need high-quality pictures of lab or manufacturing processes for analytical and sales work.

To encourage the school and industrial trade, Photo Supply offers a graphics consultation service. If a customer wishes to construct a display, whether large or small, professional advice is readily available. Along with this free service, Photo Supply carries a full line of graphic arts supplies.

Photo Supply employs four full-time clerks and two outside sales reps. These sales reps make calls on industry, attend trade shows, make presentations for schools, and assist both present and potential customers in their use and choice of visual aids.

The people who make most of the over-the-store-counter purchases are serious amateur photographers and some professional photographers who buy in small quantities. Price discounts of up to 25 percent of the suggested retail price are given to customers who purchase more than $500 worth of goods per year. Most regular customers qualify for the discount.

In the last few years, many more "amateurs" have been taking 35 mm slide pictures. Because of this, Andrew Machey, the manager of Photo Supply, felt that there ought to be a good demand for some way of viewing them. Therefore he planned a special pre-Christmas sale of inexpensive slide projectors, viewers, and home-sized projection screens. Hoping that most of these would be purchased as Christmas gifts, Machey selected some products which offered good value and discounted the prices to competitive levels, for example, projectors at $29.95, viewers at $3.95, and screens at $11.95. To promote the sale, large signs were posted in the store windows and ads were run in a Christmas gift suggestion edition of the local newspaper. This edition appeared each Wednesday during the four weeks preceding Christmas.

At these prices and with this promotion, Machey hoped to sell at least 150 projectors and screens, and 200 viewers. When the Christmas returns were in, total sales were 22 projectors, 15 screens, and 48 viewers. He was most disappointed with these results, especially because trade estimates suggested that sales of projection equipment in this price and quality range were up 300 percent over last year.

Evaluate what happened. What should Machey do in the future?

14. Mead Company

John Mead graduated in business from a large midwestern university in 1974. After a year as a car salesman, he decided to go into business for himself. In an effort to locate new opportunities, John placed several advertisements in his local newspaper—in Toledo, Ohio—explaining that he was interested in becoming a sales representative in the local area. He was quite pleased to receive a number of responses. Eventually he became the sales representative in the Toledo area for three local manufacturers: the Sampson Drill and Press Co., which manufactured portable drills; the J. C. Peterson Co., which manufactured portable sanding machines; and the Gilbert Lathe Co., which manufactured small lathes. All of these companies were relatively small and were represented in other areas by other sales representatives like John Mead.

Mead's main job was to call on industrial customers. Once he made a sale, he would send the order to the respective manufacturer, who would, in turn, ship the goods directly to the particular customer. The manufacturer would bill the customer, and Mead would receive a commission varying from 5 to 10 percent of the dollar value of the sale. It was Mead's responsibility to pay his own expenses.

Mead called on anyone in the Toledo area who might use the products he was handling. At first, his job was relatively easy, and sales came quickly because there was little competition. There are many national companies making similar products, but at that time they were not well represented in the Toledo area.

In 1976 Mead sold $150,000 worth of drills, earning a 10 percent commission; $50,000 worth of sanding machines, also earning a 10 percent commission; and $75,000 worth of small lathes, earning a 5 percent commission. He was most encouraged with his progress and was looking forward to expanding sales in the future. He was especially optimistic because he had achieved these sales volumes without overtaxing himself. In fact, he felt he was operating at about 70 percent of his capacity.

Early in 1977, however, a local manufacturer with a very good reputation—the Porter Electrical Equipment Company—started to manufacture a line of portable drills. It had a good reputation locally, and by April 1977 Porter had captured approximately half of Sampson's Toledo drill market by charging a substantially lower price. Porter was using its own sales force locally, and it was likely that it would continue to do so.

The Sampson Company assured Mead that Porter could not afford to continue to sell at such a low price and that shortly Sampson's price would be competitive with Porter's. Mead was not nearly as optimistic about the near-term prospects, however. He began looking for other products he could handle in the Toledo area. A manufacturer of hand trucks had recently approached him, but he was not too enthusiastic about this offer because the commission was only 2 percent on potential annual sales of $150,000.

Now Mead is faced with another decision. The Howard Paint Company in Cleveland, Ohio, has made what appears to be an attractive offer. They heard what a fine job he was doing in the Toledo area and felt that maybe he could help them solve their present problem. Howard is having difficulty with its whole marketing effort and would like Mead to take over.

The Howard Paint Company has been selling primarily to industrial customers in the Cleveland area and is faced with many competitors selling essentially the same product and charging the same low prices. Howard Paint is a small manufacturer. Last year's sales were $80,000. They would like to increase this sales volume and could handle at least twice this sales volume with ease. They have offered Mead a 12 percent commission on sales if he will take charge of their pricing, advertising, and sales efforts in the Cleveland area. John was flattered by their offer, but he is a little concerned because there would be a great deal more traveling than he is doing at present. For one thing, he would have to spend a couple of days each week in the Cleveland area, which is 110 miles distant. Further, he realizes that he is being asked to do more than just sell. But he did have some marketing courses in college and thinks the new opportunity might be challenging.

What should Mead do? Why?

15. Miller Sales Company

Frank Miller, now 55 years old, has been a salesman for over 30 years. He started selling in a department store but gave it up after ten years to work in a lumber yard because the future looked much better in the building materials industry. After drifting from one job to another, he finally settled down and worked his way up to be the manager of a large wholesale building materials distribution warehouse in Kansas City, Kansas. In 1959, he decided to go into business for himself, selling carload lots of lumber to large retail yards in the western Missouri, eastern Kansas area.

He made arrangements to work with five large lumber mills on the West Coast. They would notify him when a carload of lumber was available to be shipped, specifying the grade, condition, and number of each size board in the shipment. Frank was not the only person representing these mills, but he was the only one in his area. He was not obligated to take any particular number of carloads per month, but once he told the mill he wanted a particular shipment, title passed to him and he had to sell it to someone. Frank's main function was to buy the lumber from the mill as it was being shipped, find a buyer, and have the railroad divert the car to the buyer.

Frank has been in this business for 18 years, so he knows all of the lumber yard buyers in his area very well and is on good working terms with them. Most of his dealings are made over the telephone from his small office, but he tries to see each buyer about once a month. He has been marking up the lumber between 4 and 6 percent, the standard markup, depending on the grade, and has been able to make a good living for himself and his family.

In the last few years, however, interest rates were raised for home loans and the building boom slowed down. Frank's profits did, too, but he decided to stick it out, figuring that people still needed housing and business would pick up again.

Six months ago, a new, aggressive salesman, much younger than Frank, set up in the same business, covering approximately the same area but representing different mills. This new salesman charged about the same prices as Frank, but would undersell him once or twice a week in order to get the sale. Many lumber buyers, knowing that they were dealing with a homogeneous product, seemed to be willing to buy from the least expensive source. This has hurt Frank financially and personally, because even some of his "old friends" are willing to buy from the new man if the price is lower. The near-term outlook seems dark, as Frank doubts there is enough business to support two businesses like his, especially if the markup gets shaved any more.

One week ago, Frank was contacted by Mr. White, representing the Pope and Talbott particleboard manufacturing plant. White knew that Frank was well acquainted with the building supply dealers in the area and wanted to know if he would like to be the sole distributor for Pope and Talbott in that area, selling carload lots, just as he did lumber. White gave Frank several brochures on particleboard, a product introduced about 20 years ago, describing how it can be used as a cheaper and better subflooring than the standard lumber usually used. The particleboard is also made with a wood veneer so that it can be used as paneling in homes and offices. He told Frank that the lumber yards could specify the types and grades of particleboard they wanted. Therefore, they could get exactly what they needed, unlike lumber where they choose from carloads that are already made up. Frank knew that a carload of particleboard cost about 30 percent more than a carload of lumber and that sales would be less frequent. In fact, he knew that this product has not been as well accepted in his area as in many others, because no one has done much promotion in his area. But the 20 percent average markup looks very tempting, and the particleboard market is expanding.

Frank has three choices:

1. Take White's offer and sell both products.
2. Take the offer and drop lumber sales.
3. Stay strictly with lumber and forget the offer.

White is expecting an answer within another week, so Frank has to decide soon.

Evaluate what Frank has been doing. What should he do now? Why?

16. The Neil Company

The Neil Company is a full-line department store chain operating in and around Akron, Ohio. The company began in the 1920s in the downtown business district of Akron, and has now grown and expanded until it operates not only the downtown store but also branches in eight major shopping centers around Akron.

One of the more successful departments in the Neil Company stores is the Cosmetic and Drug Sundries Department. This department sells a wide range of products, ranging from face powder to vitamins. But it has not been in the prescription business and does not have a registered pharmacist in the department. Its focus in the drug area has been on "proprietary" items rather than the ethical drugs which are normally dispensed only under the supervision of a registered pharmacist.

The Neil Company is now considering the proposal of the Miller Drug Company, which is seeking to introduce a wholesale prescription service into Neil's Cosmetic and Drug Sundries Departments. The Miller Company is a well-established drug wholesaler which is now seeking to expand its business by serving retailers such as the Neil Company.

Basically, the Miller Drug Company's proposal is as follows:

1. Neil's customers would leave their prescriptions in the Drug Sundries Department one day and then pick up their medicines the following day.

2. A representative of the Miller Drug Company would pick up the prescriptions every evening at closing time and return the filled prescriptions before each store opened the following day. The Neil Company would not have to hire a pharmacist or carry any drug inventory.

3. The Neil Company could offer a savings of 30 to 35 percent to their customers. This savings would be due to the economies of the operation, including the absence of a pharmacist and the elimination of local inventories.

4. The Neil Company would receive a 35 percent commission on the selling price of each prescription sale.

5. The Neil Company's name could be identified with the service and be imprinted on all bags, bottles, and other materials associated with the prescription drug business. In other words, the Miller Drug Company would serve as a wholesaler in the operation, and would not be identified to Neil's customers.

The representatives of the Miller Drug Company pointed out that retail drug sales were expanding and were expected to continue to expand. Further, they noted that prescription drug prices were rising, and that therefore the Neil Company would have an opportunity to participate in an expanding business. Further, by offering cost savings to its customers, Neil could provide another service for them and also build return business and stimulate traffic. Also, since the Neil Company would not have to hire additional personnel or carry inventory, the 35 percent margin would be almost all net profit.

The Miller Drug Company is anxious to begin offering this service in the Akron area and has asked the Neil Company to make a decision one way or another very soon. If the Neil Company agrees to work with Miller, the Miller executives have agreed not to offer the service to any other Akron stores. On the other hand, if the Neil Company chooses not to offer the service, Miller does plan to approach other Akron retailers.

Evaluate the Miller proposal. What should the Neil Company do?

PROMOTION

17. Arrow National Bank

Dan Arrow was recently appointed director of marketing by his father, Michael Arrow, president of the Arrow National Bank. Dan is a recent graduate of a marketing program at the nearby state college. He has worked in the bank during summer vacations, but this is his first full-time job.

The Arrow National Bank is a profitable, family-run business located in Brown, a small county seat. The town itself has only about 7,000 population, but it caters to farmers located as far away as 20 miles. About ten miles south are surburban towns surrounding a metropolitan area of 150,000. Banking competition is quite strong in the metropolitan area, but in Brown there is only one other bank, of about the same size. The Arrow National Bank has been quite profitable, last year earning about $300,000—or 1 percent of assets—a profit margin that would look very attractive to big-city bankers.

Arrow National Bank has prospered over the years by emphasizing a friendly, small-town atmosphere. The employees are all local residents and are trained to be friendly with all customers, greeting them on a first-name basis. Even Dan's father tries to know all the customers personally and regularly comes out of his office to talk with them. The bank has generally followed a conservative policy, for example insisting on 25 percent down payments on homes and relatively short maturities on loans. The interest rates charged are competitive or slightly higher than those in the nearby city, but they are similar to those charged by the other bank in town. In fact, the two local banks seem to be following more or less the same approach. And given that they both have fairly convenient downtown locations, Dan feels that it is likely that the two banks will continue to share the business equally unless some change is made.

Dan has developed an idea which he feels might attract a greater share of the local business. At a recent luncheon meeting with his father, he presented his idea and was disappointed that it was not enthusiastically received. Nevertheless, he has continued to push the idea.

Basically, Dan's idea involves trying to differentiate the bank using a visual appeal. In particular, his proposal is to try to get all of the people in town to "Think Pink." Dan wants to paint the inside and outside of the bank pink and have all the bank's advertising and printed materials refer to the "Think Pink" campaign. The bank would give away pink shopping bags, offer pink deposit slips, mail out pink interest checks, advertise on pink billboards, and have pink stationery for the bank's correspondence. Dan realizes that his proposal is "far-out" for a conservative bank. But that is exactly why he thinks it has merit. He wants people to be startled into thinking about the Arrow National Bank, instead of just accepting the status quo and assuming that both banks are similar. He feels that after the initial surprise, the local citizens will think even more positively about the Arrow National Bank. Now, its reputation is very good, but he would like it to be recognized as "different." Dan feels that this would help attract a larger share of new residents and businesses. Further, Dan hopes that his "Think Pink" campaign would cause people to talk about the Arrow National Bank, and given that word-of-mouth comments are likely to be positive, the bank might win a bigger share of the present business.

Dan's father is less excited about his son's proposal. He feels the bank has done very well under his direction, and he is concerned about changing a "good thing." He worries that some of the older farmers who are loyal customers might question the integrity of the bank or even wonder if it had gone "big city." Further, he feels that Dan is talking about an important change which would be hard to undo once the decision had been made. His initial suggestion to Dan was to come up with some other way of differentiating the bank without running the risk of offending present customers. At the same time, he liked the idea of making the bank appear quite different from its sole competitor. People are continuing to move into Brown and he would like to get an increasing share of this business. But he was having difficulty accepting "Think Pink."

Evaluate Dan's proposal. Should it be accepted?

18. Sports Sales Company

Two years ago Harry Ranebow purchased the inventory, supplies, equipment, and business of Washington Sport Sales, which was located in one of the suburbs of Spokane, Washington. The business was in an older building along a major highway leading out of town, but it was several miles from any body of water. The previous owner had achieved sales volumes of about $100,000 a year, just breaking even. For this reason, plus the desire to retire to southern California, the owner had been willing to sell to Harry for roughly the value of the inventory. Washington Sport Sales had been selling two well-known brands of small pleasure boats, a leading outboard motor, two brands of snowmobiles, and a line of trailer and pickup truck campers. The total inventory was valued at about $28,000, and Harry used all of his own savings and borrowed some from two friends to buy the inventory. At the same time, he took over the lease on the building so he was able to begin operations immediately.

Harry had never operated a business of his own before, but he was confident that he would be able to do well. He had worked in a variety of capacities as an auto repairman, service man, and generally a jack-of-all-trades in the maintenance departments of several local businesses.

Soon after beginning operations, Harry hired a friend who had had a similar background. Together, they handled all selling and setup work on new sales, and maintenance work as necessary. Sometimes, they were extremely busy—at the peaks of each sport season. Then both sales and maintenance kept them going up to 16 hours a day. At these times it was difficult to have both new and repaired equipment available as soon as desired by customers. At other times, however, Harry and his friend Jim had almost nothing to do.

Harry generally charged the prices suggested by the various manufacturers, except at the end of a weather season when he was willing to make deals to minimize his inventory. Harry was a little annoyed that some of his competitors sold principally on a price basis, generally offering 10 to 20 percent off of the manufacturer's suggested list prices. Harry did not feel he wanted to get into that kind of business, however, because he wanted to build a loyal following based on friendship and personal service. And he did not feel he really had to cut price, because all of the lines he carried were "exclusive" for him in the area. No dealers within a ten-mile radius carried any of his brands.

To try to build a favorable image for his company, Harry occasionally placed advertisements in local papers and purchased some radio spots. The basic theme of this advertising was that Sports Sales Company was a good place to purchase the equipment needed for that season of the year. Occasionally he mentioned the brand names he carried, but generally he was attempting to build his own image. He decided in favor of trying to build his own image because, although he had exclusives on the brands he carried, there generally were 10 to 15 different manufacturers' goods being sold in each product category at any one time and most of the products were quite similar. Harry felt that this degree of similarity among competing products almost forced him to try to differentiate himself on the basis of his own store's service.

The first year's operation was not profitable. In fact, after paying minimal salaries to Jim and himself, the business just about broke even. And this was without making any provision for return on his investment. In hopes of improving his profitability, Harry jumped at a chance to add a line of lawn tractors and attachments as he was starting into his second year in business. This line was offered by a well-known equipment manufacturer who was expanding into his market. The equipment was similar to that offered by other lawn equipment manufacturers but had a number of unique features and specialized attachments. Harry was also attracted by the manufacturer's willingness to do some local advertising on his own and to provide some point-of-purchase displays. And he also liked the idea that customers probably would be wanting this equipment sometime earlier than they would become interested in boats and other summer items. Therefore, he would be able to handle this business without interfering with his other peak selling seasons.

Now it is two years after Harry started the Sports Sales Company and he is still only breaking even. Sales have increased somewhat, but he had to hire some part-time help. The lawn equipment line did help to expand sales as he had expected, but unfortunately it did not appear to increase profits. The part-time helpers were needed to service this business, in part because the manufacturer's advertising had generated a lot of sales inquiries. Relatively few of these resulted in sales, however, and so it is possible that Harry may have even lost money handling the new line. He is reluctant to give up this line, however, because he has no other attractive alternatives on the horizon and he does not want to give up that sales volume. Further, the manufacturer's sales rep has been most encouraging, assuring Harry that things will get better and that they will be glad to continue their promotional support for Harry's business during the coming year.

Evaluate Harry's overall strategy. What should he do in the future, especially regarding the lawn tractor line?

19. Cabco Corporation

The Cabco Corp. produces wire rope and cable ranging from ½ inch to 4 inches in diameter. The Chicago-based company produces and sells on a national basis. Principal users of the products are manufacturing firms using cranes and various other overhead lifts in their operations. Ski resorts have become customers, as cables are used in the various lifts. However, the principal customers are still cement plants, railroad and boat yards, heavy equipment manufacturers, mining operations, construction companies, and steel manufacturers.

Cabco employs its own sales specialists to call on the purchasing agents of potential users. All the sales reps are qualified engineers who go through an extensive training program covering the different applications, strengths, and other technical details concerning rope and cable. Then they are assigned a region or district, the size depending on the number of customers.

Charles Roste went to work for Cabco in 1952, immediately after receiving a civil engineering degree from Purdue University. After going through the training program, he was assigned, along with one other representative, to the Ohio, Indiana, and Michigan region. His job was to service and give technical assistance to present customers of rope and cable. He was expected to solicit new customers when the occasion arose. But his primary duties were to: (1) supply the technical assistance needed to use rope or cable in the most efficient and safe manner, (2) handle complaints, and (3) provide evaluation reports to customers' management regarding their use of cabling.

Roste became one of Cabco's most successful representatives. His exceptional ability to handle customer complaints and provide technical assistance was noted by many of the firm's customers. He also brought in a considerable amount of new business, primarily from the automobile manufacturers and ski resorts in Michigan.

Roste's success established Michigan as Cabco's largest-volume state. As a result, Michigan was designated as a separate district, and Roste was assigned as the representative for the district in 1959.

Although the company's sales in Michigan have not continued to grow in the past few years, the replacement market has been steady and profitable. This fact is primarily due to the ability and reputation of Roste. As one of the purchasing agents for a large automobile manufacturer mentioned, "When Charles Roste makes a recommendation regarding use of our equipment and cabling, even if it is a competitor's cable we are using, we are sure it is for the best for our company. Last week, for example, a cable of one of his competitors broke and we were going to give him a contract. He told us it was not a defective cable that caused the break, but rather the way we were using it. He told us how it should be used and what we needed to do to correct our operation. We took his advice and gave him the contract as well!"

Four years ago, Cabco introduced an expensive wire sling device for holding cable groupings together. The sling makes operations around the cable much safer and its use could reduce hospital and lost-time costs due to accidents. The profit margin for the sling is high, and Cabco urged all its representatives to push the sling.

The only sales rep to sell the sling with any success was Roste. Eighty percent of his customers are currently using the wire sling. In other areas, sling sales are negligible.

As a result of his success, Cabco is now considering

forming a separate department for sling sales and putting Roste in charge. His duties would include traveling to the various sales districts and training other representatives in how to sell the sling. The Michigan district would be represented by a new person.

The question confronting Cabco management is: Should they gamble on losing profitable customers in Michigan in hopes that sling sales will increase.

What should you advise? Why?

20. Bishop Furniture Company

Ann Alden has been operating the Bishop Furniture Co. for ten years and has slowly built the sales to $375,000 a year. Her store is located in the downtown shopping area of a city of 150,000 population. This is basically a factory town, and she has deliberately selected "blue-collar" workers as her target market. She carries some higher-priced furniture lines but places great emphasis on budget combinations and stresses easy credit terms.

Alden is most concerned because she feels she has reached the limit of her sales potential; at least it would seem that way because sales have not been increasing during the last two years. Her newspaper advertising seems to attract her target customers, but many of these people come in, shop around, and then leave. Some of them come back, but the majority do not. She feels her product selections are very suitable for her target market and is concerned that her sales personnel do not close more sales with potential customers. She has discussed this matter several times with her sales personnel. They respond that they feel they ought to treat all customers alike, the way they personally would want to be treated—that is, they feel their role is merely to answer questions when asked and not to make suggestions or help customers arrive at their selections. They feel that this would be too high-pressure.

Alden feels her sales personnel's attitudes are interpreted as indifference by the customers who are attracted to the store by her advertising. She feels that customers must be treated on an individual basis—and that some customers need more encouragement and suggestion than others. Moreover, she feels that some customers will actually appreciate more help and suggestion than the sales people themselves might. In sup-

Table 1

In shopping for furniture I found (find) that:	Demographic groups				Marital status	
	Group A	Group B	Group C	Group D	Newly-weds	Married 3–10 yrs.
I looked at furniture in many stores before I made a purchase	78%	57%	52%	50%	66%	71%
I went (am going) to only one store and bought (buy) what I found (find) there	2	9	10	11	9	12
To make my purchase I went (am going) back to one of the stores I shopped in previously	48	45	39	34	51	49
I looked (am looking) at furniture in no more than three stores and made (will make) my purchase in one of these	20	25	24	45	37	30
No answer	10	18	27	27	6	4

Table 2
The sample design

Demographic status

Upper class (Group A), 13% of sample
    This group consisted of managers, proprietors, or executives of large businesses. Professionals, including doctors, lawyers, engineers, college professors and school administrators, research personnel. Sales personnel, including managers, executives, and upper-income sales people above level of clerks.
    Family income over $20,000
Middle class (Group B), 37% of sample
    Group B consists of white-collar workers including clerical, secretarial, sales clerks, bookkeepers, etc. It also includes school teachers, social workers, semiprofessionals, proprietors or managers of small businesses; industrial foremen and other supervisory personnel.
    Family income between $10,000 and $20,000
Lower middle class (Group C), 36% of sample
    Skilled workers and semiskilled technicians were in this category along with custodians, elevator operators, telephone linemen, factory operatives, construction workers, and some domestic and personal service employees.
    Family income between $10,000 and $20,000
    No one in this group had above a high school education
Lower class (Group D), 14% of sample
    Nonskilled employees, day laborers. It also includes some factory operatives, domestic and service people.
    Family income under $10,000
    None had completed high school; some had only grade school education.

port of her opinion, she showed her sales people the data from a study about furniture store customers (Tables 1 and 2). She tried to explain to them about the differences in demographic groups and pointed out that her store was definitely trying to cater to specific groups. She argued that they (the sales people) really had differ-ent attitudes than their target customers and that as a result, the sales people ought to cater to the needs and attitudes of their customers and think less about how they would like to be treated.

Evaluate Alden's thinking and suggest implications for her promotion.

PRICE

21. Kennedy Dance Studio

Kathy Kennedy has been operating the Kennedy Dance Studio for five years in a suburban community of about 50,000. Slowly, she has built a clientele—mostly young girls whose mothers want them to have some ballet experience.

The studio is conveniently located downtown and within walking distance of two grade schools (grades 1–5) and one middle school (grades 6–8). Some of Kathy's customers come from these schools, but even more come from more remote schools. Most are driven and picked up by their mothers.

Kathy has a few competitors offering classes in their "rec rooms" to neighborhood children, but no serious competitors offer comparable facilities or quality of instruction. The school district offers some classes at lower prices on Saturday and during the summer, but these have not been seen as real competition by Kathy.

Most of Kathy's students come only one hour a week and slowly make enough progress so that Kathy can schedule spring recitals which show off the girl's accomplishments to their parents and friends. Even first-year students are able to make a reasonable showing, and "success" in the spring recital tends to encourage mothers to re-enroll their daughters in the fall classes.

Kathy has not had much luck developing an interest in summer classes and last year she stopped trying. She decided that her clientele associated ballet with the nine-month school year. So Kathy took off for a three-month summer vacation. Fortunately, there had been enough business in the previous nine months so she could afford to do this.

Now it is February 1974, and Kathy is very much concerned about her financial prospects for the future. The "energy crisis" caused the local school system to change the opening and closing hours of school to save energy—moving the opening from 8:00 to 8:40 A.M. and the closing from 3:00 to 3:40 P.M. This has drastically cut into Kathy's after-school business. Further, Kathy just heard that the school plans to continue with the late schedule for the coming year.

The reason for changing the school schedule was to start later so the students would be getting up later and going to school later, thereby saving energy during the dark morning hours. There is some doubt whether this really did accomplish its purpose, but the school system has decided that the new schedule will be continued indefinitely.

Kathy did not immediately see the implications for her business when the change was announced for January 1974. But it quickly became clear that her 3:30–4:20 class was at the wrong time when no one signed up for the class during the first week of January. Not only did she lose many of the girls who were formerly enrolled in her 3:30 class, but enrollment in the later classes dropped almost in half. Some of the 3:30 girls did move to the 4:30 and 5:30 classes, but probably only about 20 percent of them. It is hard to get exact figures on enrollment because there is usually at least a 20 percent turnover from fall to winter to spring terms. Kathy has gotten used to a continual flow of new girls. Few girls stay more than a couple of years, because the program is not designed to build serious ballet students, but rather to cater to the "recreational" ballet student. But, it is quite clear to Kathy that the change in school schedule has drastically cut her business and she is trying to decide what to do for the spring term and beyond.

Given that most parents seem to need about one-half hour to get their children from school to the studio, she could move the starting time of the first class to about 4:15 (from 4:30) to try to use a little more after-school time. But this would still mean that she could offer only two "prime-time" classes after school (instead of the three which she offered before) because

classes starting after 6:00 P.M. would be viewed as being "too late." Alternately, she could forget about trying to change the after-school schedule and try to fill later times with older, more serious students. Kathy has the credentials and training for offering more advanced courses, but thus far there has not been much demand for them. The local school district does offer some "adult education" classes at lower prices and this may take care of the older market.

Another possibility that Kathy is considering is to persuade the local school system to allow "early release" of interested students—with a view to filling the 3:30–4:20 or a 3:10–4:00 slot. Kathy has heard that some children are now being released an hour early for advanced training in figure skating. But the number of students involved is quite small, and Kathy fears that such an arrangement for ballet is not likely.

Now that the total amount of time available between the end of school and dinner time is almost an hour shorter, some parents may feel that there just isn't enough time for extra recreation activities. This may help account for the substantial drop in business after school. Kathy's Saturday business has not been affected by the change in school schedule, but very few of the weekday students have moved to Saturday either. This concerns Kathy for the long run, because total revenue has dropped about one quarter, bringing her studio below the break-even point. Clearly, the studio needs more students to break even because it cannot cut costs very easily. Rent, light, taxes, insurance, and other fixed costs can't be changed. Further, her two part-time assistants are paid a fixed amount for the five after-school periods and Saturday. Saturday classes are full, so it is clear that something must be done after school if the business is to survive. Before and after the school schedule change, the following numbers of students were enrolled in the various classes at approximately $3 per class.

Class	Fall 1973	Winter 1974
3:30–4:20	20	0
4:30–5:20	20	9
5:30–6:20	18	9
6:30–7:20	10	6

What has happened to the Kennedy Dance Studio? What would you recommend Kathy Kennedy do?

22. Wire Specialties, Inc.

Wire Specialties, Inc., located in Minneapolis, Minnesota, is a custom producer of industrial wire products. The company has a great deal of experience bending wire into many shapes and also has the facilities to chrome- or gold-plate finished products. The company was started ten years ago and has slowly built its sales volume to $1 million a year. Just one year ago, Robert Thomas was appointed sales manager of the consumer products division. It was his responsibility to develop this division as a producer and marketer of the company's own branded products, as distinguished from custom orders which the industrial division produces for others.

Thomas has been working on a number of different product ideas for almost a year now, and he has developed several unique designs for letter holders, flowerpot holders, key and pencil holders, and other novelties. His most promising product is a letter holder in the shape of a dog. It is very similar to one that the industrial division produced for a number of years for another company. In fact, it was experience with the seemingly amazing sales volume of this product which interested the company in the consumer market and led to the development of the consumer products division.

Thomas has sold hundreds of units of his various products to local chain stores and wholesalers on a trial basis, but each time the price has been negotiated and no firm policy has been established. Now he is faced with the decision of what price to set on the dog-shaped letter holder which he plans to push aggressively wherever he can. Actually, he has not yet decided on exactly which channels of distribution he will use, but the trials in the local area have been encouraging, and, as noted above, the experience in the industrial division suggests that there is a large market for the product.

The manufacturing cost on this product is approximately 10 cents if it is painted black and 20 cents if it is chromed or gold-plated. Similar products have been selling at retail in the 75 cents to $2.50 range. The sales and administrative overhead to be charged to the division would amount to $25,000 a year. This would include Thomas' salary and some office expenses. It is expected that a number of other products will be developed in the near future, but for the coming year it is hoped that this letter holder will account for about half the consumer products division's sales volume.

Evaluate Thomas' marketing strategy. What price should he set?

23. Acme Photo Corporation

Organized in 1948, the Acme Photo Corp. soon became one of the four major Colorado-based photofinishers, each with annual sales of about $2.5 million.

Acme was established by three people who had had considerable experience in the photofinishing industry, working in Kodak's photofinishing division in Rochester, New York. Acme started in a small rented warehouse in Boulder, Colorado. Today it has seven company-owned plants in five cities in Colorado and western Kansas. The two color processing plants are located in Boulder and Hays, Kansas. Black-and-white processing plants are located in Boulder and Hays, as well as Pueblo, Denver, and Colorado Springs, Colorado.

Acme does all of its own processing of black-and-white films, slides, prints, and movies. While they do own color processing capability, Acme has found it more economical to have most color film processed by the regional Kodak processing plant. The color film processed by Acme is of the "off-brand" variety or is special work done for professional photographers. Despite this limitation in color finishing, Acme has always given its customers fast, quality service. All pictures, including those processed by Kodak, can be returned within three days of receipt by Acme.

Acme was established originally as a wholesale photofinisher. It later developed its own processing plants in an effort to achieve greater profit. Its customers are drugstores, camera stores, department stores, photographic studios, and any other retail outlets where photofinishing is offered to consumers. These retailers insert film rolls, cartridges, negatives, and so on, into separate bags, marking on the outside the kind of work to be done. The customer is handed a receipt but seldom sees the bag into which the film has been placed. The bag has the retailer's name on it, not Acme's.

Each processing plant is fronted by a small retail outlet for drop-in customers who live in the immediate vicinity of the plant. This is a minor part of Acme's business.

The company is also engaged in direct-mail photofinishing within the state of Colorado. Each processing plant in Colorado is capable of receiving direct-mail orders from consumers. All film received is handled in the same way as the other retail business.

A breakdown of the dollar volume by type of business is shown in Table 3.

Table 3

Type of business	Percent of dollar volume
Sales to retail outlets	80
Direct-mail sales	17
Retail walk-in sales	3
	100

All processing is priced at the level established by local competition. Acme establishes a retail list price, and each retailer then is offered a trade discount based on the volume of business generated for Acme. The pricing schedule used by each of the major competitors in the Colorado-Kansas market is shown in Table 4. All direct-mail processing for final consumers is priced at the 33⅓ percent discount off retail price, but this is done under a disguised name so that retailer customers are not antagonized. Retail walk-in accounts are charged the full list price for all services performed.

Table 4

Monthly dollar volume (12-month average)	Discount (2/10 net 30)
$ 0–$ 100	33⅓%
$ 101–$ 500	40
$ 501–$1000	45
$1,001–above	50

Retail stores offering photofinishing are served by Acme's own sales force. Each processing plant has at least three people servicing accounts. Their duties include daily visits to all accounts to pick up and deliver all photofinishing work. These sales reps also make daily trips to the Greyhound bus terminal nearby to pick up and drop off color film that is being processed by Kodak.

Since the consumer does not come in contact with Acme, the firm has not found it necessary to advertise its retail business. To reach retailers, Acme is listed in the Yellow Pages of all telephone books in cities and towns served by its seven plants. There has been no attempt to make the consumer aware of Acme's service, since all consumers are served through retail stores.

The direct-mail portion of Acme's business is generated by regular advertisements in the Sunday pictorial sections of newspapers servicing Pueblo, Denver, Colorado Springs, and Boulder. These advertisements usually stress the low-price service, two-week turnaround, and fine quality. Acme does not use its own name for these markets. Mailers are provided for the consumer to send to the plant. Some people in the company felt this part of the business might have great potential if pursued more aggressively.

Recently, the president of Acme, Mr. Humma, has become worried about the loss of several retail accounts in the $500–$1,000 discount range. He has been with the company since its beginning and has always stressed quality and rapid delivery of the finished product. Demanding that all plants produce the finest-quality reproductions, Humma personally conducts periodic quality tests of each plant through its direct-mail service. Plant managers are called on the carpet for any slips in quality.

To find out what is causing the loss in retail accounts, Humma has been reviewing sales reps' reports and talking to various employees. In their weekly reports, Acme's sales reps have reported a possible trend toward higher trade discounts being offered to retail customers. Insty-Film, a competitor of equal size that offers the same services as Acme, is offering an additional 5 percent discount in each sales volume category. This price differential really makes a difference at some stores, because these retailers feel that all the major processors can do an equally good job. Further, they note, consumers apparently feel that the quality is acceptable, because there have been no complaints so far.

Acme has encountered price cutting before, but never by an equally well-established company. Humma cannot understand why these retail customers would leave Acme, because it is offering higher quality and the price difference is not that large. He is considering a direct-mail and newspaper campaign to consumers to persuade them to demand Acme's quality service from their favorite retailer. Humma feels that consumers demanding quality will force retailers to stay with or return to Acme. He says: "If we can't get the business by convincing the retailer of our fine quality, we'll get it by convincing the consumer."

Evaluate Acme's strategies and Humma's present thinking. What would you do?

24. The King Manufacturing Company

The King Manufacturing Co. of Los Angeles, California, is a leading manufacturer in the wire machinery industry. It has patents covering over 200 machine variations, but it is rare for King's customers to buy more than 30 different types in a year. Its machines are sold to wire and small-tubing manufacturers when they are increasing production capacity or replacing outdated equipment.

Established in 1865, the company has enjoyed a steady growth to its present position with annual sales of $27 million.

About ten firms compete in the wire machinery market. Each is about the same size and manufactures basically similar machinery. Each of the competitors has tended to specialize in its own geographic area. Five of the competitors are in the East, three in the Midwest, and two, including King, on the West Coast. All of the competitors offer similar prices and sell F.O.B. their factories. Demand has been fairly strong in recent years, and as a result, all of the competitors have been satisfied to sell in their geographic areas and avoid price cutting. In fact, there is an aversion to price cutting because about 20 years ago one firm tried to win additional business and found that others immediately met the price cut, but industry sales (in units) did not increase at all. Within a few years prices had returned to their earlier level, and since then competition has tended to focus on promotion.

King's promotion has depended largely on company sales reps who cover the West Coast. They usually are supported by sales engineers when the company is close to making a sale. Some advertising is done in trade journals and direct mailings are used occasionally, but the primary promotion emphasis is on personal selling. Personal contact outside of the West Coast market, however, is through manufacturers' agents.

Andrew Lunter, president of King Manufacturing Co., is not satisfied with the present situation. Industry sales have begun to level off and so have King's sales, although King has continued to hold its share of the market. He would like to find a way to compete more effectively in other regions, because he is coming to see that there is great potential outside of the West Coast if only he can find a better way of reaching it.

King has been acknowledged by competitors and buyers as one of the top-quality producers in the industry. Its machines have generally been somewhat superior to others in terms of reliability, durability, and productive capacity. The difference, however, has not been great enough to justify a higher price because the others are able to do the necessary job. In short, if a buyer had a choice between King's and another machine at the same price, King would probably get the business. But it seems clear that King's price must be at least competitive.

The average wire machine sold by King (or any of the competitors) sells for about $115,000, F.O.B. shipping point. Shipping costs within any of the three major regions averages about $1,500, but then another $1,000 must be added on shipments from the West Coast to the Midwest (either way) and another $1,000 from the Midwest to the East.

Lunter is considering the possibility of expanding his market by being willing to absorb the extra freight costs which would be incurred if a midwestern or eastern customer were to buy from his West Coast location. In other words, he would absorb the additional $1,000–$2,000 in transportation costs. By so doing, he would not be cutting price in those markets, but rather reducing his net return. He felt that his competitors would not see this as price competition and therefore would not resort to cutting prices themselves. Further, he felt that such a move would be legal, because all the customers in each major region would be offered the same price.

The sales manager, Bernard Chelps, felt that the proposed freight absorption plan might actually stimulate price competition in the midwestern and eastern markets and perhaps on the West Coast. He proposed instead that King hire some sales reps to work the midwestern and eastern markets, rather than relying on the manufacturers' agents. He felt that an additional three sales reps would not increase costs too much and could greatly increase the sales from these markets over that brought in by the agents. With this plan, there would be no need to absorb the freight, and therefore there would be no need to gamble on disrupting the status quo with respect to competitive methods. He felt this latter matter was especially important, because competition in the Midwest and East was somewhat "hotter" than that on the West Coast because of the number of competitors in these regions. The situation had been rather quiet in the West because only two firms were sharing this market.

Lunter agreed that Chelps had a point, but in view of the leveling off of industry sales, he felt that competitive situations might change drastically in the near future

and that he would rather be a leader in anything that was likely to happen rather than a follower. He was impressed with Chelp's comments regarding the greater competitiveness in the other markets, however, and therefore was unsure about what should be done, if anything.

Evaluate King's strategy planning in the light of its market situation, and explain what it should do now.

MARKETING MANAGEMENT

25. Riverside Processing Company

The Riverside Processing Co. is a well-established manufacturer in the highly seasonal vegetable canning industry. It packs and sells canned beans, peas, carrots, corn, peas and carrots mixed, and kidney beans. Sales are made primarily through food brokers to merchant wholesalers, supermarket chains (such as Kroger, Safeway, A&P, Jewel), cooperatives, and other outlets, mostly in the Chicago area. Of secondary importance, by volume, are sales in the immediate local market to institutions, grocery stores, and supermarkets, and sales of dented canned goods to "walk in" customers at low prices.

Riverside is the second largest vegetable canner in the Devil's River Valley area of Wisconsin, with sales in excess of $10 million annually (exact sales data is not published by the closely held corporation). Plants are located in Riverside, Portertown, and Williamston, Wisconsin, and Clearview, Minnesota, with main offices in Riverside. The Riverside brand is used only on canned goods sold in the immediate local market; in most other cases, the goods are sold and shipped under the retailer's label or the broker's/wholesaler's label.

Operating since 1905, Riverside has established an excellent reputation over the years for the consistent quality of its total product offering. And it is always willing to offer competitive prices. Strong channel rapport was built by Riverside's chairman of the board and chief executive officer, H. E. Edwards. Edwards, who owns controlling interest in the firm, had "worked" the Chicago area as an aggressive company salesman in the firm's earlier years before he took over from his father as president in 1931. He was an ambitious and hard-working executive, active in community affairs, and the firm prospered under his direction. He

became well known within the canned food processing industry for technical/product innovations, and during World War II was appointed to a position in Washington, D.C., on the board that formulated wartime food rationing policies.

During the "off-canning" season, Edwards traveled extensively. In connection with his travels, he arranged several significant business deals. His 1968 and 1970 trips culminated in the following two events: (1) inexpensive pineapple was imported from Formosa and marketed in the central United States through Riverside, primarily to expand the product line; (2) a technically advanced continuous-process cooker (65 feet high) was imported from England and installed at the Riverside plant in February/March 1975. It was the first of its kind in the United States and cut process time sharply.

Edwards retired in 1975 and named his son-in-law, the 35-year-old Mr. Evans, as his successor. Evans is intelligent and hard-working. As a member of the firm, he had been engaged primarily with financial matters but more recently with marketing problems. During his seven-year tenure as financial director, the firm had received its highest credit rating ever and was able to borrow working capital ($3 million to meet seasonal seed, fertilizer, can stockage, and wage requirements) at the lowest rate ever received by the company.

The fact that the firm isn't unionized allows some competitive advantage. However, minimum wage law changes have increased costs. And these and other rising costs have caused profit margins to narrow. The narrowed profit margins prompted the recent closing of the Williamston plant and then the Portertown plant, as they became comparatively less efficient to operate. The remaining two plants were considerably expanded in capacity (especially warehouse facilities), so that they could operate more profitably due to maximum use of existing processing equipment.

Shortly after Edward's retirement, Evans reviewed the company's current situation with his executives. He pointed out narrowing profit margins, debts contracted for new plant and equipment, and an increasingly competitive environment. Even considering the temporary labor-saving competitive advantage of the new cooker system, there seemed to be no way to improve the "status quo" unless the firm could sell direct, as it does in the local market, absorbing the food brokers' 5 percent commission on sales. This was the plan of action decided upon, and Mr. Burns was directed to test the new method for six months.

Burns is the only full-time salesman for the firm. Other top executives do some selling, but not much. Being a relative of Edwards', Burns is also a member of the board of directors. He is especially competent in technical matters as he has a college degree in food chemistry. Although Burns formerly did call on some important customers with the brokers' sales reps, he is not well known in the industry or even by Riverside's usual customers.

Five months later, after Burns has made several selling trips and hundreds of telephone calls, he is unwilling to continue sales efforts on his own. He is insisting that a sales staff be formed if the current operation is to continue. Orders are falling off in comparison to both expectations and the previous year's operating results. And sales of the new pineapple products are practically nil. Even in normal channels, Burns sensed a reluctance to buy, though basic consumer demand had not changed. Further, some potential customers had demanded quantity guarantees considerably larger than the firm can supply. Expanding supply would be difficult in the short run because the firm typically must contract with farmers for production acreage, to assure supplies of the type and quality they normally offer.

Edwards, still the controlling stockholder, has scheduled a meeting in two weeks to discuss the status of Riverside's current operations.

Evaluate Evans' strategy planning. What should he tell Edwards? What should be done next?

26. Nagel Mfg. Company

Bob McMahon is currently employed as a sales representative for a plastics goods manufacturer. He calls primarily on large industrial accounts, such as refrigerator manufacturers, who might need large quantities of custom-made products. He is on a straight salary of $15,000 per year, plus expenses and a company car. He expects some salary increases but does not see a great long-run opportunity with this company. As a result, he is seriously considering changing jobs and investing $20,000 in the Nagel Mfg. Co., an established midwestern thermoplastic molder and manufacturer. Harry Mack, the present owner is nearing retirement age and has not developed anyone to run the business. He has agreed to sell the business to John O'Gorman, a lawyer-entrepreneur, who has invited Bob McMahon to invest and become the sales manager. O'Gorman has agreed to give McMahon his current salary plus expenses, plus a bonus of 1 percent of profits. However, Bob must invest to become part of the new company. He will obtain a 5 percent interest in the business for his $20,000 investment.

The Nagel Mfg. Co. is well established and last year had sales of $1.5 million, but no profits. In terms of sales, costs of materials was 46 percent; direct labor, 13 percent; indirect factory labor, 15 percent; factory overhead, 13 percent; and sales overhead and general expenses, 13 percent. The company has not been making any profit for several years but has been continually adding new machines to replace those made obsolete by technological developments. The machinery is well maintained and modern, but most of it is similar to that owned by its many competitors. Most of the machines of the industry are standard. Special products are then made by using dies in conjunction with these machines.

Sales historically have been approximately two-thirds custom-molded products (that is, made to order for other producers or merchandising concerns) and the balance proprietary items, such as housewares, and game items, such as poker chips and cribbage sets. The housewares are copies of articles initiated by others and indicate neither originality nor style. Harry Mack is in charge of the proprietary items distributed through any available wholesale channels. The custom-molded products are sold through three full-time sales engineers who receive a 5 percent commission on sales up to $10,000 and then 3 percent above that level, as well as three independent representatives working part-time on a similar commission plan.

Financially, the company seems to be in fairly good condition, at least as far as book value is concerned, as the $20,000 investment would buy approximately $30,000 in assets.

O'Gorman feels that, with new management, the company offers great opportunity for profit. He expects to make some economies in the production process and hold custom-molding sales to approximately the present $1 million level. The other major expectation is that he will be able to develop the proprietary line from a sales volume of about $500,000 to $2 million a year. McMahon is expected to be a real asset here because of his sales experience. This will bring the firm up to about capacity level, but of course it will entail hiring additional employees. The major advantage of expanding sales would be spreading overhead. Some of the products proposed by the lawyer for the expansion of the proprietary line are listed below.

New products for consideration

Women's tool kit—molded housewares
Six-bottle soft drink cases
Laminating printed film on housewares—molded
Short legs for furniture—molded, $0.5 million minimum market
Home storage box for milk bottles, $0.5 million minimum market
Step-on garbage can without liner
Importing and distributing foreign housewares
Black-nylon-handled table utensils
Extruded and embossed or formed wall coverings
Extruded and formed wall decorations—nursery rhyme figures, etc.
Formed butyrate outside house shutters
Formed inside shutters in lieu of venetian blinds
School and toy blackboards
Translucent bird houses
Formed holder for vacuum cleaner attachments
Formed household door liners
Formed "train terrain" table topography for model trains
Formed skylights

There is a great deal of competition in these markets, and most retailers expect a wide margin, sometimes 40 to 50 percent, but even so, manufacturing costs are such that there is some room for promotion while still keeping the price competitive. Apparently many customers are willing to pay for the novelty of new products

How would you advise McMahon? Explain your reasoning.

27. The Ross Tool Company

The Ross Tool Co. is a manufacturer of industrial cutting tools. These tools include such items as lathe blades, drill press bits, and various other cutting edges used in the operation of large metal cutting, boring, or stamping machines. The president of the company, Ray Gillespie, takes great pride in the fact that his company, whose $1,759,000 sales in 1976 is small by industry standards, is recognized as a producer of the highest-quality line of cutting tools to be found.

Competition in the cutting tool industry is intense. Ross Tool must contend with competition not only from the original manufacturers of the machines, but also from many other relatively powerful companies offering cutting tools as one of many diverse product lines. This situation has had the effect, over the years, of standardizing the price, specifications, and in turn, the quality of the competing products of all manufacturers.

Approximately one year ago, Gillespie was tiring of the tremendous financial pressure of competing with companies enjoying economies of size. At the same time, he noted that more and more potential cutting tool customers were turning to small custom tool and die shops because of specialized needs that were not met by the mass production firms. Gillespie then considered a basic change in strategy. Although he was unwilling to become strictly a custom producer, Gillespie felt that quite possibly the recent trend toward buying customized cutting edges was a good indication of the development of new markets which would be too small for the large, multiproduct-line companies to serve profitably. He thought that the new markets might be large enough so that a flexible company of Ross Tool's size could make a good profit.

An outside company, Brook Marketing Research Associates, was asked to study the feasibility of serving this potential new market. The initial results were encouraging. It was estimated that Ross Tool could increase sales by 50 percent and double profits by serving the emerging market.

The next step taken by Ross Tool was to develop a team of technical specialists to maintain continuous contact with potential cutting tool customers. They were supposed to identify any present or future needs that might exist in enough cases to make it possible to profitably produce a specialized product. The technical specialists were not to take orders, nor to "sell" Ross Tool to the potential customers. Gillespie felt that only through this policy could these representatives easily gain access to the right persons.

The initial feedback from the technical specialists was most encouraging. The company, therefore, decided to constantly adapt its high-quality products to the ever-changing, specialized needs of users of cutting tools and edges.

The potential customers of Ross Tool's specialized tools are widely dispersed. The average sale per customer is not expected to exceed $250 at a time, but the sale will be repeated several times within a year. Because of the widely dispersed market and low sales volume per customer, Gillespie does not feel that selling the products direct, as would be done by small custom shops, is practical. At the present time, the Ross Tool Company distributes 90 percent of its regular output through a large industrial supply wholesaler which serves the entire area east of the Mississippi River. This wholesaler, although very large and well known, is having trouble moving cutting tools. It is losing sales of cutting tools in some cities to newer wholesalers specializing in the cutting tool industry. The new wholesalers are able to give more technical assistance to potential customers and therefore better service. The Ross Tool wholesaler's chief executive is convinced that the newer, less experienced concerns will either realize that a substantial profit margin cannot be maintained along with their aggressive tactics, or will eventually go broke trying to "overspecialize."

From Gillespie's standpoint, the present wholesaler is an established landmark and has served Ross Tool well in the past. The traditional wholesaler has been of great help to Ross Tool in holding down Ross Tool's inventory costs by increasing the amount of inventory maintained in the 34 branch wholesale locations operated by the wholesaler. Although he has received several complaints regarding the lack of technical assistance given by the wholesaler's sales reps, Gillespie feels that the present wholesaler is providing the best service it can, and he discounts the complaints as "the usual trouble you get into from just doing business."

Gillespie feels that there are more pressing problems than a few complaints—profits are declining. Sales of the new cutting tool line are not nearly so high as anticipated, even though all indications are that the company's new products should serve the intended market perfectly. The high costs involved in the high-quality product line and the technical specialist research team, in conjunction with less than expected sales, have significantly reduced the firm's profits. Gillespie is seriously wondering whether it is wise to continue catering to the needs of specific target markets when the results are this discouraging. He also is contemplating an increase in advertising expenditures in the hope that customers will "pull" the new products through the channel.

Evaluate Ross Tool's strategy. What should Gillespie do now?

28. "Save-A-Life" Franchise

Bob Miller and Lyle Ryan are partners in several small businesses. They are now seriously considering whether they should take on the local franchise for "Save-A-Life" products. Bob saw an advertisement in *The Wall Street Journal* and called for more information about the product and the franchise possibility. Now he and Lyle are considering whether they should take on the local franchise and hire two more salespersons to do the direct selling which is required. Lyle feels confident that he could hire and supervise the right kind of sales personnel without taxing his available time. In fact, the partners are looking for something more for Lyle to do because his current responsibilities to the partnership do not completely consume his time.

So supervision and personnel are not the problem. What is bothering the partners is whether this particular franchise is the right thing for them to do. Even more, Lyle is concerned whether there is an ethical problem. Is it "right" to send sales people with a "good story" to call on vulnerable people.

The main "Save-A-Life" product is a small radio transmitter that a person can carry around the house and a larger receiving unit that can be placed anywhere in the house. Just a push of a button on the transmitter will cause the receiver to dial up to four telephone numbers and play a pre-recorded message. Depending on the situation, these calls could be to the police, fire, or an emergency service, the person's doctor, and/

or relatives. An obvious market is older people who live alone and are worried about what happens to them if they get sick, have an accident, or are bothered by intruders. Further, women of all ages might be interested in the product if they are concerned about their personal safety. It seems likely that there would be more potential customers in urban areas where there is great concern about crime.

The national distributor of the franchise has found that it is possible to get leads for prospective customers by running advertisements in local newspapers—with pictures stressing emergency situations. Then personal sales follow-up is necessary. Sometimes several calls are needed. The system sells for $600. Bob and Lyle would have to pay $300 for each system, leaving $300 to cover the cost of sales, advertising, and general overhead. The national organization indicates that some franchise holders pay direct sales people a commission of $100–$150 per unit sold. In addition, paying about $25 per installation seems to be adequate for proper installation by "handymen" who are willing to make the necessary connections to the telephone system. The national organization is willing and able to train technical people and sales people in all the necessary functions as part of the original franchise fee. To get started, a franchise fee of $7,000 is required to cover the purchase of 15 systems, all necessary sales and promotion aids, and the right to unlimited home-office training of sales and technical personnel.

Bob and Lyle operate in a metropolitan area of about 450,000 people with a higher than average percentage of upper-income people. So they feel the economic potential may be adequate, although it is quite clear that an aggressive sales effort is required. The national distributor's sales rep feels that Bob and Lyle's sales people (they are thinking of hiring two) ought to be able to sell at least 20 units each per month after a break-in period, but of course no guarantee can be made.

Clearly, aggressive sales people will be necessary. That is why the relatively "generous" return to the sales people is suggested by the national distributor. But Lyle wonders if it is really fair to appeal to sick, old people or those who are concerned about their safety? Further, is it right to take such a big markup? Lyle realizes that without the $300 markup, there may not be any profit in it for the partners, but still he has nagging doubts about the whole idea.

Evaluate the "Save-A-Life" possibility for Bob and Lyle. Is this a good economic opportunity? Would it be "socially responsible" for them to take on this line?

29. Phoenix Steel Corporation

The troubled U.S. steel industry has been characterized by falling profits and overcapacity in recent years. Some firms have actually gone out of business. The Phoenix Steel Corporation has lost millions of dollars. Money has been poured into the company over the last ten years to try to modernize its outdated facilities and improve its productivity. None of these efforts was effective, so in 1976 the lenders and owners were quite willing to sell a controlling interest to Creusot-Loire (C-L), France's largest specialty steel maker. C-L's strategy is to move into the U.S. market by buying ailing steel companies. Besides Phoenix, C-L purchased several other smaller steel operations. None of these operations, however, are related, except that they were acquired at a low price.

C-L's move into the U.S. market was encouraged by weak sales in France, where the company is involved in steel making and construction for the nuclear industry—a market that has not yet been profitable. As a result, the firm lost a few million dollars in 1976 on over $1 billion in sales. The move into the United States was part of its worldwide expansion effort to counteract the uncertainties of the French market as well as the possibility that protectionist attitudes will arise around the world. Moreover, high taxes and employment legislation in the Common Market, together with the threat of political and economic instability in some world markets, make the United States look attractive.

C-L's strategy for the U.S. market is to use the production facilities in the United States as a place to apply French technology, not just as a route for selling French-made products. Further, C-L top management felt that if protectionist walls were to rise, then C-L would be located in a very large market which might restrict or prohibit imports from Common Market countries and Japan.

C-L's special interest in Phoenix arose from its conclusion that the company had the equipment to produce good-quality specialty plate and other specialty products. As C-L took over, however, they found that there were some serious problems. They immediately fired most of the old management and replaced it with French executives. Then they shifted the product mix away from emphasis on commercial-grade sheet and structural steel, where it was a weak competitor against Bethlehem Steel and U.S. Steel, industry giants. Production emphasis was shifted toward lower-volume, higher-profit specialty-steel markets in which C-L was a world leader. In particular, it offered steel plates used in ship building, power plants, and mining equipment. To help in this shift, C-L brought in many French experts and sent Phoenix technicians to France for training.

Besides upgrading the personnel and production methods, plans were made for increasing maintenance expenditures and plant expansion to increase production efficiencies. To increase revenues, prices were raised approximately 30 percent by eliminating discounts and other price concessions. In spite of these moves, Phoenix lost $9 million on sales of $38 million in 1977. But compared with a loss of $29 million in 1976, this was encouraging to top management, which was predicting a profit in 1978. Following this "turnaround," C-L began hiring U.S. citizens to run the company. The plan was to run the company by Americans in "the American way." Some of the Americans coming in were lured away from competing steel companies and brought steel industry expertise with them. Also, some new sales people were hired because they had a loyal customer following which might provide a quick increase in Phoenix's sales.

C-L management feels that government (U.S.) decisions on an energy policy are quite important to Phoenix's survival. The company makes seamless tubing which is used in strip mining of coal, and there are only one or two other companies in this market. So growth in this market or in similar specialty markets could spell the difference between success and failure. It is clear to all that some increase in volume is needed to get beyond the break-even point. Phoenix's chances, however, are impaired by its past bad image with steel buyers. It has a long-time reputation for low-quality products, undependable delivery, and high prices when demand is strong.

Hopefully, C-L has turned Phoenix Steel around with respect to product quality, image, and pricing. It must reckon, however, with several major competitors in its specialty steel markets. Further, it is handicapped by the fact that its production facilities are in the northeast part of the country where there is chronic overcapacity. Worse, its major competitors include Lukens and Armco—well-established specialty-steel makers with good reputations. Some other specialty-steel makers have given up on this market, closing down plants or selling them to others.

Industry specialists doubt there is any way that Phoenix can compete with the established firms, given that its plant is old and relatively unproductive. This, coupled with excess capacity in the eastern states, will probably doom C-L's efforts, they feel. There is a possibility that general market demand will rise, of course. There's also some possibility of expanding beyond the northeastern market. But then C-L would encounter entrenched competitors and have to absorb freight cost to enter these markets.

What are the prospects for C-L's current strategy? What strategy would you pursue to maximize the chance for long-run profit?

30. Auto Specialties Manufacturing Company

Auto Specialties Manufacturing Company is a supplier of malleable iron castings for several automobile and aircraft manufacturers and a variety of other users of castings. Last year's sales of castings amounted to over $50 million on a volume of over 50,000 tons of castings.

In addition to the foundry operations which produce the iron castings, Auto Specialties also produces roughly 50 percent of all the original-equipment bumper jacks installed in new automobiles each year. This is a very price-competitive business, but Auto Specialties has been able to obtain this large share of the market by relying on close personal contact between the company's sales executives and its customers, supported by extremely cooperative collaboration between the company's engineering department and its customers' buyers. This has been extremely important in this market, because the wide variety of models and model changes frequently requires alterations in the specifications of the bumper jacks. All bumper jacks are sold directly to the automobile manufacturers. No attempt has been made to sell bumper jacks to final consumers through hardware and automotive channels, although they are available through the manufacturers' automobile dealers.

Mr. Burns, Auto Specialties production manager,

would now like to begin producing hydraulic jacks for sale through automotive parts wholesalers to garages, body shops, and (in the case of one specialized design with some extra accessories) fire and police departments to aid them in rescuing accident victims in those cases where risks of fire prevent the use of cutting torches. Burns saw a variety of hydraulic jacks at a recent automotive show, and could see immediately that his plant could produce these products. This especially interested him because of the possibility of utilizing excess capacity. Further, he feels that "jacks are jacks," and that the company would merely be broadening its product line by introducing hydraulic jacks. As he became more enthusiastic about the idea, he found that his engineering department already had a design which appeared to be technically superior to the products now offered on the market. Detailed analysis indicates that the company might be able to produce a product which is made better than the competition (i.e., smoother castings, etc.), although it is not likely that customers will notice the differences. It appears that the production department could produce products comparable in cost to those currently offered by competitors at about one-half of the current retail prices.

Jack Witco, the sales manager, has just received a memo from Jim Roberts, the president of the company, explaining the production department's enthusiasm for broadening its jack line into hydraulic jacks. Roberts seems enthusiastic about the idea, too, noting that it may be a way to make fuller use of the company's resources and increase its sales. Recognizing this enthusiasm, Witco wants to develop a well-thought-out explanation of why he cannot get very excited about the proposal. He knows he is already overworked and could not possibly promote this new line himself. But more basically, he feels that the proposed hydraulic jack line is not very closely related to the company's present emphasis. He has already indicated his lack of enthusiasm to Burns, but this has made little difference in Burns' thinking. Now, it is clear that Jack will have to convince the president or he will soon be responsible for selling hydraulic jacks.

What would you advise Jack to say and do?

NOTES

CHAPTER 1

1. Reavis Cox, *Distribution in a High-Level Economy* (Englewood Cliffs, N.J.: Prentice-Hall, Inc. 1965), p. 149; and Paul W. Stewart and J. Frederick Dewhurst, *Does Distribution Cost Too Much?* (New York: Twentieth Century Fund, 1963), pp. 117–18.

2. Malcolm P. McNair, "Marketing and the Social Challenge of Our Times," in Keith Cox and Ben M. Enis, eds., *A New Measure of Responsibility for Marketing* (Chicago: American Marketing Association, 1968).

3. Peter F. Drucker, *Management: Tasks, Responsibilities, Practices* (New York: Harper & Row, 1973), pp. 64–65.

4. For more on this topic, see Reed Moyer, "Marketing in the Iron Curtain Countries," *Journal of Marketing,* October 1966, pp. 3–9; and G. Peter Lauter, "The Changing Role of Marketing in the Eastern European Socialist Economies," *Journal of Marketing,* October 1971, pp. 16–20.

5. See, for example, Milton Friedman, *Capitalism and Freedom* (Chicago: University of Chicago Press, 1962); and Murray L. Weidenbaum, *Business, Government, and the Public* (Englewood Cliffs, N.J.: Prentice-Hall, Inc., 1977). For a contrasting point of view, see John Kenneth Galbraith, *Economics and the Public Purpose* (Boston: Houghton Mifflin Company, 1973).

6. Wroe Alderson, "Factors Governing the Development of Marketing Channels," in Richard M. Clewett, ed., *Marketing Channels for Manufactured Products* (Homewood, Ill. Richard D. Irwin, Inc., 1954), p. 7.

7. Adapted from Wroe Alderson, "Factors Governing the Development of Marketing Channels."

8. Peter F. Drucker, "Marketing and Economic Development," *Journal of Marketing,* January 1958, p. 253. Reprinted from the *Journal of Marketing,* national quarterly publication of the American Marketing Association.

9. Ragnar Nurkse, *Problems of Capital Formation in Underdeveloped Countries* (Oxford: Basil Blackwell, 1953), p. 4.

10. This discussion is based largely on William McInnes, "A Conceptual Approach to Marketing," in Reavis Cox, Wroe Alderson, and Stanley J. Shapiro, eds., *Theory in Marketing,* second series (Homewood, Ill.: Richard D. Irwin, Inc., 1964), pp. 51–67; see also J. F. Grashof and A. Kelman, *Introduction to Macro-Marketing* (Columbus, Ohio: Grid, Inc., 1973); and Robert Bartels and Roger L. Jenkins, "Macromarketing," *Journal of Marketing,* October 1977, pp. 17–20.

11. Adapted from William McInnes, "A Conceptual Approach to Marketing," in Reavis Cox, Wroe Alderson, and Stanley J. Shapiro, eds., *Theory in Marketing,* second series (Homewood, Ill.: Richard D. Irwin, Inc., 1964), pp. 51–67.

12. "Forging America's Future: Strategies for National Growth and Development," Report of the Advisory Committee on National Growth Policy Processes, reprinted in *Challenge,* January/February 1977.

CHAPTER 2

1. Robert J. Keith, "The Marketing Revolution," *Journal of Marketing,* January 1960, pp. 35–38. See also "International (Harvester) Tries to Cut Its Truck Losses," *Business Week,* February 16, 1976, pp. 98–99; "Why Philip Morris Thrives," *Business Week,* January 27, 1973, pp. 48–54; and Philip Kotler, "From Sales Obsession to Marketing Effectiveness," *Harvard Business Review,* November–December, 1977, pp. 67–75.

CHAPTER 2

2. Adapted from R. F. Vizza, T. E. Chambers, and E. J. Cook, *Adoption of the Marketing Concept—Fact or Fiction?* (New York: Sales Executive Club, Inc., 1967), pp. 13–15.

3. Benson P. Shapiro, "Marketing for Nonprofit Organizations," *Harvard Business Review,* September–October 1973, pp. 123–32; Philip Kotler, *Marketing for Nonprofit Organizations* (Englewood Cliffs, N.J.: Prentice-Hall, Inc., 1976); Cecily Cannan Selby, "Better Performance from 'Nonprofits,'" *Harvard Business Review,* September–October 1978 pp. 92–98; and Thomas J. C. Raymond and Stephen A. Greyser, "The Business of Managing the Arts," *Harvard Business Review,* July–August 1978, pp. 123–32.

4. The Helpless Housewife describes a segment of the English market as seen by this marketing manager. In the United States there appears to be a "Helpless Homeowner" market (male and female) which is not fully satisfied with the typical "paint store." Some large paint manufacturers and retailers are now trying to cater to this market.

5. Alfred P. Sloan, Jr., *My Years with General Motors* (New York: MacFadden Books, 1965), Introduction, chaps. 4 and 9.

6. Daniel Yankelovich, "Psychological Market Segmentation," in Jack A. Sissors, ed., *Some Bold New Theories of Advertising in Marketing* (Evanston, Ill.: Northwestern University, 1963), pp. 23–25.

7. "The Great Digital Watch Shake-Out," *Business Week,* May 2, 1977, pp. 70–80; "The Digital Watch Becomes the World's Cheapest Timepiece," *The Wall Street Journal,* April 18, 1977, p. 11; "Gruen Industries Asks Chapter 11 Status," *The Wall Street Journal,* April 15, 1977, p. 9; "Why Gillette Stopped Its Digital Watches," *Business Week,* January 31, 1977, pp. 37–38; and "Digital Wristwatch Business Is Glowing, but Rivalry Winds Down Prices, Profits," *The Wall Street Journal,* August 24, 1976, p. 6.

CHAPTER 3

1. "The Graying of America," *Newsweek,* February 28, 1977, pp. 50–55.

2. Based on the U.S. Census, *Newsweek,* February 28, 1977, p. 52.

3. U.S. Department of Commerce, *Household Money Income in 1976,* Current Population Reports, Series P-60, no. 109, January 1978, p. 2; and Alfred L. Malabre, "Despite Inflation and Taxes, Take-Home Pay Buys More and More, Reversing a Steep Drop," *The Wall Street Journal,* February 8, 1978, p. 36.

4. "Business Out of Sync with Public, Pollster Says," *Advertising Age,* May 23, 1977, p. 4.

5. "Crash Suit Costs Ford $450,000," *Detroit Free Press,* December 14, 1972.

6. "Packaging Firm Is Found Guilty of Price Conspiracy,"

The Wall Street Journal, January 21, 1977, p. 3. See also T. McAdams and R. C. Milgus, "Growing Criminal Liability of Executives," *Harvard Business Review,* March–April 1977, pp. 36–40; Jeffrey Sonnenfeld and Paul R. Lawrence, "Why Do Companies Succumb to Price Fixing?" *Harvard Business Review,* July–August 1978, pp. 145–57; "Stiff Penalties for Price Fixing Levied by Court," *The Wall Street Journal,* February 6, 1978, p. 11; and "Borden, Dean Foods Unit Agree to Fines, Prison Sentences," *The Wall Street Journal,* December 28, 1977, p. 2.

7. "Antitrust: A Hotline to Nab Price Fixers," *Business Week,* May 30, 1977, p. 34; and G. David Hughes, "Antitrust Caveats for the Marketing Planner," *Harvard Business Review,* March–April 1978, pp. 40–58, 186–94.

8. Adapted from L. P. Feldman, *Consumer Protection: Problems and Prospects* (St. Paul: West Publishing Co., 1976), pp. 283–86.

9. Paul Busch, "A Review and Critical Evaluation of the Consumer Product Safety Commission: Marketing Management Implications," *Journal of Marketing,* October 1976, pp. 41–49.

10. "A Rancorous Bout with Chapter XI," *Business Week,* August 1, 1977, pp. 22–23; "Louisiana—Pacific's Change in Strategy," *Business Week,* May 24, 1976, pp. 50–53; "How Philips Industries Successfully Adjusted to a Smaller Market," *The Wall Street Journal,* December 31, 1976, p. 1; Theodore Levitt, "Marketing When Things Change," *Harvard Business Review,* November–December 1977, pp. 107–13; and "Home-Grown Woes: Zenith's Own Actions, As Well as Imports, Prompted Its Troubles," *The Wall Street Journal,* October 25, 1977, pp. 1, 16.

11. George C. Sawyer, "Social Issues and Social Change: Impact on Strategic Decisions," *MSU Business Topics,* Summer 1973, pp. 15–20.

12. "Oranges Start Coming Up Roses," *Business Week,* May 4, 1968, pp. 127–30.

13. *Business Week,* June 24, 1967, p. 85.

14. Based on Charles H. Kline, "The Strategy of Product Policy," *Harvard Business Review,* July–August 1955, pp. 91–100.

15. Charles H. Granger, "The Hierarchy of Objectives," *Harvard Business Review,* May–June 1964, p. 63.

16. Adapted from Peter F. Drucker, "Business Objectives and Survival Needs: Notes on a Discipline of Business Enterprise," *Journal of Business,* April 1958, pp. 181–90.

17. "A Painful Attempt to Aid Ampex," *Business Week,* February 12, 1977, p. 17; "Ford Motor Company Adopts New Tactics to Boost Its 'Big Three' Standing," *The Wall Street Journal,* May 15, 1973, p. 1; "RCA's New Vista: The Bottom Line," *Business Week,* July 4, 1977, pp. 38–44; "The Luster Dims at Westinghouse," *Business Week,* July 20, 1974, pp. 53–63; "The Old-Line Meatpackers Struggle to Survive," *Business Week,* November 13, 1978, pp. 78–80; and "At Johns-Manville, It's Back to Basics," *Business Week,* October 31, 1977, pp. 76–80.

CHAPTER 4

1. Harper W. Boyd, Jr., Ralph Westfall, and Stanley F. Stasch, *Marketing Research: Text and Cases,* 4th ed. (Homewood, Ill.: Richard D. Irwin, Inc., 1977).

2. J. G. Keane, "Some Observations on Marketing Research in Top Management Decision Making," *Journal of Marketing,* October 1969, pp. 10–15; B. A. Greenberg, Jac L. Goldstucker, and D. N. Bellenger, "What Techniques Are Used by Marketing Researchers in Business?" *Journal of Marketing,* April 1977, pp. 62–68; R. J. Small and L. J. Rosenberg, "The Marketing Researcher as a Decision Maker: Myth or Reality?" *Journal of Marketing,* January 1975, pp. 2–7; and Calvin L. Hodock, "Only Researcher Acting As 'Internal Consultant' Is Worth It to Self, Company," *Marketing News,* January 27, 1978, pp. 1, 20–21.

3. Arthur P. Felton, "Conditions of Marketing Leadership," *Harvard Business Review,* March–April 1956, pp. 117–27.

4. "Scouting the Trail for Marketers," *Business Week,* April 18, 1964, pp. 90–116.

5. Donald F. Mulvihill, "Marketing Research for the Small Company," *Journal of Marketing,* October 1951, pp. 179–82.

6. *The Role and Organization of Marketing Research, Experiences in Marketing Management,* no. 20 (New York: National Industrial Conference Board, 1969), 65 pp.

7. William A. Marsteller, "Can You Afford a Market Research Department?" *Industrial Marketing,* March 1951, pp. 36–37. See also "Top Executives Keep Tabs on the Consumer—Or Contend They Do," *The Wall Street Journal,* July 1, 1976, p. 1.

8. For more discussion see P. E. Green and D. S. Tull, *Research for Marketing Decisions,* 2d ed. (Englewood Cliffs, N.J.: Prentice-Hall, Inc., 1970), chap. 1.

9. David B. Montgomery, *Marketing Information and Decision Systems: Coming of Age in the '70s* (Cambridge, Mass.: Marketing Science Institute, August 1973), pp. 29–30; see also David B. Montgomery, "The Outlook for MIS," *Journal of Advertising Research,* June 1973, pp. 5–11; L. D. Gibson, C. S. Mayer, C. E. Nugent, and T. E. Vollmann, "An Evolutionary Approach to Marketing Information Systems," *Journal of Marketing,* April 1973, pp. 2–6; Richard H. Brien and James E. Stafford, "Marketing Information Systems: A New Dimension for Marketing Research," *Journal of Marketing,* July 1968, p. 21; and Steven L. Alter, "How Effective Managers Use Information Systems," *Harvard Business Review,* November–December 1976, pp. 97–104.

CHAPTER 5

1. "Young Market Becoming More Conventional," *Advertising Age,* May 16, 1977, p. 84; David S. Rogers and Howard L. Green, "Changes in Consumer Food Expenditure Patterns," *Journal of Marketing,* April 1978, pp. 14–19; and "Big Changes in How People Live—New Official Look," *U.S. News & World Report,* January 16, 1978, pp. 42–44.

2. Adapted from William D. Wells and George Gubar, "Life Cycle Concept in Marketing Research," *Journal of Marketing,* August 1968, p. 267.

3. "Motorcycles: The Dip Continues," *Business Week,* May 3, 1976, pp. 80–81.

4. "Why Gerber Makes an Inviting Target," *Business Week,* June 27, 1977, pp. 26–27.

5. Marcus Alexis, "Some Negro-White Differences in Consumption," *American Journal of Economics and Sociology,* January 1962, pp. 11–28. See also Andrew A. Brogowicz, "Race as a Basis for Market Segmentation: An Exploratory Analysis," Ph.D. Thesis, Michigan State University, 1977.

6. *The Nielsen Researcher,* no. 1, 1977, p. 7.

7. T. F. Bradshaw and J. F. Stinson, "Trends in Weekly Earnings: An Analysis," *Monthly Labor Review,* August 1975, pp. 25–26; W. Lazer and J. E. Smallwood, "The Changing Demographics of Women," *Journal of Marketing,* July 1977, pp. 14–30; Rena Bartos, "The Moving Target: The Impact of Women's Employment on Consumer Behavior," *Journal of Marketing,* July 1977, pp. 31–37; Suzanne H. McCall, "Meet the "Workwife" *Journal of Marketing,* July 1977, pp. 55–65; David Ignatius, "Women at Work: The Rich Get Richer as Well-to-Do Wives Enter the Labor Force," *The Wall Street Journal,* September 8, 1978, pp. 1, 27; Myra H. Strober and Charles B. Weinberg, "Working Wives and Major Family Expenditures," *Consumer Research,* December 1977, pp. 141–47; and Rena Bartos, "What Every Marketer Should Know about Women," *Harvard Business Review,* May–June 1978, pp. 73–85.

8. K. H. Chung, *Motivational Theories and Practices* (Columbus, Ohio: Grid, Inc. 1977), pp. 40–43; and A. H. Maslow, *Motivation and Personality* (New York: Harper & Brothers, 1954).

9. Robert Ardrey, *African Genesis* (New York: Atheneum, 1961), chap. 4.

10. This discussion is based on J. Pavasars and W. D. Wells, "Measures of Brand Attitudes Can Be Used to Predict Buying Behavior," *Marketing News,* April 11, 1975, p. 6; and F. E. Webster, Jr., *Social Aspects of Marketing* (Englewood Cliffs, N.J.: Prentice-Hall Inc., 1974), pp. 44–46.

11. William D. Wells and Douglas J. Tigert, "Activities, Interests, and Opinions," in James F. Engel et al., eds., *Market Segmentation* (New York: Holt Reinhart & Winston Inc., 1972), p. 258.

12. *Marketing News,* December 31, 1976, p. 8. See also "Life-Style Research Inappropriate for Some Categories of Products," *Marketing News,* June 17, 1977, p. 9; M. E. Goldberg, "Identifying Relevant Psychographic Segments: How Specifying Product Functions Can Help," *Consumer Research,* December 1976, pp. 163–69; W. D. Wells, "Psychographics: A Critical Review," *Journal of Marketing Research,* May 1975, pp. 196–213; Elizabeth A. Richards and Stephen S. Sturman, "Life-Style Segmentation in Apparel Marketing," *Journal of Marketing,* October 1977, pp. 89–91; Fred D. Reynolds, Melvin R. Crask, and William D. Wells, "The Modern

CHAPTER 5

Feminine Life Style,'' *Journal of Marketing,* July 1977, pp. 38–45; and Susan P. Douglas and Christine D. Urvan, ''Life-Style Analysis to Profile Women in International Markets,'' *Journal of Marketing,* July 1977, pp. 46–54.

13. W. H. Reynolds and James H. Meyers, ''Marketing and the American Family,'' *Business Topics,* Spring 1966, pp. 58–59. See also G. M. Munsinger, J. E. Weber and R. W. Hansen, ''Joint Home Purchasing Decisions by Husbands and Wives,'' *Consumer Research,* March 1975, pp. 60–66; E. P. Cox III, ''Family Purchase Decision Making and the Process of Adjustment,'' *Journal of Marketing Research,* May 1975, pp. 189–95; R. T. Green and I. C. M. Cunningham, ''Feminine Role Perception and Family Purchasing Decisions,'' *Journal of Marketing Research,* August 1975, pp. 325–32; I. C. M. Cunningham and R. T. Green, ''Purchasing Roles in the U.S. Family, 1955 & 1973,'' *Journal of Marketing,* October 1974, pp. 61–64; Harry L. Davis, ''Decision Making within the Household,'' *Consumer Research,* March 1976, pp. 241–60; and John Scanzoni, ''Changing Sex Roles and Emerging Directions in Family Decision Making,'' *Consumer Research,* December 1977, pp. 185–88.

14. P. Martineau, ''The Pattern of Social Classes,'' in R. L. Clewett, ed., *Marketing's Role in Scientific Management* (Chicago: American Marketing Association, 1957), pp. 246–47.

15. Adapted from P. Martineau, *Motivation in Advertising* (New York: McGraw-Hill Book Co., 1957), p. 164.

16. Bureau of Applied Social Research, Columbia University.

17. James A. Carman, *The Application of Social Class in Market Segmentation* (Berkeley: Institute of Business and Economic Research, University of California, 1965) pp. 21 and 61; and Elihu Katz and Paul E. Lazarsfeld, *Personal Influences* (Glencoe, Ill.: Free Press, 1955). See also John O. Summers, ''The Identity of Women's Clothing Fashion Opinion Leaders,'' *Journal of Marketing Research,* May 1970, pp. 178–86; and Charles W. King and John O. Summers, ''Overlap of Opinion Leadership across Consumer Product Categories,'' *Journal of Marketing Research,* February 1970, pp. 43–50.

18. Walter A. Henry, ''Cultural Values Do Correlate with Consumer Behavior,'' *Journal of Marketing Research,* May 1976, pp. 121–27; and John I. Reynolds, ''Developing Policy Responses to Cultural Differences,'' *Business Horizons,* August 1978, pp. 28–35.

19. Adapted from James H. Myers and William H. Reynolds, *Consumer Behavior and Marketing Management* (Boston: Houghton Mifflin Co., 1967), p. 49.

20. John A. Howard and Jagdish N. Sheth, *The Theory of Buyer Behavior* (New York: John Wiley & Sons, Inc., 1969), pp. 46–48. See also C. Whan Park, ''Students and Housewives: Differences in Susceptibility to Reference Group Influence,'' *Consumer Research,* September 1977, pp. 102–10.

21. Adapted from E. M. Rogers, *The Diffusion of Innovations* (New York: Free Press of Glencoe, 1962); and E. M. Rogers with F. Schoemaker, *Communication of Innovation: A Cross Cultural Approach* (New York: Free Press of Glencoe, 1968).

22. For further discussion on this topic, see James H. Myers and William H. Reynolds, *Consumer Behavior and Marketing Management* (Boston: Houghton Mifflin Co., 1967); and J. F. Engel, D. T. Kollat, and R. D. Blackwell, *Consumer Behavior* (New York: Holt Reinhart & Winston, Inc., 1968).

CHAPTER 6

1. Patrick J. Robinson and Charles W. Faris, *Industrial Buying and Creative Marketing* (Boston: Allyn & Bacon, Inc., 1967), p. 33. Reprinted by permission of the publisher.

2. Ibid., chap. 2. See also Frederick E. Webster, Jr., and Yoram Wind, ''A General Model for Understanding Organizational Buying Behavior,'' *Journal of Marketing,* April 1972, pp. 12–19; Urban B. Ozanne and Gilbert A. Churchill, Jr., ''Five Dimensions of the Industrial Adoption Process,'' *Journal of Marketing Research,* August 1971, pp. 322–28; and Donald R. Lehmann and John O'Shaughnessy, ''Difference in Attribute Importance for Different Industrial Products,'' *Journal of Marketing,* April 1974, pp. 36–42.

3. Donald F. Istvan, *Capital-Expenditure Decisions: How They Are Made In Large Corporations,* Indiana Business Report no. 33 (Bloomington: Indiana University, 1961), p. 97; James D. Edwards, ''Investment Decision Making in a Competitive Society,'' *MSU Business Topics,* Autumn 1970, pp. 53–70; and E. Raymond Corey, ''Should Companies Centralize Procurement?'' *Harvard Business Review,* November–December 1978, pp. 102–10.

4. For a detailed discussion of supermarket chain buying, see J. F. Grashof, ''Information Management for Supermarket Chain Product Mix Decisions,'' (Ph.D. thesis, Michigan State University, 1968). See also David B. Montgomery, ''New Product Distribution: An Analysis of Supermarket Buyer Decisions,'' *Journal of Marketing Research,* August 1975, pp. 255–64.

5. ''What's the Sales Potential of Those Products Taking Up Space on a Store's Valuable Shelves,'' *Systems Management,* January 1962, p. 35.

6. ''Why Sears Stays the No. 1 Retailer,'' *Business Week,* January 20, 1968, pp. 65–73.

7. ''Monsanto Moves into Farmers' Back Yard,'' *Business Week,* February 6, 1965, pp. 60–62. See also ''Agricorporations Run into Growing Criticism as Their Role Expands,'' *The Wall Street Journal,* May 2, 1972, p. 1; ''How the Family Farm Can Harvest Millions,'' *Business Week,* July 4, 1977, pp. 68–70; ''The Billion-Dollar Farm Co-ops Nobody Knows,'' *Business Week,* February 7, 1977, pp. 54–64; and Ray A. Goldberg, ''U.S. Agribusiness Breaks Out of Isolation,'' *Harvard Business Review,* May–June 1975, pp. 81–95.

CHAPTER 7

1. For a classic article on the subject, see Russell I. Haley, ''Benefit Segmentation: A Decision Oriented Research Tool,'' *Journal of Marketing,* July 1968, pp. 30–35. See

CHAPTER 7

also Richard M. Johnson, "Market Segmentation: A Strategic Management Tool," *Journal of Marketing Research*, February 1971, pp. 13–18; James H. Myers, "Benefit Structure Analysis: A New Tool for Product Planning," *Journal of Marketing*, October 1976, pp. 23–32; and Roger J. Calantone and Alan G. Sawyer, "The Stability of Benefit Segments," *Journal of Marketing Research*, August 1978, pp. 395–404.

2. Adapted from *House and Home*, April 1965, pp. 94–99.

3. The details of these techniques are beyond our scope, but for discussion see: William L. Wilkie, "The Product Stream and Market Segmentation: A Research Approach," American Marketing Association Combined Conference Proceedings, Spring and Fall 1971, Series no. 33, pp. 317–21; and R. E. Frank, W. F. Massy, and Y. Wind, *Market Segmentation* (Englewood Cliffs, N.J.: Prentice-Hall, 1972). This book has an extensive bibliography. See also Paul E. Green and Frank J. Carmone, *Multi-Dimensional Scaling and Related Techniques in Marketing Analysis* (Boston: Allyn and Bacon, Inc., 1970); and Yoram Wind, "Issues and Advances in Segmentation Research," *Journal of Marketing Research*, August 1978, pp. 317–37.

4. S. Arbeit and A. G. Sawyer, "Benefit Segmentation in a Retail Banking Environment," presented at the American Marketing Association Fall Conference, Washington, D.C., August 1973.

5. *Sales and Marketing Management*, July 25, 1977, pp. C-60, 62, and 67, © 1977, Sales and Marketing Management Survey of Buying Power; further reproduction is forbidden.

6. Checking the accuracy of forecasts is a difficult subject. See R. Ferber, W. J. Hawkes, Jr., and M. D. Plotkin, "How Reliable Are National Retail Sales Estimates?" *Journal of Marketing*, October 1976, pp. 13–22; D. J. Dalrymple, "Sales Forecasting Methods and Accuracy," *Business Horizons*, December 1975, pp. 69–73; P. R. Wotruba and M. L. Thurlow, "Sales Force Participation in Quota Setting and Sales Forecasting," *Journal of Marketing*, April 1976, pp. 11–16; R. Shoemaker and R. Staelin, "The Effects of Sampling Variation on Sales Forecasts for New Consumer Products," *Journal of Marketing Research*, May 1976, pp. 138–43; R. Staelin and R. E. Turner, "Error in Judgmental Sales Forecasts: Theory and Results," *Journal of Marketing Research*, February 1973, pp. 10–16; Charles Waldo and Dennis Fuller, "Just How Good Is the Survey of Buying Power?" *Journal of Marketing*, October 1977, pp. 64–66; and Robert C. Turner, "Should You Take Business Forecasting Seriously?" *Business Horizons*, April 1978, pp. 64–72.

CHAPTER 8

1. John M. Rathmell, "What is Meant by Services?" *Journal of Marketing*, October 1966, pp. 32–36; T. Levitt, "The Industrialization of Service," *Harvard Business Review*, September–October 1976, pp. 63–74; R. W. Obenberger and S. W. Brown, "A Marketing Alternative: Consumer Leasing and Renting," *Business Horizons*, October 1976, pp. 82–86; Richard B. Chase, "Where Does the Customer Fit in a Service Operation?" *Harvard Business Review*, November–December 1978, pp. 137–42; Dan R. E. Thomas, "Strategy Is Different in Service Industries," *Harvard Business Review*, July–August 1978, pp. 158–65; Paul F. Anderson and William Lazer, "Industrial Lease Marketing," *Journal of Marketing*, January 1978, pp. 71–79; Robert E. Sabath, "How Much Service Do Customers Really Want?" *Business Horizons*, April 1978, pp. 26–32; "Sony's U.S. Operation Goes In for Repairs," *Business Week*, March 13, 1978, pp. 31–32; and Bernard Wysocki, Jr., "Branching Out: Major Retailers Offer Varied Services to Lure Customers, Lift Profits," *The Wall Street Journal*, June 12, 1978, pp. 1, 21.

2. Robert C. Blattberg, Peter Peacock, and S. K. Sen, "Purchasing Strategies across Product Categories," *Consumer Research*, December 1976, pp. 143–54; J. B. Mason and M. L. Mayer, "Empirical Observations of Consumer Behavior as Related to Goods Classification and Retail Strategy," *Journal of Retailing*, Fall 1972, pp. 17–31; Arno K. Kleinhagen, "Shopping, Specialty, or Convenience Goods?" *Journal of Retailing*, Winter 1966–67, pp. 32–39; Louis P. Bucklin, "Testing Propensities to Shop," *Journal of Marketing*, January 1966, pp. 22–27; William P. Dommermuth, "The Shopping Matrix and Marketing Strategy," *Journal of Marketing Research*, May 1965, pp. 128–32; Richard H. Holton, "The Distinction between Convenience Goods, Shopping Goods, and Specialty Goods," *Journal of Marketing*, July 1958, pp. 53–56; Perry Bliss, "Supply Considerations and Shopper Convenience," *Journal of Marketing*, July 1966, pp. 43–45; S. Kaish, "Cognitive Dissonance and the Classification of Consumer Goods," and W. P. Dommermuth and E. W. Cundiff, "Shopping Goods, Shopping Centers, and Selling Strategies," *Journal of Marketing*, October 1967, pp. 28–36; Edward M. Tauber, "Why Do People Shop?" *Journal of Marketing*, October 1972, pp. 46–49; and Fred D. Reynolds and William R. Darden, "Intermarket Patronage: A Psychographic Study of Consumer Outshoppers," *Journal of Marketing*, October 1972, pp. 50–54.

3. M. Alexis, L. Simon, and K. Smith, "Some Determinants of Food Buying Behavior," in M. Alexis, R. Hancock, and R. J. Holloway, eds., *Empirical Foundations of Marketing: Research Findings in the Behavioral and Applied Sciences* (Skokie, Ill.: Rand McNally & Co., 1969).

4. L. P. Feldman, "Prediction of the Spatial Pattern of Shopping Behavior," *Journal of Retailing*, Spring 1967, pp. 25–30.

5. "If You Don't Give the Lady What She Wants, She'll Go Elsewhere," *Marketing News*, January 1, 1968, p. 11.

6. This figure was suggested by Professor Y. Furuhashi of the University of Notre Dame.

7. "Switching the Charge on Batteries," *Business Week*, March 13, 1965, pp. 132–34.

8. "RCA to Cut Prices on Eight Color TVs in Promotion Effort," *The Wall Street Journal*, December 31, 1976, p. 16; "Decline in Color TV Sales Brings Worry That

CHAPTER 8

More Makers May Fall by Wayside," *The Wall Street Journal*, April 2, 1974, p. 36; "Sales of Major Appliances, TV Sets Gain; But Profits Fail to Keep Up. Gap May Widen," *The Wall Street Journal*, August 21, 1972, p. 22; "What Do You Do When Snowmobiles Go on a Steep Slide?" *The Wall Street Journal*, March 8, 1978, pp. 1, 33; "Price of a Home Videotape Recorder Cut to $795 as U.S. Sales Efforts Accelerate," *The Wall Street Journal*, September 26, 1977, p. 8; and "IBM Announces 2 New Processors for Big Systems," *The Wall Street Journal*, October 7, 1977, p. 4.

9. "The Short Happy Life," *Time*, March 29, 1963, p. 83.

10. Ibid.

11. "Good Products Don't Die," P&G Chairman Declares, *Advertising Age*, November 1, 1976, p. 8. See also, "Detroit Brings Back the Fast, Flashy Auto to Aid Sluggish Sales," *The Wall Street Journal*, December 9, 1976 p. 1.

CHAPTER 9

1. Chester R. Wasson, "What Is 'New' About New Products?" *Journal of Marketing*, July 1960, pp. 52–56; Patrick M. Dunne, "What Really Are New Products?" *Journal of Business*, December 1974, pp. 20–25; and S. H. Britt and V. M. Nelson, "The Marketing Importance of the 'Just Noticeable Difference,'" *Business Horizons*, August 1976, pp. 38–40.

2. *Business Week*, April 22, 1967, p. 120.

3. Adapted from Philip Kotler, "What Consumerism Means for Marketers," *Harvard Business Review*, May–June 1972, pp. 55–56; and "Some of the pre-sweetened cereals are 50 percent sugar," *Detroit Free Press*, April 9, 1978, p. 15D, 20D.

4. "Inflation in Product Liability," *Business Week*, May 31, 1976, p. 60.

5. Adapted from Richard M. Johnson, "Market Segmentation: A Strategic Management Tool," *Journal of Marketing Research*, February 1971, p. 160. See also Henry Assael, "Perceptual Mapping to Reposition Brands," *Journal of Advertising Research*, February 1971, pp. 39–42; John P. Maggard, "Positioning Revisited," *Journal of Marketing*, January 1976, pp. 63–66; and H. E. Brown and J. T. Sims, "Market Segmentation, Product Differentiation, and Market Positioning as Alternative Marketing Strategies," in Kenneth L. Bernhardt, ed., *Marketing: 1776–1976 and Beyond*, 1976 Educators' Proceedings, Series No. 39 (Chicago: American Marketing Association, 1976).

6. *Money*, September 1976, p. 108.

7. W. A. French and L. O. Schroeder, "Package Information Legislation: Trends and Viewpoints," *MSU Business Topics*, Summer 1972, pp. 39–42. See also J. A. Miller, D. G. Topel, and R. E. Rust, "USDA Beef Grading: A Failure in Consumer Information?" *Journal of Marketing*, January 1976, pp. 25–31; Richard Staelin, "The Effects of Consumer Education on Consumer Product Safety Behavior," *Consumer Research*, June 1978, pp. 30–40;

Ronald Faber and Scott Ward, "Children's Understanding of Using Products Safely," *Journal of Marketing*, October 1977, pp. 39–46; Carl McDaniel and R. C. Baker, "Convenience Food Packaging and the Perception of Product Quality," *Journal of Marketing*, October 1977, pp. 57–58; Jacob Jacoby, Robert W. Chestnut and William Silberman, "Consumer Use and Comprehension of Nutrition Information," *Consumer Research*, September 1977, pp. 119–28; and Kenneth G. Schneider, "Prevention of Accidental Poisoning Through Package and Label Design," *Consumer Research*, September 1977, pp. 67–74.

8. J. E. Russo, "The Value of Unit Price Information," *Journal of Marketing Research*, May 1977, pp. 193–201; and K. B. Monroe and P. J. LaPlaca, "What Are the Benefits of Unit Pricing?" *Journal of Marketing*, July 1972, pp. 16–22

9. Frank Presbrey, *The History and Development of Advertising* (New York: Doubleday & Co., Inc., 1929).

10. *Business Week*, February 20, 1960, p. 71. See also Kent B. Monroe, "The Influence of Price Differences and Brand Familiarity on Brand Preferences," *Consumer Research*, June 1976, pp. 42–49.

11. "DuPont's Teflon Trademark Survives Attack," *Advertising Age*, July 14, 1975, p. 93; and George Miaoulis and Nancy D'Amato, "Consumer Confusion and Trademark Infringement," *Journal of Marketing*, April 1978, pp. 48–55.

12. *Marketing Communications*, August 1970, p. 13; "Is the Private Label Battle Heating Up?" *Grey Matter*, vol. 44, no. 7, July 1973.

13. E. Dichter, "Brand Loyalty and Motivation Research," *Food Business*, January–February 1956.

14. "Private Label Products Gain Increased Space on Many Retailers' Shelves," *The Wall Street Journal*, February 11, 1971, p. 1; "A&P's Own Brand of Consumerism," *Business Week*, April 11, 1970, p. 32; Victor J. Cook and T. F. Schutte, *Brand Policy Determination* (Boston: Allyn & Bacon, Inc., 1967); Arthur I. Cohen and Ana Loud Jones, "Brand Marketing in the New Retail Environment," *Harvard Business Review*, September–October 1978, pp. 141–48; "The Drugmakers' Rx for Living with Generics," *Business Week*, November 6, 1978, pp. 205–8; and "No-Name Goods Catching On with Grocers," *Detroit Free Press*, April 9, 1978, p. 16D.

15. See T. Levitt, "Innovative Imitation," *Harvard Business Review*, September–October 1966, pp. 63–70; and Roger A. Kerin, Michael G. Harvey, and James T. Rothe, "Cannibalism and New Product Development," *Business Horizons*, October 1978, pp. 25–31.

16. Edgar A. Pessemier, "Managing Innovation and New-Product Development," Marketing Science Institute Report No. 75–122, December 1975; Philip R. McDonald and Joseph O. Eastlack, Jr., "Top Management Involvement with New Products," *Business Horizons*, December 1971, pp. 23–31; John H. Murphy, "New Products Need Special Management," *Journal of Marketing*, October 1962, pp. 46–49; and E. J. McCarthy, "Organization for

CHAPTER 9

New Product Development?'' *Journal of Business of the University of Chicago,* April 1959, pp. 128–32.

17. Benton & Bowles Research and *Printers' Ink,* April 13, 1962, pp. 22–23.

18. Paul Stillson and E. Leonard Arnof, ''Product Search and Evaluation,'' *Journal of Marketing,* July 1957, pp. 33. See also Frank R. Bacon, Jr. and T. W. Butler, Jr., *Planned Innovation* (Ann Arbor: Institute of Science and Technology, The University of Michigan, 1973); and Yoram Wind, John F. Grashof and Joel D. Goldhar, ''Market-Based Guidelines for Design of Industrial Products,'' *Journal of Marketing,* July 1978, pp. 27–37.

19. C. Merle Crawford, ''Marketing Research and the New Product Failure Rate,'' *Journal of Marketing,* April 1977, pp. 51–61; ''Marketing Experts Help Sift Ideas, Weeding Out 99% and Garnering Big Fees,'' *The Wall Street Journal,* August 23, 1978, p. 1, 27; and J. Hugh Davidson, ''Why Most New Consumer Brands Fail,'' *Harvard Business Review,* March–April 1976, pp. 117–22.

20. Victor P. Buell, ''The Changing Role of the Product Manager in Consumer Goods Companies,'' *Journal of Marketing,* July 1975, pp. 3–11.

CHAPTER 10

1. Edwin H. Lewis, ''Distributing Electrical Products in a Dynamic Economy,'' *Electrical Wholesaling,* June 1958, p. 111.

2. D. Philip Locklin, *Economics of Transportation,* 4th ed. (Homewood, Ill.: Richard D. Irwin, Inc., 1954), p. 35.

3. D. Philip Locklin, *Economics of Transportation,* 7th ed. (Homewood, Ill.: Richard D. Irwin, Inc., 1972), p. 57.

4. Michael Etgar, ''Selection of an Effective Channel Control Mix,'' *Journal of Marketing,* July 1978, pp. 53–58; Michael Etgar, ''Intrachannel Conflict and Use of Power,'' *Journal of Marketing Research,* May 1978, pp. 273–74; and Robert F. Lusch, ''Intrachannel Conflict and Use of Power; A Reply,'' *Journal of Marketing Research,* May 1978, pp. 275–76. For further discussion on channel control, see Robert F. Lusch, ''Sources of Power: Their Impact on Intrachannel Conflict,'' *Journal of Marketing Research,* November 1976, pp. 382–90; William P. Dommermuth, ''Profiting from Distribution Conflicts,'' *Business Horizons,* December 1976, pp. 4–13; Shelby D. Hunt and John R. Nevin, ''Power in a Channel of Distribution: Sources and Consequences,'' *Journal of Marketing Research,* May 1974, pp. 186–93; Louis P. Bucklin, ''A Theory of Channel Control,'' *Journal of Marketing,* January 1973, pp. 39–47; Ronald Michman, *Marketing Channels,* (Columbus, Ohio: Grid Publishing, Inc., 1974); and Joseph B. Mason, ''Power and Channel Conflicts in Shopping Center Development,'' *Journal of Marketing,* April 1975, pp. 28–35.

5. D. J. Bowersox and E. J. McCarthy, ''Strategic Development of Planned Vertical Marketing Systems,'' in Louis Bucklin, ed., *Vertical Marketing Systems* (Glenview, Ill.: Scott, Foresman & Co., 1970).

6. Bert C. McCammon, Jr. ''The Emergence and Growth of Contractually Integrated Channels in the American Economy,'' a paper presented at the Fall Conference of the American Marketing Association, Washington, D.C., September 2, 1965.

7. ''The Court Switches Franchise Signals,'' *Business Week,* July 11, 1977, pp. 30–31. See also James R. Burley, ''Territorial Restriction and Distribution Systems: Current Legal Developments,'' *Journal of Marketing,* October 1975, pp. 52–56; Louis W. Stern et al., ''Territorial Restrictions and Distribution: A Case Analysis,'' *Journal of Marketing,* April 1976, pp. 69–75; ''Soft-Drink Bottlers Choke on FTC Ruling against Exclusive-Territory Restrictions,'' *The Wall Street Journal,* April 25, 1978, p. 6; and Michael B. Metzger, ''Schwinn's Swan Song,'' *Business Horizons,* April 1978, pp. 52–56.

CHAPTER 11

1. For more discussion of these ideas, see Louis Bucklin, ''Retail Strategy and the Classification of Consumer Goods,'' *Journal of Marketing,* January 1963, pp. 50–55.

2. ''Convenience Stores: A $7.4 Billion Mushroom,'' *Business Week,* March 21, 1977, pp. 61–64.

3. ''Why Profits Shrink at a Grand Old Name,'' (Marshall Field), *Business Week,* April 11, 1977, pp. 66–78; Louis H. Grossman, ''Merchandising Strategies of a Department Store Facing Change,'' *MSU Business Topics,* Winter 1970, pp. 31–42; and ''Suburban Malls Go Downtown,'' *Business Week,* November 10, 1973, pp. 90–94.

4. ''Vendors Pull Out All Stops,'' *Business Week,* August 15, 1970, pp. 52–53.

5. Douglas J. Dalrymple, ''Will Automatic Vending Topple Retail Precedence?'' *Journal of Retailing,* Spring 1963, pp. 27–31.

6. ''Supermarkets Eye the Sunbelt,'' *Business Week,* September 27, 1976, pp. 61–62; ''Safeway: Selling Nongrocery Items to Cure the Supermarket Blahs,'' *Business Week,* March 7, 1977, pp. 52–58; and ''How a Long Price War Dragged On and Hurt Chicago Food Chains,'' *The Wall Street Journal,* July 19, 1976, p. 1.

7. ''Mass Merchandisers Move Toward Stability,'' *The Nielsen Researcher,* no. 3, 1976, pp. 19–25.

8. ''Those 1,215 K's Stand for Kresge, K marts, and the Key to Success,'' *The Wall Street Journal,* March 8, 1977, p. 1.

9. Walter J. Salmon, Robert D. Buzzell, and Stanton G. Cort, ''Today the Shopping Center, Tomorrow the Superstore,'' *Harvard Business Review,* January–February 1974, pp. 89–98; ''Super-Stores May Suit Customers to a T—A T-Shirt or a T-Bone,'' *The Wall Street Journal,* March 13, 1973, p. 1; and *The Super-Store—Strategic Implications for the Seventies* (Cambridge, Mass.: The Marketing Science Institute, 1972).

10. Stanley C. Hollander, ''Retailing: Cause or Effect?'' in William F. Decker, ed., *Emerging Concepts in Marketing,* (Chicago: American Marketing Association, December

CHAPTER 11

1962), pp. 220–30; and Malcolm P. McNair and Eleanor G. May, "The Next Revolution of the Retailing Wheel," *Harvard Business Review,* September–October 1978, pp. 81–91.

11. For more discussion on gridding of retail markets, see "Fast-Food Franchisers Invade the City," *Business Week,* April 22, 1974, pp. 92–93; "Korvettes Tries for a Little Chic," *Business Week,* May 12, 1973, pp. 124–26; Philip D. Cooper, "Will Success Produce Problems for the Convenience Store?" *MSU Business Topics,* Winter 1972, pp. 39–43; "Levitz: The Hot Name in 'Instant' Furniture," *Business Week,* December 4, 1971, pp. 90–93; David L. Appel, "Market Segmentation—A Response to Retail Innovation," *Journal of Marketing,* April 1970, pp. 64–67; Steven R. Flaster, "A Consumer Approach to the Specialty Store," *Journal of Retailing,* Spring 1969, pp. 21–31; and A. Coskun Samli, "Segmentation and Carving a Niche in the Market Place," *Journal of Retailing,* Summer 1968, pp. 35–49.

12. E. H. Lewis and R. Hancock, *The Franchise System of Distribution* (Minneapolis: University of Minnesota Press, 1963). See also the special issue on franchising in the *Journal of Retailing,* Winter 1968–69.

13. Albert D. Bates, "The Troubled Future of Retailing," *Business Horizons,* August 1976, pp. 22–28; William R. Davidson, Albert D. Bates, and Stephen J. Bass, "Retail Life Cycle," *Harvard Business Review,* November–December 1976, pp. 89–96; "Investigating the Collapse of W. T. Grant," *Business Week,* July 19, 1976, pp. 60–62; "Shopping Center Boom Appears to Be Fading Due to Overbuilding," *The Wall Street Journal,* September 7, 1976, pp. 1; and "Jewel Co. Discloses Operations Review in Search of a More Successful Strategy," *The Wall Street Journal,* March 23, 1977, p. 12.

CHAPTER 12

1. "Food Brokers: A Comprehensive Study of Their Growing Role in Marketing," *Grocery Manufacture,* December 1969. This and others available from the National Food Brokers Association, 1916 M Street, N.W., Washington, D.C. 20036.

2. Paul D. Converse, "Twenty-Five Years in Wholesaling: A Revolution in Food Wholesaling," *Journal of Marketing,* July 1957, pp. 40–41; and Richard S. Lopata, "Faster Pace in Wholesaling," *Harvard Business Review,* July–August 1969, pp. 130–43.

3. For more discussion, see F. E. Webster, Jr., "The Role of the Industrial Distributor in Marketing Strategy," *Journal of Marketing,* July 1976, pp. 10–16; and "Wetterau: A Maverick Grocery Wholesaler," *Business Week,* February 14, 1977, pp. 121–22.

CHAPTER 13

1. Robert S. Mason, "What's a PR Director For, Anyway?," *Harvard Business Review,* September–October 1974, pp. 120–26.

2. Roger A. Strang, "Sales Promotion—Fast Growth, Faulty Management," *Harvard Business Review,* July–August 1976, pp. 115–24.

3. Ibid., pp. 116–19.

4. For more discussion on sales promotion activities, see Alfred Gross, *Sales Promotion,* various editions (New York: The Ronald Press Co.); and Ovid Riso, *Sales Promotion Handbook,* 6th ed. (Chicago: Dartnell, Inc.).

5. "More Firms Turn to Translation Experts to Avoid Costly Embarrassing Mistakes," *The Wall Street Journal,* January 13, 1977, p. 32.

6. M. S. Heidingsfield and A. B. Blankenship, *Marketing* (New York: Barnes & Noble, Inc., 1957), p. 149.

7. This curve is generally thought of as a normal curve. Here it is shown in its cumulative form.

8. For further discussion, see Gerald Zaltman, *Marketing: Contributions from the Behavioral Sciences* (New York: Harcourt, Brace and World, Inc., 1965), pp. 45–56 and 23–37; Everett M. Rogers, *The Diffusion of Innovations* (New York: Free Press, 1962); Kenneth Uhl, Roman Andrus, and Lance Poulsen, "How Are Laggards Different? An Empirical Inquiry," *Journal of Marketing Research,* February 1970, pp. 51–54. See also C. W. King and J. O. Summers, "Overlap of Opinion Leadership Across Consumer Product Categories," *Journal of Marketing Research,* February 1970, pp. 43–50; Joseph R. Mancuso, "Why Not Create Opinion Leaders for New Product Introductions?" *Journal of Marketing,* July 1969, pp. 20–25; Thomas S. Robertson, "The Process of Innovation and the Diffusion of Innovation," *Journal of Marketing,* January 1967, pp. 14–19; and Frank M. Bass, "The Relationship between Diffusion Rates, Experience Curves, and Demand Elasticities for Consumer Durable Technological Innovations," Krannert Graduate School of Management, Purdue University, West Lafayette, Indiana, Paper no. 660 (March 1978), pp. 1–25.

9. *Sales & Marketing Management,* February 27, 1978.

10. *Business Week,* December 11, 1978, p. 145.

11. Edwin H. Lewis, "Sales Promotion Decisions," *Business News Notes* (Minneapolis: School of Business Administration, University of Minnesota, November, 1954).

CHAPTER 14

1. Michael F. Lennon, "Don't Limit Customer's Horizon," *Printers' Ink,* June 30, 1961, p. 43.

2. "Making Sure the Goods Get on the Shelves," *Business Week,* July 22, 1972, pp. 46–47.

3. Adapted from Harold C. Cash and W. J. E. Crissy, "Ways of Looking at Selling," *Psychology of Selling,* 1957.

4. Ibid.

5. Ibid.

6. For more discussion, see F. E. Webster, Jr., "Rationalizing Salesmen's Compensation Plans," *Journal of Marketing,* January 1966, pp. 55–58; R. L. Day and P. D. Bennett, "Should Salesmen's Compensation Be Geared to Profits?" *Journal of Marketing,* October 1962, pp. 6–9; and John P. Steinbrink, "How To Pay Your Sales Force," *Harvard Business Review,* July–August 1978, pp. 111–22.

CHAPTER 15

1. *Advertising Age,* July 18, 1977, p. 31.

2. Exact data on this industry are elusive, but see "Showing Ad Agencies How to Grow," *Business Week,* June 1, 1974, pp. 50–56; and "How Many People Work in Advertising?" *Printers' Ink,* December 6, 1957, p. 88.

3. *Advertising Age,* September 18, 1967, pp. 77–78.

4. "A Pained Bayer Cries 'Foul,'" *Business Week,* July 25, 1977, p. 142.

5. "Product Pitches That Knock the Competition Create New Troubles," *The Wall Street Journal,* April 16, 1976, p. 1; "The FTC Broadens Its Attack on Ads," *Business Week,* June 20, 1977, pp. 27–28; William L. Wilkie and Paul W. Farris, "Comparison Advertising: Problems and Potential," *Journal of Marketing,* October 1975, pp. 7–15; and V. K. Prasad, "Communications Effectiveness of Comparative Advertising: A Laboratory Analysis," *Journal of Marketing Research,* May 1976, pp. 128–37.

6. "Will Defense-Contractor Ads Run Into New Snags in Washington?" *Printers' Ink,* January 4, 1963, p. 7; and Nugent Wedding, "Advertising, Mass Communication, and Tax Deduction," *Journal of Marketing,* April 1960, pp. 17–22.

7. "Why Jockey Switched Its Ads from TV to Print," *Business Week,* July 26, 1976, pp. 140–42.

8. "Mailing-List Brokers Sell More Than Names to Their Many Clients," *The Wall Street Journal,* February 19, 1974, p. 1.

9. "How Agencies Should Get Paid: Trend Is to 'Managed' Systems," *Advertising Age,* January 17, 1977, pp. 41–42.

10. Scott Ward, "Compromise in Commercials for Children," *Harvard Business Review,* November–December 1978, pp. 128–36; Jerry C. Olson and Philip A. Dover, "Cognitive Effects of Deceptive Advertising," *Journal of Marketing Research,* February 1978, pp. 29–38; Marvin E. Goldberg, Gerald J. Gorn, and Wendy Gibson, "TV Messages for Snack and Breakfast Foods: Do They Influence Children's Preferences?" *Consumer Research,* September 1978, pp. 73–81; Marvin E. Goldberg and Gerald J. Gorn, "Some Unintended Consequences of TV Advertising to Children," *Consumer Research,* June 1978, pp. 22–29; and Richard L. Gordon, "FTC Judge Gives Anacin $24,000,000 Headache," *Advertising Age,* September 18, 1978, pp. 1, 122.

CHAPTER 16

1. W. Warren Haynes, *Pricing Decisions in Small Business* (Lexington: University of Kentucky Press, 1962); and Alan Reynolds, "A Kind Word for 'Cream Skimming,'" *Harvard Business Review,* November–December 1974, pp. 113–20.

2. For more discussion of the behavior of satisficers, see Herbert A. Simon, *Administrative Behavior,* 2d ed., (New York: Macmillan Co., 1961).

3. "Squeeze on Product Lines," *Business Week,* January 5, 1974, p. 50; and "Pricing Strategy in an Inflation Economy," *Business Week,* April 6, 1974, pp. 43–49.

4. Joseph W. McGuire, John S. Y. Chiu, and Alvar O. Elving, "Executive Incomes, Sales and Profits," *American Economic Review,* September 1962, pp. 753–61; "For the Chief, Sales Sets the Pay," *Business Week,* September 30, 1967, p. 174; and Alfred Rappaport, "Executive Incentives vs. Corporate Growth," *Harvard Business Review,* July–August 1978, pp. 81–88.

5. For an interesting discussion of the many variations from a one-price system in retailing, see Stanley C. Hollander, "The One-Price System—Fact or Fiction?" *Journal of Retailing,* Fall 1955, pp. 127–44.

6. See, for example, "The Airline that Thrives on Discounting," *Business Week,* July 24, 1971, pp. 68–70. See also Zarrel V. Lambert, "Product Perception: An Important Variable in Pricing Strategy," *Journal of Marketing,* October 1970, pp. 68–76; and "Price and Choice Behavior," *Journal of Marketing Research,* February 1972, pp. 35–40.

7. For more discussion on price dealing, see Charles L. Hinkle, "The Strategy of Price Deals," *Harvard Business Review,* July–August 1965, pp. 75–85; B. C. Cotton and Emerson M. Babb, "Consumer Response to Promotional Deals," *Journal of Marketing,* July 1978, pp. 109–13; Robert Blattberg, Thomas Buesing, Peter Peacock and Subrata Sen, "Identifying the Deal Prone Segment," *Journal of Marketing Research,* August 1978, pp. 369–77; and Joe A. Dodson, Alice M. Tybout, and Brian Sternthal, "Impact of Deals and Deal Retraction on Brand Switching," *Journal of Marketing Research,* February 1978, pp. 72–81.

8. For discussion concerning European countries, see *Market Power and the Law* (Washington, D.C.: Organization for Economic Cooperation and Development Publication Center, 1970), 206 pp.

9. Morris L. Mayer, Joseph B. Mason, and E. A. Orbeck, "The Borden Case—A Legal Basis for Private Brand Price Discrimination," *MSU Business Topics,* Winter 1970, pp. 56–63; and Jacky Knopp, Jr., "What Are Commodities of Like Grade and Quality?" *Journal of Marketing,* July 1963, p. 63.

10. T. F. Schutte, V. J. Cook, Jr., and R. Hemsley, "What Management Can Learn from the Borden Case," *Business Horizons,* Winter 1966, pp. 23–30.

11. Peter G. Peterson, "Quantity Discounts in the Morton Salt Case," *Journal of Business of the University of Chicago,* April 1952, pp. 109–20; "Is the Cost Defense Workable," *Journal of Marketing,* January 1965, pp. 37–42; and B. J. Linder and Allan H. Savage, "Price Discrimination and Cost Defense—Change Ahead?" *MSU Business Topics,* Summer 1971, pp. 21–26.

12. "Guides against Deceptive Pricing," Federal Trade Commission, October 10, 1958, and January 8, 1964.

13. *FTC* v. *Mary Carter Paint Co.* 382 U.S. 46, 1965.

14. A. Haring and W. O. Yoder, eds., *Trading Stamps Practice and Pricing Policy,* Indiana Business Report no. 27, Bureau of Business Research (Bloomington: Indiana University, 1958), p. 301.

15. "Buyer's Choice: Stamps or Savings," *Business Week,* February 7, 1970, p. 106; and "Sharp Drop in Gas-Sta-

CHAPTER 16

tion Business Brings Trading-Stamp Industry More Profit Woes," *The Wall Street Journal,* March 1, 1974, p. 26.

16. "Grocery Coupons Are Seen Threatened by Growth of Fraudulent Redemptions," *The Wall Street Journal,* April 12, 1976, p. 26.

CHAPTER 17

1. Super-Valu Study (New York: Progressive Grocer, 1957), p. S-4–7.

2. John J. Wheatley and John S. Y. Chiu, "The Effects of Price, Store Image, and Product and Respondent Characteristics on Perceptions of Quality," *Journal of Marketing Research,* May 1977, pp. 181–86; Arthur G. Bedeian, "Consumer Perception of Price as an Indicator of Product Quality," *MSU Business Topics,* Summer 1971, pp. 59–65; David M. Gardner, "An Experimental Investigation of the Price/Quality Relationship," *Journal of Retailing,* Fall 1970, pp. 25–41; Kent B. Monroe, "Buyers' Subjective Perceptions of Price," *Journal of Marketing Research,* February 1973, pp. 70–80; and N. D. French, J. J. Williams, and W. A. Chance, "A Shopping Experiment on Price-Quality Relationships," *Journal of Retailing,* Fall 1972, pp. 3–16.

3. Dik W. Twedt, "Does the '9 Fixation in Retailing Really Promote Sales?" *Journal of Marketing,* October 1965, pp. 54–55; and H. J. Rudolph, "Pricing and Today's Market," *Printers' Ink,* May 29, 1954, pp. 22–24.

4. E. R. Hawkins, "Price Policies and Theory," *Journal of Marketing,* January 1954, p. 236; see also B. P. Shapiro, "The Psychology of Pricing," *Harvard Business Review,* July–August 1968, pp. 14–25; C. Davis Fogg and Kent H. Kohnken, "Price-Cost Planning," *Journal of Marketing,* April 1978, pp. 97–106; and Benson P. Shapiro and Barbara B. Jackson, "Industrial Pricing To Meet Consumer Needs," *Harvard Business Review,* November–December 1978, pp. 119–27.

5. Stephen Paranka, "Competitive Bidding Strategy," *Business Horizons,* June 1971, pp. 39–43; Wayne J. Morse, "Probabilistic Bidding Models; A Synthesis," *Business Horizons,* April 1975, pp. 67–74; and Kenneth Simmonds and Stuart Slatter, "The Number of Estimators: A Critical Decision for Marketing Under Competitive Bidding," *Journal of Marketing Research,* May 1978, pp. 203–13.

CHAPTER 18

1. "How Coke Runs a Foreign Empire," *Business Week,* August 25, 1973, pp. 40–43.

2. "Multinational Companies," *Business Week,* April 20, 1963, pp. 62–86; "Multinational Firms Now Dominate Much of World's Production," *The Wall Street Journal,* April 18, 1973, p. 1; "ITT Europe Rings Up Profits; A Low Profile Keeps Troubles Minor," *The Wall Street Journal,* January 9, 1974, p. 1.

3. "Why So Many French Are Tackling the U.S.," *Business Week,* July 4, 1977, p. 30; and "An Appliance Maker Scouts for U.S. Sites," *Business Week,* May 30, 1977, pp. 38–39.

4. Franklin R. Root, "Public Policy Expectations of Multinational Managers," *MSU Business Topics,* Autumn 1973, pp. 5–12; "Domesticating the Multinationals," *Business Week,* May 26, 1963, p. 15; "Multinationals: The Public Gives Them Low Marks," *Business Week,* June 9, 1973, pp. 42–44; "The Unions Move against Multinationals," *Business Week,* July 24, 1971, pp. 48–52; John Kenneth Galbraith, "The Defense of the Multinational Company," *Harvard Business Review,* March–April 1978, pp. 83–93; Lawrence G. Franko, "Multinationals: The End of U.S. Dominance," *Harvard Business Review,* November–December 1978, pp. 93–101; and Frank Meissner, "Rise of Third World 'Demands Marketing Be Stood on Its Head,'" *Marketing News,* October 6, 1978, pp. 1, 16.

5. Adapted from Warren J. Keegan, "Multinational Product Planning: Strategic Alternatives," *Journal of Marketing,* January 1969, p. 59.

6. "McDonald's Brings Hamburger (with Beer) to Hamburg," *Advertising Age,* May 30, 1977, p. 61.

7. Warren J. Keegan, "A Conceptual Framework for Multinational Marketing," *Columbia Journal of World Business,* November 1972, pp. 67–78.

8. This discussion is based on William Copulsky's "Forecasting Sales in Underdeveloped Countries," *Journal of Marketing,* July 1959, pp. 36–37. Another set of stages is interesting although less marketing oriented. See W. W. Rostow, *The Stages of Economic Growth—A Non-Communist Manifesto* (New York: Cambridge University Press, 1960).

9. *The Statistical Abstract of the United States* and the U.S. Department of Commerce Bureau of International Commerce would be good places to start locating current data. In its publication, *International Commerce,* the Department of Commerce issues a semiannual checklist of material it feels will be helpful to business people interested in the world market. The *Statistical Year Book* of the Statistical Office of the United Nations is also a good source of basic data.

10. Drawn by Joe F. McCarthy.

11. Adapted from Norton Ginsburg, *Atlas of Economic Development* by permission of the University of Chicago Press. Copyright 1961 by the University of Chicago.

12. Donald G. Halper, "The Environment for Marketing in Peru," *Journal of Marketing,* July 1966, pp. 42–46.

13. *State Journal,* Lansing, Michigan, February 10, 1970, p. D-7.

14. *The Wall Street Journal,* August 8, 1968, p. 1.

15. Norton Ginsburg, *Atlas of Economic Development* (Chicago: University of Chicago Press, 1961); and *Statistical Abstract of the U.S.,* 1976, pp. 874–75.

16. Edward Marcus, "Selling the Tropical African Market," *Journal of Marketing,* July 1961, p. 30.

17. Robert L. Brown, "The Common Market: What Its New Consumer Is Like," *Printers' Ink,* May 31, 1963, pp. 23–25.

CHAPTER 19

1. James U. McNeal, "Consumer Satisfaction: The Measure of Marketing Effectiveness," *MSU Business Topics,* Summer 1969, p. 33.

2. For an extensive discussion of the problems and mechanics of measuring the efficiency of marketing, see Stanley C. Hollander, "Measuring the Cost and Value of Marketing," *Business Topics,* Summer 1961, pp. 17–26; and Reavis Cox, *Distribution in a High-Level Economy* (Englewood Cliffs, N.J.: Prentice-Hall, Inc., 1965). See also Robert L. Steiner, "Marketing Productivity in Consumer Goods Industries—A Vertical Perspective," *Journal of Marketing,* January 1978, pp. 60–70.

3. "New Harris Consumer Study Causes Few Shocks in Adland," *Advertising Age,* May 30, 1977, p. 2.

4. B. Charles Ames, "Trappings vs. Substance in Industrial Marketing, *Harvard Business Review,* July–August 1970, pp. 93–102; and Merchant's Service, National Cash Register Co., *Establishing a Retail Store,* p. 3.

5. F. M. Nicosia, *Consumer Decision Processes* (Englewood Cliffs, N.J.: Prentice-Hall, Inc., 1966), p. 39.

6. E. H. Chamberlin, "Product Heterogeneity and Public Policy," *American Economic Review,* May 1950, p. 86.

7. Arnold J. Toynbee, *America and the World Revolution* (New York: Oxford University Press, 1966), pp. 144–45; see also John Kenneth Galbraith, *Economics and the Public Purpose* (Boston: Houghton Mifflin Co., 1973), pp. 144–45.

8. Russel J. Tomsen, "Take It Away," *Newsweek,* October 7, 1974, p. 21.

9. Robert F. Hartley, *Marketing Mistakes* (Columbus, Ohio: Grid, Inc., 1976).

10. Jack L. Engledow, "Was Consumer Satisfaction a Pig in a Poke?" *MSU Business Topics,* April 1977, p. 92.

11. "Intellectuals Should Re-Examine the Marketplace; It Supports Them, Helps Keep Them Free; Prof. Stigler," *Advertising Age,* January 28, 1963; see also E. T. Grether, "Galbraith versus the Market: A Review Article," *Journal of Marketing,* January 1968, pp. 9–14; and E. T. Grether, "Marketing and Public Policy: A Contemporary View," *Journal of Marketing,* July 1974, pp. 2–7.

12. Frederick Webster, *Social Aspects of Marketing* (Englewood Cliffs, N.J.: Prentice-Hall, Inc., 1974), p. 32.

13. See Richard P. Lundy, "How Many Service Stations Are 'Too Many'?" in Reavis Cox and Wroe Alderson, eds., *Theory in Marketing* (Homewood, Ill.; Richard D. Irwin, Inc., 1950), pp. 321–33; and Steven E. Goodman, "Quality of Life: The Role of Business," *Business Horizons,* June 1978, pp. 36–37.

14. Paul M. Mazur, "Does Distribution Cost Enough?" *Fortune,* November 1947.

15. John E. Smallwood, "The Product Life Cycle: A Key to Strategic Marketing Planning," *MSU Business Topics,* Winter 1973, pp. 29–35.

16. Irving Kristol, "The Corporation and the Dinosaur," *The Wall Street Journal,* February 14, 1974.

17. R. E. Wilkes and J. B. Wilcox, "Recent FTC Actions: Implications for the Advertising Strategist," *Journal of Marketing,* January 1974, pp. 55–61.

18. James T. Roth and Lissa Benson, "Intelligent Consumption: An Attractive Alternative to the Marketing Concept," *MSU Business Topics,* Winter 1974, pp. 30–34; and Robert E. Wilkes, "Fraudulent Behavior by Consumers," *Journal of Marketing,* October 1978, pp. 67–75.

19. "Dictating PRODUCT Safety," *Business Week,* May 18, 1974, pp. 56–62; Y. Hugh Furuhashi and E. Jerome McCarthy, *Social Issues of Marketing in the American Economy* (Columbus, Ohio: Grid, Inc., 1971); James Owens, "Business Ethics: Age-Old Ideal, Now Real," *Business Horizons,* February 1978, pp. 26–30; Steven E. Goodman, "Quality of Life: The Role of Business," *Business Horizons,* June 1978, pp. 36–37; William F. Dwyer, "Smoking: Free Choice," *Business Horizons,* June 1978, pp. 52–56; Stanley J. Shapiro, "Marketing in a Conserver Society," *Business Horizons,* April 1978, pp. 3–13; and Johan Arndt, "How Broad Should the Marketing Concept Be?" *Journal of Marketing,* January 1978, pp. 101–103.

PHOTO CREDITS

AUTHOR INDEX

A

Alderson, W., 461, 471
Alexis, M., 463, 465
Alter, S. L., 463
Ames, B. C., 471
Anderson, P. F., 465
Andrus, R., 468
Appel, D. L., 468
Arbeit, S., 465
Arndt, J., 471
Arnof, E. L., 467
Assael, H., 466

B

Babb, E. M., 469
Bacon, F., 467
Baker, R. C., 466
Bartels, R., 461
Bartos, R., 463
Bass, F. M., 468
Bass, S. J., 468
Bates, A. D., 468
Bedeian, A. G., 470
Bellenger, D. N., 463
Bennett, P. D., 468
Benson, L., 471
Bernhardt, K. L., 466
Blackwell, R. D., 464
Blankenship, A. B., 468
Blattberg, R. C., 465, 469

Bliss, P., 465
Bowersox, D. J., 467
Boyd, H. W., Jr., 463
Brien, R. H., 463
Britt, S. H., 466
Brogowicz, A. A., 463
Brown, H. E., 466
Brown, S. W., 465
Bucklin, L. P., 465, 467
Buell, V. P., 467
Buesing, T., 469
Burley, J. R., 467
Busch, P., 462
Buzzell, R. D., 467

C

Calantone, R. J., 465
Carman, J. A., 464
Carmone, F. J., 465
Chambers, T. E., 462
Chance, W. A., 470
Chase, R. B., 465
Chestnut, R. W., 466
Chiu, J. S. Y., 469–70
Churchill, G. A., 464
Clewett, R. M., 461
Cohen, A. I., 466
Cook, E. J., 462
Cook, V. J., 466, 469
Cooper, P. D., 468

Copulsky, W., 470
Corey, E. R., 464
Cort, S. G., 467
Cotton, B. C., 469
Cox, E. P., III, 464
Cox, K., 461
Cox, R., 461, 471
Crask, M. R., 463
Crawford, C. M., 467
Crissy, W. J. E., 468
Cundiff, E. W., 465
Cunningham, I. C. M., 464

D

Dalrymple, D. J., 465, 467
D'Amato, N., 466
Darden, W. R., 465
Davidson, J. H., 467
Davidson, W. R., 468
Davis, H. L., 464
Day, R. L., 468
Dichter, E., 466
Dodson, J. A., 469
Dommermuth, W. P., 465, 467
Douglas, S. P., 464
Dover, P. A., 469
Drucker, P. F., 461, 462
Dunne, P. M., 466
Dwyer, W. F., 471

SUBJECT INDEX

*This book has been set VideoComp in 10 and
9 point Spectra Light, leaded 2 points. Chapter
numbers are 48 point Memphis Bold and chapter
titles are 36 and 42 point Memphis Bold. The
size of the text area is 27 by 47½ picas.*

Customer franchise A loyal following of customers for a product or service.

Customer service level The percent of customers served within some time period.

Dealer brands Brands created by middlemen, sometimes called "private brands."

Decoding The receiver translating the message.

Demand-backward pricing Starts with an acceptable final consumer price and works backward to what a producer can charge.

Demand curve A "picture" of the relationship between price and quantity in a market—assuming all other things stay the same—for a time period.

Department stores Larger stores, organized into departments.

Description buying Buying from a written (or verbal) description of a product.

Direct competitive advertising Competitive advertising which aims for immediate buying action.

Direct-mail advertising Selling directly to the customer via his mailbox.

Discount houses Offer "hard goods" at substantial price cuts—to customers who go to the discounter's low-rent store, pay cash, and take care of any service or repair problems themselves.

Discounts Reductions from list price given by a seller to a buyer who either gives up some marketing function or provides the function himself.

Discrepancy of assortment The difference between what the typical producer makes and the assortment wanted by final consumers or users.

Discrepancy of quantity The difference between the quantity of goods it is economical for a producer to make and the quantity normally wanted by final users or consumers.

Dissonance Tension growing out of uncertainty about the rightness of a decision.

Distribution center A warehouse designed to speed the flow of goods and avoid unnecessary storage.

Diversification Moving into totally different lines of business.

Door-to-door selling Going directly to the consumer's home.

Drive A strong stimulus which causes tension which the individual tries to reduce by finding ways of satisfying this drive.

Drop-shippers Own the goods they sell, but do not handle, stock, or deliver them.

Dual distribution A manufacturer using several competing channels to reach the same target market.

Early adopters Adopters who are relatively high in social status, and probably opinion leaders—see adoption curve.

Early majority Adopters who are above average in social status—see adoption curve.

Economic men People who logically weigh choices in terms of cost and value received—to obtain the greatest satisfaction from spending their time, energy, and money.

Economic needs Needs which are concerned with making the best use of a customer's limited resources—as the customer sees it.

Economies of size As a company produces more of a particular product, the cost for each unit goes down.

Elastic demand If prices were dropped, the quantity demanded would "stretch" enough to increase total revenue.

Elastic supply The quantity offered by suppliers would "stretch" a lot if the price is raised.

Emergency goods Consumer convenience goods which are purchased when the need is great.

Glossary

(continued)

Encoding The source deciding what it wants to say and translating it into words that will have the same meaning to the receiver.

Equilibrium point Where the quantity and the price that sellers are willing to offer are equal to the quantity and price that buyers are willing to accept.

Exclusive distribution Selling through only one middleman in each geographic area.

Expense items Short-lived goods and services which are charged off as they are used—usually in the year of purchase.

Expenses Costs subtracted from the gross margin to get the net profit on an operating statement.

Experimental method Research method using experiments to test hypotheses.

Exporting Selling some of what the firm is producing to foreign markets.

Export agents Manufacturers' agents.

Export brokers Brokers.

Export commission houses Brokers.

Extensive problem-solving Involved when a need is completely new to a person—and much effort is taken to understand the need and how to satisfy it.

Factor method A sales forecasting method which tries to find a relation between a company's sales and some other factor(s).

Family brand A brand name which is used for several products.

Farm products Raw materials grown by farmers.

Federal Trade Commission (FTC) The federal government agency which polices antimonopoly laws.

Fertility rate Number of children per woman.

Financing function Provides the necessary cash and credit to manufacture, transport, store, promote, sell, and buy products.

Fishy-back service Ships combined with trucks (like rail piggy back).

Flexible-price policy The same products and quantities are offered to different customers at different prices.

F.O.B. "Free on board" some vehicle at some place.

Food broker Manufacturers' agent who specializes in grocery distribution.

Form utility Utility provided when a manufacturer makes something out of other materials.

Franchise operations A franchiser develops a marketing strategy and the franchise holders carry out the strategy in their own units.

Freight-absorption pricing Absorbing freight cost so that a firm's delivered price meets the nearest competitor's price.

Full-line pricing Setting a price for a whole line of products.

Functional discount A list price reduction given to channel members for the job they are going to do.

General-line (or single-line) wholesalers Merchant wholesalers who carry a narrower line of merchandise than general merchandise wholesalers.

General merchandise warehouses Store almost any kind of manufactured goods.

General merchandise wholesalers Merchant wholesalers who carry a wide variety of nonperishable items.

General store Sells anything the local consumers will buy in enough volume to justify carrying it.

Grading and standardization functions The sorting of products according to size and quality.

Gross margin (Gross profit) is the money left to cover the cost of selling the goods and managing the business—and hopefully, leaving a profit—after subtracting the cost of goods sold from net sales.

Gross national product (GNP) The total market value of goods and services produced in a year.

Gross sales The total amount a company charges to all customers during some time period.

Heterogeneous shopping goods Shopping goods that the customer sees as different and wants to inspect for quality and suitability.

Homogeneous shopping goods Shopping goods that the customer sees as basically the same and wants at the lowest price.

Hypotheses Educated guesses about the relationships between things or what will happen in the future.

Ideal market exposure Should make a product widely enough available to satisfy target customers' needs—but not exceed them.

Import agents Manufacturers' agents.

Import brokers Brokers.

Import commission houses Brokers.

Impulse goods Consumer convenience goods which are bought as unplanned purchases but customers don't shop for them at all.

Indirect competitive advertising Competitive advertising which points out product advantages—to affect future buying decisions.

Industrial goods Products meant for use in producing other products.

Inelastic demand Means that if a product's price were decreased, the quantity demanded would not "stretch" enough—that is, it is not elastic enough—to increase total revenue.

Inelastic supply The quantity supplied does not stretch much (if at all) if the price is raised.

Innovators First to adopt, young and high in social and economic status—see adoption curve.

Inspection buying Looking at every item.

Installations Important, long-lasting capital goods.

Institutional advertising Tries to develop goodwill for a company or even an industry instead of a specific product.

Intensive distribution Selling a product through any responsible and suitable wholesaler or retailer who will stock and/or sell the product.

Intermediate customers Any buyers between the owners of basic raw materials and final consumers.

Introductory price dealing Temporary price cuts to speed new products into a market.

Job description Shows what a salesperson is expected to do

Joint venturing A domestic firm entering a partnership with a foreign firm.

Jury of executive opinion A sales forecasting method which combines the opinions of experienced executives.

Laggards or nonadopters Lowest social status and income—see adoption curve.

Late majority Adopters who are below average in social status and income—see adoption curve.

Law of diminishing demand If the price of a product is raised, a smaller quantity will be demanded and if the price of a product is lowered, a greater quantity will be demanded.

Leader pricing Setting some very low prices—real bargains—to get customers into retail stores.

Licensing Selling the right to use some process, trademark, patent, or other right, for a fee or royalty.

Limited-function wholesalers Merchant wholesalers who provide only some wholesaling functions.

Limited-line stores Retail stores which specialize in certain lines rather than the broad assortment carried by general stores.

Limited problem solving Involves some effort to understand a person's own need and how best to satisfy it.

Lower-lower class Includes unskilled laborers and people in nonrespectable occupations.

Lower-middle class The white-collar workers—small trades people, office workers, teachers, technicians, and most sales people.

Lower-upper class Socially prominent new rich.

Macro-marketing A social process which directs an economy's flow of goods and services from producers to consumers in a way which effectively matches supply and demand and accomplishes the objectives of society.

Mail-order retailing Allows customers to "shop by mail"—using the mail-order retailers' catalogs to "see" their offerings.

Mail-order wholesaler Limited-function merchant wholesaler who sells out of a catalog which may be distributed widely to industrial customers or retailers.

Management contracting The seller provides only management skills while the production facilities are owned by others.

Manufacturer brands Brands which are created by manufacturers, sometimes called "national brands."

Manufacturers' agent An agent middleman who sells similar products for several noncompeting manufacturers—for a commission on what is actually sold.

Manufacturers' sales branches Separate wholesaling businesses which manufacturers set up away from their factories.

Glossary

(continued)

Markdown   A retail price reduction because the customers will not buy some item at the originally marked-up price.

Markdown ratio   A tool used by many retailers to measure the efficiency of various departments and their whole business.

Market   A group of sellers and buyers bargaining the terms of exchange for goods and services.

Market development   Trying to increase a firm's sales by selling its present products in new markets.

Market-directed economic system   One in which the individual decisions of the many producers and consumers make the macro-level decisions for the whole economy.

Market growth stage (of product life cycle)   When industry sales start growing fast.

Market information function   Involves the collection, analysis, and distribution of information needed to plan, carry out, and control marketing activities.

Market introduction stage (of product life cycle)   When a new idea is introduced to a market.

Market maturity stage (of product life cycle)   When industry sales level out and competition gets tougher.

Market penetration   Trying to increase a firm's sales of its present products in its present markets.

Marketing company era   A time when—in addition to short-run marketing planning—the total company effort is guided by the marketing concept.

Marketing concept   A firm aims all its efforts on satisfying its customers—at a profit.

Marketing department era   A time when there is heavy emphasis on short-run policy planning—to tie together the firm's activities.

Marketing information system (MIS)   An organized way of gathering and analyzing data to obtain information to help marketing managers make decisions.

Marketing manager's job   Consists of three basic tasks: planning, implementing, and control.

Marketing mix   The controllable variables which the company puts together to satisfy a target market.

Marketing orientation   The viewpoint that tries to carry out the marketing concept.

Marketing program   A blend of all of a firm's strategic plans into one "big" plan.

Marketing research (department)   Gathers and analyzes data to help marketing managers make decisions.

Marketing strategy   A "big picture" of what a firm will do in some market.

Markup   The dollar amount added to the costs of goods to get the selling price (usually expressed as a percentage of selling price).

Mass marketing   The typical production-oriented approach which focuses on "everyone."

Mass merchandisers   Large self-service stores with many departments which tend to emphasize "soft goods" but still follow the discount house's emphasis on lower margins to get faster turnover.

Mass merchandising concept   Retailers should offer low prices to get faster turnover and greater sales—by appealing to larger markets.

Mass selling   Communicating with large numbers of customers at the same time.

Merchant wholesalers   Own (take title to) the goods they sell.

Message channel   The carrier of the message.

Micro-marketing   The performance of activities which seek to accomplish a firm's objectives by anticipating customer needs and directing a flow of need-satisfying goods and services from producer to customer.

Middleman   Someone who specializes in trade rather than production.

Missionary sales people   Employed by a manufacturer to work with its middlemen and their customers to develop goodwill and stimulate demand, help the middlemen train their sales people, and often take orders for delivery by the middlemen.

Modified rebuy   The in-between buying process where some review of the buying situation is done—though not as much as in new-task buying.

Monopolistic competition   A market situation which develops when a market has different (heterogeneous) products—in the eyes of some customers—but sellers feel they do have some competition.

Multinational corporations Have a direct investment in several countries and run their businesses depending on the choices available anywhere in the world.

Multiple buying influences The buyer shares the purchasing decision with several managers—perhaps even top management.

Natural products Raw materials which occur in nature.

Needs The basic forces which motivate an individual to do something.

Need-satisfaction approach A sales presentation which involves developing a good understanding of the prospective customer's needs before trying to close the sale.

Negotiated contract buying Writing an adaptable contract that allows for changing the purchase requirements.

Neighborhood shopping center A planned shopping center made up of several convenience stores.

Net Payment for the face value of the invoice is due immediately.

Net profit What the company has earned from its operations during a particular time period (i.e., sales minus costs).

Net sales The sales dollars the company will receive for a particular time period.

New product A product that is new in any way for the company concerned.

New-task buying The buying process which occurs when a firm has a new need and the buyer wants a lot of information.

New unsought goods Consumer goods offering really new ideas that potential customers don't know about yet.

Noise Any factor which reduces the effectiveness of the communication process.

Noncumulative quantity discounts Quantity discounts which apply to individual orders only.

Nonprice competition Aggressive action on one or more of the Ps other than Price.

Nonrecognition (brand) A brand is not recognized by customers at all—even though middlemen may use the brand name for identification and inventory control.

Observation method A research method which involves observing potential customers' behavior.

Odd-even pricing Setting prices which end in certain numbers.

Oligopoly A market situation which develops when a market has essentially homogeneous products, relatively few sellers (or a few large firms and many smaller ones who follow the lead of the larger ones) and fairly inelastic industry demand curves.

One-price policy Offering the same price to all customers who buy goods under basically the same conditions and in the same quantities.

1/10 net 30 A 1 percent discount off the face value of the invoice is allowed if the invoice is paid within 10 days.

Open to buy The retail buyer has budgeted funds which he can spend in the current time period.

Operating ratio The ratio of an item on the operating statement to net sales.

Operating statement A summary of the financial results of the operation of a company for a specified time period.

Opinion leaders People who influence others.

Order getters Sales people concerned with developing new business.

Order getting Aggressively seeking out possible buyers with a well-organized sales presentation designed to sell a product, service, or idea.

Order takers Sales people concerned with selling to the regular or typical customers.

Order taking The routine completion of sales made regularly to the target customers.

Penetration pricing policy Trying to sell the whole market at one low price.

Personal needs Concerned with the need of an individual to gain personal satisfaction—unrelated to what others think or do.

Personal selling Direct face-to-face relationships between sellers and potential customers.

Phony list prices Prices that customers can be shown to suggest that the price they are to pay has been discounted from "list."

Glossary

(continued)

Physical distribution (PD)   Transporting and storing of physical goods within individual firms and along channel systems.

Physiological needs   Concerned with satisfying hunger, thirst, rest, sex, and other biological needs.

Piggy-back service   Puts truck trailers on rail cars to provide speed and flexibility at lower cost.

Pioneering advertising   Product advertising which tries to develop primary demand.

Place   Concerned with the selection and use of marketing specialists to provide target customers with time, place, and possession utilities.

Place utility   Having the product available where the customer wants it.

Planned economic system   One in which government planners decide what and how much is to be produced and distributed by whom, when, and to whom.

Planned shopping center   A group of stores planned as a unit to satisfy some market needs.

Possession utility   Completing a transaction and gaining possession so that one has the right to use the product.

Prestige pricing   Setting a rather high price to suggest high quality or high status.

Price discrimination   Selling the same goods to different buyers at different prices.

Price fixing   Competitors getting together to set higher than competitive prices.

Price-lining   Setting a few price levels for given classes of goods and then marking all items at these prices.

Primary data   Information which is gathered specifically to solve a current problem.

Primary demand   Demand for a product type rather than a specific brand.

Private warehouses   Storing facilities owned by companies for their own use.

Producers' cooperatives   Operate almost as full service wholesalers—with the "profits" going to the cooperatives' customer-members—but some of the wholesaling functions may be cut out because the producers don't want them.

Product   A good and/or service.

Product advertising   Advertising which tries to sell a product.

Product development   Offering new or improved products for present markets.

Product life cycle   The stages a new product goes through from beginning to end.

Product managers   Manage specific products.

Product positioning   A research tool which tries to show where proposed and/or present brands are located in a market.

Production era   A time when few manufactured products are available and the company's focus is on production.

Production-orientation   Making products which are easy to produce, and then trying to sell them.

Profit maximization objective   The firm seeks to get as much profit as it can.

Promotion   Communicating information between seller and buyer—to change attitudes and behavior.

Promotion objectives   Inform, persuade, and/or remind target customers about the company and its marketing mix.

Prospecting   Sales people following down all the "leads" in the target market.

Psychological pricing   Setting prices which have special appeal to target customers.

Public warehouses   Independent storing facilities that provide all the services that could be obtained in a company's own warehouse.

Publicity   Any *unpaid* form of nonpersonal presentation of ideas, goods, or services.

Pulling   Getting consumers to ask middlemen for the product.

Purchase discount   A reduction of the original invoice amount for some business reason.

Purchasing agents   Buying specialists for manufacturers.

Pure competition   A market situation which develops when a market has homogeneous products, many buyers and sellers who have full knowledge of the market, and ease of entry for buyers and sellers.

Push money (or prize money) allowances   Money given to retailers by manufacturers or wholesalers to pass on to the retailers' sales clerks for aggressively selling particular items.

Pushing Using normal promotion effort—personal selling and advertising—to help sell the whole marketing mix to possible channel members.

Quantity discounts Discounts offered to encourage customers to buy in larger quantities.

Quotas Set the specific quantities of goods which can move in or out of a country.

Rack-jobber A limited-function merchant wholesaler who specializes in nonfood items sold through grocery stores and supermarkets, often displaying them on his own wire racks.

Raw materials Basic goods—such as logs or iron ore—that are processed only as much as needed to move them to the next step in the production process.

Receiver A potential customer (and target of a communication effort).

Reciprocity Trading sales for sales.

Reference group The people to whom the individual looks when forming attitudes about a particular topic.

Regional shopping center A planned shopping center which includes one or two large department stores and as many as 200 small stores.

Regrouping activities Marketing activities which adjust the quantities and/or assortments of goods handled at each level in a channel of distribution.

Regularly unsought goods Consumer goods that may stay unsought but not unbought forever.

Reinforcement The satisfaction which follows a satisfying response, reducing a drive tension.

Rejection (brand) Potential customes won't buy a brand—unless its current image is changed.

Reminder advertising Advertising which tries to keep the product's name before the public.

Requisition A request to buy something.

Resident buyers Independent buying agents who work in central markets for several retailer or wholesaler customers in outlying markets.

Response An effort to satisfy a drive.

Retailing Activities involved in the sale of goods and/or services to final consumers for their own use.

Return A customer sends back purchased goods.

Risk-taking function Marketing function concerned with bearing the uncertainties that are a part of the marketing process.

Robinson-Patman Act Makes any price discrimination illegal.

Routinized response behavior Buying which involves mechanically selecting a particular way of satisfying a need whenever it occurs.

Safety needs Concerned with protection and physical well-being.

Sales decline stage (of product life cycle) When new products replace the old.

Sales era A time when a company emphasizes selling to its middlemen and final customers.

Sales managers Manage personal selling.

Sales presentation A salesperson's effort to make a sale.

Sales promotion Those promotion activities—other than personal selling and mass selling—that encourage customers to buy.

Sales promotion managers Fill the gaps between the sales and advertising managers.

Sampling buying Looking at only part of a potential purchase.

Scientific method A research approach consisting of: observation, developing hypotheses, prediction of the future, and testing the hypotheses.

Scrambled merchandising Retailers carrying any product line which they feel they can sell profitably.

Seasonal discounts Discounts offered to encourage buyers to stock earlier than present demand requires.

Secondary data Information which is already published.

Segmenters Aim at one homogeneous subset of a market (at a time) and try to develop a marketing mix that will satisfy that smaller market very well.

Segmenting A gathering process.

Selective demand Demand for a specific brand rather than a product category.

Selective distribution Selling through only those middlemen who will do a good job with the product.

Selective exposure Our eyes and minds notice only information that interests us.

Selective perception We screen out or modify ideas, messages, and information that conflict with previously learned attitudes and beliefs.

Glossary

(continued)

Selective retention We remember only what we want to remember.

Selling agent An agent middleman who takes over the *whole* marketing job of a manufacturer—not just the selling function.

Selling formula approach A sales presentation which uses a prepared outline, building on the stimulus-response model.

Selling function Promotion of the product.

Service wholesalers Merchant wholesalers who provide all the wholesaling functions.

Services (industrial goods) Expense items which support the operations of a firm.

Shopping goods Consumer goods that a customer feels are worth the time and effort to compare with competing products.

Shopping stores Retail stores which attract customers because of the width and depth of their assortments.

Stimulus-response model People respond in some predictable way to a stimulus.

Single-line (or general-line) wholesalers Merchant wholesalers who carry a narrower line of merchandise than general merchandise wholesalers.

Single-line (or limited-line) stores Retail stores which specialize in certain lines rather than the broad assortment carried by general stores.

Skimming pricing policy Tries to get the "cream" of a market (the top of a demand curve) at a high price before aiming at the more price-sensitive segments of that market.

Social class Concerned with how an individual fits into the social structure.

Social needs Concerned with things that involve a person's interaction with others.

Sorting-out process Grading or sorting products.

Source The sender of a message.

Specialty goods Consumer goods that the customer really wants and will make a special effort to buy.

Specialty shop A type of limited-line retail store—usually small, with a distinct "personality."

Specialty stores Retail stores for which customers have developed a strong attraction.

Specialty wholesalers Service (merchant) wholesalers who carry a very narrow range of products.

Standard Metropolitan Statistical Area (SMSA) An economic and social unit with a fairly large population at the center.

Standardization (and grading) functions Sorting of products according to size and quality.

Staples Consumer convenience goods which are bought often and routinely—without much thought.

Status quo objectives "Don't-rock-the-*pricing*-boat" objectives—e.g., "meeting competition" or "avoiding competition" or "stabilizing prices."

Stockturn rate The number of times the average inventory is sold in a year.

Storing The marketing function of holding goods.

Straight rebuy A routine purchase (intermediate buying) which may have been made many times before.

Strategic plan Includes the time-related details for carrying out a strategy.

Substitutes Goods or services that offer a choice to the buyer.

Supermarket A large retail store specializing in groceries—with self-service and wide assortments.

Superstores Very large retail stores that try to carry not only foods, but all goods and services which the consumer purchases routinely.

Supplies (industrial goods) Expense items that do not become a part of the final product.

Supply curve Shows the quantity of goods that would be offered at various possible prices by all suppliers together.

Supporting sales people Help the order-oriented sales people—but don't try to get orders themselves.

Survey method A research method which asks potential customers questions.

Target market A fairly homogeneous (similar) group of customers to whom a company wishes to appeal.

Target marketing Focuses on some specific target customers.

Target return objective A pricing objective which sets a specific profit-related goal.

Tariffs Taxes on imported goods.

Technological base The technical skills and equipment which affect the way the resources of an economy are converted to output.